ASP.NET MVC 4 Recipes

A Problem-Solution Approach

John Ciliberti

ASP.NET MVC 4 Recipes

ISBN-13 (pbk): 978-1-4302-4773-9

ISBN-13 (electronic): 978-1-4302-4774-6

President and Publisher: Paul Manning
Lead Editor: Jonathan Hassell
Developmental Editor: Tom Welsh
Technical Reviewer: Damien Foggon
Editorial Board: Steve Anglin, Mark Beckner, Ewan Buckingham, Gary Cornell, Louise Corrigan, Morgan Ertel,
    Jonathan Gennick, Jonathan Hassell, Robert Hutchinson, Michelle Lowman, James Markham,
    Matthew Moodie, Jeff Olson, Jeffrey Pepper, Douglas Pundick, Ben Renow-Clarke, Dominic Shakeshaft,
    Gwenan Spearing, Matt Wade, Tom Welsh
Coordinating Editor: Anamika Panchoo
Copy Editor: Kimberly Burton-Weisman
Compositor: SPi Global
Indexer: SPi Global
Artist: SPi Global
Cover Designer: Anna Ishchenko

Distributed to the book trade worldwide by Springer Science+Business Media New York, 233 Spring Street, 6th Floor, New York, NY 10013. Phone 1-800-SPRINGER, fax (201) 348-4505, e-mail orders-ny@springer-sbm.com, or visit www.springeronline.com. Apress Media, LLC is a California LLC and the sole member (owner) is Springer Science + Business Media Finance Inc (SSBM Finance Inc). SSBM Finance Inc is a Delaware corporation.

For information on translations, please e-mail rights@apress.com, or visit www.apress.com.

Apress and friends of ED books may be purchased in bulk for academic, corporate, or promotional use. eBook versions and licenses are also available for most titles. For more information, reference our Special Bulk Sales–eBook Licensing web page at www.apress.com/bulk-sales.

Any source code or other supplementary materials referenced by the author in this text is available to readers at www.apress.com. For detailed information about how to locate your book's source code, go to www.apress.com/source-code/.

This book is dedicated to all of the developers who stay up to 3AM for weeks at a time turning their ideas into reality and improving the lives of millions of people around the world.

Contents at a Glance

Contents

About the Author

John Ciliberti is an enterprise software architect who has been designing and developing web applications and enterprise scale solutions for more than 15 years. John has been creating web applications using Microsoft technologies since the early days of classic ASP development in the late 1990s. In addition to his work as a consultant and software architect, John contributes to several open-source projects and is the founder of the MyOnlineBand.com online musician collaboration community.

He is currently employed at KPMG LLC in Montvale, New Jersey, as an associate director in the KPMG US Enterprise Architecture group. In his role as an enterprise architect, John helps guide the firm's strategic technical direction and advises IT leadership on major technical initiatives. John also works closely with project teams by providing initial architectural design and architectural guidance and technical assistance throughout the project.

About the Technical Reviewer

Damien Foggon is a developer, writer, and technical reviewer in cutting-edge technologies. He has contributed to more than 50 books on .NET, C#, Visual Basic, and ASP.NET. He is the co-founder of the Newcastle-based user group NEBytes (www.nebytes.net) and he is a multiple MCPD in .NET 2.0 and .NET 3.5. Damien can be found online at http://blog.fasm.co.uk.

Acknowledgments

This book would not be possible without the help and understanding of many people. At the top of my list is my wife Kathy for putting up with me leaving her alone while I stayed up until 2 a.m. coding and writing for nights on end. I would like to thank my kids Katrina and Maria for forgiving all the missed playdates and bedtime stories. I would also like to thank my old friend Greg Orsulak for allowing me to reference our early computer inspirations as part of the book's introduction.

I would like to thank my technical reviewer Damien Foggon and the staff at Apress, especially Tom Welsh, for all their hard work and attention to detail.

I cannot forget my colleagues at KPMG, especially Chris Marshall and Mike Soranno, who have supported and encouraged me throughout this long and intense process.

Last but not least, I would like to thank Fareed Shaikh, whose philosophy lessons at Taco Bell have raised both my state of consciousness and my cholesterol.

Introduction

The first time I saw a computer that could connect to a network was back in the late '80s when my friend Greg showed me how we could use his Apple IIe to download the Anarchy Cookbook from a bulletin board service. That first experience, which included a misguided crash course in chemistry, eventually led Greg to a career as a pharmacist and got me hooked on the potential of computers.

Fast-forward to 2013 and the Internet is everywhere. It's in your home, at your job, in your car, and in your pocket. You can access the Web from your PC, your phone, your music player, your tablet, and you can even stream movies to your TV. Terrestrial radio is gradually being replaced by Internet music services, cable TV by services from Netflix and Amazon, paper maps by GPS systems, magazines and newspapers by e-readers and tablets. You surf the Web using touch screens, your voice, and TV remotes. Web pages adapt to fit your iPad's orientation, your screen dims automatically to account for room lighting, your game console and your phone can recognize your face, and your tablet can read your handwriting.

As software developers, you need to be three steps ahead of this changing world. You are on the front lines. The world expects that not only will your software work but also that it will get smarter, faster, more reliable, and easier to use. These goals are only possible with improved techniques and better tools.

Adopting new techniques and learning new tools can be challenging, especially when you are on a tight schedule. When learning new technologies, many developers can spend more time searching Google and reading blogs and forum posts than writing code. Many times, they end up using a code snippet from some random source without a full understanding of what it does. The code may seem to fit the need at that time but if it ever breaks, they do not know how to fix it because they don't understand it.

This book was written to help ASP.NET MVC developers like you to quickly find the code you need to move your project forward. More importantly, this book also will help you understand how each solution works. Each solution is broken down step by step and each code sample is explained in detail. In many cases, the explanation will go beyond the code and will discuss what is happening behind the scenes.

CHAPTER 1

■ ■ ■

The Need for Modern Web Applications

All around the world, people are spending less and less time on their PCs, and more time on tablets and smartphones. This trend is dramatically changing how we all collect, share, and work with information. As a web developer working with Microsoft technologies, you need to understand exactly what this means for your applications.

A modern web application is designed for the demands of the post-PC world. It can be deployed to a cloud infrastructure, is resilient to unreliable network conditions, is accessible from any device—anywhere—and provides a beautiful and responsive user experience.

While the basic fundamentals of modern web applications remain unchanged, the ways in which the content is consumed and experienced by the end user have evolved considerably. Modern web applications still use HTTP and HTTPS to send requests and receive responses, and most web applications still use HTML for presentation. On the other hand, the explosion of mobile devices, tablets, and hybrid PCs such as the Microsoft Surface Pro are making touch screens almost as pervasive as the mouse and keyboard. The popularity of social media has spawned a massive expansion of user-generated content that is made relevant by cutting-edge statistical algorithms paired with virtually boundless computing power. HTML5 and modern web browsers such as Google Chrome and Internet Explorer 10 have allowed developers to create dynamic, immersive user interfaces that rival native applications in sophistication and responsiveness.

The following is a list of increasingly common features and characteristics in modern web applications, along with references to recipes in this book that will help you understand how to implement these features.

- *Cross-browser compatibility*: The application experience is constant across all modern web browsers, including Google Chrome, Mozilla Firefox, Internet Explorer 9 and 10, Safari, and Opera. All of the recipes in this book have been designed and tested to work cross-browser.

- *Adaptive design*: The application automatically adapts to work on many screen resolutions, from huge 30-inch monitors to tiny 3.4-inch cell phones. This technique is covered in Recipe 11-1.

- *Natural user interfaces*: The application accepts input from natural user interfaces (NUI) such as touch, voice, NFC, video cameras, GPS, and other sensors. Meeting this requirement means that you have not only the right software but the hardware to test how the application behaves on these devices, as discussed in Recipe 3-1.

- *Social network integration*: The application seamlessly interacts with social networks. Recipes 12-1 and 12-2 demonstrate how easy Visual Studio makes it to integrate your web site with Facebook.

- *Cloud-ready*: The application can use cloud-based infrastructure and scales on demand, adding new servers when needed and scaling down when traffic slows. Chapter 6 describes architectural techniques for designing applications that can take advantage of these capabilities. Chapter 12 describes how to use Visual Studio to create an application that can be deployed to Windows Azure.

- *Resiliency*: The application can adapt to challenging network conditions and, in some cases, can work in a disconnected state. The application is designed to tolerate failures of one or more subsystems and still operate at limited but acceptable capacity. Chapter 6 talks about how to architect systems to meet this requirement. Recipe 12-5 demonstrates how to use some of the built-in features on the Windows Azure APIs to enable resilient file uploads in an ASP. NET MVC 4 application that uses Azure BLOB storage.

- *Extensible*: The application is extensible by way of RESTful APIs and its functionality can be augmented by third-party developers. Chapter 11 shows how to use ASP.NET Web API to design RESTful services and how to consume them using jQuery and Knockout.

- *Reliable*: The application is reliable and supports multiple levels of automated and manual testing before being deployed. Many recipes in this book describe not only how to develop solutions using MVC, but also how to test them. Chapter 9 is entirely dedicated to testing.

- *Maintainable*: The application is easy to maintain and can be upgraded frequently and seamlessly with minimal disruption of the service. Several recipes in this book take this into account. Recipe 1-5 shows how Microsoft Web Deploy can simplify your deployment process. Recipes 7-9 and 10-9 explain how to use the Area feature of ASP.NET MVC to keep your project organized.

- *RESTful*: The application is built on established standards and protocols, and takes advantage of network optimization appliances, load balancers, and monitoring packages. Chapter 11 demonstrates using ASP.NET Web API to create RESTful web services.

- *Secure*: The application has been designed to protect itself from evolving security threats using a layered system of counter measures. If a breach occurs, only the compromised subsystems will be affected; confidential and personally identifiable information will not be exposed. Several recipes discuss security best practices, including Recipe 3-11, which shows you how to use the IIS Application Identity feature, and Recipes 10-2 and 10-3, which demonstrate how to protect against cross-site scripting attacks when creating custom HTML helpers.

- *Scalable*: The application should be able to support thousands of concurrent users. Recipe 6-7 explains how to architect an ASP.NET MVC 4 application for Internet scale. Chapter 8 has several examples that demonstrate how to use .NET Task-based asynchronous programming to create a highly scalable application.

Although not all applications will implement all the features listed here, as frameworks evolve and these features become easier to create, consumers will begin to expect them in the same way that car buyers expect a satellite navigation system to be an option in most new cars.

1-1. Developing Modern Web Applications on the Microsoft Platform

Microsoft ASP.NET MVC Framework 4 is a solid web application framework with a growing developer community. Both the framework and its accompanying tools are actively developed and improved upon. If you have read the notoriously anti-Microsoft article, "Microsoft's Lost Decade," in *Vanity Fair*'s August 2012 issue, or other similar articles, you may have the impression that Microsoft is in big trouble. Although this article is not untrue, it does not tell the whole story.

Contrary to what some media commentators have been suggesting, Microsoft is actually in a pretty good place. Products such as Kinect, Windows Phone 8, Windows 8, Skype, Direct X 11, and Windows Azure are not only keeping pace but are breaking new ground. Microsoft is perhaps the only vendor with enough technical depth for an ecosystem that starts in the consumer space—with technologies such as Xbox—and extends all the way into corporate applications and servers.

Windows 7 was the fastest-selling desktop operating system in history and Windows 8 sold over 60 million copies in its first few months. Kinect for Xbox holds a world record as the fastest-selling consumer product, and one year later had a one million–unit sales lead over the brand-new console from Nintendo.

With the Microsoft Surface and other Windows 8 tablets, Microsoft has a created a true challenger to the iPad and Android-based tablets. On the mobile front, even though Windows Phone 7 sales were poor, Windows Phone 8 has experienced better than expected results, with Nokia selling more than 4.4 million Lumia smartphones over the 2012 holiday season. The Windows desktop operating system still enjoys more than a 90 percent market share, even with an onslaught of new competitors. Microsoft Office is still the standard productivity suite for the vast majority of businesses around the world.

Microsoft's ASP.NET is the most popular commercial web application framework and, after PHP, the second-most popular web application framework overall. According to BuiltWith (`http://trends.builtwith.com/framework/ASP.NET`), ASP.NET is used on more than 20 million public web sites.

Unfortunately, it's not all good news. Over the past few years, the number of web sites that use ASP.NET and IIS has been slowly drifting south. Frameworks such as Django CSRF, a Python-based web framework, and Ruby on Rails have been slowly eating into Microsoft's market share.

Is ASP.NET a Dying Technology?

ASP.NET is not a dying technology but rather a technology going through a transformation. ASP.NET Web Forms, which was all there was to ASP.NET before the MVC Framework came into existence, is in an undeniable decline. While Microsoft is continuing to support and improve Web Forms, the momentum is clearly moving toward the ASP.NET MVC Framework. In the same period that the overall ASP.NET platform saw a general decline, the ASP.NET MVC Framework has grown in usage by over 110 percent. The fastest growth in this trend is in the top 10,000 most popular web sites.

Figure 1-1 shows a chart by BuiltWith, which depicts the number of web sites that are using ASP.NET MVC over a one-year period. It is based on statistics taken from over 90 million web sites. The chart has three line graphs, each representing a set of web sites grouped by popularity ranking. The bottom line shows growth as a percentage of sites ranked in the top one million web sites. The next two lines show the top 100,000 sites and the top 10,000 sites, respectively.

ASP.NET MVC Usage Trends

Model View Controller Framework for ASP.NET

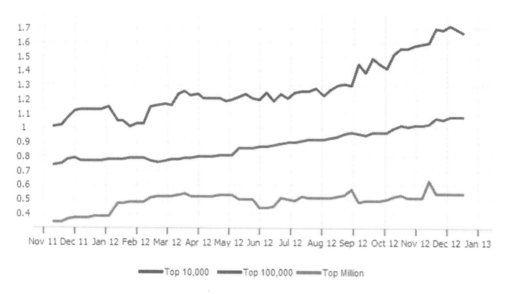

Figure 1-1. *ASP.NET MVC Usage Statistics (Source: BuiltWith.com)*

With ASP.NET 4.5 and the MVC Framework 4, Microsoft has merged its innovations in web server technologies and development tools, and has incorporated lessons learned from many competing web development technologies. From Ruby on Rails, they have taken page routing, scaffolding, and the "convention over configuration" philosophy.

Microsoft answered Sinatra, which provides a simple framework for creating RESTful web services, by introducing Web API. Node.js is a relatively new web development framework based on Google's open-source V8 JavaScript runtime engine, which is the same engine built into the Google Chrome browser. It has been making major inroads on web sites because its event-driven, nonblocking I/O model makes it easier to design highly scalable applications. Microsoft's response to Node.js is a new set of enhancements in the core .NET Framework and the new C# language features that make asynchronous programming with C# almost as simple as synchronous programming.

When you combine the advances Microsoft has made in ASP.NET and the .NET Framework with its new set of front-end development tools, including its embrace of HTML5 and inclusion of third-party open-source JavaScript frameworks (Kinect API, WinRT, XNA Studio, and Expression Blend), you begin to see a picture of a modern development stack that is extremely competitive.

Two common criticisms of Microsoft's web technologies are that everything is a closed black-box system and that Visual Studio is too expensive. This is in major contrast to the platforms that it competes against, in which most of the tools and frameworks are open source and the development tools are free.

Microsoft's response to these criticisms was to open the MVC Framework source code to the community on CodePlex and to expand the capabilities of the free version of Visual Studio. Microsoft also created several programs for students, startups, and small businesses that grant free licenses for the commercial versions of Visual Studio, Windows Server, and SQL Server, and that offers free hosting in some cases.

When you put it all together, the Microsoft platform and the ASP.NET MVC Framework provide a great foundation for developing modern web applications.

1-2. Learning Through Recipes

Unlike most programming books that are designed to be read cover to cover in a sequential order, a recipe book like this one lets you read whatever you need in any order you wish. Each recipe is completely self-contained and, in most cases, does not assume that you have read other material in the book. Occasionally, recipes reference one another to minimize unnecessary replication of content, but most often the referenced content is not essential to complete the task described.

Each recipe is broken into three sections. The first section is the Problem; it is the challenge that you face, such as how to create an MVC model using the Entity Framework Code First approach (Recipe 7-6). The second section, the Solution, provides a brief overview of the solution at a conceptual level; it is usually limited to one or two paragraphs. The bulk of the discussion, including the source code, follows in the How It Works section.

1-3. An Outline of This Book

In the first few chapters, many of the recipes focus on the fundamentals of development with ASP.NET, the ASP.NET MVC architecture, and how to get the most out of Visual Studio. The remainder of the book deals with requirements solved by writing code.

Chapter 2: Understanding ASP.NET MVC

In Chapter 2, you will find recipes that help you understand the fundamentals of the Microsoft development ecosystem and the underlying concepts behind the MVC Framework. Recipes discuss the MVC Pattern (Recipe 2-3); the differences between MVC, MVVM, and MVP (Recipe 2-4); and the architecture of the MVC Framework (Recipe 2-6).

Each of the main components of the MVC Framework, including the Model (Recipe 2-7), controllers and actions (Recipe 2-8), page routing (Recipe 2-9), and view engines (Recipe 2-10) is described in detail.

Recipe 2-12 is a must-read for developers new to the Razor engine. It demonstrates each of the Razor syntax elements through examples. It can be used as a handy cheat sheet as you begin your development.

The last recipe in this chapter demonstrates how to install an alternative third-party view engine called Spark.

Chapter 3: Setting Up Your Environment

Chapter 3 is a collection of recipes that tackle setting up your development environment, including choosing which version of the Windows OS to install (Recipe 3-2), setting up a virtual machine for development (Recipe 3-5), and installing Visual Studio 2012 (Recipe 3-7).

Chapter 4: Visual Studio 2012 Overview

The recipes in Chapter 4 cover the Visual Studio IDE in detail. Each recipe looks at a different feature, such as the Page Inspector (Recipe 4-8), the debugger (Recipes 4-9 and 4-10), and the Extension Manager (Recipe 4-13). Recipe 4-14 contains a comprehensive list of Visual Studio's keyboard shortcuts.

Chapter 5: Getting the Most from the Built-in Templates

The ASP.NET MVC Framework 4 comes with many rich templates—each containing many files and referenced assemblies. The recipes in Chapter 5 dissect each template by looking at each assembly and NuGet package included, and by describing what the templates do and how you can use them to help implement your solution.

Chapter 6: Architecting Applications with ASP.NET MVC

In Chapter 6, the recipes take a step back from the code and look at how to apply the MVC Framework from the perspective of a solutions architect. Recipe 6-1 describes the role of the architect and why it is important for large projects. Recipe 6-2 looks at the decision on whether you should build a new solution or buy a packaged product. Recipe 6-3 discusses the decision of deploying to a private data center or a public cloud. Other recipes in the chapter look at different scenarios and describe reference architectures for each.

Chapter 7: Solution Design

This chapter looks at configuring the ASP.NET membership providers for real-world deployment (Recipe 7-10) and designing a model with the Entity Framework, as well as improving application startup performance (Recipe 7-7), and organizing your project into Areas (Recipe (7-9).

Recipe 7-4 looks at what is needed to build a project that uses the Entity Framework for Oracle Data Provider and demonstrates how to set up your development environment to connect to an Oracle database. Recipe 7-6 shows how you can generate a database from your C# classes using Entity Framework Code First. Recipe 7-3 shows how to create an entity model from an SQL Server database. Recipe 7-5 shows the model-first approach.

Chapter 8: Asynchronous Programming with ASP.NET MVC

Chapter 8 takes a deep look at asynchronous programming with ASP.NET MVC and how multithreading is handled in Microsoft Internet Information Server (IIS) 7 and 8. With .NET 4.5, Microsoft has greatly simplified asynchronous programming. Unfortunately, without a firm understanding of how this technology works, using it can lead to problems that are difficult to diagnose and fix. The recipes in this chapter give you everything you need to start programming right away and they also teach the architecture, tradeoffs, and benefits of the technology so that you can better apply it.

Recipe 8-1 shows how to create an asynchronous action using the Task-based asynchronous style with the async and await keywords.

Recipe 8-3 demonstrates how to asynchronously consume a WCF service from an MVC controller action. Recipe 8-5 looks under the covers to help you understand the code generated by the C# compiler when using the async and await keywords.

The last recipe in this chapter looks at how to troubleshoot performance problems using the built-in reporting features in IIS. It also looks at the differences between synchronous and asynchronous action under load by comparing the results of multiple performance tests.

Chapter 9: Test-Driven Development with ASP.NET MVC 4

Chapter 9 is a collection of eight recipes dedicated to unit testing. Recipe 9-1 outlines how to create a testing strategy and how it can improve the quality of your application. Recipe 9-2 looks at creating unit tests for a controller action using MS Test. Recipe 9-3 demonstrates how to build an ASP.NET MVC application using a test-first approach and shows how to modify your application for testability using the tools built into Visual Studio.

Recipes 9-6 and 9-7 discuss the NUnit unit-testing framework and demonstrate how to integrate it into Visual Studio to test an ASP.NET MVC application. Recipe 9-8 demonstrates creating a mock repository using the Moq library.

Chapter 10: Moving from Web Forms to ASP.NET MVC

In Chapter 10, the recipes address everyday tasks such as creating data grids that allow sorting , filtering, and paging, and demonstrate how the technique is done using ASP.NET Web Forms and how to convert the Web Forms code to functionally-equivalent ASP.NET MVC code. The chapter has recipes for data lists (Recipe 10-1), grid views (Recipes 10-3 and 10-4), master/details views (Recipe 10-5), and custom validation (Recipe 10-6).

Recipe 10-7 is the Rosetta stone that shows the differences between Web Forms master pages and Razor layouts. Recipe 10-8 describes two techniques for creating a wizard in ASP.NET MVC.

Recipe 10-9 shows how to add ASP.NET MVC to an existing Web Forms project and how to modify the Visual Studio project file to allow you to access the MVC tools inside the project.

Chapter 11: Creating Modern User Experiences Using jQuery, Knockout, and Web API

In Chapter 11, you roll up your sleeves to write client-side code that interacts with web services built with ASP.NET Web API. The recipes show adaptive rendering with media queries (Recipe 11-1), a client-side solution for paging and sorting (Recipe 11-2), two-way data binding with Knockout (Recipe 11-3), and how to debug Web API using Fiddler 2 (Recipe 11-5).

Chapter 12: Mobile, Social, and Cloud Technologies

In Chapter 12, the recipes cover working with Facebook (Recipes 12-1 and 12-2), working with Windows Azure (Recipes 12-3 through 12-6), and creating and testing mobile web applications using jQuery Mobile (Recipes 12-7 through 12-9).

Recipe 12-2 shows how to use the new template deployed with the ASP.NET fall update, first shown at the BUILD 2012 conference to create a Facebook Canvas page.

1-4. Finding the Recipes That You Need

If, like many of us, you have a day job with a tight deadline and a spouse who wants you to change diapers and take out the trash, you don't always have the time to read a book cover to cover. You want recipes that fit your immediate needs.

This book gives you several ways to find what you are looking for. The table of contents lists all the recipes, and the index allows you to find information on a particular subject. Neither tells you what you should be looking at if you are an absolute beginner or what you need if you are a veteran Web Forms developer. The following section offers a list of recipes divided by general category, so that you can dive in to find what is most relevant to your needs.

Recommended Recipes for People New to Web Development

The following recipes are best for people who are new to web development, or who have some web development experience but are new to web development on the Microsoft platform.

- 2-1. Understanding the Microsoft Development Ecosystem
- 2-3. Understanding the MVC Pattern
- 2-4. Understanding the Differences Between MVC, MVVM, and MVP
- 2-5. Deciding Between MVC and Web Forms
- 2-6. Understanding the ASP.NET MVC Framework Architecture
- 2-9. Understanding Page Routing
- 2-8. Understanding Controllers and Actions

- 2-10. Understanding View Engines

- 2-12. Understanding Razor Syntax

- 3-7. Installing Visual Studio 2012

- 3-8. Installing Visual Studio MVC 4 Add-on for Visual Studio 2010

- 3-9. Installing IIS

- 4-1. Understanding Visual Studio

- 4-8. Using the Page Inspector to Troubleshoot CSS Layout Bugs

- 4-10. Understanding Visual Studio's Debugging Windows

- 4-18. Using the Extension Manager

- 5-1. Choosing an ASP.NET MVC 4 Project Template

Recommended Recipes for Experienced ASP.NET Web Forms Developers

The following recipes are most useful to experienced Microsoft Web Forms developers who are looking to learn MVC. These are especially useful to someone who wishes to migrate a Web Forms solution to the MVC Framework.

- 2-1. Understanding the Microsoft Development Ecosystem

- 2-3. Understanding the MVC Pattern

- 2-4. Understanding the Differences Between MVC, MVVM, and MVP

- 2-5. Deciding Between MVC and Web Forms

- 2-6. Understanding the ASP.NET MVC Framework Architecture

- 2-9. Understanding Page Routing

- 2-8. Understanding Controllers and Actions

- 2-10. Understanding View Engines

- 2-12. Understanding Razor Syntax

- 4-8. Using the Page Inspector to Troubleshoot CSS Layout Bugs

- 4-9. Using the Page Inspector While Debugging

- 5-1. Choosing an ASP.NET MVC 4 Project Template

- 5-3. Creating a Simple Form with Validation

- 5-4. Creating an Intranet Site That Uses Windows Authentication

- 9-3. Understanding Test-Driven Development Strategies

- 9-8. Mocking a Repository with Moq

- 10-1. Creating a Simple Data List Using ASP.NET MVC

- 10-2. Creating a Multiple-Column Data List Using a Custom HTML Helper Extension

- 10-3. Creating a Data Grid with Paging, Sorting, and Filtering Support

- 10-4. Creating a Data Grid That Allows Inline Editing

- 10-5. Creating a Master/Details View in ASP.NET MVC
- 10-6. Custom Validators in ASP.NET MVC
- 10-7. Moving from Master Pages in ASP.NET Web Forms to Layout Pages in Razor
- 10-8. Creating a Multipage Wizard Using ASP.NET MVC
- 10-9. Adding MVC to a Web Forms Project
- 11-2. Creating a Data Grid That Can Page and Sort Without Full-Page Postbacks

Recommended Recipes for Architects and Technical Leads

The following recipes are most useful to advanced developers, solution architects, and technical leads. These recipes focus on architecting your application, designing for scalability and performance, and configuring your development environment for large teams.

- 2-3. Understanding the MVC Pattern
- 2-4. Understanding the Differences Between MVC, MVVM, and MVP
- 2-6. Understanding the ASP.NET MVC Framework Architecture
- 3-11. Configure an Application Pool to Use an Application Identity
- 6-7. Architecting an ASP.NET MVC Application for the Internet
- 6-8. Architecting a Large-Scale Internet Application
- 6-9. Architecting a Line-of-Business Application with ASP.NET MVC
- 7-1. Designing a View That Requires Data from Multiple Models
- 7-2. Using Partial Views to Construct a Composite User Interface
- 7-5. Creating a Model Using Entity Framework Code First
- 7-9. Using Areas to Organize a Large ASP.MVC Project
- 8-2. Running Several Asynchronous Calls in Parallel Inside an Action Method
- 8-6. Understanding Threading in IIS
- 9-1. Using Testing to Improve the Quality of Your ASP.NET MVC Application
- 9-3. Understanding Test-Driven Development Strategies
- 9-5. Selecting a Unit Test Framework
- 9-8. Mocking a Repository with Moq
- 12-5. Using Fiddler 2 to Help Debug Azure Calls to the Storage Emulator

Recommended Recipes for Cloud Developers

The following recipes are helpful for developers looking to create a new application or migrate an existing application to the Microsoft Windows Azure platform.

- 3-5. Installing Hyper-V and Setting Up a Virtual Machine
- 3-6. Connecting to a Remote Development Machine Using RDP

- 6-3. Deciding Between a Public Cloud and a Private Data Center
- 6-4. Determining the Size of Your Application's Local Network
- 6-5. Determining Which Operating System to Deploy
- 6-8. Architecting a Large-Scale Internet Application
- 12-3. Setting Up Your Development for Working with Windows Azure
- 12-4. Storing and Retrieving Files on Windows Azure from an ASP.NET MVC 4 Application
- 12-5. Using Fiddler 2 to Help Debug Azure Calls to the Storage Emulator

Recommended Recipes for Developers New to jQuery and Knockout

If you are a developer coming from the ASP.NET Web Forms world and you have not worked with jQuery, it may be one of the steepest learning curves you face. Although this book is by no means an exhaustive jQuery reference, it does provide several recipes that demonstrate some of the key capabilities of the library in the context of MVC development.

Knockout.js is the client-side templating and data-binding library that is included with several out-of-the-box Visual Studio MVC project templates. Because this library is relatively new and has not been adopted as widely as some of the other libraries, I think you will probably find the following set of recipes useful.

- 4-8. Using the Page Inspector to Troubleshoot CSS Layout Bugs
- 4-9. Using the Page Inspector While Debugging
- 4-10. Understanding Visual Studio's Debugging Windows
- 5-8. Customizing the Registration Page on an Internet Site Created with the ASP.NET MVC 4 Internet Template
- 11-1. Creating an Adaptive Multicolumn Layout Using CSS Media Queries
- 11-2. Creating a Data Grid That Can Page and Sort Without Full-Page Postbacks
- 11-3. Implementing Two-Way Data Binding Using Web API and Knockout
- 11-4. Creating a Custom Route for an API Controller
- 11-5. Using Fiddler to Debug a Web API
- 12-5. Enabling Large File Uploads in an ASP.NET MVC Application Using HTML5, File API, and Windows Azure Blob Storage
- 12-8. Creating a Mobile Web Application Using jQuery Mobile and ASP.NET MVC 4

1-5. The Code Samples

Most of the recipes come with corresponding code samples that can be downloaded from the book's web site. Wherever possible, the recipes are designed to work with Visual Studio 2012's new Run Recipe feature. This feature allows Visual Studio to generate solution-specific code. It can be installed using the NuGet console. This will allow you to apply a specific recipe to your project.

▓ **Note**　You should avoid simply cutting and pasting the code samples without first reading the material that goes with it. I know you have a deadline, but I guarantee that if you do not understand the code that you are pasting into your project, you will not only miss your deadline but may introduce problems in the application that will be difficult to troubleshoot. This is true not only for the code samples in this book, but for code from blogs and forum sites as well.

Here are some words to live by:

There is no such thing as quick and dirty. Only dirty.

Taking shortcuts will almost always lead to issues later on.

Take the time to understand the code that you are adding to your project.

About the Sample Database

To complement the code samples used in this book, I have included a fairly complex database that is made up of over 30 tables and contains thousands of records. The data is based on publicly available data from a real music collaboration web site that is used by thousands of people around the world.

　　The sample database is used in many of the examples in this book, starting in Chapter 7. It is highly recommended that you download the sample database, which is distributed as an SQL Server backup file, and then restore it on your development database server running SQL Server 2005 or higher. If you do not have access to a database server, I have provided instructions on how you can download and install SQL Server Express 2012. SQL Server Express is a free version of Microsoft's flagship database server and it provides all the functionality needed to execute the examples in this book.

Install SQL Server Express with Tools

The following steps explain how to install SQL Server Express with Tools.

1. Go to www.microsoft.com/en-us/download/details.aspx?id=29062.

2. Download ENU\x64\SQLEXPRWT_x64_ENU.exe (670MB), or ENU\x86\SQLEXPRWT_x86_ENU.exe (706MB) if you are running 32-bit OS.

3. Run the installer.

4. From the SQL Server Installation Center window, click New SQL Server Stand-Alone Installation or Add Features To An Existing Installation.

5. On the License Terms screen, tick the "I accept the license terms" check box, and then click Next.

6. Click Next on the Product Update page.

7. On the feature selection page, ensure Database Engine Services and Management Tools –Basic is selected. You can uncheck SQL Server Replication tools since they are not needed. You can then click Next.

8. On the Instance Configuration screen, select Default Instance and verify that the instance root directory is appropriate for your computer. For example, if you are running low on space on your C: drive, you may want to select another disk for your instance root. Click Next to continue.

9. On the Service Accounts screen, in most cases, you can accept the default settings. This will create a service account NT Service\MSSQLServer with an Automatic Startup type for the SQL Server Database engine service. The SQL Server Browser service is disabled by default. It is recommended that you keep this setting for security reasons.

10. On the Database Engine Configuration page, it is recommended that you use the default setting of Windows Authentication Mode, which is more secure than Mixed Mode. You should also add yourself to the SQL Server administrators account by clicking the Add Current User button. On the Data Directories, adjust the settings as appropriate for your machine. Click Next to continue.

11. On the Error Reporting screen, click Next.

12. At this point, installation will proceed. It will take between 5 and 20 minutes for the installation to complete, depending on the speed of your computer.

13. On the Complete screen, click the Close button.

Installing the Sample Database

The following steps explain how to install the sample database.

1. Download the sample database backup file from the Downloads tab on the Apress web site (www.apress.com/9781430247739).

2. The database backup file is available under the Shared folder. Unzip the file to a location on your local hard disk.

3. Open SQL Server Management Studio. This is a tool that should have been installed with the SQL Server 2012 installation.

4. When prompted to connect to a server, your local machine should be selected by default and Windows Authentication should be selected. Click OK to connect.

5. In the Microsoft SQL Server Management Studio application, right-click the Databases node in the Object Explorer and select Restore Database.

6. Under Source in the Restore Database window, select Device, and then click the Ellipse button.

7. In the Select Backup Devices window, select File as the Backup Media Type, and then click the Add button.

8. Browse to the location where you unzipped the database backup file, and then select Ch7SharedDatabase.bak and then click OK.

9. Click OK in the Select Backup Devices window.

10. In the Restore Database window, the database name should be set to Ch7SharedDatabase and the last full backup should be checked in the Backup Sets To Restore list. Click the OK button to begin the restore process.

11. When completed, a message should state that the database was restored successfully. Click the OK button to dismiss the message.

12. Confirm that the database exists and is accessible by expanding the Databases node in the Microsoft SQL Server Management Studio Object Explorer.

About the Shared Library

In Chapter 7, I discuss several strategies for creating models that consume data from a back-end database. As a result of one of these recipes, we will use the Entity Framework model-first technique to map the sample database to an Entity Data Model.

For the sake of convenience, I have packaged this library into an external DLL that is also available in the Shared folder in the book's code samples. In addition to the code shown in Chapter 7, the library has some other useful utilities that are designed to make the sample applications more visually palatable. For example, rather than packaging 5000 profile pictures, the library has been modified to use a constrained sample image set that uses a random image to replace the URL of the image associated with a user.

CHAPTER 2

■ ■ ■

Understanding ASP.NET MVC

2-1. Understanding the Microsoft Web Development Ecosystem

Problem

You are new to the Microsoft platform and need to know how to get started. You are confused by the myriad of product offerings. You don't know if you should be using WebMatrix, LightSwitch, ASP.NET MVC, ASP.NET Web Forms, ASP.NET Web Pages, Napa, or Silverlight. You would like to understand all these tools and determine which tool you should learn more about.

Solution

The ever-growing selection of developer products from Microsoft has grown substantially over the past few years. The current list of products has become confusing, even for experienced Microsoft developers. To clear up this confusion, it is helpful to have a general understanding of the platforms, which include servers, productivity suites, programming frameworks, and languages. Once you understand the platforms and the types of applications that you can create on them, you can then explore the development tools to get an understanding of how each is applied to the ecosystem.

How It Works

The Microsoft web development ecosystem works by leveraging the building blocks on the Windows operating system. These building blocks include the Windows APIs (Win32), Component Object Model (COM), Object Linking and Embedding (OLE), Component Services (COM+), and the Microsoft .NET Framework.

Built from these foundational layers is Microsoft's Web Server Internet Information Services (IIS). IIS 7, which was a complete rewrite of past versions of the web server, provides a flexible extensibility model that divides its functionality into a collection of loosely-coupled modules.

This architecture allows any component to be replaced by a custom version if needed and allows additional functionality to be created by both Microsoft and third-party independent software vendors. IIS 7 ships with more than 40 modules, which include authentication, response compression, configuration, and application frameworks such as ASP.NET. They also provide backward compatibility with older versions of IIS, which allows older application frameworks such as Classic ASP.

In addition to application frameworks developed by Microsoft, IIS supports many third-party and open-source web platforms, including PHP, CGI, Perl, Node.js, Ruby on Rails, and Java development technologies such as J2EE.

Microsoft Development Platforms and Frameworks

This section introduces each of the major platforms and frameworks that have been developed by Microsoft and run on IIS.

Classic ASP

Active Server Pages (ASP) was a Microsoft web development framework released in 1998 as part of the Windows NT 4.0 Option Pack. It was extremely successful, and even though it has been superseded by ASP.NET, it continues to power hundreds of thousands of web sites. It can still be installed all versions of Windows Server, including Windows Server 2012.

ASP was also implemented on Unix and Linux systems by ChiliSoft (later acquired by Sun and now part of Oracle).

Classic ASP's popularity was driven by the fact that it was very simple and easy to learn. It allowed developers to use either VBScript or JavaScript as the programming language.

The main issue with it is was that it mixed together business logic with presentation and often led to applications that became impossible to maintain. It was also very difficult to debug. Many teams attempted to remedy ASP's shortcomings by putting the business logic into COM components written in C++ or VB. This practice was later officially recommended by Microsoft in what was called Windows DNA.

Ultimately, the rise of Java technologies and the growing complexity of business requirements led to the development of Microsoft .NET and ASP.NET, which replaced Classic ASP.

Although Classic ASP is still officially supported on the Windows Server platform, I would not recommend using it for new projects.

ASP.NET Web Forms

ASP.NET Web Forms, which was first released in 2002, is now in its seventh version. It has been the primary web development technology used on the Microsoft platform for more than ten years. Web Forms abstracts the web and uses a programming model that is very similar to programming Windows Forms. It follows a model where a developer would design a screen by dragging controls such as text boxes and drop-down lists to the design surface, and then double-clicking the control to create an event handler on a code-behind page. For example, double-clicking on a button would create an `OnClick` event handler where you would put your code to be executed when the button was clicked.

The main benefits of Web Forms is that it was easy to learn for VB programmers looking to move away from fat, client programming and start building web applications. It also saved developers time with features such as form validation controls and web site security.

The drawbacks are that is was designed for the web of 2002, when it was acceptable for every UI manipulation to result in a post back to the server. They remedied this with some success in 2008 with the release of ASP.NET Ajax, but developers who attempt to create rich user interfaces may find themselves fighting the framework.

Web Forms may still be ideal for teams that need to rapidly put together a small application that does not need a highly sophisticated user interface. However, as technologies such as SharePoint and LightSwitch become more sophisticated, and tools like business process management systems become more prevalent, the need for developers to hand-develop these types of systems are diminishing.

ASP.NET MVC

ASP.NET MVC was first released in March 2009. It shares a common infrastructure with ASP.NET Web Forms, but breaks away from the server control, drag-and-drop paradigm of the web forms world and provides a more natural model for creating Ajax-driven, rich end-user experiences.

A detailed comparison between ASP.NET Web Forms and ASP.NET MVC is provided in Recipe 2-5.

ASP.NET MVC is well suited for most web applications, and perhaps the paradigm of choice for all new development. ASP.NET MVC requires that the developer invest time into understanding the Model View Controller (MVC) pattern. Compared to some of Microsoft's other frameworks, ASP.NET MVC may not be as easy for inexperienced developers to learn.

ASP.NET Web Pages

ASP.NET Web Pages is a simple web development framework that provides a mechanism for creating custom web applications with the WebMatrix IDE. It shares some underpinnings with ASP.NET MVC, including page routing and the Razor view engine. While it is possible to create sophisticated applications using ASP.NET web pages, it is less suitable for enterprise scale than ASP.NET MVC.

It may be ideal for experienced developers looking to create a simple application. For example, let's say that you need to create a web site for your softball team and would like to expose a database of batting averages. The simplicity of WebMatrix allows you to do this faster than if you did the same application using MVC in Visual Studio. ASP.NET Web Pages is less ideal for a team of developers working on a large project.

For enterprise developers, ASP.NET Web Pages and Web Matrix can be a great prototyping tool. Its rapid application development environment allows you to quickly put together a demo and deploy it to a staging server where it can be demonstrated to end users. The project can later be ported into Visual Studio and the full MVC Framework, where you can apply enterprise development best practices and generate unit tests and other recommended artifacts.

LightSwitch

LightSwitch is a RAD (rapid application development) tool that simplifies the creation of data entry–centric applications. The initial release of LightSwitch used Silverlight to create the end-user experience. It exploited Silverlight's rich data-binding capabilities to create data-driven applications with minimal or no coding. LightSwitch applications can be run either as a browser Silverlight application or as an out-of-browser application that runs on the desktop. The latest version supports project output in HTML5 as well as Silverlight.

LightSwitch is a good solution for very simple applications. It has several major limitations, such as the inability to support forms that need to update data from multiple database tables, which prevent it from being used for anything other than trivial "peak and poke" applications.

Silverlight

Silverlight is a rich Internet application (RIA) tool that competes with the Adobe Flash plug-in. It is used primarily for creating rich media streaming experiences by web sites such as Netflix.

Even though Microsoft has pledged to continue supporting Silverlight until 2021, Microsoft's RIA strategy has shifted to HTML5. Silverlight still has some advantages over HTML, such as the ability to run on legacy enterprise desktops that have standardized on browsers such as Internet Explorer 7, which does not support HTML5 and has poor JavaScript performance. It also is superior to HTML5 in that it can deliver richer streaming experiences with an extensible codec framework and support for 3D graphics. Silverlight can run outside the browser and be granted permission to access the local file system.

I recommend that architects and tech leads avoid using Silverlight for new applications. If possible, they should either opt for an Ajax/HTML5 application or consider using a native Windows technology such as Windows Presentation Foundation (WPF). If Silverlight is used, I recommend an "islands of richness" model over a full-browser-window Silverlight application. An example of "islands of richness" is a Silverlight-based media player that allows playback of Digital Rights Management (DRM)–protected content. In a full-browser Silverlight application, the entire user experience is created in Silverlight.

SharePoint

SharePoint is one of Microsoft's most successful products. It provides a portal that teams can use to share files, and has document and records management capabilities. It also offers the ability for end users to create simple applications using nothing but a web browser, including simple forms and workflows. Advanced users can use SharePoint Designer to create more-advanced forms and workflows.

The underpinnings of SharePoint are ASP.NET Web Forms, Windows Workflow Foundation, and other Microsoft technologies. SharePoint is very extensible and there are many places for developers to add customized functionality.

Some corporations have adopted SharePoint as an application platform where many teams can deploy their custom solutions onto a shared SharePoint infrastructure. In many cases, the value-added functionality of SharePoint can dramatically reduce the amount of code that is required to create the solution.

There are several drawbacks to using SharePoint as a development platform. The largest is the overall complexity of the product. Tracking down bugs and performance problems in a SharePoint application can be extremely painful. In other cases, adding what would be trivial functionality in other Microsoft web technology would require weeks of pasting GUIDs into 900-line XML files and having to reset IIS every time you make a minor change.

SharePoint can be a powerful tool, but be sure to have a firm understanding of SharePoint development. Also, be certain that your application is using enough native SharePoint functionality to offset the complexity of development in the SharePoint ecosystem.

For Office 2013, which includes SharePoint 2013 and Office 365, Microsoft has created a new application model code named Napa, which simplifies the development experience by allowing you to use HTML, JavaScript, and CSS to create your front end, and use C#, PHP, and VB.NET to create server-side code. The new framework supports RESTful APIs, which allow you to develop your service using the platform of your choice and then use the Office JavaScript API to create a user interface to consume your service.

Figure 2-1 shows the major Microsoft web development tools and the targeted audience for each. The tools listed on the left side of the diagram are designed for a broader audience, which includes relatively nontechnical business power users. The tools on the right side are designed for professional developers and architects.

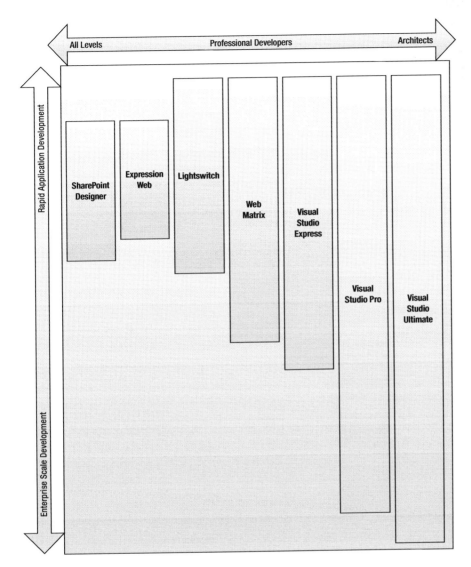

Figure 2-1. *Microsoft Web Development Tools matrix*

Microsoft Web Development Tools

The diagram shown in Figure 2-1 makes a distinction between rapid application development and enterprise scale development. On the RAD side, the tools are optimized to quickly develop a solution, but are less optimized for creating highly scalable, reliable, and maintainable applications. There are many situations where a RAD tool is "good enough." For example, if you have a customer that wants to build a web site for his small business and, in addition to his marketing capital, he would like a way to collect some customer information on his web site. In this case, tools like WebMatrix will be a good fit. On the other hand, if you are developing a trading floor application for a major brokerage firm, you would want to use the more robust toolset offered by Visual Studio. The Visual Studio products span the entire vertical axis of the diagram in Figure 2-1 since they allow developers to target the entire Microsoft stack.

Table 2-1 lists the various tools from Microsoft that can be used for web development, a brief description for each tool, and the pricing of the product at the time of this writing.

Table 2-1. *Microsoft Web Development Tools*

Tool	Description	Price (Aug 2012)
SharePoint Designer	SharePoint Designer is a free addition to Microsoft Office. It allows power users to build and enhance web sites hosted in Microsoft SharePoint. Users can create and customize SharePoint lists, create InfoPath Forms, and create workflows. They may also alter the look and feel of the SharePoint sites.	Free with Microsoft Office
	With this tool, a SharePoint power user can create somewhat sophisticated departmental scale applications without needing to write code. Advanced users that understand some basic HTML programming can create interesting user experiences.	
	There are several limitations that prevent SharePoint Designer from being a true enterprise development tool:	
	• It does not really support the concept of environment propagation. While it is possible to export a SharePoint .stp file, and then publish that file to another environment, it is not a completely reliable method since the .stp may have external dependencies not available on the target site.	
	• It does not support source control systems.	
	• It cannot unit test workflows.	
	• It is limited in flexibility and has no mechanism for writing custom code.	
Expression Web	Expression Web is a lightweight editor targeted at designers and front-end developers. It allows you to create static web pages and simple applications in ASP.NET and PHP. For ASP.NET Web Forms and PHP pages, it has basic functionality that allows you to connect to data sources.	$149
	Probably the coolest feature of Expression Web is its Web Super Preview. It allows you to view a web page from several web browsers using any local rendering engine installed on your machine, as well as remote rendering engines, and then view the different outputs side by side. For example, on a machine running Windows 7, you can compare how the page will render on Safari 4 on a Mac and several versions of Internet Explorer.	
Expression Blend	Expression Blend is a tool for creating XAML-based Silverlight, WPF, and Windows Phone applications. It can be purchased as part of Expression Studio, which includes Expression Web, a vector graphics editor called Expression Design, and Expression Encoder (which provides audio and video enhancement and encoding capabilities). It is also available as a download for MSDN subscribers.	$599
	Expression Blend 5 also allows you to create touch-friendly HTML5 applications that run as full-screen native applications on Windows 8. It does not allow you to create HTML5 applications that target web browsers.	
	For web developers, Expression Blend is useful for creating the user interface of Silverlight applications, usually in conjunction with Visual Studio.	

(continued)

Table 2-1. (*continued*)

Tool	Description	Price (Aug 2012)
WebMatrix	WebMatrix is an IDE introduced in 2011 as a lightweight alternative to Visual Studio. It is integrated with the web platform installer. It allows developers to select an open-source application from a gallery, and use that as the starting point for the application. You can then customize the configuration of the application and deploy it to a hosting provider. It also allows you to create custom web applications from scratch using the ASP.NET Web Pages framework. The WebMatrix IDE is available for free at www.microsoft.com/web/webmatrix/.	Free
	In additional to ASP.NET, Web Matrix also supports Node.js and PHP development.	
	WebMatrix can be installed side by side with Visual Studio and is well suited for consultants that work with many small clients and need to quickly customize an application such as the Drupal content management system.	
LightSwitch	LightSwitch is a RAD-based tool that can be used to create applications in Microsoft Silverlight and HTML5. It exploits Silverlight's rich data binding capabilities to create data-driven applications with minimal or no coding. LightSwitch Silverlight applications can be run either as in-browser applications or as out-of-browser applications that run on the desktop.	Included with Visual Studio 2012 Professional, Premium, and Ultimate.
	HTML5 support for LightSwitch was added with Visual Studio 2012, and at the time of this writing, was not as robust as the support for Silverlight.	
	LightSwitch is a good solution for very simple applications. It has several major limitations, such as the inability to support forms that need to update data from multiple database tables, which would prevent it from being used for anything other than trivial "peak and poke" applications.	
Visual Studio Express 2012 for Web	The express edition of Visual Studio is free. It provides hobbyist and student developers with many of the core features of the professional and ultimate versions, and shares the same project format. With the 2012 version, unit-testing tools are available along with the core web development tools. The following are the main differences between the express editions and full Visual Studio:	Free

- Several Express editions to each feature rather than a single install. For example, if you wish to develop for both IIS and Windows Phone, you need to download and install two separate products.

- No Server Explorer

- No integrated source control support.

- Limited report development support.

- Limited deployment support.

- No mobile device support.

(*continued*)

Table 2-1. (*continued*)

Tool	Description	Price (Aug 2012)
Visual Studio	There are four versions of Visual Studio 2012.	Professional: $499
	• *Test Professional*: Manual testing tools, Team Foundation Server support, and lab management.	Professional with MSDN: $1,199
	• *Professional*: Basic debugging tools, unit-testing development, platform development support, tools for Windows, Windows Server, and SQL Server.	Test Professional with MSDN: $2,169
	• *Premium*: All Professional's features plus advanced testing and diagnostics tools, code clone, basic architecture modeling tools, MS Office, Dynamics, and other Microsoft Server development support. $2,100 worth of Windows Azure cloud services.	Premium with MSDN: $6,119
	• *Ultimate*: Includes all the Premium features plus additional architecture and modeling tools, load testing, web performance testing, and IntelliTrace features. $3,700 worth of Windows Azure cloud service.	Ultimate edition with MSDN: $13,299
	With the exception of Professional, all versions of Visual Studio are packaged with MSDN subscriptions. MSDN subscriptions give you access to a large percentage of the Microsoft product catalog, including servers such as SQL Server 2012 and SharePoint, operating systems, and desktop software.	
	A comparison of different MSDN subscription levels can be downloaded from `http://download.microsoft.com/download/4/1/0/4100640B-A19F-4278-9CC3-09BD9B713111/Compare-MSDN-subscriptions.pdf`.	

After reviewing Table 2-1, you can see that Microsoft has a large variety of tools available at many different price points. Most of the examples in this book work in all versions of Visual Studio 2012, including Visual Studio Express 2012 for Web.

2-2. Understanding the Differences Between the Versions of the MVC Framework
Problem

The MVC Framework has gone through a lot of churn since its inception, and it seems as the rate that new versions are released as accelerated. You would like a better understanding of the MVC Framework versions and the differences between them.

Solution

ASP.NET MVC's first production release was in March of 2009. The initial version provided the basic plumbing: the extensibility model and a view engine based on ASP.NET Web forms.

In March 2010, version 2 was released and included more than 15 new features, such as API improvements and support for ASP.NET 4. MVC 3 was released in January 2011.

MVC 3 introduced the Razor view engine and many other features that simplified the creation of views and made it easier to maintain a separation of concerns.

In August 2012, MVC 4 was released, along with a massive wave of Microsoft products, including Visual Studio 2012. MVC 4 includes a new framework for creating HTTP services, a mechanism for allowing MVC application to change which view is selected based on the user agent, seamless deployments to Windows Azure, and bundling and minification, which can improve performance by reducing the number and size of the HTTP requests made by the client in order to render your page.

How It Works

The ASP.NET MVC Framework was first released by Microsoft as a Community Technology Preview (CTP) back in December of 2007.

■ **Note** A CTP (in Microsoft release naming-convention terminology) is a very rough prerelease that usually only includes a subset of the full planned functionality. After the CTP, Microsoft usually releases a beta version. The beta version is then typically followed by one or more release candidates (RC) that is a nearly complete version of the product. The final version is known as the release to manufacturing (RTM), but sometimes is called a release to web (RTW).

The final version, or RTM, of MVC Framework version 1 was released as an add-on to ASP.NET 3.5 on March 9, 2009. The first version introduced features such as page routing, which provides clean, search engine–friendly URLs, as well as the controller classes and a view engine based on ASP.NET Web Forms. A key component of the new MVC Framework was its extensibility points, which allowed for major components such as the view engine to be replaced with a custom design.

A year later, on March 10, 2010, Microsoft released version 2 of the MVC Framework. Version 2 could be installed alongside version 1 so that developers could maintain an existing MVC 1 application while working on an MVC 2 application at the same machine. It also allowed a web server to host both MVC 1 and MVC 2 apps without causing any problems. When you were ready to upgrade, a Visual Studio 2010 add-in for MVC provided a conversion wizard. Version 2 of the MVC Framework was a huge release, with more than 15 significant new features. The most notable new features were

- Support for asynchronous controllers.
- Support for data annotation attributes.
- Model-Validator Providers.
- Client-side validation.
- Template headers.
- Many API improvements.
- Support for ASP.NET 4 and Visual Studio 2010.

On January 13, 2011, MVC 3 was released along with a significant set of new products, including NuGet, IIS Express 7.5, Web Deploy and the Web Farm Framework 2.0, Orchard 1.0, and WebMatrix 1.0.

In addition to the normal install packages, Microsoft also released the source code for the MVC Framework under the Apache 2.0 open-source license. Major features in the 3.0 release included

- The Razor view engine.

- Unobtrusive JavaScript.

- Integration with jQuery UI and jQuery Validate plug-ins.

- Validation improvements, including remote validation.

- Entity Framework Code First support.

- Partial-page output caching.

- A new ViewBag, which used .NET 4's dynamic feature to allow late-bound data to be passed from controllers to views.

- Page Routing was no longer part of the MVC Framework; it became a part of the core ASP.NET stack.

The most significant new feature of MVC 3 is the Razor view engine. This fundamentally changes the way views are constructed. If you are coming from an ASP.NET Web Forms background, this may be the most disruptive change to the way you are used to working. Fortunately, Razor is very simple and easy to learn. Most people are able to "beat down" the learning curve and reap the productivity benefits of Razor's terse syntax within the first few weeks of using it.

In early 2012, the first beta of MVC Framework 4 was released as part of the Visual Studio 2012 beta. In March 2012, the source code to the framework—including the Web API and the Razor view engine—was released under the Apache open-source license. This is a much less restrictive license than the license issued for the 3.0 source code, and permits third parties to modify the source code and even submit their contribution to the project.

In August 2012, Microsoft released the final version of MVC 4. It is available as a downloadable add-in for Visual Studio 2010, and is included by default with Visual Studio 2012. This is the first time that a new version of the MVC Framework has been released as part of a major version of Visual Studio. This is a clear indication from Microsoft that the MVC Framework is now considered both mature and mainstream. The growth in interest and activity in the MVC developer community is another sign that ASP.NET MVC is now ready for mass adoption.

The top new features for ASP.NET 4 include

- ASP.NET Web API.

- Modernized project templates that employ cutting edge design methodologies such as adaptive rendering.

- A plethora of new features for developing mobile applications, including mobile project templates.

- A new "Recipes" feature that allows NuGet packages to generate project specific code.

- Expanded support for asynchronous programming, including support for the new Await keywords.

- Bundling and minification of script and CSS files.

- A Display Mode feature that allows a separate view to be used, depending on specified criteria. If an iPhone is detected, for example, a view optimized for that device is supplied.

- Support for the Windows Azure SDK.

2-3. Understanding the MVC Pattern

Problem

You would like to begin working with ASP.NET MVC Framework, but you do not understand the MVC pattern and why it is beneficial.

Solution

The Model View Controller (MVC) pattern is a popular design pattern used in many software systems. The pattern was first documented in 1978 by Trygve Reenskaug in regard to a project at Xerox PARC in which the MVC pattern was implemented for the Smalltalk-80 class library. MVC separates a software module into three distinct layers each with a specific role (see Figure 2-2).

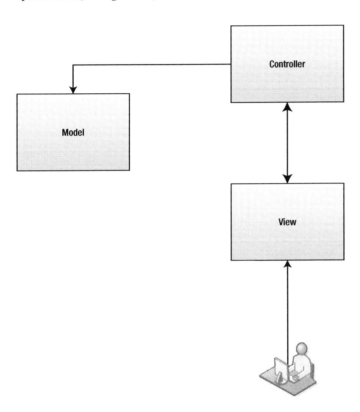

Figure 2-2. *Model View Controller*

- *Model*: Models represent data. A model can be as simple as a single object or a complex type with many collections of objects within it. The model should not include implementation details. A model may have many associated views.

- *View*: The view typically represents a user interface component that is bound to a model. The view can display the data and allow a user to modify the data. The view should always reflect the state of the model.

- *Controller*: The controller provides a mechanism for the user to interact with a system by defining how the user interface reacts to user input. It is responsible for exchanging and interpreting messages between the view and the model.

How It Works

In addition to defining the layers themselves, the MVC pattern also provides rules on how the layers are allowed to communicate.

Allowed Communication Patterns

- Users may interact with a view.

- Views may interact with controllers.

- Controllers may interact with views.

- Controllers may communicate with other controllers.

- Controllers may communicate with the model.

Restricted Communication Patterns

- Users may not interact directly with controllers.

- Users may not interact directly with a model.

- Views may not interact with other views.

- Views may not interact directly with the model.

- Models may not interact with other models.

Benefits of the MVC Design Pattern

If this is your first time reading about the MVC pattern, you may be saying to yourself, "Why bother with this approach? It seems like a lot of extra work."

The first benefit is that your view and model are decoupled. This means that you can have many views associated with a given model. For example, with one model, you may have a separate view for each CRUD (create, read, update, delete) operation.

- A read-only view that displays the record but does not allow it to be changed.

- A view for creating new records.

- A view for modifying a record.

In fact, Visual Studio has built-in features that simplify creating applications that follow the MVC pattern. In addition to your standard CRUD views, you may also want to create views that target specific devices. Perhaps you may need another view that returns the data as an Excel spreadsheet. In addition to views created for humans, you can also provide web services that are accessed by other applications or client-side scripts.

The second main advantage is the view/controller decoupling. This allows you to change the way an application responds to user input without changing the view. It also allows the user interface (the view) to be changed without changing the way the application responds to user input. In web applications, the user interface will likely change more often than the business rules. This is especially true when the user interface is controlled by a marketing department. By keeping the controller logic separate from the presentation, you can reshuffle your page layouts as often as marketing requires, without inadvertently breaking your business logic.

Another advantage of using the MVC pattern is that separating concerns allows different team members to focus on the part of the application that best aligns with their respective skill sets. For example, very few people possess both the skills for creating an attractive front-end interface using HTML and CSS, and also know the intricacies of C# programming. It also allows team members to simultaneously work on their respective parts of the page, since the code and the presentation are in different files. For the team that engages in test-driven development, the MVC pattern lends itself well to creating automated unit tests.

Other Technologies That Use the MVC Pattern

ASP.NET MVC is not the only product that uses the MVC pattern and it is not the first web development framework to utilize it. There are thousands of frameworks and applications that implement the MVC pattern. The following list describes several of the most popular frameworks that use the MVC pattern.

- *Apple iOS Development*: If you plan on creating a native application for the iPhone or iPad using Apple Xcode, you need to implement the MVC pattern. Xcode employs a drag-and-drop interface that allows you to define the various UI components and then drag a connector to the controller to define its relationship to the view.

- *Apache Struts*: First released in May 2000, Apache Struts is an open-source framework that extends the Java Servlet API for creating Java Enterprise Edition web applications. Struts is probably the most mature MVC-based application framework. It has been used on thousands of enterprise-scale applications at Fortune 500 companies.

- *Spring Framework*: Spring is another Java framework that features an MVC Framework in addition to its Inversion of Control container and aspect-oriented programming features. The Spring Framework's MVC Framework was created to address architectural deficiencies in Apache Struts by providing better separation between the MVC layers.

- *Yii*: The Yii Framework is one of the most popular PHP frameworks. It is noted for being fast, secure, and well documented. The framework has a web-based code generator that turns a database table into a model class. The code generator will also generate PHP code to perform CRUD operations that follow the MVC pattern. You can then modify the generated code to meet your needs.

- *Ember.js*: Ember.js is a JavaScript MVC Framework and templating engine. It has support for UI Bindings, composed views, provides a web presentation layer, and plays nicely with other JavaScript libraries. Ember can be used in conjunction with a server-side MVC Framework to extend the MVC benefits to the ever-increasing complexity of the modern web application presentation tier.

- *Ruby on Rails*: Ruby on Rails is a popular MVC web development framework used by thousands of web sites. In Rails, the model is implemented as the `ActiveRecord` that maintains the relationship between the model and the database. Ruby method names are generated automatically based on the field names in the database. The view is implemented by the `ActionView` library and the `ActionController` subsystem that implements the controller. Much of Microsoft's MVC Framework is inspired by Ruby on Rails, including its dynamic data scaffolding technology. In Rails, scaffolding generates major pieces of the application based on a model definition that includes the model class, forms, CSS style sheets, and tests.

2-4. Understanding the Differences Between MVC, MVVM, and MVP
Problem

In addition to the MVC pattern, you often hear allot about MVVM and MVP but you are confused about what the differences are between them and where they should be applied.

Solution

The three patterns—Model-View-Controller (MVC), Model-View-Presenter (MVP), and Model-View-ViewModel (MVVM)—have many similarities, but also are very different. All three patterns have an underlying goal, which is to separate the view from the model. All three patterns contain the concepts of the model and the view. The main difference between the patterns is the way changes are propagated between the view and the model. The view model, the presenter, and the controller all share the responsibility of communicating state changes between the view and the model, but they employ a different mechanism to do it.

How It Works

In MVC, events fired in the view result in actions being called on the controller. In the MVC Framework, this is implemented by HTTP requests routed to the appropriate controller by the ASP.NET request routing subsystem. Each unique URL is mapped to a special method in the controller, known as an *action*. Inside the action method, the view data is processed and the model is updated. MVC controllers also have the additional responsibility of determining which view should be displayed.

In the MVP pattern, the controller has been replaced by the presenter. The presenter is similar to the controller in that it is the only entity that should manipulate the model. Presenters differ from the controllers in three ways:

1. They do not play the role of the traffic cop as controllers do, but instead are instantiated by a view.

2. The view and the presenter are completely decoupled and communicate by way of an interface.

3. The presenter handles all UI events on behalf of the view.

The MVP pattern is commonly used by Enterprise ASP.NET Web Forms developers who need to create automated unit tests for their code-behind pages, but do not want to run the tests inside of a web server process. By modeling the properties and events defined in the Web Forms page into an interface, a mock implementation of the page can be used when running unit tests. Figure 2-3 shows a conceptual diagram of the MVP pattern implemented in an ASP.NET Web Forms application.

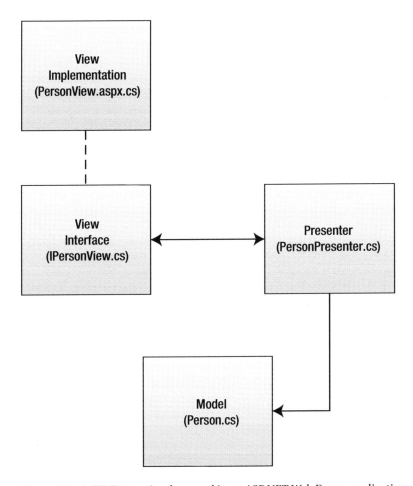

Figure 2-3. *MVP Pattern implemented in an ASP.NET Web Forms application*

In the MVVM pattern, two-way data binding is used to communicate state changes in the view to the view model. In application frameworks such as WPF and Silverlight, this is done by setting the view model as the data context on the view. Because the data binding is bidirectional, when the view model's data is changed, the updates value is automatically propagated to the view, and changes to the view are automatically propagated to the view model.

The view model typically uses the observer pattern, in which an event is fired every time an exposed property is modified—notifying subscribers that a change has occurred.

The main advantage of this pattern is that it eliminates the need to explicitly write code such as `PersonNameTextbox.Text = myViewModel.Person.Name` in order to update the user interface with data from the view model. It also removes the necessity of writing code such as `myViewModel.Person.Name = PersonNameTextBox.Text` to update the model with changes made by the end user in the view.

I will show you how to use the MVVM pattern in your client-side code with Knockout.js in Chapter 12's "Client-Side Data Binding" section.

2-5. Deciding Between MVC and Web Forms

Problem

You're a veteran ASP.NET Web Forms developer that has been using web forms for several years. You are assigned to a new project that is wrapping up requirements gathering, and you are about to begin your design. You need help deciding whether to stick with Web Forms or dive into MVC. If MVC is not yet a standard development framework in your organization, you may need to justify this design decision to management or an enterprise architecture team.

Solution

We briefly discussed both ASP.NET Web Forms and MVC in Recipe 2-1—"Understanding the Microsoft Web Development Ecosystem." In the current recipe, we take a detailed look at the advantages and disadvantages of each, and make the case for MVC.

First, I have to say that Web Forms gave us a pretty good run. I have used Web Forms on many successful projects. Many of them are still in active use almost ten years after they were initially deployed. So I guess you can say, if it's not broken, don't fix it. I guess you can say the same thing about Windows XP. Windows XP came out at about the same time as ASP.NET Web Forms, and like Web Forms Windows XP, it is continually used by millions of Microsoft customers around the world. Indeed, many organizations are sticking with Windows XP even though it is now three additions off from the latest and greatest. On the other hand, if you are still on Windows XP, you are missing out on many of the innovations and productivity improvements that have come with each new edition of Windows. You are also not able to take advantage of some of the new improvements in hardware, such as USB 3, multicore CPUs, and super-capacity hard drives. The plain truth is, even though Windows XP and ASP.NET Web Forms are good systems, they were both designed for a different age of computing.

How It Works

No technology is perfect. They all have things they can do very well, and areas where they lack and can use improvement. This section takes an honest look Web Forms and MVC, and discusses the benefits and drawbacks of each.

Web Forms Advantages

Let's start by reminiscing on the good things about Web Forms:

- *Large talent pool*: If you are building a new team or are looking to expand your current team, it is relatively easy to find developers who are familiar with ASP.NET Web Forms. This is not necessarily true for MVC Framework.

- *Familiar programming model*: The programming model of dragging UI components to a design surface and then double-clicking them to implement the event handler is familiar to developers who have worked with traditional desktop technologies such as Visual Basic.

- *Only a limited knowledge of HTML and JavaScript is required*: Developers do not need to have a deep understanding of HTML, JavaScript, and CSS. Most of the gory details are hidden by the framework.

- *Large control library*: It comes with a huge library of UI components known as *controls*. Everything from text boxes to menus is just a drag-and-drop away from being part of your application.

- *Easy-to-create user controls*: It is very easy to create composite or custom controls using the User Controls feature.

- *Simplified form validation*: Validation controls allow you to create user-friendly forms that ensure that user input is correct before the form is submitted to the server. If the user is a nonhuman bot or a human that has purposely disabled JavaScript to bypass your form validation, the validation controls automatically check the input on the server.

- *Navigation and sitemaps*: Site map providers can be coupled with a breadcrumb control to automatically generate second-level navigation for your site.

- *Separation of concerns*: Code-behind pages separate C# code from the presentation logic.

- *Easy Ajax*: ASP.NET Ajax allows for a modern client-side experience while maintaining the abstraction layer provided by Web Forms.

Web Forms Disadvantages

The preceding list shows that Web Forms has many compelling traits. There are reasons it has been so popular for so long. On the other hand, as the web has evolved, many of the traits that made Web Forms so popular are now becoming its weakness.

- *Talent pool has an outdated skill set*: While it may be true that finding people that know the MVC Framework and Razor syntax are harder to find than those that know Web Forms, the other side of the story is that if you are trying to create a fresh user experience, Web Forms skills may not be able to provide what you need. The people who are creating the next-generation web experience have embraced the web, know HTML, love JavaScript, and can use CSS as their canvas. For this next generation of web developers, Web Form's abstraction is an alien abomination. The MVC Framework, on the other hand, with its clean HTML output and familiar development pattern that is similar to other popular frameworks, such as Rails and Yii, will have a more natural transition.

- *Drag-and-drop programming model less relevant*: While the traditional Visual Basic drag-and-drop programming model is still alive, it is no longer thriving. Most desktop developers have moved on from Win Forms to the XAML-based UI development of WPF. XAML-based desktop applications have as much in common with web development as they do with VB Programming. While you can create a form by dragging and dropping controls to the design surface, if you are creating a UI with any complexity, you are skipping the designer built into Visual Studio, and jumping into a tool like Expression Blend or just switching to code view. Windows 8 and WinRT are moving the Windows UI paradigm even further to the web model by allowing Windows user interfaces to be created using HTML5 and JavaScript. So even though the VB programming model has not completely died, it is fading from relevance in favor of a web-based approach.

- *ASP.NET controls are not as effective as modern client-side libraries*: The large library of UI widgets that come with Web Forms, which seemed like such an asset a few years ago, are also falling out of favor. The JavaScript UI libraries that are freely available from jQuery and others are just plain better than what is available in ASP.NET. They render faster, do not rely on the dreaded ASP.NET view state, and are beautiful. While many of the controls have been updated in the latest release of ASP.NET, most of them still use deprecated rending techniques such as using HTML tables for layouts. They are also difficult, if not impossible, to program against from client-side code.

- • *ASP.NET validation controls less effectively than client-side frameworks*: The ASP.NET validation controls still have one advantage over alternative client-side validation components in that they validate the input server-side as well as the client-side. However, if you are using best practices such as protecting your back-end code from SQL Injection and Cross Site Scripting attacks, the server-side validation is not as critical. On the other hand, client-side libraries such as the jQuery Validation plug-in are very powerful, flexible, and easy to use. It offers 19 built-in validation methods compared to the five built-in validation types in ASP.NET Web Forms. The jQuery plug-in is somewhat easy to extend, whereas creating custom validators in Web Forms can be a tedious task that is difficult to debug. In addition, the markup required to apply validation to your form using the ASP.NET validation controls is cumbersome and makes the HTML difficult to read. This problem is compounded if you use ASP.NET Ajax toolkit validation extenders. Listing 2-1 shows a simple form that is validated using ASP.NET validation controls. Listing 2-2 shows the same form using jQuery validation.

Listing 2-1. Markup for Adding Validation Rules to a Single Form Element Using the Web Forms Validation Controls

```
<asp:TextBox ID="UserName" runat="server" MaxLength="50" CssClass="RegFormFields"
        ToolTip="User names may only contain numbers and letters and must begin with a letter.
Spaces are not allowed in user names." ></asp:TextBox>
<asp:RequiredFieldValidator ID="UserNameRequired" runat="server"
      ControlToValidate="UserName" ErrorMessage="User Name is required."
      ToolTip="User Name is required."
      ValidationGroup="CreateUserWizard1">*</asp:RequiredFieldValidator>
<cc2:ValidatorCalloutExtender
     ID="ValidatorCalloutExtender6"
     runat="server"
     CloseImageUrl="Images/close.gif"
     Enabled="True"
     HighlightCssClass="highlight"
     TargetControlID="UserNameRequired"
     WarningIconImageUrl="Images/alert-large.gif"
     Width="300px">
</cc2:ValidatorCalloutExtender>
<asp:RegularExpressionValidator
     ID="UserNameRegExValidator"
     runat="server"
     ControlToValidate="UserName"
     Display="None"
     ErrorMessage="User names may only contain numbers and letters and must start with a letter."
     Text="*"
     ValidationExpression="^([a-zA-Z])[\w]*$"></asp:RegularExpressionValidator>
<cc2:ValidatorCalloutExtender
     ID="ValidatorCalloutExtender8"
     runat="server"
     CloseImageUrl="Images/close.gif"
     Enabled="True"
     HighlightCssClass="highlight"
     TargetControlID="UserNameRegExValidator"
     WarningIconImageUrl="Images/alert-large.gif"
     Width="300px">
</cc2:ValidatorCalloutExtender>
```

Listing 2-2. HTML Helpers Reduce the Markup in the View to Just a Few Lines. The Validation in This Case Is Applied As Data Annotations on the Model.

```
@Html.TextBoxFor(m => m.UserName)
```

In listing 2-3 you can see the HTML markup that is output by the `Html.TextBoxFor` helper. Notice that the code it generates includes the required HTML attributes required for jQuery validation. You may also notice that all the form data including the contents of the `data-val-regex` property are encoded. This encoding helps prevent malicious users from attacking your web site using techniques such as cross-site-scripting.

Listing 2-3. The HTML Rendered by the HTML Helpers Shown in Listing 2-2

```
<input data-val="true" data-val-regex="User&#32;names&#32;may&#32;only&#32;contain&#32;numbers&#32;
and&#32;letters&#32;and&#32;must&#32;start&#32;with&#32;a&#32;letter." data-val-regex-pattern="
^([a-zA-Z])[\w]*$" data-val-required="The&#32;User&#32;name&#32;field&#32;is&#32;required."
id="UserName" name="UserName" type="text" value="" />
```

- *The code-behind pages often break separation of concerns*: While a disciplined programmer can create clean code-behind pages, in many cases, developers break the separation of concerns by manipulating the user interface in the code-behind page, or even worse—directly manipulating the database from the code behind. This often leads to huge, fragile, unmaintainable, and untestable code.

- *View State*: Web Forms uses a concept known as *view state*, in which a hidden field contains the values of all server-side controls, encoded in a big nasty string. This data is sent on every postback, which slows response times and increases bandwidth usage. For pages that use controls such as a grid view, the view state can be hundreds of kilobytes.

- *Client-side code is difficult to work with*: The client-side code generated by Web Forms is difficult to read and very difficult to code against. First, each UI Widget that you drag onto a page is attached to a DLL with possibly 20 embedded script files. In many cases, using just one of these controls on a page will lead to all 20 of these scripts being included on your page in the form of `<script src="/ScriptResource.axd?d=JzFjHNVTNSRvxnyOuI_HmzgpeGgm-le_2D eNc7ub5pZUcy9A8M9scHh3p580Af72CFevs-15tBuSlQYGR8Y6jhCLDnQaQ1K84GPCFXjTaKWxU1eVz t8qVZ8mueqHNb4FDLOkRw2&amp;t=ffffffff8a8533f5" type="text/javascript"></script>`. When a JavaScript error occurs because of something in one of these mysterious files, it can be very difficult to track the root cause.

- *Another pain point for client-side developers is the automatic naming convention used for client-side elements*: With the default setting, you get ids in the form of `ctl00_LoginView1_ LoginName1`. For nested UI elements, it gets even worse. ASP.NET 4 offers a mechanism to aid in this situation by allowing you to specify how the client ID can be generated.

- *Code-behind pages can't be tested with automated testing tools*: Code-behind pages are simply not designed for this scenario. There is no easy way to abstract the code-behind pages so that a unit test framework can be used. If you were planning on using a test-driven development (TDD) approach with Web Forms, you will have a difficult time.

To summarize, Web Forms' past strengths have become its weaknesses, its abstraction of the web alienates it from the new generation of web developers, and its tightly coupled architecture makes it unusable with modern agile programming techniques.

Another problem with Web Forms, which may have become apparent to you after reading Recipe 2-1, is that there are better alternatives for building quick departmental applications in the Microsoft stack. For example, if you need to create an intranet portal or a simple file-sharing site with workflow s for approval and review, you may want to consider using SharePoint. If you need to quickly put together an application that replaces an Access database currently used by your department, you may want to consider using LightSwitch.

For many of the remaining use cases, the MVC Framework is simply a better fit.

So that we can end this recipe with the positive attributes of the MVC Framework, let's begin with its negatives.

MVC Disadvantages

- *Learning curve*: If you are coming from Web Forms, there is a substantial learning curve associated with moving to MVC. Having to learn a new technology on a deadline is never fun.

- *More complex*: The MVC code separates the code that makes up a page into a minimum of three files. If you are not planning on doing unit testing, and don't like HTML coding, MVC may not be the best choice

- *No drag-and-drop form creation*: If you use the MVC Framework, you will be hand-coding your HTML. In fact, Visual Studio does not even offer a visual designer for MVC Views when using the Razor view engine.

For most teams, the learning curve may be the hardest con to move past. In many corporate environments, the first requirement to be documented is the deadline. The client doesn't know what they want, but they know they need it done by September 1st. Unfortunately, this is a fact of life for developers. There is always going to be new technologies and there will always be the first project using it. The thing to keep in mind is on the long-term impact of the decision. Successful projects typically have a shelf life between five and ten years. The time lost to learning curves is insignificant over the course of the bigger picture. Selecting the wrong framework (just because it's the one you know) can have a significant impact—especially if the application needs to be rewritten in a few years once the inherent problems with Web Forms rears its ugly head.

For the complexity con, I would categorize it as relative. Over the course of a project, a Web Forms code behind that has grown into a 5,000-line catastrophe is much more complex to maintain than the separate files forced upon you by the MVC Framework.

The lack of the drag-and-drop form creation and the lack of server controls will only hurt for the initial prototyping of your forms. If you really rely on this functionality, there are alternatives—such as creating the base HTML in an HTML editor such as Expression Web or even Visual Studio, and then copying the HTML code into the view.

MVC Advantages

- Clean separation of concerns.

- Full control over HTML.

- Fully testable/can use TDD.

- Easy-to-create REST APIs.

- Can use any JavaScript UI Framework.

- Clean HTML, no view state or postback events.

- Extensibility framework presents many opportunities for third-party developers to enhance the framework.

- Built-in scaffolding allows for the rapid creation of maintainable data entry forms. This provides a single point of maintenance when used in conjunction with the Entity Framework.

2-6. Understanding the ASP.NET MVC Framework Architecture

Problem

You have heard a lot about the ASP.NET MVC Framework and you are eager to jump in and start coding, but you don't know where to start. You need a 10,000-foot view on what it is and how to use it.

Solution

The ASP.NET MVC Framework is a web application development framework that leverages the Microsoft .NET Framework managed runtime environment and the core infrastructure provided by ASP.NET. For the users of the systems created using the framework, it provides rich, descriptive URLs and clean client-side code that downloads and renders quickly in a browser. For development teams, it provides agility through rapid application development enabled by Visual Studio, and the stability and maintainability facilitated by using architectural best practices and proven design patterns.

The MVC Framework utilizes the tried-and-true MVC pattern to provide testability and separation of concerns.

If you are not familiar with the MVC pattern or concepts such as "separation of concerns" don't worry—we will go over these in detail later in this chapter.

In the MVC Framework, the ASP.NET MVC model can be any .NET class. It is usually mapped to some sort of persistence store, such as a database, but does not have to be. The model can be as simple as a single primitive type or a complex data structure with many nested collections of types.

ASP.NET MVC views are server-side templates that can be associated with a model. The view is interpreted by the ASP.NET runtime engine to generate the HTTP response that is sent to the web browser. This is usually in the form of HTML, CSS, and JavaScript, but may also be XML—or whatever else you need to send to the client.

ASP.NET MVC controllers are special .NET classes that derive from the `System.Web.Mvc.Controller` class. The controller is the glue that binds the view to the model. It is also responsible for exchanging data between the model and the view.

Visual Studio provides project templates and wizards to help you get started, as well as built-in tools that aid in the process of creating new controllers and views, and binding them to models.

Unlike ASP.NET Web Forms development, MVC does not attempt to abstract the web. This approach gives the developer coarse-grained control of the rendered front-end code. Since the web is no longer abstracted, to get the most out of MVC, you or someone on your team really needs to have a working understanding of HTML, JavaScript, CSS, and jQuery, in addition to knowledge of the .NET Framework.

How It Works

Now that we have the 10,000-foot view, we can dig a little deeper and look at the MVC Framework architecture. Figure 2-4 shows a high-level architecture of an MVC application. In the first block of the diagram, we have custom application code created by you. This consists of your models, controllers, and views. In most applications, we would also have additional, user-created components, such as a data abstraction layer (DAL) and a persistence layer.

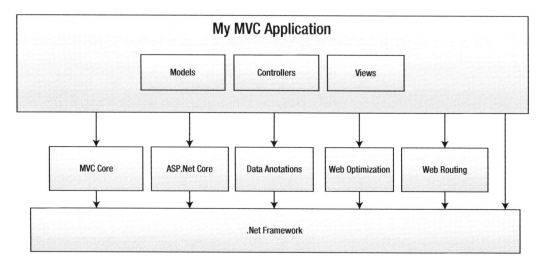

Figure 2-4. MVC conceptual architecture

The next section of the diagram shows major components of ASP.NET and the MVC Framework.

One important feature of the architecture is the loose coupling of components. The dependency structure is very flat, with no hierarchy between components. For example, the MVC Framework components do not have any direct dependencies on the ASP.NET Core. Later in this book, I will show how this architecture makes it easier to apply TDD methodologies with the MVC Framework.

One interesting exercise that you can do, if you happen to have a copy of Visual Studio 2012 Ultimate, is use the Architecture Explorer feature to create a dependency graph of the application. In Figure 2-4, I took a very simple MVC application generated by one of the built-in templates, and then used the Architecture–Create Dependency Graph command to create the diagram. Inside Visual Studio, the graph is interactive and allows you to expand and collapse the different components. When you click any component, Visual Studio draws arrows that show the dependencies for each of the components.

You can also use Visual Studio's object explorer to dig even deeper and see all the classes and methods available inside of each assembly.

Looking at Figure 2-4, you see the following components:

- .NET Framework assemblies

  - *mscorelib.dll*: Contains many of the core libraries for the .NET Framework including system types, reflection, security principals, collections, and system diagnostics.

  - *Microsoft.CSharp*: C# Language constructs.

  - *System.Core*: LINQ and runtime compilation services.

- ASP.NET assemblies

  - *System.Web*: Contains the `HttpApplication` class, web routing, and the security provider framework.

  - *System.ComponentModel.DataAnnotations*: Provides a declarative programming model that allows you to decorate a model with attributes that can be used by the dynamic data scaffolding infrastructure.

36

- MVC Specific assemblies

  - *System.Web.Http*: Contains routing extensions for the MVC Framework.

  - *System.Web.Optimization*: Contains libraries for bundling and compressing CSS and JavaScript files to speed page download and execution times on the client.

  - *System.Web.Mvc*: Contains base classes and default implementations controllers, filters, action results, and other core functionality of the MVC Framework.

In Figure 2-5, you see the diagram from Figure 2-3 with the custom code section expanded. Here the template has created two controllers, three models, and a number of configuration classes that are used for setting up page routing and bundling.

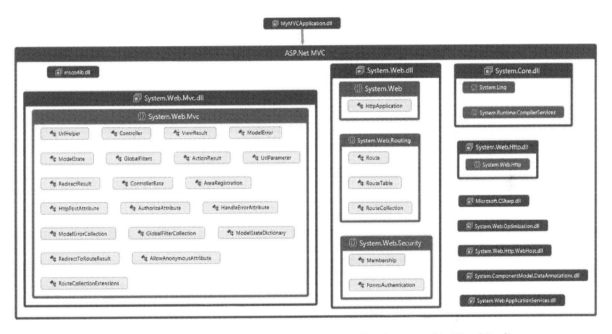

Figure 2-5. *Screenshot of dependency graph for an ASP.NET MVC application created in Visual Studio*

The views are not shown in the diagrams. By default, views are compiled at runtime the first time a page is requested. If these were included, you would see the views shown as a separate assembly on the top section of the diagram, and System.Web.WebPages grouped in the externals section of the diagram.

Figure 2-6 shows a dependency graph created using Visual Studio that shows the dependencies between the components added to a project using the ASP.NET MVC Basic template.

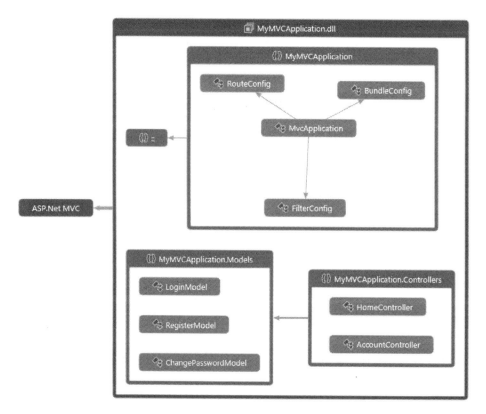

Figure 2-6. *Dependency graph for basic MVC application*

2-7. Understanding Models

Problem

You know that *models* are the M in MVC, but are not sure how they differ from regular C# classes. You would like to get a better understanding of what models are.

Solution

The MVC Framework can use any .NET class as a model. If you wish, you could even use a simple primitive as your model. More often, the model is a complex class that contains many complex types and collections of types.

Although you could use any class, it is usually better to create classes that fulfill the model role. While the primary function of the model is to describe your domain, it can also provide functionality such as calculations, complex validation logic, and managing the state of the entities it describes. You do not want to create classes that perform a dual role and mix together model and controller logic. Please refer to Recipe 2-3—"Understanding the MVC Pattern"—and review the section on allowed communication patterns for general guidelines on how the model should interact with your application.

When you create a project using Visual Studio, it creates a Models folder, and depending on what template you use, it may place several models in the folder for you. When you create your models, you can follow this pattern or, if the complexity of the model warrants it, you can place your model in a separate project.

There are several patterns that you can use when creating your models. Some of the most popular methods include

- Creating simple classes.

- Creating composite classes.

- Using the Entity Framework.

How It Works
Creating Simple Classes

If you follow the pattern used by the Visual Studio team, you can create a set of simple classes with no complex types that consist of nothing but public properties and data annotations. In the Internet application template for example, they have created a file, AccountModel.cs, which contains several model classes. Each class has only enough properties to support the view that it is used with. Each property is decorated with a set of data annotations. These attributes—when used with the HTML helpers—automatically generate the HTML needed to support form validation using jQuery Validation. Listing 2-4 shows the model for the sample registration page found in the MVC Internet Application Template.

Listing 2-4. RegisterModel from MVC Internet Application Template

```
public class RegisterModel
    {
        [Required]
        [Display(Name = "User name")]
        public string UserName { get; set; }

        [Required]
        [DataType(DataType.EmailAddress)]
        [Display(Name = "Email address")]
        public string Email { get; set; }

        [Required]
        [StringLength(100, ErrorMessage = "The {0} must be at least {2} characters long.",
MinimumLength = 6)]
        [DataType(DataType.Password)]
        [Display(Name = "Password")]
        public string Password { get; set; }

        [DataType(DataType.Password)]
        [Display(Name = "Confirm password")]
        [Compare("Password", ErrorMessage = "The password and confirmation password do not match.")]
        public string ConfirmPassword { get; set; }
    }
```

RegisterModel is a very simple class with four properties. It uses data annotations to apply certain attributes to each property. The advantage of this approach is that information such as the field name (whether or not the field is required) and validation errors messages can be maintained in a single file and used with many views. For example, if this model is has a view designed for a PC, another one designed for a tablet, and a web API for a native iPhone application, the information can be applied uniformly across all views.

Creating Composite Models

If a simple model like the one mentioned in the last section will not meet the needs of your views, you can create a composite model. This method is useful in cases when you are displaying a view that needs data from several objects. It may also be useful in situations where you are working with an existing library that does not map well to your view. In this case, the external library that defines your view is not in your project's model folder but in another project.

Rather than trying to using the external classes as your model or jamming random objects into the ViewBag, you can add a class that references one or more classes in your external library. Listing 2-5 shows a simple example of a model that describes items in a guitar case.

Listing 2-5. The WhatsInMyGuitarCaseModel

```
public class WhatsInMyGuitarCaseModel
{
    public List<GuitarPick> Picks { get; set; }
    public List<GuitarCable> Cables { get; set; }
    public Guitar MyGuitar { get; set; }
}
```

One problem that may jump right out at you when viewing this example is that since the external class does not use data annotations, you are not able to benefit from the declarative syntax used in Listing 2-4. We will go over this and other issues in detail in Chapter 7's "Designing a Model" recipes.

Using the Entity Framework

Another way of defining a model is to use the Entity Framework or another object-relational mapper (ORM) to define the model. With this option, your model is also connected to your data abstraction layer. The Entity Framework provides several ways to design your model.

- *Model first*: Uses a designer to define a model, and then generates a database based on the model.

- *Database first*: Creates a model based on a database schema.

- *Code first*: Allows you to use a plain old C# object (POCO) as a model, and then connect it to the Entity Framework using a class derived from DbContext.

We go over these options in detail in Chapter 7.

2-8. Understanding Controllers and Actions
Problem

You need some help understanding the role of the controller in an ASP.NET MVC application.

Solution

Controllers are classes that extend System.Web.Mvc.Controller. By convention, all controllers are placed inside a folder named Controllers inside of the MVC web application project. Inside of the controller are one or more methods that return an ActionResult. These methods are known as Actions.

The controller provides three roles in the MVC application.

- It selects what view should be displayed.

- It allows clean separation between the view and the model by acting as an intermediary between the two.

- It processes data before it is passed along.

How It Works

The process of determining what view is to be displayed can be done in a number of ways. The first is based on a combination of convention and routing logic. By convention, each MVC project has a Views folder. Inside the Views folder, there is a subfolder that matches the name of a controller. For example, the AccountController.cs file that is placed in MVC projects created using the Internet application template has a corresponding views folder named Account. Figure 2-7 shows AccountController.cs and its corresponding view folder.

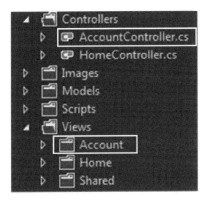

Figure 2-7. *The Account Controller and corresponding view folder*

Inside the account view folder are four views. Each of the views maps to an action inside of the AccountController class. For example, the Login action maps to the view defined in the file Login.cshtml. When the ASP.NET request routing component maps a given URL to an action, unless the logic in the action states otherwise, the view with a file name that matches the method name of the action is displayed.

The second method used to determine what view should be displayed, shown in Listing 2-6, is when logic inside an action method explicitly calls one of the redirect methods and returns the ActionResult instance that results from the method call.

Listing 2-6. Login Action from the AccountController

```
[AllowAnonymous]
[HttpPost]
public ActionResult Login(LoginModel model, string returnUrl)
{
    if (ModelState.IsValid)
    {
        if (Membership.ValidateUser(model.UserName, model.Password))
        {
```

```
                FormsAuthentication.SetAuthCookie(model.UserName, model.RememberMe);
                if (Url.IsLocalUrl(returnUrl))
                {
                    return Redirect(returnUrl);
                }
                else
                {
                    return RedirectToAction("Index", "Home");
                }
            }
            else
            {
                ModelState.AddModelError("", "The user name or password provided is incorrect.");
            }
        }

        // If we got this far, something failed, redisplay form
        return View(model);
}
```

Notice the attributes that precede the action method definition for the Login action. The first attribute—
[AllowAnonymous]—tells ASP.NET that anonymous users may execute this method. It is needed to override the
[Authorize] attribute set on the class definition. The [HttpPost] attribute tells the routing engine to only call this
Action if—in addition to the correct routing data being available—the HTTP verb used in the request is POST. This
allows a separate action to be called on a GET request.

The Redirect(someUrl) method takes any URL as a parameter and returns an ActionResult. It's an
ActionResult that forces the browser to redirect.

The call to RedirectToAction("Index", "Home") takes the name of the action and the name of the controller
as parameters. It instructs the browser to redirect to the URL corresponding to the Controller and Action specified. In
this example, it instructs the browser to redirect the URL to the Index action of the HomeController. ASP.NET MVC is
not returning a view directly when we use either Redirect or RedirectToAction. A new request is then made to that
URL by the browser.

2-9. Understanding Page Routing
Problem

You understand the basics of how MVC controllers work, but are unsure about how the ASP.NET routing engine is
able to map a URL to the correct Controller and execute the proper action.

Solution

The ASP.NET MVC Routing System uses a series of rules listed in a routing table to determine which controller
and action are executed in response to a request. The routing engine intercepts each request and determines if the
URL specified matches a pattern in the routing rules list. Each routing rule contains placeholders that can match
a controller, an action, and any number of variables. When a URL is found to match a pattern, the routing engine
attempts to match the text in the placeholders with a controller. If it cannot find a match, the routing engine throws an
error. The routing engine is also responsible for constructing URLs that can be used to create callbacks to the correct
controller and action that are used in forms and Ajax calls.

How It Works

Starting with MVC 4, the Visual Studio template adds a folder called App_Start to each project. Inside that folder are three classes. Each class contains a static method that is called from inside the global.asax file each time the web application is started. One of the classes, RouteConfig.cs, contains the default routing rules for the application. The code for this file is shown in Listing 2-7.

Listing 2-7. Routes Defined by the Visual Studio MVC Web Application Template

```
public static void RegisterRoutes(RouteCollection routes)
        {
            routes.IgnoreRoute("{resource}.axd/{*pathInfo}");

            routes.MapHttpRoute(
                name: "DefaultApi",
                routeTemplate: "api/{controller}/{id}",
                defaults: new { id = RouteParameter.Optional }
            );

            routes.MapRoute(
                name: "Default",
                url: "{controller}/{action}/{id}",
                defaults: new { controller = "Home", action = "Index", id = UrlParameter.Optional }
            );
        }
```

The first line in the method adds an exclusion pattern that tells the ASP.NET routing component to ignore all paths that start with a file name ending in an .axd extension. In ASP.NET, .axd files represent embedded resource requests that are usually associated with web controls that contain resources such as images and JavaScript files. Since these files would never be associated with a controller, it is best to let the routing engine ignore them.

The next line creates the default routing rules for Web API requests. It defines a routing template for "api/{controller}/{id}" and declares the id parameter as optional. An important thing to notice is that for Web API routes, we use MapHttpRoute rather than MapRoute.

The last line creates a similar route for standard controllers. It defines a routing template for "{controller}/{action}/{id}" and declares the id parameter as optional. This routing template specifies the controller to be used and the action to be called for the route.

For API requests, the URL pattern follows the following convention:

- /api/controllerName: Returns an API result for all items for a given model associated with the controller. For example, an HTTP GET request for the /api/Account URL should contain a list of accounts.

- /api/controllerName/id: Returns an API result for a particular item. For example, the /api/Account/jciliberti URL should return information only for the jciliberti account. Notice that unlike the standard routes, the HTTP routes do not take an Action as a parameter. This is because the API actions are mapped to HTTP verbs such as GET, POST, DELETE, and PUT. We will learn more about the web API features in Chapter 11.

With standard routes, an action is specified in addition to the controller. In some cases, an HTTP verb can also play a role in deciding what action is called.

Another important thing to note about routing rules is that they are processed in order. The first route that matches the URL is the one that is used. Any routes found after the matched route are completely ignored. When adding routes to the routing label, be sure to add specific routes prior to general ones. We cover this topic in greater detail in Chapter 5.

2-10. Understanding View Engines

Problem

You may have heard the term "view engine" used in this book and in other media regarding MVC, but you do not really understand what they are and how they fit into the MVC Framework.

Solution

The MVC Framework has a modular design and allows for each of the modules to be replaced or enhanced by a custom implementation. Of all the modules in MVC, the one that has the most developer interest is the view engine. Many view engines have been created by the community. Some of them emulate popular templating systems from other platforms and others are unique to ASP.NET.

How It Works

A view engine is the MVC Subsystem that defines the expressive syntax for authoring views and a rendering engine that converts the server-side template into HTML markup. MVC 4 ships with two view engines, web forms (.aspx) and Razor (.cshtml).

Each view engine has three main functional components.

- *View engine class*: Implements the IViewEngine interface and provides a mechanism for locating view templates.

- *View class*: Implements the IView interface and provides a method for combining the template with data from the current context and the model to output HTML markup.

- *Template parsing engine*: Parses the template and compiles the view into executable code.

On other platforms, a view engine is sometimes referred to as a *template engine*. This is a component that takes a text file that usually contains a mix of HTML markup and scripts, parses the file, and then executes the code in the file to render the results. On development platforms that do not use the MVC pattern, the templating engine is the primary interface for developing the application. An example of a templating engine is Classic ASP.

By making the view engine modular, the MVC team has made it possible to completely change the way views are constructed and rendered without impacting the rest of the infrastructure. For example, if you install the NHaml view engine, you could create views in a similar fashion to creating Haml views on Ruby on Rails.

The first component of the trio that makes up a view engine is a class that implements the IViewEngine interface. This interface is defined in Listing 2-8.

Listing 2-8. The View Engine Interface

```
public interface IViewEngine
{
   ViewEngineResult FindPartialView(
      ControllerContext controllerContext,
      string partialViewName,
      bool useCache
   );
```

```
ViewEngineResult FindView(
    ControllerContext controllerContext,
    string partialViewName,
    string masterName,
    bool useCache
);

    void ReleaseView(ControllerContext controllerContext, IView view);
}
```

The IViewEngine interface is pretty simple. It consists of three methods. Two of them are for finding views and the last is for releasing the view from memory. Notice both of the Find methods contain an argument for bool useCache. An implementation can use this mechanism to allow the view engine to pull a previously rendered version of the view from the cache so that it does not need to be rendered again.

There are two find methods, one for finding a view and another for finding a partial view. A partial view is a normal view that can be nested inside a parent view. Another thing to notice is that the only difference between the method definitions is that one does not include an augment for the masterName. Both methods return a type of ViewEngineResult. With this in mind, it is possible to have any view act as a partial view.

The second component that the view class implements is the IView interface (see Listing 2-9). This interface has a single method called Render.

Listing 2-9. The IView Interface

```
public interface IView
{
    void Render(
        ViewContext viewContext,
        TextWriter writer
    };
)
```

The ViewContext contains all the data that needs to be passed to the template parsing engine component, including the controller context, the form context, the HTTP context, route data, view data, and information about any parent actions.

The final component, the template parsing engine, does not implement any predefined interface. This allows developers to do whatever they want. This component is typically by far the most complex of three components and may consist of hundreds of classes. If you ever endeavor to create your own view engine, you will spend the majority of your time with this component.

2-11. Choosing a View Engine
Problem

You have decided to use MVC for your next project. You heard that there are many view engines that can be used with the framework. You would like to know which engines are available and which one you should select for your project. You also would like to know if it is better for your organization to standardize on a particular view engine, or should you always pick the best view engine to meet the particular requirements.

Solution

Since the release of MVC 3.0, Microsoft and most of the development community have championed the Razor view engine. It has become the de facto default for ASP.NET MVC development. It is also the view engine of choice for WebMatrix's ASP.NET Web Pages. For most people looking to start a new project using MVC, the Razor view engine is probably the best choice. Teams that are porting an MVC 2.0 application to MVC 4.0 are probably better-off staying with the Web Forms view engine. I do not recommend mixing multiple view engines in a single project. This is because it will make the project more difficult to maintain and require members of the team to know both view engines.

As far as standardizing on an enterprise scale, I do believe that there are tangible benefits to having your organization standardize on not only a view engine, but also coding standards and development methodologies. While you can argue that a certain view engine may fit a particular problem better than Razor, in the long run, having the ability to move team members across projects and across organizations will in most cases reap greater benefits. It also fosters opportunities to create shared components, libraries, and documentation that can be used across your organization. For example, it is possible to create a corporate NuGet repository and then create commands that can do things such as apply the corporate branding to your site.

The one downside of this approach is its possible impact on agility, especially when you need to incorporate new technologies into the standard. This problem is addressable by ensuring that standards are reviewed and updated by a cross-organizational architecture review board on a quarterly basis. It is also important to have an exception policy that allows teams to try new approaches, technologies, and languages when adequate justification is presented. The exception policy should encourage innovation but discourage "résumé-driven development." Résumé-driven development is an anti-pattern where developers select new technologies either out of personal curiosity or because they want to be able to add it to the skills section of their resume, even though it does necessarily fit the needs of the project.

Even though Razor will meet the needs of most, it is not the only game in town. If fact, view engines have been created to cater to many programming styles and languages. Next, I'll describe many of the more popular view engines, their pros and cons, and the situations where they make the most sense to use.

How It Works

This section will help you to understand the advantages and disadvantages of some of the major view engines.

Web Forms View Engine

The Web Forms view engine was the only view engine supported by Microsoft in the first edition of the MVC Framework and the default engine for MVC 1.0. It used the same parsing engine and syntax as regular ASP.NET Web Forms.

The main advantage of this view engine is that it is familiar to experienced web forms developers. It is also mature and robust. It is installed by default along with a set of project templates that use it when you install the MVC Framework or use one of the newer versions of Visual Studio that come with MVC by default. It also has strong IntelliSense support and supports any language with an associated CodeDom provider. This includes Boo, C#, F#, Nemerle, and VB.NET.

The main disadvantages of this view engine is that since it looks like regular ASP.NET Web Forms, it may invite some old habits, especially with web forms developers just starting to use MVC. For example, a developer may add a web control to a page rather than standard markup. In some cases, the page may actually compile but it will not have the expected behavior since MVC does not support the page life cycle that most controls depend on. Another detractor for the Web Forms view engine is that it does not always encourage the rendering of well-formed HTML. While it is possible to create messy HTML with any view engine, the Web Forms engine is more inclined to create what some call "tag soup." For example, nested HTML tables and inline styles mixed with randomly inserted script tags and JavaScript.

Another weakness of Web Forms is its relative verbosity when compared to some of the other engines. In some cases, when compared to an engine such as Razor, you may need to write substantially more code to achieve the same objective.

Razor View Engine

As stated earlier, Razor is now the first choice for most people. It first shipped with MVC Framework 3.0 and is included in the new versions of Visual Studio. The following are a few reasons why you may want to choose this engine as your standard.

- *Simple syntax*: It's compact, expressive, fluid, and easy to learn. The parser is smart. It can automatically infer server-side code blocks without the need to explicitly encapsulate them in special characters.

- *Supports C# and VB.NET*: Server-side code blocks can be written in either C# or VB.NET.

- *Great IntelliSense*: Visual Studio provides surprisingly good statement completion for Razor.

- *Automatic XSS protection*: XSS is a technique used by hackers to inject code into your application. Razor protects against this type of attack by HTML encoding output emitted from server-side code blocks.

- *Layout pages*: This is a similar concept to Master Pages in web forms. It allows you to create a layout page that contains the boilerplate code that needs to be made available across a set of pages.

- *Unit testable*: The Razor parser and view engine can be instantiated directly inside a unit test without running into problems like missing dependencies. This can be used to verify that the expected HTML code is output when a test model is passed in. This does not help with unit testing any JavaScript embedded in the page, however.

- *Lots of example code*: Most of the code samples you find on the web and in books have examples in Razor. You may have a bit more luck Googling your way out of a coding jam using Razor rather than a less popular engine such as Spark.

The only real disadvantage for Razor is that if you are coming from the Web Forms world, it will take you a few weeks of coding before you get your bearings straight. For people new to web development or new to ASP.NET, most find Razor easier to learn than Web Forms.

The Spark View Engine

Before Razor was selected as the default view engine by Microsoft, the Spark view engine was a close second in terms of popular alternatives to Web Forms. The Spark engine attempts to allow HTML rather than blocks of server code dominate. It allows the server code to fit seamlessly into the HTML. It is a mature engine and one of the most feature-rich of the alternative view engines available.

One of the nice things about the Spark engine is that it allows for the creation of clean, readable views. Its binding feature can potentially remove all inline code from your view. It avoids the use of escape characters, placing all language constructs into HTML elements and attributes. For example, an `if` statement would be written as follows:

```
<if condition="Model.HasNextPage">
...
</if>
```

If you have ever used Cold Fusion (an old server-side templating engine created by Macromedia), the Spark view engine syntax engine would feel very familiar.

The only major criticism of Spark is that it can be difficult to differentiate server-side template logic from normal HTML. This can cause headaches when working with a designer.

You can learn more about the Spark view engine at http://sparkviewengine.com.

There is an example later in this chapter that shows how to add Spark to your project.

NHaml

NHaml (pronounced enamel) is a .NET port of the Haml view engine for Ruby on Rails. Haml, which stands for HTML Abstraction Markup Language, was designed to replace inline templating systems such as PHP and Classic ASP. Unlike most view engines, the mark up does not require the use of angle brackets at all. It instead relies on the level of indentation to determine where elements and code blocks begin. The primary principle of Haml is that "markup should be beautiful." There is a saying that beauty is in the eye of the beholder, but for many Rails developers, Haml is an invaluable tool.

Even though NHaml is a port of Haml, the actual syntax differs quite substantially. In the .NET version, in addition to using % symbols to designate elements, NHaml also makes use of the HTML helpers that are part of the MVC Framework.

The main benefit of NHaml is that the markup is very compact, and once you get used to it, easy to read. Out of all the view engines currently available for MVC, NHaml is arguably the most compact.

The NHaml port is a good fit if you ever need to port a Rails project to MVC. Even though most of the views would not work out of the box, it is a matter of tweaking the syntax rather than a complete rewrite.

Unfortunately, other than a basic syntax highlighter add-in, there is limited support for NHaml in Visual Studio. There is no IntelliSense, and the user community for NHaml is relatively small.

You can find out more about NHaml at http://code.google.com/p/nhaml/.

You can get more information about the original Haml from http://haml.info/.

Other View Engines

The following lists a few other view engines that are available for download.

- *Bellevue*: Uses pure HTML without any additional tags or syntax, and uses CSS-like syntax to inject dynamic content into the HTML. Bellevue is still in the prototype stage, and according to the author, it "contains hacks." More information about Bellevue can be found www.ope.ag/Bellevue/Page/intro.

- *Brail*: A port from the MonoRail project, Brail is designed to use the Boo programming language. Boo is a new object-oriented statically-typed language with a Python-inspired syntax. More information about Brail can be found at http://mvccontrib.codeplex.com/wikipage?title=Brail&ProjectName=mvccontrib.

  Information about Boo can be found at http://boo.codehaus.org.

- *Hasic*: A view engine for people who love Visual Basic. It essentially makes your views into VB.NET classes and uses VB.NET XML literals for the page markup. More information about Hasic can be found at www.assembla.com/wiki/show/hasic.

- *NDjango*: A view engine based on the popular Python-based template engine Django, but uses F# rather than Python. It may be a good choice for functional programming aficionados. More information about NDjango can be found at http://ndjango.org/index.php?title=NDjango_Home.

- *SharpTiles*: A partial port of the JavaServer Pages Standard Tag Library (JSTL). It works with both ASP.NET and MonoRail. It can also be used as a standalone template engine. SharpTiles is fast, testable, and provides high usability of components. More information about SharpTiles can be found at www.sharptiles.org.

2-12. Understanding Razor Syntax

Problem

You decided that you want to use the Razor view engine for you new project, but are intimidated by the new syntax. You would like to gain a solid grasp of the fundamentals before jumping into coding.

Solution

Razor was designed to be easy to learn. It builds on your knowledge of HTML and C#, and includes simple syntax for adding variables and code blocks to your page. The easiest way to demonstrate razor's syntax is to walk you through the basic syntax elements using a series of short examples. This section will serve as a basic Razor primer. More advanced examples are presented throughout the book.

How It Works

In this section, we review the major syntax elements used in Razor.

Variables

To include a variable into a view, simply prefix the variable name with an @ symbol.

```
<span>It is now @DateTime.Now</span>
```

This code prints the date and the time on the page.

Control Statements

Listing 2-10 shows a simple if-else statement. Notice the lack of explicit code block delimiters. Razor's smart parser is able to automatically determine sever-side script blocks from HTML.

Listing 2-10. If Statement

```
@if (Model.MyGuitar.HasWhammyBar)
    {
        <span>My Guitar has a @Model.MyGuitar.WhammyBarType Whammy Bar</span>
    }
    else
    {
        <span>No Whammy bars on this guitar</span>
    }
```

In this statement, not only is the Razor engine able to detect the `if` statement, but it was also able to detect the variable embedded in the `<span>` tag.

Loops

Listing 2-11 shows a simple loop statement. This time, I am showing a list of cables in my guitar case.

Listing 2-11. The foreach Statement

```
<ol>
@foreach(var cable in Model.Cables)
{
    <li>
        Brand : @cable.Vendor<br />
        Type : @cable.ConnectorType<br />
        Length : @cable.Length

    </li>
}
</ol>
```

In this example, we see that the opening tags for the unordered list are defined outside of the loop; the data regarding our cables is displayed inside of the loop. The amazing thing about using Razor with Visual Studio is that the IntelliSense experience is similar to working in a .cs file. It automatically determined that the cable variable was of the GuitarCable type and automatically suggested the available members.

HTML Helpers

The MVC Framework comes with a number of HTML helpers that work with the data annotations defined on your model to significantly reduce the amount of code your solution requires.

Listing 2-12 shows the code from the Register view that comes with the Internet Application template.

Listing 2-12. Using HTML Helpers to Simplify Creating a Form

```
@using (Html.BeginForm()) {
    @Html.ValidationSummary()

    <fieldset>
        <legend>Registration Form</legend>
        <ol>
            <li>
                @Html.LabelFor(m => m.UserName)
                @Html.TextBoxFor(m => m.UserName)
            </li>
            <li>
                @Html.LabelFor(m => m.Email)
                @Html.TextBoxFor(m => m.Email)
            </li>
            <li>
                @Html.LabelFor(m => m.Password)
                @Html.PasswordFor(m => m.Password)
            </li>
            <li>
                @Html.LabelFor(m => m.ConfirmPassword)
                @Html.PasswordFor(m => m.ConfirmPassword)
            </li>
        </ol>
        <input type="submit" value="Register" />
    </fieldset>
```

The first line of the example shows use of the @using(Html.BeginForm()). The @using statement is a wrapper that can be used with helpers that feature begin and end tags. In this case, it renders the beginning and end tags of the HTML form.

The @Html.ValidationSummary helper generates the code that displays the validation summary created by jQuery validation or validation done from the controller.

The @Html.LabelFor and @Html.TextBox take a Lambda expression as a parameter. The HTML helper uses reflection to pull data from the data annotations that decorate the RegisterModel and combine them with the data contained in the object passed into the Lambda expression to generate a form element. For this to work, data annotations must be added to the model that specifies the validation rules.

The HTML code in Listing 2-13 is output as a result of Listing 2-12.

Listing 2-13. HTML Code Generated by the Razor Markup in Listing 2-12

```
<form action="/Account/Register" method="post"><div class="validation-summary-valid" data-valmsg-
summary="true"><ul><li style="display:none"></li>
</ul></div>    <fieldset>
        <legend>Registration Form</legend>
        <ol>
            <li>
                <label for="UserName">User name</label>
                <input data-val="true" data-val-required="The&#32;User&#32;name&#32;field&#32;is&#32
;required." id="UserName" name="UserName" type="text" value="" />
            </li>
            <li>
                <label for="Email">Email address</label>
                <input data-val="true" data-val-required="The&#32;Email&#32;address&#32;field&#32;is
&#32;required." id="Email" name="Email" type="text" value="" />
            </li>
            <li>
                <label for="Password">Password</label>
                <input data-val="true" data-val-length="The&#32;Password&#32;must&#32;be&#32;a
t&#32;least&#32;6&#32;characters&#32;long." data-val-length-max="100" data-val-length-min="6"
data-val-required="The&#32;Password&#32;field&#32;is&#32;required." id="Password" name="Password"
type="password" />
            </li>
            <li>
                <label for="ConfirmPassword">Confirm password</label>
                <input id="ConfirmPassword" name="ConfirmPassword" type="password" />
            </li>
        </ol>
        <input type="submit" value="Register" />
    </fieldset>
</form>
```

Code Blocks

Code blocks are sections of the view that contain only C# code and no markup. While inside a code block, all rules of the project's programming language must be followed. With C# projects, for example, a semicolon is required at the end of each statement.

CHAPTER 2 ■ UNDERSTANDING ASP.NET MVC

Code blocks begin with @{ and end with }. There is no predefined limit on the number of lines of code in a code block. Keep in mind that the only code that we should add to our views is view logic. You should not perform calculations or manipulate the model while in the view. An example of a code block is shown in Listing 2-14.

Listing 2-14. Example of a Code Block

```
@{
    ViewBag.Title = "Details";
}
```

Explicit Code Nuggets

As smart as Razor is, it can get confused when we do silly things like attempt to use a variable inside of an HTML attribute. Suppose, for example, that you had an image that used productId as the file name.

```
<img src=/media/products/guitars/gibson/lespaul/@model.ProductId.png />
```

In this case, Razor will fail to recognize that @model.ProductId is a variable name, and incorrectly renders the variable name instead of the value.

This can be corrected by wrapping the variable with a set of parentheses.

```
<img src=/media/products/guitars/gibson/lespaul/@(model.ProductId).png />
```

Explicit Markup

Sometimes you may want to have plain text mixed in with your code. Without the presence of angle brackets, Razor has a difficult time finding the end of your code block. To get around this problem, the Razor team invented the @: and the <text> block. The @: symbol is used for single-line explicit markup. <text> is used for multiple lines of markup. An example of explicit markup is shown in Listing 2-15.

Listing 2-15. Example of Explicit Markup

```
@if(12==12){
    @: I have @Model.Picks.Count in my guitar case
};
<text>
Only the best guitar players play @Model.MyGuitar.Model
    and we know who we are.
</text>
```

The syntax allows code nuggets to be mixed with the explicit markup.
It should be noted that the markup shown in Listing 2-16 will fail.

Listing 2-16. Example of Invalid Explicit Markup

```
@if(12==12){
    @: I have @Model.Picks.Count in my guitar case};
```

Since the @: symbol states that all content on this line is markup, the "};" is rendered as markup and the page will have a validation error because the if statement is missing a closing brace.

52

Comments

Every coding language needs a way to add comments. In Razor, we use the following syntax to create a comment:

```
@* This is my comment. *@
```

All code and markup between the symbols is commented out. This is useful for when you want to add a comment to your code, but do not want it to appear in the markup sent to the client.

2-13. Installing an Alternative View Engine

Problem

You have a set of challenges in your current project that could be better met with a different view engine. You have done some research and found that the Spark view engine best meets your need. Now you need to know how to add the view engine to your project.

Solution

To use the Spark view engine, first you need to create an ASP.NET MVC project in Visual Studio. You can then use the NuGet package manager to add Spark to your project. Once Spark has been added, you need to modify your configuration to apply settings for Spark, and add Spark to the MVC view engines collection in the application_start method of your project. Once this has been done, you can begin using Spark rather than Razor or ASPX for all your new views.

How It Works

This section provides step-by-step instructions on how to get started using Spark in Visual Studio 2012.

1. Launch Visual Studio and use the Ctrl+Shift+N keyboard shortcut to launch the New Project dialog box.

2. In the New Project dialog box, select the ASP.NET MVC 4 Web Application template and call the project **SparkDemo**.

3. On the Select a Template screen, choose the Basic template, keeping the Razor view engine selected. Since Visual Studio does not have built-in templates for Spark, you will need to use one of the built-in template types. Razor has been selected in this example since it is slightly easier to modify for use with Spark than the ASPX template. Click OK to create your project. Visual Studio processes the request for several minutes until your project is ready.

4. In the Solution Explorer, right-click References, and then select Manage NuGet Packages.

5. On the left-hand side, expand the Online node and select "NuGet official package source". Once the list of packages appears, click in the search box and type **Spark**. After a few moments, the list should show something like Figure 2-8.

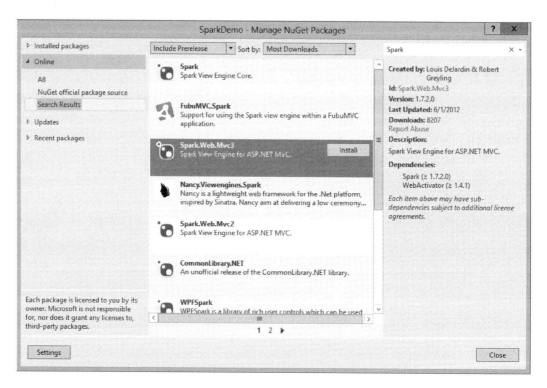

Figure 2-8. *Find Spark in NuGet*

6. Select the Spark.Web.Mvcx package that matches your project type. If you are targeting MVC 4, you need to choose the Spark.Web.MVC4 package. Click Install. If all goes well, it should see a message stating that you have successfully installed the package. Green check marks appear next to the packages that you have installed. Notice, as shown in Figure 2-9, that in addition to Spark.Web.MVC4, the Spark view engine core has also been added to your project.

Figure 2-9. *NuGet after Spark is installed*

7. Close the NuGet Package Manager. You can now use Solution Explorer to see the changes that the Spark NuGet packages made to the project. If you expand the References node in Solution Explorer, notice that the assemblies Spark and Spark.Web.MVC have been added to the project. Inside the App_Start folder's Views\Shared folder is a file named _global.spark.

8. In order for ASP.NET MVC to use the Spark view engine, it must be added to the application's view engine list. To do this, open the global.asax.cs file by double-clicking global.asax in Solution Explorer. Change the Application_Start() method to look like Listing 2-17.

Listing 2-17. Adding the Spark View Engine to Application_Start()

```
//using statements removed for brevity
using Spark.Web.Mvc;

namespace Ch2.R_13SparkDemo
{
    public class MvcApplication : System.Web.HttpApplication
    {
        protected void Application_Start()
        {
            AreaRegistration.RegisterAllAreas();
```

```
        ViewEngines.Engines.Add(new SparkViewFactory());
        FilterConfig.RegisterGlobalFilters(GlobalFilters.Filters);
        RouteConfig.RegisterRoutes(RouteTable.Routes);
        BundleConfig.RegisterBundles(BundleTable.Bundles);
      }
    }
  }
```

Two lines of code have been added to Global.aspx.cs. The first change is to add a reference to Spark.Web.MVC. The second adds a new SparkViewFactory to the view engines list.

9. Next, you need to modify the web.config file so that it adds a configuration section for any configuration settings you wish to make for the Spark engine. To do this double-click, web.config from Solution Explorer and modify it to look like Listing 2-18.

Listing 2-18. Adding a Configuration Section

```
...
<configSections>
    ...
    <section name="spark" type="Spark.Configuration.SparkSectionHandler, Spark"/>
</configSections>
    <spark>
            <compilation debug="true"/>
            <pages automaticEncoding="true">
                    <namespaces>
                            <add namespace="System"/>
                            <add namespace="System.Collections.Generic"/>
                            <add namespace="System.Linq"/>
                            <add namespace="System.Web.Helpers" />
                            <add namespace="System.Web.Mvc" />
                            <add namespace="System.Web.Mvc.Ajax" />
                            <add namespace="System.Web.Mvc.Html" />
                            <add namespace="System.Web.Optimization" />
                            <add namespace="System.Web.Routing" />
                            <add namespace="System.Web.WebPages" />
                    </namespaces>
            </pages>
    </spark>
    ...
```

Listing 2-18 adds a configuration for Spark and adds a number of settings, such as enabling debug mode and enabling automatic HTML encoding to all dynamic output. This setting helps prevent malicious users from injecting harmful client-side code into your site. It also adds a set of name spaces that will be automatically included in all your views. A full list of possible settings can be found on the Spark web site (http://sparkviewengine.com/documentation/).

10. You can now begin creating your site. For this example, we will create a simple Hello World site. To do this, first create the Home controller by right-clicking the Controllers folder in Solution Explorer. Select Add ➤ New Controller from the pop-up menu. Change the controller name to **HomeController**. Select the Empty MVC Controller template, and then click the Add button. A new class that extends Controller will be added to the project. The class will contain a single method named Index.

11. Now you can create your first Spark view. To do this, right-click the Views folder and then select Add ➤ New Folder. Name the folder **Home**. Right-click the folder you just created, and then select Add ➤ View. Name the view **Index**. Notice in the View Engine drop-down list there is no option for Spark. In fact, there is no built-in support at all for Spark in Visual Studio. Uncheck the "Use a layout or master page" check box. This ensures that the new view contains boilerplate HTML, including html, head, and body tags. Click the Add button. Visual Studio creates a new file, Index.cshtml, and opens the file for you.

12. Remove any Razor code that the template added to the file, then right-click the file in Solution Explorer and rename it from Index.cshtml to **Index.spark**. Click Yes in the "Are you sure" check box. ASP.NET MVC uses the file extension to decide which view engine to use to process the file.

13. Modify Index.spark so that it looks like Listing 2-19, and then press the F5 key. After a few moments, your web browser will open, showing the simple web page you just created.

Listing 2-19. Index.spark

```
<!DOCTYPE html>
<html>
<head>
    <meta name="viewport" content="width=device-width" />
    <title>Hello World Spark</title>
</head>
<body>
    <div>
        Hello World from the Spark View Engine
        <br />
        The current time in our data center is : ${DateTime.Now}.
    </div>
</body>
</html>
```

From this example, you can see that it is relatively easy to use an alternative view engine. In some cases, view engines such as Spark may be a better fit for your project. Unfortunately, for most of the view engines not officially supported by Microsoft, you will not have the rich experience inside of Visual Studio.

One important thing to take note of from this recipe is that other than the creation and syntax used for the views, other aspects of the project, such as creation of the controllers, are unchanged.

CHAPTER 3

Setting Up Your Environment

3-1. Acquiring the Ideal Developer Hardware

Problem

You are new to Microsoft development and want to know what you need to get started. You are unsure if your current computer will make a good developer machine. If you need to upgrade, how do you justify the cost of this hardware to your management?

Solution

The ideal developer machine has a powerful multicore CPU, fast and abundant disk drives, and copious amounts of RAM; is attached to multiple large flat-screen monitors; and needs a video card powerful enough to drive them.

As an ASP.NET MVC developer, you are writing software that runs on the server or in the cloud. The software that you create may someday be used by thousands of people, and it may become an essential asset to your company. The tools that you use to create and test this software will put a much greater demand on your PC than a typical word processor or web browser. For certain development activities, you may need to run several operating systems at once inside of virtual machines. Your development tools will have many windows and toolbars, and you will often need to work with many open documents at once. To avoid the introduction of bugs that appear in production but can't be reproduced on your developer machine, your development environment should match your deployment environment as closely as possible.

Businesses make technology purchasing decisions based on return on investment (ROI). To justify your ideal developer hardware, you need to write a business case that demonstrates how ROI will be achieved through better developer productivity.

How It Works

Having a proper development machine is an important factor in being successful as a developer. If you are developing on an underpowered machine running the wrong operating system and do not have proper rights on that environment, you and your team may waste a lot of time fighting your environment.

The low-cost machine that your company is giving out to its sales force is not necessarily a good fit for a developer. If it's been five years since your last PC upgrade, chances are the machine you are using may not be the best fit either.

Proper hardware for a developer is not difficult to justify. According to PayScale (www.payscale.com), the average salary for a .NET developer is around $87,000 per year. Assuming you work five days a week and eight hours a day, this would work out to approximately $42 per hour. If having proper development hardware saves you two hours per day, your company would save $420 per week. For a large project that is scheduled to take six months, your saving would be over $10,000. Since the delta between the laptops purchased for your sales force and a proper developer machine is less than $500, it should be a no-brainer for your company to approve a hardware upgrade, especially for senior developers and architects who are likely making considerably more than $42 per hour.

The following are a few other things that you can add to your nonstandard hardware acquisition justification proposal:

- Your deployment targets are 64-bit servers with dual six-core, hyper-threaded CPU and 128GB of RAM. You plan to use advanced asynchronous and parallel programming techniques, but they are impossible to debug properly on your current machine.

- Your deployment target is a 64-bit operating system. With the current 32-bit OS on your laptop, it is impossible for you to know how garbage collection will affect your application when it is consuming a large amount of memory.

- You would like to use Visual Studio's performance profiling tools, but the results of the profiling are inconclusive on your current environment.

Having the right hardware is an important part of a developer's toolkit. It keeps you motivated and allows you to get your work done faster. The people who make hardware purchasing decisions at your company may not be aware of your special requirements. In most cases, it does not hurt to ask for what you need. The worst thing they can do is say no.

If you are an independent developer who buys your own hardware, the augment stated previously applies to your budget as well. The only difference is that the equation changes to how many projects can you complete within a given time period. If anything, this is more critical to you if you are working on fixed-price engagements.

Developer Machine Hardware

Before you come up with your justification document, you need to spec out your development machine.

The first decision you need to make is whether to get a desktop computer or a laptop. Well, in a perfect world the answer would be, "Yes! One of each, please." At companies like Microsoft and Google, this is actually standard issue. If you do have to choose, for most of us, a laptop computer is the best choice. Laptops are less powerful and more expensive than the equivalent desktops, but the flexibility they bring you is well worth the compromise. This is especially true if your employer allows you to work from home.

The laptop should have a compatible docking station, a good video card, fast CPU, lots of disk space and RAM, and it should have a high-definition display.

For CPU, you should favor power over battery life. In most situations, you code with your laptop plugged in. If you go with an Intel processor, this means at least a Core i5, but the Quad Core i7 is best. Much of the two hours saved will come from the smaller amount of time it takes between hitting F5 and having your page appear on the screen. A powerful CPU is a major part of that equation.

A large amount of RAM is also important, especially if you plan to run one or more virtual machines locally. Four gigabytes is the absolute minimum, but try to get 12GB or more if you can.

Disk space is the next major concern. This is where a desktop is great. Many of the high-end desktops have built-in RAID controllers. In a perfect world, you would have a 250GB SSD for your system drive and three 1TB drives configured as RAID 5. On a laptop, you should choose an option that has both an SSD and a standard hard disk. By using an SSD, boot times are significantly faster. On a laptop with an SSD running Windows 8, you can have a cold boot time of less than seven seconds. This is amazing when you consider the fact that many corporate machines take as long as three minutes to boot. In addition to the built-in hard drives, it is also nice to have an external drive connected via a USB 3 or Thunderbolt. You can get a 4TB external drive for under $150. These are ideal for archiving your virtual machines and backing up your PC. Even if you have adequate network storage, your network administrator will never be happy to see you copying a 200GB VHD over the LAN.

The laptop does not need to be aesthetically pleasing. This is a machine for getting work done, not for impressing the baristas at your local coffee shop. You should not care if your PC is ugly, but you should pay attention to the overall build quality. Your high-end laptop is useless if it breaks every time you sneeze.

Touch Screens

Another feature that will become increasingly common on Windows PCs is touch screens. In the past, this was a novelty, and even people who bought a PC with a touch screen never actually used the touch part. All this has changed with Windows 8. With the Microsoft Surface and hundreds of other touch-friendly Windows 8 devices hitting the market, millions of iPads, and 100 million smartphones and iPod touch devices, you can almost guarantee that someone will access your application with a touch-first device. If you are developing an application that will be exposed to the public over the Internet, there will likely be a significant number of touch users.

Whether or not you should have a touch screen on your development machine has to do with how much time you spend developing user interface components. My rule of thumb is if you spend more than 30 percent of your time developing user interface components, you should have a touch device. This does not necessarily mean that your main developer box has a touch screen. You could have a secondary device like an iPad or similar device to use for sanity checks that ensure your application is usable in touch-only or touch-first use cases.

Displays

Last but not least is your display. On the laptop itself, I recommend a 15-inch display. Seventeen-inch screens are OK, but in my opinion, a 17-inch laptop is just too clunky to carry around. In addition to the laptop display, you should have a docking station that supports two external monitors. Be careful and be sure that the connectors are either DVI or DisplayPort. This is required get the full resolution of your display. VGA ports simply do not cut the mustard for high-resolution displays.

In a perfect world, you would have two, 24-inch 1080p high-definition displays. You use one for Visual Studio maximized in its full glory and the other monitor for everything else.

Figure 3-1 shows an ideal developer workstation. It includes a high-power desktop powering two 24-inch monitors. On the left side, there is an MS Build edition of the Samsung Series 7 Slate running Windows 8. On the right side, there is an older, clunky laptop running a standard corporate machine image.

Figure 3-1. A "perfect world" developer setup

Having the two large displays gives you a lot of real estate for all your windows. It allows you to have everything you need right in front of you. It saves a lot of time that is often wasted Alt-Tabbing around looking for a particular window.

The touch-screen computer allows you to do some basic touch-compatibility testing on your application's user interface.

Having the clunky laptop is an important part of the perfect world setup scenario. It helps you avoid the dreaded "but it works on my machine" syndrome. This is a common problem where testers and sometimes users find problems with your application, but the developer is unable to reproduce the problem on a development machine. It should not be difficult to acquire an old laptop that has recently retired from the field. An alternative to having a physical laptop is to have a virtual machine running the desktop image. Having the extra laptop is beneficial because in addition to giving you an accurate testing PC, it is also provides additional screen real-estate.

In addition to what is shown here, you can also have a number of virtual machines running in the data center to use for specific tasks such as testing on old web browsers.

Every bug found by the developer and fixed on the spot saves hours of extra work compared to when it is sent to QA (quality assurance), where it needs to be documented, sent back to you to be verified, and so forth.

Mouse and Keyboard

A quality mouse and keyboard are often overlooked components of the developer workstation. They should be ergonomic and comfortable to use for long periods. Wireless peripherals should be avoided in favor of wired devices that plug into your docking station or USB hub. Wireless keyboards require batteries that seem to always die at the worst times. They are also subject to interference, which can result in typos and latency.

Summary

To summarize everything we've covered thus far, Table 3-1 shows a hardware inventory list to give to your manager.

Table 3-1. *A Hardware Inventory List*

Quantity	Item	Description
1	Developer Laptop	CPU: Intel Quad Core i7 12GB RAM 250GB SSD & 500GB standard hard drive 15-inch display USB 3 or Thunderbolt support Touch screen (optional) 8 points or more capacitive touch Windows 8 Professional 64-bit
1	Docking Station	Supports 2 DVI or DisplayPort for external displays
2	LCD Display	24-inch, 1920 ×1080 high-definition display
1	External Hard Drive	2TB–4TB with either USB 3 or Thunderbolt support
1	Test Laptop	Company standard-build (should be of quality equal to the worst machine in the field)
1	USB Keyboard	Ergonomic full-sized keyboard comfortable to use for long periods
1	USB Mouse	A mouse with programmable extra buttons (you can configure them to map to hotkeys in Visual Studio)

3-2. Choosing an Operating System for Your Development Machine

Problem

In a perfect world, your developer machine uses the same operating system and configuration as your production server. Unfortunately, this is not always possible. For example, if you are deploying your application to Windows Azure, there is no option for installing Azure on your desktop. Another problem you may have is that you are supporting several applications that are running on several different versions of Windows Server. You may also be developing desktop or even Windows 8–style applications. What is a developer to do? You need to know which operating system you should run on your development machine.

Solution

The solution to this broader problem is operating system virtualization. There are several products that allow you to run several operating systems at the same time as virtual machines on top of Windows. However, you still need to choose a host operating system. As an ASP.NET MVC developer, Windows 8 Professional is probably the best choice for the host operating system on your development machine.

How It Works

Windows 8 is the first desktop operating system with a built-in hypervisor. Microsoft's Hyper-V, which has been available on Windows Server, is now available on desktop Windows as well. The hypervisor allows you to run virtual machines on your local desktop computer at near raw hardware speeds. In the past, you were able to have a similar capability using VMWare Workstation, Virtual PC, or Oracle VirtualBox. The difference with Hyper-V is that your VMs run closer to the metal and incur lower I/O overhead than user-mode applications such as Virtual PC.

If you are unable to run Windows 8, the next-best option is VMWare Workstation on either Windows 7 or Mac OS. Even though VMWare Workstation runs in user mode, meaning it is an application running on top of Windows, it does offer strong support for hardware-assisted virtualization and can even run 3D graphics.

In almost all cases, you should use a virtual machine for your development environment. The following are the reasons why:

- You can have a virtualized version of the development environment with an operating system that matches the configuration of your deployment target for all the systems you maintain.

- As you are going through the phases of development, you sometimes need to experiment with risky components and configurations that can potentially FUBAR your machine. Hyper-V and VMWare both have snapshot capabilities. With snapshots, you can take a picture of your machine at a given time and then restore back to that point later. For example, before starting a SharePoint installation, you take a snapshot. During the installation, you click the wrong button. SharePoint freaks out and wreaks untold havoc on your machine. Rather than rebuild your entire machine from scratch, you can restore from the snapshot—and everything is OK again. Another great use for snapshots is testing installation programs. You can run your installer, verify that it didn't work, fix the problem, roll back to snapshot, and then try again.

- Having a consistent developer machine image for all members of your team. VMWare and Hyper-V both support creating machine templates. This allows you to create a base image with all the tools you need for a project. When a new team member comes on board, you can spin up a new VM and get him or her productive almost immediately.

- Testing across different versions of Internet Explorer. Since it is not possible to have two versions of Internet Explorer installed on the same machine at the same time, using virtual machines solves this issue. This technique can also be used with MS Office or other tools with the same limitation.

- Virtual machines also have the unique ability to use virtual hardware such as network cards and iSCSI. With iSCSI, for example, you can create Windows server clusters that require shared storage. Without virtualization, you would need to purchase expensive specialized hardware and software licensing for SAN packages such as EMC PowerPath.

- Most companies are virtualizing their production servers. This makes it very likely that your code is eventually deployed to a virtual machine. Developing and testing your code on an environment that is almost identical to production reduces the number of issues you run into when you deploy your application.

I recommend that you set up your development environment to mimic production as much as possible. The following is a sample virtual machine setup.

- RAM: 4GB
- CPU: 2
- Disk 1: C: System 60GB
- Disk 2: E: Logs 10GB
- Disk 3: F: Data 30GB
- OS: Windows Server 2012 Standard Edition

3-3. Choosing Between IIS Express, IIS 8, and the Visual Studio Development Server

Problem

When you are developing a web application using ASP.NET MVC, you need to have a local web server that you can use to test and debug your application. Visual Studio gives you several choices, including its own built-in development server, IIS Express, or a full version of IIS. You need to know which web server you should use and what the differences are between them.

Solution

The full version of Internet Information Services (IIS) should almost always be your first choice for a development environment. Although Visual Studio 2012 ships with a light version of IIS called IIS Express and the even less-capable Visual Studio Development Server, both are missing some features and have some limitations. You may also find that some things that work well on IIS Express fail when deployed to production.

How It Works

Depending on what project template you select, Visual Studio 2012 defaults to either IIS Express or the Visual Studio Development Server. IIS Express 8 is bundled with Visual Studio 2012 and is installed by default as part of the installation. For earlier versions of Visual Studio, IIS Express can be downloaded and installed separately.

Even though these light web servers are not as full-featured as the full version of IIS, they can be very useful in the following scenarios:

- You are developing ASP.NET applications on Windows XP. If your company is still forcing you to develop on Windows XP and you do not have access to a virtual development environment, you have no choice but to use the ASP.NET Developer Server or IIS Express 7.5 since the full version of IIS is not supported on Windows XP.

- Your company's security policy prohibits the installation of a web server on desktop computers or do not permit users to have administrative access to their machines. Since IIS Express does not run as a service and requires no administrative rights, you are still able to use it without violating your company's policy.

- You need to have multiple users work independently on the same computer.

- You are lazy and just want to do F5 debugging without needing to worry about configuring a web server.

- You do not have administrative access to your development machine.

Since the scenarios listed are not uncommon, and many development teams are saddled by these constraints, Microsoft has put some effort into providing a development server that is based on IIS and supports many of the code features, but eliminates the administrative burden and potential security issues of running a web server on your desktop.

Other developers do need the full functionality of IIS, particularly teams that are working on complex applications.

Table 3-2 shows the major differences between IIS and IIS Express. The most important differences are the process model and the support for application pools and application identities. These are very important differences that will affect your application's behavior when it is deployed. For anything other than trivial applications, I highly recommend using the full version of IIS on your development machines.

Table 3-2. Major Differences Between IIS and IIS Express

Feature	IIS	IIS Express
Deployment Method	Windows feature	Included with WebMatrix and Visual Studio 2012. Can also be downloaded as a standalone.
Supported Versions of Windows	Windows Vista, Windows 7, Windows 8, as well as all editions of Windows Server	All editions of Windows after Windows XP
Support for non-Administrators	No	Yes
Supported Protocols	HTTP, HTTPS, WebDAV, FTP, and WCF support for HTTP, TCP, Named Pipes, and Microsoft Message Queues	HTTP, HTTPS, and WCF Support for HTTP
IIS Extension Support	Support for hundreds of IIS add-ins, including smooth media streaming, the search engine optimization toolkit, and more.	IIS Express has two, built-in extensions. One for Fast CGI and another for URL Rewriting. No other add-in can be installed.
Process Model	Uses Windows Process Activation Service (WAS)	The process is launched by the developer, usually by beginning a debugging session in Visual Studio.
Support for Application Pools	Yes	Runs in the context of the end user. It does not use application pools.

If possible, running the full version of IIS gives you more consistent results and helps you avoid the "but it works on my machine" syndrome. As for Windows Vista, Windows clients can now install IIS on their local desktops. Table 3-3 shows how the client operating system maps to the server versions. I have also listed the version of IIS Express that can be installed on each client operating system.

Table 3-3. *Client OS Versions and Associated Server and IIS Versions*

Client OS Version	Server OS Version	IIS Version	IIS Express Version
Windows XP	Windows Server 2003	6 (server only)	7.5
Vista	Windows Server 2008	7.0	7.5
Windows 7	Windows Server 2008 R2	7.5	7.5, 8
Windows 8	Windows Server 2012	8	7.5, 8

3-4. Filling Your Development Toolbox
Problem

Once you have your developer server/workstation ready to go, you need to install your development tools. You need to know which tools need to be installed on your workstation.

Solution

The following are a list of tools that are recommended for MVC development.

- *Visual Studio 2012*: For most developers, the professional version should be adequate. Students and others who are learning Microsoft development can use Visual Studio 2012 Express for Web.

- *Google Chrome*: For testing cross-browser compatibility.

  - *Chrome Web Developer Tools*: Useful developer toolbar.

  - *Firebug Lite*: Like Firebug for Firefox, but not as good.

- *Mozilla Firefox*: For testing cross-browser compatibility.

  - *Firebug add-on for Firefox: An essential debugging tool.*

  - *Web Developer add-on: A toolbar with many useful tools for developers.*

  - *YSlow add-on*: A tool developed by Yahoo that helps diagnose client-side performance issues.

- *Fiddler 2*: A web proxy that is essential for debugging client-side code.

- *Wireshark*: A network protocol analyzer. If you need to dig deeper into a network-related issue with your application, Wireshark allows you to monitor all network interfaces on your computer and inspect individual network packets.

- *IIS*: Microsoft's web server. It is a Windows feature that needs to be enabled.

- *SQL Server*: You should have a local copy of SQL Server available on your local machine where you can manipulate data and modify schemas at will without affecting other team members. Your team should also have a dedicated SQL Server for integration testing. Depending on your needs, SQL Server Express should be perfectly OK for your local development environment unless you need to a use a feature that is not available on Express.

- *Evernote or OneNote*: A way to take and share notes with your team members is an essential communication tool and a helpful way to keep track of things.

- *Notepad ++*: A free text editor that provides color-coding for many different types of files.

- *Komodo Edit*: A free text editor that supports many file types and programming languages, including CoffeeScript, PHP, Python, Ruby, HTML5, and JavaScript.

- *Windows Sysinternals tools*: An amazing set of tools originally created by Mark Russinovich in 1996, but it has been continuously updated and improved.

- *Remote Desktop Connection Manager*: A console that helps you manage connections to many remote computers.

- *Classic Start menu*: For those of you running Windows 8 but missing your Start menu, this application adds a Windows XP–style Start menu to your screen. It includes many options for customizing the menu, including changing the graphics used for the Start menu, and creating custom themes.

- *Stardock Start8*: This is another Start menu add-in for Windows 8. Rather than recreating a Windows XP Start menu experience like the classic Start menu, Start8 merges the Start menu concept with the Windows 8 Start screen.

- *VirtualCloneDrive*: A utility for Windows 7 that allows you to mount ISO images. It is helpful if you have an MSDN subscription and often download Microsoft products in the ISO or IMG format.

3-5. Installing Hyper-V and Setting Up a Virtual Machine
Problem

You would like to run Windows Server on your local computer but you still need to have a desktop version of Windows installed for various reasons. You think that virtualization is the answer, but you are not sure how to set this up.

Solution

There are two ways you can solve this problem.

- Run VMWare Workstation, Virtual Box, or Hyper-V on your local PC.

- Set up a dedicated VMWare or Hyper-V server and access the VMs using a remote desktop.

If you have access to a Hyper-V or VMWare server, creating the virtual machine on the server hardware has some advantages over local VMs. These advantages include the ability to run a larger number of machines, create bigger machines with more CPU and memory that are available locally and the fact that the VMs can be running all the time. With the VM running all the time, you can use Remote Desktop to access it at any time. Unfortunately, not all development teams will have access to a Hyper-V server or cluster. In some cases, you may have access but since the environment is administered by another group, you may have trouble administering your server, taking and restoring snapshots, attaching ISO images to install software and other common tasks.

The work around to this issue is to run the virtual machines on your local development computer. The main advantages of this approach are that you have full control of the environment, you can take and restore snapshots at will, and since the machine is running locally, you won't have problems caused by network latency. This option does require that you have a fairly beefy PC with a lot of RAM.

If you are running Windows 8, you have the option of installing Hyper-V, which gives you almost bare-metal performance and is probably the best performing virtual machine option for the desktop. It is also included as part of Windows so you do not need to purchase any additional software.

How It Works

In this section, I discuss installing and configuring the Hyper-V hypervisor and setting up a virtual machine running Windows Server 2012. If you are not running Windows 8, you will not be able to follow along in this section. There are alternatives to Hyper-V that run on older versions of Windows, as well as Mac OS and Linux. Of these, Oracle's VirtualBox is a good choice since it is fairly robust, can run on almost any hardware, and is available for free. Step-by-step instructions for installing VirtualBox can be found on the VirtualBox web site at `https://www.virtualbox.org/manual/ch01.html#intro-installing`.

Install Hyper-V Step-by-Step

Hyper-V is a built-in feature for Windows 8 Pro. It is not available in WinRT, the ARM-based version of Windows 8, and it is not available on previous versions of Windows. System requirements for running Hyper-V are as follows:

- A 64-bit system that supports Second Level Address Translation (SLAT). This feature is available on all current-version Intel and AMD processors, but may not be available if you have an older PC.

- Windows 8 Professional 64-bit or Windows Server 2012.

- 4GB of RAM (realistically, you should have 12GB or more).

Since Hyper-V is a Windows feature, you can install it using the Turn Windows Features On and Off application. To get to this on Windows 8, hit the Windows key on your keyboard, and then type **turn fe**. On the Search sidebar, tap or click Settings to search within Settings. Your screen should look similar to Figure 3-2.

***Figure 3-2.** Searching Settings*

In the search results section, you see the Turn Features On or Off application. Tap or click the app to launch it.

After clicking the app, Windows switches into desktop mode and the Windows Features box appears. In the Windows Features application, click Hyper-V. Clicking the outermost node automatically selects all the subcomponents. You expand the node to verify that all subcomponents are selected, as shown in Figure 3-3.

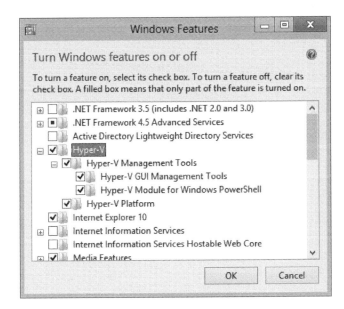

***Figure 3-3.** Windows Features application*

Click the OK button to begin the installation.

After several minutes, the Wizard notifies you that installation is complete. You may need to reboot your workstation.

After Windows completes its restart, you should see two new tiles on your Start screen: Hyper-V Manager and Hyper-V Virtual Machines. To avoid needing to search through the Start screen the next time you need to run Hyper-V, right-click (or down swipe if you have a touch screen) the Hyper-V Manager tile and click Pin to Taskbar. Your screen should resemble Figure 3-4.

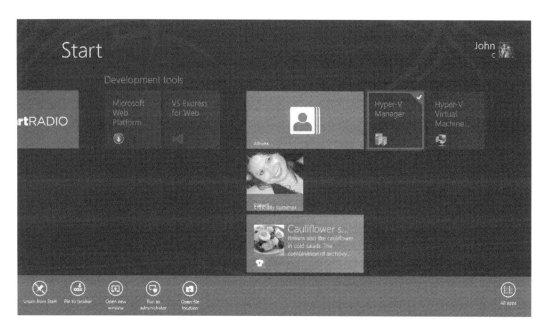

***Figure 3-4.** Pinning an app to the desktop taskbar*

The Hyper-V icon is now pinned to the desktop's taskbar. The Windows 8 taskbar is identical to the taskbar introduced in Windows 7, which combines the quick-launch toolbar with the taskbar.

Now that we have Hyper-V installed, we need to create our developer machine image.

The first thing you need is an ISO image of the operating system. An ISO image is a file that contains the contents of a CD or DVD. If you work for a large company, they may have a custom build of Windows Server that, in addition to the base Windows installation, has standard setup management tools and configurations. If this is available, you should use it. The goal is to make your development machine as production-like as possible.

If you do not have a company-specific build of Windows Server but have an MSDN subscription, you can download the image from the MSDN web site.

In this example, I am using Windows Server 2012—the latest server operating system from Microsoft. Just to clarify, ASP.NET MVC does not require Windows Server 2012, and works on any Windows operating system that supports the .NET Framework 4.5.

Once the ISO file is downloaded, you need to use the Hyper-V Manager to create a new virtual machine. Click the Hyper-V Manager icon that we created earlier to open Hyper-V. The Hyper-V Manager screen, shown in Figure 3-5, is split into three main sections, including a server list pane, a content area that consists of information about the virtual machines, and an Actions pane that contains a list of actions that can be taken for a selected virtual machine. On the left side is a tree view that lists all the Hyper-V servers. After a fresh install, the Hyper-V Manager only lists your local computer. Other computers can be added to this list by right-clicking Hyper-V Manager and selecting Connect to Another Computer.

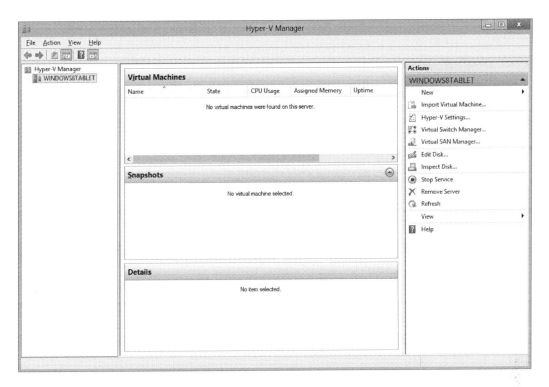

Figure 3-5. *Hyper-V Manager*

If you click your local sever, you see a list of machines in the center section under Virtual Machines. Since you have not created any VMs yet, nothing is displayed.

Creating a Virtual Switch

Before you create your first virtual machine, you need to create a virtual switch to enable network connectivity for your VMs. A virtual switch is a software-based layer-2 network device. It allows your virtual machine to connect to a physical network by mapping it to a network adaptor installed on your PC. It is also possible to use this functionality to create private networks that are only accessible to other virtual machines connected to the switch.

To create your virtual switch, click Virtual Switch Manager . . . , which is located on the Actions Panel. This opens the Virtual Switch Manager dialog box.

On the right side of the Virtual Switch Manager dialog box, ensure that External is selected for the What type of switch do you want to create? check box. An External Switch allows your virtual machine to access the network as if it were a physical machine on your network. Click the Create Virtual Switch button.

In the Virtual Switch Properties dialog box, name the switch **ExternalSwitch1**. In the notes field, enter **Connects to external network**.

For this demo, I am creating the VM on a Samsung Series 7 Slate, which is a Windows 8 Professional powered tablet. Since this PC is mobile, I may use this VM in many places that do not have a wired network. Because of this, I am taking advantage of a new capability of Hyper-V on Windows 8 that allows me to choose a Wi-Fi adapter for my external network. On your machine, you can select any of the available network adapters.

Keep the remaining default settings so that your screen looks similar to Figure 3-6, and then click the OK button. Hyper-V will begin configuring your new adapter.

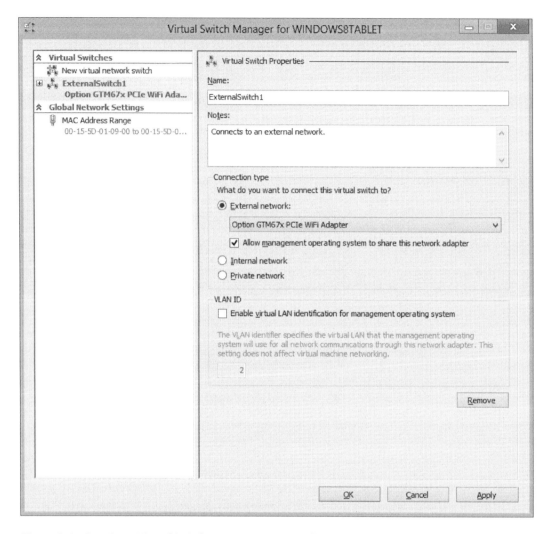

Figure 3-6. Creating a Virtual Switch using Hyper-V Virtual Switch Manager

A pop-up box may notify you that this change may disrupt network connectivity. Click Yes if prompted.

After a few moments, the settings are applied and the window closes.

Now that you have a switch created, let's go ahead and create the virtual machine. On the Action Panel, click New and select Virtual Machine.

The New Virtual Machine Wizard appears. Click Next on the Before You Begin page.

In the name field, enter **ASP.NET MVC Dev Machine**. Optionally, you can click the "Store the virtual machine in a different location" check box, and select a location that has adequate disk space. You should select a location that has at least 30GB free. If you take a lot of snapshots, the space needed for the VM can be quite large. In the example, I am using a USB 3 1TB external hard disk for my VM location. This configuration screen is shown in Figure 3-7.

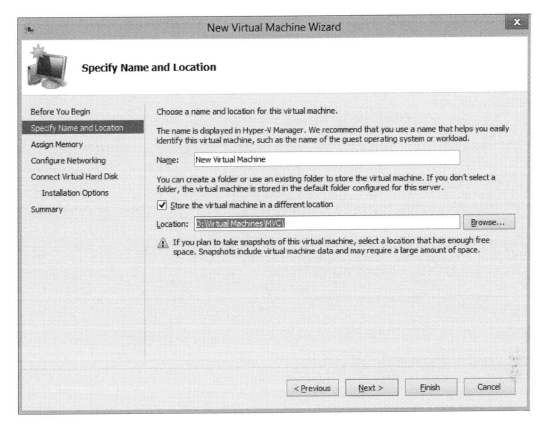

Figure 3-7. *Specify name and location for your VM*

Click Next on the Specify Name and Location screen.

For Start-up memory, you need at least 2GB. If you check the "Use Dynamic Memory for this virtual machine" check box, Hyper-V automatically adjusts the amount of memory allocated for the machine. For example, if I allocate 2GB of RAM for the virtual machine, but only a fraction of that is actually allocated, Hyper-V tricks the VM into thinking it still has 2GB available—but silently steals some of that unallocated RAM and gives it to other running VMs or to the host itself. The Assign Memory configuration screen is shown in Figure 3-8.

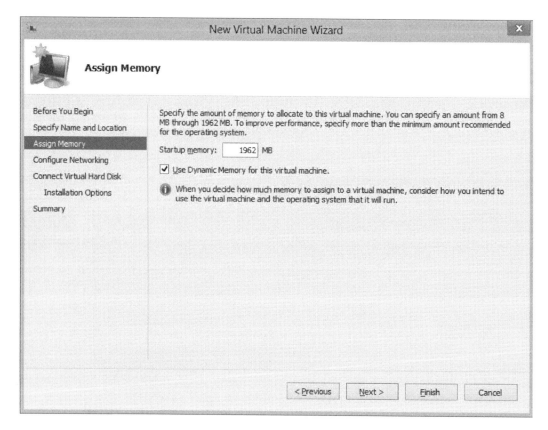

Figure 3-8. *Specify startup memory*

Click Next on the Assign Memory page to move on to configuring the network.

■ **Note**   One thing that is different about running Hyper-V compared to user-mode virtualization technologies such as Virtual PC is that once the Hyper-V role is installed, the host operating system is actually virtualized and runs on top of the hypervisor. The host virtual machine does have some special rights and can talk to the hardware in ways that the other VMs cannot, but it is still a virtual machine. Because of this, when dynamic memory is enabled, Hyper-V may actually take unused memory from your virtual machine and give it to the host.

For the Connection, select ExternalSwitch1, the switch we created. Click Next to move on to connecting the virtual hard disk.

On the Connect Virtual Hard Disk screen, we change the name of the disk to **MVCSystem** and change the size to 60GB. This disk will dynamically expand, so it will only take the physical space it actually needs. You should make note of the fact that the default option is using the new .vhdx format. This format is not compatible with older versions of Hyper-V. If you think that you may use this VM with an older version of Hyper-V, select Attach a Virtual Disk Later. Figure 3-9 shows the Connect Virtual Hard Disk configuration screen.

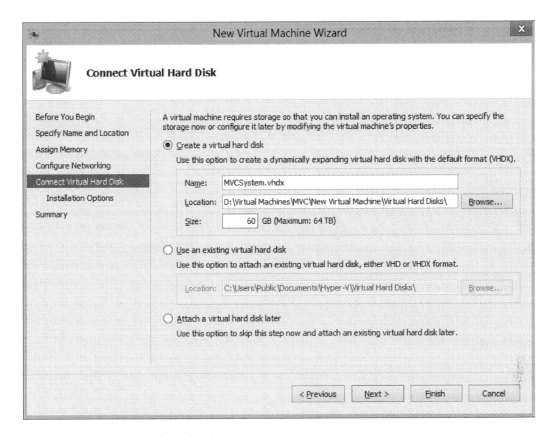

Figure 3-9. *Connect Virtual Hard Disk*

Click the Finish button to begin creating the VM. After a few moments, your VM is created and you should see it listed under the Virtual Machines section of the Hyper-V Manager.

■ **Note**   One interesting thing to note about virtual hard disks is that starting in Windows 7, VHDs can be mounted to a physical machine and used just like any other hard drive attached to the system.

Next, we add hard disks to your VM. We are doing this so that our new server matches our production server specifications. We will create two drives: an E: drive, which contains our IIS, SQL Server, and Application log files; and an F: drive, which contains our application files and data.

Within Hyper-V Manager, right-click your virtual machine and select Settings . . . from the pop-up menu. Take a look at the settings that you can change. You can adjust memory and the number and type of processor, add IDE and SCSI controllers, create COM ports, and even change your BIOS settings.

To add an additional disk drive to your VM, click IDE Controller 0 under Hardware in the left pane of the Settings window, and then click Add with Hard Drive selected, as shown in Figure 3-10.

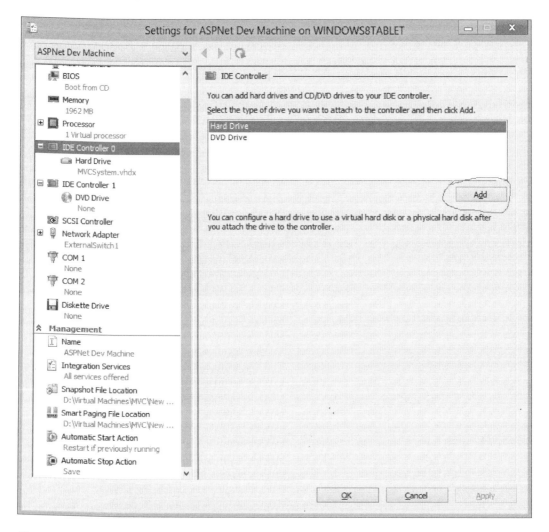

Figure 3-10. *Adding additional hard drives*

On the New Hard Drive screen, ensure that the Location Setting for IDE Controller 1 is not in use. If it is, select the next location on the list. In the Media section, make sure Virtual Hard Disk is selected, and then click the New button.

Follow the wizard, keeping the default values. At Specify Name and Location, name the disk **ASPMVCLogs.vhdx** and specify the same folder that we saved our system drive. On the Configure Disk page, set the size to 10GB.

Repeat the steps from earlier, but this time select IDE Controller 1, Location 1, name the disk **ASPMVCData.vhdx**, and configure the size of the disk to 30GB. If you think you need additional space for your data, feel free to add it. Remember, the goal with this setup is to match what you are considering for production.

Installing the Operating System

Now that you have created the virtual machines and added the hard disks, you are now ready to begin installing the operating system. To install the operating system, you first need to mount the ISO image containing Windows Server 2012 onto the DVD drive. To do this under IDE Controller 1, select DVD Drive. Under Media, select Image File. Click Browse . . . and then select your ISO file. The Settings dialog box should look similar to Figure 3-11.

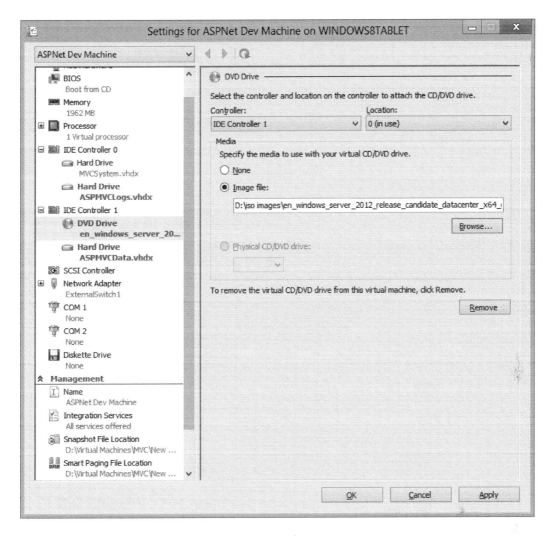

Figure 3-11. *Mounting the ISO image to the CD-ROM drive*

Click OK. Changes are applied and the window closes.

In the Hyper-V Manager console, click your virtual machine and choose Connect . . .. A window with a black screen shows you a message that lets you know that the virtual machine is in the off state.

On the left side of the Virtual Machine Connection window's toolbar, click the green Start button to turn on your machine. The VM boots from the CD and begins the Windows installation process.

After several minutes, the installation sequence begins. When prompted to select what version of the operating system to install, be sure to install Server with GUI. We need the GUI for our development environment. Click Next.

When asked where you want to install Windows, select Drive 0, as shown in Figure 3-12.

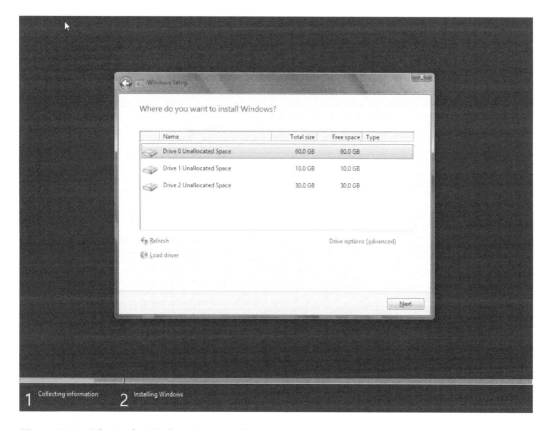

Figure 3-12. *Selcting the Windows System volume*

Once the installation starts, it takes about an hour to complete. You are then prompted to create an administrative password.

Once you enter the password, Windows completes the installation and eventually displays the login screen. Log in to Windows and try opening Internet Explorer to verify you have network connectivity.

Although you can continue to use the Hyper-V Virtual Machine connection (HVVMC) application, you will have more capabilities if you use the Remote Desktop client to connect. HVVMC has advantages like taking control of special Windows keys and allowing you to watch the machine boot, but RDP allows you to permit the VM to use both of your monitors, and supports more colors and higher screen resolutions.

Once you are connected, there are some changes you can make to the servers configuration that make it easier to use as your development environment. These tasks include:

- Going into Disk Management and assigning drive letters to the other disk drives you created in earlier. This should match your production machine specifications. In this example, I am using C for drive 0, E for drive 1, and F for drive 2. If you wish, you can take advantage of Windows Server 2012's support for GUID Partition Table disks and the ReFS file system format.

- Under System Properties' Advanced tab, opening the Performance Options dialog box. From its Advanced tab, select Programs for Adjust for Best Performance of:. This makes applications such as Visual Studio run better on the server OS.

- Configuring Windows Update. If your company has a server-patching solution (other than Windows Update) such as Lumension, ensure that it is installed and configured.

- Turning off IE Enhanced Security Configuration. You can do this from the Server Manager. Click Local Server, and then under Properties, click the link next to IE Enhanced Security Configuration. This setting is useful for production servers but is far too restrictive for a development machine.

3-6. Connecting to a Remote Development Machine Using RDP

Problem

You have created a new virtual machine in Hyper-V and you would like to connect to it using Remote Desktop. You have entered the computer's name into the RDP client, but it will not connect. You need to fix this so that you can work.

Solution

Windows Server is secure by default. This means that when you first set up your server, almost everything is disabled, including Remote Desktop. You need to enable remote access before you can access the VM using RDP.

How It Works

To enable this, connect to your machine from the Hyper-V Manager console. Log in and then tap the Windows key. This brings up the Windows 8 Start screen. Type **remote**, and then click Settings on the Search pane. Click "Allow remote access to your computer" (see Figure 3-13).

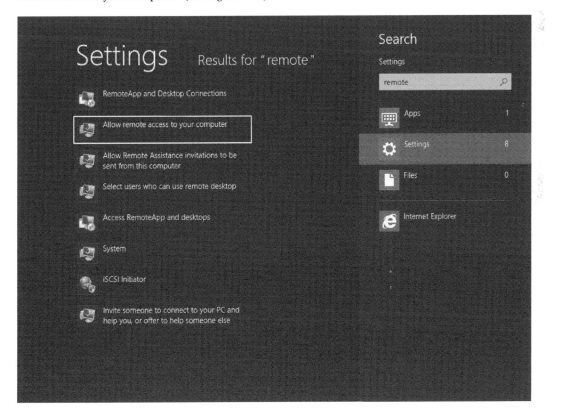

Figure 3-13. *Finding the Allow Remote Access applet using the Windows Server 2012 Start screen*

The system properties applet is displayed on the desktop with the Remote tab selected. Click "Allow remote connections to this computer". An alert pops up to let you know that a new firewall exception will be enabled. Click OK.

Then click OK on the System Properties applet.

Now that you have allowed RDP, you can connect. The RDP client has had some substantial improvements since Windows 7. The Windows 8 version is touch-optimized, so that mobile admins can easily manage servers using a touch-enabled device such as a tablet. It also has the ability to automatically detect connection quality and adjust the experience as needed. If you are using a system with multiple monitors, (starting with Windows 7) the remote desktop client allows you to use all of your monitors for a remote session. To enable this, click the display tab, and then slide the display configuration bar all the way to the right so that it says Full Screen. You can then click the "Use all my monitors for the remote session" check box.

3-7. Installing Visual Studio 2012

Problem

You are new to Microsoft development and have never installed a Microsoft development tool. You need some help to get up and running.

Solution

Installing Visual Studio is actually pretty easy. Before you begin, there are a few decisions you need to make.

1. Which version of Visual Studio you would like to install?

2. Do you want to install it on your local computer or on a virtual machine?

If you are just starting out in Microsoft development, Visual Studio Express for Web may be your best choice. In Chapter 2, there are several recipes that go over the Microsoft developer ecosystem in detail. If you have not read that chapter, I suggest you review it before selecting a product.

In Recipe 3-1, I discuss the merits of using virtual machines over installing on your local operating system. In most professional development scenarios, the virtual machine approach is preferred, but both approaches are valid. If you are just starting out, installing Visual Studio on your local computer may be a lot easier for you.

How It Works

Before installing Visual Studio 2012, ensure that your system meets the requirements.

Supported Operating Systems

- Windows 7 (x64 and x86)

- Windows 8 (x64 and x86)

- Windows Server 2008 R2

- Windows Server 2012

Notice that Windows XP, Windows Server 2003, Windows Vista, and Windows Server 2008 are not supported.

Hardware Requirements

- 1.6 GHz or faster processor

- 1GB of RAM (1.5GB if running on a virtual machine)

- 10GB of available disk space

- 5400 rpm hard drive

- DirectX 9–capable video card running at 1024 × 768 or higher resolution

Notice the requirement for a DirectX 9–compatible video card. This may exclude some low-end business laptops. The 1.6 GHz requirement could mean that Visual Studio performs poorly with some aggressive, power-saving modes that are configured on some laptops to boost battery life. To avoid these issues, ensure that you adjust your power settings to maximum performance when you are plugged in. Also, even though the minimum RAM requirements are 1GB, realistically you need at least 4GB of RAM to be productive. In most cases, Visual Studio is not the only application that you are running.

Installing Visual Studio Using Web Platform Installer

To install Visual Studio 2012 Express for Web, visit the following web page, using the computer on which you want to install the product: www.microsoft.com/visualstudio/11/en-us/downloads#express-web.

There are two main options on the page for the installation: using the Web Platform Installer or downloading the ISO image file. The Web Platform Installer allows you to install a variety or tools including WebMatrix, the Azure SDK, and hundreds of other free tools and libraries. The ISO file is useful if you do not want to use the Web Platform Installer or if you want to configure an automated install across multiple computers.

For this exercise, we will use the Web Platform Installer.

Once you click the install link, a small executable is downloaded. Depending on the browser you are using, you may have to click through one or more warning links before the installer launches.

Once the executable is launched, if Web Platform Installer (WebPI) is not installed or out-of-date, it prompts you to install or update WebPI. Once WebPI is up-to-date, it prompts you to begin the installation of Visual Studio.

■ **Note** If while running IE10 you are prompted to select a program to open the file, IE10 may have renamed the file so that it ends with an _EXE rather than an .EXE. This is a new "feature" in Internet Explorer that helps to protect you from executable programs that may have downloaded from an untrusted source. To correct this issue, cancel out of the Select a Program dialog box and then rename the file so that it ends in an .EXE.

The first screen of the installation wizard should show that you are about to install Visual Studio Express for Web with Windows Azure SDK. Click Install. The next screen shows a list of the items that will be installed. Click I Accept to acknowledge that you accept the licensing terms.

The installation should take about 15 minutes. When it is finished, it displays screen details of the products and where they were installed. You can click the Finish button to continue. You can then exit the Web Platform Installer.

You should now have a new item on your Start screen (Windows 8) or folder on your Start menu for VS Express for Web. After launching the application for the first time, it may take a minute or two for Visual Studio to load your settings. Once this is done, you can review the Visual Studio start page where there are access links to documentation and tutorials or create a new project.

3-8. Installing Visual Studio MVC 4 Add-on for Visual Studio 2010

Problem

You are a user of Visual Studio 2010 and do not want to upgrade, or you are using an operating system that does not support Visual Studio 2012 but would like to target MVC Framework 4 for your next project. You need to know how to upgrade Visual Studio so that it can support the new version of the MVC Framework.

Solution

Visual Studio 2012 is not the only version of Visual Studio that supports web development in Visual Studio. It is also supported in Visual Studio 2010. It can be downloaded and installed using the Web Platform Installer (WebPI). If you have WebPI installed, you can launch it from the Windows Start menu; otherwise, you can download the latest installation package from `www.asp.net/mvc/mvc4`.

The installation can be performed using the Web Platform Installer or via a standalone installer. MVC 4 can be installed side-by-side with older versions of MVC.

How It works

Before installing the MVC 4 Tools for Visual Studio, make sure that any older versions of the MVC 4 framework or tools for Visual Studio have been removed. This is only for older versions of MVC 4, such as the beta or release candidate. It is perfectly fine to install the new version of MVC 4 side-by-side with older versions of MVC, such as MVC 3. The MVC 4 installer also requires that Visual Studio 2010 Service Pack 1 or Visual Web Developer Studio Express 2010 with Service Pack 1 be installed prior to install. If these prerequisites are missing, they will be added by WPI during the install.

If you are installing the product from WebPI, you can use the search box in the top left of the screen to search for MVC 4. Locate ASP.NET MVC 4 Installer (Visual Studio 2010), then click the Add button. You may then click the Install button on the bottom of the screen.

On the Prerequisites screen, confirm that you are installing the correct package, and then click the I Accept button. The installation should take about 15 to 20 minutes, depending on how fast your computer and network connection are.

Once the installation is complete, you can close WebPI and open Visual Studio. If you create a new project, you will see a new project type for ASP.NET MVC 4 Web Application.

3-9. Installing IIS

Problem

You would like to develop your code against the same version of IIS that you will use in production. Visual Studio comes with IIS Express, but since this is not exactly the same, it is possible that some features may work differently in production.

Solution

IIS is a feature of the Window operating system and can be installed by using the Add Windows Features Control Panel applet. I will show the procedure for installing IIS for Windows 7 and Windows 8 server.

How It Works
IIS 7.5 on Windows 7

IIS 7.5 is the version of IIS that ships with Windows 7 and Windows Server 2008 R2. It can be installed using the Turn Windows Features On or Off applet. Make sure you have your Windows installation media available before performing these tasks. To launch the installer on Windows 7, click the Start button and type **Windows Features** (see Figure 3-14).

Figure 3-14. *How to find the Add or Remove Features applet on Windows 7*

Click Turn Windows Features On or Off to launch the applet.

▓ **Note**   The IIS installation procedure for IIS 8 on Windows 8 is almost identical to Windows 7, with the exception of the procedure to locate the Add or Remove Features applet. In both cases, the search is initiated by first tapping the Windows key and typing **Windows Feature**. The difference is that on Windows 8, rather than a Start menu, you have a Start screen, and you need to click or tap the Settings button under search on the left side of the screen to include Windows Settings in the search results.

Locate Internet Information Services in the list of Windows Features and ensure the following components are selected:

- *Web Management Tools*: You need this to administer IIS. In most cases, all you need is the IIS Management Console. However, if you are migrating an existing application or writing an application that requires compatibility with IIS 6, you need to include IIS 6 Metabase compatibility. Other tools in this category include WMI compatibility and IIS 6 scripting tools. As always, you should install only what you need. The more components you install, the greater the amount of system resources required and the larger the attack surface on your server.

- *ASP.NET*: You need this to support MVC (model-view-controller) development.

- *ISAPI Extensions*: You need this to support ASP.NET in classic mode.

- *Performance Features*: Provides content compression support.

- *Security*: Provides several authentication mechanisms.

Figure 3-15 shows the Windows Features, Turn Windows features on or off screen with the Internet Information Services feature partially selected.

Figure 3-15. *Enabling IIS 7.5 on Windows 7*

Click OK to begin the install. If prompted, insert the Windows Installation CD or browse to the equivalent file, such as a mounted ISO file.

IIS 8 on Windows Server 2012

On Windows Server 2012, Microsoft has graced us with the new Server Manager application. This new application allows administrators and developers to administer groups of servers from a single convenient user interface. Here I show you how to use this tool to add the application role to your development server.

When you log in to Windows Server, the Server Manager opens by default. If it does not, you can launch it by clicking the shortcut on your taskbar. Figure 3-16 shows how the Server Manager may appear on a typical Windows Server installation.

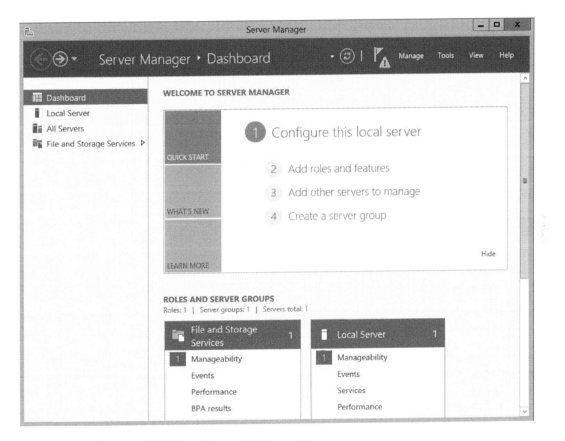

Figure 3-16. *The Microsoft Windows Server 2012 Server Manager*

On the Server Manager dashboard, click Add Roles and Features under the Configure This Local Server section. This launches the Add Roles and Features Wizard.

Click through the Before You Begin page, select Role-based or Feature-based Installation as shown in Figure 3-17, and then click Next.

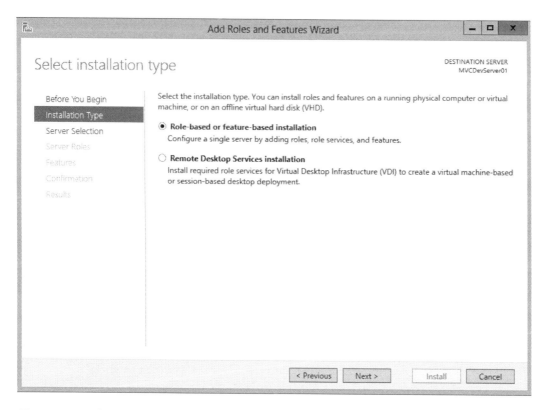

Figure 3-17. *Select Role-based feature installation*

On the next screen, you are prompted to select your server. A new feature introduced with Windows Server 2012 is the ability to install services and roles on many servers at once. For example, if you had a web farm that consisted of five front-end servers, you could create a server group and administer all the servers at once using the server manager. In the case of our development server (shown in Figure 3-18), we only have a single server to manage. Select your server and click Next.

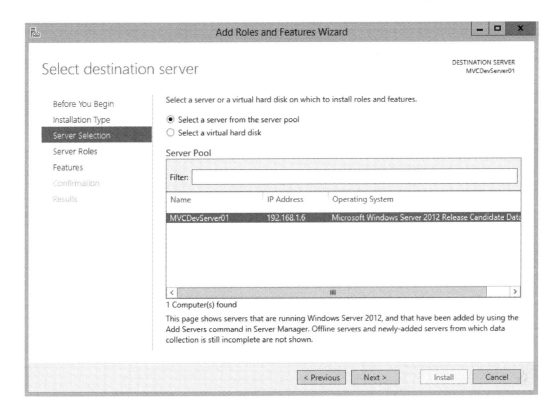

Figure 3-18. *Selecting servers to manage in the Add Roles and Features wizard*

On the next screen, you select the server roles you wish to install. We are going to install the Application Server role, which includes IIS along with support for ASP.NET. IIS is a module system that allows you to be very specific about which components to install. From a security and performance perspective, it is very important to only install the features you need. This lowers the amount of potential vulnerabilities installed on your machine that can be exploited by hackers, and reduces the number of components that are consuming system resources. Figure 3-19 shows the Select Server Roles screen with the Application Server role selected.

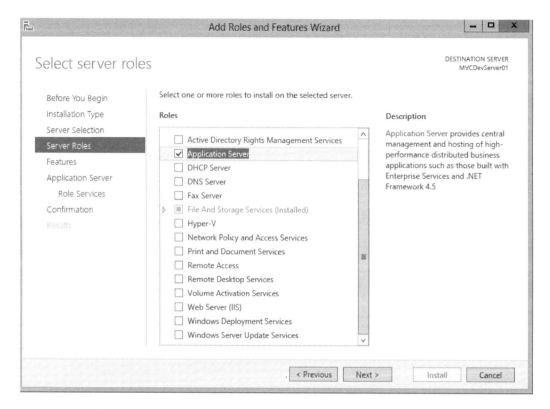

Figure 3-19. *Selecting the Application Server role*

Click Next. You are taken to the Features tab. If you need additional features for your application, such as older versions of the .NET framework, you can use this screen to add them. Some common features that many application use are Message Queuing, SMTP, Windows Identity Foundation, and Media Foundation. If you are not familiar with these features, you can click the name of the feature, and a description of the feature is displayed on the right panel. For this exercise, we will not install any additional features. Do not check any boxes on this screen. Click Next.

Click Next again on the Application Server Role screen. Then you can select which components of the application role you wish to install on the Role Services screen. In addition to IIS, we will add distributed transaction support, WS-Atomic transaction support, and HTTP Activation. I show you how to use these features later on in this book. Check the boxes next to the features you need. When you click the Web Server role, you see a pop-up window similar to Figure 3-20 informing you that additional features will be installed. Click Add Features to dismiss the window.

Figure 3-20. Confirmation prompt

You receive a similar pop-up window after clicking Windows Process Activation Services. Click Add Features on this dialog box as well. When you are done, your screen should look similar to Figure 3-21.

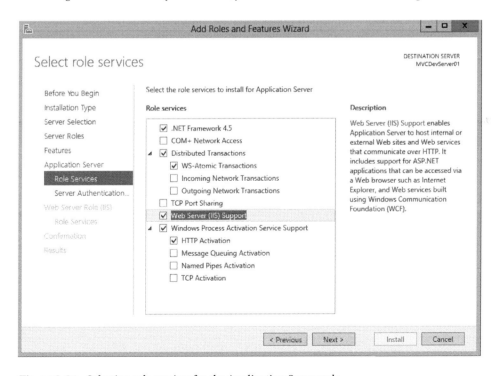

Figure 3-21. Selecting role services for the Application Server role

Because we selected the WS-Atomic Transactions component, on the next phase of the wizard, we are prompted to import an SSL certificate, which is needed for this feature. Select the Create a Self-Signed Certificate option. Self-signed certificates are useful for development. For a production deployment, you use a certificate from a trusted certificate authority such as VeriSign, or if your application is running on your intranet, you use one from your corporate issuing authority.

It is extremely important to include security considerations such as SSL certificates in the earlier phases of development. I have seen major issues result from development teams never testing their application using SSL until it was deployed to production.

Click Next through the information screen to get to the Role Services page. Select Application Initialization and WebSocket Protocol in addition to the items already selected. These components are found under the Application Development category. The Select role services screen is show in Figure 3-22.

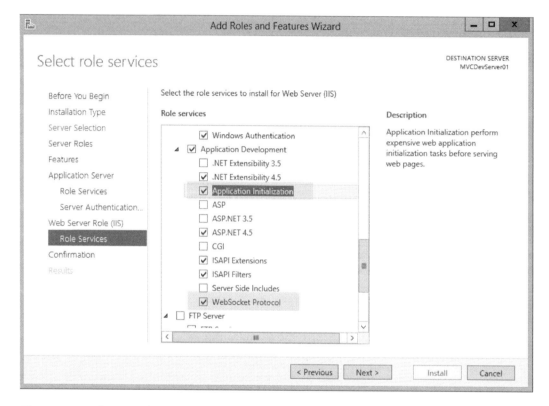

Figure 3-22. *Selecting Role Services for the Web Server Role*

Application Initialization allows you to run code when your application starts to warm the cache and precompile pages so that the performance of the application is not poor for the first few people to access your application after a deployment or server reboot.

The WebSocket Protocol is a new feature of IIS that allows you to create real-time interactions such as chat applications without the need to use techniques such as polling.

I demonstrate how to use these features later in the book.

Click the Next button through to the confirmation page. Review all the services that will be installed. The list should include all the roles and features you have selected, as well as any dependencies they may have. Click the Install button to begin the installation process. If you wish, you can close the window and allow the tasks to complete in the background.

3-10. Configure Your MVC Project to Use IIS Rather Than IIS Express

Problem

You have installed IIS on your development machine, but when you create a new project, Visual Studio is still using either IIS Express or the Visual Studio Development Server. You want to use the full version of IIS so that your development machine is a better match for production. You need to configure your project to use your full version of IIS.

Solution

The MVC Project templates, like all project templates in Visual Studio, use either the Visual Studio Development Server or IIS Express by default. If you want to use the full version of IIS, you need to change the configuration of your project.

To do this, open your MVC Project in Visual Studio. Make sure you run Visual Studio as an administrator. You need to be running under elevated privileges in order to make changes to IIS. By default, Windows uses a feature called User Account Control that makes most of the actions you perform run under a lower security context. This helps prevent you from inadvertently installing malicious applications such as viruses and spyware. To run an application as an administrator, you can right-click the application's icon and select Run As Administrator.

How It Works

If you have not yet created a project, you can create one by selecting New Project from the Visual Studio file menu, and then selecting ASP.NET MVC 4 Web Application from the available templates.

Figure 3-22 shows the New Project dialog box. On the left side of the screen under Visual C#, select Web. This will filter the project templates that appear in the center pane to show only C# ASP.NET application projects. Notice that you can choose between several project types, including ASP.NET Web Forms, MVC 3, MVC 4, Dynamic Data Entities Web Application, AJAX Server Controls, AJAX Server Control Extender, Server Control, and an empty ASP.NET project. Select the ASP.NET MVC 4 Web Application, and give the application a name in the name field. Figure 3-23 shows the default name, MvcApplication1. Change the project name to **MVCApplicationInIIS**.

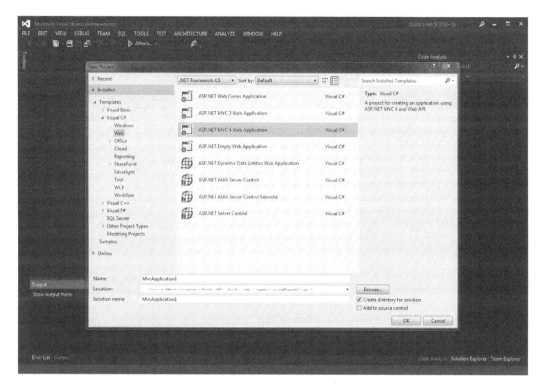

Figure 3-23. *Creating a new ASP.NET MVC 4 project in Visual Studio 2012*

In the Location field, you should select a location that is not under your personal user directory. We need to configure IIS to access this path. It is running under a different security context. My personal preference is to create a directory structure similar to how the solution will be deployed in production. For example, if your production server standard installs web applications on the E: drive, you should select a path such as E:\WebRoot\MvcApplication1.

In the Solution Name, enter a name for the solution. Ensure the Create Directory for Solution check box is checked, and then click OK.

Now you see the New ASP.NET MVC Project dialog box, which displays a list of project templates. The templates include Empty, Basic, Internet Application, Intranet Application, Mobile Application, and Web API. We go over the project templates in detail in Chapter 5. Select the Basic template and ensure the Razor view engine is selected in the View Engine dialog box. Leave the "Create a unit test project" unchecked. Your screen should look similar to Figure 3-24. Click OK to create your project.

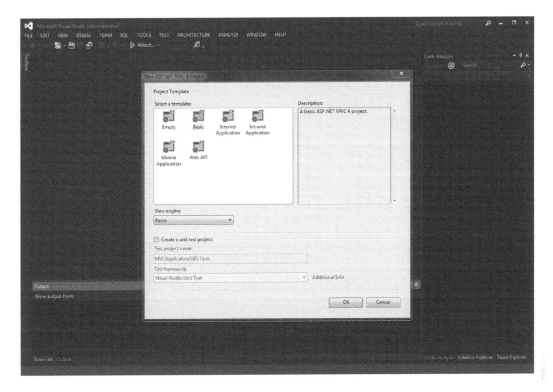

Figure 3-24. *Selecting an ASP.NET MVC 4 project template*

Once your solution is created, you should see the project files that were created in the Solution Explorer. To access the project's Settings page, right-click the web application project node in Solution Explorer, and select Properties from the pop-up menu. The properties page is shown in Figure 3-25.

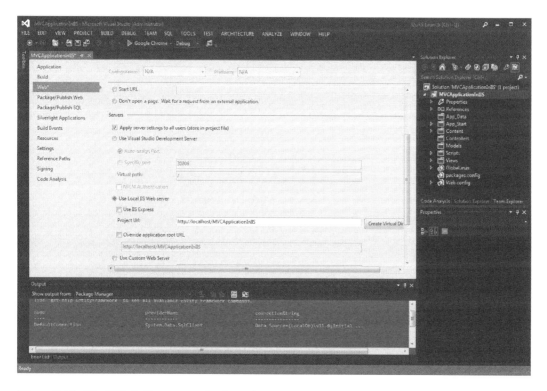

Figure 3-25. *The Web Settings screen for the project*

The project's properties window appears. On the left side of the page, click Web to see the Web Property page. Scroll down to the servers section and click Use Local IIS Web Server. If a Window appears warning you about using LocalDB, click Cancel.

■ **Note** LocalDB is a simple database created specifically for developers. Unfortunately, by default, each user account that accesses this database gets a private instance that cannot be accessed by other users. Because of this, a database that was created in Visual Studio under your user context cannot be accessed from IIS, which is running under an Application Pool identity. To get around this issue, you can either create a shared LocalDB instance or use another database engine, such as SQL Server Express.

By default, Visual Studio attempts to create a virtual directory under the root web site. In many cases, this setting is fine, but there are several scenarios where a virtual directory may not suit your needs. Take the following, for example:

- Your application may need to use custom bindings. In IIS, a binding is a combination of protocol, IP address, port, and sometimes the hostname. Bindings are set at the site level and affect all virtual directories and applications under the site.

- Your application may need to have a different autostart preference from the parent site, and you may want to enable the preload feature. The preload feature allows an IIS application to be initialized as soon as the worker process starts. This can significantly reduce the response times of the first request. As a developer, you may need to customize this feature so that in addition to loading dependencies such as the .NET Framework and performing just-in-time compilation of ASP.NET applications, you can load data into the application's cache. Application Initialization was available as an add-in for IIS 7.5 via WebPI, and is included as a role service for IIS 8.

- Your application uses SSL Mutual Authentication and you would like to configure a certificate for a specific URL. SSL certificates are bound at the site level.

- Your application uses some sort of URL processing and may behave slightly differently when the root of the site appears as a subdirectory. If you're programming defensively, your application should be able to account for both conditions; but it's nice to test the functionality from the browser as well as in unit tests.

- You prefer not to have your application appear as a subdirectory.

If you wish to deviate from the default and create a new root web site rather than a virtual directory, you can continue following along with this example. If a virtual directory meets your needs, click the Create Virtual Directory button. IIS creates a new virtual directory under the default web site and creates a new application in IIS.

▓ **Note**   IIS configuration is organized in a hierarchy. A site is the root container with several applications and virtual directories within it. In addition to its bindings, the site configuration can contain configuration settings for logging, failed request tracing, and limits such as the amount of bandwidth that can be used by applications contained within the site.

A site must have at least one application that functions as the root. An application is responsible for delivering content and providing services. Sites can have many other applications in addition to the root, which can each be configured to belong to separate application pools used to isolate the sites from each other. They can run different versions of the .NET Framework and run under different security contexts.

Applications can contain one or more virtual directories. Virtual directories are paths associated with a physical directory that can be located either on the same machine or on a remote server. Applications require that a root virtual directory that contains the application's content be defined. Virtual directories can be added to the application so that content can be included in an application from several physical locations.

Let's start by creating a fake domain name that we can use for our project. While this is not required and it is perfectly OK for you to access your application using either localhost, the loopback address (127.0.0.1), or the actual IP address of your machine, it can be beneficial to use a friendly DNS name to access a development web site. For example, you may have several root web sites configured on your development machines and you would like to access all of them on port 80. In this case, you need to configure the site bindings in IIS to use a host header and create host entries on your PC, or if possible, add a DNS entry.

Assuming that you do not have access to a DNS server, you can fool your computer by creating a new entry in our Hosts file.

To do this from the Start menu, type **Notepad**. When Notepad appears in the list, right-click it and select Run As Administrator. Now that we have Notepad running in elevated privilege mode, we can use the file menu to browse to the following location:

`C:\Windows\System32\Drivers\etc`

Since there are no text files in this directory, it appears empty. In the file type drop-down list, select "All Files (*.*)". The dialog box should now look similar to Figure 3-26. Select Hosts and click Open.

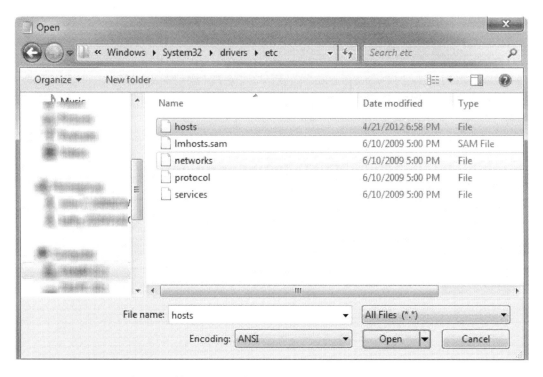

Figure 3-26. *Opening the Hosts file in Notepad*

The Windows DNS system, which is used to turn friendly names such as **Apress.com** into internet IP addresses, uses the host file as the first place to look before going out and querying a DNS server. Because of this, you can come up with arbitrary hostnames and map them back to the loopback address. The loopback address is a special IP address that always means your local machine.

Add the following entry into your host file:

```
::1 dev.mvcapp1.apress.com
```

In this line, we are using the IPV6 notation for the loopback address, and creating a friendly name for that address (dev.mvcapp1.apress.com). This friendly name only works on our machine.

Save the host file and close Notepad.

Back in Visual Studio, change the project URL field to look like what's shown in Figure 3-27.

Figure 3-27. *The Project URL in Visual Studio*

Do not click the Create Virtual Directory button. Clicking this button creates a new virtual directory at the root of the web site using the default settings. If another virtual directory is mapped to this location, an error will be thrown. In any case, for the sake of this exercise, we will configure the web site manually so it can be bound to the root application using the host entry created earlier.

Open the Internet Information Services (IIS) Manager. You can do this by hitting the Windows key on your keyboard and typing **IIS Manager**. Make sure the Internet Information Services (IIS) Manager is selected, and then press the Enter key to launch the application.

On the left panel, expand your server. Then right-click Sites and select Add Web Site from the pop-up menu, as shown in Figure 3-28.

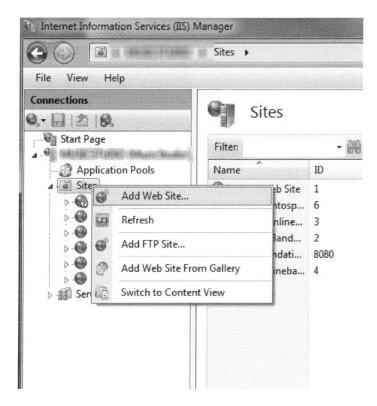

Figure 3-28. *Adding a web site in the Internet Information Services (IIS) Manager*

In the hostname box, enter the fake DNS name we came up with when we hacked the Hosts file. For site name, enter **mvcapp1**. For the physical path setting, browse to your project's directory. When you're done, the Add Web Site window should look similar to Figure 3-29.

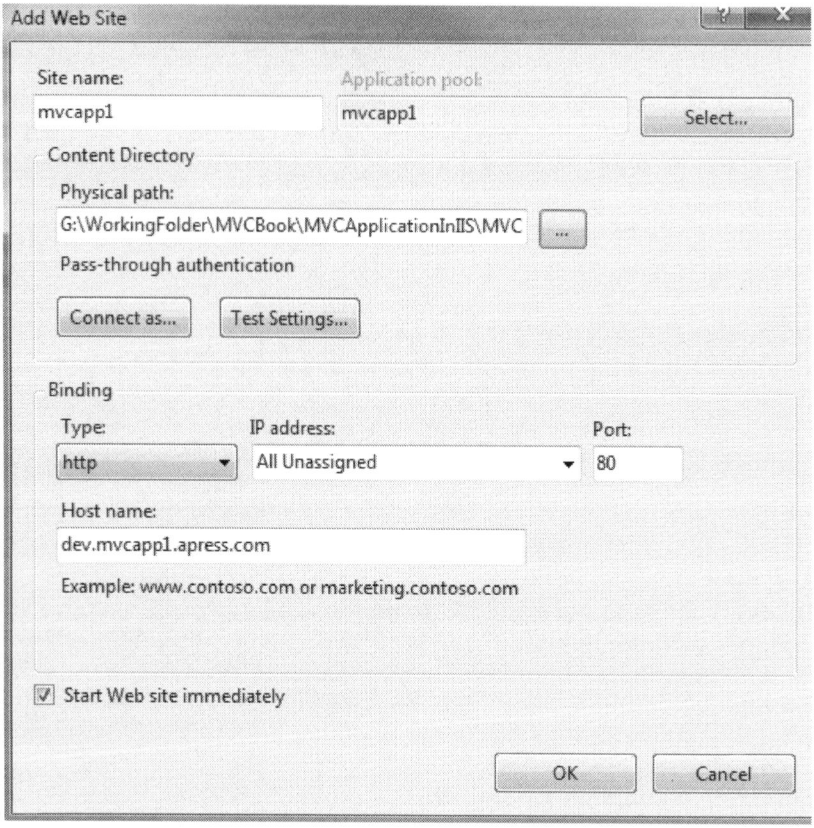

Figure 3-29. *Adding a web site, step 2*

Click OK to create the web site.

Now that you have created the web site, you can go back into Visual Studio and save your project's settings. Now that your web site is using IIS, you need to perform some additional configuration in order to get your site working again. See Recipe 3-11 for more information.

3-11. Configure an Application Pool to Use an Application Identity
Problem

You have created a new web site in IIS and you have your MVC Project to use for debugging, but Visual Studio returns an error when you try to debug it. When you open the site directly in a web browser, you see an error page similar to Figure 3-30.

Server Error in Application "MVCAPP1"

Internet Information Services

Error Summary

HTTP Error 403.14 - Forbidden

The Web server is configured to not list the contents of this directory.

Detailed Error Information

Module	**DirectoryListingModule**	Requested URL	**http://dev.mvcapp1.apress.com:80/**
Notification	**ExecuteRequestHandler**	Physical Path	**G:\WorkingFolder\MVCBook\MVCApplicationInIIS\MVCApplicationInIIS**
Handler	**StaticFile**	Logon Method	**Anonymous**
Error Code	**0x00000000**	Logon User	**Anonymous**

Most likely causes:

- A default document is not configured for the requested URL, and directory browsing is not enabled on the server.

Figure 3-30. *Expected error message*

Solution

The page is not displaying and Visual Studio cannot debug the page because the IIS Application Pool identity has not been configured properly. We will create a new Application Pool for our web site and ensure it has the proper rights to execute.

How It Works

Open IIS Manager. Expand the server node, and then click your web site. On the Actions pane on the right side of the window, click Advanced Settings.

Make note of the Application Pool name for the application. The advanced settings page is shown in Figure 3-31.

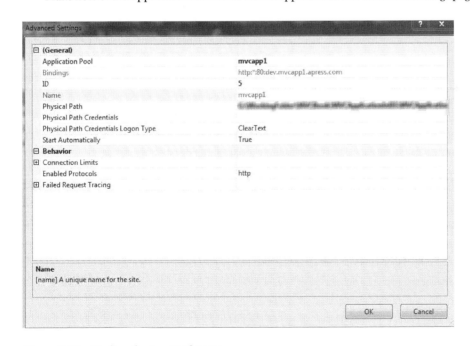

Figure 3-31. *Finding the App Pool name*

Hit Cancel to close the window.

On the Connections panel, click Application Pools. The list of application pools appears in the main pane. Find your application pool. There are probably a few thing wrong with it.

1. It is using the wrong version of the .NET Framework.

2. It is using Classic Managed Pipeline Mode.

3. It is using Network Service as its identity.

We will now correct these errors.

Click the Application Pool name to select it. In the Actions pane, click Advanced Settings. In the Advanced Settings dialog box, make the following changes:

-   Change .NET Framework Version to 4.0.

-   Change Managed Pipeline Mode to Integrated.

-   Change the Process Model Identity Property to ApplicationPoolIdentity.

When you are done the Advanced Setting screen should look like Figure 3-32.

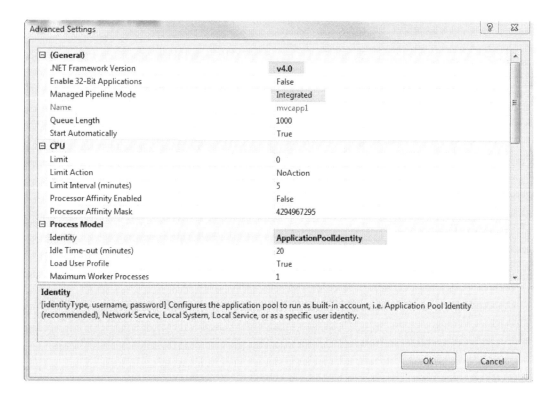

Figure 3-32. *Application Pool Advanced Settings*

Click OK to save your settings.

Open your web browser and navigate to your site to verify that it works. Now you are ready to begin developing your solution.

3-12. Configuring Visual Studio to Automatically Launch As Administrator

Problem

You are using the full version of IIS with your application. In order for you to debug your application, Visual Studio needs to run under elevated privileges. You keep forgetting to launch Visual Studio as an administrator. You wish there was a way that it could be set up to do this automatically.

Solution

Windows has several features that allow programs designed for legacy versions of the operating system to continue working on latest versions. One of these features can be exploited to create a short cut that will always launch Visual Studio as an administrator.

How It Works

To configure this setting, assuming you have pinned a shortcut for Visual Studio to your taskbar, right-click the shortcut. In the Jump List, locate the icon for launching Visual Studio, and right-click that. Then select properties from the pop-up menu.

On the Shortcut Properties dialog box, select the Compatibility tab. Under Privilege Level, choose "Run this program as an administrator". Click OK to save your settings.

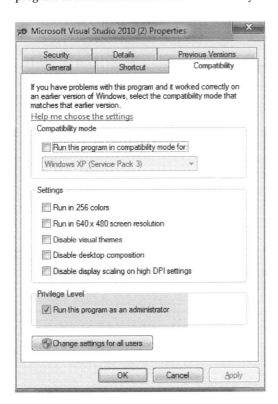

Figure 3-33. *Setting compatibility settings*

From now on, whenever you launch Visual Studio from the modified shortcut, it will run as an administrator. Depending on your user account control settings, you may be prompted with a warning message each time you launch Visual Studio. If you receive the warning message, click Yes.

3-13. Setting Up a Shared Instance of LocalDB
Problem

You have configured Visual Studio to use IIS and now your application is no longer able to connect to the LocalDB instance in Visual Studio. If you switch your project back to using the Visual Studio Development Server, you can connect and all works as designed. When you switch to IIS, it fails and Visual Studio continues to prompt you to switch to SQL Server Express. You do not want to use SQL Server Express because you like the simplicity of LocalDB. You would like to understand why this is failing and how you can correct the problem.

Solution

The reason IIS cannot connect to your LocalDB instance but Visual Studio Development Server can is because LocalDB, by default, creates a private database instance that can only be accessed by the user that created it. When you run your application using the Visual Studio Development Server, the server runs under your user context and has access to the database. Since IIS is running under a different user account, it does not have access to the database—even though it is using the same connection string.

You can correct this problem in two ways. The first way is to change the IIS worker process to run under your account. In general, this not a good idea since your user account has much broader access rights on your server than the IIS Application Pool identity normally has, which can lead to bugs that you will not find until you deploy your application. The second option is to use the LocalDB command-line application to share your LocalDB instance with all users on your local machine, and then modify your web.config file to access it.

How It works

The first step in this process is to create the share for your LocalDB instance on your computer. To do this, open a command window as an administrator. From the desktop on Windows 8, mouse over the lower-left corner of the screen until you see the Start icon. Right-click to reveal the power user menu and select Command Prompt (Admin).

On Windows 7, from the Start menu, type **Comm**. When you see Command Prompt appear under Applications, right-click it and select Run As Administrator.

Click Yes to the user account control prompt, and then enter the code from Listing 3-1 into the command window.

Listing 3-1. Creating a Shared LocalDB Instance

```
Sqllocaldb share v11.0 SHARED_LOCAL_DB
```

LocalDB responds by confirming that the instance was created as a shared database with a message such as: `private LocalDB instance v11.0 shared with the shared name: SHARED_LOCAL_DB`.

`v11.0` is the private name of the LocalDB instance created by default for your user account. `SHARED_LOCAL_DB` is the shared name of your database instance that can now be accessed by any account on your machine.

The next step is to modify your connection string in your web.config file so that it resembles Listing 3-2.

Listing 3-2. Web.config File Connection String for Shared LocalDB

```
<connectionStrings>
   <add name="DefaultConnection" providerName="System.Data.SqlClient" connectionString="Data
Source=(LocalDb)\.\SHARED_LOCAL_DB;Initial Catalog=aspnet-Chapter3-20120630230638;Integrated
Security=SSPI;AttachDBFilename=|DataDirectory|\aspnet-Chapter3-20120630230638.mdf" />
   </connectionStrings>
```

The code in bold shows the change made to the connection string. The final step is to grant permission for the IIS account to access the LocalDB. To do this, you first need to start the instance. This is accomplished simply by connecting to it, which is done using Visual Studio 2012's Database Explorer.

In Visual Studio, use the Ctrl+Alt+S keyboard shortcut to open the Database Connections window.

Right-click the Default Connection, then click Modify Connection. In the Modify Connection dialog box, click OK. If you have not yet created the database, it will ask if you want to create it now. Click Yes if prompted.

Now that the database has been created, we can add the IIS account as a user in the database. To do this, create a query similar to Listing 3-3, and then click the Execute button on the toolbar.

Listing 3-3. Granting the IIS Application Pool Identity Rights to Your LocalDB Instance

```
create login [IIS APPPOOL\myappname] from windows;
exec sp_addsrvrolemember N'IIS APPPOOL\myappname', sysadmin
```

You should now be able to run your application. Verify that you can connect to the LocalDB.

CHAPTER 4

Visual Studio 2012 Overview

4-1. Understanding Visual Studio 2012

Problem

You just installed Visual Studio and you are completely overwhelmed by its many toolbars and menus. You would like a simple explanation of what it all does and what features are most relevant for ASP.NET MVC developers.

Solution

Visual Studio is an Integrated Development Environment (IDE) that provides tools for creating solutions for Windows Server, Web Application, Windows Client, Windows Store, Windows Phone, and Windows Azure. For ASP.NET MVC Framework developers, Visual Studio provides the following features:

- Intelligent code editors that understand language syntax for managed languages such as C# and VB.NET, as well as web standards such as JavaScript and CSS. It also understands the APIs used in your project (including ones that you may have created) and automatically completes your code as you type. The code editor makes your code more readable by color coding keywords, variable names, and literals, and by automatically formatting your code as you write it. The code editors will also detect errors in your syntax as you type, and help you to detect and remove errors from your code.

- A powerful debugging engine that allows you to step forward and backward through your code, examining the values of variables, setting breakpoints and executing code in the immediate window. The debugger allows you to use IIS Express, a built-in lightweight web server, or the full version of IIS. It also allows you to attach to and debug processes on remote servers.

- An extensible library of templates and add-ins that you can use to jump-start your project and increase your productivity.

How It Works

At its core, Visual Studio is a composite application framework. It provides a shell with placeholders for docking child windows, menus, and toolbars. The user interface is divided into six main areas.

- *Menu*: Standard windows menus that allow you to dive into the many areas of the application.

- *Toolbar*: A set of toolbars (docked under the menu) that provide quick access to many commonly-used features.

- *Left pane*: Typically contains the Toolbox, which is normally filled with UI components that can be dragged to a design surface. May also contain the Server Explorer, which allows you to connect to application and database servers on your local network.

- *Center pane*: Contains open documents such as C# files and Razor views. May also contain property pages.

- *Right pane*: Contains the Solution Explorer and Properties windows.

- *Bottom pane*: Contains a compiler output window and error list.

In some ways, Visual Studio is like a simple operating system that allows multiple applications to run together. Each of the editions of Visual Studio comes with a different set of plug-in applications. Additional plug-in applications can be added to Visual Studio using the Extension Manager or by side-loading them using third-party installers.

The Express edition and the Ultimate edition both share the same core, but are differentiated by the add-ins. This architecture allows Visual Studio to be used to develop not just web applications—but just about any software in any programming language.

We will now look at each of the five sections in detail, discussing the default windows and toolbars in each section and how they are used in ASP.NET MVC development.

A Lap Around the User Interface

Figure 4-1 shows Visual Studio 2012 Ultimate Edition with an MVC 4 project loaded. Going from top to bottom, and from left to right, I will point out the major user interface elements.

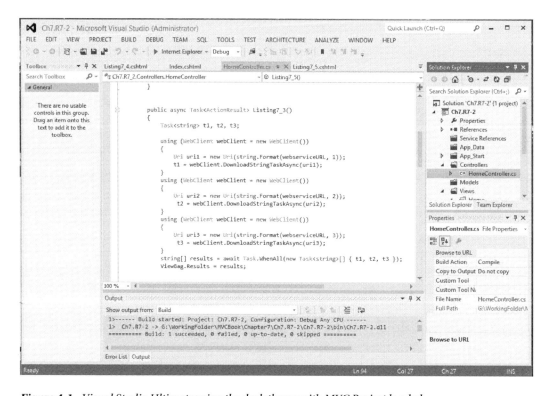

Figure 4-1. *Visual Studio Ultimate using the dark theme with MVC Project loaded*

At the very top is the title bar. It tells us the name of the solution and the user context it is currently running under. Figure 4-1 shows the solution name is MVCApplicationIIS and that Visual Studio is running under the context of Administrator . On the right side of the title bar is the Quick Launch search box. This feature acts very much like the search box on the Windows 7 Start menu. If you click inside the search box or use the Ctrl+Q keyboard shortcut, the Quick Launch bar becomes active and starts listening for input. As you type, it searches Visual Studio's list of menus, options, and open documents, and returns a list of items that match your result. Pressing the Enter key automatically launches the first item that appears in the search result.

For example, if you would like to view the Visual Studio Start page, press Ctrl+Q, and then type **start page**. A list of matching items appears below the search box. Items are removed from the list as you type additional characters to narrow the search. If you use this feature often, it remembers the items that you chose and automatically brings them to the top of the list.

In Figure 4-2, you can see that the Start page is selected after typing just a few characters of a search.

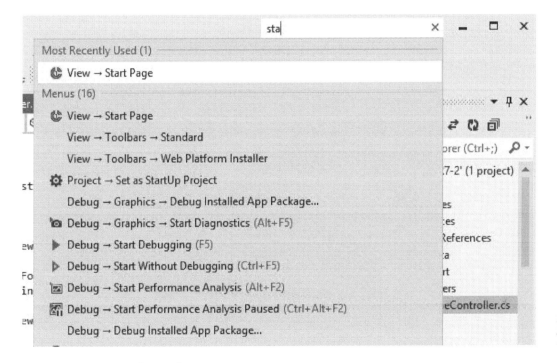

Figure 4-2. *Using Quick Launch*

Moving down from the title bar is the menu bar. In a celebration of topography, Visual Studio screams at us with a myriad of menu choices.

In compliance with decades-old Windows UI standards, the first menu listed is the FILE menu. A with most of the menu items, its specific contents will vary based on what window or item currently has focus in the IDE. FILE contains commands for saving files, creating new items, loading files and solutions, and for printing.

The next item is EDIT, which, in addition to the standard cut, copy, and paste commands, also has several search and code navigation utilities and advanced formatting commands.

The VIEW menu contains a list of all the Windows and toolbars available to you. We will go over some of these items in detail later in the chapter.

The PROJECT menu contains a list of commands that affect the currently active project. Inside a solution, you may have many projects. A project becomes active when you select the project or project item in Solution Explorer or an editor window containing a project item has focus. The PROJECT menu lets you add items to the project, access the project's properties pages, and manage NuGet packages for the project.

The BUILD menu, like the PROJECT menu, pertains only to the active project or solution. When the solution is selected, the build command will be applied to the entire solution rather than an individual project. The BUILD menu contains commands for compiling your project, running code analysis, and for deploying your solution. The BUILD menu is not available on the Express edition of Visual Studio.

The TEAM menu contains commands relevant to Microsoft Team Foundation Server (TFS), a source control and work item tracking system. It provides robust source-control system capabilities such as check-out/check-in, versioning, branching and merging, and conflict resolution. TFS also provides project management capabilities, requirements management, test case management, and bug tracking. All this functionality is integrated with source control. It also integrates with SharePoint, SQL Server Analysis Server (SSAS), and SQL Server Reports Server (SSRS) to offer a project dashboard containing team documents, active work items, and reports showing the project's progress.

The SQL menu contains commands that allow you to connect to SQL Server databases and perform actions such as schema comparisons and running queries. The SQL menu is not available on Visual Studio Express.

The TOOLS menu contains commands for connecting to databases and servers, managing library packages and extensions, and customizing Visual Studio. It also allows you to launch tools such as the WCF configuration editor and the handy-dandy Create GUID tool.

The TEST menu contains commands for running automated unit tests, debugging unit tests, and modifying the settings of a test.

The ARCHITECTURE menu, which is exclusive to the Premium and Ultimate editions, allows access to Visual Studio's architectural modeling tools.

The ANALYZE menu provides access to Visual Studio's performance profiling, concurrency visualizers, static code analysis, and code metrics tools. This menu is also exclusive to the Premium and Ultimate editions.

The WINDOW menu allows you to dock, float, hide, and rearrange all of your Visual Studio windows. My favorite command is Auto Hide All. This collapses all Visual Studio's windows, dedicating all of your screen real-estate to your code.

The HELP menu gives you access to all the Visual Studio, C#, and MVC Framework documentation. Depending on your setup, it can utilize a local copy of the MSDN library or simply link to the MSDN content on the Internet.

The title bar, menu bar, and toolbars for Visual Studio 2012 Ultimate edition are shown in Figure 4-3.

Figure 4-3. *Visual Studio Ultimate menus and toolbars in debug mode*

Toolbars

In Visual Studio 2012, Microsoft has substantially changed the appearance of toolbars. It has replaced colorful icons used in past versions with flat, solid-colored icons. They have also removed the bevels and other visual flare around the toolbars to create a seamless flush look. They have also made an effort to hide potentially unnecessary toolbars in order to provide additional real-estate to the code window.

Figure 4-4 shows Visual Studio 2012 side by side with its predecessor, Visual Studio 2010.

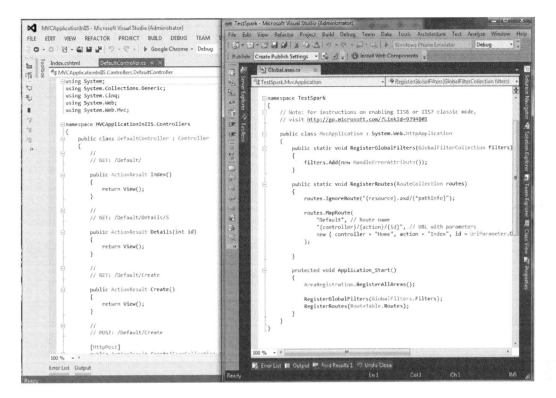

Figure 4-4. *Visual Studio 2012 and 2010 side by side*

The toolbars that are displayed depend on the type of document that currently has focus. Directly under the menu bar is the Standard toolbar. When editing certain types of documents, a toolbar specific to the document type appears below or to the right of the Standard toolbar.

Figure 4-5 shows the default toolbar layout on the Visual Studio 2012 Ultimate edition with a .CS file active in the document pane. In this view, there are four toolbars, including the Standard toolbar, the Text Editor toolbar, and the work item tracking toolbar. On the Standard toolbar, the leftmost items are a pair of Document History Navigation buttons. They work similar to the button on a web browser and allow you to navigate to the last document you had open. If you closed that document, Visual Studio reopens it. This is handy when you have many documents open and need to move back and forth through several of them frequently.

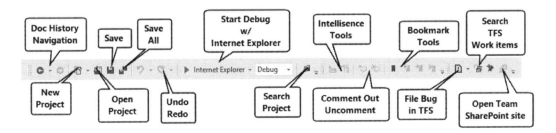

Figure 4-5. *The Visual Studio 2012 standard toolbar*

Next on the toolbar is the New Project button followed by the Open Project and Save buttons. The Start Debugging button, which looks like a green Play button, allows you to configure it so that any installed web browser can be used. Figure 4-5 shows Internet Explorer, which is the default. If you click the Down arrow to the right of the currently selected browser name, a drop-down list of available web browsers will be displayed.

The next toolbar shown in Figure 4-5 is the Text Editor toolbar. By default, this toolbar only appears when a code file such as a .CS file is active in the document pane. It contains the following buttons:

- *Display Quick Info*: Shows syntax information for the currently active object in the open code file. You can also see the same information by hovering the mouse over the item.

- *Toggles between suggestions and standard completion modes*: When enabled, pressing the Enter key always inserts a new line at the current location in the text editor. When disabled (the default), hitting the Enter key autocompletes whatever code you are typing, based on the selected value in the IntelliSense overlay that is automatically displayed as you type.

- *Comment out the selected lines*: Clicking this button turns the selected text in the editor into a code comment.

- *Uncomment the selected lines*: Clicking this button removes the code comment markup from the selected lines.

- *Toggle bookmark on the current line*: Very useful for navigating a large code file. By using this item, you can place bookmarks on sections of code you are working on. Once you create several bookmarks, you can use the next two buttons to move back and forth between them.

If you are using Microsoft's Team Foundation Server source control and work item tracking system and you are currently connected to a team project, the Work Item Tracking toolbar will appear to the right of the other toolbars. This toolbar allows you to create new work items such as bugs and tasks, search work items, or open the team project SharePoint portal site.

Like most Microsoft products, the toolbar can be completely customized to your needs. For example, if you do not find the Work Item Tracking toolbar useful, you can remove it and add other tools that better meet your needs. You may also add and remove buttons from existing toolbars and even create your own custom toolbars.

The Left Pane

On the left-hand side is a pane that contains your toolbox and Server Explorer. In Web Forms, the toolbox contains a list of server controls that you can drag to the design surface. When using the Razor view engine, there are no web server controls and there is no designer. That's right, there is no WYSIWYG drag-and-drop design surface in Visual Studio for MVC view development with Razor.

In the absence of server controls, all that appears in the toolbar is standard HTML input elements. You can drag them from the toolbox to the editor window to insert the HTML markup that makes up the element.

The Server Explorer is another tool that typically sits in your left panel. It allows you to connect to databases and servers. For databases, it allows you to view and edit tables, views, stored procedures, and even database diagrams. It provides some of the same functionality as SQL Server Management Studio right inside Visual Studio. This includes visual editors for creating and editing table definitions, query editors, and data grids that allow you to edit data.

The Server Explorer also allows you to peer into many of the administrative aspects of the servers you are connected to. You can view event logs, management classes that include things like disk volumes and network adaptors, message queues, performance counters, and even running services. This tool saves you time by letting you dig into the heart of a server without ever needing to leave Visual Studio. For example, if your program writes log entries to a message queue, you can use Server Explorer to verify the messages are being written as expected.

All the windows and toolbars including the Server Explorer can be undocked. An undocked window can be moved anywhere—even to another screen if you are using more than one display. It can be resized, maximized, closed, or docked to another position in Visual Studio. Figure 4-6 shows the Server Explorer undocked and expanded. You can see a connection to a database under the Data Connection with the tree of objects that can be accessed.

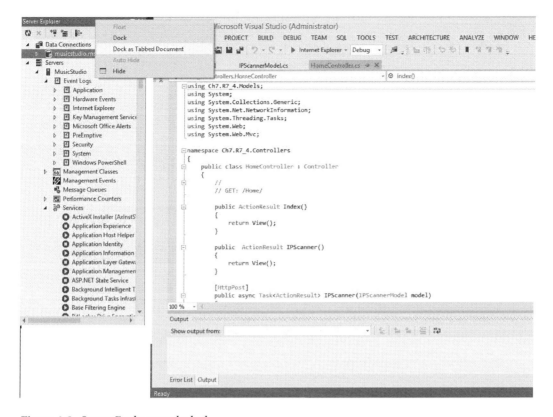

Figure 4-6. *Server Explorer undocked*

Under Servers, you see the available objects, including the Windows Services running on the server.

In the upper-right corner of Figure 4-6, you can see the pop-up menu that appears when you right-click the title bar. The following commands are available:

- *Float*: Undocks the current window.

- *Float All*: This command only works in the central pane that normally houses the code editors. It will undock not only the current tabbed document, but the entire tabbed document container. This is useful when you are working on a system attached to multiple displays and would like to use one display for all of your code windows and another display for Visual Studio.

- *Dock*: Docks the floating window. Unfortunately, it does not always redock the window to its original position.

- *Dock as Tabbed Document*: Docks the window into the central pane as a tabbed document.

- *Auto Hide*: This command automatically hides a docked window, minimizing along the outer edge of the dock area. The minimized window can be expanded by clicking the minimized title bar. When the window loses focus, it is automatically minimized again. This is extremely useful when working on a small screen or when using a projector with a poor resolution.

- *Hide*: Closes the window. If you want to view the window again, you will need to reopen it using the VIEW menu.

The Center Pane

The center pane is the main stage area of Visual Studio. It contains all of your open documents and allows you to navigate between them using tabs placed along the top of the area.

Figure 4-7 shows some of the main features of the Visual Studio tabbed document pane. In this screenshot, the _Layout.cshtml file is pinned. When a document is pinned, it is always visible and stays docked to the left side of the window. You can pin as many documents as useful. To pin a document, mouse over the tab. It becomes highlighted and a small icon that looks like a pushpin appears to the left of the Close icon. Click the Pin icon and your document becomes pinned. Perform the inverse of this procedure to unpin the document.

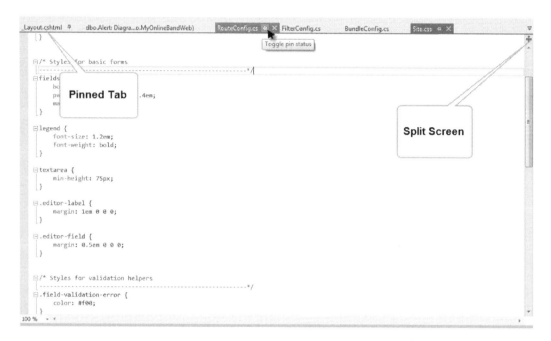

Figure 4-7. *Tabbed documents in Visual Studio 2012*

If you have opened more documents than can be displayed as tabs along the top of the tabbed document pane, you can access the remaining documents by clicking the small Down arrow on the top-right corner of the pane. This will show you a list of open documents.

Also shown in Figure 4-7 is the Screen Splitter tool. It allows you to view two sections of a single document at once.

Visual Studio 2012 includes a new, file preview feature that opens a document in a Preview tab when it is selected in the Solution Explorer window. Preview tabs are aligned to the right side of the tabbed document pane; they have purple tabs when active. Only one document can be previewed at once. The contents of the Preview tab are replaced by the next document selected. You can promote a previewed document to an open one by right-clicking the tab and selecting Keep Tab Open from the pop-up menu.

The Solution Explorer

The Solution Explorer is a tree view of all your solution's projects and files. You can use Solution Explorer to open files for editing, checking files in and out of source control, adding new files and folders to your project, and to browse the members of a class. There are several new productivity features added to the Solution Explorer since Visual

Studio 2010. If you installed the Visual Studio Power Tools pack, some of these features may be familiar. A screen shot showing Solution Explorer with an ASP.NET MVC application loaded is shown in Figure 4-8. Figure 4-8 shows the how the integrated class viewer allows you to drill down into the contents of a file.

Figure 4-8. *Solution Explorer*

The Solution Explorer's toolbar has three sets of tools. The first set consists of Back, Forward, and Home buttons. These buttons work with the Search Solution Explorer box. The Back and Forward buttons allow you to navigate back and forth between search results. The Home button clears the search and returns Solution Explorer to its default view.

The next set of buttons affect what is displayed in Solution Explorer independent of the search results. The first button in this set allows you to filter what is displayed in Solution Explorer based on one of two criteria. The default filter will show only files that have been modified since being checked out of source control. The purpose of the second filter option is to only show files that are currently open. This is a great feature to use when you have a large number of open files and it is difficult to navigate between then using the tabbed documents pane.

The next button in this section syncs Solution Explorer with the active document. In cases where you have applied filters or collapsed elements, clicking this button will expand the collapsed node and select the active document in Solution Explorer. Also in this section are Refresh buttons that update the display to include changes to the file system. The Collapse All button collapses the entire Solution Explorer tree structure. The last button in this section shows or hides files that exist in the solution directory on the file system but are not included in the project.

113

In the last section of the toolbar, there are two buttons. The first button, which looks a wrench, displays the properties window for the selected item. The last button toggles on the "Preview selected item" feature. With this enabled, when an item is clicked, it appears in the tabbed document window but with its tab on the right-hand side of the pane. If you are using Visual Studio 2012 Ultimate Edition, an additional toolbar button is available, which when clicked, generates a dependency graph of the selected document.

The real power of Solution Explorer is the tree view itself. Many features can be found by right-clicking items in the tree view. For example, right-clicking the solution file allows access to a menu of commands that can be executed across the entire solution. Right-clicking a project displays a list of commands that can be executed against the project. The number of items that appear vary depending on what edition of Visual Studio you are using and which add-ins are installed. Figure 4-9 shows the commands available after right-clicking a project in Solution Explorer.

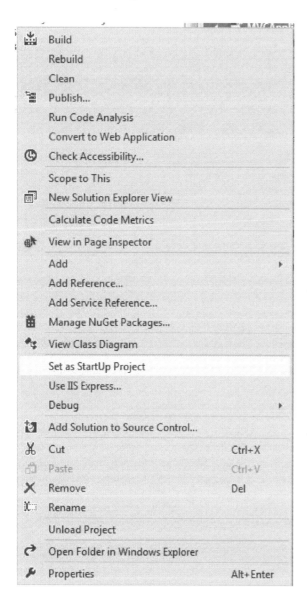

Figure 4-9. *Solution Explorer pop-up menu for a project*

Another nice new feature is the New Solution Explorer View menu item. It opens a new Solution Explorer window that shows a portion of the tree, starting with the selected item. You can then dock this new view so that you can easily switch between trees of items. This becomes very useful when you have solutions containing thousands of items. It will save you a lot of time that you would have otherwise wasted scrolling through the Solution Explorer.

The Bottom Pane

The last thing to discuss in this quick tour of Visual Studio is the bottom pane. This section contains two main items. The Output pane, which contains compiler outputs as well as diagnostics data that your program may generate using `Debug.Write` statements. The other window is the Error List. It shows you all the compiler errors and warnings, as well as errors in warnings about your JavaScript, HTML, and CSS files that are in the active window.

If you are in debug mode, the bottom pane contains many of your debugging windows, such as your Locals, Watch, and Immediate windows. The debugging windows are discussed in detail in Recipe 4-9.

4-2. Changing the Style of the Visual Studio Menu
Problem

For Visual Studio 2012, Microsoft added some Windows 8–type styling to the IDE. One of these changes made the menu text all capital letters. You and your team really dislike this visual style and find it distracting. You would like the menus to appear as they did in previous versions of Visual Studio.

Solution

With Visual Studio 2012, Microsoft has made a somewhat radical transformation of the user interface. For many veteran .NET developers, this change is a bit disorienting. Although Visual Studio is not itself a Windows Store application, it does borrow some of the basic design principles, such as content over chrome, simple flat appearances, and emphasis on typography. Many people in the community have expressed disappointment regarding some of the design choices. By far, the "all caps" menu has drawn the greatest amount of criticism. Even though it is a silly aesthetic issue that you will most likely get used to in time, it does add additional pixels to the menu bar and can be distracting. Luckily, several extensions that allow you to change this look are available in the Visual Studio Gallery.

Of the available extensions, I have found that VSCommands for Visual Studio 2012 works the best. In addition to allowing you to modify the menu bar to use normal capitalization, it also allows you to hide the menu bar all together. If you choose this option, you can set it up so that the menu will appear only when the mouse hovers between the toolbar and the title bar, or you can keep it hidden completely and use the Alt key on your keyboard to display the menu when needed. The latter setting is similar to the default setting on both Internet Explorer and Firefox.

How It Works

To install VSCommands for Visual Studio 2012, perform the following steps:

1. From the Tools menu, click Extensions and Updates.
2. In the left sidebar, click Online. Visual Studio Gallery is selected by default.
3. In the Search Visual Studio Gallery text box (located in the upper-right of the Extensions and Updates dialog box), type **VSCommands**.
4. Click the Download button to install the add-in.
5. Restart Visual Studio.

Once the add-in is installed, you need to configure it to change your menu style. Restart Visual Studio. From the Tools menu, select VSCommands ➤ Options. This is a new menu item created by the VSCommands extension. Under IDE Enhancements, click Main Menu. You can then change the settings from Default (ALL CAPS) to Sentence Case. Figure 4-10 shows the VSCommands configuration screen.

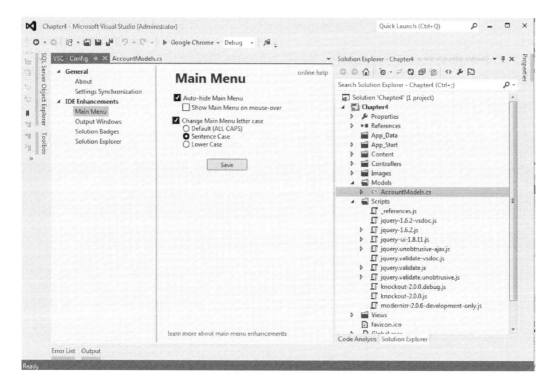

Figure 4-10. *VSCommands settings*

In this example, the menu is hidden and can only be displayed by pressing the Alt key and setting the menu case to Sentence Case. Notice in Figure 4-10 that the menu bar is hidden.

4-3. Changing the Visual Studio Color Scheme

Problem

You find the default color scheme to be hard on your eyes and you would prefer an alternative overall look for Visual Studio.

Solution

Visual Studio comes with two color themes: light and dark. The light theme is the default setting and features gray and black topography against a white background. The dark theme is essentially the inverse of the light, with a dark background and light text.

How It works

Let's change the theme. From the Tools menu, select Options. In the options dialog box, expand Environment and then click General. Under Visual Experience, you can change the color theme, as shown in Figure 4-11.

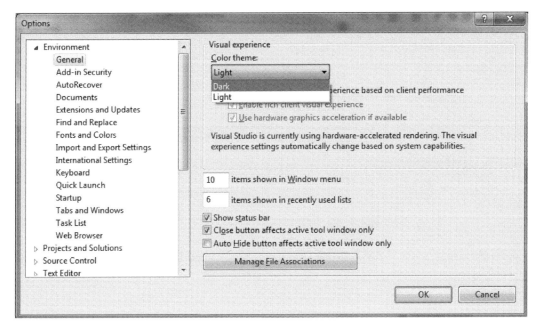

Figure 4-11. *Changing the Visual Studio color theme*

In addition to the themes, Visual Studio offers more than 100 options for customizing the colors of virtually every editor and window. Under the Fonts and Colors section of the Environment options, you will find a litany of configurable properties. These settings override the settings from the themes. It is important to note that even after switching to another theme, your color choices will remain. In some cases, this makes the text difficult to read. Luckily, Visual Studio has a failsafe that allows you to revert from the original theme by clicking the Use Defaults button on the Fonts and Colors screen.

4-4. Installing Visual Studio Documentation for Offline Use
Problem

You need to work in a location with limited access to the Internet but still need to access documentation regarding Visual Studio, C#, the MVC Framework, and the .NET class libraries.

Solution

When you first install Visual Studio, you are given a choice about whether to store help on your local computer or to use the online help hosted on MSDN.com. If you choose the default settings, some of the core documentation will be stored locally but the remainder will be online. For most people, the online version of help is optimal since it is continually kept up-to-date and is augmented by a number of blogs, forums, and articles. The online-only option also saves you several gigabytes of disk space. However, if you know you will be working in a location with limited connectivity to the Internet, you can perform the following steps to install the MSDN documentation on your local computer.

1. From the Visual Studio Help menu, select Add and Remove Help Content.

2. The Microsoft Help Viewer window will be displayed. If you have a connection to the Internet, you can select Online as the Installation source. If you do not have an Internet connection, the Visual Studio installation media will be required.

3. For Local store path, select a disk location that has enough space. The entire library will require several gigabytes of disk space.

4. Select the documentation that you wish to install locally by clicking the Add action. As you add selections, they will appear in the Pending Changes section. On bottom of the window, a counter will show the amount of disk space required and how much free space is available. You should download only what you require. For ASP.NET MVC developers, the following packages are recommended:

   - NET Framework 4.5 (Local by default)

   - Visual Studio 2012 Fundamentals (Local by default)

   - JavaScript

   - Visual Basic and Visual C#

   - Books Online for SQL Server 2012

   - Patterns & Practices Web Development

   - Patterns & Practices Service Development

   The total size of the recommended packages is around 4.8GB.

5. Click Update to begin the download.

Once the packages have downloaded, you will be able to access them though the Visual Studio help menu. The help viewer application will notify you when updates are available for your installed content. It is generally a good idea to open the help viewer and update your content before leaving for any engagement where you will not be able to access the Internet. For example, before you depart on a 15-hour flight from New York to Hong Kong, make sure your spare laptop battery is charged and your help documents are up-to-date for more productive flight time.

4-5. Resetting the Default Visual Studio Window Layout
Problem
You have accidentally closed some of the windows in Visual Studio and you are unable to put them back to their original positions. You would like to restore Visual Studio to its original settings.

Solution
As with the colors schemes, Visual Studio has a fallback solution to reset the window layouts to their default settings.

How It works

To reset the layouts to their default positions, from the Window menu, select Reset Window Layout. Visual Studio will prompt you to confirm that you really want to remove all of your customizations and return to the default settings. Click the Yes button. After several minutes, your settings will be restored.

4-6. Creating a Custom Toolbar

Problem

You have installed several add-ins and frequently use Visual Studio features that are not available on the main toolbar. You would like to create a custom toolbar that will give you quick and easy access to these features.

Solution

Visual Studio's menus and toolbars are very customizable. You can add custom toolbars and menus, or change the contents of existing ones.

How It Works

To demonstrate this feature, we will add a custom toolbar that appears whenever we have a Razor view open in the editor. On the toolbar, we will add buttons that show the Page Inspector, CSS Properties, the Document Outline button, and buttons for a third-party add-in, the JavaScript Parser extension.

To edit the Visual Studio layout for Razor views, open a Razor view and click inside it to ensure that it is the active window. Razor views should be found inside the Views folder in your MVC solution; they have a .cshtml file extension.

Notice that the HTML editor toolbar is now present above the editor. If you have a wide-screen monitor, you can drag the toolbar so that it appears beside your main toolbar rather than under it. Now you are ready to add your new toolbar.

1. From the Tools menu, click Customize.

2. On the Customize dialog box, click New. On the New Toolbar dialog box, enter **Razor Tools**, and then click OK. Razor Tools now appears checked in the Toolbars list.

3. Click on the Commands tab, and then click Toolbar to select it.

4. Select Razor Tools from the drop-down list. The Controls list will be empty.

5. Click Add Command.

6. Select View as the category, then Page Inspector, and then click OK.

7. Repeat this to add additional commands. Figure 4-12 shows the Customize dialog box with the Page Inspector and some additional third-party controls added to the toolbar. Figure 4-13 shows how the toolbar looks inside Visual Studio.

Figure 4-12. *Creating a custom toolbar*

Figure 4-12 shows the completed Razor Tools configuration in the Customize dialog box. The toolbar contains a link to the JS Parser, a third-party add-in that simplifies navigation of large, complex JavaScript files. It also contains a link to the Document Outline tool, the CSS Properties window, the Page Inspector, and the Split tool.

4-7. Navigating a Large Razor View or HTML File
Problem

You have a large View that is made up of hundreds of elements. Navigating this page is difficult. You would like to have a better way to navigate through the file.

Solution

Visual Studio has a built-in Document Outline tool. This tool generates an outline of the document based on the HTML elements, which are displayed in a tree-view format.

How It Works

Clicking an element in the tree view will navigate to that element in the document and highlight it in the code window. Figure 4-13 shows the Document Outline tool docked in the left pane and a Contact.cshtml View docked in the tabbed document pane.

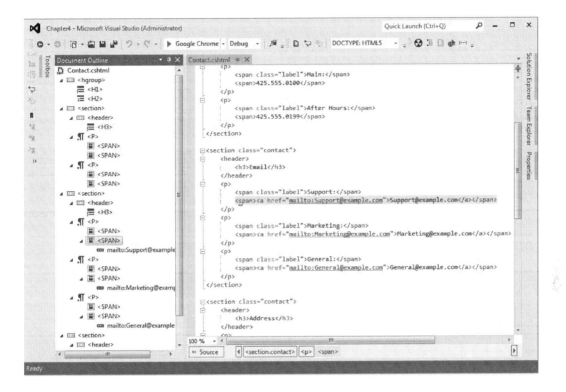

Figure 4-13. *Document Outline tool*

The right pane is hidden. A SPAN element has been selected in the document outline and the corresponding element has been selected in the document.

You can open the Document Outline window via the View menu under Other Windows submenu.

We demonstrated how to create a custom toolbar that included a quick link to this feature in Recipe 4-6. In Figure 4-13, a shortcut to this feature has been added to a custom toolbar.

4-8. Using the Page Inspector to Troubleshoot CSS Layout Bugs
Problem

You are troubleshooting a layout issue. You have applied a style to an element, yet it does not behave as you expect. You need to view the HTML output from your Razor code to see which styles are applied. Since the code that defines the style is spread across several style sheets, it makes this problem very difficult to solve.

Solution

The Page Inspector is a new tool that is bundled with all editions of Visual Studio 2012. The tool helps developers troubleshoot layout issues by highlighting all the code that contributes to the rendering of a selected section of a web page. The Page Inspector allows you to view the rendered output of your MVC View in an integrated browser window, and then select a particular element on the page by clicking it. Once an element is selected, the tool opens all the files in your solution that make up your page and automatically highlight the code in each file that takes part in rendering the selected section. The Page Inspector also shows the dynamically generated HTML that is sent to the web browser, and all the CSS style rules that are relevant to the selected section of the page.

You can open the Page Inspector by right-clicking the view in Solution Explorer and selecting View in the Page Inspector.

How It Works

The functionality of the Visual Studio Page Inspector is similar in to the Inspect Element feature found in the developer tools included in most major browsers. In Firefox, for example, if you right-click an element on a web page and select Inspect Element from the pop-up menu, an element inspection overlay is displayed. The Firefox Inspect Element feature, like the Visual Studio Page Inspector, will display the HTML Markup and the style rules. It also allows you to view the computed styles. While the Firefox Inspect Element feature has functional overlap with Page Inspector, it also has a major disadvantage: it does not have knowledge of the server-side code that makes up the element. Figure 4-14 shows the Firefox Inspect Element feature in action.

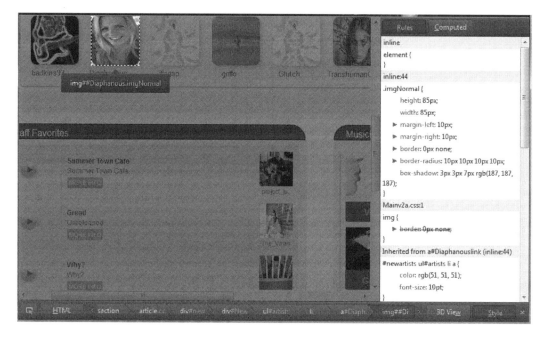

Figure 4-14. *The Firefox Inspect Element feature*

Along the top of the screen, you can see the selected element clearly outlined with the element markup displayed below the element in a callout bubble. Along the bottom of the browser window, you can see the element hierarchy, which allows you to navigate backward though the parent elements. Along the right side of the window is a box that shows the CSS code that defines the style for the element. Notice that it displays both inline styles as well as styles defined in external files. Overridden styles appear crossed out.

If we were using static HTML rather than ASP.NET MVC, the Firefox feature may have solved our problem. It has shown us that the style rule `border` was applied on both the `img` element in the `Main2a.css` file and in an inline style in the `.imgNormal` class. We clearly see the rule defined in `.imgNormal` has overridden the rule applied to `img`. Even though this is valuable insight, Firefox does not tell me what server-side file is generating the inline style. In fact, Firefox has no idea that this page is dynamically generated. It does not know that ASP.NET's bundling feature has combined and compressed several CSS files. It will show you where the style is defined in the combined and minified CSS file, but has no knowledge of what server-side CSS file the style was defined in.

The Visual Studio Page Inspector, on the other hand, does know about your dynamic pages. It knows which views are being called, and it knows about bundling. It even knows about the HTML helpers that you are using inside your Views.

Page Inspector Prerequisites

There are several prerequisites to running the Page Inspector. If your system is not configured properly or does not have the prerequisites installed, the Page Inspector will happily inform you of your missing dependencies. The Page Inspector's requirements include:

- Internet Explorer 9 or higher.

- Internet Explorer Enhanced Security Configuration must be disabled. This feature is enabled by default for Windows Server–based operating systems. You can disable it from the Server Manager. Click Local Server, and then under Properties, click the link next to IE Enhanced Security Configuration. This setting is useful for production servers, but is far too restrictive for a development machine.

- Debugging must be enabled in your project's `Web.config` file or the PageInspector. ServerCodeMappingSupport must be added to the application settings section of the `Web.config` file.

- The Page Inspector assemblies must be deployed to your development machine's global assembly cache (GAC). This should have been done for you when you installed Visual Studio.

- If your project is configured to use a local IIS web server, the IIS Worker Process must be configured to use .NET 4. If you are using IIS Express or the Visual Studio Development Server, you must also verify that these are running .NET version 4.

- The project must be using ASPX or Razor version 2 or higher. Page Inspector will not work with MVC 3. You will need to upgrade your project in order to take advantage of this feature.

- The URL being analyzed must map to a project in the current solution.

Using the Page Inspector

To begin using the Page Inspector, right-click a view in Solution Explorer and select View in Page Inspector. You can also open it by selecting Other Window–Page Inspector from the View menu.

When the Page Inspector opens, it will be docked in the left panel of Visual Studio. On most displays, this will make the Page Inspector too narrow to be useful. You will likely need to hide the Solution Explorer and manually resize the Page Inspector window in order to easily access all the UI elements available in the Page Inspector. Alternatively, if you have a second display, you can right-click the Page Inspector's title bar and select Float to float the window. You then drag it to your second monitor screen and resize it according to your needs.

Figure 4-15 shows the home page of MyOnlineBand in the Page Inspector.

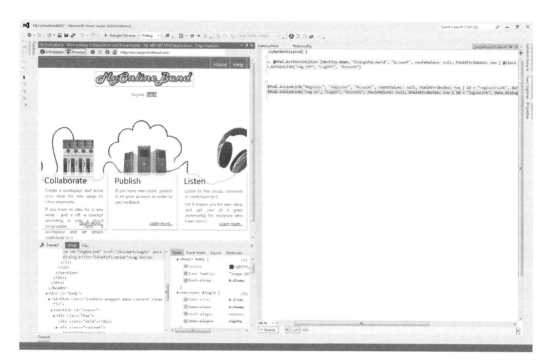

Figure 4-15. *Page Inspector*

In Figure 4-15, the Login link has been selected for inspection. In the HTML frame in the bottom left of the Page Inspector, the full rendered output of the page is displayed and the markup for the selected element is highlighted. We can clearly see the generated output for the element.

```
<a id="loginLink" href="/Account/Login" data-dialog-title="Identification">Log in</a>
```

The Page Inspector's HTML frame contains the entire dynamically-generated HTML that was sent to the browser. This is the same markup you would see if you opened the page in Internet Explorer and viewed the source. You can expand and collapse groups of HTML elements, and when Inspection Mode is enabled, you can click an HTML element and it's rendered visual output will appear in the browser window. This window is useful for ensuring your HTML output has been rendered as expected.

Also in the lower left frame of the Page Inspector is the Files viewer. If you click the Files tab, a list of the Views and Partial Views that make up the page will be shown. If you click on the page name, the document will open in the code editor.

The real power of the Page Inspector is its knowledge of your server-side code. In the example shown in Figure 4-15, when the link was selected in the Inspector, the _LoginPartial.cshtml partial view was automatically opened in preview mode and the source code that generated the output was automatically highlighted. This is very powerful. With one click, not only can I see the HTML output, but also the Razor code that is being executed. In this example, I see the following code called from the _LoginPartial.cshtml partial view:

```
@Html.ActionLink("Log in", "Login", "Account", routeValues: null, htmlAttributes: new
{ id="loginLink", data_dialog_title="Identification" })
```

On the bottom left is the Styles frame, which shows CSS rules that have been applied to the selected element. As with the Firefox example, the overridden rules are crossed out. Next to each style rule is a check box. If you uncheck a particular style rule, it is no longer applied to the page loaded in the browser window. This is very helpful when debugging layout issues. Figure 4-16 shows the Style Frame of the Page Inspector. It shows all the style rules that affect the Login link. You can clearly see that the inline style has been applied to the element, while several inherited styles are being ignored.

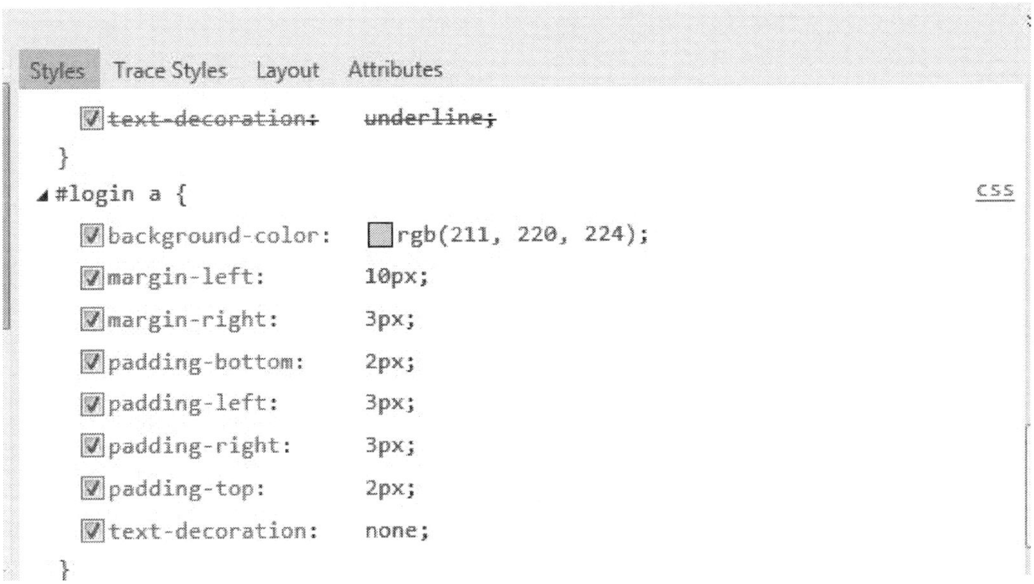

```
Styles   Trace Styles   Layout   Attributes

     ☑ text-decoration:    underline;
  }
  ◢ #login a {                                             CSS
     ☑ background-color:    ▢ rgb(211, 220, 224);
     ☑ margin-left:         10px;
     ☑ margin-right:        3px;
     ☑ padding-bottom:      2px;
     ☑ padding-left:        3px;
     ☑ padding-right:       3px;
     ☑ padding-top:         2px;
     ☑ text-decoration:     none;
  }
```

Figure 4-16. *The Styles Frame of the Page Inspector*

In addition to the main Styles viewer, the lower-right frame of the Page Inspector also has a Trace Styles tool, a Layout viewer, and an Attributes viewer.

The Trace Styles tool is similar to the Styles viewer, but allows you to drill down by properties. For example, if you are trying to troubleshoot the background color of an element, you can open the Style Trace tool and find the background-color property. You can then expand the node and see all the style rules that are influencing the background color of your selected element.

The Layout viewer shows a graphical box model of the computed CSS properties on your selected element. The tool shows the offset, margin, border, padding, and dimensions of the element.

The Attributes viewer lists all the HTML attributes that have been applied to the selected element. In addition to viewing the current settings, this tool allows you to edit the attribute values and add further attributes. The changes are immediately displayed in the Page Inspector's browser. This is helpful because it allows you to quickly experiment with attribute settings without needing to save and reload the page.

4-9. Using the Page Inspector While Debugging
Problem

You suspect that a flaw in a custom HTML Helper extension is resulting in a layout issue during certain conditions. You would like to be able to use the Page Inspector as your default browser when you initiate debugging.

Solution

Visual Studio 2012 allows you select any browser installed on your computer as the default browser for debugging. In addition, you may also select the Page Inspector as your debug browser. On the main Visual Studio toolbar, select the drop-down list next to the Start Debug button and select Page Inspector.

How It Works

As shown in Figure 4-17, Visual Studio allows you to debug using any browser installed on your computer. From Visual Studio's standard toolbar, click the Down arrow on the right side of the Start Debugging button, and then select Page Inspector from the drop-down list. You can then either click the button or press the F5 key on your keyboard to begin debugging in the Page Inspector.

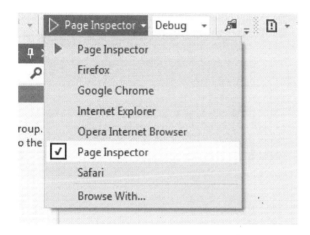

Figure 4-17. *Selecting Page Inspector as your browser for debugging*

This is helpful for debugging client-side layout issues that may have origins in server-side code. Unfortunately, the client-side JavaScript debugging feature only works with Internet Explorer. Also, JavaScript breakpoints are not hit when debugging in the Page Inspector.

This feature offers substantial benefits when writing a custom HTML helper. HTML helper can be somewhat tricky to debug because you often have a mix of C# code, Razor, or ASPX markup and client-side CSS and HTML. By using the Page Inspector as your debug browser, you can step though your HTML helper code and ensure that it is generating the output you expect. You can then continue to walk through the view logic until the page is rendered, and then use the Trace styles tool and Attributes viewer to examine how the rendered output affects the page layout.

4-10. Understanding Visual Studio's Debugging Windows
Problem

You would like to watch how the value of a variable changes during the execution of your application. You are unsure of how to use debugging windows in Visual Studio, and you would like to understand what each window does and how they work together.

Solution

Visual Studio has five main debugging windows: the Locals window, the Watch window, the Call Stack window, the Immediate window, and the Output window.

The Locals window shows all the variables that are in currently in scope. It shows the name of the variable, its current value, and the type of variable. For complex types, the value is displayed as a tree of objects. You can expand the tree to inspect the values of the nested types contained within the object.

If you have a complex page with many variables, tracking a value in the Locals window can become cumbersome. The Watch window helps solve this issue by allowing you to "add a watch" for a particular variable.

The Call Stack window allows you to view the functions that are currently on the stack. It displays the name of the function and the programming language it is written in. The Call Stack window can be configured to show additional information, such as the byte offset, line number, parameter names, and module name. It also allows you to insert breakpoints on a specific call to a function.

The Immediate window allows you to execute code in the current context of a breakpoint. You can enter any code that is valid during that moment in the program. The statement will be executed when you type **Enter**.

How It Works

Visual Studio has a powerful debugger. It allows you to set breakpoints in all of your server-side code, including your models, views, and controllers. If you are debugging with Internet Explorer as your default browser, you can set breakpoints in your JavaScript files. Visual Studio also allows you to debug your SQL Server–stored procedures, native code, GPU code, DirectX graphics, Silverlight applications, and WCF services. While it is unlikely that you will need to debug GPU or DirectX graphics in an ASP.NET project, in many cases, you may need to walk through a page execution that starts in controller class, calls stored procedures in a SQL Server database, copies the data from SQL Server into a model, displays the data in a view, and then allows the user to interact with that data using client-side JavaScript and Silverlight. The Visual Studio debugger allows you to step through this page execution from cradle to grave. It allows you set breakpoints anywhere in the program flow and dig into the details of the application state.

■ **Tip**　Visual Studio does not allow you to debug JavaScript and Silverlight at the same time. Breakpoints in your script files are ignored while the Silverlight debugger is enabled. If you do come across a situation where you need to debug both Silverlight and JavaScript on the same page, there is a workaround. You can include a debugger command in your script file above the line of code that you would like to break on. You will get a warning message informing you that an unhandled exception occurred (Script Breakpoint) and that administrative permission is required in order to invoke the Just-In-Time debugger. You can then step through the JavaScript code in a new Visual Studio window.

The first step in debugging a project is setting breakpoints. A breakpoint is a place in your code where you want the debugger to pause your application's execution. The most common way to set a breakpoint is to click the margin in the left side of the code editor window. You may also set breakpoints using the Call Stack window or by using the New Breakpoint dialog box. These alternative methods are sometimes required when it not possible to set a breakpoint on code that you are targeting because there is more than one statement in a single line.

Once your breakpoint is set, you can edit it by right-clicking the breakpoint (as shown in Figure 4-18). The breakpoint pop-up menu allows you to delete the breakpoint, disable the breakpoint, change the position of the breakpoint, and offers a number of options that can change when the breakpoint will cause the debugger to pause your application's execution.

Figure 4-18. *The Edit Breakpoint pop-up menu*

You can start debugging by clicking the Start Debug button from the main toolbar or by pressing the F5 key on your keyboard. After you start the debugger, it will open your application in the web browser. The debugger will attach itself to the IIS worker process, the web browser (if using Internet Explorer), and, if configured, your SQL Server Database. It will pause execution when a breakpoint is hit.

In Figure 4-19, we can see the Visual Debugger in action. In this example, it has paused execution in the HomeController inside an action method called DbTest. In the code editor, the debugger will highlight the current line of code to be executed. The breakpoint is highlighted in red and the line to be executed in yellow. You can view the values of the variables in the current view directly in the code editor by placing your mouse over a variable.

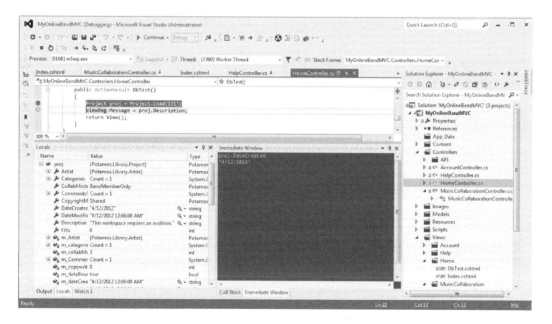

Figure 4-19. *Visual Studio debugging windows*

Figure 4-19 also shows the Locals window. In this example, it is showing two variables—proj, which is a custom type, and ViewBag, which is a dynamic type that is included in all controller actions. The ViewBag variable is not shown in Figure 4-19 because proj has been expanded, which pushes ViewBag below the scroll line. Because proj is a complex type, its value is shown as a tree view. The tree view has been expanded to view the contents of the variable.

In the Immediate window, we are allowed to enter any code that is executable in the current context. In Figure 4-19, proj.DateCreated was entered in the Immediate window, and when the Enter key was pressed, the value "4/12/2012" was displayed.

The Immediate window is not limited to printing variables. You may also call methods and change values of objects. This can be handy when you would like to see how changes in input will affect the operations you are debugging.

Another feature worth mentioning is the ability to pin a mouse over pop-up in the code window. This allows you to make the pop-up window that appears when you mouseover always visible while debugging. While debugging and stopped at a breakpoint (in break mode), mouse over a variable that you wish to pin. On the right side of the pop-up, click the Pin icon. You can then click the double Down Arrow icon to view or enter a comment about that variable. When you are done, it looks similar to Figure 4-20.

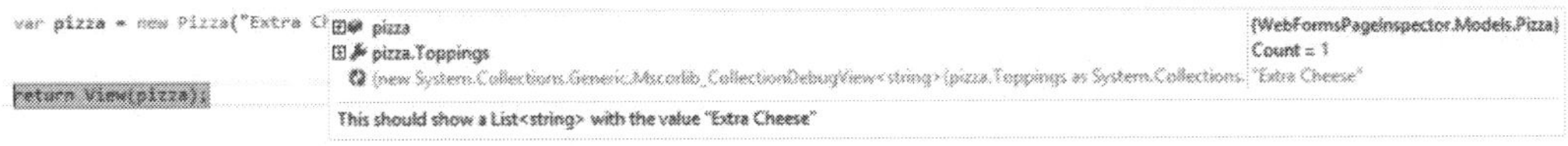

Figure 4-20. *Pinning a break mode viable pop-up on a complex type*

When the variable is out of scope, such as at the beginning of the next debugging session before the variable has been initialized, the pinned pop-up will display the last value assigned to it during the last debugging session. In the case of a complex type, you are able to expand each variable and then individually pin each member. In Figure 4-20, in addition to the main pizza variable, pizza.toppings, one of its members is also pinned so that multiple levels are shown for each debug session.

4-11. Setting a Conditional Breakpoint
Problem

You are debugging an issue that occurs inside a loop. You think that the unexpected behavior is occurring only when a certain variable is set to a value above the expected range. You set a breakpoint inside the loop, but need to step though over 100 iterations of the loop before you loop over an object that matches your suspected condition. This is an extremely time-consuming process. You need to find a better way.

Solution

The Visual Studio debugger has a great feature called *conditional breakpoints*. To use this feature, create a new breakpoint by clicking in the margin on the left side of the code window. The breakpoint will appear as a red dot. Right-click the red dot and select Condition... from the pop-up menu. In the Breakpoint Condition dialog box, check the Condition check box, enter an expression in the text box, and then click OK. Now the breakpoint will only be hot when the condition is true.

How It works

The conditional breakpoint dialog has two options. The first is to break when a specified condition is true. For example, let's say we have some action method that iterates through hundreds of numbers and prints out a statement that specifies whether the number is odd or even. You have an if statement that prints out a statement that you are half way there when the count hits 50. You would like to set a conditional breakpoint that pauses execution only when the count is equal to 50.

To do this, do the following.

1. Click the left margin next to the line of code where you would like to place the breakpoint.

2. Right-click the new breakpoint and select Condition from the pop-up menu.

3. In the dialog box, enter **i==50** and make sure the Is True option is selected.

4. Click OK, and then press the F5 key to debug your application.

The breakpoint should now be hit only once.

The second option used to create a breakpoint condition is to specify a variable name as the expression in the Condition text box, and then click the Has Changed option. For example, suppose that you have a code path that updates a variable named isHalfDone when i==50. You would like to watch changes made to this variable each time it is changed. In this case, you could create the breakpoint and then add the breakpoint condition with isHalfDone in the condition text box, as shown in Figure 4-21. The debugger should stop on loop iterations only where the isHalfDone variable is modified.

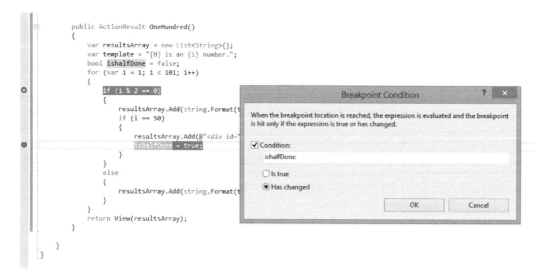

Figure 4-21. *Setting a conditional breakpoint*

This is a simplified example, but it should give you a general idea how the feature works. It is extremely useful when you have a global variable that can be updated by several places in your code and you need to determine which one is causing an erroneous value to be written.

4-12. Using the Output Window

Problem

While being able to pause a program's execution and step through your code is a very powerful feature, it can also be a very time-consuming exercise. Rather than manually stepping though line by line, you would prefer to output certain data to a log window so that you can analyze it later.

Solution

The Visual Studio Output window can be a powerful member of your debugging toolset. When you are debugging your application, the Output window automatically alters its behavior so that it shows output from the debugger. You can route messages to the debugger in two ways:

- Modifying your source code to include calls to the System.Diagnostics.Debug namespace.

- Setting breakpoint conditions that send messages to the output window.

How It Works
Using the System.Diagnostics.Debug Namespace

The System.Diagnostics.Debug namespace has a number of useful methods that you can use to aid in your debugging process. Among the most powerful are the Debug.WriteLine and Debug.Assert methods. Many renowned .NET coding experts, including John Robbins and Juval Lowy, are enthusiastic advocates of using this technique. In his book *Debugging Applications for Microsoft .NET and Microsoft Windows* (Microsoft Press, 2010), John Robbins calls assertions "the most important proactive programming tool in your development arsenal." Juval Lowy has often been heard to say that you can tell the quality of an application's code by the number of assertions used in the code. In his IDesign C# coding standard, Lowy states that all assumptions should be asserted and that one out of every five lines of code in your application should be an assertion.

The Debug.Assert method has four overloads, all of which take a condition resulting in a Boolean value as the first parameter. The additional parameters can be used to add messages that can describe the condition. If the Boolean condition returns false, the assertion will fail, and in addition to the message that you have added to the assertion, a stack trace of where the assertion occurred will be written to the output window.

The Debug.WriteLine statements are used to log information about the execution of the method. The logged statements are categorized as either Normal—indicating an expected application flow, or Error—indicated an error condition.

Listing 4-1 shows an action method that is using Debug.WriteLine and Debug.Assert to send messages about the program execution to the Output window. A Debug.Assert call is made after a call is made to the Project.Load method. The assumption asserted is that the proj object has been initialized. If this assumption is false, then the assertion message will be logged to the Output window.

Listing 4-1. An Example of Using Debug.Assert

```
public ActionResult DbTest()
{
   Debug.WriteLine("Attempting to load project data.", "Normal");
   try
   {
      Project proj=Project.Load(121);
      Debug.Assert(proj != null, "The project object was not initialized");
      if (proj != null)
```

```
        {
            ViewBag.Message = proj.Description;
Debug.WriteLine("Project loaded and the description has been written to the view bag.", "Normal");

        }
    }
    catch
    {
        Debug.WriteLine("An error occurred.", "Error");
    }
    return View();
}
```

Listing 4-2 shows the messages written to the Output window. The messages explicitly set in the Debug.Writeline and Debug.Assert calls are shown in bold.

Listing 4-2. Results of Assert and Writeline Statements in Output Window

Normal: Attempting to load project data.
A first chance exception of type 'System.InvalidOperationException' occurred in System.dll
A first chance exception of type 'System.FormatException' occurred in mscorlib.dll
A first chance exception of type 'System.InvalidCastException' occurred in System.Data.dll
---- DEBUG ASSERTION FAILED ----
---- Assert Short Message ----
The project object was not initialized
---- Assert Long Message ----

    at MyOnlineBandMVC.Controllers.HomeController.DbTest() in g:\WorkingFolder\MyOnlineBand 5\
MyOnlineBandMVC\MyOnlineBandMVC\Controllers\HomeController.cs:line 26
    at lambda_method(Closure , ControllerBase , Object[])
    at System.Web.Mvc.ReflectedActionDescriptor.Execute(ControllerContext controllerContext,
IDictionary'2 parameters)
    at System.Web.Mvc.ControllerActionInvoker.InvokeActionMethod(ControllerContext controllerContext,
ActionDescriptor actionDescriptor, IDictionary'2 parameters)
    at
    ...[Content ommitted for brevity]
    at System.Web.Hosting.PipelineRuntime.ProcessRequestNotificationHelper(IntPtr
rootedObjectsPointer, IntPtr nativeRequestContext, IntPtr moduleData, Int32 flags)
    at System.Web.Hosting.PipelineRuntime.ProcessRequestNotification(IntPtr rootedObjectsPointer,
IntPtr nativeRequestContext, IntPtr moduleData, Int32 flags)

Normal: Project loaded and the description has been written to the view bag.

Using "When Hit" to Print Statements to the Output Window

After you create a breakpoint, you can change its behavior so that rather than pausing program execution, you can have the debugger write the desired information to the Output window. To enable this feature, perform the following steps.

1. Right-click a breakpoint and select When Hit... from the pop-up menu.

2. Ensure that both the Print a Message: and Continue Execution check boxes are checked. Modify the message as desired.

3. Click OK. The breakpoint will now appear as a diamond rather than a circle.

Figure 4-22 shows the When Breakpoint Is Hit dialog box with the default settings. It will print the name of the function, the thread id, and the thread name to the Output window when the breakpoint is hit.

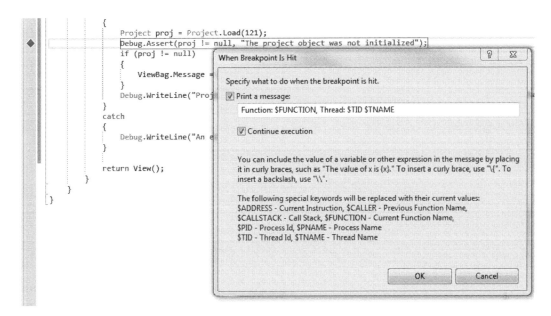

Figure 4-22. *When Breakpoint Is Hit dialog box*

The When Breakpoint Is Hit has its own set of keywords that can be used to create an expression. The expression can include plain text, one or more of the special keywords, and C# expressions surrounded by curly braces.

For example, if you are unconcerned about the name of the function or what thread you are on, you can replace the default expression with something like the following:

```
The value of proj.DateCreated is {proj.DateCreated}
```

Listing 4-3 shows an example of what the debugger will send to the Output window when using the When Hit feature. The first line in bold shows the output for the default expression. The second is the results of the preceding sample expression.

Listing 4-3. Results of Using When Hit Expressions in the Output Window

```
Normal: Attempting to load project data.
Function: MyOnlineBandMVC.Controllers.HomeController.DbTest(), Thread: 0x22BC Worker Thread
...
'w3wp.exe' (Managed (v4.0.30319)): Loaded 'C:\Windows\assembly\GAC_MSIL\Microsoft.VisualStudio.
Debugger.Runtime\11.0.0.0__b03f5f7f11d50a3a\Microsoft.VisualStudio.Debugger.Runtime.dll'
The value of proj.CreateDate is "4/12/2012"
```

4-13. Using the Extension Manager to Find and Install Add-ons for Visual Studio

Problem

You would like to understand how to use the Visual Studio extension and update manager, and you would like to know what extensions you should install.

Solution

The Extension Manager is a tool that allows you to find and install add-ins for Visual Studio. You can think of it as an app store for Visual Studio. To launch the Extension Manager from the Tools menu, select Extensions and Updates.

The initial view shows you a list of updates that you currently have installed. If an update is available for the add-in, you are notified and given a chance to upgrade.

You can search for new add-ons by clicking the Online button and drilling down to Visual Studio Gallery. There are thousands of extensions available. These extensions include Visual Studio project templates, samples, controls, SDKs, and tools.

How It Works

Although you do not need to use the Extension Manager to manage your Visual Studio extensions, it is a good idea for several reasons.

1. It's convenient. You have one place to go to manage all of your extensions, see reviews of the extensions, and in most cases, you can install the add-on with one click.

2. When updates are made to an installed extension, Visual Studio will alert you and give you the option to upgrade. The alert will persist in the system tray until it is dismissed.

3. You can easily see the extensions that you have installed and easily disable them if you notice that Visual Studio is exhibiting unexpected behavior or has begun to perform poorly after an add-in has been installed.

4. In addition to the Microsoft Visual Studio Gallery, it is possible to set up a custom repository where only approved add-ins can be downloaded.

There are few things to keep in mind before installing add-ons from the gallery.

- Many of the extensions have been created by the community and some are supported by an individual developer. If you and your team become dependent on an extension, you may not be able to get support for it.

- Before installing the extension, read the reviews and pay attention to the ratings. You should also make note of the publisher. You will need to click the More Information link, which opens the extensions information page on the Visual Studio Gallery web site.

- Anyone can submit an extension to the gallery. Microsoft does not test, certify, or make any claims regarding the quality of any extensions in the gallery.

- If you are installing multiple extensions, be aware that they may have never been tested together. You may find cases where two extensions each got a large number of positive reviews and work fine when installed alone, but cause Visual Studio to run slowly and occasionally hang when installed together. Imagine two add-ins that both want to change the color of the same item in the code window.

- The more extensions you add to Visual Studio, the longer it will take to load and the more memory it will take up.

You should only install extensions that solve a particular problem. Don't install extensions that you really do not need. If you are not using an extension, disable it. For example, if you installed Matthew Manela's Snippet Designer and used it to create several snippets but are not planning on creating any addition snippets in the near future, you should disable it.

Useful Extensions for MVC Development

Table 4-1 lists some useful extensions for ASP.NET MVC development. This is by no means an exhaustive list. New extensions are added all the time. Be sure to check it often and to read ratings and reviews before installing an extension.

Table 4-1. Useful Visual Studio Templates for MVC Developers

Extension Name	Publisher	What It Does
Image Optimizer	Mads Kristensen	The Image Optimizer adds an Optimize images command to the Solution Explorer context menu. It allows you automatically optimize all PNG, GIF, and JPEG files in a particular folder using Yahoo! Smush.it and PunyPNG. It can significantly reduce the size of your image files without any noticeable degradation in quality.
VSCommands	Squared Infinity	The VSCommands extension adds several new capabilities to Visual Studio. • It allows you to change the visual style of Visual Studio's main menu. • Adds Solution Badges, which are custom overlays that replace the default window thumbnail with one that clearly indicates what solution is loaded in Visual Studio. This is very useful when running several projects at once. • Adds the ability to copy and paste references between projects to Solution Explorer. • The ability to Zip a solution from inside Solution Explorer. This is very handy if you happen to be writing a book about Visual Studio and need to zip and upload code samples. • Improves the visual style of the Output Window and color-codes important messages. • Adds the ability to synchronize Visual Studio settings across several computers.

(continued)

135

Table 4-1. (*continued*)

Extension Name	Publisher	What It Does
Indent Guides	Steve Dower	Improves the Visual Studio code editor by adding vertical lines at each indent level in your code. The indent lines help improve yours code's readability and makes it easier to understand the flow of the code.
JavaScript Parser	MegaBoich	Improves Visual Studio experience for working with large JavaScript files. • Simplifies navigation by creating a tree of functions. • Creates a task list by locating TODO comments inside the JavaScript file.
Snippet Designer	Matthew Manela	Greatly simplifies the creation and management of Visual Studio snippets. Snippets are small code templates that can be used inside a code file.
Web Essentials 2012	Mads Kristensen	Suite of helpers for useful for HTML and CSS authoring. An especially useful feature is its ability to synchronize vendor-specific property settings for CSS properties such as border-radius and transform. It also improves CSS IntelliSense with support for custom fonts, regions, !Important, and CSS animation.

4-14. Visual Studio Keyboard Shortcuts
Problem

You would like to have a cheat sheet of all the most useful keyboard shortcuts available in Visual Studio.

Solution

There are literally hundreds of keyboard shortcuts in Visual Studio. In addition to the default set of shortcuts, Visual Studio allows you to create your own. Memorizing the shortcuts to some of the most common commands will increase your productivity by reducing the amount of time spent clicking through menus.

How It Works

Microsoft has kindly compiled an exhaustive list of keyboard shortcuts, which is available at http://msdn.microsoft.com/en-us/library/da5kh0wa%28v=vs.110%29.aspx (or http://tinyurl.com/6lv8vp4).

   The following tables list the most useful shortcuts.

Debugging

Keyboard Shortcut	Description
F5	Start debugging.
Ctrl + F5	Starts the application without debugging.
Shift + F5	Stops the current debug session.

Keyboard Shortcut	Description
F10	Step Over command. While in debug mode will move to the next step in the code in the local method. It will step over code in outside methods unless the external code contains a breakpoint.
Ctrl+F10	When in break mode, will resume execution of the code from the current statement to the statement at current cursor position.
F11	Step Into command. While in debug mode, it will move to the next step in the code even if the next executable line of code is defined in another assembly as long as debug symbols are available.
F9	Creates or removes a breakpoint at the current line in the code editor.
Ctrl+B	Displays the new breakpoint dialog window.
Ctrl+Alt+B	Displays the Breakpoints dialog window, which allows you to view and edit all breakpoints defined in the current solution.

Testing

The following shortcuts use complex keyboard shortcuts known as *chords*. They are a sequence of key stroke combinations. They are notated as [key1],[key2].

Keyboard Shortcut	Description
Ctrl+R, Ctrl+A	Debug all tests in the solution.
Ctrl+R, Ctrl+C	Debug all tests in current class.
Ctrl+R, T	Run all tests in the current context.
Ctrl+R, Ctrl+T	Debug all tests in the current context.
Ctrl+R, Ctrl+D	Debug all tests in the current result set that are checked.
Ctrl+R, F	Run all tests in the current result set that are checked without the debugger.

Help

Keyboard Shortcut	Description
F1	Display a topic from help related to the user interface element that currently has focus.

Window Management

Keyboard Shortcut	Description
Shift+Alt+Enter	Toggles full screen mode.
Ctrl+F4	Closes current open document.
Ctrl+Shift+F6	Moves to the next document.

Build and Save

Keyboard Shortcut	Description
Ctrl+Shift+B	Build solution.
Ctrl+Break	Cancel build.
Ctrl+S	Save current document.
Ctrl+Shift+S	Save all documents.

Project

Keyboard Shortcut	Description
Ctrl+Shift+N	New Project
Ctrl+N	New File
Ctrl+Shift+O	Open project or solution.
Ctrl+O	Open file.
Ctrl+M, Ctrl+C	Create new controller.
Ctrl+Shift+A	Add new item.
Shift+Alt+A	Add existing item.
Shift+Alt+C	Add new Class item.

CHAPTER 5

Getting the Most from the Built-in Templates

5-1. Choosing an ASP.NET MVC 4 Project Template

Problem

You are about to start a new ASP.NET MVC project. You have opened Visual Studio and selected ASP.NET MVC 4 as your project type. You are now presented with a screen that lists several templates. You are not sure which one to choose and what the major differences are between them.

Solution

The Visual Studio templates provide a starting point for your project by including a basic web site structure, layout pages, and commonly used JavaScript libraries. The names of the templates clearly indicate each templates purpose and how you should use them. For example, if you need to create an Internet-facing application with a forms login and registration, use the Internet Application template. If you are building a line of business applications (LOB) that will be deployed on your company's local intranet, use the Intranet Application template.

How It Works

ASP.NET MVC 4 comes with six built-in Visual Studio templates: Empty, Basic, Intranet Application, Intranet Application, Mobile Application, and Web API. The following is a quick breakdown of each template and where to use them.

- *Empty*: Bare bones MVC Project. Use for projects that do not require authorization and do not need forms with validation. Perfect for projects that need to provide read-only access to content such as marketing capital.

- *Basic*: Similar to Empty, but adds jQuery and validation support. It is a good template for creating applications that use Anonymous Authentication and need basic input forms.

- *Intranet Application*: Provides an application structure that includes several default controllers, models, and views. It also provides instructions on how to enable Windows Authentication in IIS. A perfect starting point for a corporate line of business applications.

- *Internet Application*: Provides an application structure that includes controllers and views for home and account setup. It has views for registration and login. It is configured to use the Universal Providers and configured for Forms Authentication.

- *Web API*: Provides an application structure that includes a `Values` controller that creates a simple RESTful API with actions for each of the HTTP verbs: `GET`, `POST`, `PUT`, and `DELETE`. It also includes a home controller and corresponding view that gives a brief explanation of ASP.NET Web API.

- *Mobile Application*: Creates a project that targets mobile devices, and like the Internet template, has an Account controller that uses forms authentication.

The Empty Template

The Empty template is the most basic of the templates. It comes with a set of folders that make up a basic application structure that includes the following:

- `Controllers`: Should contain all of your application's controller classes.

- `Models`: Should contain your application's models.

- `Views`: Should contain your views.

- `App_Start`: Contains static classes that are used for application initialization.

- `App_Data`: Can contain data files for SQL Express or other small file based databases. In general, you need to be careful about using web server local storage for data. You can run into issues if you need to scale out or if you have an unexpected volume of data.

These folders are common to all the MVC templates. The Empty template does not include `Scripts` and `Content` directories, as do most of the other templates.

Inside the `App_Start` folder are two C# files: `FilterConfig.cs` and `RouteConfig.cs`. Both contain static helper classes that are called in the `Application_Start()` method of the `Global.asax` file—a file inherited from ASP.NET Web Forms that defines a number of events that fire throughout the lifecycle of an application. The `Application_Start()` method is called when the application is started, and usually performs application initialization tasks. In our Empty MVC Application template, the `Application_Start()` method calls the required `RegisterAllAreas` method and the two static initialization methods defined in the `App_Start` folder.

Listing 5-1 shows the `Application_Start()` method from `global.asax`. The first line inside `Application_Start()` calls `AreaRegistration.RegisterAllAreas()`. This is a required method that registers all areas defined in the application with the MVC engine. In ASP.NET MVC, Areas are a way to partition large MVC applications into more manageable subsystems.

Listing 5-1. Global.asax Application_Start Method

```
public class MvcApplication : System.Web.HttpApplication
{
    protected void Application_Start()
    {
        AreaRegistration.RegisterAllAreas();

        FilterConfig.RegisterGlobalFilters(GlobalFilters.Filters);
        RouteConfig.RegisterRoutes(RouteTable.Routes);
    }
}
```

The second line calls the `FilterConfig.RegisterGlobalFilters` method, which is defined on the `FilterConfig.cs` file shown in Listing 5-2. This method registers global filters with the MVC engine. Filters provide a mechanism for inserting processing logic either before or after an action method has been called. Global filters are filters that can be applied to all action methods in an MVC application.

The last line in Listing 5-1 calls `RouteConfig.RegisterRoutes`. This method defines the routes used by the application. In MVC, routes are used to define the URL structure of the application.

Listing 5-2 show the contents of the `FilterConfig.cs` file. It defines a class with a single static method: `RegisterGlobalFilters`. In the Empty project template, this method registers a single filter called `HandleErrorAttribute`.

Listing 5-2. FilterConfig.cs from App_Start Folder

```
public class FilterConfig
{
    public static void RegisterGlobalFilters(GlobalFilterCollection filters)
    {
        filters.Add(new HandleErrorAttribute());
    }
}
```

The `HandleErrorAttribite` filter adds default error behavior to each action method, which, in case of an error, will attempt to display a view named Error—which should be located in the `/Views/Shared` folder of your project. Since this view does not exist in the Empty template, a default error message that explains how to configure custom errors in the `Web.config` file will be displayed. It should also be noted that the default behavior for ASP.NET MVC applications is to display a detailed error message when a page is viewed from the local web server. Because of this, you will see the detailed error message rather than the custom page.

Another element that is common for all the MVC templates, including the Empty template, is the inclusion of `packages.config`. This file is used by Visual Studio's NuGet package manager to keep track of the NuGet packages installed in the project.

In Listing 5-3, the contents of `packages.config` is shown. It is an XML file that contains a list of assemblies included in the project that are managed by NuGet. The NuGet package manager allows you to search for and include .NET components and JavaScript libraries in your project. In addition, it also offers you a simple way to keep these files and their dependencies up-to-date. Before NuGet, developers needed to scour the Internet for a component, download it, sometimes compile it, and then add it as a reference to the project. NuGet simplified this process.

Listing 5-3. Empty Project's Package.config

```
<?xml version="1.0" encoding="utf-8"?>
<packages>
  <package id="Microsoft.AspNet.Mvc" version="4.0.20710.0" targetFramework="net45" />
  <package id="Microsoft.AspNet.Razor" version="2.0.20710.0" targetFramework="net45" />
  <package id="Microsoft.AspNet.WebApi" version="4.0.20710.0" targetFramework="net45" />
  <package id="Microsoft.AspNet.WebApi.Client" version="4.0.20710.0" targetFramework="net45" />
  <package id="Microsoft.AspNet.WebApi.Core" version="4.0.20710.0" targetFramework="net45" />
  <package id="Microsoft.AspNet.WebApi.WebHost" version="4.0.20710.0" targetFramework="net45" />
  <package id="Microsoft.AspNet.WebPages" version="2.0.20710.0" targetFramework="net45" />
  <package id="Microsoft.Net.Http" version="2.0.20710.0" targetFramework="net45" />
  <package id="Microsoft.Web.Infrastructure" version="1.0.0.0" targetFramework="net45" />
  <package id="Newtonsoft.Json" version="4.5.6" targetFramework="net45" />
</packages>
```

Each package listed in the configuration file contains an id, which is a unique value that should match an entry in the package repository. It also includes the version and the target framework. The target framework is usually the same as the target framework for the project. For MVC 4, the target framework will always be .NET 4.5.

You should not modify this file directly. It is managed by the NuGet package manager. It is useful to browse in order to see which packages are installed for the project. Another way you can view this information is to right-click either the project node or the References folder in Solution Explorer and select Manage NuGet Packages… from the pop-up menu. In the NuGet window, click Installed Packages. This shows you a list of the installed packages. You can click each package and read its description.

We will now take a brief look at each of the packages included in the Empty template. These packages are core components for all MVC projects and are included in the other templates. Understanding what each of them does will give you a deeper understanding of the framework.

- *Json.NET*: This package provides a serialization mechanism for converting .NET objects to and from JavaScript Object Notation (JSON). Even though there is a built-in JSON serializer in the .NET Framework, the MVC team has selected Json.NET because it is faster and more feature-rich than Microsoft's implementation. In addition to basic serialization capabilities, it also offers a LINQ to JSON capability for manually reading and writing JSON, and the ability to convert XML to JSON and JSON to XML.

- *Microsoft .NET Framework 4 HTTP Client Libraries*: Provides interface for sending, receiving, and processing HTTP messages. It is essential for consuming RESTFul services from your server-side code.

- *Microsoft ASP.NET MVC 4*: The primary runtime engine for MVC Framework. Including it as a NuGet package allows you to upgrade projects independently.

- *Microsoft ASP.NET Razor 2*: Contains the core runtime assemblies for ASP.NET Web Pages, which includes the Razor view engine.

- *Microsoft ASP.NET Web API*: Allows you to create RESTFul services on top of the MVC Framework infrastructure. There are three additional libraries included because the Microsoft ASP.NET Web API is dependent on them. These include Microsoft ASP.NET Web API Client Libraries, Microsoft ASP.NET Web API Core Libraries, and Microsoft ASP.NET Web API Web Host.

- *Microsoft ASP.NET Web Pages 2*: Contains assemblies shared by both ASP.NET MVC and ASP.NET Web Pages. This package has dependencies on both Microsoft ASP.NET Razor 2 and `Microsoft.Web.Infrastructure`.

- *Microsoft.Web.Infrastructure*: Allows you to dynamically register HTTP Modules at runtime.

The Basic Template

Building off the Empty template, the Basic template adds infrastructure to your application. This includes directories for Script and Content. It also adds a Shared folder (under the Views folder) that contains the _Layout.cshtml and Error.cshtml files. Under the Views folder, the template adds the _ViewStart.cshtml file, which sets Shared/_Layout.cshtml as the default page template for the project. It also adds additional NuGet packages.

As discussed in the last section, `Error.cshtml` is the default custom error page that is used by the `ErrorHandelAttribute` global filter. You can modify this file to create a richer landing page for end users when errors occur.

`_ViewStart.cshtml` lets the Razor engine know the location of the default layout page. Razor layout pages provide a place to define templates that will contain all of your web application's boilerplate structure, including the page header and navigation. If you are familiar with ASP.NET Web Forms, the layout concept shares the same basic function as a master page. Listing 5-4 shows the contents of `_ViewStart.cshtml`. It is a very simple file with a single line that sets the Layout property to `_Layout.cshtml`.

Listing 5-4. _ViewStart.cshtml

```
@{
    Layout = "~/Views/Shared/_Layout.cshtml";
}
```

_Layout.cshtml defines the default page template for your web site. It defines several areas that are placeholders for viewing specific content. It also can be used to include default script libraries and CSS. Listing 5-5 shows the _Layout.cshtml file included in the Basic template.

Listing 5-5. _Layout.cshtml from the Basic Template

```
<!DOCTYPE html>
<html>
<head>
    <meta charset="utf-8" />
    <meta name="viewport" content="width=device-width" />
    <title>@ViewBag.Title</title>
    @Styles.Render("~/Content/css")
    @Scripts.Render("~/bundles/modernizr")
</head>
<body>
    @RenderBody()

    @Scripts.Render("~/bundles/jquery")
    @RenderSection("scripts", required: false)
</body>
</html>
```

Let's take a look at the code in Listing 5-5. While this is a very simple layout page, it tells us a lot about the MVC team's design philosophy. It also introduces you to some layout page concepts, as well as some of the new HTML5 capabilities.

In the first line, we see `<!DOCTYPE html>`. This is an HTML declaration that tells the browser which version of the HTML specification the document is written. In this case, it is telling the browser that our page is using HTML5. If you have ever worked with HTML, you are likely familiar with the DOCTYPE declaration, but may be surprised by how simple it is with HTML5. In past versions of the specification, DOCTYPE included reference to a DTD hosted at W3.org. It's great to see that the standardization boards have finally listened to people who actually write code for a living rather than giving in to the lure of compromise. This is the first DOCTYPE in history that a normal human can actually memorize.

The next tag of interest is `<meta name="viewport" content="width=device-width"/>`. This tag was first used on the iPhone to tell the phone where on the page it should pan and zoom to by default. The tag (as shown in Listing 5-5) will set the width of the page to match the width of the device. Once you add a controller and a corresponding view to your project, you can test this out by accessing your site using a device emulator or by changing the size of your browser window. The content will fill the screen of the mobile device and should not require the user to use a zoom gesture to make it readable.

The next section of Listing 5-5 introduces some basic Razor code. In the `title` tag, you see a Razor expression that prints the contents of the `@ViewBag.Title` between the beginning and ending title tags. The `ViewBag` is a *dynamic method bag*, which are objects that can add and remove properties and methods at runtime. `Title` is a dynamic property. It is not a special name. You could just as easily call it `PageTitle` or anything else you want, and it will function exactly the same. In views that use _Layout.cshtml, you can either set the value of `@ViewBag.Title` in your controller or use a code block inside the view.

`@Styles.Render` and `@Scripts.Render` work with ASP.NET 4.5's bundling and minification feature. Both methods allow you to pass in collection bundles that have been registered as part of your application initialization sequence. It will take all the script and CSS tags that are defined in the bundles, combine them all into a single file, then minify them by removing unneeded white space and comments—making variable names shorter.

`@RenderBody()` is a placeholder that contains the body of your view. This is followed by an additional call to `@Scripts.Render` that adds the jQuery bundle to the pace. The final Razor markup is a call to `@RenderSection`. This creates an optional section for your views, where you can add additional client-side JavaScript code.

The Basic template contains all the NuGet packages used in the empty template, and adds the following:

- *Entity Framework*: Microsoft's recommended data access technology, which includes powerful, object relational-mapping features. The template uses version 5 of the Framework, which includes built-in support for code-first development and support for enums.

- *jQuery*: jQuery is one of the web's most popular JavaScript frameworks. It simplifies many complex client-side programming tasks, including traversing the HTML document object model, event handling, and animation.

- *jQuery UI (Combined Library)*: An open-source JavaScript library built on top of jQuery, which contains user interface components such as data input widgets, animation effects, and themes support.

- *jQuery Validation*: A jQuery plug-in that simplifies client-side form validation.

- *knockoutjs*: A JavaScript library that uses the MVVM pattern to simplify the creation of dynamic user interfaces with clean code that is easier to maintain.

- *Microsoft ASP.NET Universal Providers Core Libraries*: Provides support for all editions of SQL Server from 2005 and up, including LocalDB. In addition, the Universal Provider is compatible with Windows Azure and is designed to allow developers to easily switch between traditional SQL Server and the cloud-hosted version. The Universal Providers are not backward compatible with the database schema used for the SQL providers introduced with ASP.NET 2.0.

- *Microsoft ASP.NET Web Optimization Framework*: Provides infrastructure for bundling and minification.

- *Microsoft jQuery Unobtrusive Ajax and Microsoft jQuery Unobtrusive Validation*: A jQuery plug-in that aids in developing pages that do not need to use inline JavaScript. These add-ins help enforce separation of concerns in your client code.

- *Modernizr*: Helps you take advantage of HTML5 and CSS 3 while maintaining compatibility with older browsers.

- *WebGrease*: A component used by the ASP.NET Web Optimization Framework to optimize JavaScript and CSS files. It also has a number of command-line utilities that can be accessed via the NuGet command window.

When added together, the Basic template is made up of 37 .NET assemblies and seven JavaScript libraries. Looking at this, you may be saying, "Wow. I have not even started my project yet, and it's already bloated." On the other hand, you have a whole lot of high-quality infrastructure code that you no longer need to write and maintain. You also have the right to remove packages that you do not need; simply use the NuGet package manager.

Inside the App_Start folder, the Basic template added another file: BundleConfig.cs. This file defines the script and CCS files that should be bundled and minified by the ASP.NET Web Optimization Framework. Listing 5-6 shows the contents of BundleConfig.cs. It is similar to the other files in the App_Start directory. It has a class with a single static method: RegisterBundles. When this method is called from Global.asax, the BundleCollection is passed in as a parameter.

Listing 5-6. BundleConfig.cs from the Basic Template

```
public class BundleConfig
{
    // For more information on Bundling, visit http://go.microsoft.com/fwlink/?LinkId=254725
    public static void RegisterBundles(BundleCollection bundles)
    {
        bundles.Add(new ScriptBundle("~/bundles/jquery").Include(
                    "~/Scripts/jquery-{version}.js"));
```

```
bundles.Add(new ScriptBundle("~/bundles/jqueryui").Include(
            "~/Scripts/jquery-ui-{version}.js"));

bundles.Add(new ScriptBundle("~/bundles/jqueryval").Include(
            "~/Scripts/jquery.unobtrusive*",
            "~/Scripts/jquery.validate*"));

// Use the development version of Modernizr to develop with and learn from. Then, when you're
// ready for production, use the build tool at http://modernizr.com to pick only the tests you need.
bundles.Add(new ScriptBundle("~/bundles/modernizr").Include(
            "~/Scripts/modernizr-*"));

bundles.Add(new StyleBundle("~/Content/css").Include("~/Content/site.css"));

bundles.Add(new StyleBundle("~/Content/themes/base/css").Include(
            "~/Content/themes/base/jquery.ui.core.css",
            "~/Content/themes/base/jquery.ui.resizable.css",
            "~/Content/themes/base/jquery.ui.selectable.css",
            "~/Content/themes/base/jquery.ui.accordion.css",
            "~/Content/themes/base/jquery.ui.autocomplete.css",
            "~/Content/themes/base/jquery.ui.button.css",
            "~/Content/themes/base/jquery.ui.dialog.css",
            "~/Content/themes/base/jquery.ui.slider.css",
            "~/Content/themes/base/jquery.ui.tabs.css",
            "~/Content/themes/base/jquery.ui.datepicker.css",
            "~/Content/themes/base/jquery.ui.progressbar.css",
            "~/Content/themes/base/jquery.ui.theme.css"));
    }
}
```

A total of six bundles are defined. The first call creates a bundle for the jQuery library. The second creates a bundle for the jQuery UI library. The third adds bundles for Microsoft's Unobtrusive Ajax and Unobtrusive Validation libraries. At runtime, it will create a new file that contains minified versions of the combined libraries. Next, a bundle is created for the Modernizr libraries, which helps provide backward compatibility with non-HTML5-compliant web browsers, such as Internet Explorer 8. This is followed by a bundle is for site.css. This is the main style sheet used for the template. The last statement takes each of the CSS files used by the jQuery UI default theme.

Inside the Content directory, you find the site.css files along with the CSS files used by jQuery UI.

The Intranet Application Template

The Intranet Application template builds on the foundation of the Basic template. It includes all the files, folders, and NuGet packages that Basic does.

After you create your project and open it for the first time, you are treated to a readme.txt file that explains how to enable Windows Authentication on your web site. If you do not follow these instructions, you will see an accessed-denied message when you attempt to run the application.

The Intranet Application template includes a Home controller that is defined in the HomeController.cshtml file. This controller includes three action methods: Index(), About(), and Contact(). The action methods have three corresponding views under the Views\Home directory: Index.cshtml, About.cshtml, and Contact.cshtml.

_Layout.cshtml is a bit more complex than the one in the Basic template. It starts with the same construct, but adds some boilerplates, including a header with navigation and a "Hello" message that uses @User.Identity.Name to get the user's login name from the current security context.

An Images directory is also included with the template. It contains all the images and icons used in the views.

The Internet Application Template

The Internet Application template builds on the Intranet Application template. It adds an additional controller called the Account Controller in the /Controllers/AccountController.cs file along with a set of views and partial views to correspond to the actions defined in AccountController . It also has a model defined in the /Models/AccountModel.cs file that is used by the controller and the views. This creates a complete web site with a forms-based login and a registration page using Microsoft's Forms Authentication, with the Universal Provider configured to use SQL Server LocalDB.

The AccountController makes use of several techniques, such as using data annotations along with HTML helpers that create code that work with the jQuery Validation libraries to automatically add validation to your forms. We will go over these techniques in detail in Recipes 5-8 and 5-10.

In addition to Forms Authentication, the Internet Application template also supports a number of third-party authentication providers for open OpenID and OAuth. This allows you to use external authentication providers, including Microsoft LiveID, Twitter, Facebook, and Google. Added to the App_Start folder is a file called AuthConfig.cs, which lets you configure the use of these services for your site. The Account controller has implemented much of the integration code required for associating and disassociating accounts. The core infrastructure for the external authentication providers is contained in a series of NuGet packages.

The Web API Template

The Web API template is similar to the Basic template, but adds a controller that extends ApiController. It also provides a home controller that includes some links to tutorials for Web API.

Listing 5-7 shows the code inside the Web API template's ApiController. Notice in the class declaration that the class extends the ApiController class rather the Controller class. Also, the return statements in the action methods do not return ActionResults. The Get() method returns an IEnumerable<string> and Get(int id) returns a string. In fact, the action methods can return any .NET type. The framework will automatically serialize the result to the requested format, which can either be SOAP or JSON. The method names used in the Web API controller are not arbitrary. Each of them is mapped to a corresponding HTTP verb. The Get() action, for example, is an HTTP GET request for the URL /api/values. Using the conventions of REST, the expectation would be that the method would respond with a list of values.

Listing 5-7. The Values Controller

```
public class ValuesController : ApiController
{
    // GET api/values
    public IEnumerable<string> Get()
    {
        return new string[] { "value1", "value2" };
    }

    // GET api/values/5
    public string Get(int id)
    {
        return "value";
    }
```

```
    // POST api/values
    public void Post(string value)
    {
    }

    // PUT api/values/5
    public void Put(int id, string value)
    {
    }

    // DELETE api/values/5
    public void Delete(int id)
    {
    }
}
```

The Mobile Application Template

The Mobile Application template is very similar to the Internet Application template in that it shares the basic site structure. The main difference is the implementation of the views, which have simplified content tailored for smaller screens. The views and have been enhanced with jQuery Mobile. This provides a mobile experience that is comparable to native applications. Like the other JavaScript libraries included in the project, jQuery Mobile has been added as a NuGet package.

5-2. Creating a Simple Web Site Using the ASP.NET MVC 4 Empty Template

Problem

You have volunteered to create a web site for a local charity. They want the site to similar to the fliers that they have been using. The web site will be open to the general public and will not require authentication. You will not be using jQuery UI nor will you be creating any custom forms. You want to make the page as search engine accessible as possible. You have decided that the Empty project template meet your needs. After creating your project, you need help creating the page taxonomy and setting up page routing.

Solution

Use the empty template to create your new solution. Add a controller named **JoeyBellaMemorialFund**. You then add three action methods that include the following:

- Index: The home page.

- TrickyTray: Shows information about an upcoming tricky tray.

- BeefSteakDinner: Shows information about an upcoming beefsteak dinner event.

Next, you create views to correspond with the action methods and then add the appropriate content. Since the content is static, you will not need to create a model for this project.

How It Works

The following are step-by-step instructions for creating the simple web site. The full code for this recipe is available on the Apress web site.

Creating the Project

To create your web site:

1. Open Visual Studio. From the File menu, select New ➤ Project.

2. In the New Project dialog box, select the ASP.NET MVC 4 project template if it is visible. Otherwise, in the search box in the upper-right side of the New Project dialog window, type **ASP.NET MVC 4 C#**. Then click the ASP.NET MVC 4 Web Application project template. Visual Studio will remember that you selected this template and will show it as part of your default project template list the next time you create a project.

3. Next, give your project a name, and assign a name and a location for your solution.

4. In the New ASP.NET MVC 4 Project window, select the Empty template. Ensure that the selected view engine is Razor. Click the OK button to create the project.

■ **Note**   For this book, I am using the following convention for naming Visual Studio projects related to the recipes. For the project names, I am using the following convention:

Ch<chapter number>.R<recipe number>.<Short Name>

For this recipe, the solution name is Ch5.R2.SimpleWebApp.

The solution name consists of only the chapter number and the recipe number with the project name omitted.

Creating the Controller

The first step in creating our controller is to consider our URL scheme. Since the names of our controller and actions will appear in the URL, it is important to put some thought into naming them.

Since we want this project to be easy for search engines to find, we want to use keywords in the name of the URL. For the web site's URL, the charity has purchased the domain JBMF-NJ.org. Web search engines such as Goggle sort search results from a complex algorithm that determines which items appear first. One important factor is the domain name. Keywords in the domain name have a major impact on search ranking. It is important to have localized search results. Since this charity is located in New Jersey (NJ), adding the state abbreviation to the domain name is helpful. The charity's acronym is also in the domain name. Google Analytics found that most people searched for the charity using its acronym. Other people searched using the full name of the charity. To accommodate these searches, we want the full name of the charity—Joey Bella Memorial Fund—to appear in all URLs on our simple web site. To meet this requirement, we name the controller JoeyBellaMemorialFundController. You also have the option of creating a custom route by modifying the RouteConfig.cs file in the App_Start folder.

To create the controller:

1. In Solution Explorer, right-click the Controllers folder then select New and then Controller. Alternatively, use the Visual Studio Ctrl+M, Ctrl+C keyboard shortcut chord. To do this, press the Ctrl key, and then type **M** followed by **C**. The Add Controller dialog box will appear.

2. Rename the controller **JoeyBellaMemorialFundController**.

3. Click the Add button to create the controller.

4. Visual Studio will create the controller class and add an action method called Index().

5. Add two additional actions names: TrickyTray and BeefSteakDinner.

The controller class should look like Listing 5-8.

Listing 5-8. JoeyBellaMemorialFundController.cs

```
public class JoeyBellaMemorialFundController : Controller
{
    //
    // GET: /JoeyBellaMemorialFund/

    public ActionResult Index()
    {
        return View();
    }

    //
    // GET: /JoeyBellaMemorialFund/TrickyTray
    public ActionResult TrickyTray()
    {
        return View();
    }

    //
    // GET: /JoeyBellaMemorialFund/BeefSteakDinner
    public ActionResult BeefSteakDinner()
    {
        return View();
    }

}
```

In this example, I placed comments to show the URL that will correspond to each action. The comments are not required but can be helpful. Since this is a very simple web site, we will not have any processing inside the controller. We will just return an ActionResult, which corresponds to a view. This is done by calling the Controller.View() method.

Creating the Views

Now that we have created the controller and added actions, we need to create views for each action. The first step is to create a new subfolder under the project's view directory that has the same name as the controller. To be in compliance with the convention, we will name the folder JoeyBellaMemorialFund.

1. In Solution Explorer, right-click the Views folder and select Add, and then Folder from the pop-up menu. The folder will appear in rename mode under the Views folder. Type the controller name, and then press Enter. If you accidentally click away from renaming the folder, you can rename the folder by right-clicking it and selecting Rename from the pop-up menu.

2. You now need to create the views. Right-click your newly created folder and select Add, and then View.

3. In the Add View dialog box, enter **Index** for the view name. Uncheck "Use a layout or master page" and ensure that the Razor view engine is selected.

4. Click the Add button. Visual Studio will create the view and open it for editing.

5. Repeat this process and create two additional views for TrickyTray and BeefSteakDinner.

6. Press the F5 key on your keyboard to compile your application and launch it in your default web browser.

7. You will see a 404 (Not Found) error on the default page. This is expected since we have not changed the default routing to use our controller. Verify that the pages are available at the URLs we have mapped out in the controller (for example, /JoeyBellaMemorialFund/BeefSteakDinner). If you have not modified the views, each will be displayed as a blank page. The Title specified in the Table tag on each view should appear in the browser tab name.

8. Close the browser window and return to Visual Studio. If you are running a web browser other than Internet Explorer, you need to hit the Stop button on the debug toolbar to stop debugging.

Modifying the Default Route

In order for our Index action to be invoked when a user enters the root of the web site, we need to change the configuration of the routing engine so that the JoeyBellaMemorialFundController is the default.

1. Open the App_Start/RouteConfig.cs file. Modify the second routes MapRoute method so that the default controller is renamed to **JoeyBellaMemorialFund**. When you are done, it should look like Listing 5-9.

2. Press the F5 key to verify that the default route is working as expected. Since you have not added any content to your Index view, it will show a blank web page.

Listing 5-9. Changing the Default Route in the RouteConfig.cs File

```
public class RouteConfig
{
    public static void RegisterRoutes(RouteCollection routes)
    {
        routes.IgnoreRoute("{resource}.axd/{*pathInfo}");

        routes.MapHttpRoute(
            name: "DefaultApi",
            routeTemplate: "api/{controller}/{id}",
            defaults: new { id = RouteParameter.Optional }
        );

        routes.MapRoute(
            name: "Default",
            url: "{controller}/{action}/{id}",
```

```
                    defaults: new { controller = "JoeyBellaMemorialFund", action = "Index",
        id = UrlParameter.Optional }
                );
        }
    }
```

It should be noted that because of the default route configuration, there are actually three possible routes to your home page:

- \: This is the root URL for your web site. The first route found that matches this URL is the Default. This route expects the first part of the URL to match the name of a controller. Since no data exists in this URL, it maps it to the default controller, which has been configured to use JoeyBellaMemorialFund. Since it also lacks an action, it will use the Index default action.

- \JoeyBellaMemorialFund: This URL will match on the controller name, but since it lacks the action, it will be mapped to the Index default action.

- \JoeyBellaMemorialFund\Index: In this case, since the URL matches both a controller and an action name it is routed as you would expect.

You are now ready to add the content to your views. Since this solution only requires static content, you can add any HTML, CSS, Flash, or Silverlight and JavaScript that meets your needs. Even if you are not using a database to dynamically create, you can still benefit from using MVC Framework features such as layout pages and partial views to make your web site easier to maintain.

5-3. Creating a Simple Form with Validation Using the ASP.NET MVC 4 Basic Template

Problem

Your brother is an electrician who just started his own business, Victory Lighting. He gently reminds you about the fact that he helped you install the overhead lighting in your living room three summers ago and then asks you to help him create a web site for his business. He wants a home page that gives the basics about his business and a form that prospective customers can fill out to request a quote. Since you have a day job and do not want to spend the next three weekends writing code, you need to find a fast way of creating the web site, including a form with validation.

Solution

Since this web site is very simple and is open to the public, but needs some infrastructure to handle form validation, you have selected the Basic template. After creating your project, you add a Home Controller with several actions:

- Index: The home page.

- RequestAQuote: Hosts the quote request form.

- ThankYou: Displays a thank-you message after the quote has been requested.

- An additional action method to your home controller to handle the POST condition for your RequestAQuote form.

In addition to the controller, you need to create views for each of the actions and model names that use data annotations.

How It Works

In this recipe, we will be creating a model that uses data annotations and HTML helpers that automatically wire this form with jQuery Validation. This design will allow you to create the form with a minimal amount of code.

Creating the Project

The first step is to create the Visual Studio project.

1. Open Visual Studio. Select New ➤ Project from the File menu.

2. In the New Project window, expand C#, click Web, and then click the ASP.NET MVC 4 Web Application project template.

3. Give the project and solution a name, and then click OK.

4. In the New ASP.NET MVC 4 Project window, select the Basic template. Ensure that the selected view engine is Razor. Click the OK button to create the project.

Create the Home Controller

Now that the project has been created, you need to add the HomeController that will contain the actions for the home page and the request-a-quote form.

1. Click the controller node in Visual Studio and then use the Visual Studio Ctrl+M, Ctrl+C keyboard shortcut chord to create a new controller.

2. In the Add Controller dialog window, name the controller **HomeController**.

3. Click the Add button.

4. Add actions for Index(), RequestAQuote(), and ThankYou().

5. Create an additional RequestAQuote action, but decorate it with the [HttpPost] attribute.

6. Modify the body of the RequestAQuote with the HttpPost attribute so that it will redirect the user to the ThankYou action.

When you are done, the controller should look like Listing 5-10.

Listing 5-10. The HomeController

```
public class HomeController : Controller
{
    //
    // GET: /Home/ and Website Root

    public ActionResult Index()
    {
        return View();
    }

    //
    // GET: /Home/RequestAQuote
```

```
public ActionResult RequestAQuote()
{
    return View();
}

//
// POST: /Home/RequestAQuote

[HttpPost]
public ActionResult RequestAQuote(FormCollection collection)
{
    try
    {
        // TODO: Add insert logic here

        return RedirectToAction("ThankYou");
    }
    catch
    {
        return View();
    }
}

//
// GET: /Home/ThankYou

public ActionResult ThankYou()
{
    return View();
}
}
```

As a placeholder, we have passed a FormCollection as a parameter for the HttpPost RequestAQuote. You can change this to use a custom model class after you have created one. The placeholder is required because in a controller class (as with all C# classes), you cannot have two methods with the same name and parameters. Use the Ctrl+Shift+B keyboard shortcut to build the solution.

Creating the Model

You now need to create the model. Since this data will not be saved to a database but rather just sent in an email, we can use a simple .NET class. We will use data annotations to describe the display name and validation requirements for each field.

1. In Solution Explorer, right-click the Models folder. Click Add, and then Class.

2. In the Add New Item window, change the name of the class to **RequestAQuoteModel**, and then click the Add button.

3. Modify the RequestAQuoteModel class so that it looks like Listing 5-11.

Listing 5-11. RequestAQuoteModel.cs

```
public class RequestAQuoteModel
{
    public string ProjectType { get; set; }

    public string ZipCode { get; set; }

    public string ContactName { get; set; }

    public string Email { get; set; }

    public string DayTimePhone { get; set; }

    public string ProjectDescription { get; set; }
}
```

There is nothing special about this class. For now, it is just a simple .NET class with a handful of properties.

Modify the RequestAQuote action in HomeController so that the RequestAQuoteModel class is passed in. The home controller should now look like Listing 5-12.

Listing 5-12. HomeController Modified to Use the Model

```
using System.Web.Mvc;
using Ch5.R5_3.BasicFormValidation.Models;

namespace Ch5.R5_3.BasicFormValidation.Controllers
{
    public class HomeController : Controller
    {
        ...

        //
        // POST: /Home/RequestAQuote

        [HttpPost]
        public ActionResult RequestAQuote(RequestAQuoteModel quote)
        {
            try
            {
                // TODO: Add insert logic here

                return RedirectToAction("ThankYou");
            }
            catch
            {
                return View();
            }
        }

        //
        // GET: /Home/ThankYou
```

```
        public ActionResult ThankYou()
        {
            return View();
        }
    }
}
```

I made several changes in Listing 5-12. First, a using statement was added for the project's Model namespace. Second, the POST action for RequestAQuote now takes the RequestAQuoteModel as a parameter. Finally, the call to RedirectToAction was modified to send the user to the thank-you page after the form is submitted.

Creating the Views

There are three views that need to be created for this project: an Index view that will be the home page for the web site, the RequestAQuote view that will host the request input form, and a ThankYou view that will be displayed after the form has been submitted.

1. In Solution Explorer, right-click the Views folder. Click Add, and then New Folder. Name the new folder **Home**.

2. Right-click the Home folder, click Add, and then View.

3. In the Add View window, change the View Name to **Index**. Make sure "Use a layout or master page" is checked.

4. Click the Add button to create the view.

5. Repeat steps 1-4 for the RequestAQuote and ThankYou views.

6. Change the contents of Index.cshtml to look like Listing 5-13.

    Listing 5-13. Index.cshtml

    ```
    @{
        ViewBag.Title = "Victory Lighting Design & Electrical Design";
    }

    <h2>Victory Lighting Design & Electrical Design</h2>
    You need an electical work? We make you an offer you can't refuse.<br />

    @Html.ActionLink("Request a free quote.","RequestAQuote");
    ```

7. Change the contents of RequestAQuote.cshtml to look like Listing 5-14.

8. Press the F5 key to compile and launch your project. Verify that clicking the "Request a free quote link" will bring up the form. Try submitting a form to see what happens.

Listing 5-13 is a very simple home page. On a real page, you would spend time making this page look professional. For the purposes of this recipe, however, we will not. Since this is a layout page, we need to set the ViewBag.Title property in order for the page title to be set. There is also a link to the RequestAQuote page. For this example, the Html.ActionLink HTML helper is used to create the link. There are several overloads for the Html.ActionLink helper. For this example, we are passing in two parameters: the first contains the text we would like to have displayed on the link and the second is an action we would like to link to. Since this overload does not specify a controller, it will assume that the action is in the current controller. Other possible overloads for Html.ActionLink allow you to specify a controller, route data, and HTML attributes to be added to the rendered anchor tag.

The main advantage of using the `Html.ActionLink` helper is that if you decide to change your page routing to use a different URL scheme, you do not have to worry about updating all of your links. A second advantage is that they save you some typing.

Listing 5-14. RequestAQuote.cshtml

```
@model Ch5.R5_3.BasicFormValidation.Models.RequestAQuoteModel
@{
    ViewBag.Title = "Request a Free Quote";
    List<string> ProjectTypes = new List<string>();
    ProjectTypes.Add("Electrical Wiring");
    // add additional drop down list items here
}

<h2>Request A Quote</h2>
@using (Html.BeginForm()){
    @Html.ValidationSummary()
    <fieldset>
        <legend>Request Quote Form</legend>
        <ol>
            <li>
                @Html.LabelFor(m=>m.ProjectType)
                @Html.DropDownListFor(m=>m.ProjectType, new MultiSelectList(ProjectTypes))
            </li>
            <li>
                @Html.LabelFor(m=>m.ContactName)
                @Html.TextBoxFor(m=>m.ContactName)
            </li>
            <li>
                @Html.LabelFor(m=>m.DayTimePhone)
                @Html.TextBoxFor(m=>m.DayTimePhone)
            </li>
            <li>
                @Html.LabelFor(m=>m.Email)
                @Html.TextBoxFor(m=>m.Email)
            </li>
            <li>
                @Html.LabelFor(m=>m.ProjectDescription)
                @Html.TextBoxFor(m=>m.ProjectDescription)
            </li>
        </ol>
        <input type="submit" value="Request Quote" />
    </fieldset>

}
```

Listing 5-14 shows the request feedback form. The very first line of the form is a reference to the model. By binding our view to the model, Visual Studio will allow us to use IntelliSense for the model, which makes typing a bit easier. Next, a code block sets the title of the page and creates a `List` that will hold the options for the drop-down list. There are a number of ways that this list is created, such as either as part of the model or inside the controller. Since the list is static in this particular instance and I only have one view, placing this code inside a Razor code block may be

OK. If the same list of items was needed for additional views or if you needed to pull the values from a database, you should consider refactoring this code so that it is moved to the model.

The next bit or Razor code wraps a call to `Html.BeginForm()` inside a `@using(){}` block. This shorthand method ensures that the `Html.EndForm()` method is called.

Next, a series of `@Html.LabelFor` and `@Html.TextBoxFor` statements are used to create the form. Using the HTML helpers will allow us to use data annotations on the model to provide much of the details on how the fields are rendered. The `LabelFor` and `TextBoxFor` HTML helpers follow a similar pattern.

If you are not familiar with LINQ and the use of lambda expressions in C#, the syntax used with the HTML helpers may seem confusing. To explain it, we will break down some of the expressions used in the `RequestAQuote` view. Lambda expressions are shorthand syntax for creating anonymous functions.

On the left side of the lambda operator ("`=>`") is the list of parameters. On the right side of the lambda is the body of the function. In the expression `@Html.TextBoxFor(m=>m.DayTimePhone)`, a call is made to the `TextBoxFor` HTML helper that passes the lambda expression `m=>m.DayTimePhone`. The `m` represents the model passed to the view and is of the type specified in the `@model` directive. The model type is automatically inferred by the compiler and does not need to be set explicitly. Visual Studio's IntelliSense engine will also infer the type and will provide autocompletion for the `m` variable's properties on the right side of the lambda. The variable name used for the left side of the lambda does not need to be `m`. In fact, it can be any legal variable name; `m` is used by convention.

On the right side of the lambda, the `TextBoxFor` method expects a property of the model. At runtime, the `TextBoxFor` method will use reflection to get information about the model and the property passed as a parameter. It then uses that data to create the HTML input element as well as several custom data attributes. Custom data attributes are a new feature in HTML5 that permits the addition of attributes that begin with `data-` to be added to an HTML element. These data attributes are then treated as storage containers for data related to the element. The addition of this data does not affect presentation.

`@Html.DropDownListFor` is a slightly more sophisticated example HTML helper that was used in Listing 5-14. In this case, not only do you pass in the property but also a `MultiSelectList` that contains the values of the drop-down list. There are several overloads to this method, which let you specify which properties are used for the value and display text. In this example, we are passing in a string that is used for both the display name and the value.

Adding Data Attributes to the Model

If you run the project now, you will notice that it is missing some functionality. There is no form validation, and the labels match the property names written in camel case. Another problem is that the project description text box is rendered as an input element rather than a text area. Because we are using the HTML helpers to render the form, both of these problems can be corrected using data attributes. Open `RequestAQuoteModel.cs` and modify it so it looks like Listing 5-15.

Listing 5-15. RequestAQuoteModel with Data Attributes

```
using System.ComponentModel;
using System.ComponentModel.DataAnnotations;

namespace Ch5.R5_3.BasicFormValidation.Models
{
    public class RequestAQuoteModel
    {
        [Required]
        [DisplayName("Type of Project")]
        public string ProjectType { get; set; }

        [Required]
        [DataType(DataType.PostalCode)]
```

```
        [RegularExpression(@"^\d{5}$|^\d{5}-\d{4}$", ErrorMessage="The postal code should be in the
format 00000 or 00000-0000")]
        [DisplayName("Postal Code")]
        public string ZipCode { get; set; }

        [StringLength(50,MinimumLength=2)]
        [DisplayName("Contact Name")]
        public string ContactName { get; set; }

        [Required]
        [DataType(DataType.EmailAddress)]
        public string Email { get; set; }

        [DataType(DataType.PhoneNumber,ErrorMessage="Please provide the phone number area code first
in the format (000) 000-0000")]
        [DisplayName("Daytime Phone Number")]
        public string DayTimePhone { get; set; }

        [Required]
        [DisplayName("Project Description")]
        [StringLength(5000, MinimumLength = 10)]
        [DataType(DataType.MultilineText)]
        public string ProjectDescription { get; set; }
    }
}
```

In Listing 5-15, a number of data validation attributes have been added. The attributes describe the display names, the minimum and maximum length of each property, a data type, and even regular expressions that describe the expected format. If you run the project and try the form again, you will notice that a few things have changed. For one, the form labels now reflect the values from the DisplayName attributes in your form. The project description is still rendered as an input field and the validation still does not work. We need to make some adjustments to the view in order to correct these issues. Open RequestAQuote.cshtml and modify to look like Listing 5-16.

Listing 5-16. Changing RequestAQuote.cshtml So That It Provides Validation

```
...
<!-- content removed for brevity -->
@using (Html.BeginForm()){
    @Html.ValidationSummary()
    <fieldset>
        <legend>Request Quote Form</legend>
        <ol>
            <li>
                @Html.LabelFor(m=>m.ProjectType)
                @Html.DropDownListFor(m=>m.ProjectType, new MultiSelectList(ProjectTypes))
            </li>
            <li>
                @Html.LabelFor(m=>m.ZipCode)
                @Html.EditorFor(m=>m.ZipCode)
            </li>
```

```
            <li>
                @Html.LabelFor(m=>m.ContactName)
                @Html.EditorFor(m=>m.ContactName)
            </li>
            <li>
                @Html.LabelFor(m=>m.DayTimePhone)
                @Html.EditorFor(m=>m.DayTimePhone)
            </li>
            <li>
                @Html.LabelFor(m=>m.Email)
                @Html.EditorFor(m=>m.Email)
            </li>
            <li>
                @Html.LabelFor(m=>m.ProjectDescription)
                @Html.EditorFor(m=>m.ProjectDescription)

            </li>
        </ol>
        <input type="submit" value="Request Quote" />
    </fieldset>

}

@section scripts{
    @Scripts.Render("~/bundles/jqueryval")
}
```

In Listing 5-16, the code in bold has been modified to enable validation. The last lines of the view include the script bundle defined for the jQuery Validation and Microsoft's Unobtrusive Validation libraries. Adding this script file is all you need to do to enable validation. The other change made to the form was the replacement of the `TextFor` HTML helper with `EditorFor`, an HTML helper that uses the data type attribute defined in the model to determine how to render the field. Since the `ProjectDescription` property was decorated with `[DataType(DataType.MultilineText)]`, it is now rendered as a `textarea` element. Since the email field was decorated with `[DataType(DataType.EmailAddress)]`, it is now rendered as an input element with the "email" type attribute. Email is a new form attribute type in HTML5. Modern browsers will automatically validate that the input is an email address. Since older browsers do not recognize "email" as a valid attribute value for an input element, they fall back to the text box default value.

The remaining properties are rendered as `<input type="text" ...` even though some of them have been decorated with data type attributes. This is because ASP.NET knows that there is no HTML input type that matches the data type. The zip code, for example, required a regular expression attribute in order to support validation.

Listing 5-17 shows a fragment of the HTML rendered by the ASP.NET for `RequestAQuote.cshtml`. Note the custom data attributes added to the form's input elements. You may also notice that the email field is now of the "email" type.

Listing 5-17. The HTML Rendered for the RequestAQuote.cshtml

```
<li>
<label for="ZipCode">Postal Code</label>
<input class="text-box single-line"
data-val="true"
data-val-regex="The postal code should be in the format 00000 or 00000-0000"
data-val-regex-pattern="^\d{5}$|^\d{5}-\d{4}$"
```

```
data-val-required="The Postal Code field is required."
id="ZipCode"
name="ZipCode"
type="text"
value="" />
</li>
...
<label for="Email">Email</label>
<input class="text-box single-line" data-val="true" data-val-required="The Email field is required."
id="Email" name="Email" type="email" value="" />
</li>
<li>
<label for="ProjectDescription">Project Description</label>
<textarea class="text-box multi-line" data-val="true" data-val-length="The field Project Description
must be a string with a minimum length of 10 and a maximum length of 5000." data-val-length-
max="5000" data-val-length-min="10" data-val-required="The Project Description field is required."
id="ProjectDescription" name="ProjectDescription">
</textarea>

</li>
```

Figure 5-1 shows the form validation in action. Notice how the validation for the email addresses does not match the rest of the validation. The error is rendered automatically by Firefox because we have specified the email input type. You can see the validation summary on the top of the screen.

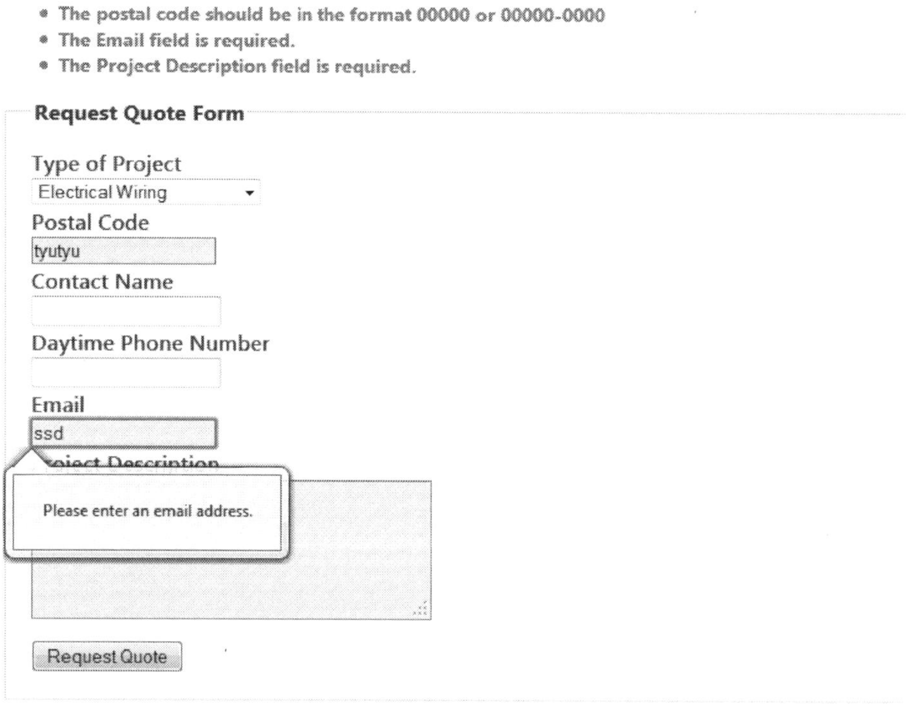

Figure 5-1. *The form validation in action*

If you are unhappy with the default behavior and styling of the HTML5 form validation, you have two main options. The first is not to use them at all and fall back to using the regular expression-based validation as with the postal code field. This is also backward compatible with older browsers. The other option is to use CSS to style the overlay so that it is consistent with the rest of your validation markup. For example, to remove the thick line and the drop shadow for the invalidated email field, you can add style for the `input:invalid` selector in your `site.css` file and change it to match the style defined for `.input-validation-error`. For the pop-up message, this is a bit more complex since each browser has designed this a little differently. As of this writing, Google Chrome is the only browser that has a documented way of modifying the styles of the pop-ups. It allows you to create CSS declarations for two WebKit-specific pseudo-elements: `::-webkit-validation-bubble-message`, which represents the body of the bubble, and `::-webkit-validation-bubble-arrow`, which is used for the callout arrow.

5-4. Creating an Intranet Site That Uses Windows Authentication Using the ASP.NET MVC 4 Intranet Template

Problem

You need to create a web site to be hosted on your intranet and you need to use Windows Authentication so that office workers can seamlessly access your application without be prompted for credentials.

Solution

To create a site that works with Windows Authentication, all you need to do is create a new project using the Intranet Application template. Once the site has been created, you will need to modify the web site so that Anonymous Authentication is disabled and Windows Authentication is enabled.

How It Works

For this recipe we first need to create the project in Visual Studio and then configure Internet Information Services (IIS). This recipe assumes that you have a full version of IIS and the Windows Authentication feature installed on your development machine and are running either Windows 8 Professional or Windows 7 Professional, Enterprise or Ultimate. The Windows Authentication module is not available for the home editions of Windows. If you are using a professional or enterprise version of Windows client or Windows Server but have not installed IIS, please refer to Recipe 3-9 for instructions on setting up IIS. IIS Express does not come with the IIS Windows Authentication module.

Creating the Project

To create your web site:

1. Open Visual Studio with elevated privileges. From the File menu, select New ➤ Project. You must run Visual Studio with elevated privileges in order to work with IIS. To do this, launch Visual Studio by right-clicking the icon in the Start menu or Start screen, and select Run As Administrator.

2. Type **ASP.NET MVC 4 C#** in the search box inside the New Project dialog box, and then click the ASP.NET MVC 4 Web Application project template.

3. In the New Project dialog box, give your project a name and assign a name to your solution. Click OK to continue.

4. In the New ASP.NET MVC 4 Project window, select the Intranet Application template. Ensure that the selected view engine is Razor. Click the OK button to create the project.

5. In Solution Explorer, right-click your project and select Properties.

6. The Project Properties editor will appear as a tabbed document. Click Web on the left-side navigation to access the web settings.

7. Under Servers, make sure that Use Local IIS Web Server is selected, and that Use IIS Express is unchecked.

8. If you get a pop-up message telling you that you need to use SQL Server Express, check the "Don't ask me again for this project" check box, and then click the Cancel button. You can configure this manually later if needed.

9. Click the Create Virtual Directory button to create a new virtual directory under the root web site.

10. Press Ctrl+F5 to run your project. Confirm that you get an Access Denied message.

11. Open Internet Information Services (IIS) Manager. You can do this by pressing the Windows key and typing **IIS**. On Windows 8, you need to click Settings from the categories on the right side of the screen.

12. In IIS Manager, expand the Sites node under Connections on the left side of the screen. Expand the Default Web Site node, and then click your new virtual directory.

13. Under the IIS Section, double-click Authentication, which should be the first icon under the IIS Section in the IIS Manager's features view.

14. Click Anonymous Authentication, and then click Disable, which is under Actions on the right side of the screen.

15. Click Windows Authentication, and then click Enable on the Actions pane.

16. Refresh the web site. You should now be prompted for your Windows credentials. Once you enter them, you should be able to see the Welcome page.

Alternatively, if you want to create a new web site rather than a virtual directory, follow the instructions in Recipe 3-10 to set up a new web site in IIS. See Recipe 3-11 to configure the Application Pool.

5-5. Configuring Windows Authentication Using the Web.config File

Problem

You are deploying your web application on a large web farm and do not want to manually configure Windows Authentication across all the web servers. You wish to be able to control the IIS settings inside the Web.config file rather than through IIS.

Solution

Microsoft has several solutions that are helpful for managing the configuration of a web farm, including IIS Shared Administration, PowerShell commandlets, and the ability to create automated installers. While the IIS Shared configuration is a very powerful way to manage your server farm, it is possible that your support organization may not be ready for it. The other two options simplify the setup, but would still need to be run across all the servers. Many developers prefer to control some aspects of the IIS configuration using the `Web.config` file.

This solution requires two steps:

1. Have an administrator unlock the configuration sections in the `applicationHost.config` file.

2. Modify the `Web.config` file in your application root.

How It Works

The default configuration for IIS is locked down. A set of rules applied at the machine level prevents many of the IIS settings from being overridden in downstream `Web.config` files. The master file that controls these settings is the `applicationHost.config` file. You can find this file at the following path:

`%windir%\system32\inetsrv\config\applicationHost.config`

▓ **Caution**   If you make a mistake editing this file, you will break every web site on your machine. It is recommended that you make a backup of this file before making any changes.

In their infinite wisdom, Microsoft has made it so that it is not possible to load this file inside Visual Studio. If you jumped right in and tried to open `applicationHost.config` in Visual Studio, you will be disappointed. Visual Studio will refuse to open the file and, in fact, will even hide the file in the browse dialog box. To edit this file, you will need a good text editor (such as Notepad) running in elevated mode. From the Start menu, type **notepad** in the search box, and then right-click the Notepad icon and select Run As Administrator. On Windows 8, the process is similar, but you need to right-click the file in the Start screen and then click Run As administrator in the bottom toolbar.

Once Notepad is open, type Ctrl+O to access the Open dialog box. Make sure that All Files is selected in the File Type dialog box, and then open the file. Use the Ctrl+F keyboard shortcut to display the Find dialog box, and search for **anonymousAuthentication**. Modify the file so that it looks like Listing 5-18.

Listing 5-18. Modified ApplicationHost.config File

```
<sectionGroup name="security">
    <section name="access" overrideModeDefault="Deny" />
    <section name="applicationDependencies" overrideModeDefault="Deny" />
    <sectionGroup name="">
        <section name="anonymousAuthentication" overrideModeDefault="Allow" />
        <section name="basicAuthentication" overrideModeDefault="Deny" />
        <section name="clientCertificateMappingAuthentication"
overrideModeDefault="Deny" />
        <section name="digestAuthentication" overrideModeDefault="Deny" />
        <section name="iisClientCertificateMappingAuthentication"
overrideModeDefault="Deny" />
        <section name="windowsAuthentication" overrideModeDefault="Allow" />
    </sectionGroup>
    <section name="authorization" overrideModeDefault="Allow" />
    <section name="ipSecurity" overrideModeDefault="Deny" />
    <section name="isapiCgiRestriction" allowDefinition="AppHostOnly"
overrideModeDefault="Deny" />
```

```
                <section name="requestFiltering" overrideModeDefault="Allow" />
            </sectionGroup>
```

Note that the configuration settings for anonymousAuthentication and windowsAuthentication have been modified. The overrideModeDefault attribute has been changed from Deny to Allow. You can now add the settings to the Web.config file.

Listing 5-19 shows how to configure Windows Authentication in the Web.config file.

Listing 5-19. Modified Web.config File

```
...
<system.webServer>
    <validation validateIntegratedModeConfiguration="false" />
        <security>
                <>
                        <anonymousAuthentication enabled="false" />
                        <windowsAuthentication enabled="true"/>
                </>
        </security>
    </system.webServer>
...
```

The following are a few things that you should watch out for before making this change.

- Talk to members of your information security practice and let them know you are considering making this change. There may be security implications if others are allowed to upload code to the same set of web servers.

- Talk to your systems administration team to ensure that there are no Group Policy Objects (GPO) in place that will override your configuration. Many organization use GPOs to lock down production servers. These settings are applied every time the server is restarted. If there is a GPO in place that enforces the section lock, you will find that your application will not function after your next reboot. IIS will start, but you will see an error message complaining about a configuration error when you attempt to load your application in a browser. If you are not sure whether there is a GPO in place, reboot your server after you make the change to ensure that the application still functions.

5-6. Creating an Internet Site That Uses Forms Authentication Using the Internet Application Template

Problem

You need to create an application that will be exposed to the Internet. You would like some parts of your application to only be accessible by registered users. To enable this, you need a registration page, a login page, and a way for users to manage their passwords.

Solution

You're in luck! The ASP.NET MVC Internet Application template gives you all this out of the box without the need to write a single line of code. Just open Visual Studio and create a new project using the Internet template—and you are off to a good start.

How It Works

First, you need to create the project. To do so, perform the following actions.

1. Open Visual Studio and select New ➤ Project from the File menu.

2. In the New Project window, expand C#, click Web, and then click the ASP.NET MVC 4 Web Application project template.

3. Give the project and solution a name, and then click OK.

4. In the New ASP.NET MVC 4 Project window, select the Internet Application template. Ensure that the selected view engine is Razor. Click the OK button to create the project.

Understanding Forms Authentication

Most public facing Internet applications feature some sort of registration form to allow new members to sign up for the site. They then have an HTML-based form that allows them to log in with a username and password. Developers have been creating this functionality in their applications from scratch since the early days of the web. There are likely hundreds of thousands of implementations of this idea. Unfortunately, many of these custom security frameworks have led to thousands of breaches with millions of passwords being exposed, money stolen, and reputations tarnished. While you can develop your own security, it is usually a bad idea, and as of ASP.NET 2.0, almost completely unnecessary.

There are two main components that make up the Microsoft Forms Authentication implementation: the FormsAuthenticationModule and the ASP.NET provider model.

The FormsAuthenticationModule is an HTTP module that processes each request sent to IIS. This includes not only calls to ASP.NET MVC controller actions, but also images and other static items. The module knows which parts of the application require a password and which parts are open to the general public. It examines the incoming request and checks to see if the user is authenticated, whether the content is restricted, and whether the user is a member of a security role that has been granted access to a particular resource. If an unauthenticated user attempts to access a restricted resource, the FormsAuthenticationModule will redirect the user to a configured login page.

The following lists the steps used by the FormsAuthenticationModule to enable access to a restricted resource.

1. A request is sent from the web browser to a restricted page.

2. IIS returns an HTTP 302 redirect to the configured login page with the URL of the original requested page in the query string.

3. The user fills out the login form and submits it. The form submission is an HTTP POST request, and in addition to the username and password, the original URL is posted. It is important that this GET request be sent over a secure connection, otherwise the password will be sent in clear text. It is also very important that a POST is used and not a GET, otherwise the username and passwords will end up in the IIS log.

4. The server passes the username and password to the Membership Provider, which validates it against a data source.

5. The server generates an authorization cookie and sends it back to the client as an HTTP 302 redirect, which indicates to the browser that the file has been temporarily moved and provides the redirection URL.

6. The client browser then makes a new request with the authorization cookie to the original requested page.

7. The server passes the cookie to the `FormsAuthenticationModule`, which will then create a Generic Principle object that represents the user's security context and attaches it to the HTTP Context.

Steps 6 and 7 are repeated for each request sent to the server.

Understanding the ASP.NET Provider Model

Starting with ASP.NET 2.0, Microsoft introduced the concept of providers. The providers are based on a pattern that allows the implementation of the API be separate from the API itself. In Microsoft's provider model, this is accomplished by having providers derive from an abstract base class. ASP.NET uses this provider pattern for several pluggable components, including:

- *Membership Provider*: Enables registration, password management, and user account management.

- *Role Provider*: Used in conjunction with the Membership Provider to implement role-based authorization.

- *Site Map Provider*: Used for creating maps of a site's contents, which is helpful for creating navigation breadcrumbs and menus.

- *Session State Provider*: Used in ASP.NET applications to keep information about a particular user in memory for the duration of a user session.

- *Profile Provider*: Allows personalization information about a user to be stored on the site.

- *Cache*: Allows the ASP.NET cache mechanism to be replaced with alternative implementations, such as the App Fabric Caching Service.

For Forms Authentication in ASP.NET, the Membership Provider and the Role Provider are the most critical components to understand. These providers implement the typical business logic needed for site registration and authorization. ASP.NET also made the providers easy to work with by providing a number of server controls that you can drag onto your page. In the MVC world, there are no server controls. Microsoft has instead provided a rich sample on how to get started with the providers in the Internet Application template.

The provider model separates interface from implementation. It allows you to swap out the backend without needing to change any of your application code. Microsoft has implemented several of the most common solutions with providers that use Active Directory and SQL Server. It is also possible for you to implement your own providers.

Which provider your application is currently using is determined by the configuration in the project's `Web.config`, as well as the system-wide configuration files. For the Internet Application template, Microsoft uses the SQL Server Providers and configures them to store their data in a LocalDB instance. This setting is inherited from the root `Web.config` file located in `<systemdrive>\Windows\Microsoft.NET\Framework\v4.0.30319\Config`. The database connection string is overridden in the `Web.config` in your application's root directory. The relevant settings are shown in Listing 5-19.

Listing 5-19. *Relevant Sections of Default Web.config for the Internet Template*

```
<connectionStrings>
  <add name="DefaultConnection"
      connectionString="Data Source=(LocalDb)\v11.0;Initial Catalog=aspnet-InternetRTM-
20120903142944;Integrated Security=SSPI;AttachDBFilename=|DataDirectory|\aspnet-InternetRTM-
20120903142944.mdf"
      providerName="System.Data.SqlClient" />
</connectionStrings>
```

```
...
<authentication mode="Forms">
    <forms loginUrl="~/Account/Login" timeout="2880" />
</authentication>
...
  <entityFramework>
    <defaultConnectionFactory type="System.Data.Entity.Infrastructure.LocalDbConnectionFactory,
EntityFramework">
        <parameters>
          <parameter value="v11.0" />
        </parameters>
    </defaultConnectionFactory>
  </entityFramework>
```

The first relevant section of the Web.config file is the connection strings section. It defines a connection called DefaultConnection, which is using the System.Data.SqlClient provider to connect to a LocalDB database. The LocalDB stores its data in a file that is stored in the aspnet-InternetRTM-20120903142944.mdf file. The actual file name is generated by Visual Studio based on the name of your project and followed by a unique numeric identifier.

In older versions of ASP.NET, you were required to use a utility to create your ASP.NET database with the correct schema. With ASP.NET 4, the provider now automatically creates the database the first time you use it. When you first create your application, no database exists. Once you run your application and perform an operation such as attempting to login or register, the database is created for you with the required schema elements.

Once the database has been created, you can explore and modify it using Visual Studio. By default, this database file is hidden in Visual Studio. To view the file in Solution Explorer, you can click the Show All Files button. If you wish to browse the database, you can examine the schema, and browse and edit the data using Visual Studio Server Explorer or Visual Studio SQL Server Object Explorer.

To open Server Explorer, use the Ctrl+Alt+S keyboard shortcut. You should then see the DefaultConnection(you rprojectname) listed under Data Connections.

The next item of interest is the authentication element. It sets the authentication mode to Forms authentication and specifies a login URL and timeout. When users access a restricted part of a web site, they will be redirected to a URL specified in the loginUrl attribute. This URL should display a form that prompts the user for a username and password. The timeout attribute describes the time in minutes until the authentication cookie will expire. If you keep the value generated by the Internet template, the cookie will be valid for two days.

▓ **Note** When using IIS configured in Integrated mode, the authentication section of the Web.config file is completely independent of the system.webServer section. It is possible to configure the site to require Windows Authentication at an IIS level and have it configured for Forms Authentication in ASP.NET. The results would be that the user is authenticated twice. The Windows Authentication would allow the user to access IIS and the Forms Authentication would then provide the authentication required for the application.

Missing from the Web.config file is the Membership and Role provider configurations. Since no values have been added, the web site will inherit the values set in the root Web.config file. If you would like to modify your application to use an alternative provider such as the Microsoft ASP.NET Universal Providers, you can add it to your project using the NuGet package manager. When you install the package, it will automatically add the required assemblies to your application and modify your application's Web.config file to include the necessary settings.

Understanding the AccountController

If you run the application, you will notice it contains forms for registration, login, and changing your password. All this functionality is contained in the `AccountController`. The `AccountController` uses models defined in the `Models\AccountModels.cs` file. It has seven associated views and three partial views. Inside `AccountModel.cs`, you will find several classes, which in most cases directly correspond to the views.

To get an understanding of how this works, we will look at the code that makes up the site registration. We will start by examining the `RegisterModel` class that is defined inside `Models\AccountModel.cs`. This class is shown in Listing 5-20.

Listing 5-20. The RegistrationModel Class

```
public class RegisterModel
{
    [Required]
    [Display(Name = "User name")]
    public string UserName { get; set; }

    [Required]
    [StringLength(100, ErrorMessage = "The {0} must be at least {2} characters long.",
MinimumLength = 6)]
    [DataType(DataType.Password)]
    [Display(Name = "Password")]
    public string Password { get; set; }

    [DataType(DataType.Password)]
    [Display(Name = "Confirm password")]
    [Compare("Password", ErrorMessage = "The password and confirmation password do not match.")]
    public string ConfirmPassword { get; set; }
}
```

The class consists of four properties decorated with data annotations. The annotations specify whether or not the property is required, the display name of the field, as well as validation logic and error messages.

In the `Views\Account\Register.cshtml` file, these attributes are put to use by the `@Html.xxxFor` helper methods, as shown in Listing 5-21.

Listing 5-21. Registration.cshtml

```
@model Internet.Models.RegisterModel

@{
    ViewBag.Title = "Register";
}

<hgroup class="title">
    <h1>@ViewBag.Title.</h1>
    <h2>Create a new account.</h2>
</hgroup>

@using (Html.BeginForm()) {
    @Html.AntiForgeryToken()
    @Html.ValidationSummary()
```

```
    <fieldset>
        <legend>Registration Form</legend>
        <ol>
            <li>
                @Html.LabelFor(m => m.UserName)
                @Html.TextBoxFor(m => m.UserName)
            </li>
            <li>
                @Html.LabelFor(m => m.Password)
                @Html.PasswordFor(m => m.Password)
            </li>
            <li>
                @Html.LabelFor(m => m.ConfirmPassword)
                @Html.PasswordFor(m => m.ConfirmPassword)
            </li>
        </ol>
        <input type="submit" value="Register" />
    </fieldset>
}

@section Scripts {
    @Scripts.Render("~/bundles/jqueryval")
}
```

The HTML helpers use reflection to read information in the data annotations. They then use this information to generate the HTML with attributes that can be used, in conjunction with the jQuery Validation and Microsoft's Unobtrusive Validation libraries, to implement the validation logic on the client. In addition, the data annotation—in conjunction with the ASP.NET MVC Framework—also performs validation on the server. You can try this out by disabling JavaScript in the browser and then trying to submit the registration form without providing any values. You will see the form post data back to the server and the page return with validation error messages rendered in the HTML.

Another item of interest in Listing 5-21 is the inclusion of @Html.AntiForgeryToken(). This helper function works in conjunction with the ValidateAntiForgeryToken filter to prevent cross-site request forgery (CSRF) attacks. CSRF attacks are considered one of the biggest threats facing modern web applications.

In a CSRF attack, the bad guy takes advantage of the fact that you are using a cookie-based forms authentication. In most cases, it uses social engineering tactics to trick a user into submitting a form from a site hosted by the hacker. The form submits the data to a controller on your web site. As long as the authentication cookie that was set the last time the user logged into your site is still valid, the form post can be used to modify data on your web site. This is usually targeted at user account data. In one highly publicized case, it was used to exploit a banking web site to transfer money from the account of the user to an account controlled by the hacker.

The ValidateAntiForgeryToken filter works by adding a hidden field to forms that use the @Html.AntiForgeryToken() helper along with a cookie. The form field and the cookie are both named _RequestVerificationToken and include identical values. When a form post is submitted, the filter verifies that both the cookie and the form field exist and that they contain matching values.

So far, we have looked at pretty standard MVC code that does not have much to do with the Forms Authentication and ASP.NET Membership Provider. All the logic for interacting with the membership provider is found in the controller. Listing 5-22 shows an abbreviated version of the Controllers\AccountController.cs file.

Listing 5-22. AccountController.cs

```
namespace Internet.Controllers
{

    [Authorize]
    public class AccountController : Controller
    {

        //
        // this section has been removed for brevity
        //

        [AllowAnonymous]
        public ActionResult Register()
        {
            return View();
        }

        //
        // POST: /Account/Register

        [HttpPost]
        [AllowAnonymous]
        [ValidateAntiForgeryToken]
        public ActionResult Register(RegisterModel model)
        {
            if (ModelState.IsValid)
            {
                // Attempt to register the user
                try
                {
                    WebSecurity.CreateUserAndAccount(model.UserName, model.Password);
                    WebSecurity.Login(model.UserName, model.Password);
                    return RedirectToAction("Index", "Home");
                }
                catch (MembershipCreateUserException e)
                {
                    ModelState.AddModelError("", ErrorCodeToString(e.StatusCode));
                }
            }

            // If we got this far, something failed, redisplay form
            return View(model);
        }

        //
        // This section has been removed for brevity
        //

    }
}
```

In Listing 5-22, the interesting lines of code have been highlighted in bold text. The first line of interest is the inclusion of the [Authorize] attribute. In ASP.NET Web Forms, you can specify which parts of your application are available to the general unauthenticated masses, and which parts are members-only by placing Web.config files with the relevant authorization rules in your site's subdirectories. In MVC, the directory structure is dynamic, based on the routing rules defined in your App_Start/RouteConfig.cs file. Because of this, there are no subdirectories to place configuration files into. Another method was needed. The solution was a set of action filters that can be applied to entire MVC controller classes or individual action methods. An action filter is similar in concept to an HTTP Module in that it can insert logic into a processing pipeline, but unlike modules, action filters only apply to actions inside controllers. In this example, the [Authorize] attribute is applied to the entire controller. It states that all actions in this controller require that the user be authenticated.

You may be asking yourself how the [Authorize] attribute knows the user has been authenticated. This is where the FormsAuthenticationModule comes in. As discussed earlier in this recipe, the module will check every request to verify the existence of a valid token. If the token is found, the module will construct a Generic Principle object and place it in the application context.

The code inside the Authorize filter has access to the HTML context and can see not only that the user is logged in, but also what roles the user is a member of. If the user is not authenticated or is authenticated but not authorized to access the requested action, the MVC Framework will return an HTTP 302 status code and a location header containing the URL of the login page with the page you were attempting to request appended as a query string. The web browser then uses this information to automatically redirect you to the login page listed in the Web.config file.

Moving down though Listing 5-22, you can see that there are two actions for the registration: a GET action that returns an empty registration form to the user, and a POST action that processes the form data. Both actions are decorated with the [AllowAnonymous] attribute. This attribute overrides the class level [Authorize] attribute and allows anonymous access to the actions.

Inside the POST action, you see a call to ModelState.IsValid. The ModelState class is bound to the model and can use the data annotations to validate that the model meets the criteria specified. For veteran ASP.NET Web Forms developers, this may seem a lot like the Page.IsValid property, but it is more powerful since it is bound to a model that can be used with multiple views.

In the highlighted line, we see the WebSecurity.CreateUserAndAccount method being called. This is part of SimpleMembership security provider that is built into ASP.NET Web Pages. The SimpleMembership is built on top of the core ASP.NET abstract base classes for the Membership Provider and Role Provider. It invokes the configured Membership Provider. They contain the business logic for creating users, managing passwords, and authenticating logins.

5-7. Modifying an Internet Site to Use a Custom SQL Server Database

Problem

You have created a new web site using the Internet Application template and it works great. Now you need to deploy it to the Internet and are expecting to get thousands of people signing up once the marketing campaign is in full swing. While the LocalDB was convenient for prototyping, you want to use a full version of SQL Server running on a dedicated SQL Server machine for production.

Solution

First, you will need to create an ASP.NET database on your database server or add the ASP.NET schema to an existing database. Once this is done, you need to modify your application's configuration file to use your new database rather than LocalDB.

How It Works

First, you need to create a database with the ASP.NET database schema. There are several approaches to doing this, including backing up the database and then restoring it on another machine, having SQL Server Manager script the database and then running the script on the destination server, using web deploy to migrate the data to production, or using the aspnet_regsql.exe tool.

Once the database is ready, we can change the Web.config file. This seems like a straightforward task, but there are a few little things that may surprise you.

Creating the ASP.NET Schema Using aspnet_regsql.exe

The best approach to creating this schema depends a lot on the number of changes you have made to the database. If you have just started your project, the best approach is to use the aspnet_regsql.exe tool. This tool can also remove the schema from a database if it is no longer required. To run the tool, perform the following steps.

1. Open the Visual Studio Command Prompt by pressing the Windows key on your keyboard, typing **Visual Studio Com**, and then clicking the Visual Studio Command Prompt icon.

2. Enter **aspnet_regsql.exe** in the Command window, and then click OK.

3. In the ASP.NET SQL Server Setup Wizard:

    -   Click Next on the Welcome Screen.

    -   On the Select a Setup Option screen, select Configure SQL Server for application Services, and then click the Next button.

    -   On the Select a Server and Database screen, enter the name or IP Address of your SQL Server, and then enter the required credentials.

    -   In the Database drop-down, you can: (a) accept <default>, which will create a database named aspnetdb, (b) select an existing database, or (c) type in the name you would like for a new database.

    -   Click Next. Confirm your settings, and then click Next again.

You can confirm that the database has been created by viewing the database using the SQL Server Object Explorer in Visual Studio or by using SQL Server Manager.

Understanding the Default Setting in Machine.config

One thing that you need to understand before changing Web.config is that all Web.config files are part of a machine-wide hierarchy. In order to simplify the Web.config file in individual projects, Microsoft has taken the liberty to move many default settings to the Machine.config file and the root Web.config files located in the %WINDIR%\Microsoft.Net\Framework\v4.0.30319\Config directory.

▓ **Note**   On 64-bit versions of Windows, you will find two Framework folders: Framework, which contains the 32-bit versions of the binaries for the .NET Framework, and Framework64, which includes the 64-bit version. In cases where you need to modify these files, you will need to understand which version of the files to edit. Unless you have configured the web site to run in 32-bit mode, the 64-bit framework will be used for applications hosted in IIS.

In most cases, I do not recommend modifying these files, but you may want to take a look at them to understand what is inside of them. For example, Listing 5-23 shows the connectionStrings setting from the Machine.config file.

Listing 5-23. Machine.config Connection Strings

```
<connectionStrings>
        <add name="LocalSqlServer"
connectionString="data source=.\SQLEXPRESS;Integrated
Security=SSPI;AttachDBFilename=|DataDirectory|aspnetdb.mdf;User Instance=true"
providerName="System.Data.SqlClient"/>
    </connectionStrings>
```

Since your application's configuration file inherits the settings in machine.config file, this connection string is automatically included with your configuration. While this connection may not actually harm anything, it may not be something you require.

Included in machine.config are a number of default providers, as shown in Listing 5-24.

Listing 5-24. Providers in the Machine.config File

```
<system.web>
        <processModel autoConfig="true"/>
        <httpHandlers/>
        <membership>
            <providers>
                <add
                        name="AspNetSqlMembershipProvider"
                        type="System.Web.Security.SqlMembershipProvider, System.Web,
                        Version=4.0.0.0, Culture=neutral, PublicKeyToken=b03f5f7f11d50a3a"
                        connectionStringName="LocalSqlServer"
                        enablePasswordRetrieval="false"
                        enablePasswordReset="true"
                        requiresQuestionAndAnswer="true"
                        applicationName="/"
                        requiresUniqueEmail="false"
                        passwordFormat="Hashed"
                        maxInvalidPasswordAttempts="5"
                        minRequiredPasswordLength="7"
                        minRequiredNonalphanumericCharacters="1"
                        passwordAttemptWindow="10"
                        passwordStrengthRegularExpression=""
                />
            </providers>
        </membership>

        <profile>
            <providers>
                <add
                        name="AspNetSqlProfileProvider"
                        connectionStringName="LocalSqlServer"
                        applicationName="/"
                        type="System.Web.Profile.SqlProfileProvider, System.Web,
                        Version=4.0.0.0, Culture=neutral, PublicKeyToken=b03f5f7f11d50a3a"
                />
```

```
                </providers>
            </profile>

        <roleManager>
            <providers>
                <add
                        name="AspNetSqlRoleProvider"
                        connectionStringName="LocalSqlServer"
                        applicationName="/"
                        type="System.Web.Security.SqlRoleProvider, System.Web, Version=4.0.0.0,
                        Culture=neutral, PublicKeyToken=b03f5f7f11d50a3a"
                />
                <add
                        name="AspNetWindowsTokenRoleProvider"
                        applicationName="/"
                        type="System.Web.Security.WindowsTokenRoleProvider, System.Web,
                        Version=4.0.0.0, Culture=neutral, PublicKeyToken=b03f5f7f11d50a3a"
                />
            </providers>
        </roleManager>
    </system.web>
```

Listing 5-24 shows that in machine.config, there are providers for membership, roles, and profiles. All the profile settings are using the connection string specified in the connectionString sections. You should note the settings for the membership provider. These determine many of the details about how your login and registration work, and how the passwords are stored inside your database. All these settings can be overridden in your application's Web.config file, if necessary. If you are OK with the default setting, you do not need to include any additional configuration.

Modifying Your Web.config File

Now that we understand what is in the machine configuration file, we can modify your application's configuration to use the database created earlier.

1. Open your project in Visual Studio. Open your Web.config file.

2. Use the <clear/> command inside the <connectionStrings> section to remove any connection strings that you may have inherited from Machine.config.

3. Change the connection string so that it points to the desired database. When you are done, it should look similar to Listing 5-25.

4. Modify the default providers so that they look like Listing 5-26.

5. Save your project and press the F5 key to verify that it works as expected.

6. Use the SQL Object Explorer in Visual Studio to verify that the data has been saved to the correct database.

Listing 5-25. *The connectionStrings Section of the Web.config File*

```
<connectionStrings>
          <clear/>
    <add name="connstr"
              providerName="System.Data.SqlClient"
              connectionString="Data Source=reallymassivedatabaseserver;Initial
Catalog=aspnetdb;Integrated Security=True;Connect Timeout=15;Encrypt=False;
TrustServerCertificate=False" />
  </connectionStrings>
```

The first thing that has been changed in Listing 5-26 is the inclusion of `<clear/>`. It removes any connection strings that may have been inherited from machine.config and other configuration files. By including it, we know that the connection string that we have added is the only one in the collection and removes the possibility of connecting to an incorrect data source.

Next, the connection string is modified to point to the desired database. If you have trouble remembering the syntax for connection strings, an easy way to acquire it is to use Visual Studio's SQL Server Object Explorer. You can acquire the connection string by performing the following actions.

1. Open the SQL Server Object Explorer by selecting it from the View menu or by using the Ctrl+\, Ctrl+S keyboard shortcut.

2. In the SQL Server Object Explorer toolbar, click the Add SQL Server icon.

3. Enter the server name or select it from the drop-down list, and then select the authentication method. If required, enter the appropriate credentials.

4. The server should now appear in the SQL Server Object Explorer. Expand the server and databases nodes, and locate the database that you would like to connect to.

5. Right-click the database and select Properties from the pop-up menu.

6. The Properties window is docked on the right-hand panel. The connection string is listed as one of the properties. You can click inside the property and use the Ctrl+A keyboard shortcut to select all, and then Ctrl+C to copy.

7. You can then paste it into the `connectionString` property of the connection string entry in the `Web.config` file.

Before we move on, we will take a quick look at the properties of the connection string so that you understand them.

- *Data Source*: The name of the database server. If you are connecting to a local database, you can use a period as the data source name (*"."*)

- *Initial Catalog*: The name of the individual database that you wish to connect to. If this is not included, your application will need to specify a database name in its code.

- *Integrated Security*: Allows you to use Windows Authentication when connecting to the database. If this is set to false, then the username and password must be specified in the connection string. Using Windows Authentication is a best practice and is significantly more secure than using SQL Server Authentication. It also offers the benefit of not having a clear-text password in the configuration file. When using Integrated Security, you need to make sure that the account used by your application pool has appropriate rights on the database.

- *Connect Timeout*: The amount of time in seconds that your application should wait for the database server to respond before terminating the connection and throwing an error.

- *Encrypt*: If set to true, SQL Server will use SSL encryption when communicating with the server. This setting requires that a valid certificate be installed on SQL Server. You should always use SSL when connecting to a remote data source such as the one stored in SQL Azure.

- *TrustServerCertificate*: When set to true, it will bypasses a security check that validates the certificate. This may be required in situations where the mechanism that is used to verify the certificate cannot succeed because of firewall rules. The certificate validation step helps protect your application from "man-in-the-middle" attacks. You should only use this setting when you have to either set it or not use SSL at all.

Listing 5-26 shows a custom provider configuration. In the default configuration, Visual Studio uses a new set of providers known as the *Universal Providers*. In this configuration, the default providers have been replaced with the legacy SQL Server Providers and the connectionStringName has been set to the custom connection string.

Listing 5-26. Provider Configuration

```
<membership defaultProvider="SqlProvider">
    <providers>
                <clear/>
                <add name="SqlProvider"
                        type="System.Web.Security.SqlMembershipProvider, System.Web,
Version=4.0.0.0, Culture=neutral, PublicKeyToken=b03f5f7f11d50a3a"
                        connectionStringName="connstr"
                        enablePasswordRetrieval="false"
                        enablePasswordReset="true"
                        requiresQuestionAndAnswer="false"
                        requiresUniqueEmail="false"
                        maxInvalidPasswordAttempts="5"
                        minRequiredPasswordLength="6"
                        minRequiredNonalphanumericCharacters="0"
                        passwordAttemptWindow="10"
                        applicationName="/" />
    </providers>
  </membership>
  <roleManager>
    <providers>
                <clear/>
                <add connectionStringName="connstr"
                        applicationName="/" name="AspNetSqlRoleProvider"
                        type="System.Web.Security.SqlRoleProvider, System.Web,
Version=4.0.0.0, Culture=neutral, PublicKeyToken=b03f5f7f11d50a3a" />
        </providers>
  </roleManager>
```

The Universal Providers have been designed to provide broader compatibility at the expense of removing dependencies on SQL Server features that may not be available in all database types. The Universal Providers are not backward compatible with the legacy SQL Server Providers and have a different database schema. The major differences are as follows:

- With the new Universal Provider, you no longer need to use the aspnet_regsql.exe to create your schema. On the positive, this is convenient and saves you around two minutes of extra work. It creates the schema for you on your first access. The downside of this is that your service account requires elevated rights on the database in order to perform DDL commands. This breaks the security concept of least privilege, which could allow an attacker to drop and create tables at will if he happens to come across an SQL Injection vulnerability in your application.

- The Universal Provider does not use stored procedures. Some may argue that with modern query optimizers such as the one in SQL Server 2012, this is no longer a great performance problem. However, stored procedures do offer some undeniable benefits:

  - Precompiled SQL statements and execution plans.

  - Improved security by limiting user access to certain procedures rather than granting broad read access to tables and views.

  - Reduced network usage between clients and the database server.

  - Allows for incremental performance optimizations without needing to write your own SQL Provider.

- The Universal Provider does not use views.

- The Schema no longer prefixes the table names with aspnet_. This change is also unfortunate since it is no longer easy to distinguish tables used by the ASP.NET providers from other tables in your database.

5-8. Customizing the Registration Page on an Internet Site Created with the ASP.NET MVC 4 Internet Template

Problem

You have created a new application using the Internet Application template, but need to add a few custom fields to your registration form. You are using the default Membership Provider and need to understand how to customize this feature without writing a custom provider.

Solution

To customize the registration form, you will need to change several files—including the account models, the registration views, and the controller. You will also need to create a custom mechanism for storing any additional user information you are collecting.

How It Works

While the template provides a good starting point in most custom applications, it will not likely meet all of your requirements. In many cases, you will need to collect much more information about your users than their usernames and email addresses. One of the first design challenges is how to store the additional information. There are several possible ways to solve this problem:

- Write a custom Membership Provider or extend the built-in provider so that it holds all additional user data.

- Use the Profile Provider to store the additional fields in a name/value pair format.

- Use the Membership Provider to track usernames, passwords, and email, and then create custom objects to store your additional information.

Of the three choices, you will probably find that the custom object will give you the most flexibility and be the easiest to implement. The Profile Provider is good for storing user preference information, but it is cumbersome to work with for general needs.

In this example, we will create a registration form for a musician's collaboration web site. As part of the initial registration, you like to gather additional information, such as the type of instrument the new user plays. This web site will use an external SQL Server database, and since we want to make sure that our custom objects and the membership database tables do not go out of sync, we want to use the System.Transactions TransactionScope features, which require the Microsoft Distributed Transaction Coordinator (MSDTC) service to be running.

The first step is to add a new Visual Studio project the solution to hold the custom objects.

1. In Solution Explorer, right-click the solution name. Select Add, and then New Project from the pop-up menu.

2. In the Add New Project dialog box, select Class Library as the project type. Name the library **MusicCollaborationLib**, and then click OK.

3. In Solution Explorer, right-click Class1.cs and rename it.

4. Right-click the MusicCollaborationLib project. Select Add, and then New Folder. Name the new folder **Domain**.

5. Right-click the Domain folder and select Add, and then Class. Name the class **Artist**. Repeat for another class named **Skill**.

6. Create another folder under the project, and name it **Repository**.

7. Create a new interface named **IArtistRepository** and a class named **SampleArtistRepository**.

8. Modify the new files so that they look like Listing 5-27.

9. Right-click the References folder in the web site project in Solution Explorer. Select Add Reference.

10. In the reference manager, click Solution and select MusicCollaborationLib.

11. Click OK.

12. Modify the AccountModel as shown in Listing 5-28.

13. Modify the AccountController as shown in Listing 5-29.

14. Modify the Register.cshtml file as shown in Listing 5-30.

15. Modify the connection stringWeb.config file as shown in Listing 5-31.

Listing 5-27 shows a very simple class library with a repository interface and a mock implementation. In your real application, you have an implementation that stores this in a database. It may be helpful to create a mock implementation, but in most cases, you would use a mocking framework such as RhinoMock to aid in this. For simplicity in this example, we are using a class with hard-coded values.

Listing 5-27. The Custom Class Library

```
//Artist.cs
namespace MusicCollaborationLib.Domain
{
    public class Artist
    {
        public string FirstName { get; set; }
        public string LastName { get; set; }
        public Skill PrimarySkill { get; set; }
    }
}

//Skill.cs
namespace MusicCollaborationLib.Domain
{
    public class Skill
    {
        public string SkillName { get; set; }
        public int SkillLevel { get; set; }
    }
}

// IArtistRepository.cs
using MusicCollaborationLib.Domain;
namespace MusicCollaborationLib.Repository
{
    public interface IArtistRepository
    {
        Artist Create(Artist artist);
        void Delete(int id);
        Artist GetArtist(int id);
        IEnumerable<Artist> GetArtists();
    }
}

//SampleArtistRepository.cs
namespace MusicCollaborationLib.Repository
{
    public class SampleArtistRepository: IArtistRepository
    {
        #region IArtistRepository Members

        public Artist Create(Artist artist)
        {
            return new Artist { FirstName = "John", LastName = "Ciliberti", PrimarySkill = new Skill
{ SkillLevel=11, SkillName="Guitar"} };
        }
```

```
        public void Delete(int id)
        {
            //code to delete artist
        }

        public Artist GetArtist(int id)
        {
            return new Artist { FirstName = "John", LastName = "Ciliberti", PrimarySkill = new Skill
{ SkillLevel = 11, SkillName = "Guitar" } };
        }

        public IEnumerable<Artist> GetArtists()
        {
            //code that returns a list of artists
            return new List<Artist>();
        }

        #endregion
    }
}
```

In Listing 5-28, an additional read-only property has been added to the register model—that will hold information about the primary musical instrument our new site-member plays. In addition, a new class called InstrumentItem has been created to hold items that will be used to populate a drop-down list in the Register view. The Get method of the Instrument item property contains the values for the drop-down list.

Data annotations have been added. This will be used for both client-side and server-side validation of the form data.

Listing 5-28. Modified AccountModel.cs

```
public class RegisterModel
    {
        [Required]
        [Display(Name = "User name")]
        public string UserName { get; set; }

        [Required]
        [Display(Name = "Email address")]
    [RegularExpression(@"^([0-9a-zA-Z]([-.\w]*[0-9a-zA-Z])*@([0-9a-zA-Z][-\w]*[0-9a-zA-Z]\.)+[a-
zA-Z]{2,9})$",
            ErrorMessage="Please enter a valid email address")]
        public string Email { get; set; }

        [Required]
        [StringLength(100, ErrorMessage = "The {0} must be at least {2} characters long.",
MinimumLength = 6)]
        [DataType(DataType.Password)]
        [Display(Name = "Password")]
        public string Password { get; set; }
```

```
[DataType(DataType.Password)]
[Display(Name = "Confirm password")]
[Compare("Password", ErrorMessage = "The password and confirmation password do not match.")]
public string ConfirmPassword { get; set; }

[Required]
[Display(Name = "Primary Instrument")]
public string SelectedPrimaryInstrument { get; set; }

public IEnumerable<InstrumentItem> InstrumentItems
{
    get {
        return new List<InstrumentItem>
        {
            new InstrumentItem{ Text="Please Select", Value=""},
            new InstrumentItem{ Text="Bass Guitar", Value="Bass Guitar"},
            new InstrumentItem{ Text="Clarinet", Value="Clarinet"},
            new InstrumentItem{ Text="DJ", Value="DJ"},
            new InstrumentItem{ Text="Drums", Value="Drums"},
            new InstrumentItem{ Text="Flute", Value="Flute"},
            new InstrumentItem{ Text="Guitar", Value="Guitar"},
            new InstrumentItem{ Text="Harmonica", Value="Harmonica"},
            new InstrumentItem{ Text="Keyboards", Value="Keyboards"},
            new InstrumentItem{ Text="Lyricist", Value="Lyricist"},
            new InstrumentItem{ Text="Producer", Value="Producer"},
            new InstrumentItem{ Text="Saxophone", Value="Saxophone"},
            new InstrumentItem{ Text="Songwriter", Value="Songwriter"},
            new InstrumentItem{ Text="Trumpet", Value="Trumpet"},
            new InstrumentItem{ Text="Vocal", Value="Vocal"},

        };
    }
}
}
```

In Listing 5-29, we made several changes to the controller. In the GET version of the Register action, we passed in a copy of the model that contains our list used to populate the drop-down list. Since we need to pass data to the Register view on the initial get request, the model needs to be passed to the view.

For the POST action, we have made several key changes. First, the ValidateAntiForgeryToken attribute has been added. This is a security feature that when used in conjunction with anti-cross-site scripting, attack countermeasures can help prevent cross-site request forgery attacks. It is recommended that you use these techniques whenever practical.

In the method body itself, we first validate the model state using ModelState.IsValid. If any of the posted form data fails, the validation tests we stipulated in our model's data annotations will return false. In this case, the user is sent back to the Register view where they can see the error messages.

Next, we initialize a MembershipCreateStatus variable. We will use this as an output parameter to the Membership.CreateUser method. We can later check the value of this variable to see if the registration was successful.

This action will modify two sets of tables. The first are database tables updated by the ASP.NET membership provider; the second is done by our custom object. Since we would like all the database changes to be rolled back in the event of a failure, we wrap all the save operations in a `TransactionScope`. This ensures that both SQL Server calls are included in the transaction, and if an error occurs, all changes are rolled back.

Since our transaction involves more than one object, `System.Transaction` will escalate this to the MSDTC. In order for this to work, the MSDTC service must be running. This service is not running by default, and needs to be started using the Services application. On Windows 8, this can also be enabled using the Services tab on the task manager.

It is also important to note that MSDTC only works with the SQL Server providers and is not compatible with LocalDB.

For the `CreateUser` method call itself, we are passing in the model data that was binded to the form data filled in by the user, including the username, password, and email address. For our form, we are not using a question-and-answer password, so we pass null values for both. The question and answer can be used with the password reset feature if the membership provider is configured to use `enablePasswordReset="true"` and `requiresQuestionAndAnswer="true"` in the `Web.config` file. For our configuration, both values are set to false.

After the user has been created, we test the `CreationStatus` variable to ensure that the account was created successfully. We then create our custom Artist object and populate it with data from the model. We then use the Create method from the SampleArtistRepository to save the artist data.

The last step is to create the user's authentication cookie and redirect him or her back to the home page.

Listing 5-29. Changes to the AccountController

```
[AllowAnonymous]
public ActionResult Register()
{
    var model = new RegisterModel();

    return View(model);
}


[AllowAnonymous]
[HttpPost]
[ValidateAntiForgeryToken]
public ActionResult Register(RegisterModel model)
{
    if (ModelState.IsValid)
    {
        // Attempt to register the user
        MembershipCreateStatus createStatus;
        using (TransactionScope scope = new TransactionScope())
        {
            Membership.CreateUser(model.UserName,
                model.Password,
                model.Email,
                passwordQuestion: null,
                passwordAnswer: null,
                isApproved: true,
                providerUserKey: null,
                status: out createStatus);
            IArtistRepository artistManager = new SampleArtistRepository();
```

```
            if (createStatus == MembershipCreateStatus.Success)
            {
                Artist artist = new Artist
                {
                    PrimarySkill = new Skill
                    {
                        SkillName = model.SelectedPrimaryInstrument,
                        SkillLevel = 5
                    }
                };
                artistManager.Create(artist);
                scope.Complete();
                FormsAuthentication.SetAuthCookie(model.UserName,
createPersistentCookie: false);
                return RedirectToAction("Index", "Home");
            }
            else
            {
                ModelState.AddModelError("", ErrorCodeToString(createStatus));
            }
        }
    }

    // If we got this far, something failed, redisplay form
    return View(model);
}
```

The drop-down list has been added to the registration form in Listing 5-30. We do this using the
Html.DropDownListFor HTML helper. Like most of the helpers, it uses a lambda expression to bind the HTML
objects in the view to the model data. The delegate in the Html.DropDownListFor method takes two parameters:
m.SelectedPrimaryInstrument and Model.InstrumentItems. It renders the items as list items in the drop-down, and
if the item passed in the first parameter is found in the IEnumerable passed as the second parameter, if will add the
selected HTML attribute to that element.

Listing 5-30. Modifications Made to Register.cshtml

```
@using (Html.BeginForm()) {
    @Html.ValidationSummary()
    @Html.AntiForgeryToken()
    <fieldset>
        <legend>Registration Form</legend>
        <ol>
            <li>
                @Html.LabelFor(m => m.UserName)
                @Html.TextBoxFor(m => m.UserName)
            </li>
            <li>
                @Html.LabelFor(m => m.Email)
                @Html.TextBoxFor(m => m.Email)
            </li>
```

```
            <li>
                @Html.LabelFor(m=>m.SelectedPrimaryInstrument)
                @Html.DropDownListFor(m => m.SelectedPrimaryInstrument, new SelectList(Model.
InstrumentItems, "Value", "Text"))
            </li>
            <li>
                @Html.LabelFor(m => m.Password)
                @Html.PasswordFor(m => m.Password)
            </li>
            <li>
                @Html.LabelFor(m => m.ConfirmPassword)
                @Html.PasswordFor(m => m.ConfirmPassword)
            </li>
        </ol>
        <input type="submit" value="Register" />
    </fieldset>
}
@section Scripts {
    @Scripts.Render("~/bundles/jqueryval")
}
```

If you run the application, you should see the modified registration form with the drop-down list. You can experiment with entering invalid data into fields and see how it reacts. This example does not link your custom object with the membership provider object. When a user is created by the membership provider, a unique key is generated. You can query this value using the MembershipUser.ProviderUserKey property.

If this were a real system, you would need to add an id field to the Artist object and then populate it with the ProviderUserKey. The SQLServerMembership provider uses an SQL Server UniqueIdentifier data type for this field.

For the convenience of the developer, Microsoft has configured the web site to use SQL Server LocalDB to store your application's data. While this is fine for getting started, you will not be able to use this database when you deploy your application.

Luckily, changing the database used for your project is very easy. All you need to do is modify the connection string in your Web.config file to point to a SQL Server database. Listing 5-31 shows the connectionStrings section of Web.Config modified to use a database named Ch5.R5-8 on the default SQL Server instance installed on the local machine.

Listing 5-31. Modified Connection String in the Web.config file

```
<connectionStrings>
  <add name="DefaultConnection"
      connectionString="Data Source=.;Initial Catalog=Ch5.R5-8;Integrated Security=True;"
      providerName="System.Data.SqlClient" />
</connectionStrings>
```

If you do not have a database server running locally on the web server you can replace the "." specified in the Data Source property with the name of the remote server. To use integrated security with a remote server you need to change the Identity used by your web site's application pool to NETWORK SERVICE and then grant the required permissions on the database server for your server's domain account.

CHAPTER 6

Architecting Applications with ASP.NET MVC

This chapter will use recipes to introduce several architectural concepts. The recipes in the first part of the chapter will walk you though some of the key decision points that need to be made early in a project. The remainder of the recipes will focus on reference architectures for some common use-cases. The solutions feature both traditional web application architectures, as well as more modern approaches that include the use of cloud services.

6-1. Understanding the Role of the Architect

Problem

You have just begun reviewing the requirements for a new project. The project is larger in scope than other projects you have done in the past, but you are confident that you can solve the problem using your skills as an ASP.NET MVC developer. However, the business sponsor for the project is unsure of your proposed approach, so decides to bring in a software architect to help guide the design of this project. You have never worked with an architect before, so you would like to understand what role he plays and how he differs from a senior developer or technical lead.

Solution

In the world of information technology, the term "architect" is used rather loosely. Many people in different roles at different levels in the organization claim to be architects. The official definition of a software architect and the role he or she plays differs from organization to organization. You see this when looking at job listings for architect positions on various internet job boards. The common thread between the various definitions is that the architect is central to the overall design of something. Depending on your skill set and level in an organization, that something may be a subsystem, a database, an enterprise-scale application, a network, or even an IT strategy for an entire company. Some companies are creating nontechnical architecture roles such as a business architect and a service architect. These nontechnical roles focus on designing business processes rather than technology. Job titles for technical roles include solution architect, enterprise architect, information architect, infrastructure architect, and even cloud architect.

For the purposes of this chapter, the recipes will focus on the domain of the *solution architect*. A solution architect is responsible for the overall design of a software system. Solution architects work with business analysts to gain an overall understanding of the requirements for a system. They then determine the technologies that should be used for the system, design the physical topology of the system, and consult with the lead developer on the detailed design.

Since this book is focused on Microsoft technology, the solutions presented here will be Microsoft-centric with an emphasis on web-based solutions using ASP.NET MVC.

How It Works

Many from around the world have watched the rebuilding effort in Lower Manhattan with anxious curiosity. From the early conceptual drawings to the scale models, the laying of foundation, and then finally, One World Trade Center emerging prominently in the New York City skyline.

It has been over ten years since construction began at the site, and still hundreds of workers labor night and day on what seems like something so large and so complex that it should be impossible. Can you imagine such a project being undertaken without the planning and design work of skilled architects? Would the skills of the steel workers and carpenters alone be enough to complete a project like this one?

Most solution architects start their careers as developers, but many come from other IT disciplines, such as system administrators and networking engineering roles. Most people do not start their careers as an architect, but graduate into the role after five to ten years in the trenches. Solution architects typically do not write production code. If an architect writes code at all, it is usually for proof-of-concept projects that will teach them enough about a technology to understand if it is suitable for a proposed use.

Architects require training on the latest technologies in order to understand what tools are available and how they should be used. Their knowledge is broad rather than deep, but most will have deeper knowledge in a particular specialization. For example, Microsoft-centric IT shops may favor hiring architects that, in addition to general architecture skills, have a deep knowledge of ASP.NET MVC.

In addition to software development technologies, solution architects should have a broad understanding of network topologies, servers, storage technologies, and security appliances such as intrusion detection and prevention systems. Solution architects must develop strong written and verbal communication skills, and have a professional appearance and demeanor. Solution architects may move on to become enterprise architects, where their role will broaden and they will function as advisors to the IT executive staff, helping to shape overall IT strategy.

The Difference Between a Solution Architect and a Development Lead

A *development lead*, also known as a technical lead, is the most senior developer on a project team. He or she is responsible for detailed system design, including the API design, domain model, database, and project structure. The technical lead may participate in coding, but in most cases, it is a secondary role with the majority of time spent performing management functions. The development lead is usually only assigned to one or two projects at a time. In contrast, a solution architect may be assigned to many projects at once. The majority of the solution architect's time is spent at the beginning of a project, but he or she will usually participate in consulting, and in some cases, troubleshooting activities.

The development lead is normally aligned with a business unit and has domain knowledge relevant to that organization. Solution architects are normally part of a multifunction shared services group in a centralized IT organization. Increasingly, both roles are being externalized, but in most cases, onshore consultants are preferred to offshore roles. Whether or not the role is externalized has a lot to do with how closely the architect and development leads are aligned with the business and how important domain knowledge is to their job function.

In smaller organizations, the line between solution architect and development lead may be blurred—with a single individual performing both roles. Smaller organizations may not have enough work to justify a full-time solution architect. In most cases, they bring in external resources to fill this gap, especially if there is a skill gap in a technical area. For example, if an organization is new to ASP.NET MVC, they may bring in an architecture consultant to help frame out the first project, while performing knowledge transfer with internal staff.

Other Architect Roles

As the architecture role has evolved, several specializations have begun to emerge. Table 6-1 lists the different variations on the architect role.

Table 6-1. *Architecture Roles*

Role	Description	Prevalence
Infrastructure Architect	Focuses on network infrastructure, virtualization, storage technologies, and other IT infrastructure. This role may be rebranded as a cloud architect as IT infrastructure evolves to include both public and private cloud technologies. In a Microsoft-centric IT shop, skills may include Windows Server, Microsoft Exchange, Windows Azure, and Active Directory.	High
Information Architect	Focuses on information management and collaboration. Has skills in data warehousing, data visualization, management of unstructured data analytics. In a Microsoft shop, has knowledge of Microsoft SQL Server, Microsoft SharePoint, Microsoft SQL Server Master Data Management, Microsoft SQL Server Reporting Services, Microsoft PowerPivot, and Microsoft SQL Server Analysis Services (SSAS).	Medium
Enterprise Architecture	Possesses a deep understanding of an organization's technical assets from a holistic point of view. Helps to shape technical strategy through research of emerging technologies coupled with insight into an organization's processes and data. Should have broad knowledge of the entire Microsoft software infrastructure, including technologies such as ASP.NET MVC.	Medium
Service Architect	Creates business services that integrate with technology offerings. This role is less focused on technology.	Emerging
Business Architect	Focuses on creating an understanding of the structure of the business. This is not a technical role.	Emerging

6-2. Understanding the Buy or Build Decision

Problem

You are given a set of requirements for a system that will manage contracts for construction projects occurring across your company's many locations. After reading the requirements, it seems that the problem to solve is not unique to your company. You need to know whether you should propose a custom system or look for a packaged product in the marketplace.

Solution

There are products in the marketplace for almost every common business problem you can think of. Very often it is more economical to purchase and deploy than to custom-develop the system from scratch. In some cases, you can find a Software as a Service (SaaS) provider that not only provides a solution, but also hosts the solution. In other cases, you may construct a solution that consists of one or more vendor products that you can integrate with a custom solution based on ASP.NET MVC.

The first step in deciding whether to buy or build is to understand the market you are targeting. For the sample use case, there may be several product categories that fit. Once you narrow the product category, you need to do some research on the products in the space and determine who the product leader is. The maturity of a product segment is important since immature product segments tend to be volatile. You do not want to purchase a product from a vendor who may be out of business in a year. In some cases, you can purchase research from companies such as Gartner and Forrester. Once you narrow your vendor list to three vendors or less, you can bring the products into your lab to see how they perform.

Based on your lab analysis and paper research, you will be able to provide a recommendation on whether to build or buy, and if buying, which vendor you prefer.

How It Works

Many developers and architects fall into the habit of using what is comfortable rather than what is needed. This behavior is sometimes referred to as the Golden Hammer AntiPattern. When all that you have is a hammer, everything looks like a nail. You need to be mindful that custom-built web applications are not the best solution to every problem. Many times, if you have a common business problem, there will be many solutions. The following are some examples of common problems for which you should almost never build a custom solution:

- Blog

- Content Management System

- Wiki

- Customer Relationship Management System (CRM)

- Bulk Email System

- Enterprise Single Sign-On System

For each of these types of systems, there are hundreds of canned solutions, including open-source, commercial solutions, add-ins for products like Outlook and SharePoint, and SaaS solutions. There are solutions written in every programming language and platform. Most of them are highly configurable and customizable. In most cases, a custom solution will be less effective and more expensive to implement and maintain.

You should push for a custom ASP.NET MVC solution when the system requirements are unique to your company's business model or in cases where the proposed system is critical for your company to gain a competitive advantage.

In some cases, it may be advantageous to select a product from the marketplace that has been developed using a familiar platform such as ASP.NET. If you and others at your firm know this technology well, it can make the platform easier for you to deploy, maintain, and troubleshoot. If the product offers extensibility points, they will be easier for you and your team to exploit.

However, you should be careful not to let the system platform completely cloud your judgment. There are many fine products written in Java and other languages. In the end, the product selection should be based on how well the product meets your requirements.

Understanding the Market Segment

The first step in this process is to get a clear understanding of the requirements. If the business requirements document is too vague, ask for clarification. Talk with the business analyst and paraphrase your understanding of the requirements. Be sure you have it right. Other things to watch for are business requirements that are contradictory or illogical. Many design flaws can be traced back to the requirements. As the architect, you are often the first person to look at the requirements in a practical way. It is your job to take this from an abstraction and turn it into a design. You need to point out flaws when you see them.

Going back to our use case from the problem statement, you know that you work for are a large enterprise or government institution with many physical locations. You know that there are many construction projects occurring at many different locations. You also know that the business is looking for a way to manage the contracts with the various construction contractors. Is a solution to this problem going to improve the overall competitiveness of your company? Is your company's business process of managing construction projects so unique that no other company would have similar requirements? The answer is most likely, "no."

Bases on the requirements, you find two categories of projects that meet your needs. The first one is general-purpose contract management systems. You find that this is a project segment that has been growing in maturity with many established vendors that offer highly configurable solutions, some of which can integrate with your company's enterprise resource planning (ERP) system. The bad news is that the price for most of these systems is much higher than your customer's budget, and the better ones are so complex to configure that you will need to pay premium professional service dollars to have one of their consultant's set it up for you. The second product category is more specific to managing construction contracts. The problem with this space is that it is a much smaller market and the vendors in the space are not as mature as in the Enterprise Contract Management space. Out of the ten or so vendors, you are able to narrow down to the choice two vendors that best meet your requirements and seem to have firm financials and a stable technology.

Bringing the Products into the Lab

Even if you are able to purchase a research paper, it is sometimes still advantageous to bring each product in-house for a test drive. Many products look great on paper and may demo well, but unless you bring them into the lab and do a thorough component analysis, there is no way to really know what you are getting. You should always push for this type of analysis when applicable. This is especially true if a product was selected by the business. Business users often select products based on things like the user experience (UX) and the color schemes. The goals of your component analysis are as follows:

- *Ensure that the product is deployable in your environment.* For example, if the product will only work on Firefox 14 or better, but your company has standardized on IE 6, this may be an issue. On the other hand, if the product only works on Windows 2000, which has been out of support for years, the product probably has bigger problems.

- *Ensure that the product is supportable.* Many products require a Java application server such as JBoss. If the JBoss is installed for you automatically, and updates to JBoss are supplied by the vendor as part of the normal patching process, this may be OK. On the other hand, if JBoss requires a manual installation and needs to be maintained separately, you will need to define a process for doing so. It also may be possible that your company has a Java application server standard. Is the software certified to run on your standard platform?

- *Look for odd mismatches in the technology stack.* If you see that some components are written in classic ASP, other parts are using PHP, and yet another section uses Ruby with some Java thrown in for good measure, chances are the system is poorly architected.

- *Gain an understanding of the application's communication patterns.* If the software requires inbound connections that originate outside of your firewall, your company may have policies in place that forbid this pattern.

- *Pay attention to performance.* Does the application run poorly, even with small amounts of data and no concurrency? If so, how do you think it will run in production? You should always get scalability statistics for the application from the vendor. You need to understand how many concurrent users can be supported for each front-end server. For example, if they can only support 20 users per server, and the system will need to support 20,000 users, you may want to look at another product.

Falling Back to Custom Development

Sometimes, even if there are many vendors in a market segment, you can still justify custom development over a software purchase in the following cases:

- None of the vendors are able to meet your requirements, and the cost of customizing the product to meet your needs would be greater than developing your own.

- The price of the package greatly exceeds the planned budget, and you only need a small portion of the features the package provides. Many vendor packages may meet your requirements but are more than what you need.

- If you work in a large enterprise, it is possible that none of the vendors has ever worked with a company your size and will be ill-equipped to meet your demands.

- Your organization has stricter security requirements than what the vender product was designed for. For SaaS providers, your information security policies may require ISO 27001 certification, for example.

- The one vendor that meets your requirements is run by a single developer out of his mother's basement. All kidding aside, you should only select vendors that have a proven track record for supporting an organization of your size. You need to know with a high degree of confidence that the vendor can support you once your service goes into production.

There are many cases where vendor solutions fall flat. Bringing in the wrong product can spell disaster, especially if the product was expensive. Even if your management is pushing hard for a vendor-based solution, if the solution is wrong, hold fast in your recommendation. Back up your recommendation by documenting the pros and cons of each approach in an honest and non-biased way.

6-3. Deciding Between a Public Cloud and a Private Data Center
Problem

While reviewing possible deployment scenarios with a client, you were asked if you thought the application should be deployed to the cloud. The client seemed to think that the cloud was "magical" and by using it, the application would be able to do all kinds of things automatically. You need to know if a public cloud deployment is a good idea and how to explain the benefits and risks of this decision to the client.

Solution

In most cases, the answer to whether a cloud offering is a good fit can be determined by two factors: data privacy and cost. For data privacy and security, both Amazon and Microsoft have solid offerings—but in some cases, contractual obligations that limit the storage of confidential client information at third-parties may restrict you from using cloud services. From a cost perspective, cloud providers will only charge you based on what you use, and since they buy and deploy hardware at such large volumes, their unit prices are reduced due to economies of scale. There are some circumstances where reusing an existing asset can be more cost effective, but in most cases, cloud vendors will be less expensive. Cloud vendors also offer the ability to scale on demand, and create the illusion of unlimited storage capacity and computing power.

As cloud vendors evolve and mature, many of the concerns that have prevented firms from moving to the cloud have been evaporating. If your client is open to cloud deployment and the system requirements, risk profile and costing make sense; you should consider deploying the application to the cloud.

How It Works

Like many buzzwords in information technology, the meaning of the term "cloud" has been hijacked and twisted by almost every technology vendor on the planet. Because of this, the term "cloud" is being used to describe services, hardware platforms, and even storage appliances. Many service providers call their offering "The Cloud." Apple, for example, calls their ability to store your files and settings on Apple's servers the "iCloud." The term is also used to describe privately-hosted clusters of virtual machines, hosting solutions in external data centers, and complete applications hosted in a vendor's data center.

Most cloud services can be categorized into one of three service models: hosting services known as Infrastructure as a Service (IaaS), publicly-hosted APIs known as Platform as a Service (PaaS), and externally-hosted software solutions, or Software as a Service (SaaS). From the perspective of someone developing a custom software solution based on ASP.NET MVC, when customers are asking about a potential cloud deployment, they are usually thinking about either an IaaS or PaaS deployment—likely from Amazon AWS for IaaS or Microsoft Azure for PaaS.

Microsoft has recently become an IaaS provider by adding virtual machines based on their Hyper-V technology to their Azure portfolio. Amazon has also been expanding its services. Amazon now offers a Simple Queue Service (SQS), Elastic Map Reduce (EMR), and Simple Workflow Service (Amazon AWS), in addition to its mature IaaS services. Amazon and Microsoft are not the only players in the space. Other vendors include Rackspace, Nirvanix, Google, IBM, Flexscale, and `Force.com`.

Choosing Between PaaS and IaaS

According to Gartner's article "On Demand: From Capacity to Capability" (`www.gartner.com/id=1508715`), 50 to 80 percent of a typical company's IT budget is spent on infrastructure provisioning and operations. This process of ordering hardware, allocating resources to install the hardware, racking and cabling, installing the operating system, and server configuration and patching can sometimes takes weeks, if not months, in some organizations. Once the servers are set up, additional time is spent configuring routers, firewalls, and load balancers. In IaaS solutions, this entire hardware provisioning workflow has been done for you. A façade has been build that masks this complexity and gives the illusion of unlimited computing power. The process of provisioning a server that once took weeks is now done in the click of a button. If you get an unexpected spike in traffic, services such as Amazon's Auto Scaling and Paraleap Technologies' AzureWatch for Windows Azure can automatically create new instances to meet the demand, and then deprovision them once they are no longer required.

If you are porting an existing codebase, an IaaS solution would likely be the best choice. The IaaS vendor supplies you with computing power, hypervisor clustering, and network infrastructure. You have total control over the VM and can install whatever software you require. Both Amazon and Microsoft allow you to create custom machine images and create new machines using a web-based administration tool. With both IaaS offerings, you are responsible for purchasing the licensing for all software that you install on your machines, including the operating system. You are also responsible for patching the operating system and for monitoring conditions such as low disk space and low memory, and catching and removing malware.

PaaS solutions, on the other hand, abstract away the idea of a traditional operating system. You no longer need to worry about server patches and upgrades. You create and package your software, and then deploy it to the appropriate role. Your software can consume storage services, relational database services, queues, and other services offered by the provider's API. With Windows Azure, the ASP.NET MVC 4 role will allow you to deploy most ASP.NET MVC applications with only minor configuration changes. If you need more capacity, you no longer need to spin up an entire new operating system—you only need to spin up another instance of your application. In the IaaS world, you may need to consider how the service is load balanced. On Amazon, you may need to spin up an instance of Elastic Load Balancing, another billable service to manage your traffic routing. In the PaaS world, this is managed for you and included in the price. The downside of PaaS is that you do not have control over the environment. You may have problems leveraging certain third-party tools that cannot run on a web or worker role. Another risk is that if you invest too much in APIs specific to a certain cloud offering, it may make it difficult to migrate from the service.

It is also possible to use both PaaS and IaaS together to create a hybrid solution. For example, you can consume Microsoft's IaaS offering by purchasing a subscription and adding several VM roles on Azure to host a custom SharePoint configuration. You can then use several web and SQL roles to host an ASP.NET MVC application that is surfaced on SharePoint using web parts or SharePoint apps if you are using SharePoint 2013. If you are expecting that your SharePoint site will need to host a large number of documents, you can use a remote BLOB storage provider, such as Metalogix StoragePoint, which can offload the BLOB storage to Windows Azure BLOB storage.

6-4. Determining the Size of Your Application's Local Network
Problem

You have been given requirements for a system. The business sponsor estimates that the new service will attract ten to twenty thousand visitors a day, and that number will grow significantly over the course of a two-year period. A company security policy mandates that each application be isolated in its own private virtual network(PVLAN). You are asked how large the network should be. Your network admin asks in an email if you need a /28 network or a /27 network. You are expected to provide an answer before the next status meeting.

Solution

In many projects, the first architectural decision you need to make is to size your network. This roughly translates into the maximum number of unique IP addresses you will need for your application's private network, plus additional address reserved for your gateway and other network services. You can estimate this by first determining the number of servers you will need to deploy in the first few years of your application's lifetime, and then multiplying by two so that you can account for extra network adapters installed on each server for use in backups.

How It Works

In the human world, when people need to drive to a house they have never been to, they generally need two bits of information: the street address and directions for how to get there. In IP networking, you have a similar concept but you use an IP address rather than a street address, and instead of using Google Maps, you use something called a routing table.

When your networking team designed your network, they were given a finite set of addresses to work with. If this pool of addresses is not properly managed, the pool can run dry and they will not be able to provision IP addresses to new devices without first removing an existing device from the network. In order to reduce the amount of unique IP addresses needed, and to reduce the complexity or the routing tables, they use a technique known as *network addresses aggregation*. The most common method used for network address aggregation is called Classless Inter-Domain Routing (CIDR).

With this in mind, you may need to supply your network administrator with an address space aggregation type in the format of /xx, where xx is the number of bits in the network part of the IP address. This notation is called a *routing prefix mask*.

So as not to get lost in an in-depth TCP/IP discussion, Table 6-2 shows how the routing prefix mask translates to the number of hosts you can have in your PVLAN.

Table 6-2. *Using CIDR Address Space Aggregations*

Available Hosts Addresses	Routing Prefix Mask
16	/28
32	/27
64	/26
128	/25
256	/24
512	/23
1024	/22
2048	/21
4096	/20

As shown in Table 6-2, each time you reduce the prefix mask size, the number of available host addresses doubles.

Looking back at the requirements from the problem statement, you are expecting ten to twenty thousand visitors a day, as well as significant growth over a two-year period. Using this as a baseline, you need to estimate the peak number of concurrent users and then determine how many of them can be supported by a single server.

What makes this tricky is that the growth projections are usually just high-level estimates based on your customer's expectations, which are normally over-optimistic. Over-estimating will cause you to waste valuable IP addresses and add complexity for your network administrators. On the other hand, underestimating may result in a fire drill at some later date, in which you need to create a larger PVLAN and then migrate your application to it. This is a significant amount of work and will likely result in downtime. What you need to do is give yourself a buffer. If service is growing rapidly, you should be able to project when your pool of IP addresses will be exhausted and plan accordingly.

If the service does well and you are peaking at 20,000 visitors a day, and that traffic triples over the next two years, you would have 60,000 visitors a day. If your service is targeting customers in the United States and most of these visits will occur during business hours, you can estimate an average concurrency rate based on a 12-hour day when you compensate for the four US time zones. This comes to an average of around 5,000 users per hour during your active period.

The next statistic to integrate into your estimate is the average length of each visit. For each of the 5,000 users per hour, how long will they be sticking around the site? For this estimate, you need to look at the use cases in the requirements document. Depending on the type of service you are developing, this can be anywhere from a few seconds to 45 minutes.

For the sake of this estimating exercise, let us assume that the average length per visit is 5 minutes. Based on this rate, the average concurrency rate for the application would be around 5000/(60/5) or 416.6. Unfortunately, your traffic will not always be uniform and you will have spikes in traffic. You may have a daily spike, let's say many users log in at around 5PM and 6PM every day. You also may have seasonal spikes, such as around the holiday season when the average number of visitors a day triples to 180,000. Based on these numbers, you can construct a perfect storm scenario in which 50 percent of your 180,000 peak-season users all log in at your peak traffic hour. Thankfully, the magic of time zones will spread out this peak across a four-hour period. This gives you (180000/2)/4=22500.

To recap, at some point two years after the deployment of your service, if the service is as popular as the customer expects, and traffic triples over the course of the two-year period, you will be faced with a traffic spike of around 22,000 concurrent visitors that lasts for around four hours. Of course, all of this is a high-level estimate. Since you are not psychic, you have no way of knowing for sure. In most cases, your customer will not even get a tenth of the traffic they are expecting. For this excise, since we are only trying to determine the number of IP addresses that we will need (and not ordering servers), it is OK to go for the optimistic estimate.

6-5. Determining Which Operating System to Deploy

Problem

As a developer, you like to be on the cutting edge. Windows Server 2012 is a huge release for Microsoft. It is perhaps the most significant change to the Windows Server ecosystem since Windows 2000 Server. Your application is going live soon, but the server team does not yet support Windows Server 2012. Should you push your management to allow you to deploy on 2012, or should you concede and stay with Windows Server 2008 R2?

Solution

Generally speaking, when possible, you should always opt for the latest version of the server operating system that has been validated and is fully supported by your company's server operations staff. This will help ensure that your software will be stable and secure. You should not push to move to the latest version unless your software has a dependency on a new Windows feature. In that case, you still should work with your server operations group to validate the server build before you deploy. You should avoid deploying on beta and release candidate versions of the OS.

How It Works

When deploying a new system, there are several benefits to being on the latest version of the operating system. In the Microsoft world, it ensures that you will have four years of mainstream operating system support and an additional five years of extended support. It also ensures that you will have the best foundation for your application, allowing you to take advantage of new capabilities on the platform.

There are also dangers of rushing to deploy on the latest bits. For one, you run the risk of being the first Microsoft customer to find their latest bug. When you call Microsoft support, you may be surprised to discover that they do not have a fix for your problem in the knowledge base. In fact, they have no idea how to solve your problem but they will try to reassure you by issuing a ticket with premier services. A few weeks later, you may be informed that they have a "hotfix" that solves your problem. To put this in perspective, Windows Server 2008 R2 SP 1 contains 970 hotfixes and security updates. In other words, Microsoft has corrected 970 bugs since the launch of the OS. Many of these bugs were found by Microsoft customers. The full list of these bug fixes, along with links to the knowledge base articles about them, can be found on the Microsoft download website at www.microsoft.com/en-us/download/details.aspx?id=269.

Most organizations have a standard, server build procedure, which may include a custom Windows installer. This ensures that operating systems are deployed in a consistent and supportable way. It also streamlines the installation process. In some cases, the process can be completely automated, especially when server builds are coupled with virtualization. Since it will take your organization a month or so to prepare, test, and build a custom server, you will most likely not have a custom build for the latest OS available on the day the operating system is released. With this in mind, when possible, you should plan your deployments to align with your company's operating system release cycles.

It is a best practice to consume the services on your server and development platform rather than writing custom code. The less code you have to write, the less code you need to maintain, and the faster you can get to market. There are times when the new version of Windows will offer a capability that can save you months of coding. If you intend on using this new feature, you need to plan ahead. Let your server operations team know what your plans are. If they know well in advance that you need the new version of Windows Server, they may be able to prioritize having a build ready that coincides with your project plan.

Having a dependency on a new, prerelease feature is risky. Sometimes features that exist in a prerelease version of Windows may not make it to the final version. When defining your project charter, you need to ensure that these risks are accounted for in the risk register and that you have a realistic contingency.

6-6. Documenting Your Architecture

Problem

You have thought through all of your design decisions and now need to document your architecture. You are not sure if you need to learn UML or if you should buy an expensive diagramming tool.

Solution

When creating your diagrams, UML can be very helpful but it is not required. Ultimately, you should follow whatever documentation standard your company has adopted. If your company has not instituted a documentation standard, then you should strive to make your diagrams simple and easy to understand.

A common technique used to document a system is to use the concept of architectural views. Using this approach, you will segment your architecture document into several sections that each emphasizes a unique aspect of the system. The sections can include the enterprise architecture context, architectural constraints, principles and assumptions, a logical view, an interface view, a physical view, and a deployment view.

How It Works

For the purposes of this chapter, we will focus on the enterprise architecture context view, the physical view, and the deployment view. These views show how the application is deployed on the infrastructure and how it integrates with other systems in the enterprise.

UML vs. Freestyle

Universal Modeling Language (UML) can be an effective way of communicating a design, but it is not the only way a design can be documented. One key principle from the Manifesto for Agile Software Development is, "Individuals and interactions over processes and tools." From this perspective, the tools and methodologies used to create your design are less important than how effectively your design is communicated to your intended audience. UML's benefit is based on the assumption that because of its universal nature, everyone is familiar with its conventions and that its diagrams do not require much explanation. The problem with this assumption is that this is not always the case. In many organizations, a significant percentage of developers and IT staff have not had exposure to UML, and most business users probably never heard of it. If this is the case in your organization, would UML be the best format to express your design?

Even if people in your organization have not had training on UML, you can still benefit from the fact that the industry has put a lot of effort into defining the UML specification. There has been a lot of thought put into the types of diagrams and the symbols used in them. Because of this, many UML diagrams can be easily read and understood without any special training.

On the other hand, freestyle documents just work better sometimes. For example, if you ever need to present your design to a group of business users or executives using a PowerPoint slide deck, many times the UML diagram will be too complicated. In this case, a simplified and possibly colorful diagram may be more effective than a UML diagram.

Modeling and Documentation Tools

There are many tools available for documenting application and network architectures. These tools vary greatly in price and capabilities. I recommend evaluating several of them to determine which tool best suits your needs. The following is a list of some tools that you may want to consider:

- *OpenText ProVision*: A very robust tool that stores all of your diagrams in an SQL database and lets you create maps of your entire enterprise, which can be viewed from different perspectives and correlated not only with technologies, but also with functional capabilities. It can also give insight to the dependencies between applications. For example, if you are looking to retire or replace a system, Provision can be used to create reports that show what systems depend on it and the nature of the integration. The cons of ProVision are its pricing and learning curve. There is also a lot of upfront work required before Provision can be used to create any useful reports.

- *Sparx Systems Enterprise Architect*: Another robust tool that allows for end-to-end modeling and has an option for a server-based repository. Simple installation with a small 38MB download. It also provides tools for generating code from the diagrams. It is also somewhat complex to learn, but it's pricing is more reasonable than Open Text.

- *IBM Rational Rhapsody*: Provides UML diagramming, code generation, and simulation. It is a feature-rich and mature product. It integrates with IBM's full suite of requirements management and modeling tools. It also has the ability to integrate with Visual Studio, where it can generate Windows Workflow Foundation applications. Cons are complexity, learning curve, and price.

- *Microsoft Visual Studio Ultimate Edition*: Provides UML Diagramming, code generation for class diagrams, and diagram generation from existing code. It does not provide round-trip generation, meaning that if you generate code from your diagram and then modify the code, the diagram will not be updated. It also provides a layer diagramming feature that allows code to be validated against the design during a build. When used in conjunction with Team Foundation Server, diagrams can be linked with work items that can be associated with code checked into the source control system. Cons are that it is not as mature as competing products in its price range and that only team members with VS Ultimate or VS Premium may view the diagrams.

- *Microsoft Visio*: If you have an MSDN subscription, Microsoft Visio is included. Visio comes with several templates and stencil sets for creating network and software diagrams. A Visio stencil is a scalable diagram component that can be used in your diagram. In addition to the stencils included, there are many available on the web, including stencils for the most common network hardware. Visio 2013 includes support for UML 2.4, Business Process Model Notation 2.0, and Windows Work Flow Foundation 4.0. When used in conjunction with Microsoft SharePoint, remote team members can collaborate on a document in real time. Cons are that it is not as robust as some of the other solutions. For example, it does not have a comprehensive server-side solution for end-to-end enterprise architecture documentation as do the Open Text and IBM solutions.

- *diagram.ly*: Free, web-based, and easy to use. No install or sign up required. Built using the mxGraph JavaScript diagramming library. It works well for creating basic diagrams. Allows you to save the diagrams on your local PC as an XML file. It does not offer any advanced features such as code generation.

Architectural Views

When documenting your architecture, readability and simplicity are important to making your design easy to understand. One way to accomplish this is to create several diagrams, each of which shows a unique view of the system. The first of these views is the physical view. This is a high-level diagram that shows how your application is physically deployed on the network. Figure 6-1 shows an Internet-facing application that consists of two web servers load balanced by a dedicated hardware device and a dedicated database server.

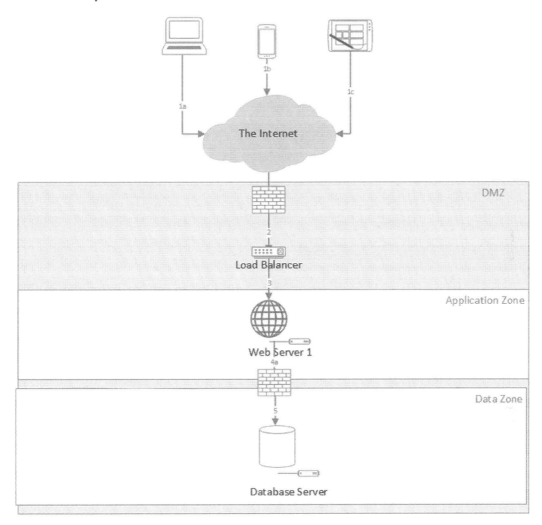

Figure 6-1. *Physical view for a simple Internet application*

Figure 6-1 tells us a lot about the design. It shows that the application will be deployed to the DMZ and will be accessible over the Internet by PCs, tablets, and smartphones. It shows that traffic is routed through an external firewall to a load balancer. The load balancer then routes the traffic to two web servers. Early in the design phase, you will not know the name of the web servers and can use generic names such as Web Server 1. Later on, after the servers have been deployed, the placeholder names can be replaced with the real server names and IP Addresses. Figure 6-1 also shows that there is another firewall sitting between the web servers and the database, and that the application has a single database server.

The diagram does not tell us what type of software is running on the servers. It also does not provide much detail about network infrastructure. It also does not tell or show which ports or protocols are being used.

Figure 6-2 shows a UML Deployment diagram. This is describing the same system as Figure 6-1, but focuses on what is being deployed rather than where it is deployed. It shows that a personal computer running a web browser is communicating using the HTTP protocol with a web server running IIS 8. It also shows that there is a component named "sample web app," which is an ASP.NET MVC application running in the IIS 8 execution environment. The diagram also shows that the web server is connected to a database server that is also running on a virtual machine. The database server's operating system is Windows Server 2012 Standard edition and it is running an SQL Server 2012 Web edition database system. A database named SampleDB is running inside the SQL Server 2012 execution context.

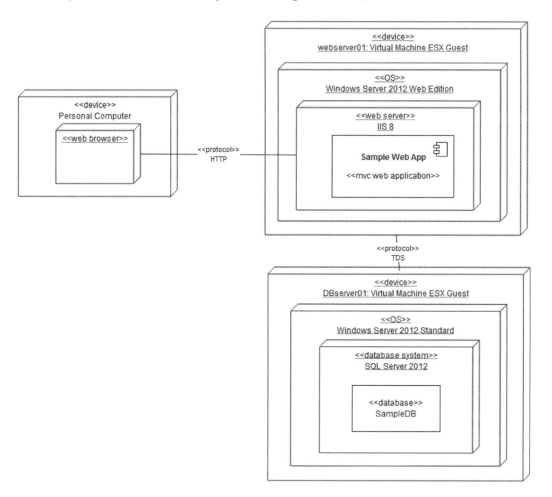

Figure 6-2. *UML deployment diagram*

Note that Figure 6-2 only shows a single web server rather than two, as in Figure 6-1. This is because the intent of the diagram is to show what components are deployed on each server role rather than network topology. It is perfectly fine for both servers, but in this case, I have chosen not to since all servers in the web role will have the same components. Also, in cases where you have many web servers, trying to put them all on one diagram would not be practical.

Also omitted from Figure 6-2 are the port numbers used for communication. Again, this is a matter of style, personal preference, or organizational documentation standards—adding the port numbers is not incorrect. My preference in this case is to omit this information here and include it on a diagram showing network topology.

The UML deployment diagram in Figure 6-2 is made up of *nodes*, which are represented by 3D boxes. In Figure 6-2, the parent node is a device that is implied by the <<device>> prototype declaration. Directly below the prototype are attributes that describe it. In this case, the name of the device—webserver01—is shown followed by a colon and a description of the server. Nested inside the device is another node that describes the operating system. Inside the operating system, you can see the web server node. The web server and OS are examples of specializations of the node symbol. Another way this could have been expressed would have been to show the OS type and an attribute of the server rather than an execution environment node.

The UML specification also provides a convention for showing which software components and artifacts are installed. A component is usually used to describe a conceptual software element such as subsystem. In this example, "sample web app" is the component. If you wish, you can add more detail that shows that "sample web app" is made up of several artifacts. An *artifact* is a deployable component. It could be a .dll, a web deployment package, or even an .aspx or .cshtml page. Many of the modeling tools—such as Provision—allow the documents to be interactive, so rather than showing this as a static diagram, users can navigate through the many layers. In Figure 6-2 for example, you would be able to double-click the "sample web app" component to see the various artifacts that make it up.

Figure 6-3 shows an example of how an application fits into the overall architecture of the enterprise. This diagram is completely abstract. It does not show servers or networks. It shows each application as a simple box with a name in it, and then has arrows pointing out of each box indicating a dependency hierarchy. In this case, there is a new application being deployed: E-Commerce Application. It has dependencies on Email Marketing, Inventory, Invoicing, and Vendor Management. Email Marketing has a dependency on CRM. CRM, Vendor Management, and Invoicing have dependencies on the ERP system. This type of documentation is very valuable, especially when a system needs to be upgraded or replaced. Think about the ERP system in this example. What systems will be affected if the ERP system has to be replaced?

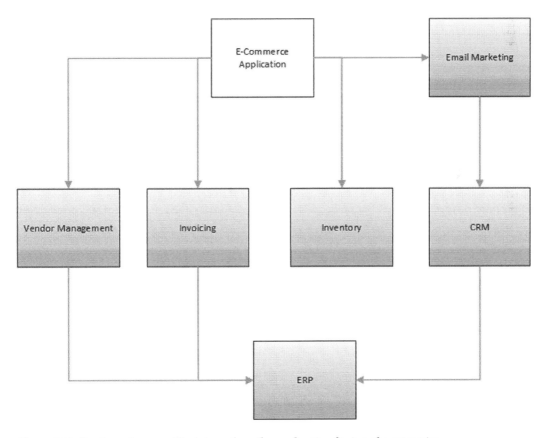

Figure 6-3. Freeform document that shows how the application fits into the enterprise

6-7. Architecting an ASP.NET MVC Application for the Internet

Problem

You have been given requirements for a system that needs to be exposed to the Internet. The business sponsor estimates that the new service will attract several thousand visitors a day, and that number will grow significantly over the course of a two-year period. Your client does not allow his system data to be stored offsite, which restricts you from using a public cloud vendor such as Amazon or Microsoft. You need to know how the system should be architected.

Solution

In order for the application to be accessible to the Internet, it will need to be deployed in a network segment commonly known as a DMZ. The DMZ is a no man's land that sits between the protected corporate intranet and the open Internet. Inside the DMZ, applications are usually segmented into separate, private virtual local area networks (PVLAN). Servers in one PVLAN will not be able to access servers in other PVLANs unless access is explicitly allowed using access control lists (ACL) on the router. This design will restrict a compromised application from exposing other applications in the DMZ to attack.

The application servers and the database servers for the application should be separated by firewalls. Communication between the SQL Server and application server is encrypted. For added security, you can configure SQL Server to listen on a nonstandard port. Using a nonstandard port can help prevent attacks—such as from the SQL Slammer worm.

The application servers can be virtualized and are configured to sit behind a network load balancer. Additional front-end servers can be added as needed.

How It Works

Before you can deploy your servers, you need to have infrastructure in place to build upon. As a developer or architect, you may not be directly involved in setting up the network or racking and cabling the servers, but may be involved in making decisions about their size, number, and configuration.

You then need to determine how many front-end web servers you will need, whether to deploy a stand-alone SQL Server or a cluster, and if you will need any additional servers to fill utility roles such as queuing and batch processing. You also need to determine disk space; the type of disk configuration; and whether to use local storage, network-attached storage (NAS), or a storage area network (SAN).

When designing your service, you should assume that it needs to run on multiple web servers, even if you are deploying to a single front-end server for the initial launch. With this in mind, you should not be dependent on any local machine resources. You should not save data to local hard drives. You should also avoid using session variables. By default, session state is stored in the memory assigned to your application's process on the local machine. If the user is sent to another machine on the next request, the session data will not be available. This can be mitigated by using a dedicated session state server or by storing session data inside SQL Server, but these options have their own drawbacks. You also need to be mindful about your use of caching. Don't assume the value you wrote to the cache on the last request will be available on the next request. Even if the user is sent to the same machine, it is possible that ASP.NET has flushed the cache because the process is running low on memory.

Reference Architecture

In the problem statement, the customer is claiming that they are expecting several thousand visitors a day. Let's suppose that the business analyst had drilled down and refined the estimate to between 2,000 and 3,000 visitors a day. Of these users, around 50 percent will be nonregistered users who are simply browsing the web site for information. The remaining 50 percent will be logging in and performing transactions. Around 5 percent will be running process intensive reporting functions. Most of the users will be from North America. Usage of the service will peak at around

4PM, with an estimated maximum concurrency rate of 200 users. The web application is primarily just pulling data from a database, doing some minor data manipulation, and sending the data as JSON to the client where client-side JavaScript performs most of the rendering functions. The customer can tolerate a moderate amount of downtime and does not require high availability.

Based on this information, a basic two-tier web application should be enough to meet the demand. From a pure capacity perspective, it may even be possible to host the database on the same server, but for security reasons, the database server should never be on the same machine as the web server when a service is exposed to the Internet.

Even though only one web server will be deployed initially, it is placed behind a hardware load balancer so that it can scale horizontally if required. Both the web and database tier will be virtualized, meaning they will be running inside virtual machines rather than dedicated physical hardware. For the initial deployment, the web server will be assigned a single CPU and 2GB of RAM. This may seem low, but based on the requirements, it should be more than what is needed for this application. If it is found that the application needs additional RAM, the virtual machine infrastructure allows RAM and CPU to be easily upgraded.

This design has the following benefits:

- In most production deployments, the hypervisor environment is clustered and *has the capability to seamlessly migrate your virtual machine to another physical machine without any downtime.* This capability provides redundancy to your application and prevents a single hardware event from disabling your service.

- In most production deployments, *the hypervisor environment stores the virtual hard disks on a storage area network (SAN).* This provides additional redundancy to your application's storage.

- *A substantially lower cost.* Physical machines require space in a datacenter. If you purchase a physical machine, you need to pay a recurring cost for that space on top of the initial cost of the server. With virtual machines, you will pay only a fraction of this cost.

- *It's greener.* Overall, virtual machines consume less power than physical machines. Virtual machines do not need to be sent to a landfill when they are no longer needed.

- *Virtual machines can scale on demand.* With a short outage, a virtual machine can easily add RAM and CPU. In our example, if the user base doubles, additional CPUs and RAM can be added in minutes.

- *Lower software licensing costs.* Many vendors calculate the cost of the software license by the number of physical cores. Many new servers are configured with two CPU sockets, each with six cores. If you do not actually need all the processing power, this can be a significant waste of money.

Figure 6-4 shows the physical view of the web application reference architecture. The main communication paths are explained in Table 6-3. The purpose of this diagram is to show how the application is deployed on the network, and to illustrate the ports and protocols it uses to communicate. This type of diagram would be useful to members of the network team and the security team, as well as for development and quality assurance (QA). It omits detailed network information such as the model numbers for network hardware, routers, and switches. Unless dedicated network hardware was deployed specifically for your application, that level of detail is usually not required.

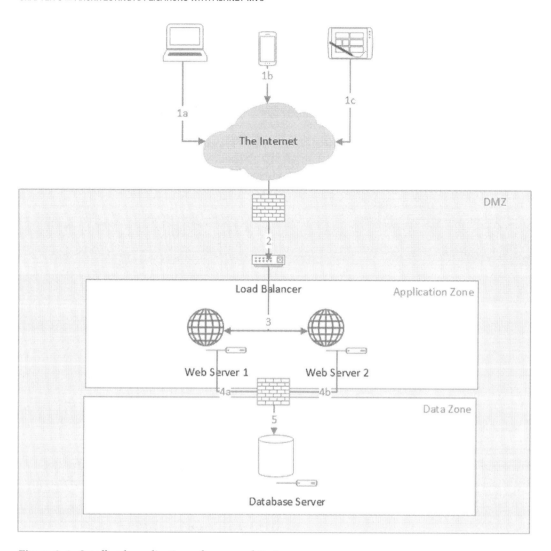

Figure 6-4. *Small web application reference architecture*

Table 6-3. *Communication Paths Used in the Reference Architecture Shown in Figure 6-4*

	Ports	Protocol	Description
1	80, 443	HTTP, HTTPS	HTTP requests are initiated on standard ports by the various endpoints, which may include PCs, tablets, and smartphones.
2	80,443	HTTP, HTTPS	The traffic traverses the external firewall. If this is an advanced device, the incoming traffic has been analyzed to ensure it is not using a known attack vector.

(*continued*)

Table 6-3. (*continued*)

	Ports	Protocol	Description
3	80,443	HTTP	The traffic has passed through a hardware load balancer. If this is a modern load balancer such as an F5 Local Traffic Manager (LTM), it comes equipped with SSL acceleration capabilities. If the traffic comes over SSL, the SSL traffic will be terminated at LTM and only HTTP traffic will be sent to the balanced web servers. This design simplifies certificate management and offloads the SSL decryption. It also allows the load balancer to modify the request. In some instances, it can be used for scenarios where a large number of users are accessing the site from a proxy server and the application requires sticky connections. In this case, the load balancer can append a cookie to the requests and use that to uniquely identify each user, rather than attempting to do so using an IP address. If you do not use an advanced load balancer or do not use the SSL feature, the HTTPS data will pass through the LTM and be handled by the web server.
4	1433 or custom port	TDS	The data passes through the internal firewall. The firewall has been configured to allow traffic only from the web server on the specific port. By default, SQL Server uses TCP port 1433, but it is recommended that a nonstandard port be used to protect your database from potential worms and other threats that could take advantage of potential zero-day security vulnerabilities in SQL Server. Although an attack is less likely in this scenario since all the servers are isolated in dedicated zones, it is still possible. A zero-day vulnerability is an exploitable flaw in an application that an attacker can use to damage a system in which no patch currently exists. Depending on the firewall's capability, it may inspect the traffic to ensure it is the correct protocol and verify that it is not following a known attack pattern.
5	1433 or custom port	TDS	The web server opens several connections to SQL Server. For extra security, it can be configured to use a custom port. SQL Server uses the Tabular Data Stream (TDS) protocol to send and receive information.

Server Configuration

The reference architecture consists of two servers: a web server and a database server. Both servers are virtualized and are running on a Hyper-V or VMWare cluster. Redundancy for the servers is provided by the virtual machine infrastructure. VMWare has a technology called VMotion. It allows your virtual machine to move between hosts without a noticeable gap in accessibility. Microsoft has a similar feature called Live Migration. Since all virtual machine images are stored on a SAN, the virtual machine infrastructure also provides a level of high availability as well as redundancy for storage.

Table 6-4. *Server Configuration for Web Server*

OS:	Windows Server 2012 Standard Edition
RAM:	2GB
CPU:	1 CPU
Disk Configuration:	C: (SYSTEM) 40GB, E: (LOGS) 4GB, F: (Data) 30GB
Software Installed:	IIS 8 Web Deployment Manager Antivirus software

Table 6-5. *Server Configuration for Database Server*

OS:	Windows Server 2012 Standard Edition
RAM:	4GB
CPU:	2 CPU
Disk Configuration:	C: (SYSTEM) 60GB, E: (LOGS) 10GB, F: (Data) 60GB
Software Installed:	Microsoft SQL Server 2012 Web Edition Antivirus software

6-8. Architecting a Large-Scale Internet Application
Problem

Your client has big plans. They have just secured funding from an angel investor and are ready to start building the latest social mega app. They are planning Super Bowl ads, branded monster trucks, and are even thinking about hiring some attractive women to hand out T-shirts at the next big tech trade show. They are expecting millions of users and thousands of transactions per second. You have been hired as the architect. You need some direction on how to design this solution.

Solution

For a startup company that hopes to target consumers on a massive scale, a public cloud vendor is going to be the best option. If your client can scale out the solution as needed and pay only for what he needs, he will be able to start on a solid foundation without needing to make a huge upfront capital investment.

In order to deal with the potentially massive number of transactions, you will need to attack the problem from multiple angles. This includes the following:

- Caching static content such as images, CSS, and script files on a content delivery network (CDN).

- Using a distributed cache to reduce redundant SQL Server calls.

- Employing a queuing mechanism to help you stay responsive during large spikes in transactions.

- Designing the data tier so that in addition to a primary database, several read-only replicas are available to handle large numbers of read requests.

- Using a BLOB storage service to handle storage of any large objects such as documents, images, audio, and video that may be uploaded to the service.

- Splitting the application into web and application tiers so that it is easily and appropriately scaled.

- Employing a monitoring system that works in conjunction with autoscaling components so that the application can scale up and down automatically.

- Keeping your server software as simple as possible and pushing complex UI rendering logic to the client whenever possible.

How It Works

After deciding on a public cloud-based architecture, the next big decision will be whether to use a Platform as a Service (PaaS) offering or to use the cloud only for infrastructure. If you are planning to build your application using ASP.NET MVC, a PaaS offering will likely be the best choice since it will allow you to scale out without needing to manage licensing for Microsoft Windows Server.

Microsoft and Amazon both have solid offerings for ASP.NET developers. Microsoft has Azure, which includes a specialized role for ASP.NET MVC. Amazon offers a service called AWS Elastic Beanstalk, which is a PaaS solution built on top of their leading IaaS solution. Amazon is somewhat new to the PaaS space, and whereas it does support Microsoft development technologies, it is less responsive to changes in the Microsoft stack than Azure.

Reference Architecture

Figure 6-5 shows a vendor agnostic reference architecture for a large-scale web application hosted in a public cloud. Table 6-6 explains the communication paths in detail.

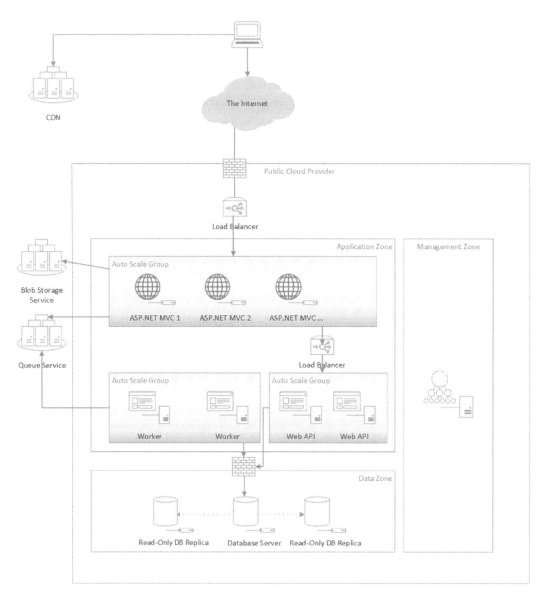

Figure 6-5. *Reference architecture for high-volume web application*

Table 6-6. *Communication Paths used in Figure 6-5*

Components	Ports	Protocol	Description
Client to External Firewall	80, 443	HTTP, HTTPS	HTTP requests are initiated on standard ports by the various endpoints, which may include PCs, tablets, and smartphones. The traffic traverses the external firewall. If this is an advanced device, the incoming traffic has been analyzed to ensure it is not using a known attack vector.
Client to CDN	80, 443	HTTP, HTTPS	Client connects to the Content Delivery Network (CDN) servers to download static files. The CDN are a set of globally distributed content servers that provide clients with a fast/low latency download of static files.
Firewall to Load Balancer	80, 443	HTTP, HTTPS	The traffic has passed through a load balancer. Amazon and Microsoft both have load-balancing solutions in the cloud. Amazon Elastic Load Balancers, for example, can detect unhealthy EC2 instances and stop routing traffic to them. They also have the ability to manage SSL certificates and support sticky sessions.
Load Balancer to ASP.NETMVC Servers	80, 443	HTTP, HTTPS	The load balancer routes traffic to a set of autoscaling web servers or ASP.NET MVC 4 roles, which process the incoming requests and return results to the user.
ASP.NET MVC Servers to BLOB Storage	443	HTTPS	When users upload files to the service, the web servers save the data to a BLOB storage service, such as Amazon's S3 or Microsoft's Azure BLOB Storage, using a RESTful API over SSL.
ASP.NET MVC Servers to Queue Service	443	HTTPS	In order to handle large numbers of incoming write transactions, the ASP.NET application sends the incoming requests to a queue where they can be processed later by the worker roles.
Worker to Queue Service	443	HTTPS	The worker servers pull data from the queue and process it. The management server can monitor the size of the queue and provision more worker servers if required.
ASP.NET Application to Web API via Load Balancer	443	HTTPS	The ASP.NET MVC servers pull data from the Web API tier. The Web API tier handles data access from the data tier and passes the data to the ASP.NET MVC application. The Web API can also be exposed directly to the web over HTTPS so that customers can consume the API directly and write their own front-ends. In general, you should always use SSL for communications when using a public cloud.
Worker to Data Tier	(TBD)	TDS	The worker servers save data to the primary database after processing it in the queue. The SQL Server service is configured to run on a nonstandard port for security reasons.
Web API to Data Tier	(TBD)	TDS	The Web API can read and write to the data tier. Since the majority of the requests are reads, these requests are offloaded to read-only replicas. This allows the main database to maximize its throughput for processing incoming transactions.

6-9. Architecting a Line-of-Business Application with ASP.NET MVC

Problem

You have been assigned to build a new HR application that will replace your company's performance management system. The system will guide employees and their management through an annual goal-setting and review process. It will need to support your company's 30,000 employees and handle spikes in traffic that occur during review submission deadlines. Employees will be able to upload up to 40 documents per review period. All data must be retained for seven years. You need to know how the system should be architected.

Solution

For this solution, you will deploy your application behind the safety of your company's firewall and manage access to the system through Active Directory. You will also use Active Directory to retrieve information regarding employee and manager relationships. You application will be deployed to two virtual machines running an ASP.NET MVC application and two physical servers in a cluster configuration for the database.

How It Works

For this application, usage for most of the year will be nominal—with all the usage coming in big spikes corresponding with the annual review cycle. This usage pattern is not uncommon for line-of-business applications. Applications such as this are perfect candidates for cloud deployment. Since you only pay for what you use in the cloud model, the system resources can be throttled back to the bare minimum for most of the year, and then ramped up again for peak. Unfortunately, many companies are not ready to move to the public cloud because of privacy and security concerns. These companies can still gain some cost advantages through virtualization, however. With virtualization technology—even with the RAM on each virtual machine configured for 4GB during the offseason when unitization is low—the hypervisor will reclaim assigned but unused memory from the VMs using techniques such as transparent page sharing, ballooning, and swapping.

For front-end web servers and application server roles, virtual machines should almost always be your first choice. Virtualization provides versatility and cost savings not possible with physical hardware. For database servers, this choice is not always as simple. A few challenges with databases include high I/O utilization, greater disk space and memory requirements, and limited options for horizontal scaling. While modern virtualization environments can give you nearly bare-metal performance, the fact that a server's I/O resources are shared by many guest OS, means that an I/O-heavy database can degrade the performance of an entire node. If a database requires a large amount of disk space, it can also negatively affect cost effectiveness of the Hyper-V cluster by reducing the number of virtual machines that can use a storage array on the SAN. It is possible to mitigate this by configuring the VM to use direct disk access rather than a virtual hard disk file. With direct disk access, the VM disk is mapped to a physical volume rather than using a file on a shared volume. The problem with direct access volumes is that there are a finite number of them that can be configured for a hypervisor cluster.

With these challenges in mind, while it may be OK to virtualize a small- to medium-sized database, it may not be the best design for a large, heavily utilized database. In this example use case, the system will be storing a large number of documents related to the review process and will need to process a large number of transactions during peak loads. Because of this, while it may be possible to deploy the database to a virtual machine, the potential cost saving is not worth the risk of possible performance issues caused by an underpowered database server.

Since this is a high-profile application used by the entire company, downtime would cause a major disruption if it occurred during the peak usage period. To reduce the likelihood of a prolonged period of downtime, it is necessary to mitigate any single points of failure in the system design. For this reason, the database is configured as an active/passive database cluster. In an active/passive configuration, one server is configured as active and processes all queries, and the other is passive and does not process queries. Both servers share a logical disk drive. In case of a failure in the active server (node), the cluster service will fail over to the passive node.

Reference Architecture

Figure 6-6 shows the reference architecture for a line-of-business application deployed to a corporate intranet.

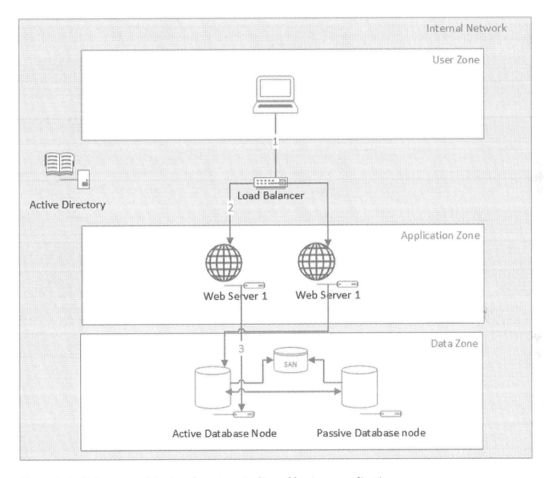

Figure 6-6. *Reference architecture for enterprise line-of-business application*

The communication paths shown in Figure 6-6 are described in detail in Table 6-7.

Table 6-7. *Communication Paths Used in the Reference Architecture Shown in Figure 6-6*

Step	Ports	Protocol	Description
1	443	HTTPS	HTTPS requests are initiated on the standard port by the various endpoints, which may include PCs, tablets, and smartphones. All traffic between the client and the load balancer is over SSL.
KDC	88	TCP	The system uses Kerberos for authentication. When an application is configured to use Kerberos, the server uses the SPNEGO protocol to determine if it is supported by the browser. If supported, the client contacts the Key Distribution Center on the domain controller. In a series of steps, the domain controller validates the user's credentials and sends the client a service ticket. This service ticket is passed to the server, which decrypts the ticket and validates that the user has access rights to the application. IIS then creates an access token for the user, which is used in all future requests.
2	80	HTTP	The traffic has passed through a hardware load balancer. If this is a modern load balancer such as an F5 Local Traffic Manager (LTM), it comes equipped with SSL acceleration capabilities. The SSL traffic is terminated at LTM, and only HTTP traffic is sent to balanced web servers. This design simplifies certificate management and offloads the SSL decryption.
3	(TDB)	TDS	The web server opens several connections to SQL Server using a custom port. SQL Server uses the Tabular Data Stream (TDS) protocol to send and receive information. The firewall has been configured to allow traffic only from the web server on the specific port. By default, SQL Server uses TCP port 1433 but it is recommended that a nonstandard port be used to protect your database from potential worms and other threats that could take advantage of potential zero-day security vulnerabilities in SQL Server. A zero-day vulnerability is an exploitable flaw in an application that an attacker can use to damage a system in which no patch currently exists. The database is a cluster that is using a SAN to store its data. The servers are typically connected to the SAN using a fiber-optic connection by way of a host protected area (HPA) card.

Server Configuration

The reference architecture consists of four servers: two web servers and two database servers. Both web servers are virtualized and are running on a Hyper-V or VMWare cluster. Redundancy for the servers is provided by the virtual machine infrastructure. VMWare has a technology called VMotion. It allows for your virtual machine to move between hosts without a noticeable gap in accessibility. Microsoft has a similar feature called Live Migration. Since all virtual machine images are stored on a SAN, the virtual machine infrastructure also provides a level of high availability as well redundancy for storage. The database servers are physical. For this application, mid-sized servers could be used.

Table 6-8. *Server Configuration for Web Servers*

OS:	Windows Server 2012 Standard Edition
RAM:	4GB
CPU:	2 CPU
Disk Configuration:	C: (SYSTEM) 40GB, E: (LOGS) 4GB, F: (Data) 30GB
Software Installed:	IIS 8 Web Deployment Manager Antivirus software Windows Server App Fabric for distributed cache

Table 6-9. *Server Configuration for Database Servers*

OS:	Windows Server 2012 Standard Edition
RAM:	24GB
CPU:	2 six-core CPUs, such as the Intel Xeon 5600 series
Attached Disk Configuration:	C: (SYSTEM) 120GB
SAN Configuration:	E: (LOGS) 120GB X2 RAID 1, F: (Data) 1.3 TB using 6 500GB drives configured as Raid 0+1, G: (TempDB) 120GB X2 RAID 1
Software Installed:	Microsoft SQL Server 2012 Standard Edition Antivirus software

The database server has been configured for high I/O throughput. The disks subsystem has been designed so that separate physical disk arrays are used for each logical drive. This design maximizes the number of spindles available, which increases the amount of I/O operations that can be performed concurrently.

The E: drive is used for the SQL Server transaction log and is optimized for writes. The data drive is configured to use to use a RAID 0+1 configuration, which offers fast read/write operations but requires more disks. In this example, it is using six 500GB drives, which will result in around 1.3TB of usable disk space.

Another drive is dedicated for TempDB, which is write-intensive. When designing a disk subsystem, you should always try and use separate physical drives for the transaction logs and data drives so that SQL Server can write to both concurrently.

The database server has two CPU sockets, each with six cores. The Intel Xeon series supports hyper-threading, which will result in a total of 24 logical CPUs. The server has also been loaded up with 24GB of RAM. It is generally recommended that 2GB of RAM be allocated for each CPU core.

With this configuration, the SQL Server should avoid many of the common performance bottlenecks, including CPU, memory, and I/O.

6-10. Configuring SQL Server to Use a Custom Port
Problem

Starting in 2003, a number of high-profile security issues caused by viruses and worms that exploited buffer overflow vulnerabilities in Microsoft's SQL Server caused widespread mayhem. The most destructive of these was the SQL Slammer worm. The bug that allowed this worm to spread has long since been corrected, but this does not mean that new, undiscovered bugs are not lurking in the SQL Server code. By default, SQL Server listens for incoming queries on port 1433. Since future worms and viruses would likely use the default configuration as an attack vector, many companies use alternate ports for SQL Server. You would like to follow this practice and need to know how to configure SQL Server and your client applications.

Solution

To change the default ports used by SQL Server, you must use the SQL Server Configuration Manager to change the TCP ports used by SQL Server. On client configurations, you must specify the port number in the connection string.

How It Works

After installing SQL Server, communication over TCP is disabled by default. If your application server is not on the same machine as your database server, you must enable the TCP protocol using the SQL Server Configuration Manager.

To change this setting, you must perform the following steps.

1. Tap the Windows key on your keyboard and begin to type **SQL Server Configuration Manager**. When the item appears in the program list, click it to open the configuration manager.

2. In the console pane of the SQL Server Configuration Manager, expand SQL Server Network Configuration, and then expand Protocols for [instance name]. Make sure you are not selecting the 32-bit version.

3. Double-click TCP/IP. If TCP/IP is disabled, enable it, and then click the IP Addresses tab.

4. Click each of the addresses listed and change the port number to the desired port.

Make sure that you change the port to an unused port below 49151. Ports between 49152 and 65535 are dynamic ports used by Windows for server-to-server RPC traffic. You should refer to the following documents to help ensure that you do not configure your app to use a common port number, which can lead to conflicts:

- `www.iana.org/assignments/port-numbers`: Shows common services and port numbers.

- `http://support.microsoft.com/kb/929851`: Discusses the default dynamic port ranges for Windows 8 and Windows Server 2012.

Client Configuration

When configuring a third-party application, it will attempt to use the default SQL Server port to communicate with the database. If you have set SQL Server to run on an alternative port, the installations of these products will fail. To correct this, you must specify the port number during product installation. The common convention used by most third-party application installers is to append the server name with a comma followed by the port number. For example "myservername,1440".

In some cases, the installer will not understand this convention. You can get around this problem by using the SQL Server Client configuration utility on pre- 2012 versions of SQL Server or the SQL Server Configuration Manager for SQL Server 2012 to create an alias. You can configure the alias to use your default port.

For SQL Server 2012, this can be done by performing the following steps.

1. Tap the Windows key on your keyboard and begin to type **SQL Server Configuration Manager**. When the item appears in the program list, click it to open the configuration manager.

2. In the console pane of the SQL Server Configuration Manager, expand SQL Native Client 11.0 Configuration. For applications such as SQL Server Management Studio, you also need to configure an alias for SQL Native Client 11.0 Configuration (32-bit).

3. Right-click Aliases and select New Alias.

4. Provide an alias name. This is the name that you will use in your ASP.NET MVC application's connection string. Enter your custom port number and the name of the SQL Server.

5. Click OK.

You should now be able to connect to the server using the alias. This technique is also useful for when you have an application that you cannot or do not want to change the configuration, but the database needs to be moved to a new server. In this case, you can use the old server name for the alias.

CHAPTER 7

Solution Design

7-1. Designing a View That Requires Data from Multiple Models
Problem

You have to design a complex view that contains data from many sources. You would like to use a strongly-typed view so that you can take advantage of IntelliSense in Visual Studio. You want to use an existing class library for your model, but it is made up of many classes. You do not see a way to add multiple models to a view. You want to know what is the best way to do this.

Solution

There are three possible approaches to solving this problem. One is to define a new model in the Model folder of your MVC project that is a composite that will contain all the data sources needed for your view. Another approach is to create several partial views, each with its own model, and then mash them all together in one super-view.

The advantage of the first approach is that it is very customable to your use case and you can accommodate for unique data relationships that may only appear in your view. The downside is that you will not be able to reuse the model and may end up repeating code such as data annotations in multiple places. The second approach would be more attractive if you foresee using the partial views in several places in your application.

Rather than sending the data to the view via server-side code, the third approach is to make the data available via a Web API and then have script blocks on the page call the services and render the user interface client-side. This approach works well if you are expecting to support mobile devices and Windows Store applications in addition to your web application. It also provides an additional benefit of gained scalability since you are pushing the rendering logic to the client. The downside of this approach is that it can result in a large amount of difficult-to-maintain-and-test client code. This problem can be partially mitigated with the use of client-side MVC Frameworks and unit test libraries.

How It Works

Many applications will need to consume domain models from other .NET projects and even third-party libraries. It is simply not practical to create your entire solution inside a single Visual Studio project file, especially when working with a team.

The MVC programming model dictates that each view is associated with exactly one model. You cannot have multiple models. This is very confusing for many developers coming from non-MVC coding experiences. The best way to think of this is that the ASP.NET MVC application is part of the presentation layer. With this is mind, your model represents the data needed for a view, and in many cases may be different from your domain model.

To demonstrate how this works, we will show an example user-dashboard page for a musician collaboration web site. The page shows several pieces of information about the artist, including a news feed, personal messages alerts, a to-do list, a list of songs exposed via an HTML-based media player, and a list of collaboration spaces that the artist has either started or contributed to. It also shows statistics, including profile views and song plays.

For this recipe, we will implement a composite mode where most of the business logic and data access code is defined in an external project. In our model, we will reference the external library and create a custom class that acts as a wrapper. We will then create a strongly-typed view based on this model.

As discussed in the solution section, this is one of three possible approaches for solving this problem. The other approaches are using partial views, as described in Recipe 7-2, and using JavaScript to make several calls to a RESTful web service, as shown in Recipe 11-7.

Creating the Project

For this example, we will use the ASP.NET MVC 4 Internet Application template. To create the project with this template, perform the following steps:

1. Open Visual Studio 2012 and click the New Project link from the Start screen.

2. In the New Project window, select the C# ASP.NET MVC 4 Web Application template. If you have not used this template before, you can use the search box located in the upper-right of the window to find it.

3. Give the project a name, select a location, and provide a solution name. The examples in this book follow a convention of Ch<chapter number>.R<recipe number> for the project name, and use the default solution name. For this example, the project is named Ch7.R1.

4. Click OK. Select Internet Application on the Select a Template screen. Make sure that the Razor view engine is selected.

5. Click OK to create the project.

Adding an External Class Library

This solution references an external class library. If you are following along, you can download the code from the Apress web site. Also included is a sample database that can be used with the examples. The database is distributed as an SQL Server backup file. If you wish to use it, you will need to restore the database either by using SQL Server Management Studio or the command line. For example, to restore the backup to a new database named MVCExampleDB, you can type the following at the command line:

```
sqlcmd -S . -Q "RESTORE DATABASE MVCExamplesDB FROM DISK ='G:\MVCBook\Shared\SharedAPI.bak'"
```

Please refer to the Microsoft documentation located at http://msdn.microsoft.com/en-us/library/ms177429.aspx if you are not familiar with the procedure.

To add the external library to your solution, right-click your Solution node in Solution Explorer and select Add, and then Existing Project from the pop-up menu. From the downloaded source code, browse to the \Chapter7\Ch7.SharedAPI\Ch7.SharedAPI folder, select Ch7.SharedAPI.csproj, and click Open.

Once the Shared API project has been added to the solution, you need to add it as a reference to your Internet Application project. To do this, right-click the project node for your Internet Application project and select Add Reference from the pop-up list. In the Reference Manager window, click the Solution node in the left panel and then check the box next to the Ch7.SharedAPI project. Click OK to add the reference.

■ **Note** Make the sure that the check box is selected. Clicking the project name to select it does not select the check box. If the check box is not selected the reference will not be added to your project.

Setting up the Database Connection Strings

The Ch7.SharesAPI project uses the Entity Framework and requires that a specially formatted connection string be added to the Internet Application project's Web.config. To do this, open the App.config file from the Ch7.SharedAPI project and locate the MobEntities connection string from the connectionStrings section. The connection string in App.config was created automatically by Visual Studio when the Entity Data Model was added to the project. Copy this connection string.

Once the connection string has been copied, open the Web.config file in your Internet Application project, locate the connectionStrings section, and paste the connection string after the connection string that was included with the template. Click the Save button on the Visual Studio toolbar to save your changes. When you are done, the connection strings section should look similar to Listing 7-1.

Listing 7-1. Entity Framework Connection String in the Web.config file

```
<connectionStrings>
    <add
name="DefaultConnection"
connectionString="Data Source=(LocalDb)\v11.0;Initial Catalog=aspnet-Ch7.R7_1-
20120911084121;Integrated Security=SSPI;AttachDBFilename=|DataDirectory|\aspnet-Ch7.R7_1-
20120911084121.mdf"
providerName="System.Data.SqlClient" />

<add
name="MobEntities"

connectionString="metadata=res://*/Mob.csdl|res://*/Mob.ssdl|res://*/Mob.msl;provider=System.Data.
SqlClient;provider connection string=&quot;data source=.;initial catalog=Ch7SharedDatabase;integrated
security=True;MultipleActiveResultSets=True;App=EntityFramework&quot;"

providerName="System.Data.EntityClient" />
    </connectionStrings>
```

In Listing 7-1, the connection string uses data source=.. The dot is shorthand that refers to the default SQL Server instance on the local machine. If you do not have an SQL Server instance installed on your local computer, you will need to adjust this setting accordingly. The Initial catalog property has been configured to use Ch7SharedDatabase. For this to work correctly, I am assuming that you have installed this database by restoring the database from the backup file supplied with the source code. In addition to the schema needed for the exercise, the database contains sample data that will be useful for testing the examples.

Changing the Connection String Used by the Account Controller

Since this solution will use the built-in Account controller that is part of the Internet Solution template, we will need to modify the default connection string so that it uses the same database as the rest of the application. By default, this points to a LocalDb instance that creates a database file stored in your application's App_Data folder, which is created the first time you run the application.

Modify the connection string section of your Web.config file so that it looks similar to Listing 7-2.

Listing 7-2. Customizing the Connection String for the DefaultConnection in Web.config

```
<add
    name="DefaultConnection"
    connectionString="data source=.;Initial Catalog=Ch7SimpleMembership;Integrated Security=SSPI;"
    providerName="System.Data.SqlClient"
    />
```

In Listing 7-2, the data source has been changed to "." and the Initial Catalog has been changed to Ch7SimpleMembership. The AttachDBFileName attribute has been removed because it is no longer required since the database is no longer using a local file.

We need to make one more change to the project before we can move to the model. We need to change the initialization parameters for the simple membership provider so that it will work with a custom user table used by the external library. The SimpleMembershipProvider is installed by default with the ASP.NET MVC 4 Internet Application template. It works in conjunction with the Account controller to provide the ability for users to register, login using ASP.NET Forms Authentication, and to integrate with third-party identity providers.

Modifying the Simple Membership Initializer

To modify the initialization of the simple provider to work with our custom table, open the Filter/ InitializeSimpleMembershipAttribute.cs file and modify its SimpleMembershipInitializer subclass to look like Listing 7-3.

Listing 7-3. InitializeSimpleMembershipAttribute.cs Modified to Use a Custom User Profile Table

```
private class SimpleMembershipInitializer
{
    public SimpleMembershipInitializer()
    {

        try
        {
            WebSecurity.InitializeDatabaseConnection("DefaultConnection", "Artist", "ArtistId",
"ArtistDisplayName", autoCreateTables: true);
        }
        catch (Exception ex)
        {
            throw new InvalidOperationException("The ASP.NET Simple Membership
database could not be initialized. For more information, please see
http://go.microsoft.com/fwlink/?LinkId=256588", ex);
        }
    }
}
```

We have changed the data connection initialization code so that it will use our custom table. Now when we use any WebSecurity API calls such as WebSecurity.CreateUserAndAccount, our Artist table will be used to store the username and the unique identifier. Our custom table will be the source for the identifier used in the other tables used by the simple membership provider.

Creating the Model

Our model for our dashboard page will pull data from several sources. The main source is the `Artist` entity from the external library. This is a large and complex entity with many navigation properties linking the Entity to related entities in the data model. The second source is a list of news feed topics. The news feed is based on data in the web site but has been denormalized into a schema optimized for reading. In addition, it will contain data from the ASP. NET membership provider.

The first version of our model shown in Listing 7-4 was very simple. It exposed two properties: one for the Artist object and the other for our news feed.

Listing 7-4. First Version of the ArtistDashboard Model

```
public class ArtistDashboardModel
{
  public Artist Artist { get; set; }
  public List<Alert> NewsFeed { get; set; }
  public DateTime PasswordLastChangedDate { get; set; }
}
```

While this will work, there are a number of problems with it. First, since no data annotations have been applied, all the text such as labels, validation rules, and any other customizations needed would need to be added elsewhere in the application.

This type of design can lead to a view with many inline code blocks and other poor practices that can make your application more difficult to test and maintain.

The second problem is that it is somewhat incomplete and lacks data for many of the elements, such as custom URLs and messages—including error messages that may need to be passed to the view.

The third problem is that this model exposes only the `Artist` entity and expects that all the needed information will be accessible via its navigation properties. Although this is possible, you may end up needing to write LINQ queries inside the view in order to get to all your data. You should avoid performing LINQ queries or any other type of data access operation inside the view.

A better approach is to design a model that is better suited to the needs of the view. Listing 7-5 shows version 2 of the `ArtistDashboardModel`.

Listing 7-5. ArtistDashboardModel Version 2

```
public class ArtistDashboardModel
{
    public List<Alert> NewsFeed { get; set; }
    public List<CollaborationSpace> CollaborationSpaces { get; set; }
    public List<PlaylistItem> ArtistSongs { get; set; }
    public List<Task> Tasks { get; set; }

    [Display(Name = "Member Since")]
    public DateTime AccountCreatedDate { get; set; }

    [Display(Name = "Password last changed")]
    public DateTime PasswordLastChangedDate { get; set; }

    [Display(Name = "Profile Hits")]
    public long ProfileViews { get; set; }
```

```
    [Display(Name = "Profile Last Viewed")]
    public DateTime ProfileLastViewedDate { get; set; }

    [Display(Name = "Profile Bookmark")]
    public string ProfileBookmark { get; set; }

    public string AvatarURL { get; set; }

    public string ArtistName { get; set; }

    public string ErrorMessage { get; set; }
}
```

In the updated version, the properties or the Artist entity have been expanded and data annotations have been added to several of them. The information in the data annotations will be used in the view to display labels for the properties. The model contains three lists that will be used on the view to display grids of data.

Another advantage of the refactored model is that even though we have expanded it, we have also simplified it. Since the complex Artist entity with its many navigation properties is no longer included, you no longer need to have detailed knowledge of the entire data model in order to create the controller. In fact, now you have a direct alignment between the data exposed in your model and what you need to expose to your view.

Creating the Artist Controller

In our application, the Index action of the Artist controller will be the first screen users see after they log in. We had modified the Login action of the Account controller to redirect to this page rather than to the Home controller's Index action. The modified Login action is shown in Listing 7-6.

Listing 7-6. Customized Version of the Login Action of the Account Controller

```
public ActionResult Login(LoginModel model, string returnUrl)
{
 if (ModelState.IsValid && WebSecurity.Login(model.UserName, model.Password, persistCookie:
model.RememberMe))
    {
    if (null == returnUrl)
    {
        return RedirectToAction("Index", "Artist");
    }
    else
    {
        return RedirectToLocal(returnUrl);
    }
}
// If we got this far, something failed, redisplay form
ModelState.AddModelError("", "The user name or password provided is incorrect.");
return View(model);
}
```

The Login action now first checks to see if a return URL has been added to the query string. This will happen if a user was redirected to the login page after she attempted to access a restricted page. This allows users to be redirected to that page once they login. If no URL is present, we will redirect the user to the Index action of the Artist controller. The Artist controller is shown in Listing 7-7.

Listing 7-7. The ArtistController

```
public class ArtistController : Controller
{
  MobEntities m_context = new MobEntities();

  [Authorize(Roles="Artist")]
  public ActionResult Index()
  {
    ArtistDashboardModel model = new ArtistDashboardModel();
    try
    {
      int artistId = WebSecurity.CurrentUserId;
      var userDataCollection = from d in m_context.Artists
                               where d.ArtistId == artistId
                               select new
                               {
                                   d.CreateDate,
                                   d.LastActivityDate,
                                   d.Messages.Count,
                                   d.ProfileViews,
                                   d.Tasks,
                                   d.UserName,
                                   d.ProfileLastViewDate,
                                   d.AvatarURL,
                                   defaultPlaylist =
                                    d.PlayLists.Where(p => p.IsDefaultPlaylist == true)
                               };
      var userData = userDataCollection.FirstOrDefault();

      var workspaces =
          from w in m_context.ArtistCollaborationSpaces.Where(e => e.ArtistId == artistId)
          select w.CollaborationSpace;

      model.AccountCreatedDate = userData.CreateDate;
      model.ArtistName = userData.UserName;
      model.ProfileLastViewedDate = userData.ProfileLastViewDate.Value;
      model.ProfileBookmark = string.Concat(SharedConfig.ApplicationURL, "/",
            userData.UserName);
      model.ProfileViews = userData.ProfileViews;
      model.AvatarURL = userData.AvatarURL;
      model.PasswordLastChangedDate =
        WebSecurity.GetPasswordChangedDate(WebSecurity.CurrentUserName);

      model.NewsFeed = m_context.GetUserAlerts(artistId).ToList();


      model.Tasks = userData.Tasks.ToList();
      model.CollaborationSpaces = workspaces.ToList();
      model.ArtistSongs = userData.defualtPlaylist.FirstOrDefault().PlaylistItems.ToList();
    }
```

```
    catch (Exception e)
    {
      model.ErrorMessage = @"Sorry. Something dreadful has occurred. Please accept our sincerest
                            apology.";
    }

    return View(model);
  }


  protected override void Dispose(bool disposing)
  {
    m_context.Dispose();
    base.Dispose(disposing);
  }

}
```

The Index action of Artist relies on information about the logged in user in order to query the database. Because of this, we need to ensure that the user is logged in before accessing it. We also need to make sure that only members of the Artist role can access it since the page will contain some restricted information. To achieve this the action is decorated with the Authorize attribute with the roles parameter specifying that the Artist role is required.

Next, we instantiate a new ArtistDashboardModel object. At the point of object creation, it is not bound to any data and contains mostly null values. The rest of the controller code will populate the object before passing it to the view.

The first thing we need is the unique identifier for the artist. One limitation of using the SimpleMembershipProvider with a custom user table is that you can no longer use any of the typical ASP.NET membership provider API calls. Your interactions with the membership provider are now restricted to the methods available in the WebMatrix.WebData.WebSecurity class. We use WebSecurity.CurrentUserId, which returns an integer. We cache this value in a variable called artistId. It should be noted that the WebSecurity.CurrentUserId method will query the database each time it is called.

Now that we have an artistId, we can use it to query the required Artist data. The first operation queries against the Artist entity. It pulls back several pieces of information about the artist and some statistical information regarding the number of people who viewed his profile. It also gets a count of the messages in his inbox, a list of assigned tasks, and a list of songs in a default playlist.

Next, we get a list of collaboration spaces that the artist has either started or contributed to. We then use the data returned from the query to populate the first set of properties for the model. For the PasswordLastChangedDate property, we need to get data from the membership provider by calling WebSecurity.GetPasswordChangedDate. This is required since the data is managed by the provider and is not mapped in the Entity Data Model. We then make several other calls to the DbContext to populate the news feed, the task list, and the tasks.

Once all the assignments have been made to the model, we pass the data off to our view by calling return View(model).

The end result, shown in Figure 7-1, is a somewhat sophisticated view that uses a mix of JavaScript, HTML, and Silverlight to render the results. Since we used a strongly typed model, authoring the view was simplified since we had full IntelliSense support. The use of IntelliSense significantly reduces the number of errors caused by typing mistakes.

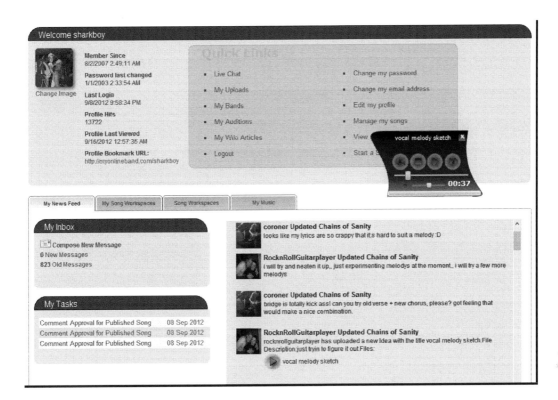

Figure 7-1. *The Artist Index view displaying data from several sources*

In Figure 7-1, you can see the main artist profile data displayed in the top-left side. The Inbox and task data displayed along the lower-left side, and the news feed on the bottom right. The remaining data is hidden in several tabs.

7-2. Using Partial Views to Construct a Composite User Interface
Problem

You have to design a complex view that contains data from many sources. You would like to use a strongly-typed view so that you can take advantage of IntelliSense in Visual Studio. You want to reuse the visual elements of this view in other parts of your application.

Solution

The best solution for this problem would be to create several partial views each with its own model and then combine them into a composite view. This would meet the requirement for creating the complex view and allow you to use the partial views in other parts of your application.

How It Works

For this example, we will use an API that is part of an external library defined in another project. We will then create models for each of the partial views that we need to create, followed by the partial views themselves. Finally, we will create a composite view that consumes all the partial views.

Creating the Project

For this example, we will be using the ASP.NET MVC 4 Internet Application template. To create the project using this template, perform the following steps:

1. Open Visual Studio 2012 and click the New Project link from the Start screen.

2. In the New Project window, select the C# ASP.NET MVC 4 Web Application template. If you have not used this template before, you can use the search box in the upper-right side of the window to find it.

3. Give the project a name, select a location, and provide a solution name. The examples in this book follow a convention of Ch<chapter number>.R<recipe number> for the project name, and use the default solution name. For this example, the project is named Ch7.R2.

4. Click OK and then select Internet Application on the select a template screen. Make sure that the Razor view engine is selected.

5. Click OK to create the project.

Adding External Class Library

This solution references an external class library. If you are following along, you can download the code from the Apress web site. Also included is a sample database that can be used with the examples. The database is distributed as SQL Server backup file. If you wish to use it, you will need to restore the database either by using SQL Server Management Studio or the command line. Please refer to the Microsoft documentation located at http://msdn.microsoft.com/en-us/library/ms177429.aspx if you are not familiar with the procedure.

1. To add the external library to your solution, right-click your Solution node in Solution Explorer, select Add, and then select Existing Project from the pop-up menu. From the downloaded source code, browse to the \Chapter7\Ch7.SharedAPI\Ch7.SharedAPI folder, select Ch7.SharedAPI.csproj, and click Open.

2. Once the Shared API project has been added to the solution, you need to add it as a reference to your Internet Application project. To do this, right-click the project node for your Internet Application project and select Add Reference from the pop-up list. In the Reference Manager window, click the Solution node in the left panel and then check the box next to the Ch7.SharedAPI project. Click OK to add.

Changing the Connection Strings

This project will use two connection strings: one required by the external library that we have added to the project, and the other used by the membership provider. To modify the connection strings, open the Web.config file and modify them to look similar to Listing 7-8.

Listing 7-8. Connection String Modifications in Web.Config

```
<connectionStrings>
    <add
    name="DefaultConnection"
    connectionString="data source=.;Initial Catalog=Ch7SharedDatabase;Integrated Security=SSPI;"
    providerName="System.Data.SqlClient"
    />
    <add name="MobEntities"
```

```
connectionString="metadata=res://*/Mob.csdl|res://*/Mob.ssdl|res://*/Mob.msl;provider=System.Data.
SqlClient;provider
connection string=&quot;data source=.;initial
catalog=Ch7SharedDatabase;integrated
security=True;MultipleActiveResultSets=True;App=EntityFramework&quot;"
providerName="System.Data.EntityClient" />
  </connectionStrings>
```

In this example, we have modified the Default connection so that it no longer uses a local file but rather a local SQL Server instance. We have also added an Entity Framework connection string called MobEntities. This is required by the external library.

Modifying the Simple Membership Initializer

Since this project is using the Internet Application template, it has been set up to use the ASP.NET Simple Membership Provider, which allows you to define a custom user-table rather than keeping this information in a separate user table, as do most of the other providers. For this to work, it needs to run some initialization code before it is used.

For the Internet Application template, assure that the initialization code is run before any calls are made to the provider by applying the InitializeSimpleMembershipAttribute to the AccountController class. InitializeSimpleMembershipAttribute is an action filter, which is defined in the Filters/InitializeSimpleMembershipAttribute.cs file.

In this recipe, we are using a custom table called Artist as our user table. We are storing the user ids in a column called ArtistId. The usernames will be stored in a column called UserName. In order for the Simple Membership Provider to use our custom table, we need to modify the initialization code as shown in Listing 7-9.

Listing 7-9. Initializing the Simple Membership Provider with a Custom Table

```
[AttributeUsage(AttributeTargets.Class | AttributeTargets.Method, AllowMultiple = false,
Inherited = true)]
    public sealed class InitializeSimpleMembershipAttribute : ActionFilterAttribute
    {
        private static SimpleMembershipInitializer _initializer;
        private static object _initializerLock = new object();
        private static bool _isInitialized;

        public override void OnActionExecuting(ActionExecutingContext filterContext)
        {
            // Ensure ASP.NET Simple Membership is initialized only once per app start
            LazyInitializer.EnsureInitialized(ref _initializer, ref _isInitialized,
            ref _initializerLock);
        }

        private class SimpleMembershipInitializer
        {
            public SimpleMembershipInitializer()
            {

                try
                {
                    WebSecurity.InitializeDatabaseConnection("DefaultConnection", "Artist",
                    "ArtistId", "UserName", autoCreateTables: true);
                }
```

```
                catch (Exception ex)
                {
                        throw new InvalidOperationException("The ASP.NET Simple Membership
database could not be initialized. For more information, please see
http://go.microsoft.com/fwlink/?LinkId=256588", ex);
                }
            }
        }
    }
```

Creating the Models

In this example, we will create a composite view that uses four models, a news feed, a song playlist, a collaboration workspace list, and an artist profile card. Each model will be placed in its own class file under the models folder in our solution. To add the classes, right-click the models folder in Solution Explorer, select Add, and then select Class. In the Add New Item window, name the first file **ArtistInfoModel.cs**. Repeat this process for NewsFeedModel.cs, SongCollaborationWorkspaceModel.cs, and SongPlaylistModel.cs.

When you are done, modify the files to look like Listing 7-10.

Listing 7-10. Models for Partial Views

```
//
// SongCollaborationWorkspaceListModel.cs
//
public class SongCollaborationWorkspaceListModel
{
        [Display(Name = "Number of Workspaces Found: ")]
        public int NumberofMatchingWorkspaces { get; set; }
        public List<CollaborationSpace> CollaborationSpaces { get; set; }
}


//
// SongPlaylistModel.cs
//
public class SongPlaylistModel
{
        [Display(Name = "Number of Songs Found: ")]
        public int NumberofMatchingSongs { get; set; }
        public List<PlaylistItem> ArtistSongs { get; set; }
}



//
// NewsFeedModel.cs
//
public class NewsFeedModel
    {
        public List<Alert> NewsFeed { get; set; }
        public string Message { get; set; }
    }
```

```
//
// ArtistInfoModel.cs
//
public class ArtistInfoModel
    {
        [Display(Name = "Member Since")]
        public DateTime AccountCreatedDate { get; set; }

        [Display(Name = "Password last changed")]
        public DateTime PasswordLastChangedDate { get; set; }

        [Display(Name = "Profile Hits")]
        public long ProfileViews { get; set; }

        [Display(Name = "Profile Last Viewed")]
        public DateTime ProfileLastViewedDate { get; set; }

        [Display(Name = "Member Since")]
        public string ProfileBookmark { get; set; }

        public string AvatarURL { get; set; }

        public string ArtistName { get; set; }
    }
```

The code in Listing 7-10 is pretty straightforward. Each file contains a single class that declares a number of public properties. Where required, we have added data annotations to some of the properties that will be used in conjunction with the @Html.LabelFor HTML helper to render labels for each data item.

Creating the Partial Views

The next step is to create the partial views. Partial views are regular views that are designed to be included in a parent view. There are two methods for using partial views. In one method, the parent view can load the partials using the @Html.Partial helper method, which instructs the view engine to load the content without rendering content from any layout pages. In this design, the model is passed as a parameter to the partial view when calling the @Html.Partial("~/Views/Partials/_MyPartialView.cshtml",Model). If you use this strategy, you will need to create a composite model as we did in Recipe 7-1.

In this example, we use the second method, which is to call the @Html.Action helper. This will execute another controller action and inject the output into the parent page.

When creating partial views, it is important to follow the prescribed naming convention for the sake of consistency. In the naming convention for partial views, the file name begins with an underscore and is suffixed by Partial. For example, the partial view for ArtistInfo would be named _ArtistInfoPartial.cshtml.

While the underscore has no technical ramifications in the MVC Framework, it does have significance in ASP.NET WebPages—where the convention originated. The Partial suffix tells other developers that the file is intended to function as a partial view.

■ **Note**   In ASP.NET Web Pages, files with names starting with an underscore are not served to the users directly. This helps eliminate possible usability or security issues that may occur from users inadvertently or maliciously using the view in an unintended and untested manner. In ASP.NET MVC, users cannot directly access .cshtml files at all, regardless of its prefix. On the other hand, ASP.NET MVC does allow direct access to actions that return partial views. This allows a user to directly browse a partial view if they can determine the URL. If you wish to prevent this, you must decorate the action method with the [ChildActionOnly] attribute.

In this example, since all the partial views will be used with a single controller—the Artist controller, we will create a new folder under Views named Artist. We will then create the partial views inside this folder. If the partial view were intended for general use, such as being used as part of a layout page, we would place it in the Views\Shared folder.

To create the partial view, first create a new folder named **Artist** under the Views folder by right-clicking the Views folder in Solution Explorer, selecting Add, and then New Folder. The new folder will appear in Solution Explorer and it will be selected for renaming. Change the name to **Artist**.

Right-click the newly created folder, select Add, and then select View from the pop-up menu. Name the view **Index**, ensure that the Razor view engine is selected and that "Use a layout or master page" is checked, and then click the Add button.

This creates the Index view that we will use as the parent for hosting our child views.

Next, right-click the Artist folder again, select Add, and then select View. This time, name the view _ArtistInfoPartial and check the Create as Partial check box. Click the Add button. The new partial view should be added to the project. Notice that the new file is completely empty. When you click the Create as Partial check box, you are telling Visual Studio not to include any of the normal boilerplate code that it normally includes when it creates the view.

Create additional partial views named _NewsFeedPartial.cshtml, _SongCollaborationWorkspacePartial.cs, _SongPlaylistPartial.cs, and _NoDataPartial.cs.

_NoDataPartial.cs will be used in cases where no data is found.

For now, modify each of them so that they contain a small amount of text that indicates the name of the partial view. We will use this to perform a quick smoke-test before adding any additional complexity.

Creating the ArtistController

For this example, we will create a controller called the ArtistController. It will contain actions for both the partial views and a parent view that will serve as a container.

To create the Artist controller, right-click the Controllers folder in Solution Explorer, select Add, and then select Controller. In the Add Controller dialog box, name the controller **ArtistController** and select Empty MVC Controller from the Template drop-down list. Click the Add button to create the new controller.

Even though we have selected the empty template, Visual Studio still adds a single action method named Index. Keep the Index method "as is" and add four more action methods named ArtistInfo, NewsFeed, SongCollaborationWorkspace, and SongPlaylist.

Modify each of the newly created action method to contain a statement that returns a partial view. To do this, use the PartialView method and pass in the name of the partial view, excluding the file extension as a parameter. For example, for the ArtistInfo method, you will call return PartialView("_ArtistInfoPartial").

When you have completed this step, your controller should look like Listing 7-11.

Listing 7-11. The Artist Controller

```
public class ArtistController : Controller
    {
        //
        // GET: /Artist/

        public ActionResult Index()
        {
            return View();
        }

        public ActionResult ArtistInfo()
        {
            return PartialView("_ArtistInfoPartial");
        }

        public ActionResult NewsFeed()
        {
            return PartialView("_NewsFeedPartial");
        }

        public ActionResult SongCollaborationWorkspace()
        {
            return PartialView("_SongCollaborationWorkspacePartial");
        }

        public ActionResult SongPlaylist()
        {
            return PartialView("_SongPlaylistPartial");
        }

    }
```

Adding References to the Partial Views in Index.cshtml

Index.cshtml will serve as the container for the partial views. It will combine all the information to create a dashboard page that will be displayed to the artist once she has logged into the web site.

To add references to the partial views, we will use the Html.Action HTML helper, which takes the name of the action as a parameter and renders an HTML anchor tag with an HREF attribute based on the route information for the action. When you are done, Artist/Index.cshtml should look like Listing 7-12.

Listing 7-12. Artist/Index.cshtml with References to the Partial Views

```
@{
    ViewBag.Title = "Index";
}

<h2>Welcome @Profile.UserName</h2>
<h3>Artist Information</h3>
@Html.Action("ArtistInfo","Artist")
<br />
```

```
<h3>Your music</h3>
@Html.Action("SongPlaylist")

<br />
<h3>News Feed</h3>
@Html.Action("NewsFeed")

<br />
<h3>Song Collaboration Spaces that you have started or have contributed to</h3>
@Html.Action("SongCollaborationWorkspace")
```

At this point, we should be able to run a quick test to verify that all the partial views are being displayed inside our Index page. To do this, click the Start Debugging button from the Visual Studio toolbar. Once the browser has opened with the home page loaded, navigate to /Artist in the web browser. Expect to see all the headings that you had added to each of the partial views earlier.

You should also be able to browse the partial views directly using the controller actions set up for each. Try navigating to /Artist/ArtistInfo. You should see the text you added to the view, without any of the content from the layout page.

Connecting the Data

Now that we have created the models, the controller, the parent view, and the partial views, we now need to put them all together.

Since the four partial views need to connect to a database, the first thing we need to do is set up a database connection. The views will use an external library with a dependency on the Entity Framework as their primary data source. In order to create a reference to this database connection, we will create an instance of the MobEntities context, which is an Entity Framework DbContext object that acts as a proxy to the database. It will track the changes to your data entities and allow you to save the changes back to the database in a batch-like manner. It also allows you to query the database via LINQ queries. MobEntities implements the IDisposable interface. It is important to ensure that it is disposed of when you are no longer using it. In this example, this is achieved by overriding the Dispose method on the Artist controller and then calling the Dispose method on the context, as shown in Listing 7-13.

Listing 7-13. Overriding Dispose in a Controller

```
// Create the DBContext object as a global member variable
MobEntities m_context = new MobEntities();
//...
//bunch of actions that use the context
//...

// Override dispose and call the Dispose method on the DBContext object
protected override void Dispose(bool disposing)
{
    m_context.Dispose();
    base.Dispose(disposing);
}
```

One thing that you may be tempted to do is to wrap the instantiation of the DbContext in a Using block inside your action method. Unfortunately, this will not work because you will be disposing of the DbContext before it has a chance to be used inside the view. This will result in an IllegalOperationException.

Since the data we want to display is targeted for a logged-in user, we need to ensure that the action methods can only be accessed by authenticated users. To achieve this, we will add the `Authorize` attribute to the `Index` action. We also need to ensure that the authorized user is in the proper security role. We can do this by using the named parameter `Roles` to the `Authorize` attribute declaration, as shown in Listing 7-14.

Listing 7-14. Modifying the Index Action So That It Is Restricted to Members of the Artist Role

```
[Authorize(Roles = "Artist")]

public ActionResult Index()
{
    return View();
}
```

Next, we begin modifying the actions used with the partial views, starting with the `ArtistInfo` action. First, we will prevent the partial view from being accessed directly by adding the `ChildActionOnly` attribute. Once this attribute is applied, the action can only be invoked when accessed via a call to `Html.Action` or `Html.RenderAction` called in a parent view.

Then we will create an instance of our model, `ArtistInfoModel`. This object will hold the data that we will pass to the `_ArtistInfoPartial` view.

We then use `WebSecurity.CurrentUserId` to get the unique identifier for the logged in user. This value will be used to query our data source for the needed information about the current user.

Once the context has been created, we can use it to create a query. In this case, since we only need some of the data from the `Artist` entity, we will save the results into an anonymous type. An anonymous type is a class that is created by the compiler that exposes the properties required by our query.

The new anonymous type that is created is wrapped inside an `IQueryable` called `userDataCollection`. To access it, we call `userDataCollection.FirstOrDefault()`. If the query has found a result, `FirstOrDefault()` will return the first instance of the anonymous type exposed; otherwise, it will return the default value for the type. The default value for nullable and reference types such as our object is `null`. Because of this, it is important to check for a `null` value before attempting to access the properties of your object to avoid a `NullReferenceException`.

If our test for `null` fails, we handle the condition by returning the `PartialViewResult` for the `_NoDataPartial` view and pass in a string as its model.

■ **Tip**   Keep your views as simple as possible. By setting up a special partial view for dealing with the no data condition, we are saving ourselves the trouble of adding server-side control logic inside the view. This will make the view easier to maintain and a lot easier for designers to work with.

Once we have ensured that our query result contains a value, we can then assign the results to our model. For the last property, `PasswordLastChangedDate`, we need a value that is only accessible from the membership provider. We access this by calling the `WebSecurity.GetPasswordChangedDate` method.

Finally, we deal with any potential error conditions using the same technique used with the no data condition. Again, we are returning a `PartialView` result and passing it a string as a model. This technique will allow the rest of the view to be rendered, but it will show the error message passes a string in place of the normal output of the page.

Listing 7-15 shows the modified `ArtistInfo` action.

Listing 7-15. ArtistInfo Action from the ArtistController

```
[ChildActionOnly]
    public ActionResult ArtistInfo()
    {
        ArtistInfoModel model = new ArtistInfoModel();
        int artistId = WebSecurity.CurrentUserId;
        try
        {

            var userDataCollection = from d in m_context.Artists
                                     where d.ArtistId == artistId
                                     select new
                                     {
                                         d.CreateDate,
                                         d.LastActivityDate,
                                         d.ProfileViews,
                                         d.Tasks,
                                         d.UserName,
                                         d.ProfileLastViewDate,
                                         d.AvatarURL
                                     };
            var userData = userDataCollection.FirstOrDefault();
            if (userData != null)
            {
                model.AccountCreatedDate = userData.CreateDate;
                model.ArtistName = userData.UserName;
                model.ProfileLastViewedDate = userData.ProfileLastViewDate.Value;
                model.ProfileBookmark = string.Concat(SharedConfig.ApplicationURL, "/",
                userData.UserName);
                model.ProfileViews = userData.ProfileViews;
                model.AvatarURL = userData.AvatarURL;
                model.PasswordLastChangedDate =
                WebSecurity.GetPasswordChangedDate(WebSecurity.CurrentUserName);
            }
            else
            {
                return PartialView("_NoDataPartial", "Error occurred.");
            }

        }
        catch (Exception)
        {
            //TODO: Log exception
            model.ErrorMessage = "Sorry could not access the data.";
        }
        return PartialView("_ArtistInfoPartial",model);
    }
```

At this point, you can debug your application to ensure that it compiles and that there are no runtime errors when you access Artist/Index.

Next, we will add code to the NewsFeed action so that it returns the required data. This will have a similar set up to the ArtistInfo action except that we will use a mapped function to get a result set in the form of a List of Alert entities. Since we are working with a number of records in this result set rather than a single entity, we call the ToList() method on the ObjectResult that is returned from our mapped function call. Mapped functions are the Entity Framework's way of allowing your code to call stored procedures in your database.

The modified NewsFeed action is shown in Listing 7-16.

Listing 7-16. NewsFeed Action in ArtistController

```
[ChildActionOnly]
public ActionResult NewsFeed()
{

  NewsFeedModel model = new NewsFeedModel();
  int artistId = WebSecurity.CurrentUserId;
  try
  {
    var obj = m_context.GetUserAlerts(artistId);
    if (obj != null )
    {
      model.NewsFeed = obj.ToList();
    }
    if(model.NewsFeed.Count()==0)
    {
      return PartialView("_NoDataPartial", "Sorry, no matching stories found.");
     }

  }
  catch
  {
      //TODO: Log exception
              return PartialView("_NoDataPartial", "Sorry could not access the data.");
  }
  return PartialView("_NewsFeedPartial", model);
}
```

In order to verify that we have results from this query, we first create a List<Alert> object by calling obj.ToList(). We then use the Count() method on the List to verify that we have at least one record. You want to call the Count method on the List object and not the ObjectResult. The count on the ObjectResult object will be will result in an error informing you that the results of a query can only be enumerated once.

For the remainder of the actions, we will use LINQ queries to return lists of workspaces and songs related to the artist. The modified SongPlaylist and SongCollaborationWorkspace() actions are shown in Listing 7-17.

Listing 7-17. The SongPlaylist and SongCollaborationWorkspace() Actions of the Artist Controller

```
[ChildActionOnly]
public ActionResult SongCollaborationWorkspace()
{
  SongCollaborationWorkspaceListModel model = new SongCollaborationWorkspaceListModel();
  int artistId = WebSecurity.CurrentUserId;
  try
  {
```

```
      var workspaces = from w in m_context.ArtistCollaborationSpaces.Where(e => e.ArtistId ==
                      artistId)
      select w.CollaborationSpace;
      if (workspaces != null && workspaces.Count() > 0)
      {
        model.CollaborationSpaces = workspaces.ToList();
      }
      else
      {
        return PartialView("_NoDataPartial", "No workspaces found.");
      }
  }
  catch
  {
    //TODO log error
    return PartialView("_NoDataPartial", "An error occurred.");
  }
    return PartialView("_SongCollaborationWorkspacePartial",model);
}

[ChildActionOnly]
public ActionResult SongPlaylist()
{
    SongPlaylistModel model = new SongPlaylistModel();
    int artistId = WebSecurity.CurrentUserId;
    try
    {
      var playlistitems = from a in m_context.PlaylistItems
                          where (a.PlayList.ArtistId == artistId)
                          && (a.PlayList.IsDefaultPlaylist == true)
                          orderby a.DisplayOrder
                          select a;
      if (null != playlistitems && playlistitems.Count() > 0)
      {
          model.ArtistSongs = playlistitems.ToList();
      }
      else
      {
          return PartialView("_NoDataPartial", "No songs found.");
      }

    }
    catch
    {
        //TODO log error
        return PartialView("_NoDataPartial", "An error occurred.");
    }
    return PartialView("_SongPlaylistPartial",model);
}
```

Accessing the Model Data from the Partial Views

The last part of this example shows how you can access the data from the model inside each of the partial views. The HTML code has been simplified for these examples so that you can see the data access code without needing to thumb through all the markup.

For the _NoDataPartial, there are a total of two lines of code. The first line declares the model is a string. The second line prints out the string inside an HTML DIV tag. Notice the casing used. In the model declaration, @model is lowercase. In all other cases, the M in model is capitalized. The code for _NoDataPartial is shown in Listing 7-18.

Listing 7-18. _NoDataPartial.cshtml

```
@model string

<div class="NoDataFound">@Model</div>
```

For the remainder of the views, we are using a @foreach statement to loop through the contents of the result set and display the required values. The code for _NewsFeedPartial.cshtml is shown in Listing 7-19. The remainder of the views are omitted from this section for the sake of brevity, but are available with the code samples that can be downloaded from the book's web site.

Listing 7-19. _NewsFeedPartial.cshtml

```
@model Ch7.R7_2.Models.NewsFeedModel
<div id="NewsPaneLeft">
    <div id="NewsWrapper">
        @foreach(var item in Model.NewsFeed){
        <div class="NewsItem">
            <a href="#">
                <span class="NewsItemImage">
                        <img src='@item.ActorAvatarUrl' alt='@item.ActorDisplayName'  />
                    </span>
                    <span class="NewsItemContent">
                        <h3>@item.Headline</h3>
                        @item.Summary
                    </span>
            </a>
        </div>
        }
    </div>
 </div>
```

7-3. Creating a Model Using Entity Framework Database First
Problem

You have an existing database that you would like to expose as an ASP.NET MVC application. You would like to be able to show your client a working prototype as quickly as possible.

Solution

The MVC Framework, when combined with the Entity Framework database-first approach, allows you to create a functioning prototype for your application very quickly. You would first need to generate an Entity Data Model from your database, compile the MVC application, and then create your controllers and strongly-typed views using the scaffolding templates. You could then customize your application to meet your needs.

How It Works

To create your project, open Visual Studio, select File, and then New Project from the File menu. Select the ASP.NET MVC 4 template, provide a name and location for your solution, and click the OK button.

On the New ASP.NET MVC 4 Project window, select the best project type for your needs. For this example, we will be using the Basic template. Click OK. Visual Studio will create the project for you.

Creating the Model

To create the model, right-click the project folder in the Visual Studio Solution Explorer, select Add, and then select New Item from the pop-up menu. On the left panel of the Add New Item window, select Data to filer the listed project templates to only data-related project types. In the center pane, select ADO.NET Entity Data Model and give the model a name. In this example, I am naming the model MobEntities. Click the Add button when you are ready. Visual Studio will start the Entity Data Model Wizard.

In the Entity Data Model Wizard Choose Model Content screen, select the "Generate from database" icon and then click Next. The Choose Your Data Connection screen will appear.

On the Choose Your Data Connection screen, you will be prompted to select a data connection from a drop-down list of available connections. If you have connected to the database that contains your schema before using Visual Studio, the connection should appear in the list. If this is your first time, you will need to click the New Connection button.

If you need to create the new connection, you will need to fill out the required information on the Connection Properties window. You can enter "." (a shorthand expression for the default SQL Server instance on your local machine) for the Server Name field if you are connecting to a local instance of SQL Server. If you need to connect to a local SQL Express instance, you can use .\SQLExpress. This is the default name for the named instance of what SQL Express creates when it is installed. Alternatively, you can use the drop-down list, which shows a list of servers on your local network. If the user interface locks up after you click the drop-down list, do not worry, this is normal. The UI will become responsive again once the dialog box has finished its port scan.

If you are connecting to a database management system other than SQL Server, you will need to download the appropriate drivers from the database vendor and verify that they offer a provider that works with ADO.NET Entity Framework.

Once you have selected a server, you can choose a database to connect to in the "Select or enter a database name" box. For this example, we will use a database named Ch7SharedDatabase. This database is available for download on the book's web site.

Once you have chosen a database, use the Test Database Connection button to verify connectivity to the SQL Server database. Click OK to continue.

Once you have created your connection, you can select it from the drop-down list. Make sure that the "Save entity connection settings in Web.config" check box is selected. Then enter a name for your connection string as you would like it to appear in the Web.config file. Click Next. The Choose Your Data Connection screen is shown in Figure 7-2.

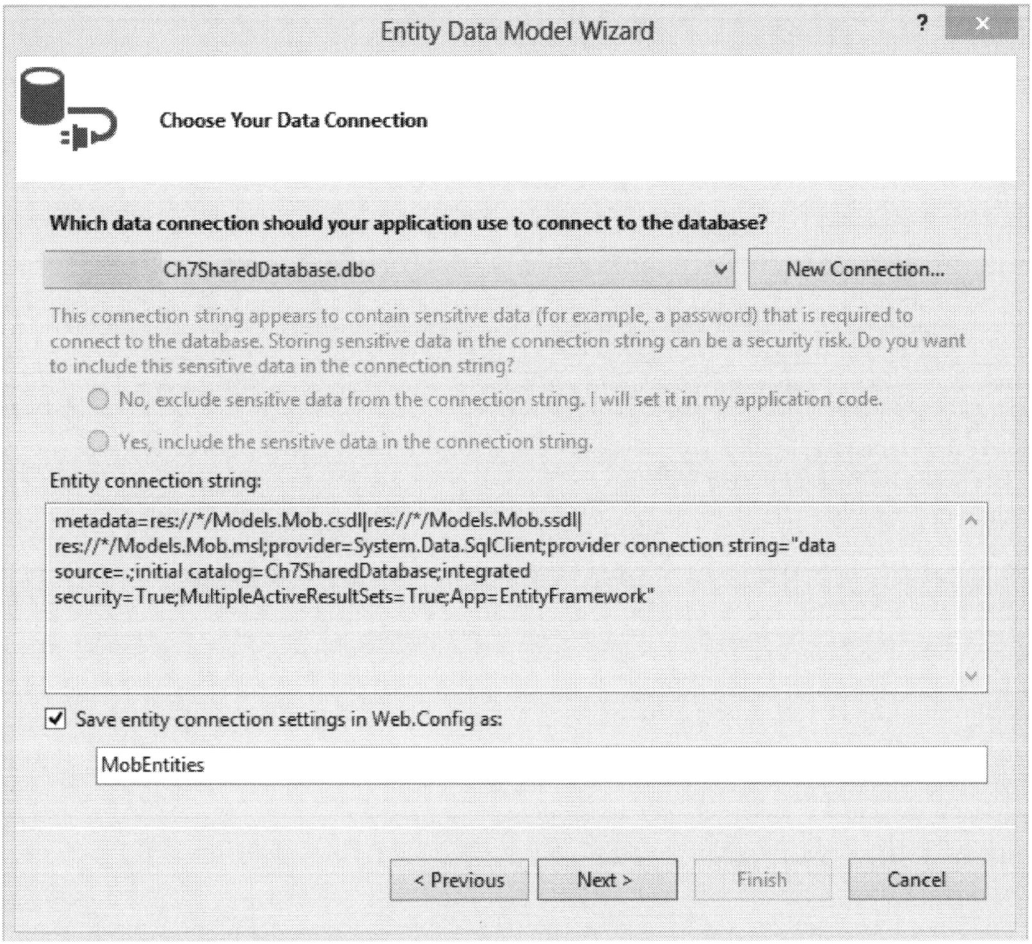

Figure 7-2. *Choosing a database connection for your data model*

After you click Next, the Choose Your Database Objects and Settings screen will appear. This screen will allow you to choose the database objects you would like to have in your model. If you check the Tables check box, all the tables in your database will be selected. If you would like to narrow down the selection, you can expand the Tables node by clicking the arrow that appears to the left side of the Tables check box when you hover the mouse over it.

For this exercise, we will expand the Tables node and the DBO schema node, and then select the following tables from the database:

- `Artist`
- `ArtistSkill`

Once you have selected the tables, review the remaining settings on this screen. There are three check boxes located under the object selection window. The first check box, "Pluralize or singularize generated object names" determines how objects are named in the code generated by the model. If this box remains checked, Visual Studio will generate an Entity named `Artist` and another named `ArtistSkill`. It will also create collections for these objects that will be available if you write LINQ queries against your model. For example, to query a list of artist objects from the model, you could write a LINQ query similar to: `var userDataCollection = from d in m_context.Artists select d;`.

The next check box allows you to decide whether or not you want to include the foreign key columns in the database model. If this is checked in addition to a *navigation property*, which is a property used by the Entity Framework to allow you to access related data across tables, the model will include the unique identifier for the parent record as a property on the child entity. This will save you a lot of work since you will not need to create the object relationships and you can just use the foreign key values.

The last check box, "Import selected stored procedures and functions into the entity model," will import any selected stored procedures as mapped functions into the model. This allows you to call the stored procedures directly from your model and optionally have the procedure return a list of entities.

For the Model Namespace, choose the .NET namespace you would like to use for this model. For this example, we will use Ch7.R73.Model.

Figure 7-3 shows the Choose Your Database Objects and Settings screen.

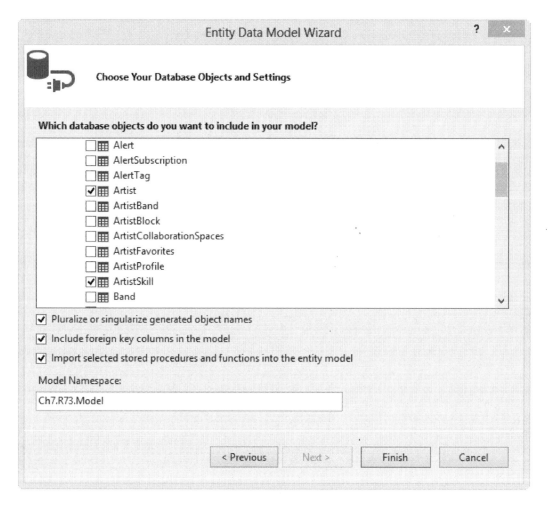

Figure 7-3. *Selecting the objects for your Entity Data Model*

Click the Finish button. Visual Studio will generate your model.

■ **Caution** There is a bug in the Entity Framework components of Visual Studio that prevents your model code from being regenerated after you make changes to the model when the .edmx file is in a subfolder inside the solution. The problem is a known issue and has been documented in the codeplex work item at http://entityframework.codeplex.com/workitem/453. The workaround for this issue is to move the .edmx file to the root of your project folder.

When you are done, the .edmx file will appear as an entity diagram in the main Visual Studio window. If you click an entity, you can see its properties. You may also click the property names of each table to view its name and type of access modifier used. You may modify these values if you wish.

If you click the line that connects the two tables, you can see the details of the relationship between the tables. In addition to the diagram view, you can also use the Model Explorer to view and modify the details of your model. Figure 7-4 shows the model diagram generated by Visual Studio.

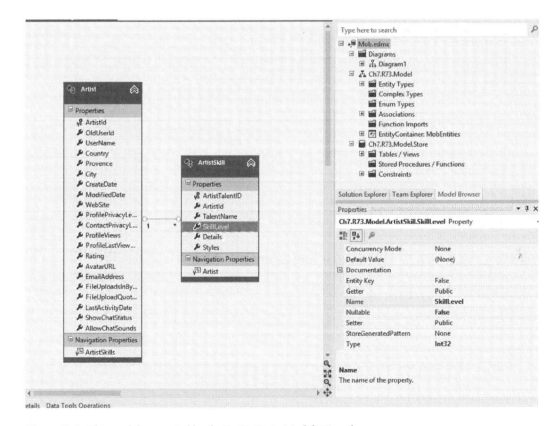

Figure 7-4. *The model generated by the Entity Data Model Wizard*

Creating the Controller

Now that our model has been created, the next step will be to compile the project. Visual Studio will not be able to display the new C# types created by the model until the project is compiled. To compile the project, select Build Solution from the Build menu.

Once the build has completed, right-click the Controllers folder in Solution Explorer, select Add, and then select New Controller.

In the Add Controller dialog window, name the controller the **ArtistController**. Under Scaffolding options, select the MVC controller with read/write actions and views, using Entity Framework. For the Model class, select Artist (Ch7.R7_3), and for the Data context class, select MobEntities (Ch7.R7_3). Ensure that Razor is selected on the Views drop-down list and then click Add.

■ **Note** If you get an error from Visual Studio informing you that the Artist class is not part of the MobEntities, you may be experiencing a bug in Visual Studio. The workaround for this is to close Visual Studio and reopen it.

When Visual Studio is done, it will have created six new files. In the Controllers directory, there is the ArtistController.cs. This file will contain eight actions. The actions include Index, which provides a list of all the items in the selected list; Details, which shows the details for a particular item; Create, which allows you to create a new record; Edit, which provides a form for editing a record; and Delete, which allows you to delete a record. Create, Edit, and Delete actions have been created for GET and POST. The GET version of the action will display the data entry form and the POST will save the changes.

In addition to the controllers, under the Views folder, a new subfolder for Artist has been created and five new views have been added that correspond with each of the actions.

Viewing the Web Site

Before we can view the web site, we need to modify the RouteConfig.cs file in the App_Start folder so that the default route points to the Artist controller rather than the Home controller. Since we did not create a Home controller, we will see an HTTP 404 error when we debug the application. To correct this, change the RouteConfig.cs file so that it looks like Listing 7-20.

Listing 7-20. Modified RouteConfig with Artist as the Default Controller

```
public static void RegisterRoutes(RouteCollection routes)
    {
        routes.IgnoreRoute("{resource}.axd/{*pathInfo}");

        routes.MapRoute(
            name: "Default",
            url: "{controller}/{action}/{id}",
            defaults: new { controller = "Artist", action = "Index", id = UrlParameter.Optional }
        );
    }
```

Once you have made this change, press the F5 key on your keyboard to launch the web site in debug mode. When the web site opens, you will see a somewhat unwieldy list. This is because the code generator includes all properties by default. Since the Artist entity has 20 properties, the list scrolls horizontally. This far from an optimal user interface. You can correct this by opening the Artist/Index.cshtml file and removing the fields that you do not want to display. When you do this, be sure to remove both the table header column and the data column. The updated version of the Artist/Index.cshtml file is shown in Listing 7-21.

Listing 7-21. Modified Scaffolding for Index View

```
@model IEnumerable<Ch7.R3.Artist>

@{
    ViewBag.Title = "Index";
}

<h2>Index</h2>

<p>
    @Html.ActionLink("Create New", "Create")
</p>
<table>
    <tr>

        <th>
            @Html.DisplayNameFor(model => model.UserName)
        </th>
        <th>
            @Html.DisplayNameFor(model => model.CreateDate)
        </th>

        <th>
            @Html.DisplayNameFor(model => model.ProfileViews)
        </th>

        <th>
            @Html.DisplayNameFor(model => model.FileUploadsInBytes)
        </th>
        <th>
            @Html.DisplayNameFor(model => model.FileUploadQuotaInBytes)
        </th>

        <th></th>
    </tr>

@foreach (var item in Model) {
    <tr>

        <td>
            @Html.DisplayFor(modelItem => item.UserName)
        </td>

        <td>
            @Html.DisplayFor(modelItem => item.CreateDate)
        </td>

        <td>
            @Html.DisplayFor(modelItem => item.ProfileViews)
        </td>
```

```
        <td>
            @Html.DisplayFor(modelItem => item.FileUploadsInBytes)
        </td>
        <td>
            @Html.DisplayFor(modelItem => item.FileUploadQuotaInBytes)
        </td>
        <td>
            @Html.ActionLink("Edit", "Edit", new { id=item.ArtistId }) |
            @Html.ActionLink("Details", "Details", new { id=item.ArtistId }) |
            @Html.ActionLink("Delete", "Delete", new { id=item.ArtistId })
        </td>
    </tr>
}

</table>
```

You do not need to stop the debugger or recompile your code to make changes to the views. This allows you to make changes to the view and then view the changes in the browser while still in debug mode. If you refresh the page after making the changes, you will see the modifications in the browser right away.

As you browse the site, you can navigate from the main list to pages that allow you to view, edit, and delete the records. You may also create new records.

In most cases, you will not be able to do this out of the box for a production application, but it does give you a good starting point.

7-4. Creating a Model Using Entity Framework Database First with Oracle

Problem

You are working on an ASP.NET MVC project that needs to connect to an Oracle database server. You would like to use the Entity Framework, but you are not sure if it is possible.

Solution

Oracle offers its own provider for Entity Framework. The required components and add-ins for Visual Studio can be downloaded from the Oracle web site by searching for **ODAC with Oracle Developer Tools for Visual Studio**.

Once this package has been installed, you can use the Entity Data Model Wizard to generate a model from your Oracle database.

How It Works

Oracle offers a number of tools for .NET developers, including an add-in Visual Studio 2012. The most important set of the tools are included in a package named ODTwithODAC1120xxx. This package includes the following:

- Oracle Developer Tools for Visual Studio (ODT)

- Oracle Data Access Components (ODAC)

- Oracle Data Provider for .NET 4 and .NET 2

- Oracle Data Provider for ASP.NET 4 and ASP.NET 2

- Oracle Database Extensions for .NET

- Oracle Services for Microsoft Transaction Server

- Oracle SQL *Plus

- Oracle SQL Instant Client

In addition to ODT for .NET, Oracle offers several other tools that are useful for .NET developers, including the Oracle Database 11g Express Edition and Oracle SQL Developer. The Oracle Express Edition database is a free, lightweight version of the Oracle database engine. It can be installed on the developer work station. In general, it is helpful to have a local instance of your application's database, over which you have complete administrative control for development purposes.

Oracle SQL Developer is an IDE for creating and managing Oracle databases and packages. This is very helpful for working with Oracle database. It allows you to create users, tablespaces, and other proprietary Oracle constructs that cannot be created using Visual Studio.

■ **Note**　The Oracle Developer Tools for .NET do not work with Visual Studio Express Edition.

Acquiring and Installing the Oracle Database and Tools

The Oracle tools are free and can be downloaded from the Oracle web site. The web site does require that you register and sign in before allowing you to download packages. Windows downloads for the Oracle database components can be found at www.oracle.com/technetwork/database/windows/downloads/index.html.

Each of the packages are around 300MB and are distributed as ZIP files. Download the files to a temporary directory on your hard drive, and then decompress them. While it is possible to run the installer from the ZIP folder, I generally do not recommend doing so. Since the unzipping process takes several minutes, it is difficult to tell if the installer application has launched.

You can launch the installer by navigating to the folder created when you unzipped each package and then launching the setup.exe file. The setup file launches a wizard that steps you through the setup package.

■ **Tip**　Even if you have a dedicated Oracle development database server, in many cases, it can be beneficial to have a local Oracle instance running on your development machine. For most developers, the Oracle Database Express Edition (XE) is the best fit because of its relatively compact size.

After launching the installation program, you can perform the following steps to install ODT.

1. Click Next on the Welcome screen.

2. Specify an inventory directory, and then click Next. The Oracle Installer uses this directory to keep track of what Oracle products are installed on your PC.

3. Make sure that the Oracle Data Access Components for Oracle Client 11.2.x is selected, and then click Next.

4. On the Install Location screen, specify paths for the Oracle configuration files (Oracle Base) and software files. Click Next.

5. Install the application components that you require. If you are only doing ASP.NET MVC development, you can uncheck the OLE DB providers and Oracle Services for Microsoft Transaction Services. Make sure that the Oracle Data Provider for .NET, Oracle Providers for ASP.NET, and Oracle Developer Tools for Visual Studio are selected. Optionally, you can install the documentation for Visual Studio 2010 and 2012. Click Next.

6. Make note of the location of the scripts listed. These scripts can be used to install the ASP.NET Membership provider schemas on your Oracle database. Click Next.

7. On the Oracle Developer Tools for Visual Studio screen, select Visual Studio 2012, and then click Next.

8. On the Summary page, confirm your settings, and then click Install to begin the installation.

9. When the installation has completed, the wizard will again remind you of the location of the scripts needed to create your schema. If you forgot to take note of this during step 6, take note now. Click Exit to close.

Once the installation is complete, you should have a number of new tools available on your Start screen (or Start menu).

Creating an Alias for a Remote Oracle Server

If you are connecting to a remote Oracle database, you need to create an alias in your tnsnames.ora file in order to connect to your database. If you are using a local connection, you can skip this step.

The tnsnames.ora file allows you to create easy-to-remember names for the various Oracle databases that you may need to connect to. The default installation of the Oracle client that was installed as part of ODT setup does not include a tnsnames.ora file, but it does provide you with a sample file. The sample file is located under your Oracle installation folder, which will be in <drive letter>:\app\<user name>\product\11.2.0\client_2\Network\Admin\Sample if you used the default settings.

You can open this sample file using Notepad. It provides you with a sample entry and gives you a template for your first entry. Listing 7-22 shows an example of an alias created for a remote Oracle instance running Oracle Database 11g Express Edition.

Listing 7-22. Tnsnames.ora File with an Alias Defined

```
HappyOracleDB =
  (DESCRIPTION =
    (ADDRESS = (PROTOCOL = TCP)(HOST = 192.168.1.15)(PORT = 1521))
    (CONNECT_DATA =
      (SERVER = DEDICATED)
      (SID = xe)
    )
  )
```

In this example, I have created an alias named HappyOracleDB. The database is on a server with the 192.168.1.15 IP address. It is running on the default Oracle port 1521.

Once you create your alias, you need to save your file to the Oracle client's Network\Admin folder. This should be in the parent directory of the Sample folder.

Creating an Entity Data Model from an Oracle Database

Open Visual Studio and click New Project from the Start page. Click Windows in the left pane that lists the template categories, and then select Class Library from the list of available templates. While you can create your Entity Data Model directly inside your ASP.NET MVC project, in most cases it is best to define this in a separate class library. Using a separate class library allows you to reuse the model in other projects and also aids in team development scenarios by helping you avoid needing to merge changes to a Visual Studio project file in your source control system.

Give the project a name. For this example, I will use the name Ch7.R4.DAL. Click the OK button to create the project.

After the project has been created, delete Class1.cs since it will not be used. After deleting the file in Solution Explorer, right-click the project node, select Add, and then select New Item. In the Add New Item window, select the Data category from the left pane, and then select ADO.NET Entity Data Model from the list of templates. Give the model a name, and then click the Add button. For this example, I am naming the file ODT.edmx.

In the Entity Data Model Wizard window, select the "Generate from database" option, and then click Next.

On the Choose Your Data Connection page of the Entity Data Model Wizard, click New Connection. The SQL Server Database is selected by default. To change the connection type to an Oracle Database (Oracle ODP.NET), click the Change button. On the Change Data Source screen, select Oracle Database and then select Oracle Data Provider for .NET as your data provider. Click OK.

In the Data Source Name field, select the name of the alias that you defined in the tnsnames.ora file, or keep the default value if you are connecting to a local instance.

Depending on how your Oracle server is configured, you can select either Windows Integrated Authentication or specify the username and password of the user account you would like to use for your application. If you have installed a local instance on your computer and have not created any additional users, you can connect using the Oracle administrative account "SYSTEM." The password for this account is set when you perform your installation.

Keep the default values for the Role and Connection names, and then use the Test Connection button to verify your connectivity. If your connectivity test fails, ensure that your tnsnames.ora file has the correct values and that the firewall settings are allowing your developer machine to connect to your database machine on port 1521.

If the connection succeeds, click the OK button.

If you are using a username and password to connect to your database, Visual Studio will warn that you have potentially sensitive information in your connection string. Click "Yes, include the sensitive data in the connection string." See Recipe 7-8 to learn how you can encrypt your connection string. Provide a name for your connection settings and then click Next.

■ **Tip** I do not recommend setting important configuration values such as database passwords in your code. Doing so will make it difficult to change once your code is in production. There are other methods that can be used to secure your connection string, such as using the aspnet_regiis command-line utility to encrypt the connection strings section of your Web.config file. Setting a password in your code is not secure. It is possible for anyone who has possession of your compiled assembly to use a tool such as JetBrains DotPeek to decompile your application and search for the code that includes the password.

In the Choose you Database Objects and Settings screen, select the schema objects that you wish to include in your Entity Data Model.

Once you have selected the tables, review the remaining settings on this screen. There are three check boxes located under the object selection window. The first check box, "Pluralize or singularize generated object names," determines how objects will be named in the code generated by the model. For example, if this box remains checked Visual Studio will generate an Entity named Artist. It will also create collections for these objects that will be available if you write LINQ queries against your model. For example to query a list of artist objects from the model you could write a LINQ query similar to: var userDataCollection = from d in m_context.Artists select d;

The next check box allows you to decide whether or not you want to include the foreign key columns in the database model. If this is checked in addition to a navigation property, the model will also include the unique identifier for the parent record as a property on the child entity.

The last check box, "Import selected stored procedures and functions into the entity model" will import any selected stored procedures as mapped functions into the model. This will allow you to call the stored procedures directly from your model and optionally have the procedure return a list of entities.

For the Model Namespace choose the .NET namespace you would like to use for this model. For this example, we will use Ch7.R4.Model for the model namespace.

Click the Finish button to create your model. Your model will be shown as a diagram. Press the F6 key to build your application.

Adding Your Entity Data Model to an ASP.NET MVC Application

Now that you have created your Entity Data Model, you can use it with an ASP.NET MVC application. To create a project using the Basic template, perform the following steps:

1. Open Visual Studio 2012 and click the New Project link from the Start screen.

2. In the New Project window, select the C# ASP.NET MVC 4 Web Application template. If you have not used this template before, you can use the search box in the upper-right side of the window to find it.

3. Give the project a name, select a location, and provide a solution name. The examples in this book follow a convention of Ch<chapter number>.R<recipe number> for the project name and use the default solution name. For this example, the project is named Ch7.R74.

4. Click OK then select Basic on the select a template screen. Make sure that the Razor view engine is selected.

5. Click OK to create the project.

6. Once the project has been created, right-click the Solution node in Solution Explorer and select Add Existing Project.

7. In the Add Existing Project Window, browse to the Ch7.R4.DAL folder and select Ch7.R4.DAL.csproj, and then click the Open button.

8. Right-click the Ch7.R4 project node and select Add Reference.

9. In the Add Reference window, expand the solution node and check the box next to Ch7.R4.DAL.

10. Build the solution by pressing the F6 key.

Creating a User Interface to View, Edit, Create, and Delete Records in the Oracle Database

The last step in this recipe will use Visual Studio to create a scaffolding for viewing, editing, creating, and deleting records from our Oracle database. This can be done using the steps outlined in this section.

1. Open the App.config file from the Ch7.R4.DAL folder and copy the connection string for your Oracle connection.

2. Open the Web.Config file in the Ch7.R4 project and paste the connection string into its connection string section.

3. In the Ch7.R4 project, right-click the Controllers folder in Solution Explorer and select Add and the New Controller from the pop-up window.

4. In the Add Controller window, name the controller **ArtistController**. Select MVC controller with read/write actions and views by using the Entity Framework from the Template drop-down box. For the Model class, select Artist. For the Data context class, select Entities.

5. Ensure that Razor is selected in the Views drop-down list, and then click the Add button.

6. Once the process is completed, Visual Studio will have created a new controller and a set of five views that provides a basic user interface for Create Read Update and Delete (CRUD) operations on your Artist table.

Press the F5 key to debug your application. Since you did not create a Home controller, you will need to append the URL with "Artist" in order to view the generated interface. You should be able to edit and view information in your Oracle database. You can then edit the files created by Visual Studio and style them using CSS.

7-5. Creating a Model Using Entity Framework Model First
Problem

You need to start a new project but you have not yet created a database. You would like to begin by designing the entity model. You would also like to use a visual tool.

Solution

In addition to helping you design your application's domain model, the Entity Framework modeling tool that is included with Visual Studio can be used to generate Data Definition Language (DDL) code for creating your database. DDL is a subset of the Structured Query Language (SQL) standard used to define the structure of the database.

You can create a new entity model by adding a new ADO.NET Entity Data Model to your project and selecting the Empty Model option. You can then proceed to use the tool to design your model. When you are ready, you can right-click the background of the model and select Generate Database from Model to make a script that can be used to create your database.

How It Works

For this example, we will start by creating an empty solution and then add two projects to it. The first project will be a class library that will contain our Entity Data Model, and the second will contain our ASP.NET MVC web application. While you can create your Entity Data Model directly inside your ASP.NET MVC project, in most cases it is best to define this in a separate class library. Using a separate class library allows you to reuse the model in other projects and aids in team development scenarios by helping you avoid the need to merge changes to a Visual Studio project file in your source control system.

Creating the Solution

To create the solution;

1. Open Visual Studio and click New Project from the Start page. In the left hand pane that lists the template categories expand the Other Project Types node, and then click Visual Studio Solutions. Select Blank Solution from the list of templates.

2. Give the solution a name. For this example, I will use the name Ch7.R5. Click the OK button to create the project.

3. After the solution has been created, right-click the Solution node in Solution Explorer and select Add and then New Project. Select the Class Library template from the template list and name the project, **Ch7.R5.DAL**.

4. After the project has been created, in Solution Explorer, right-click the project node and select Add and then New Item. In the Add New Item window select the Data category from the left pane then select ADO.NET Entity Data Model from the list of templates. Give the model a name. For this example, I am naming the file EDM.edmx. Select the Empty model option and click the Add button.

5. An empty diagram should now be displayed in the tabbed document area.

Adding Entities to Your Model

Now that you have created a model you can begin to add entities to it. To do so;

1. If the toolbox is not visible, select Toolbox from the Visual Studio View menu. The toolbox will display four items: Pointer, which allows you to select and position items on your model; Association, which allows you to define "Has a" relationships between entities; Entities, which allows you to create new entity objects; and Inheritance, which allows you to create "Is a" relationships between entities.

2. To create your first entity, click the Entity item in the toolbox, and while holding down the left mouse button, drag it onto the design surface before releasing the mouse button. A new entity named Entity1 will appear on the model. To rename your new Entity, double-click its title. Name the entity **Artist**.

3. To add a property to your model using the diagram, right-click the Artist entity, select Add New, and then select Scalar Property from the pop-up window. Name the new property **UserName**. The new property has been created as a string type, which is the default. To modify the UserName property, right-click it in the diagram and select Properties. The Properties window will appear docked under the Solution Explorer window. Change the Max Length value to **256** and set its Unicode value to **true**.

Using this technique, add a few other properties to the Artist model—with the values in Table 7-1 as your guide.

Table 7-1. Properties of the Artist Entity

Name	Entity Key	Type	Max Length	Nullable	Unicode	Default Value
ArtistId	True	Int32		False		
UserName	False	String	256	False	True	
Country	False	String	50	True	False	USA
Provence	False	String	65	True	True	New Jersey
City	False	String	50	True	True	Paterson
CreateDate	False	DateTime		False		

When you have completed adding the properties, add a second entity and name it **ArtistSkill**. Rename its id field **ArtistSkillId**, and then create its properties according to the values in Table 7-2. Do not surround your default values with quotes.

Table 7-2. *Properties of the ArtistSkill Entity*

Name	Entity Key	Type	Max Length	Nullable	Unicode	Default Value
ArtistSkillId	True	Int32		False		
TalentName	False	String	50	False	False	Guitar
SkillLevel	False	Int32		False	False	0
Details	False	String	500	True	False	
Styles	False	String	500	False	False	

Now that we have created the tables, we can create a relationship between them. To do this, click the Association tool in the toolbox. When you mouse over the diagram, your cursor should now look like the Association icon. Click the Artist entity and then click the ArtistSkill entity. A line connecting the two entities will be in the diagram. A "1" appears on the Artist side of the line and a "*" on the ArtistSkill side. This indicates a one-to-many relationship between an Artist and ArtistSkill. In other words, an artist may have many skills.

▒ **Note**   You do not need to explicitly define the foreign key field in the child table. When the designer generates the SQL code to create the database, it will add the field automatically based on the relationship.

When you are done, your model should look similar to Figure 7-5.

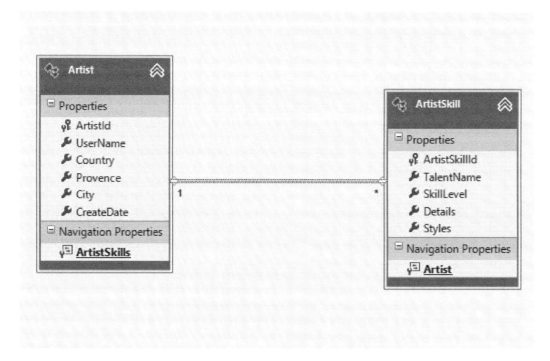

Figure 7-5. *The completed model*

Save your project by clicking the Save All icon in the Visual Studio toolbar.

Creating a Database from the Model

Now that we have created our Entity Data Model, we can use it to create a database. This is a two-step process where first we create a script and then we execute it against the database.

To create an SQL Server database from the mode;

1. Right-click anywhere in the model diagram or right-click anywhere in the Model Explorer. Select Generate Database from Model from the pop-up menu.

2. In the Generate Database Wizard, click the New Connection button.

3. In the Connection Properties window, make sure the data source is Microsoft SQL Server. If it is not, click the Change button, select SQL Server from the Change Data Source window, and select .NET Framework Data Provider for SQL Server in the Data Provider drop-down list. Click OK to return to the Connection Properties window.

4. You can enter " . " (a shorthand expression for the default SQL server instance on your local machine) for the Server Name field if you are connecting to a local instance of SQL Server. If you need to connect to a local SQL Express instance, you can use . \SQLExpress. This is the default name for the named instance that SQL Express creates when it is installed. Alternatively, you can use the drop-down list, which will show a list of severs on your local network.

5. Since we want to create a new database, do not select a database from the drop-down list but instead type in a name that you would like to use for your database, and then click OK.

6. Visual Studio will let you know that the database does not exist and will ask you if you wish to create it. Click Yes.

7. Clicking Yes closes the Connection Properties window and returns you to the Generate Database Wizard. On the choose Your Data Connection page of the wizard, tick the "Save Entity Connection settings in App.Config as:" check box, and then click Next.

8. The Summary and Settings page of the wizard will be displayed. You can leave the default value in the Save DDL As text box. Review the script that was generated by the tool. It should define two tables and create a foreign key relationship between them.

9. Click the Finish button to close the wizard. Visual Studio will add the new .sql file to your project and open it for you. The script should look similar to Listing 7-23.

Listing 7-23. SQL Server DDL Code Generated from Your Entity Data Model

```
-- --------------------------------------------------
-- Entity Designer DDL Script for SQL Server 2005, 2008, and Azure
-- --------------------------------------------------
-- Date Created: 09/21/2012 01:49:31
-- Generated from EDMX file: G:\WorkingFolder\MVCBook\Chapter7\Ch7.R5\Ch7.R5.DAL\EDM.edmx
-- --------------------------------------------------

SET QUOTED_IDENTIFIER OFF;
GO
USE [NewDatabase];
GO
IF SCHEMA_ID(N'dbo') IS NULL EXECUTE(N'CREATE SCHEMA [dbo]');
GO

-- Creating table 'Artists'
CREATE TABLE [dbo].[Artists] (
    [ArtistId] int IDENTITY(1,1) NOT NULL,
    [UserName] nvarchar(256)  NOT NULL,
    [Country] nvarchar(50)  NOT NULL,
    [Provence] nvarchar(65)  NULL,
    [City] nvarchar(50)  NULL,
    [CreateDate] datetime  NOT NULL
);
GO

-- Creating table 'ArtistSkills'
CREATE TABLE [dbo].[ArtistSkills] (
    [ArtistSkillId] int IDENTITY(1,1) NOT NULL,
    [TalentName] nvarchar(50)  NOT NULL,
    [SkillLevel] int  NOT NULL,
    [Details] nvarchar(500)  NULL,
    [Styles] nvarchar(500)  NOT NULL,
    [Artist_ArtistId] int  NOT NULL
);
GO
-- --------------------------------------------------
```

```
-- Creating all PRIMARY KEY constraints
-- --------------------------------------------------

-- Creating primary key on [ArtistId] in table 'Artists'
ALTER TABLE [dbo].[Artists]
ADD CONSTRAINT [PK_Artists]
    PRIMARY KEY CLUSTERED ([ArtistId] ASC);
GO

-- Creating primary key on [ArtistSkillId] in table 'ArtistSkills'
ALTER TABLE [dbo].[ArtistSkills]
ADD CONSTRAINT [PK_ArtistSkills]
    PRIMARY KEY CLUSTERED ([ArtistSkillId] ASC);
GO


-- --------------------------------------------------
-- Creating all FOREIGN KEY constraints
-- --------------------------------------------------

-- Creating foreign key on [Artist_ArtistId] in table 'ArtistSkills'
ALTER TABLE [dbo].[ArtistSkills]
ADD CONSTRAINT [FK_ArtistArtistSkill]
    FOREIGN KEY ([Artist_ArtistId])
    REFERENCES [dbo].[Artists]
        ([ArtistId])
    ON DELETE NO ACTION ON UPDATE NO ACTION;

-- Creating non-clustered index for FOREIGN KEY 'FK_ArtistArtistSkill'
CREATE INDEX [IX_FK_ArtistArtistSkill]
ON [dbo].[ArtistSkills]
    ([Artist_ArtistId]);
GO


-- --------------------------------------------------
-- Script has ended
-- --------------------------------------------------
```

At this point, the new database has been created but no objects have been added to it. Only the script has been created. To create your schema in the database, click the Execute button, which is located under the tab in the toolbar directly above the Code Editor window. A Connect to Server window will pop-up. Click the Connect button. The window will close and after a few moments, you will see Visual Studio's message window state "Command(s) completed successfully."

Adding Your Entity Data Model to an ASP.NET MVC Application

Now that you have created your Entity Data Model, you can use it with an ASP.NET MVC application. To create a project using the Basic template, perform the following steps:

1. Right-click the solution node in Solution Explorer, select Add, and then select New Project.

2. In the New Project window, select the C# ASP.NET MVC 4 Web Application template.

3. Name the project **Ch7.R5.Web**.

4. Click OK, and then select Basic on the Select a Template screen. Make sure that the Razor view engine is selected.

5. Click OK to create the project.

6. Once the project has been created, right-click the Solution node in Solution Explorer and select Add Existing Project.

7. Right-click the `Ch7.R5.Web` project node and select Add Reference.

8. In the Add Reference window, expand the solution node and check the box next to `Ch7.R5.DAL`.

9. Build the solution by pressing the F6 key.

You can now reference the model in your controllers and views.

7-6. Creating a Model Using Entity Framework Code First
Problem

You have just started a new project but have not created your database. You like to work with plain old C# objects (POCO), but you are not fond of the code generation concepts used by the Entity Framework's Code First and Model First strategies. On the other hand, you do not want to hand-code all of your data access code, and you would like to take advantage of *some* of the features in the Entity Framework.

Solution

Starting with Entity Framework version 4.1, a code-first approach was offered as an alternative to the model-first and database-first strategies. With code-first, the database is generated from your C# classes. There is no `.edmx` file and no generated classes.

How It Works

For this example, we will start by creating an empty solution and then add two projects to it. The first project will be a class library that will contain our class library, and the second will contain our ASP.NET MVC web application. While you can create your classes directly inside your ASP.NET MVC project, in most cases it is best to define this in a separate class library. Using a separate class library allows you to reuse the model in other projects and aids in team development scenarios by helping you avoid the need to merge changes to a Visual Studio project file in your source control system.

Creating the Solution

Open Visual Studio and click New Project from the Start page. In the left pane that lists the template categories, expand the Other Project Types node, and then click Visual Studio Solutions. Select Blank Solution from the list of templates.

Give the solution a name. For this example, I will use the name `Ch7.R6`. Click the OK button to create the project.

After the solution has been created, right-click the Solution node in Solution Explorer, select Add, and then select New Project. Select the Class Library template from the template list and name the project **Ch7.R6.Library**.

After the project has been created, in Solution Explorer, right-click `Class1.cs` and select Delete. Click OK when prompted.

Adding Your Classes

For this example, our model will consist of two classes: `Artist` and `ArtistSkill`. The first class will represent a recording artist and the second class will represent skills possessed by that artist. The classes themselves will be plain C# classes. There will be no Entity Framework–specific code required.

1. Add a new folder to your solution and name it **Entities**.

2. Right-click this folder, select Add, and then select Class.

3. In the Add New Item window, name your file `Artist.cs`, and then click the Add button.

4. Repeat this process for the second class, naming the file `ArtistSkill.cs`.

Modify the files to look like Listing 7-24.

Listing 7-24. Your Class Library

```
namespace Ch7.R6.Library.Entities
{
 ///
// Artist.cs
//


    public partial class Artist
    {
        public Artist()
        {
            this.Country = "USA";
            this.Provence = "New Jersey";
            this.City = "Paterson";
            this.ArtistSkills = new HashSet<ArtistSkill>();
        }

        public int ArtistId { get; set; }
        public string UserName { get; set; }
        public string Country { get; set; }
        public string Provence { get; set; }
        public string City { get; set; }
        public DateTime CreateDate { get; set; }
        public DateTime ModifiedDate { get; set; }
        public string WebSite { get; set; }

        public virtual ICollection<ArtistSkill> ArtistSkills { get; set; }
    }
}
namespace Ch7.R6.Library.Entities
{
```

```
///
/// ArtistSkill.cs
///
public partial class ArtistSkill
    {
        public ArtistSkill()
        {
            this.TalentName = "\"Guitar\"";
            this.SkillLevel = 0;
        }

        public int ArtistSkillId { get; set; }
        public string TalentName { get; set; }
        public int SkillLevel { get; set; }
        public string Details { get; set; }
        public string Styles { get; set; }

        public virtual Artist Artist { get; set; }
    }
}
```

Creating the DbContext

Up until now, you have created two normal C# classes. These classes by themselves do not have any knowledge of any database and have no way of persisting their values. To enable this functionality, we first need to add a reference to the Entity Framework to the project. Once the reference has been added, we can then create a class that extends the DbContext class.

To add the latest version of Entity Framework to the project;

1. Right-click the References folder in the Solution Explorer and choose Manage NuGet Packages.

2. Select `EntityFramework` from the list, and then click the Install button. If you do not see it in the list, use the search box to find it. If prompted, click the I Accept button on the License Acceptance window. All assemblies required by the Entity Framework will be added to your project.

3. Now that `EntityFramework` has been added, you can now create your `DBContext` class. To do this, first create a new folder at the root of your project and name it **Context**. Right-click the folder, select Add, and then select New Class. Name the class **ArtistContext.cs**.

Modify the class to look like Listing 7-25.

Listing 7-25. The ArtistContext Class

```
using Ch7.R6.Library.Entities;
using System.Data.Entity;

namespace Ch7.R6.Library.Context
{
    public class ArtistContext : DbContext
    {
```

```
        public DbSet<Artist> Artists { get; set; }
        public DbSet<ArtistSkill> ArtistSkills { get; set; }
    }
}
```

First, we add the System.Data.Entity and Ch7.R6.Library.Entities namespaces to the file. We then change the class's access modifier to public so that it can be accessible outside the assembly. The ArtistContext class has been modified to extend DbContext. By doing this, we have transformed this simple class into a proxy to our back-end data store, and made it implement both the repository and unit of work patterns.

Inside the body of the class are two public properties that expose a DbSet collection of Artist and ArtistSkill. A DbSet class represents a collection of entities of a given type within the context. It allows data to be queried, updated, and deleted from the back-end database.

From the perspective of the developer, we have just made a persistent ignorant pair of C# classes into an almost fully functional data access layer.

Creating the Database

Your DbContext class is the proxy that your code uses to communicate with its persistence store. The back-end store that DbContext uses is determined by one of two things: a connection string that you explicitly provide in your code or configuration, or if nothing is provided, a dynamically generated connection string based on its class name and namespace.

In Listing 7-25, we have not passed in any information telling it what connection to use and thus no Entity Framework connection strings have been added to App.config. Your DbContext class will use the Code First connection by convention approach. The convention specifies that it will attempt to connect to an SQL Express instance running on the local machine. It will then look for a database named Ch7.R6.Library.Context.ArtistContext. If this database does not exist, the DbContext class will attempt to create it. If you were to hard-code the connection string, it would look something like Listing 7-26.

Listing 7-26. The Connection String Listing 7-25 Will Use by Convention

```
Server=.\SQLExpress;Integrated Security=True;Initial Catalog=Ch7.R6.Library.Context.ArtistContext
```

However, when you use NuGet to add a reference to EntityFramework version 5 to your project, the package will add an entry to your App.config file that will override the default connection string, replacing it with one that uses SQL Server 2012 LocalDB. The actual version number for LocalDB is provided in the App.Config file under the entityFramework section. If you open the App.config file, the Ch7.R6.Library project, you should see an entry like the one shown in Listing 7-27.

Listing 7-27. Entity Framework Default Connection Factory Settings from App.config

```
  <entityFramework>
    <defaultConnectionFactory type="System.Data.Entity.Infrastructure.LocalDbConnectionFactory,
EntityFramework">
      <parameters>
        <parameter value="v11.0" />
      </parameters>
    </defaultConnectionFactory>
  </entityFramework>
```

The defaultConnectionFactory setting tells the Entity Framework the class it should use to generate the connection strings. The NuGet package–imposed configuration replaces the default setting of SqlConnectionFactory with LocalDbConnectionFactory. The classes differ by their default behaviors as well as the parameters that they accept via configuration. For example, the SqlConnectionFactory will create connections that use .\SQLExpress for the server name property of the connection string unless this value is overridden by a modifying the SqlConnectionFactory's BaseConnectionString property.

If this is OK with you and you want to use the LocalDB database, then there is nothing more you need to do to create your database. It will be created for you automatically the first time the constructor for ArtistContext is called. If you would like to use another database, you will need to change this via code, configuration, or a combination of the two.

In this example, we will use the combination approach by defining a connection string in our configuration file and then modifying our ArtistContext class so that it will use that connection string.

First, we will define a connection string and add it to our App.config file, as shown in Listing 7-28.

Listing 7-28. Adding a Connection String to the App.Config file

```
<connectionStrings>
<add name="DefaultConnection"
        providerName="System.Data.SqlClient"
        connectionString="Server=.;Integrated Security=True;Initial
Catalog=Ch7_R6;MultipleActiveResultSets=True"
        />
<connectionStrings/>
```

This connection string uses the default SQL Server instance running on the local computer and will use a database named NewDatabase. We have also enabled the Multiple Active Result Sets (MARS) feature. This allows more than one batch to be executed at once by a single connection. This setting is required by the Entity Framework.

Now that we have a connection string, we need to modify the constructor of the ArtistContext class so that it will use it. To do this, modify ArtistContext as shown in Listing 7-29.

Listing 7-29. ArtistContext Modified to Use the DefaultConnection Connection String

```
public class ArtistContext : DbContext
{
    public ArtistContext() : base("name=DefaultConnection")
    {
    }
    public DbSet<Artist> Artists { get; set; }
    public DbSet<ArtistSkill> ArtistSkills { get; set; }
}
```

In Listing 7-29, we add a constructor that calls the DbContext base constructor and passes in a named connection string.

With the current setting, if we do nothing else, simply creating an instance of our ArtistContext class will create a new database named NewDatabase on our local SQL Server default instance and add two tables with the fields defined in our classes.

Database Migrations

The default DbContext behavior of creating a new database the first time it is created is a really great feature. This may be exactly what you need if you were writing a Windows client application that needs to connect to a local SQL Server.

LocalDB is a perfect fit for that scenario, especially when the computer is used by more than one user, each wanting to keep his own settings.

A web developer, however, has a different set of problems. Our systems are under constant threat of attack. For this reason, the user account that your application uses to connect to the database should have limited rights. This is called the *principle of least privilege*. If your application's account has administrative rights on your production database, you are opening yourself to a large amount of risk. All it takes is one mistake by a developer to leave an SQL Injection vulnerability open. A skilled attacker can use your web application to create and drop databases and tables at will.

With this in mind, you should never allow your web application on a production system to have access for creating and dropping databases. In most cases, you should also restrict it from being able to create and delete database objects such as tables, indexes, stored procedures, and user accounts. Your database and the required schema should exist before deploying your application. Changes to your application in production, including its database, should be performed under a well-organized change control process.

Fortunately, the Entity Framework team has a built-in mechanism known as Database Migrations, which allows you to have control over the changes made to your system.

The Database Migrations feature, which can be enabled using the NuGet console, automatically creates a set of classes using metadata from your database to synchronize changes between your class library and your database. It also allows you to change these classes so that you have precise control of any changes that are made.

Enabling Database Migrations

To enable database migrations, first you need to display the NuGet console. To do this;

1. From the Visual Studio menu, select View ➤ Other Windows ➤ Package Manager Console.

2. The Package Manager Console will open docked in the bottom center pane below the Code Editor window.

3. To enable code migrations, enter the following command at the prompt and then press the Enter key to execute it:

    Enable-Migrations

The package manager will check to see if your project contains a DbContext class, and then it will check to see if it is targeting an existing database. When it is finished, it will tell you that Code First Migrations are enabled for your project. It will have added a new folder called Migrations to your project and add a class to that folder named Configuration, as shown in Listing 7-30.

Listing 7-30. Configuration.cs

```
internal sealed class Configuration :
DbMigrationsConfiguration<Ch7.R6.Library.Context.ArtistContext>
    {
        public Configuration()
        {
            AutomaticMigrationsEnabled = false;
        }

        protected override void Seed(Ch7.R6.Library.Context.ArtistContext context)
        {
            //  This method will be called after migrating to the latest version.

            //  You can use the DbSet<T>.AddOrUpdate() helper extension method
            //  to avoid creating duplicate seed data. E.g.
```

```
        //
        //    context.People.AddOrUpdate(
        //       p => p.FullName,
        //       new Person { FullName = "Andrew Peters" },
        //       new Person { FullName = "Brice Lambson" },
        //       new Person { FullName = "Rowan Miller" }
        //    );
        //
    }
  }
}
```

The class consists of a constructor that sets the `AutomaticMigrationsEnabled` property to false. With this setting enabled, the NuGet `Update-Database` command will require that migration scripts be created in order to make changes to your database. The migration scripts can be created for you automatically by using the NuGet `Add-Migration` command. With automatic migration disabled, you have more control over what happens to your database. You also have a record of the changes made to your database, as well as the ability to downgrade.

If you are working on the initial phase of development and are making many changes, the automatic migration feature can be helpful since you can keep your database in sync with your code changes without the need to create a specific migration for each.

The Seed method is responsible for repopulating your database with some sample data after the schema has been updated. You can hard-code some values, as shown in the example, or you can write more-elaborate code that can import data from a text file or spreadsheet, for example.

Creating Your First Migration

Now that database migrations have been enabled, you can use the `Add-Migration` and `Update-Database` command to modify the schema and seed the database.

Each migration should be given a name to help you to understand what each one does. To create your first migration, enter the following command into the Package Manager Console:

```
Add-Migration ArtistCreate
```

When the command is run, the package manager will inform you that it is creating a snapshot of your current code's first model, which it will use to calculate the changes to your model on the next migration.

It will create a new file in the `Migrations` folder that will consist of a unique identifier, followed by an underscore, and then the name you designated to the migration. The class it creates will consist of two methods: `Up()` and `Down()`. The `Up()` method is the code that is run to create or modify your schema. The `Down()` method is the steps required to downgrade your database to the state it existed in before your migration was run. The generated code is shown in Listing 7-31.

Listing 7-31. ArtistCreate Migration

```
namespace Ch7.R6.Library.Migrations
{
    using System;
    using System.Data.Entity.Migrations;

    public partial class ArtistCreate : DbMigration
    {
        public override void Up()
        {
```

```
        CreateTable(
            "dbo.Artists",
            c => new
                {
                    ArtistId = c.Int(nullable: false, identity: true),
                    UserName = c.String(),
                    Country = c.String(),
                    Provence = c.String(),
                    City = c.String(),
                    CreateDate = c.DateTime(nullable: false),
                })
            .PrimaryKey(t => t.ArtistId);

        CreateTable(
            "dbo.ArtistSkills",
            c => new
                {
                    ArtistSkillId = c.Int(nullable: false, identity: true),
                    TalentName = c.String(),
                    SkillLevel = c.Int(nullable: false),
                    Details = c.String(),
                    Styles = c.String(),
                    Artist_ArtistId = c.Int(),
                })
            .PrimaryKey(t => t.ArtistSkillId)
            .ForeignKey("dbo.Artists", t => t.Artist_ArtistId)
            .Index(t => t.Artist_ArtistId);

    }

    public override void Down()
    {
        DropIndex("dbo.ArtistSkills", new[] { "Artist_ArtistId" });
        DropForeignKey("dbo.ArtistSkills", "Artist_ArtistId", "dbo.Artists");
        DropTable("dbo.ArtistSkills");
        DropTable("dbo.Artists");
    }
  }
}
```

Take note of the fact that the Down() method is completely dropping the tables, which will delete any data in them.

▨ **Tip** Always review your migration code. Even though the Entity Framework team did a pretty good job with the code generator, it is not perfect. There are times when you may need to tweak the code so that it creates the database objects you need.

At this point, even though the scaffolding has been generated, it has not been executed. If you notice that you are missing something and need to make changes to your model, you can make the changes and then run `Add-Migration <migration number>_ArtistCreate` to regenerate the scaffolding.

Running the Migration

To run the migration, you can use the `Update-Database` command in the NuGet Manager Console. It will now use the connection string specified in your `ArtistContext` constructor. If the connection is successful, it will verify that the database exists. In this case, since we have not created the database, it will create it for us automatically using the server's default settings for new databases. Once the database is created, it will use the code in the Migration's Up method to generate the DDL code required to create the database objects.

If you would like to see the SQL code that is generated by the command, you can use the `-verbose` method. This will display all the SQL commands run for each migration.

Backing out a Migration

If you would like to back out a particular migration, you can call `Update-Database` and pass in the name of the migration you would like to revert to using the `-TargetMigration` flag. If you wish to back out all migrations and start over, you can pass in 0 for the `-TargetMigration` name.

To review how this works, first make some changes to the model to include a second migration.

Since our original model did not use any data annotations to specify the maximum length of our string values, the resulting database is using `varchar(MAX)` as the data type for each column. This is probably not a good idea since you will incur a performance penalty for using it and should only use it when you need to store values with more than 8000 characters. Another mistake is that since we did not specify otherwise, all the columns were created as nullable. To correct this, we will change the `Artist` class to look like Listing 7-32. We will also make similar changes to the `ArtistSkill` table.

Listing 7-32. The Artist Class with Data Annotations Specifying a Max Value

```
using System;
using System.Collections.Generic;
//.. other using statement ommited for brevity
using System.ComponentModel.DataAnnotations;

namespace Ch7.R6.Library.Entities
{

    public partial class Artist
    {
        public Artist()
        {
            this.Country = "USA";
            this.Provence = "New Jersey";
            this.City = "Paterson";
            this.ArtistSkills = new HashSet<ArtistSkill>();
        }

        public int ArtistId { get; set; }

        [MaxLength(256)]
        [Required]
        public string UserName { get; set; }
```

```
        [MaxLength(50)]
        [Required]
        public string Country { get; set; }

        [MaxLength(65)]
        public string Provence { get; set; }

        [MaxLength(50)]
        public string City { get; set; }

        [Required]
        public DateTime CreateDate { get; set; }

        [Required]
        public DateTime ModifiedDate { get; set; }

        [MaxLength(255)]
        public string WebSite { get; set; }

        public virtual ICollection<ArtistSkill> ArtistSkills { get; set; }
    }
}
```

After making the required changes to the `Artist` class, we can create another migration to record the changes. To do this in the Package Manager Console, type

```
Add-Migration MaxLengthAndRequiredFields
```

You will see a new migration that consists of several `AlterColumn` statements. To update your database, you can run the `Update-Database` command again. This will use check to see what migrations need to be run and then execute them one-by-one in a sequence. Since we have only added a single migration, only one migration will be run. This time when you run `Update-Database` use the `-verbose` flag so that you can see the SQL commands generated.

If you open the database using SQL Manager or Visual Studio's Database Explorer, you should see the changes applied to your database.

The first time you run the `Update-Database` command, database migration creates a new system table called `__MigrationHistory`. This table has three columns: `MigrationId`, `Model`, and `ProductVersion`. The `MigrationId` field contains a unique identifier that matches the name of the associated migration file created in Visual Studio. The `Model` column stores a binary version of the model, which includes all classes tied to the data context. The Entity Framework uses this to compare the current version of the model's code to what is stored in migration history to determine compatibility. `ProductVersion` keeps track of the version of .NET Framework and Entity Framework used to generate the migration.

To roll back this last change, we can run the following command, shown in Listing 7-33, in the Package Manager Console.

Listing 7-33. Reverting to a Specific Migration Level

```
Update-Database -verbose -TargetMigration 201209221819161_ArtistCreate
```

The Package Manager Console will inform you that it is reverting migration `201209221915330_MaxLengthAndRequiredFields` and then display the `ALTER TABLE` statements to undo the changes. If you look at the database now, you will see that all the columns are back to having `varchar(MAX)` data types, and again allow `NULL`.

To completely remove all the changes made to the database since we have started, you can run the command shown in Listing 7-34 in the Package Manager Console.

Listing 7-34. Reverting All Migrations

```
Update-Database -verbose -TargetMigration 0
```

You will see that all the tables and indexes created since we began have been deleted. The __MigrationHistory has also been removed.

You can add back all the changes by running Update-Database with no parameters. This will run all the migrations in the project's Migrations folder.

Promoting the Changes to Production

In most organizations, developers do not have direct access to production. There is usually some sort of change control process in place in which the developers create a change ticket and then attach a script that includes the needed changes.

In order to accommodate this need, the Code First Migration NuGet commands include a -Script switch for the Update-Database command. When the -Script is used, an SQL script will be created and no actions will be taken against the database. Listing 7-35 creates a new SQL Script and opens it in Visual Studio.

Listing 7-35. Generating a Script That Contains All of Your Migration Code

```
Update-Database -Script
```

This command generates a script for all of your migrations, including the script to create the __MigrationHistory table and insert the data for each migration.

If you do not want to include all the migrations, you can add two additional command-line switches: SourceMigration, which is the starting point for our migrations, and -TargetMigration, which is the newest migration to implement. Listing 7-36 shows a Package Manager Console command that uses both switches.

Listing 7-36. Generating a Script That Includes Several Migrations

```
Update-Database -Script -SourceMigration:$InitialDatabase -
TargetMigration:"MaxLengthAndRequiredFields"
```

$InitialDatabase is a variable that represents the initial state of the database prior to any migrations. By setting the -SourceMigration to it, we are saying to include all migration since we started. The -TargetMigration command switch tells us the last migration to include in the update.

If you would like to generate a script that includes only the code for the MaxLengthAndRequiredFields migration, you can modify your command to look like Listing 7-37.

Listing 7-37. Generating a Script That Targets a Specific Migration

```
Update-Database -Script -SourceMigration:"ArtistCreate" -TargetMigration:"MaxLengthAndRequiredFields"
```

For the migration, we have used ArtistCreate as the source and MaxLengthAndRequiredFields as the target. This will result in only the code for the MaxLengthAndRequiredFields being added to the script.

The Entity Framework Code First database migration is a powerful feature that makes the Code First development pattern an attractive choice. Unfortunately, Code First it is still missing some essential functionality, such as support for stored procedures. This functionality is promised to be included in Entity Framework 6, which is currently still under development.

7-7. Improving Application Startup Performance

Problem

Your new application has been deployed to production. Some users are complaining about performance. You access the application and find that it is running smoothly, as you expected. After doing some research, you find that the users who are complaining of performance problems tend to access the application early in the morning after the application has been idle for a number of hours.

Solution

Internet Information Server (IIS) is designed to manage web servers that may be running hundreds of web sites and applications. One of the optimizations added to maximize the amount of memory available to active applications is unloading inactive applications and reloading them on first access. The first person to access this application will experience a performance hit. This problem can be exacerbated if ASP.NET pages require compilation or if it needs to query the database with data that is normally cached.

There are a few things you can do to solve this problem. One is to modify the application's configuration to prevent it from being unloaded. If this solution does not provide enough relief, it can be combined with techniques such as creating a warm-up script to fill the cache as soon as the process starts, and then precompiling the views.

How It Works

We should see if we can solve the problem by preventing the application from being unloaded when it times out. This is the easiest of the solutions suggested and it can be accomplished by modifying a few settings in the Internet Information Services (IIS) Manager, as follows:

1. Open IIS Manager by tapping the Windows key on your keyboard and typing **IIS**. The Internet Information Services Manager icon should appear in the list of matching applications. Click it to launch IIS Manager.

2. If you do not know which application pool the application is using, locate your site in the Connections pane of IIS Manager, and then click your site to select it. In the Actions pane, select Advanced Settings. In the Advanced Settings window, take note of the application pool. Click Cancel to close the window.

3. Under the Connections pane in IIS Manager, click Application Pools. Locate the application pool that your web application is using, and then click it to select it.

4. In the Actions pane, click Advanced Settings.

5. Under the Process Model section, find the property for Idle Time-out. Change this value to **0**. A value of 0 indicates that the process should never be shut down, regardless of how long it has been idle.

6. Scroll back up to the General Settings section and locate the Start Mode property. Set this value to Always Running. This will ensure that the application will start when the server starts.

The two settings changed in IIS makes certain that the process will start when the server starts and that the process will not go to sleep.

7-8. Encrypting the Connection Strings in Your Web.config File

Problem

You are using a database the does not allow you to use Windows Integrated Authentication, which requires you to put the database username and password in the configuration file. Your company's security guidelines restrict user credentials from existing unencrypted in a file. You need to find a way to encrypt this information without breaking your application or changing your data access code.

Solution

The ASP.NET IIS Registration tool is a command-line tool that is shipped with the .NET Framework. It includes an option that allows you to encrypt sections of a configuration file for a specific application.

How It Works

The ASP.NET IIS Registration tool (`aspnet_regiis.exe`) performs many functions for ASP.NET, including enabling ASP.NET in IIS, installing the schema in SQL Databases for the ASP.NET SQL providers, and miscellaneous functions such as encrypting sections of your configuration files.

On a machine with Visual Studio installed on it, the easiest way to run the tool is to use the Visual Studio Developer command prompt. This is an instance of the command line initialized with the relevant paths. In this case, you can just open the command prompt and type `aspnet_regiis -?` to see a list of available options. If you scroll down, you will find an entire section dedicated to configuration encryption options.

On a server that you would not normally have Visual Studio installed, you will need to type the whole path, which is `%SYSTEMROOT%\Microsoft.NET\Framework64\v4.0.30319\aspnet_regiis`.

The ASP.NET IIS Registration tool has a few options for encrypting all or part of the configuration file. The most common method to encrypt the section uses the machine key. To do this, execute the command shown in Listing 7-38 on your production server as part of your deployment.

Listing 7-38. Encrypting the Connection Strings Section of a Web.config file

```
%SYSTEMROOT%\Microsoft.NET\Framework64\v4.0.30319\aspnet_regiis -pef "connecti onStrings"
"G:\WorkingFolder\MVCBook\Chapter7\Ch7.R8\Ch7.R8" -prov DataProtectio nConfigurationProvider
```

The -pef option allows you to specify a file name rather than a relative path that needs to be parsed by IIS, as does the -pe option. From my experience, this seems to be the most reliable method. The `-prov` specifies which encryption provider to use. If omitted, the RSA provider will be used by default.

After running the command, the contents of the connection strings section of your `Web.config` file will be replaced by a `<cipherData>` element that contains a `<cipherValue>`, which contains the encrypted connection string, as shown in Listing 7-39.

Listing 7-39. The connectionString Section of Web.config After Running aspnet_regiis -pef

```
<connectionStrings configProtectionProvider="DataProtectionConfigurationProvider">
    <EncryptedData>
      <CipherData>
        <CipherValue>AQAAANCMnd8BFd[cipher value shortened to save space]</CipherValue>
      </CipherData>
    </EncryptedData>
  </connectionStrings>
```

To decrypt the file, you can use `aspnet_regiis` with the `-pdf` option. This option does not require a provider parameter. It is able to determine this automatically. Listing 7-40 shows the syntax for the decryption command.

Listing 7-40. Decrypting the Connection String Using aspnet_regiis

```
%SYSTEMROOT%\Microsoft.NET\Framework64\v4.0.30319\aspnet_regiis -pdf "connecti onStrings"
"G:\WorkingFolder\MVCBook\Chapter7\Ch7.R8\Ch7.R8" -prov DataProtectio nConfigurationProvider
```

After running this command, the `Web.config` file should be returned to normal. You will need to decrypt the file in order to edit it. In most cases, if you need to perform this task on your production system, you should place the command inside a `.bat` file to reduce the likelihood of typing errors and to ever so slightly improve the lives or your server administrators.

7-9. Using Areas to Organize a Large ASP.MVC Project
Problem

You are designing a somewhat sophisticated ASP.NET MVC application that is made up of several subsystems. You would like to have a Home controller for each of the main subsystems. Since it is not possible to have two controllers with the same name, you have been creating controllers with names such as `ArtistHomeController`, `HelpHomeController`, `MusicHomeController`, and more. You have created new routing rules to maintain your URL structure, but you are finding this process cumbersome as your project grows. You are looking for a better way to organize your project.

Solution

ASP.NET MVC has a concept known as Areas, which allows you to define separate MVC folder structures for each subsystem. You can easily create a new Area in Visual Studio by right-clicking your application's project node, and selecting Add and then Area.

How It Works

Areas help you organize your site by separating subdivisions of your site into functionally independent sections. In this example, we will show a musicians' collaboration community web site that has divided its functionality into areas for collaboration, music, artist profiles, administration, and finding help. Each area will have its own Home controller as well as controllers specific to each area.

Creating the Project

For this example, we will use the ASP.NET MVC 4 Internet Application template. To create the project using this template, perform the following steps:

1. Open Visual Studio 2012 and click the New Project link from the Start screen.

2. In the New Project window select the C# ASP.NET MVC 4 Web Application template. If you have not used this template before, you can use the search box in the upper-right side of the window to find it.

3. Give the project a name, select a location, and provide a solution name. The examples in this book follow a convention of Ch<chapter number>.R<recipe number> for the project name, and use the default solution name. For this example, the project is named Ch7.R9.

4. Click OK and then select Internet Application on the Select a Template screen. Make sure that the Razor view engine is selected.

5. Click OK to create the project.

Creating a New Area

To create a new area, right-click the project node of your ASP.NET MVC project in Solution Explorer, and select Add and then Area.

In the Add Area window, enter the name for your area Administration. Click the Add button to create the area. Repeat this process and create additional areas for Collaboration, Help, and Music.

For each of the areas you have created, Visual Studio will create a new folder named Areas under the root of your application. It will also create subfolders under the Areas folder named for each of the areas you have created. When you are done, your project should look similar to Figure 7-6.

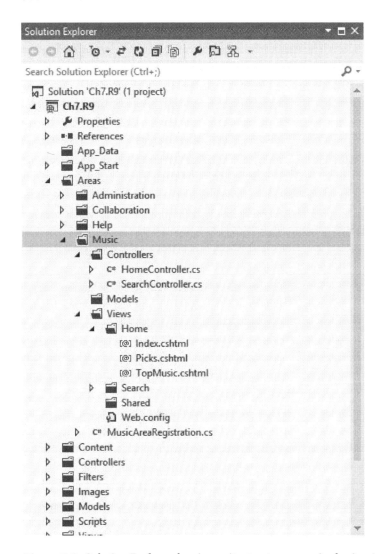

Figure 7-6. *Solution Explorer showing a site structure organized using Areas*

Inside each of your Areas folders, you have a similar structure—as in the root of the web site—with folders for Models, Controllers, and Views. Just like in the root of your site, the Views folder has a subfolder named Shared. Unlike the root, the Areas\<your area name>\Views\Shared folder is empty. The Views folder is also missing _Layout.cshtml and does not contain a _ViewStart.cshtml.

Each area will contain an area registration class. For example, in the Areas\Administration folder, you will find a file named AdministrationAreaRegistration.cs. This file contains a class that extends the AreaRegistration class and overrides its AreaName property and RegisterArea method.

The AdministrationAreaRegistration class is shown in Listing 7-41.

Listing 7-41. The Area Registration Class for the Administration Area

```
namespace Ch7.R9.Areas.Administration
{
    public class AdministrationAreaRegistration : AreaRegistration
    {
        public override string AreaName
        {
            get
            {
                return "Administration";
            }
        }

        public override void RegisterArea(AreaRegistrationContext context)
        {
            context.MapRoute(
                "Administration_default",
                "Administration/{controller}/{action}/{id}",
                new { action = "Index", id = UrlParameter.Optional }
            );
        }
    }
}
```

The primary function of this class is to register routes for your area. Depending on your requirements, you can edit this file and create additional routes to meet the needs of your application. The one provided by the template creates a default route for your area that is similar to the default route for the root of your application.

In the Global.asax (see Listing 7-42), the AreaRegistration.RegisterAllAreas(), which is included as part of all the Visual Studio ASP.NET MVC templates, is called. This method uses reflection to discover all the classes in your application that derive from the AreaRegistration class and then executes their RegisterArea methods.

Listing 7-42. Area Registration Inside Global.asax

```
protected void Application_Start()
{
    AreaRegistration.RegisterAllAreas();

    WebApiConfig.Register(GlobalConfiguration.Configuration);
    FilterConfig.RegisterGlobalFilters(GlobalFilters.Filters);
    RouteConfig.RegisterRoutes(RouteTable.Routes);
    BundleConfig.RegisterBundles(BundleTable.Bundles);
    AuthConfig.RegisterAuth();
}
```

One important thing to note about Listing 7-42 is the order in which the methods are called. Since AreaRegistration.RegisterAllAreas is called before RouteConfig.RegisterRoutes, the routes registered in AreaRegistration.RegisterAllAreas will appear first in the routing table. Because the routing engine will return the first match found in the routing table, it is possible that routes defined in the RouteConfig class may be overridden.

In cases where you have more than one area, RegisterAllAreas will call the RegisterArea method for each in alphabetical order. In this example, area registration is called in the following order: Administration, Collaboration, Help, and Music. This is helpful to know in situations where you need to debug a page routing issue.

Adding Home Controllers to Each Area

According to the problem statement for this recipe, one of the driving forces to using Areas was the ability to have multiple HomeControllers. From a C# perspective, this can be accomplished by putting the HomeControllers in separate namespaces. But even with separate namespaces, ASP.NET MVC will have issues resolving the routes to the correct types. Areas help us solve this problem.

To add a HomeController to your Administrators Area, right-click the Controllers folder of your Administrators Area, select Add, and then select Controller. In the Add Controller window, name the controller **HomeController**, and under Scaffolding options, select the Empty MVC Controller template. Click Add to create the controller. A new class file named HomeController.cs will be added to the Controllers directory. It will include a class named HomeController that is derived from System.Web.Mvc.Controller. It will contain a single method called Index.

Repeat this process for the other areas.

Adding Index Views for Each Area

We now need to create views to match each of the HomeControllers in each of our areas. To do this, starting in the Administration area, right-click the Views folder, select Add, and then select New Folder. Name the new folder **Home**.

Right-click the Home folder, select Add, and then select View. In the Add View window, name the view **Index** and keep rest of the default settings. Click Add to create the view.

Repeat this process for the remainder of the areas.

At this point, you should be able to debug the application. To do this, press the F5 key. After a few moments, a browser window will open and display your site.

Unfortunately, rather than seeing your beautiful masterpiece of HTML and CSS, you are faced with the ASP.NET error page. The error message is displayed in Listing 7-43.

Listing 7-43. Error Message on the Root Web Page

```
[InvalidOperationException: Multiple types were found that match the controller named 'Home'. This
can happen if the route that services this request ('{controller}/{action}/{id}') does not specify
namespaces to search for a controller that matches the request. If this is the case, register this
route by calling an overload of the 'MapRoute' method that takes a 'namespaces' parameter.

The request for 'Home' has found the following matching controllers:
Ch7.R9.Areas.Administration.Controllers.HomeController
Ch7.R9.Areas.Collaboration.Controllers.HomeController
Ch7.R9.Areas.Help.Controllers.HomeController
Ch7.R9.Areas.Music.Controllers.HomeController
Ch7.R9.Controllers.HomeController
```

ASP.NET is complaining that it found multiple controllers that match the given route and it does not know which one to use. Rather than potentially giving us the wrong controller, it throws an error. Luckily, it also tells us how to correct the problem.

Modifying the Default Route to Allow Multiple Home Controllers

To correct the error shown in Listing 7-43, we need to modify the default route defined in the App_Start\RouteConfig.cs so that the route specifies the route name as well as the name of the controller. We will do this by adding a value using the namespaces: named parameter, as shown in Listing 7-44.

Listing 7-44. Modifications Made to the Default Route

```
public class RouteConfig
    {
        public static void RegisterRoutes(RouteCollection routes)
        {
            routes.IgnoreRoute("{resource}.axd/{*pathInfo}");

            routes.MapRoute(
                name: "Default",
                url: "{controller}/{action}/{id}",
                defaults: new { controller = "Home", action = "Index", id = UrlParameter.Optional },
                namespaces: new[] { "Ch7.R9.Controllers" }
            );
        }
    }
```

After making the change, press the F5 key to start debugging the application. This time, we see our home page. Now try the following URLs for your areas:

- http://localhost:<port>/Administration/Home

- http://localhost:<port>/Collaboration/Home

- http://localhost:<port>/Help/Home

- http://localhost:<port>/Music/Home

All the URLs should work. You will probably notice, however, that they are not using the layout page. This is because the Views directory in each of the areas is missing the _ViewStart.cshtml file. This file defines the default layout page for all the views within the local Views folder. If you wish to have all the Views in all of your areas use the same layout page as the parent site, you will need to copy the _ViewStart.cshtml file to all the Views directories for each area.

First, if you have not done so, close the browser window to stop debugging. Visual Studio does not allow you to add new files to the project while in debug mode. Next, copy the _ViewStart.cshtml file. To do this, right-click the _ViewStart.cshtml file in the parent site's Views directory, and then select Copy. Finally, right-click the Views folder in each of the areas, and then select Paste.

If you press F5 and then browse to all the areas, you will see that all the pages are now using the layout page.

Modifying the Navigation in the Layout Page to Include Links to the Areas

Our new site is almost ready. The last step is to modify the web site's primary navigation to include links to our new areas. To do this, open Views\Shared_Layout.cshtml. Around the middle of the page, you will find a set of three action links. Add three new links to this section so that it looks like Listing 7-45.

Listing 7-45. Modifying _Layout.cshtml to Include Link to the Home Controller Index Actions in the Areas

```
<header>
 <div class="content-wrapper">
  <div class="float-left">
    <p class="site-title">
@Html.ActionLink("your logo here", "Index", "Home", new { area = "" },null)
    </p>
   </div>
```

271

```
  <div class="float-right">
    <section id="login">
       @Html.Partial("_LoginPartial")
    </section>
    <nav>
      <ul id="menu">
        <li>@Html.ActionLink("Home", "Index", "Home", new { area = "" },null)</li>
        <li>@Html.ActionLink("Collaboration", "Index", "Home", new { area = "Collaboration"
},null)</li>
        <li>@Html.ActionLink("Music", "Index", "Home", new { area = "Music" },null)</li>
        <li>@Html.ActionLink("Contact", "Contact", "Home", new { area = "" },null)</li>
        <li>@Html.ActionLink("About", "About", "Home", new { area = "" },null)</li>
        <li>@Html.ActionLink("Help", "Index", "Home", new { area = "Help" },null)</li>
      </ul>
    </nav>
  </div>
  </div>
</header>
```

Notice that all the links in Listing 7-45 have been modified to include the additional parameters for the additional route values. This overload of the ActionLink method also takes a parameter for HTML attributes that is set to null.

In each case, we pass in a new anonymous type with a property called area. To create links for the controller on the main site, we set the area property to an empty string; otherwise, we specify the name of the area.

7-10. Disabling Automatic Table Creation with the Simple Membership Provider

Problem

The ASP.NET MVC 4 Internet application template uses the Simple Membership Provider with its Account controller. By default, the first time you run your project and access functionality powered by the provider, all the database objects are created for you. Unfortunately for you, your company's security policy prohibits service accounts used by web applications to have create-table rights on the database. You need to disable automatic table creation and provide your DBA with scripts to generate the required schema.

Solution

The Simple Membership Provider was designed to make things easier for the developer. With the default settings enabled, the developer does not need to worry about installing database schemas and can even configure a completely custom user-table without writing a single line of SQL. However, in cases where you cannot allow the web site service account to create new database tables, you will need to manually create the schema.

To script the schema, you can first run your project in a nonproduction environment with the permissions necessary to generate the required objects. You can then use the SQL Server Management studio to generate SQL Scripts for the tables.

How It Works

The Simple Membership Provider is configured with the Internet Application template by default. It has been set up to create the required database on the first use. When the membership provider is initialized, it creates four tables that are required for the membership provider. In addition, the Internet Application template also creates a table called UserProfile. The template also includes a UserProfile class that is defined in the Models\AccountModels.cs file and set up to use the Entity Framework.

The UserProfile class and its Entity Framework companion are shown in Listing 7-46.

Listing 7-46. The UserProfile Class from AccountModels.cs

```
public class UsersContext : DbContext
    {
        public UsersContext()
            : base("DefaultConnection")
        {
        }

        public DbSet<UserProfile> UserProfiles { get; set; }
    }

[Table("UserProfile")]
    public class UserProfile
    {
        [Key]
        [DatabaseGeneratedAttribute(DatabaseGeneratedOption.Identity)]
        public int UserId { get; set; }
        public string UserName { get; set; }
    }
```

The UserProfile class has two fields: UserId and UserName. The class is decorated with a Table attribute, which designates it as a persistent class and maps it to a database table named UserProfile. The UserId field is decorated with two attributes: the Key attribute and the DatabaseGeneratedAttribute. The attributes tell the Entity Framework that the UserId field is a primary key that is also an Identity column. Identity columns are special fields in SQL Server tables that are automatically populated with an integer that increments for each new record.

Also defined in the AccountModel.cs file is the UserContext class. UserContext derives from DbContext. It contains a single property called UserProfiles, which is a DbSet bound to the UserProfile class.

DbContext is an essential part of the Entity Framework. It combines the unit-of-work and repository patterns, allows you to track changes made to a set of objects, and then save the changes to a database. The UserContext class manages instances of the UserProfile class. It is used in the Account controller to load and save changes to the UserProfile table in the database configured in the DefaultConnection. DefaultConnection is a connection string defined in the Web.config that by default is configured to use SQL Server LocalDB and stores its data in an .mdb file in the project's App_Data folder.

One key feature that differentiates the SimpleMembershipProvider from the legacy SQLServerMembershipProvider is its ability to use a custom user table. It allows you to use any table in the same database used by the Simple Membership Provider. It also allows you to customize that table however you like. For example, if you want expand on the data captured for the user profiles, you can modify the table in the database and then add the corresponding fields to the UserProfile class. You can also use another table entirely. You do not need to name the table **UserProfile**. In fact, the only requirement is that the table contains a column for the UserId, which must be an integer, and UserName, which should be a varchar. By default, the UserName field is defined as a nvarchar(56). Use of this data type is not compulsory but is probably a good idea, especially if you would like to allow the use of Unicode characters such as letters from the Chinese alphabet in your usernames.

The names of the user table, the primary key field, and the username field can be customized using the WebSecurity.InitializeDatabaseConnection method. In the Internet Application template, this is called in the InitializeSimpleMembershipAttribute action filter. This is an action filter that is applied to the Account controller ([InitializeSimpleMembership]). It ensures that the membership provider has been initialized, and by default will create the required database tables if they do not exist. Listing 7-47 shows the call to the `WebSecurity.InitializeDatabaseConnection` in the `Filters\InitializeSimpleMembershipAttribute.cs` file.

Listing 7-47. Initializing the Simple Membership Provider

```
[AttributeUsage(AttributeTargets.Class | AttributeTargets.Method, AllowMultiple = false,
Inherited = true)]
    public sealed class InitializeSimpleMembershipAttribute : ActionFilterAttribute
    {
        private static SimpleMembershipInitializer _initializer;
        private static object _initializerLock = new object();
        private static bool _isInitialized;

        public override void OnActionExecuting(ActionExecutingContext filterContext)
        {
            // Ensure ASP.NET Simple Membership is initialized only once per app start
            LazyInitializer.EnsureInitialized(ref _initializer, ref _isInitialized, ref
_initializerLock);
        }

        private class SimpleMembershipInitializer
        {
            public SimpleMembershipInitializer()
            {
                Database.SetInitializer<UsersContext>(null);

                try
                {
                    using (var context = new UsersContext())
                    {
                        if (!context.Database.Exists())
                        {
                            // Create the SimpleMembership database without Entity Framework
                            migration schema
                            ((IObjectContextAdapter)context).ObjectContext.CreateDatabase();
                        }
                    }

                    WebSecurity.InitializeDatabaseConnection("DefaultConnection", "UserProfile",
"UserId", "UserName", autoCreateTables: true);
                }
                catch (Exception ex)
                {
                    throw new InvalidOperationException("The ASP.NET Simple Membership
database could not be initialized. For more information, please see
http://go.microsoft.com/fwlink/?LinkId=256588", ex);
                }
            }
        }
    }
```

InitializeSimpleMembershipAttribute extends ActionFilterAttribute. Action filters allow you to inject code into the ASP.NET MVC page execution life cycle. InitializeSimpleMembershipAttribute implements an OnActionExecuting method. When a controller class is decorated with the InitializeSimpleMembershipAttribute, the code inside OnActionExecute will run each time an action method in that controller is called. Since this has been added to the Account controller, calling any of its actions will execute the code.

Inside OnActionExecuting, a call is made to LazyInitializer.EnsureInitialized. This method checks to see if the method class passed in its Target parameter has been initialized. It ensures that the code in the SimpleMembershipInitializer class is executed only once per application lifecycle.

The SimpleMembershipInitializer class performs the bulk of the work. It calls Database.SetInitialzer on the UserContext class. This sets a database initialization strategy for UserContext. Since null is passed for its strategy parameter the default strategy CreateDatabaseIfNotExist is used. At this point, a strategy has been set but nothing has been created.

Next, inside a try/catch block an instance of the UserContext class is created and context.Database.Exists() is called to verify the existence of the database. If the database does not exist, it will be created at this point. This only creates the database. It does not add the schema. Since they are not catching any specific exception, any error thrown is caught and then rethrown as an InvalidOperationException. Common causes for errors at this point can be permissions issues or configuration problems in the Web.config file.

Finally, the WebSecurity.InitializeDatabaseConnection is called. This method creates the schema for the Simple Membership Provider if it does not exist, and will create the table specified in the userTableName parameter. If this table already exists, it will not modify it. If it does not exist, it will create a new table with the name specified and it will add two columns to the table using the column names specified in the userIdColumn and the userNameColumn parameters.

■ **Note** WebSecurity.InitializeDatabaseConnection does not use the UserProfile class defined in the AccountModels.cs files when creating the schema. Modifying UserProfile will in no way change the definition of the tables created when the Simple Membership Provider is initialized. It only creates the user id and username using the values specified. If you need to change the definition of the user profile table, you must either do so manually or use the NuGet data migration functionality described in Recipe 7-6.

The WebSecurity.InitializeDatabaseConnection method takes five parameters. The parameters are explained in Table 7-3.

Table 7-3. The WebSecurity.InitializeDatabaseConnection Parameters Explained

Parameter Name	Data Type	Description
connectionString	String	The name of the connection string that will be used for the membership provider.
userTableName	String	The name of the database table that contains your user profile information. The Internet Application template uses UserProfile, but you can use any table you wish.
userIdColumn	String	The name of the column that is used as the primary key. This column must be an int data type. Using UniqueIdentifier with the legacy SQL Server provider is not supported.
useNameColumn	String	The name of the username column. The column can be any string data type, such as varchar or nvarchar.
autocreateTables	bool	If set to true, allows the required database tables to be created. It does not create the database. The database must exist, otherwise the method call will fail.

Modifying the InitializeSimpleMembershipAttribute So That It No Longer Creates or Modifies the Database

Theoretically, if the objects required by the Simple Membership Provider exist, the code as it is will not modify the database.

If you still feel the need or are required by a security mandate to remove any code that can potentially create or modify your database schema, you can do so my modifying the InitializeSimpleMembershipAttribute so that it looks like Listing 7-48.

Listing 7-48. SimpleMembershipInitializer Modified So That It Will No Longer Create or Modify Your Database

```
private class SimpleMembershipInitializer
    {
        public SimpleMembershipInitializer()
        {

            try
            {
                WebSecurity.InitializeDatabaseConnection("DefaultConnection", "UserProfile",
                "UserId", "UserName", autoCreateTables: false);
            }
            catch (Exception ex)
            {
                throw new InvalidOperationException("The ASP.NET Simple Membership
database could not be initialized. For more information, please see
http://go.microsoft.com/fwlink/?LinkId=256588", ex);
            }
        }
    }
```

In Listing 7-48, the code that verifies the existence of the database, and creates it if it does not exist, has been removed completely. The WebSecurity.InitializeDatabaseConnection method call has been modified so that it no longer creates the tables if they do not exist. It will still verify the existence of the tables and throw an InvalidOperationException if the tables are not found.

Manually Creating the Schema

Since the schema will no longer be created for you automatically, you will need to create it yourself. Luckily, the schema is very simple. It consists of four tables in addition to the table that you define to store the user profile information. Figure 7-7 shows the schema generated using the default settings in the ASP.NET MVC Internet Application template.

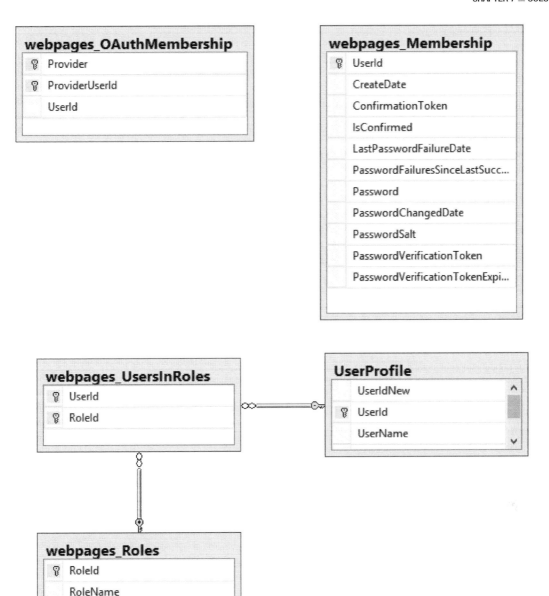

Figure 7-7. *The ASP.NET Webpages Simple Membership Provider schema*

As you can see, the schema really is as simple as advertised. All the tables that are normally generated by the provider's initialization code are prefixed with webpages_. Referential integrity constraints are provided for the user profile and roles tables, but omitted for the membership tables.

webpages_OAuthMembership

The webpages_OAuthMembership table keeps track of your user's affiliations with third-party membership providers. It contains three columns that track the provider name, the user's id from the provider, and the user's id from the UserProfile table. Listing 7-49 shows the database script required to create this table.

Listing 7-49. webpages_OAuthMembership CREATE TABLE Script

```
CREATE TABLE webpages_OAuthMembership
(Provider nvarchar(30) NOT NULL,
ProviderUserId nvarchar(100) NOT NULL,
UserId int NOT NULL,
PRIMARY KEY (Provider, ProviderUserId))
```

webpages_Membership

The webpages_Membership table contains all the information that allows a user to log in to the web site with the exception of the login name, which is stored in the user profile table. It stores a hashed version of the password, a password salt, and the number of columns that contain validation tokens for use in resetting the password and verifying a user account. An implementation has been added to the Internet Application template for performing password reset, but no implementation has been provided for account confirmation. Listing 7-50 shows the CREATE TABLE script for webpages_Membership.

Listing 7-50. webpages_Membership CREATE TABLE Script

```
CREATE TABLE [dbo].[webpages_Membership]
(
        [UserId] [int] NOT NULL  PRIMARY KEY,
        [CreateDate] [datetime] NULL,
        [ConfirmationToken] [nvarchar](128) NULL,
        [IsConfirmed] [bit] NULL DEFAULT 0,
        [LastPasswordFailureDate] [datetime] NULL,
        [PasswordFailuresSinceLastSuccess] [int] NOT NULL DEFAULT 0,
        [Password] [nvarchar](128) NOT NULL,
        [PasswordChangedDate] [datetime] NULL,
        [PasswordSalt] [nvarchar](128) NOT NULL,
        [PasswordVerificationToken] [nvarchar](128) NULL,
        [PasswordVerificationTokenExpirationDate] [datetime] NULL,
)
```

webpages_Roles

The webpages_Roles table is a simple table that tracks the names of roles and uses an Identity column for its primary key. The CREATE TABLE script for webpages_Roles is shown in Listing 7-51.

Listing 7-51. webpages_Roles CREATE TABLE Script

```
CREATE TABLE webpages_Roles
(
  RoleId  int NOT NULL PRIMARY KEY IDENTITY,
  RoleName nvarchar(256)NOT NULL UNIQUE
)
```

webpages_UserInRoles

The webpages_UserInRoles table creates a relationship between a user defined in your user profile table and your defined security roles. This relationship is used by the Simple Membership Provider to enforce authorization rules in combination with the Authorization attributes that can be applied to controller and actions. The table consists of two columns that are foreign keys to the user profile table and the roles table. The CREATE TABLE script is shown in Listing 7-52.

Listing 7-52. webpages_UsersInRoles Create Table Script

```
CREATE TABLE webpages_UsersInRoles (
                    UserId                              int             NOT NULL,
                    RoleId                              int             NOT NULL,
                    PRIMARY KEY (UserId, RoleId),
                    CONSTRAINT fk_UserId FOREIGN KEY (UserId) REFERENCES [UserProfile]
([UserId]),
                    CONSTRAINT fk_RoleId FOREIGN KEY (RoleId) REFERENCES webpages_Roles(RoleId) )
```

By using the CREATE TABLE scripts provided in this section, you can easily create the needed schema without requiring your application to have CREATE TABLE permissions in production.

Not shown here is the UserProfile table. This table has been omitted because for most applications it will need to be customized for your application. Note that if you use a table name or id column that differs from the implementation provided in the Internet Application template, you will need to modify the code in Listing 7-52 to reflect the correct table and column names in the foreign key constraint definitions.

CHAPTER 8

■ ■ ■

Asynchronous Programming with ASP.NET MVC

8-1. Using Async Actions

Problem

You have an application that is responsive most of the time but occasionally runs slow and sometimes freezes up entirely. After doing some analysis, you discover a correlation between your application's slowdowns and the performance of a remote web service that is called by one of your controllers. What seems strange is that even though the remote web service is only used by one part of your application, your entire application is effected by the slowdown. Using Internet Service Manager's active request report (see Recipe 8-7), you notice many requests stuck in the beginrequest state. You need to understand how to solve this issue.

Solution

The slow web service calls are blocking the threads in your application's worker process. If the threads are blocked for too long, new threads will need to be created in order to service incoming requests. There are limits to how many threads can be created and how fast the CLR thread pool can inject new ones. When these limits are exceeded, new requests are queued. If the queue size exceeds its limit or the number of concurrent executing requests exceeds the maximum allowed, IIS will begin rejecting new requests with a Service Unavailable (HTTP 503 code). The result of this is that your application will perform poorly and may eventually fail.

In cases where the blocking is caused by a high-latency remote call, it is sometimes possible to mitigate this issue by making the action method that calls the slow service asynchronous. In past versions of ASP.NET MVC, this was accomplished by creating controllers that derived from the AsyncController class. For ASP.NET MVC 4, Microsoft allows you to takes advantage of an easier method for performing asynchronous operations by creating awaitable action methods that use the async and await keywords.

How It Works

To convert a synchronous action method into an asynchronous one, you need to perform the following steps:

1. Modify your action method's declaration by adding the async keyword after the access modifier. The async keyword tells the C# compiler that this in an asynchronous method.

2. Change the method's return type to Task<T> where T is the type that you would like your method to return. For example, if you would like your action method to return a string, you would change it to use Task<string>.

3. Use the await keyword to call an asynchronous method. For .NET 4.5, many classes have been updated to include methods that use the Task-based asynchronous programming model introduced in .NET 4.0.

■ **Note** In most cases, Task-based asynchronous method names will have an Async suffix, such as in the HttpClient.GetStringAsync method. For classes such as WebClient, it may not be as straightforward. For example, WebClient already had a number of methods with Async suffixes that use the older asynchronous pattern. Since Microsoft did not want to break backward compatibility, they ended up creating new methods that implement the Task-based pattern. For example, WebClient has three versions of the DownloadData method. It has a synchronous version named DownloadData, DownloadDataAsync for the callback-based asynchronous pattern, and DownloadDataTaskAsync for the Task-based asynchronous version.

Listing 8-1 shows a normal Web API action method. It returns a PlaylistModel object for the given id or null if the id supplied is outside the expected range. For this example, let's imagine that the PlaylistRepository connects to a very slow back-end server that takes an average of 5 seconds to return a result. Since the Get action is synchronous, its thread will be blocked until the GetAllPlaylists method returns.

Listing 8-1. Synchronous Action Method

```
// GET api/playlist/5
public  PlaylistModel Get(int id)
{
  List<PlaylistModel> list = PlaylistRepository.GetAllPlaylists();

  if (id < list.Count)
  {
    return list[id];
  }
  else
  {
    return null;
   }
}
```

Listing 8-2 shows the same method converted to an asynchronous version. The results of the method are the same as the synchronous version, as is the perceived response time. From the perspective of the end user consuming this service from a web browser, nothing has changed. One important thing to understand is that if the GetAllPlaylistAsync method takes 5 seconds to execute, the Get action will not move to the next line until GetAllPlaylistAsync has completed. The difference is that the asynchronous version does not block the thread while waiting for the GetAllPlaylistAsync method to return as it does in the synchronous version. This allows IIS to use this thread to perform other work while it is waiting.

Listing 8-2. *Asynchronous Version of Action Method Shown in Listing 8-1*

```
public async Task<PlaylistModel> Get(int id)
{
        List<PlaylistModel> list = await  PlaylistRepository.GetAllPlaylistsAsync();

        if (id < list.Count)
        {
            return list[id];
        }
        else
        {
            return null;
        }
}
```

In Listing 8-2, the first change is to add the async keyword after the public access modifier. The return type is then changed from List<PlaylistModel> to Task<List<PlaylistModel>>. The last step is to remove the call to PlaylistRepository.GetAllPaylists and replace it with a call to the async version of the method PlaylistRepository.GetAllPlaylistsAsync.

One thing you should keep in mind is that even though the code seems simple, it is only simple because the C# compiler is writing the complex code for you. There are significant differences between the CLR intermediate language code generated for Listings 8-1 and 8-2. This difference comes with the price of a slight performance penalty that, depending on your application, may be amplified when your application is under load. For this reason, you should not make all of your code asynchronous but rather apply this technique where the performance cost is offset by the benefit of using nonblocking IO calls.

In general, if your application is performing well using synchronous methods, do not change it. On the other hand, if you do discover performance issues similar to the one described in this recipe's problem statement, you can experiment with this technique. Whether or not this technique will pay dividends for you depends on your application.

If you would like to get a deeper understanding of what is happening inside the C# compiler when you use the async and await keywords, I recommend reading Recipes 8-5 and 8-6.

8-2. Running Several Asynchronous Calls in Parallel Inside an Action Method

Problem

You have an action method in your controller that need to pull data from several remote servers. You need to make five calls in all with each taking around 1 second each. As a result your page takes an average of 5 seconds to respond which does not meet your performance requirements. You would like to run these tasks in parallel so that your page can render faster.

Solution

To solve this problem you fire any number of asynchronous operations and save each result as a Task. You can then await each Task simultaneously using the Task.WhenAll method.

How It Works

The Task.WhenAll method takes either an array of Task objects or an IEnumerable of Task as a parameter and will return an array when all the Tasks have completed. The array return type will match the type that the tasks encapsulate. The example in Listing 8-3 shows the three separate web service calls being sent in parallel.

Listing 8-3. Using Web Client to Download Three Web Pages in Parallel

```
public async Task<ActionResult> CallThreeServicesAsync()
{
    Task<string> t1, t2, t3;

    using (WebClient webClient = new WebClient())
    {
        Uri uri1 = new Uri(string.Format(webserviceURL, 1));
        t1 = webClient.DownloadStringTaskAsync(uri1);
    }
    using (WebClient webClient = new WebClient())
    {
        Uri uri2 = new Uri(string.Format(webserviceURL, 2));
        t2 = webClient.DownloadStringTaskAsync(uri2);
    }
    using (WebClient webClient = new WebClient())
    {
        Uri uri3 = new Uri(string.Format(webserviceURL, 3));
        t3 = webClient.DownloadStringTaskAsync(uri3);
    }

    string[] results = await Task.WhenAll(new Task<string>[] { t1, t2, t3 });
    ViewBag.Results = results;

    return View();
}
```

The first thing you need to do in order to use any Task-based asynchronous calls in your action method is to mark the method as asynchronous using the async keyword. Next, you need to change the return type of the action from ActionResult to Task<ActionResult>.

For this example, we make three web service calls asynchronously using the WebClient.DownloadStringTaskAsync method. This method takes a URL as a parameter and returns a Task<String>. In the Task-based API, you designate the return type for the Task by specifying it as the generic type. In this example, we are using the string type since we will be retrieving a JSON-encoded string and printing it in our view. The code for the view is available in the book's code samples, which can be downloaded from the book's web site.

Notice that each download Task has its own WebClient rather than having a single instance making all the calls. This is required since a single WebClient does not support concurrent I/O operations. If you try and use a single WebClient object, you will get the following error message:

```
[InvalidOperationException: An asynchronous module or handler completed while an asynchronous
operation was still pending.]
```

Another important thing to notice is that you need to use the DownloadStringTaskAsync method rather than DownloadStringAsync. The latter is used for the asynchronous programming pattern introduced in .NET 3.5. It requires that a separate callback method be created.

At this point, we have not yet executed any calls to the web service. We have only provided instructions that describe what work we want to perform and what type of data we are expecting in return.

In order to execute the series of DownloadStringTaskAsync, we then call Task.WhenAll, passing it a new array initialized with the three Task objects that were declared earlier. This method will complete when all the asynchronous methods have finished and returns an array of strings, since an array of Task<string> was used.

Listing 8-4 shows a bit more complex example where rather than passing in a fixed set of Task objects, a List of Task<byte[]> is created and then populated in the body of a loop. In each loop iteration, a resource is downloaded using the WebClient DownloadDataTaskAsync method. DownloadDataTaskAsync is similar to the DownloadStringTaskAsync method in that it takes a URL as a parameter and returns the contents of the page. The difference is that rather than returning a string, it returns the data as an array of bytes. You would use this in cases where you need to download binary data such as an image or a music file. Finally, WhenAll is called with the IEnumerable passed as a parameter. The WhenAll method call returns a two-dimensional byte array.

Listing 8-4. Using WhenAll with an IEnumerible

```
public async Task<ActionResult> CallTenServicesAsync()
{
    List<Task<byte[]>> dataTasks = new List<Task<byte[]>>();

    for (int i = 0; i < 10; i++)
    {
        using (WebClient webClient = new WebClient())
        {
            Uri uri = new Uri(string.Format(webserviceURL, i));
            dataTasks.Add(webClient.DownloadDataTaskAsync(uri));
        }
    }

    byte[][] allBytes = await Task.WhenAll(dataTasks);

    ViewBag.totalLength = allBytes.Sum(w => w.Length);

    return View();
}
```

Looking at Listings 8-3 and 8-4, you have probably noticed that all the Tasks passed to Task.WhenAll are of the same type. This is a requirement. If you attempt to pass in mixed types, the code will not compile. This is somewhat inconvenient. Since you are calling out to several services, it is likely that they will have different return types.

There are a few strategies that you can use to get around this. The first would be like in Listing 8-3, where the code is calling a RESTful web service and receiving the results as a JSON-encoded string. After the I/O operations are complete, you can then use a JSON serializer such as the one in Newtonsoft.Json to convert the JSON text into C# objects. Another strategy would be use an IEnumerable<Task> rather than a Task of a certain return type. In this case, you will not be able to pass the results of the await operation directly into an array, as in Listings 8-3 and 8-4. You will instead need to cast the results for each operation as shown in Listing 8-5.

Listing 8-5. Using Task.WhenAll with Tasks with Different Return Types

```
public async Task<ActionResult> GetPhotoAndComments()
{
    List<Task> tasks = new List<Task>();
```

```
using (WebClient webClient = new WebClient())
{
    Uri uri1 = new Uri(PhotoCommentServiceURL);
    tasks.Add(webClient.DownloadStringTaskAsync(uri1));
}

using (WebClient webClient = new WebClient())
{
    Uri uri2 = new Uri(DynamicImgServiceUrl);
    tasks.Add(webClient.DownloadDataTaskAsync(uri2));
}
await Task.WhenAll(tasks);

ViewBag.PhotoComments = ((Task<string>)tasks[0]).Result;
string imageBase64 = Convert.ToBase64String(((Task<byte[]>)tasks[1]).Result);
string imageSrc = string.Format("data:image/jpeg;base64,{0}", imageBase64);
ViewBag.Photo = imageSrc;

return View();
}
```

In Listing 8-5, we are awaiting two Tasks. The first will call a web service to retrieve a list of comments about a photo and will return a string. The second call will retrieve image data and has the return type of a byte array. After the await call, the results of each operation is written to the Result property of each task. An explicit cast is used to write the results to the ViewBag.

The image data is then converted to a Base64 encoded string so that it can be used as a data URI in the src attribute of an image element in the view.

8-3. Consuming WCF Service from an MVC 4 Project
Problem

You application requires that you consume WCF service from a third-party application that you are integrating with. You need to create a proxy for this service so that you can call it from inside your controller.

Solution

To consume a WCF service from your project, first add a service reference to the project and then evoke the service using the generated proxy class.

How It Works

Even though WCF services are no longer the cool new thing, there are many cases where you will still need to create and consume them, such as when you are interacting with systems that do not support RESTful interfaces or are interacting with systems that require advanced web service techniques such as cross-service transactions based on the WS-Transactions specification.

When you add a service reference to your project, Visual Studio will automatically update your project's `Web.config` with a service model configuration section that includes information such as the service's address and message format. It will also generate a proxy class that you can use in your code in order to call the service.

Setting up Your Service

The technique for consuming a WCF service is somewhat straightforward.

1. Open your project in Visual Studio, right-click the References node inside Solution Explorer, and select Add Service Reference.

2. Enter the URL of the service into the Address text box. It should in a format similar to `https://serviceurl/services/myservice.svc`.

3. Click the Go button. A list of services will appear in the Services box. If more than one service is listed, select the one you want.

4. In the Namespace text box, enter the namespace you would like to use for the generated proxy class.

5. Click the "Advanced" button. Notice that "Allow generation of asynchronous operations" and "Generate task-based operations" are selected by default. This allows you to use the new Task-based asynchronous programming model introduced in .NET 4.0. If you do not intend to call the web service asynchronously, you should uncheck this box since it would shrink the size of the proxy classes that are generated.

6. If you are consuming a service from another MVC 4 project, uncheck the "Reuse types in referenced assemblies". If you leave this checked, the reference to `Newtonsoft.Json` will cause an error to occur and your proxy class will not be generated.

7. Click OK to close the advanced dialog box, and then click OK again to create the service reference. After a few moments, the service reference will be added to your project.

8. You can now access the service, as shown in Listings 8-6 and 8-7.

Calling the WCF Service Asynchronously

Listing 8-6 shows how to call the service using the synchronous method. Listing 8-7 shows an asynchronous example.

Listing 8-6. Calling a WCF Service from a Controller

```
using Ch8.R4.ServiceReference1;

//other using statements removed for brevity

public ActionResult CallWCFService()
{
    PlaylistServiceClient client = new PlaylistServiceClient();
    PlaylistModel[] playlistArray = client.GetAllPlayLists();
    return View(playlistArray);
}
```

Listing 8-7. Calling a WCF Service from a Controller Using Task-Based Asynchronous Methods

```
public async Task<ActionResult> CallWCFServiceAsync()
{
    PlaylistServiceClient client = new PlaylistServiceClient();
    PlaylistModel[] playlistArray = await client.GetAllPlayListsAsync();
    return View(playlistArray);
}
```

In the CallWCFService action, we first create a new instance of the proxy class, PlaylistServiceClient. This is the class that Visual Studio generated for our WCF service when it was added as a service reference. We then call GetAllPlayLists(), which makes a synchronous call to the WCF service and returns an array of PlaylistModel objects. The PlaylistModel was also generated by Visual Studio when the service reference was created. All the information needed to generate the class is made available from the service metadata. The service metadata is formatted according to the Web Service Definition Language (WSDL) standard.

The code excerpts in Listing 8-6 and Listing 8-7 are very similar. The differences between them are emphasized with bold text. First, the async keyword is added to the method signature and the return type has been encapsulated inside a Task. This Task is used as a state machine that keeps track of the status of an asynchronous call.

Inside the CallWCFServiceAsync action, the GetAllPlayLists call has been replaced with its asynchronous equivalent. The await keyword has been placed between the assignment operator and the web service call. The await keyword marks the spot where execution will resume when the web service call completes.

From the perspective of the end user, there is no change in behavior between the code in Listings 8-6 and 8-7. There is still only one request and one response. If the web service takes 5 seconds to complete, the end user will still need to wait at least 5 seconds for a response. The benefit of using the async version is that rather than blocking the thread, it releases it and allows it to perform other work while we are waiting for the results from the service.

Making Several WCF Calls in Parallel Using Task.WaitAll

Listing 8-8 shows several asynchronous WCF calls performed in parallel using Task.WhenAll.

Listing 8-8. Using Task.WhenAll with WCF Services

```
public async Task<ActionResult> CallWCFWithWaitAll()
{
  PlaylistServiceClient client = new PlaylistServiceClient();
  Task<PlaylistModel> task1 = client.GetPlayListAsync(1);
  Task<PlaylistModel> task2 = client.GetPlayListAsync(2);
  Task<PlaylistModel> task3 = client.GetPlayListAsync(3);
  PlaylistModel[] playlistArray =
    await Task.WhenAll(new Task<PlaylistModel>[] { task1, task2, task3 });
        return View(playlistArray);
  }
```

Modifying the WCF Configuration in Web.config

In a many cases, the default WCF client configuration that is created by Visual Studio can meet your needs, but there are many scenarios where adjustments may need to be made. When you add a service reference, Visual Studio assumes that you want to use the least complex and most compatible binding—the basicHttpBinding. This binding is very similar in behavior and capabilities to classic ASMX web services.

Listing 8-9 shows an example of some custom WCF settings in an application's Web.config file. In this example, we have changed two settings: we increased the maximum size of messages that can be received by that client and we are allowing our WCF client to accept cookies from that service. The rest of the sample configuration in Listing 8-9 is created by Visual Studio when the service reference is added.

Listing 8-9. Web.config File Changes for WCF Client Configuration

```
<system.serviceModel>
  <bindings>
    <basicHttpBinding>
      <binding name="BasicHttpBinding_IPlaylistService"
              maxReceivedMessageSize="2097152"
              allowCookies="true" />
    </basicHttpBinding>
  </bindings>
  <client>
    <endpoint address="http://localhost/WebAPIForLoadTest/WcfServices/PlaylistService.svc"
      binding="basicHttpBinding"
      bindingConfiguration="BasicHttpBinding_IPlaylistService"
      contract="ServiceReference1.IPlaylistService"
      name="BasicHttpBinding_IPlaylistService" />
  </client>
</system.serviceModel>
```

All WCF configuration is contained in the system.serviceModel configuration section. Starting with .NET 4.0, Microsoft simplified the configuration by moving many of the common settings for WCF to the system-level configuration files. This minimizes your responsibilities so that you only need to worry about the binding you want to use and what endpoint the service is assigned to.

In the binding section of the configuration, you can configure the settings for the basicHttpBinding, or if you wish, use an alternate binding such as wsHttpBinding, netMsmqBinding, or a custom binding. In this example, we have changed two settings:

- maxReceivedMessageSize: This setting restricts the size of the incoming messages in order to help prevent denial-of-service attacks. Its default value of 65,536 bytes is often too small to handle even modest result sets. This setting can be adjusted upward to as large as 2,147,483,647 bytes (2GB). It is recommended that this setting not be made any larger than needed. In Listing 8-9, it has been configured to accept up to 2MB.

- allowCookies: This setting is useful when working with ASMX web services that may be using cookies. To include this setting ensures that cookies sent from the remote server are sent along with each subsequent request to that service.

In WCF, a binding is a set of predefined communication aspects that you can apply to a particular end point. The basicHttpBinding, for example, specifies that the application will communicate over HTTP or HTTPS, and that it will use either Text or MTOM encoding. The NetMsmqBinding, on the other hand, supports the Microsoft Message Queuing Service (MSMQ) as a transport.

8-4. Boosting the Performance of Task-Based Asynchronous Communications Using Caching

Problem

You have implemented a service that needs to make many back-end service calls using the Task-based asynchronous programming style. You notice that, when under load, the server is using more memory and CPU than you had initially anticipated.

Solution

The Task objects that are used in the Task-based asynchronous pattern work like templates which, when compiled, generate relatively complex intermediate language code that includes a state machine for tracking the lifecycle of each task. For web applications with light loads and for typical client-side application development scenarios, the extra weight gained by using Tasks is insignificant. However, on a server application that is handling thousands of requests per minute, the number of these objects can become a burden by consuming memory and creating more work for the garbage collector.

In some cases, this problem can be mitigated by reusing a set of static Task objects that contain preset values. This reduces the number of objects that need to be created at runtime, which can improve the performance of your application. You can achieve further performance gains by caching the results of network operations, thus avoiding redundant requests for items already in the cache.

How It Works

In this example, I have created a web site that allows you to enter an IP address range and then tells you which IP addresses are available by using the System.Net.NetworkInformation.Ping class. This is a bit of a contrived example since it's hard to imagine such a service being used under high-volume conditions, but it serves the purpose of demonstrating this technique.

To create this example, start by opening Visual Studio and creating a new ASP.NET MVC 4 web application using the Basic template with the Razor view engine. Once the project has been created, perform the following steps:

1. Right-click the Models folder and select Add Class. Name the new class **IpScannerModel** and modify it to look like Listing 8-10.

2. Right-click the Views folder and select Add New Folder. Name the folder **Home**.

3. Right-click the Home folder that you have just created. Select Add View. Name the view **IpScanner**. Untick the layout page check box, make sure that the Razor view engine is selected, and then click Add. Modify the view to look like Listing 8-11.

4. Right-click the Controllers folder, click Add, and then click Controller. Name the controller **HomeController** and make sure Empty MVC Controller is selected. Click the Add button. Modify the controller to look like Listing 8-12.

■ **Caution**   One of the cardinal sins in software development is premature optimization—changes made to code to avoid potential performance problems that are yet to be experienced. In most cases, this is wasteful and it can even turn out to be harmful because you are adding unnecessary complexity (and perhaps even bugs) to your code. Techniques like those shown in this recipe should only be used to solve a specific issue after it has been identified.

The Model

The model in this example is a complex type that consists of an IpRange object that has two properties: a start IP address and an end IP address. It also consists of a List of String that should contain a list of IP addresses. The model is shown in Listing 8-10.

Listing 8-10. The IPScannerModel

```
using System.Collections.Generic;
using System.ComponentModel;
using System.ComponentModel.DataAnnotations;

namespace Ch8.R4.Models
{
    public class IPScannerModel
    {
        public IPRange RangeToScan
        {
            get;
            set;
        }

        private List<string> _IpList = null;
        public List<string> IpList
        {
            get
            {
                if (null==_IpList)
                {
                    _IpList = new List<string>();
                }
                return _IpList;
            }
            set
            {
                _IpList = value;
            }
        }
    }

    public class IPRange
    {
        [Required]
        [DisplayName("Start Address")]
        [RegularExpression(ipAddressRegEx,
         ErrorMessage = "Must be a valid IP Address.")]
        public string StartAddress
        {
            get;
            set;
        }
```

```
    [Required]
    [DisplayName("End Address")]
    [RegularExpression(ipAddressRegEx,
     ErrorMessage = "Must be a valid IP Address.")]
    public string EndAddress
    {
        get;
        set;
    }
    private const string ipAddressRegEx = @"^(25[0-5]|2[0-4][0-9]|[0-1]{1}[0-9]{2}|[1-9]{1}
[0-9]{1}|[1-9])\.(25[0-5]|2[0-4][0-9]|[0-1]{1}[0-9]{2}|[1-9]{1}[0-9]{1}|[1-9]|0)\.(25[0-5]|2[0-4]
[0-9]|[0-1]{1}[0-9]{2}|[1-9]{1}[0-9]{1}|[1-9]|0)\.(25[0-5]|2[0-4][0-9]|[0-1]{1}[0-9]{2}|[1-9]{1}
[0-9]{1}|[0-9])$";
    }

}
```

Notice that the IpRange class is using data annotation. These annotations are later used in the view in conjunction with HTML helper methods and jQuery Validation to provide client-side form validation.

For the sake of simplicity, we are using a regular expression to validate the IP addresses. A string constant is used to store the regular expression. This reduces the need to plug this unpleasant string inside the data annotation, which enhances readability. It also allows the string to be defined in one place, which increases maintainability.

The use of a regular expression is not the best way to validate an IP address. This particular expression still may allow invalid addresses to be entered. A better solution for this case would be a custom validator. An example of a custom validator is available in Recipe 10-5.

The View

The view consists of a form that allows you to enter the IP address range and click a button to initiate the scan. It is a strongly-typed view that uses the IPScannerModel. It also includes the jQuery validation script bundle so that it can take advantage of the data annotations in the model. It includes a few if statements that hide the available IP address list until the Scan IP Range button is clicked. If no results are found it will inform the user that no addresses are available in the range selected. The code for the IPScanner view is shown in Listing 8-11.

Listing 8-11. IPScanner.cshtml

```
@model Ch8.R4.Models.IPScannerModel
@{
    ViewBag.Title = "IP Address Scanner";
}


<h2>IP Address Scanner</h2>
Use this tool to show available IP Addresses in our lab.
@using (Html.BeginForm(new { ReturnUrl = ViewBag.ReturnUrl })) {
    @Html.ValidationSummary(false, "The start address and end address are required and both must
be valid IP Addresses.")
<fieldset>
    <legend>Enter an Ip Address Range to scan</legend>
    <ol>
       <li>
        @Html.LabelFor(a=> a.RangeToScan.StartAddress)
```

```
        @Html.TextBoxFor(a => a.RangeToScan.StartAddress)
        </li>
    <li>
        @Html.LabelFor(a=> a.RangeToScan.EndAddress)
@Html.TextBoxFor(a => a.RangeToScan.EndAddress)
    </li>
        </ol>
    <input type="submit" value="Scan IP Range" />
</fieldset>
}
@if ((Model!=null))
{
    if ((Model.IpList != null) && (Model.IpList.Count > 0)){
        <div>
            The following IP Addresses are availible
        </div>
<ul>
@foreach (var item in Model.IpList)
{
    <li>
        @item
    </li>
}
</ul>
    }
else{
        <div>
            No Ip Addresses are available in the range provided
        </div>
    }
}


@section Scripts {
    @Scripts.Render("~/bundles/jqueryval")
}
```

The view starts out with a model binding declaration. This binds the view to Ch8.R4.Models.IpScannerModel. Then we set the title ViewBag.Title to Ip Address Scanner. This is used by the Layout page to set the HTML title element for the page.

Next, we use the Html.BeginFrom helper to create the opening and closing HTML form elements and set the form action to ViewBag.Return URL. This is a value that is set automatically by the MVC Framework. It will contain the URL of the current controller action unless you overwrite this value in your controller. By default, this method will set the form's method attribute to "post". With this setting, when the Submit button is clicked, it will invoke the IpScanner action decorated with the [HttpPost] attribute in the HomeController.

The @Html.ValidationSummary helper is used to display validation errors on the page.

In the next few lines of code, we use the @Html.LabelForm and @Html.Textbox for methods to generate the form elements and associated attributes. Special attributes are automatically added to the rendered HTML, which can be used by the jQuery validation library. The final input for the form is a submit button with text that reads "Scan IP Range".

After the closing fieldset, we use a closing curly brace to close the form that we started with the BeginForm helper.

In addition to the form, this view is also used to display the results. To do this, we add a Razor control statement that checks for the existence of the model. If the model is null, it does not render any content. If the model has a value, it makes the assumption that the model contains a valid IpList and then renders it as an unordered list.

Finally, we include the jQuery validation script bundle. This will generate the script references for all the JavaScript files needed to the jQuery Validation library, which is used for client-side form validation.

The Controller

The controller is made up of two Actions. One is for the GET operation that simply returns the view without performing any processing. The second is for the POST operation that takes the IP range and uses it to generate a list of IP addresses. It then checks to see if each address is in use by using the functionality in System.Net.NetworkInformation.Ping class. It uses a combination of asynchronous communication and caching to dramatically decrease the processing time. The HomeController's IpScanner Action is shown in Listing 8-12.

Listing 8-12. HomeController Class IpScanner HTTPPost Action

```
...
using System.Net.NetworkInformation;
...
[HttpPost]
public async Task<ActionResult> IPScanner(IPScannerModel model)
{
 if (ModelState.IsValid)
 {
    model.IpList = generateListFromRange(model.RangeToScan);
    List<Task<PingReply>> taskList = new List<Task<PingReply>>();
    Dictionary<string, Task<PingReply>> cache = getDictionaryFromCache();
    foreach (var item in model.IpList)
    {
      Task<PingReply> reply;
      if (!areResultsInCache(item, cache, out reply))
      {
        Ping pingSender = new Ping();
        reply = pingSender.SendPingAsync(item);
        cache.Add(item, reply);
      }
      taskList.Add(reply);
    }
    HttpContext.Cache.Insert("CachedPingReply",
                             cache,
                             null,
                             DateTime.UtcNow.AddMinutes(10),
                             TimeSpan.Zero);

    PingReply[] results = await Task.WhenAll(taskList);
    model.IpList = updateStatus(model.IpList, results);
    }
```

```
    else
    {
        ModelState.AddModelError("", "Please enter a valid IP Address range.");
    }
    return View(model);
}
```

When the form is submitted, the action shown in Listing 8-12 will process. The first operation performed verifies that the data in the model is valid. This is a backup mechanism to prevent the form from being processed if the client-side validation is bypassed, such as in cases where the user has disabled JavaScript.

Like the JavaScript validation, the server-side validation is based on the data annotations that have been applied to the model. The ModelState.IsValid property is calculated automatically by the framework using the data annotations. There is no additional code that you need to write.

Next, we use the generateListFromRange local helper method to attempt to generate a list of IP addresses from the data in the model's RangeToScan property. The RangeToScan property contains an instance of an IpRange class. The model's RangeToScan property should be filled with data from the form because its two text boxes were bound to the model's RangeToScan.StartAddress and RangeToScan.EndAddress properties.

Next, we begin the preparation for a series of asynchronous network operations by creating a list of Task objects that will track the state of each ping operation and then return a PingReply object if the operation completes successfully.

We also grab a list of previously executed tasks from the cache. These are stored in a Dictionary, which uses the IP address as the key and a Task of PingResult as the value.

We then loop through the list of IP addresses and prepare the System.Net.NetworkInformation.Ping class to send Internet Control Message Protocol (ICMP) echo-request packages to each host. At this point, we are not executing the Ping operations but rather defining the tasks we want to execute.

Rather than creating a new Task object for each operation, we check to see if we have one in the cache. Each time the tool is run, it will cache the resulting Task objects. This reduces the overall number of Task objects that need to be created and destroyed. We do this by using another local helper method, areResultsInCache, which will return true if the item exists, and then provide the cached copy as an output parameter. If it returns false, we prepare an asynchronous ping operation and assign a new Task object to track its status. We also add the new Task object to the cache for use in potential future operations.

After we exit the for loop, we then update the cache so that it includes any new IP addresses that may have been added.

The Cache.Insert method used here allows us to add or update values placed in the cache. The cache itself is a specialized collection type that is created for each application domain.

The Cache.Insert method has several variations. The first parameter in the version used in this example is the name for the object. This can be any string. The next parameter is the object you wish to insert. In this case, we are inserting a Dictionary object that contains key/values for our IP address results. The third parameter is for a CacheDependency object, which is a file or cache key that is monitored by the caching system. If a change is detected on the specified dependency, the object will be automatically removed from the cache. Since we are not using a dependency in this example, we simply pass in null. The next two parameters specify how long the item should remain in the cache before it is deleted. For our example, we want to use an absolute time of ten minutes. Passing TimeSpan.Zero for the sliding expiration parameter indicates that we want the object to be deleted in ten minutes regardless of the last time the item was accessed.

Finally, after all the asynchronous operations have been prepared, we use the Task.WhenAll method to send the ICMP packets to each host. We use the await keyword to mark the place where execution will resume once all the tasks in taskList have been completed.

Once the awaited tasks have been completed, the results are stored into an array of PingReply objects. We process this information to see which results had successful replies by using the updateStatus local helper method. The updateStatus method will return a list of string objects for each of the IP addresses that could not be reached by the ping requests.

We then pass this list to the model and return the ViewResult with an updated model.

In this example, we have broken the controller logic into several subroutines. This was done to make the code easier to read and maintain. The first of these private methods is shown in Listing 8-13.

Listing 8-13. HomeController generateListFromRange Helper

```
private List<string> generateListFromRange(IpRange iPRange)
{
  if (iPRange != null)
  {

    string ipTemplate =
      string.Concat
      (
       iPRange.StartAddress.Substring(0,(iPRange.StartAddress.LastIndexOf(".")+1)), "{0}"
      );

    int start, end;
    start =
      Convert.ToInt32
      (
       iPRange.StartAddress.Substring( (iPRange.StartAddress.LastIndexOf(".")+1))
      );

   end =
     Convert.ToInt32
     (
      iPRange.EndAddress.Substring((iPRange.EndAddress.LastIndexOf(".")+1))
     );

 List<string> ipp = new List<string>();
 for (int i = start; i <= end; i++)
 {
     ipp.Add(string.Format(ipTemplate, i));
 }
 return ipp;
}
return null;
}
```

The generateListFromRange private method, shown in Listing 8-13, takes an IpRange object as a parameter. It verifies that the object is not null and then does some string manipulation to create a template for the IP address range based on the first three octets of the StartAddress property. For example, if the start address were 192.168.1.1, the template would be 192.168.1.{0}.

If you are an astute developer, you probably can find a number of issues with the assumptions made in this code, but keep in mind this has been purposely simplified for the sake of this example. To make this code production-ready, at the very least you would need to add some additional validation logic to ensure that the start address and end address shared the same three octets.

Moving on, we declare two integer variables called start and end. We then use the Convert.ToInt32 method in conjunction with the String.Substring method to convert the last octet of each IP address in the IpRange variable into an integer.

We then use a for loop to create a string for each of the possible IP addresses between the start and end addresses.

When the loop completes, the list is returned.

The second helper method used in the IPScanner action is areResultsInCache, which is shown in Listing 8-14. This method takes an IpAddressProperties object and compares it to objects held in the cache. If it finds a match, it will return true and then return the matching object as an output parameter.

Listing 8-14. HomeController areResultsInCache Helper Method

```
private bool areResultsInCache(string item,
                               Dictionary<string, Task<PingReply>> cache,
                               out Task<PingReply> reply)
{
  if (cache != null)
  {
    return cache.TryGetValue(item, out reply);
  }
  else
  {
    reply = null;
    return false;
  }
}
```

In Listing 8-14, we check to see if the Dictionary object passed in the cache parameter is null. If the cache is null, then we return false and set the output parameter to null.

If the cache does exist, we use its TryGetValue method to pull the object from the collection. If the item exists, the method returns true and the matching object is assigned to the output parameter. If it is not found, the method returns false and the output parameter is set to null.

Another private helper method used in the IPScanner action is getDictionaryFromCache, shown in Listing 8-15. This method checks for the existence of the "CachedPingReply" Dictionary in the cache, and then creates it if it does not exist. It then returns the Dictionary.

Listing 8-15. The getDictionaryFromCache Helper

```
private Dictionary<string, Task<PingReply>> getDictionaryFromCache()
{
  Dictionary<string, Task<PingReply>> cache;
  if (HttpContext.Cache["CachedPingReply"] != null)
  {
    cache = (Dictionary<string, Task<PingReply>>)HttpContext.Cache["CachedPingReply"];
  }
  else
  {
    cache = new Dictionary<string, Task<PingReply>>();
  }
  return cache;
}
```

The last helper method used in the IPScanner action is updateStatus, shown in Listing 8-16. This method is used to filter out the IP addresses that have replied to our ping request. Since the goal of our IPScanner action is to determine which IP addresses are available, we don't care about the one address that did respond but rather the ones that did not.

Listing 8-16. HomeController updateStatus Helper Method

```
private List<string> updateStatus(List<string> list, PingReply[] results)
{
  foreach (var item in results)
  {
    if (item.Status == IPStatus.Success)
    {
      list.RemoveAll(s => s == item.Address.ToString());
    }
  }
 return list;
}
```

Now that the application has been built, you can try it out. First, try a small IP range such as 192.168.1.1 to 192.168.1.10. Note how long it takes for the page to return. On the first run, it should take between 10 and 15 seconds. On the next try, the results are almost instant. This is because the results were cached and it no longer needed to make the ping requests. Try it again with a larger number of requests, say 192.168.1.1 to 192.168.1.100. Notice that it will take a little longer than the first attempt but the increase in time is not expediential. This is because it is executing the requests asynchronously.

8-5. Using IL Disassembler to See Code Generated by the C# Compiler
Problem

You have started using the new .NET asynchronous programming pattern and love its relative simplicity compared to other programming models. However, you would like to have a better understanding of the code generated by the compiler so that you can improve the designs of your asynchronous methods.

Solution

There are several tools available, including the .NET IL Disassembler tool, which is installed with the .NET Framework. It allows you to reverse engineer a compiled .NET assembly and browse the IL code. Some tools. such as ILSpy, .NET Reflector, and JetBrains dotPeek allow you to go a step further and actually generate C# code from the disassembled intermediate language code.

How It Works

When you build your .NET application, the compiler generates intermediate language (IL). This architecture provides developers with a choice of programming languages and allows the compiled code to run on any Windows machine that has the correct version of the common language runtime installed.

When the .NET assembly needs to be executed, the just-in-time (JIT) compiler will convert the IL into machine code. The machine code can then be executed.

To see this in action, you can use the .NET IL Disassembler tool. This is a tool that comes with the .NET Framework. It allows you to open a .NET assembly and view the compiler-generated intermediate language code in a human-readable format. Even though you would not want to edit this code directly, viewing it is an interesting exercise that can increase your understanding of both the C# compiler and the .NET Framework.

I have included a brief tutorial here to demonstrate the differences between the IL generated for an asynchronous method and a synchronous one.

1. Open Visual Studio and create a new MVC 4 Application using the empty template.

2. Add a new Web API controller by right-clicking the Controllers folder and selecting Add and the Controller.

3. In the Add Controller dialog box, name the controller **NormalController**. Select the Empty API Controller template and then click Add to create the file. We are using Web API since the code is less complex from an IL perspective.

4. Create a second Empty Web API controller using the method described in steps 2 and 3, but name this controller **AsyncController**.

5. Enter the code from Listing 8-17 into NormalController. Enter the code from Listing 8-18 into AsyncController. The two examples are functionally equivalent and return an integer with the value of 1.

Listing 8-17. NormalController.cs

```
public class NormalController : ApiController
{
 public int Get()
 {
    int i = 1;
    return i;
 }
}
```

Listing 8-18. AsyncController.cs

```
using System.Threading.Tasks;
...
public class AsyncController : ApiController
{
  public async Task<int> Get()
  {
    int i = await Task.FromResult<int>(1);
    return i;
  }
}
```

6. Build your project by pressing the F6 key on your keyboard or by selecting Build Solution from the Build menu.

7. Open the Developer Command Prompt. This is a special shortcut for the command window. It includes paths to all the .NET Framework tools.

8. In the command window type **ildasm**.

9. Once the IL Disassembler application opens, use the File menu to browse to your MVC application's BIN directory and select the assembly for your application. By default, this will be the name of your application.

10. Once opened, IL DASM will show you all the IL included in your assembly. If you expand the node for your assembly and then the Controllers node, you should see your two controllers.

11. Expand the nodes for your controllers as shown in Figure 8-1 and note how different they are. For the code generated from Listing 8-18, there will be a value class <Get>d_0. You can now expand this node and examine the inner workings of this class. Double-click the MoveNext method. This contains the bulk of the operations for the action method. Even if you are not an expert in IL, you should get some sense of the amount of overhead required when using asynchronous operations. Simply stated, it is not magic and it is not free.

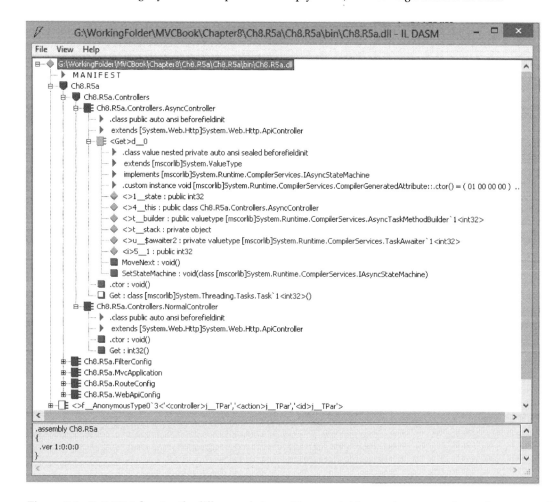

Figure 8-1. *IL DASM showing the differences between IL generated for synchronous and asynchronous methods*

Using JetBrains dotPeek

If you found the IL code difficult to understand, don't be too hard on yourself. IL was not necessarily meant to be read by humans—with the exception of the .NET Framework development team. To get a better understanding of what is going on, you can use tools such as ILSpy or dotPeek to do a complete reverse engineering of your code by converting the IL into C# code. This will show you the C# code you would have had to write if you did not use the new asynchronous framework.

In this example, we will use dotPeek, a free decompiler developed by JetBrains. JetBrains is best known for its .NET refactoring product ReSharper. The tool can be downloaded from the JetBrains web site (www.jetbrains.com/decompiler/).

Once the tool has been downloaded, you need to install it. You can then launch it by clicking its tile on the Start screen (or icon on the Start menu).

To get a better picture of the code that the C# compiler generates when using Task-based asynchronous programming with the async and await keywords, we will create a simple command-line application.

1. Open Visual Studio and select New Project from the start page.

2. In the New Project window, select Windows, and then Console Application.

3. Give the project a name and click OK.

4. Modify the code to match Listing 8-19, and then build the application.

Listing 8-19. The Wassup World Application

```
class Program
{
  static void Main(string[] args)
  {
   sayWassup();
  }
  private static void sayWassup()
  {
    Console.WriteLine("Wassup...... World");
   }
}
```

The code in Listing 8-19 is very simple. It contains one method named sayWassup, which is called inside the Main method. If you are not familiar with the term, "Wassup" is American for "Hello."

Now that you have built the project, you can reverse engineer it using dotPeek. Open JetBrains dotPeek, and then click Open from the dotPeek toolbar. Browse to the output folder for your project. There will be an .exe file located inside the debug\bin directory.

Select your application from the Assembly Explorer, and then click the "Show compiler-generated code" button on the toolbar. You should now see you're application in the main window. It will look something like Listing 8-20.

Listing 8-20. The Wassup World Application Reversed Engineered Using dotPeek

```
internal class Program
{
    public Program()
    {
      base.\u002Ector();
    }

    private static void Main(string[] args)
    {
      Program.sayWassup();
    }

    private static void sayWassup()
    {
      Console.WriteLine("Wassup...... World");
    }
}
```

Notice that other than being slightly more verbose by explicitly including the default constructor, Listing 8-20 is almost identical to Listing 8-19.

To understand the code generated by the C# compiler when we use the async keyword, we will now convert the Wassup method to include the asynchronous programming infrastructure. To do this, modify the method to look like Listing 8-21.

Listing 8-21. Async Wassup

```
class Program
{
  static void Main(string[] args)
  {
    sayWassup().Wait();
  }
  private async static Task sayWassup()
  {
    Console.WriteLine("Wassup...... World");
  }

}
```

We have added the async keyword to the sayWassup method and changed its return type from void to Task. Note that since there is no return type, you do not need to make the Task generic.

In the Main method, the Task.Wait() method is added to the sayWassup call. This is required; otherwise, the application will exit before the asynchronous task has a chance to complete.

Compile the program. Notice that you will get a compiler warning that informs you that since you did not add an await operator to your method, it will run synchronously. In other words, even though we have marked this method as async, its behavior will be unchanged.

Return to dotPeek and reload the assembly by clicking it again in the Assembly Explorer. Notice the changes. That the AsyncStateMachine attribute has been added to your sayWassup method, which associates it with a <sayWaasup>d__0 structure that implements the IAsyncStateMachine interface. The body of your method has been wrapped inside the IAsyncStateMachine.MoveNext() method of the structure—only it has been surrounded by a try/catch block and numerous calls to the AsyncTaskMethodBuilder that is in charge of maintaining the state of your task. The full dotPeek decompilation is shown in Listing 8-22.

Listing 8-22. The Async Version of Wassup World Reverse Engineered by dotPeek

```
// Type: CH7.R7_5.Program
// Assembly: CH7.R8-5, Version=1.0.0.0, Culture=neutral, PublicKeyToken=null
// Assembly location: G:\WorkingFolder\MVCBook\Chapter7\CH7.R8-5\CH7.R8-5\bin\Release\CH7.R8-5.exe

using System;
using System.Diagnostics;
using System.Runtime.CompilerServices;
using System.Runtime.InteropServices;
using System.Threading.Tasks;

namespace CH7.R7_5
{
  internal class Program
  {
```

```
    public Program()
    {
      base.\u002Ector();
    }

    private static void Main(string[] args)
    {
      Program.sayWassup().Wait();
    }

    [AsyncStateMachine(typeof (Program.\u003CsayWassup\u003Ed__0))]
    [DebuggerStepThrough]
    private static Task sayWassup()
    {
      Program.\u003CsayWassup\u003Ed__0 stateMachine;
      stateMachine.\u003C\u003Et__builder = AsyncTaskMethodBuilder.Create();
      stateMachine.\u003C\u003E1__state = -1;
      stateMachine.\u003C\u003Et__builder.Start<Program.\u003CsayWassup\u003Ed__0>(ref
stateMachine);
      return stateMachine.\u003C\u003Et__builder.Task;
    }

    [CompilerGenerated]
    [StructLayout(LayoutKind.Auto)]
    private struct \u003CsayWassup\u003Ed__0 : IAsyncStateMachine
    {
      public int \u003C\u003E1__state;
      public AsyncTaskMethodBuilder \u003C\u003Et__builder;

      void IAsyncStateMachine.MoveNext()
      {
        try
        {
          Console.WriteLine("Wassup...... World");
        }
        catch (Exception ex)
        {
          this.\u003C\u003E1__state = -2;
          this.\u003C\u003Et__builder.SetException(ex);
          return;
        }
        this.\u003C\u003E1__state = -2;
        this.\u003C\u003Et__builder.SetResult();
      }

      [DebuggerHidden]
      void IAsyncStateMachine.SetStateMachine(IAsyncStateMachine param0)
      {
        this.\u003C\u003Et__builder.SetStateMachine(param0);
      }
    }
  }
}
```

8-6. Understanding Threading in IIS

Problem

You would like to have a more detailed understanding of how ASP.NET manages its threads, and how this affects IIS's ability to respond to requests while under load. You would also like to understand how using asynchronous actions would affect your application's ability to scale.

Solution

The job of the web server is to listen for incoming requests, determine how to process those requests, and then fulfill the requests. IIS determines the number of requests it should try and process at one time based on the number of logical CPUs available on the box. By default, this value is set to 5000. On a virtual machine with two CPUs, this would allow 10,000 concurrent requests. If the number of requests exceeds the number that IIS can process at once, it will queue the requests. If the size of the queue exceeds its configured limit, IIS will begin rejecting new requests and respond with an HTTP 503 status code, which means that the server is too busy.

Using asynchronous actions in your ASP.NET applications can help in some situations, but in others, it may actually make things worse. Starting with ASP.NET 4.0, concurrency limits are based on the number of simultaneous requests rather than the number of threads. With this in mind, you should concentrate on making the duration of requests as short as possible. Using the async pattern can be helpful in this regard by being able to process several calls to back-end servers at once, which in some situations can lead to quicker overall response time. When under extreme load, however, since asynchronous calls require more overhead than synchronous ones, the overhead of garbage collecting the Task objects can make performance worse than if the workload was processed synchronously.

How It Works

Before diving into the threading model, it is essential to first understand Internet Information Servers architectural components at a deeper level. IIS has several core layers, which include protocol listeners, a Hypertext Transfer Protocol stack, the World Wide Web publishing service, and Windows Process Activation Service (WAS). All additional functionality is provided by way of modules.

HTTP.sys

Your web server's scalability is governed by several factors, including the amount of RAM, the number of CPUs and their power, disk I/O throughput, and network capacity. The operating system's primary job is to manage these resources. The intermediary between your application and the operating system is a kernel mode driver known as HTTP.sys.

As a kernel mode driver, HTTP.sys has unrestricted access to the hardware. It can execute any CPU instruction and access any memory address. Kernel mode drivers avoid the need to transition between user mode and kernel mode, which makes them very fast at performing certain types of tasks. The drawback of being a kernel mode driver is that if HTTP.sys crashes, the entire server will go down with it. Fortunately, Microsoft has invested in making HTTP.sys both stable and secure so that crashes caused by HTTP.sys are rare.

HTTP.sys has two main roles in the IIS architecture. First, it is the default protocol listener for the most common protocols used on the web: HTTP and HTTPS. As a protocol listener, HTTP.sys is responsible for handling protocol specific requests and then passing the requests to other IIS components for further processing. HTTP.sys also performs the role of a hypertext transfer protocol stack. In this role, HTTP.sys performs caching, queuing, pre-processing, and some low-level security filtering.

HTTP.sys functions as both an essential component of IIS and a core part of the Windows networking subsystem. For IIS, HTTP.sys provides the following functionality:

- *A protocol listener for the HTTP and HTTPS protocols*, which receives incoming requests and then passes them off to other IIS modules for processing.

- *Kernel-mode caching*, which allows it to respond to requests for cached resources without needing to switch to user mode. This allows IIS to respond to cached requests rapidly with minimal expenditure of system resources.

- *Kernel-mode request handling*, which allows HTTP.sys to forward a request to the correct worker process without requiring a context switch.

- *A kernel-mode queuing mechanism*, which responds when worker processes are too busy to accept new requests.

HTTP.sys makes IIS very efficient at handing requests for static resources. On the initial request for a static resource, HTTP.sys will need to grab the file from disk or from over a network if the server is using network-attached storage (NAS). This initial load of the file into memory is usually very fast but substantially slower than subsequent requests for the same static resource that is serviced direct from memory.

The bottleneck with static resources usually becomes the download of the resource to the client. To maximize the number of concurrent downloads, IIS uses an asynchronous I/O API called the Input/Output Completion Port (IOCP). IIS has a dedicated pool of threads for processing I/O and managing the IOCP queue. Starting with IIS 7 on Windows Server 2008, the IOCP was improved so that it reduced the number of context switches required. This change measurably improved scalability.

■ **Tip** Even with the improved I/O completion port handling in Windows Server 2008 and up, a large number of slow downloads can still take down even the largest server. To mitigate this effect, you should consider moving some static resources either to a dedicated web server role or to a content delivery network. When Microsoft is expecting a large number of downloads—such as when Windows 8 was made available to partners via TechNet and MSDN—they contract Akamai, which provides a global network of servers dedicated to serving static content.

The World Wide Web Publishing Service

The World Wide Web Publishing Service (W3SVC) is responsible for managing configuration for HTTP.sys and for sending notifications to the Windows Process Activation Service (WAS) when new requests are ready for processing. In earlier versions of IIS, W3SVC was also responsible for managing worker processes. Starting with IIS 7.0 on Windows Server 2008, this function was delegated to WAS.

Another important function of W3SVC is the collection of HTTP-specific performance counter data. This includes counters for the number of requests, the size of the queues, classic ASP, and more. Remember, if the service is down or not installed, you will not be able to collect performance data.

Windows Process Activation Service (WAS)

One of the biggest architectural changes introduced in IIS 7.0 was the delegation of worker process management to WAS. One of the main drivers in the development of WAS was the need to be able to process requests for non-HTTP protocol listeners inside IIS. The Windows Communication Foundation (WCF), which was introduced in .NET 3.0, provided a programming model that allowed service developers to use other protocols in addition to HTTP. This includes TCP, Named Pipes, and the Microsoft Message Queuing (MSMQ) service.

Before the WAS was introduced, using one of these communication channels required creating your own host service. While WCF gave you a few base classes to use as a starting point for your service, you could not benefit from features such as process health monitoring and rapid fail protection unless you provided this functionality yourself.

With IIS 7.0 and above, you can host your WCF components in IIS after installing the Windows Communication Foundation Non-HTTP Activation and Windows Process Activation Features.

WAS is made up of three main components:

- *The configuration manager*: Reads configuration information for web applications and application pools from the `applicationhost.config` file.

- *The process manager*: Manages mappings between application pools and worker processes. In cases where a worker process has not been started, the process manager will create a new one.

- *The unmanaged listener adaptor interface*: Provides an interface for non-HTTP protocol listeners to send activation requests to the WAS.

Modules

Outside of the core processing capabilities of HTTP.sys, W3SVC, and WAS, all other functionality in IIS is delivered by modules. This includes security, ISAPI support, GZIP compression, FastCGI, caching, and logging and diagnostics. Most importantly from the perspective of an ASP.NET MVC developer are the managed support modules that provide support for managed code to be executed in the IIS request pipeline.

This responsibility is split between two modules:

- ManagedEngine (`webengine.dll`): Primary integration point to managed code in the IIS pipeline.

- ConfigurationValidationEngine (`validcfg.dll`): Validates the configuration of module and handler declarations inside ASP.NET `Web.config` files when using an application pool running in Integrated mode.

This integration point is exploited to provide additional functionality via managed modules. The ASP.NET includes several out-of-the-box managed modules that provide features such as forms authentication, session support, and URL mapping. You may also create your own modules and handlers, which you can apply to not only your application but to other applications running on the server—including ones that are not running ASP.NET. In fact, *MSDN Magazine* has an article that demonstrates how you can create a PHP application that uses the ASP.NET Forms Authentication module (`http://msdn.microsoft.com/en-us/magazine/cc135973.aspx`). In addition, this same mechanism can also be applied to static files such as images, CSS style sheets, and PDFs.

■ **Note**   This functionality is only available in integrated pipeline mode. When in classic mode, only managed code such as ASP.NET pages will be processed by the modules. In addition, when using classic mode, processes such as authentication are performed twice on managed code. Each request is first authenticated by the IIS pipeline and then reauthenticated by the ASP.NET pipeline.

IIS Request Processing for ASP.NET

Now that you have a fundamental understanding of IIS, we can start looking at how this architecture impacts your application. The following list will walk you through the integrated processing pipeline and attempt to illustrate how the layers fit together. It will show that there are at least three thread switches for each request that requires processing by the ASP.NET engine. This includes a transition from HTTP.sys to ASP.NET and then to the Common Language Runtime (CLR).

1. On startup, HTTP.sys queries WAS for configuration data for the requested URL. The WAS configuration manager component reads the `applicationhost.config` information and gives it to W3SVC, which is the listener adapter for HTTP.sys. W3SVC then uses the information to configure HTTP.sys.

2. A user initiates a request for an ASP.NET page hosted on your server. The request is received by a protocol listener. Since this is an HTTP request, it is handled by HTTP.sys. HTTP.sys will post the request to an I/O completion port queue that WAS subscribes to. WAS uses a dedicated thread pool to process the queue. By default, this thread pool can use as many as 250 threads per available processing core and up to 1000 I/O completion threads.

3. If the worker process that the configuration data associates with the URL has not started, WAS will create a new instance of `w3wp.exe` to host the worker process.

4. Inside the worker process, ASP.NET checks to see how many requests are being processed. If this is above the default limit of 5000, the request will be placed inside a queue. If the queue size is above the limit of 1000, then the request will be rejected and a 503 error returned. You can monitor both of these values using the requests executing and requests queued performance counters. If the request is for a static file or can be handled from the cache, ASP.NET will complete the request and post the results on an IIS I/O completion port. For other requests, ASP.NET posts the request to the CLR thread pool.

5. The CLR will then execute the request. Your code is run here. As of ASP.NET 4.0, there is no longer a limit on the number of threads when running your application in IIS Integrated mode. The size of the thread pool is managed automatically. You can override this via configuration but it is not recommended. In IIS Integrated mode, ASP.NET is run as an IIS module. For classic mode, it is run as an ISAPI filter and is subject to the limitations of that model in an addition to a performance penalty created by compatibility layers.

6. When the CLR is done executing the requests, it posts the response to HTTP.sys, which then posts to an IIS I/O completion port.

7. The user receives the response.

The only place where you as a developer have control over how threads are processed is in step 7. Because of this, the use of asynchronous actions has only a limited real-world effect on scalability. In many cases, even though the CLR needs to create fewer threads to process your requests, which has a positive influence on performance, it also needs to allocate additional objects that it will eventually need to clean up via garbage collection. Garbage collection can be a very expensive process. The .NET garbage collection process will suspend all threads momentarily when it needs to run a generation 2 collection (GC2). Part of your job as a developer should be to reduce the number of objects created and ensure that they are quickly dereferenced. This is so that they can be cleaned up before being promoted to GC2.

When to Use Asynchronous Action Methods

There are two general use cases for using asynchronous actions in your application. The first is to help mitigate large spikes in traffic for services with high network latency and for sites with low to moderate traffic that need to make calls to multiple back-end services.

By far the most effective use of the asynchronous actions was when needing to make many back-end calls in parallel in a single action method under low to moderate load. Using this technique, if you have to make calls to three services that each take around 2 seconds to return, you can still have a response time of around 2 seconds. When compared to a synchronous version of the same method, the asynchronous one will perform much faster. However, when under heavy load, the additional processing and garbage collection overhead associated with the asynchronous methods can actually make the service perform worse than a synchronous version where the network calls are made one at a time.

The other example is in cases where you have a massive spike in traffic and your worker process is waiting on a slow backend. In theory, asynchronous actions should be helpful. With synchronous methods, you have a one-to-one ratio between concurrent requests and worker threads to process them. As your workload increases, the thread pool will need to increase to keep up with demand. The CLR has a built-in throttle that limits it to creating around two new threads every second. If you are getting three requests per second and it take 2 seconds to process each request—and most of that time is spent waiting on I/O, using an asynchronous action method may help you to handle the spike by freeing up existing threads rather than blocking them. If the heavy traffic is sustained, however, I/O completion ports with handles on your Task objects may cause many of your Task objects to be promoted to garbage collection level 2 (GC2). This condition can lead to a massive performance problem and even make the web application completely unresponsive.

Performance Testing Results

As part of the research performed for this chapter, I created a set of simple applications that used asynchronous action methods, and then I ran load tests against them. The results showed that you can have substantial benefits from using asynchronous controller actions, but only if you are in a situation where you have a back end with high latency and your machine has adequate resources.

The Code Being Tested

The purpose of the test was to prove the theory that you can gain scalability improvements by using asynchronous actions in situations when your application needs to communicate with a slow back-end service. If the theory was shown to be true, I also wanted to understand how many additional users could be supported per server.

The test included two new Visual Studio projects:

- A simple web application that called a back-end service

- A remote web service that included a five-second delay before returning a response

For the web application, I created a new ASP.NET MVC application using the Basic template and I added a `HomeController` with the following two actions:

- Index: Uses an asynchronous communication to call the back end

- Index2: Uses synchronous communication to call the back end

I set up the application so that I could configure the number of back-end calls made for each request. In many applications, you may need to make several calls to a back-end database or web service to render a single page. The code for the `HomeController` is shown in Listing 8-23.

Listing 8-23. HomeController for the Slow Web Application

```
public class HomeController : Controller
{
   private static string webserviceURL = ConfigurationManager.AppSettings["WebserviceUrl"];
   private  static int numberOfCalls =
           int.Parse(ConfigurationManager.AppSettings["NumberOfBackendCalls"]);

   public async Task<ActionResult> Index()
   {
     int size = 0;
     size = await CallWebServiceAsync();
     ViewBag.RequestSize = size;
     return View();
   }

   static async Task<int> CallWebServiceAsync()
    {
     int totalLength = 0;
     List<Task<byte[]>> dataTasks = new List<Task<byte[]>>();
     for (int i = 0; i < numberOfCalls; i++)
     {
        using (WebClient webClient = new WebClient())
        {
          Uri uri = new Uri(string.Format(webserviceURL, i));
          dataTasks.Add(webClient.DownloadDataTaskAsync(uri));
        }
     }
     byte[][] allBytes = await Task.WhenAll(dataTasks);
     foreach (byte[] ar in allBytes)
        totalLength = ar.Length;

    return totalLength;
   }

   public ActionResult Index2()
   {
     int size = 0;
     size = CallWebService();

     ViewBag.RequestSize = size;
     return View();
   }
   static int CallWebService()
   {
    int totalLength = 0;
    using (WebClient webClient = new WebClient())
    {
```

```
    for (int i = 0; i < numberOfCalls; i++)
    {
      Uri uri = new Uri(string.Format(webserviceURL, i));
      var data = webClient.DownloadData(uri);
      totalLength += data.Length;
    }
  }
  return totalLength;
 }

}
```

In the App Settings section of the Web.config file, the URL for the web service was set up with a placeholder for a numeric identifier. Depending on the parameter passed, you will get a different data set returned.

For the web service application, I started with the ASP.NET MVC Application Web API template. In order to make the test a little bit more realistic, I added a simple repository class that generated sample data to be returned by the web service, as shown in Listing 8-24. Two API controllers were then created with one using the asynchronous version and the other using the synchronous.

Listing 8-24. The Playlist Repository

```
public static class PlaylistRepository
    {
        public static async Task<List<PlaylistModel>> GetAllPlaylistsAsync()
        {
            await Task.Delay(5000);
            return _GetAllPlayLists();
        }

        public static List<PlaylistModel> GetAllPlayLists()
        {
            Thread.Sleep(5000);
            return _GetAllPlayLists();
        }

        private static List<PlaylistModel> _GetAllPlayLists()
        {
            List<PlaylistModel> pl = new List<PlaylistModel>();

            for (int i = 0; i < 50; i++)
            {
                PlaylistModel item = new PlaylistModel();
                item.PlayListName = string.Concat("Playlist ", i);
                for (int j = 0; j < 10; j++)
                {
                    SongModel song = new SongModel
                    {
                        AlbumName = "Test",
                        PublishedDate = DateTime.Now.AddYears(-i),
```

```
                SongArtist = new ArtistModel
                {
                    ArtistHomePageUrl = "http://apress.com",
                    ArtistName = string.Concat("Artist ", j, "-", i),
                    ArtistThumbnailImageUrl = string.Empty
                },
                SongOrder = j,
                Title = string.Concat("Song ", j, "-", i)
            };
            item.Songs.Add(song);
        }
        pl.Add(item);
    }
    return pl;
    }
}
```

The repository class shown in Listing 8-23 contained three methods:

- _GetAllPlaylists: A private method that generates a list of 50 PlaylistModel objects and returns them as a list.

- GetAllPlaylists: Uses Thread.Sleep to block the thread for 5 seconds, and then calls _GetAllPlaylists to return a list of playlists.

- GetAllPlaylists: Uses Task.Delay(5000) to suspend execution of the method for 5 seconds without blocking the thread. It then calls _GetAllPlaylists to return a list of playlists.

The API controllers each had a Get action that accepts an integer as a parameter. This will take a single item from the list generated from the repository.

Load Test Setup

The load test was created using Visual Studio Ultimate edition. It consisted of two scenarios. One scenario browsed the synchronous page from the ASP.NET web application and the other called the asynchronous one.

The ASP.NET MVC web site and the Web API application were deployed to two different virtual machines running Windows Server 2012 deployed on two separate physical computers. For the initial test, both virtual machines were given 2 CPU and 2GB of RAM. The load generator was hosted on a separate machine with 2 CPU and 4GB of RAM.

A diagram that shows the lab configuration for the test is shown in Figure 8-2.

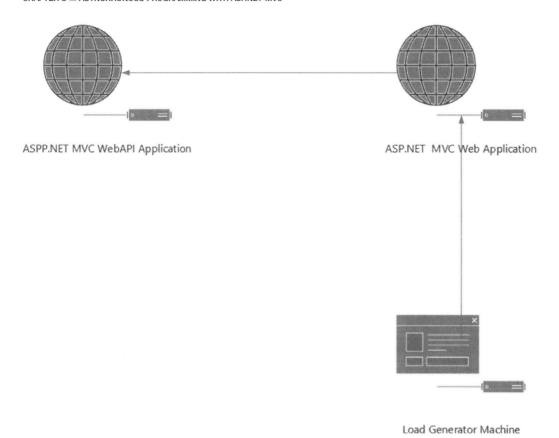

ASPP.NET MVC WebAPI Application

ASP.NET MVC Web Application

Load Generator Machine

Figure 8-2. *Load test configuration*

Testing Results for the Web Application

After running the first round of testing, it was found that when the web application was configured to make a single back-end call per request, the synchronous version was around 5 percent faster overall and that both tests maxed out at around 200 virtual users before response times jumped from 5 seconds (expected because of the artificial latency) all the way up to around 45 seconds and more. CPU usage on the MVC web application machine was very high.

Next, I added another two CPUs to the ASP.NET MVC web application virtual machine and added performance counters to watch for paging. Again, similar results were recorded, but this time the synchronous version won by a greater margin. This was likely caused by the fact that since the CPU count had been increased from two to four, the number of requests that could be processed concurrently had doubled. Since there is a one-to-one ratio between threads and requests in the synchronous version, and the CLR has a built-in throttle on the number of new threads it can create, this resulted in some built-in throttling that slowed the application's rate for processing new requests.

In the asynchronous version, since the threads are not blocked, existing threads can be used to process new requests. Because of this, IIS takes on a much greater workload and does much less queuing. This leads to additional pressure on system resources—especially memory. The system was essentially out of resources and so ground to a halt.

I then bumped the memory on the web server up to 8GB of RAM. With this configuration, I did see a positive result when using the asynchronous version of the controller. CPU was still very high but it was around 3 percent lower than in the previous test; the response times on the asynchronous version were much better.

Figures 8-3 and 8-4 show the comparative response times between the two tests.

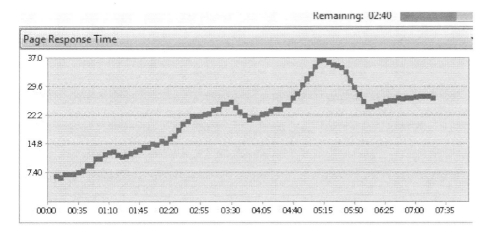

Figure 8-3. *Page response times for the synchronous action with a slow back end*

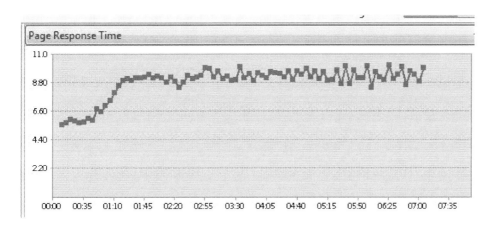

Figure 8-4. *Page response times for asynchronous action with a slow back end*

The chart shown in Figure 8-3 shows the response times in seconds for the web application when using the synchronous version of the action. For the first 3 minutes of the test, load is ramped up from 10 users to 250 users with 10 new users added every 10 seconds. Response times peaked at 37 seconds, with the majority of the requests taking around 24 seconds.

The ASP.NET Requests Queued counter averaged at around 150 requests queued. CPU usage on the web server was around 50 percent throughout the test.

The chart in Figure 8-4 shows the results for the asynchronous action. In this test, even with the ramp-up period compressed to about 1 minute, the server was able to keep pace and only added 2 seconds of additional latency to the response. Unlike the synchronous version, response times were somewhat uniform, with the majority of the responses taking around 9 seconds. The ASP.NET Requests Queued counter was less than 10 for the majority of the tests, but the percentage of time, and GC, and number of generation 2 collections was much higher. The CPU utilization was very high throughout the test, with an average utilization rate of over 90 percent. The CPU statistics are shown in Figure 8-5.

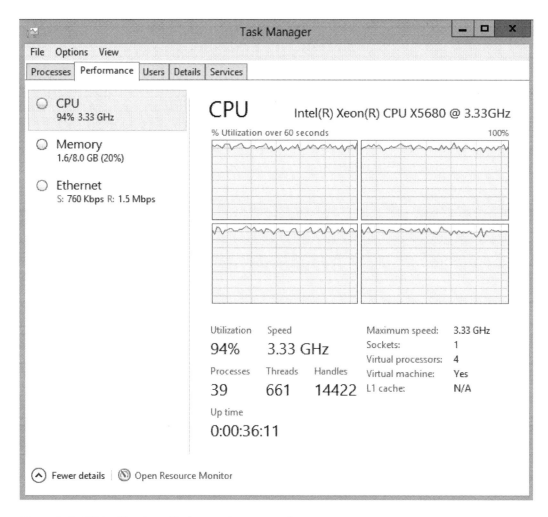

Figure 8-5. *CPU utilization with the asynchronous action*

When using the asynchronous actions, threads spend less time being blocked and more time working. This will lead to both higher throughput and very high CPU utilization.

Results for the Web API Application

The web application used for the load test was set up to send one or more requests to the Web API application. The number of back-end requests sent was determined by a configurable parameter in the Web.config file. For the first set of tests, this was configured to have a 1:1 ratio between requests and back-end calls. For this test, the Web API did a good job of keeping pace and had almost no performance problems. When this value was changed to that, ten back-end calls were made for each request. The synchronous version of the Web API controller became unresponsive, with CPU near 100 percent and most requests stuck in the Begin Request phase of the pipeline.

After making an adjustment to the Web API application so that only the asynchronous version was used, not only was it able to withstand the load, it did so with very low CPU utilization. At peak, it was processing over 2500 current requests and seemed as if it could handle much more.

In contrast to the web server, which had 4 CPU and 8GB of RAM, the server for the Web API only had 2 CPU and 1GB of RAM.

Why was the benefit of using asynchronous actions much more dramatic for the Web API application as opposed to the MVC?

After running a test about 15 times and reviewing the performance counter data, it seemed that the garbage collector was to blame. I saw a very poor ratio between Gen1 and Gen2 garbage collection and a large number of allocations. I also saw correlations between % Time in GC and CPU spikes. I did not see the same issues occurring on the Web API application.

The reason that the Web API application did not see the same problem is because its delays were induced artificially using `Task.Delay`. It had huge number of allocations, but since nothing was referencing them, they were cleaned up in generation 0 garbage collection sweeps. This was not the case for the MVC application since its delays were caused by a real service call and not a `Task.Delay`. When you make an actual network call, a lot is going on behind the scenes. `Task.Delay` does no real work.

Lessons Learned

There are three main lessons learned from this exercise:

1. Asynchronous actions are slower and more resource-intensive than normal actions in most scenarios.

2. In cases where your action is accessing a high-latency back end, using asynchronous actions can have a substantial benefit—but only if you have enough system resources to offset their higher resource consumption.

3. `Task.Delay` is not useful for testing the effectiveness of using asynchronous actions to improve scalability for systems that need to make calls to slow back-end services.

The .NET Task-based asynchronous programming API is a powerful tool that has made a once difficult programming style easy to use for almost all levels of developers. To be successful using it, it is helpful to understand how it works behind the scenes and what the limitations are. You should still use the synchronous programming style for most of your code and reserve the .NET Task-based asynchronous programming for when you know that there will be a measurable benefit. If you are expecting a heavy load, be sure to use a load-testing tool to verify that you are getting the results you expect. Modify your infrastructure to compensate for your scalability limitations.

8-7. Using Internet Information Services (IIS) Request Monitoring and Tracing

Problem

You have been tasked with troubleshooting intermittent issues on your company's web server. You have been using the Windows Application event logs, the IIS logs, and have been watching performance counters, but you still feel like you are missing something. You wish you had a real-time window into what was happening on your server.

Solution

A number of add-ons are available for Internet Information Services Manager that will allow you to see real-time activity for an IIS worker process. Among these is the IIS Request Monitor tool. It allows you to see details about the requests that are currently being executed and can give you insight into which pages are being accessed when the application is experiencing poor performance.

How It Works

The IIS Request Monitoring is an optional component that is not part of the default installation of the IIS Management tools. If the add-ons were not included in your server build, you will need to consult with your server administrator to get them installed.

If you have administrative access to your server, they can be installed by using the Web Platform Installer.

Installing IIS Request Monitoring

You can install the Request Monitoring tool either by using the Web Platform installer or by adding it as a role service when installing the Web Server Role on Windows Server.

To install the IIS Request Monitoring and Tracing tools, launch the Web Platform Installer by pressing the Windows key on your keyboard and then typing **Web Platform**. The Web Platform Installer should appear on the Start menu (or Start screen if you are running Windows Server 2012 or Windows 8). Click the Web Platform Installer icon to launch it.

After Web Platform Installer is done loading, click inside the search box, and type **IIS:**, and then press Enter. The Web Platform Installer will display a list of available extensions for IIS.

Scroll down the list until you see IIS:Tracing. If the component has not yet been installed, an Add button will appear on the right side of the screen. Click the Add button. The text on the Add button will change to "Remove".

Scroll down the list until you see IIS:Request Monitor. If it is not already installed, click its Add button.

Click the Install button on the bottom of the Window and then click the I Accept button if prompted. Web Platform Installer should promptly begin the installation process.

When the process has completed, click the Finish button. You can then click the Exit button to close the Web Platform Installer.

Using the Request Monitoring Tool

Once the Request Monitoring Tool has been installed, it can be accessed from inside the IIS Manager. To access it, open the IIS Manager and click the server node in the Connections pane.

Locate the icon labeled Worker Processes in the center panel under the IIS category, as shown in Figure 8-6. Note that this icon only appears when you click the server node. It will not be available if Sites or any of its child nodes are selected.

Figure 8-6. *Locating the Worker Processes icon in IIS Manager*

Double-click the Worker Processes icon. This will bring you to the Worker Processes screen. This screen shows a report of all the worker processes on the server that are currently active. It lists the Application Pool Name, its process id, its running state, the percentage of CPU time allocated to the process, the amount of memory allocated to the process, and how much of that memory is currently in use.

This screen is useful when you are having performance problems on a server that hosts several web applications. It should allow you to see which app pools are consuming the most system resources.

The Worker Processes screen is shown in Figure 8-7. It shows a server with only one active worker process, which is common for servers that are dedicated for a single application. In this screenshot, the process is not consuming many resources.

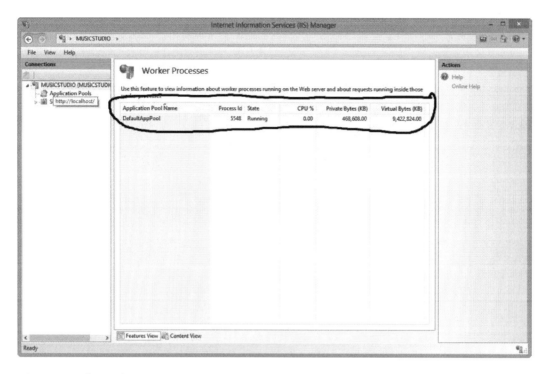

Figure 8-7. *The Worker Processes screen in IIS Manager*

If you double-click the worker process or click it once and then click View Current Requests from the Actions panel, you will navigate to the Requests page. This page will display all the requests for the current process that have been running for more than 1 second. Requests that have been running for less than a second are not displayed. Do not be alarmed if you view this page and do not see any data. If you are not seeing data, the most likely cause is that your application is running smoothly with all the requests completing in less than a second.

Figure 8-8 shows the Requests screen on a server with ten concurrent requests that have been executing for more than 1 second. Looking at the monitor, I can see that someone from the IP Address 192.168.1.7 has been sending multiple requests to the same URL over and over. I can also see that the request is in the ExecuteRequestHandler pipeline module state in the ManagedPipelineModule. This indicates that code is being executed by .NET code on my page.

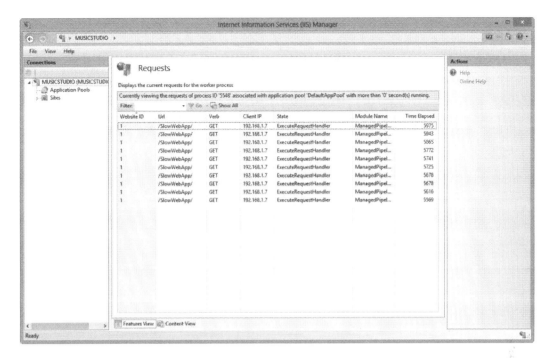

Figure 8-8. *The Requests screen in IIS Manager*

In Figure 8-8, I can also see that most of the requests have been executing for more than 5 seconds. Since I know from the Worker Processes screen that no CPU time has been allocated to this worker process, something must blocking the page, such as a slow back-end request.

This is great information. I now know which page is causing the problem and that something is blocking in the .NET code on that page. I now know exactly where to look for the next phase of troubleshooting.

In Recipe 8-1, we have a problem statement in which we use this tool to identify that many requests are stuck in the BeginRequest state. This was an indication that IIS was executing its maximum number of requests and was beginning to queue new requests. We know this because the BeginRequest state is the first event to occur during the processing of a request. At this point, the request is being created by the server and it is unlikely that any code we have written would be blocking.

You can confirm this assumption by using Performance Monitor to examine the ASP.NET Requests in the Native Queue performance counter. If the assumption is correct, you should get a similar number of items in the Request Monitor with a BeginRequest state as you did in the performance counter.

You would then look to see which requests are executing and which state they are stuck in. For example, if you see a large number of requests in the AuthenticateRequest state, it could be an indication of an issue with your authentication subsystem.

When you see many requests in the ExecuteRequestHandler state for the ManagedPipelineModule, then it is likely that the problem exists in your code. If you see mostly the same page in this step, then you can narrow your focus on that page. In cases where you see many different pages in this state, it could be a general resource constraint that is causing your problem. Many times the answer is that you need to scale out your infrastructure rather than modify your code.

CHAPTER 9

Test-Driven Development with ASP.NET MVC 4

9-1. Using Testing to Improve the Quality of Your ASP.NET MVC Application

Problem

You are part of an organization that does not follow a formal strategy for testing your applications. In most cases, testing is performed by a developer clicking through the completed application and verifying that it works as expected. In some cases, you may have a dedicated QA that does this basic click-through testing for you.

Unfortunately, you have found that this strategy fails on several levels. First of all, it relies on a completely manual process that is very time-consuming and may only cover a small percentage of your application's code. This process leaves many potential bugs to be discovered by your end users. Second, in most cases, you are finding problems late in the development cycle, which makes them more difficult and expensive to diagnose, correct, and deploy. Finally, this strategy significantly increases the risk and complexity of implementing subsequent releases because of the requirement for an end-to-end manual regression testing.

Solution

The cost of bugs that make their way into production code is difficult to measure. This is especially true if a bug (or a combination of them) results in lost customers and decreased sales. While it may not be possible to prevent all defects from reaching production, you can significantly improve the quality of your application by implementing a comprehensive quality control strategy. This strategy should consist of unit tests, static code analysis, peer code reviews, integration tests, and performance tests, topped off with manual testing and a customer feedback program.

How It Works

Successful quality assurance (QA) strategies should focus on finding the problems in your application as early in the development process as possible. Some even argue that QA should begin in the requirements gathering phase, where poorly thought through and even contradictory requirements can be corrected or eliminated before making their way to the architects canvas. The architect and technical lead are the next line of defense. They should run each of the use cases defined in the requirements documentation through their design, and ensure that the design can meet the needs of the application. They are also responsible for ensuring that the application is designed in such a way that it can be easily tested.

Assuming that the business analysts, architects, and technical leads have done their jobs properly, most of the responsibility for application quality falls squarely on the shoulders of the developers. The developer is responsible for writing quality code that meets the standards of the organization, writing unit tests that cover as much of the code as possible, and alerting the technical lead to possible flaws in the design. The developer is also responsible for identifying parts of the application that may throw exceptions, and catching and logging the exception appropriately.

Unit Tests

A *unit test* is a simple program that allows you to test specific sections of code independently. Unit tests should be isolated, fast, and test a very specific test case. They should be executed at the click of a button without any additional input from the tester. They should also support being run automatically, either alone or as part of a set of tests. These automatable unit tests can then be used as part of a nightly build or continuous integration process. If done properly, unit tests should provide coverage of the majority of your production code. The amount of your production code covered by unit tests is known as its *code coverage percentage*.

Unit testing is not a new concept. It has been around as long as people have been developing component-based applications. Before the popularization of unit testing frameworks, most unit tests were either created as either command-line applications or simple user interfaces. Today most unit tests are written using frameworks that reduce the amount of code that needs to be written for each test and provide APIs to simplify automation of test execution and results aggregation. These frameworks are often bundled with tools called *test runners* that aid in automating test execution and examining the test results.

Popular unit testing frameworks include the following:

- *MS Test*: The testing framework included as part of Microsoft's Visual Studio Quality Tools framework. It is included with all versions of Visual Studio 2012.

- *NUnit*: Originally created as a port of the Java-based JUnit framework, NUnit has become extremely popular and is now used by most .NET developers who employ test-first development. It also has a rich ecosystem of add-ons and is compatible with many third-party test runners.

- *xUnit.net*: Created by the original developer of NUnit, xUnit was specifically designed around the concept of test-driven development (TDD) and works with several test runner frameworks, including ReSharper, CodeRush, and TestDriven.NET.

- *MbUnit*: A unit-testing framework for .NET built on top of the Gallio Automation Platform.

All these tools offer similar sets of core capabilities but differ on implementation details and style. If you would like to learn more about each of these tools, you can refer to Recipe 9-5, "Selecting a Unit Test Framework."

Visual Studio offers an integrated test runner that can be used with many of the aforementioned frameworks.

Code Coverage Tools

A code coverage tool is a software component that can examine a set of unit tests and determine how much of the code under test (CUT) is executed by the tests. Some tools, such as the one built into Visual Studio, can identify production code that is not covered by unit tests and provide visual feedback to the developer by highlighting the uncovered code in the editor.

Microsoft includes an integrated code coverage tool with the Visual Studio Premium and Ultimate editions. If you are not using these top-tier editions of Visual Studio, several third-party code coverage tools are available for .NET developers. They include JetBrains dotCover, NCrunch, and NCover.

Integration Testing

Even if you cover 100 percent of your code using unit tests, it is still very possible that things will not work as expected when the units run together. In addition, unit tests are focused on your class libraries and controller actions, and do not cover the code in your views. Integration tests cover this gap. For ASP.NET MVC applications, integration tests are typically performed in the web browser layer.

One approach to this problem is to have human testers manually verify that every screen in your web application works as it should. This is a time-consuming manual process that is typically performed by a dedicated QA team late in your application life cycle. If you would like to perform integration tests more frequently, such as part of a nightly build process, manual human testing is probably not practical.

Another approach that has been growing in popularity is automated integration testing. For ASP.NET MVC applications, this usually is in the form of browser automation. Visual Studio Premium and Ultimate editions have a built-in tool for automated browser tests. It is called Coded UI Tests. This feature allows you to record actions performed in your application while selecting page elements that you want the test to keep of track of. For example, if after submitting a form you expect a page element to indicate that the data was saved successfully, you can create an assertion that will test the value of this element. Once you have completed the recording, you can generate code that can be executed by Visual Studio's built-in test runner.

If you are not using Visual Studio Premium or Ultimate, there are several open-source and commercial third-party alternatives. These tools include:

- *WatiN* (`http://watin.org`): A test automation tool inspired by the Ruby-based Watir. Like the other tools in this category, it emulates a human driving a web browser. It supports Ajax-based web sites and can even record screenshots. WatiN may be easily added to a test project using NuGet. It has a relatively simple and easy-to-follow syntax.

- *Lightweight Test Automation Framework* (`http://ltaf.codeplex.com`): An open-source automation framework designed specifically for ASP.NET applications. It was developed by the ASP.NET QA team.

- *SeleniumHQ* (`http://seleniumhq.org`): A suite of tools that can automate browsers across many platforms and generate scripts in many programming languages. As a .NET developer, you can use the Selenium IDE, which is a Firefox plug-in that allows you to record test scenarios inside the Firefox web browser. You can then use the Selenium 2.0 WebDriver for .NET, which is available from NuGet to create tests compatible with the Microsoft test runner.

Static Code Analysis

Static code analysis tools analyze an assembly and verify that the code meets a set of code quality criteria and best practices. They can automatically select issues such as security vulnerabilities, resource leaks, and improper use of `P/Invoke`. They can ensure that your code matches your organization's naming conventions and can detect misspelled method and variable names.

All versions of Visual Studio 2012 (except the Test Professional edition) include a built-in Static Code Analysis tool. Code analysis can be configured in each project's property page. The Code Analysis property page allows you to enable code analysis to run automatically for each build. You can run code analysis by selecting Run Code Analysis from the Build menu.

Visual Studio ships with a number of predefined rule sets. The Microsoft Managed Minimum Rules rule set is selected by default for each project. With the default rule set, rule violations result in compilation warnings. Each warning includes a link to a help page that describes the rule and explains how to correct the issue.

If you wish, you may select another rule set or select several of the predefined ones. You may also create your own rule sets and create rule suppression lists that will suppress warning messages for specific violations.

In addition to the static code analysis tools available in Visual Studio, many other tools are available in the marketplace, including the following:

- *Parasoft dotTEST* (`parasoft.com`): Includes a static code analysis tool in addition to peer code review and unit testing frameworks.

- *HP Fortify Static Code Analyzer (*`hpenterprisesecurity.com`*)*: A code analyzer that focuses on the security aspects of your code. It is much more in-depth and up-to-date than Microsoft's built-in code analysis tools. It is used by many US banks, the US military, and the world's top accounting firms.

- *Armorize CodeSecure (*`armorize.com`*)*: Similar to HP's Fortify, CodeSecure is focused on the security aspects of the code under test.

If you plan on using static code analysis, it is best to begin using it as early in the project as possible and to use it continuously throughout the development process. If you leave this until the end of the project, you may be unpleasantly surprised at the number of defects detected by the tool.

Peer Code Review

Another technique that has been known to improve the quality of code is a formalized peer code review process. In a *peer code review*, developers review each other's code before the application is released to QA. Code reviews can help identify bugs, can help increase a code base's readability and maintainability, and increase collaboration between team members.

Peer code reviews also have been known to improve quality because of the physiological effect it has on developers. Developers will take extra time to improve the quality of the code when they know the code will be reviewed and scrutinized by peers and perhaps their superiors.

On the other hand, if a peer review process is not handled properly, it can result in wasted time and cause resentment between developers who may not be respectful enough when offering criticism.

A peer review process does not necessarily require any specialized tools. However, several vendors have created a tool to aid in code review, to document that the review occurred, and to record metrics to assess the effectiveness of it. Among these tools is Visual Studio Team Foundation Server (TFS). With the TFS code review tool, you can send a review request to one or more of your teammates. If teammates accept the review request, they can do a side-by-side comparison of your new code and the last version checked into source control. The reviewer can make comments on specific blocks of code and on entire files, as well as offer overall comments of the review. The comments are stored in TFS and are associated with a given change set. In TFS, a change set is a set of source files, work items, and other artifacts that are modified as part of a check-in.

If your team does not use TFS, there are other tools in the marketplace, including the following:

- *SmartBear*: A peer review and collaboration tool that integrates with TFS, Perforce, Git, and other source control products.

- *Atlassian Crucible*: A web application–based code review product that integrates with Subversion, Git, Mercurial, CVS, and Perforce source control systems.

Load Testing

Load testing or *stress testing* is the process of seeing how an application performs under heavy user load. Many applications that perform well under normal conditions may fail under load. Some conditions—such as code that results in database deadlocks, excessive disk I/O, or are consequences of a resource leak such as unmanaged threads or database connections—may be difficult to detect by other means.

In a load test, one or more test cases are recorded typically by using a browser plug-in. The plug-in will record page navigation, form input, query strings, and cookies sent from the server. It then uses this information to generate a script. Testers can modify this script and parameterize certain values, such as form inputs, so that there can be variation between different simulated user sessions.

For example, if you wish to simulate many different users logging into your web site, you can use the browser plug-in record navigating to your web site and then using a login form to enter a username and password. You would then modify the generated script so that the username and password can be replaced with data from a file or a database table.

Visual Studio Ultimate edition has a built-in load-testing tool. It allows you to create one or more web performance tests, which generate a script for an individual scenario. You can then combine these scenarios to create a load test. In the load test, you can define the number of virtual users assigned to each scenario, select the web browsers to be included in the simulation, and the network connectivity type.

9-2. Creating Unit Tests for a Controller Action Using MS Test

Problem

Since you are new to automated unit testing, you are unsure how to create a test, what needs to be tested, or how to know when a test is successful. You would like to start with as simple an example as possible so that you can gain a basic understanding of the overall process of creating unit tests.

Solution

Assuming the project was initially created without any unit tests, the first thing you will have to do is create a unit test project. Within that project, you will create a test class for each controller. Each test class should have a number of tests for each action in your controller class. You should test to ensure that

1.   The controller is returning the correct view.

2.   The content of the data passed to the view is as expected.

How It Works

In this exercise, we will create a new project using the ASP.NET MVC Internet template and create unit tests for the controllers that are provided out of the box. This is to give you a fundamental understanding of the overall process of creating tests. This example purposely avoids complex topics that are covered in detail in other recipes within this chapter.

Adding a Unit Test Project to Your Solution

To begin, we will launch Visual Studio and create a new project using the following steps:

1.   Open Visual Studio and select New Project from the File menu.

2.   On the New Project screen, select ASP.NET MVC 4 Web Application. Name the project **Ch9.R2.Web** and the solution **Ch9.R2**. Then click OK.

3. In the New ASP.NET MVC 4 Project Window, select the Basic template. Ensure that the Razor view engine is selected.

4. Tick the "Create a unit test project" check box and accept the default name Ch9.R2.Web. Tests. Click OK to create the new solution that will include the web and test projects.

Exploring the Test Project

The test project created by Visual Studio automatically added several assets. In the project's references, it has added more than 20 assemblies, including your web application, the Microsoft Visual Studio Quality Tools Unit Testing framework, the core .NET system assemblies, and many assembles used by the ASP.NET MVC Framework. It should be noted that you do not actually need all of these assemblies for this example.

It had also created a folder named Controllers, which contained a class named HomeControllerTests.

Inside HomeControllerTests.cs, you will find three test methods. This is a one-to-one relationship between the controller actions in the HomeController in the web application project and the test project.

We know that this is a test class that contains test methods because the class declaration is decorated with a TestClass attribute and the methods with TestMethod attributes.

Inside the bodies of each test method are an Arrange section that creates an instance of HomeController, and Act section that executes the controller action, and an Assert section that uses the testing framework assert commands to validate each test.

Listing 9-1 shows the generated test class.

Listing 9-1. Test Code Generated by Visual Studio's Internet Template

```
using Ch9.R2.Web.Controllers;
using Microsoft.VisualStudio.TestTools.UnitTesting;
using System.Web.Mvc;

namespace Ch9.R2.Web.Tests.Controllers
{
    [TestClass]
    public class HomeControllerTest
    {
        [TestMethod]
        public void Index()
        {
            // Arrange
            HomeController controller = new HomeController();

            // Act
            ViewResult result = controller.Index() as ViewResult;

            // Assert
            Assert.AreEqual("Modify this template to jump-start your ASP.NET MVC application.",
            result.ViewBag.Message);
        }

        [TestMethod]
        public void About()
        {
```

```
        // Arrange
        HomeController controller = new HomeController();

        // Act
        ViewResult result = controller.About() as ViewResult;

        // Assert
        Assert.IsNotNull(result);
    }

    [TestMethod]
    public void Contact()
    {
        // Arrange
        HomeController controller = new HomeController();

        // Act
        ViewResult result = controller.Contact() as ViewResult;

        // Assert
        Assert.IsNotNull(result);
    }
  }
}
```

Running the Generated Tests for HomeController

Visual Studio has several features that allow you to view available tests for a given project, execute the tests, and then examine the results. To see how these features work, we will build the solution and then execute the tests, as follows:

1. From the Visual Studio Build menu, select Build Solution.

2. If the Test Explorer is not visible, open it by selecting Test ➤ Windows ➤ Test Explorer.

3. The Test Explorer will show the three tests categorized under Not Run Tests. Each of the tests will have a blue icon that denotes that it has not yet run.

4. To run the tests, click the Run All link on the top-left of the Test Explorer pane.

5. All three tests should pass. You should see green checkmark icons next to each test name.

Enhancing the Tests for HomeController

The HomeController consists of three simple actions. Each of them add data to the ViewBag and return a view. The generated unit tests ensure that the Index view contains the correct value in its ViewBag's Message property and that the About and Contact action do not return a null ViewResult.

While the generated code from the template gives you a basic foundation to get started, they are not really thorough tests. For one thing, the names of the tests method are not very descriptive. You cannot tell what conditions are being tested inside each method. The methods also are overly simplified and are not covering critical aspects of the code, such as the action returning the correct view.

■ **Tip**   When writing unit tests, it recommended that you give the test methods descriptive names. This is very helpful for making your tests easy to maintain and for reviewing results of your tests. When a test fails, you should be able to easily tell what went wrong. The tests should be very specific. You should create one test for each assertion. You should avoid adding more than one assertion per test method. See Recipe 9-4 for more information.

We will now rename the tests and add an additional test for each action. When we are done, each action will have two tests: one that verifies that it is returning the correct view and another that validates that the ViewBag contains the expected value. To do this, you need to do the following:

1. Rename the Index test method **IndexAction_ReturnsMessageInViewBag**.

2. Create a second test method named **IndexAction_ReturnsIndexView**.

3. Change the body of the method to contain an Assert.Fail call. This allows the code to compile and reminds us that we need to complete the test.

4. Create similar test methods for each of the actions in the HomeController. When you are done, your HomeControllerTest class should look like Listing 9-2.

Listing 9-2. Empty HomeControllerTests

```
using Ch9.R2.Web.Controllers;
using Microsoft.VisualStudio.TestTools.UnitTesting;
using System.Web.Mvc;

namespace Ch9.R2.Web.Tests.Controllers
{
    [TestClass]
    public class HomeControllerTest
    {
        [TestMethod]
        public void IndexAction_ReturnsMessageInViewBag()
        {
            // Arrange
            HomeController controller = new HomeController();

            // Act
            ViewResult result = controller.Index() as ViewResult;

            // Assert
            Assert.AreEqual("Modify this template to jump-start your ASP.NET MVC application.",
                    result.ViewBag.Message);
        }

        [TestMethod]
        public void IndexAction_ReturnsIndexView()
        {
            Assert.Fail("Test not complete");
        }
```

```
        [TestMethod]
        public void AboutAction_ReturnsMessageInViewBag()
        {
            Assert.Fail("Test not complete");
        }

        [TestMethod]
        public void AboutAction_ReturnsAboutView()
        {
            Assert.Fail("Test not complete");
        }

        [TestMethod]
        public void ContactAction_ReturnsMessageInViewBag()
        {
            Assert.Fail("Test not complete");
        }
        [TestMethod]
        public void ContactAction_ReturnsContactView()
        {
            Assert.Fail("Test not complete");
        }
    }
}
```

Build the test project by using the Shift+F6 keyboard shortcut or by right-clicking the test project node in Solution Explorer and selecting Build. Once the project has been built, Visual Studio should automatically detect your tests and then display them in the Test Explorer window. If the Test Explorer is not displayed, open it by selecting Test ➤ Windows ➤ Test Explorer from Visual Studio's main menu. The Test Explorer will be docked in the left pane and it will show all the tests that have been created so far.

Click the Run All link at the top of the Test Explorer window. The tests will run in background. When the tests have completed, an error icon will appear next to each—indicating that the test failed because the method asserted inconclusive.

Testing to Confirm That the Action Returns the Correct View

We will now edit the tests so that they each of them verify a specific aspect of the code in HomeController. We will start with the test method IndexAction_ReturnsIndexView. This method will verify that Index action of HomeController returns the correct action result. We will verify that the action result is not null and that the view name is Index.

In most cases, test methods should follow the Arrange, Act, and Assert (AAA) pattern. In the Arrange section of the method, we perform setup by defining variables that include the input we would like to pass to the code under test and the expected result. In the *Act* portion of the code, we execute the code under test with the input defined in the Arrange section. Finally, we assert our assumptions by comparing our actual results against the expected results we defined in the Arrange section of the code.

To implement this pattern in IndexAction_ReturnsIndexView, we will start by creating a string variable named expected and setting it to our expected view name, Index. Next, we will create an instance of HomeController. These two lines of code define the Arrange section of our test method.

Next, implement the Act section by executing the Index method of HomeController and writing the action result to a variable named result.

The final line of code in the unit test uses the UnitTesting.Assert.AreEqual method to compare the results to our expected value. When using the Assert.AreEqual method, you should always put the expected value as the first parameter and the actual value as the second parameter. The resulting test method is shown in Listing 9-3.

Listing 9-3. IndexAction_ReturnsIndexView Test Method

```
[TestMethod]
public void IndexAction_ReturnsIndexView()
{
  //Arrange
  string expected = "Index";
  var homeController = new HomeController();

  //Act
  var result = homeController.Index() as ViewResult;

  //Assert
  Assert.AreEqual(expected, result.ViewName,"Unexpected view name");
}
```

To rerun the test, we will need to first build the solution. We can then right-click the IndexAction_ReturnsIndexView test in the Test Explorer window and choose Run Selected Tests from the pop-up menu. This will result in a failed test, as shown in Figure 9-1.

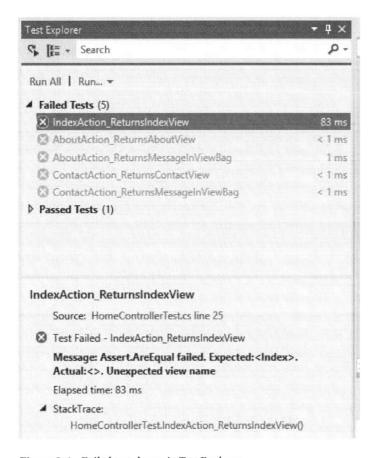

Figure 9-1. *Failed test shown in Test Explorer*

Test Explorer gives us detailed information about the failed test. First, it shows us that the IndexAction_ ReturnsIndexView test has failed and that the test took 83 milliseconds to complete. If you click the failed test, Test Explorer will provide detailed information on why the test failed, including the file name and line number, the message created from the tests assertion, and a stack trace that shows each of the methods involved in the failure. Clicking the links in the stack trace will open the associated code in Visual Studio.

Now that we know that our test has failed, we need to figure out why, and then make corrections to either our code under test or the test itself. The first thing that should draw your attention is the assertion message shown in Test Explorer:

```
Message:Assert.AreEqual failed. Expected:<Index>. Actual<>.
```

This tells us that our view name was an empty string instead of the expected value of "Index". This test result may be somewhat surprising since when we run the application, we can see that the correct view is returned. If our code works, why does our test fail?

Unfortunately, this mismatch is caused by that fact that our Index action in HomeController does not explicitly specify a view name when returning the ViewResult. Because of this, the ViewName property is never set. When the value is null or empty, the MVC Framework will derive the view name from the name of the action using reflection. Our test does not follow this same logic, but instead relies on the value of the ViewResult.ViewName property. Since this value has never been set, our test fails.

So how should we fix this? Should we implement the ASP.NET MVC convention logic into our unit test? If you did that, then you would be breaking the rule about keeping your unit tests as simple as possible. A better solution would be to modify the HomeController so that the Index action explicitly sets the name of the view.

Listing 9-4 shows the Index action modified to have a hard-coded view name passed as a parameter to the View method.

Listing 9-4. Index Action Modified to Contain a Hard Coded View Name

```
public ActionResult Index()
{
    ViewBag.Message = "Modify this template to jump-start your ASP.NET MVC application.";

    return View("Index");
}
```

After building the solution and running the test, the test should pass. The results are shown in Figure 9-2.

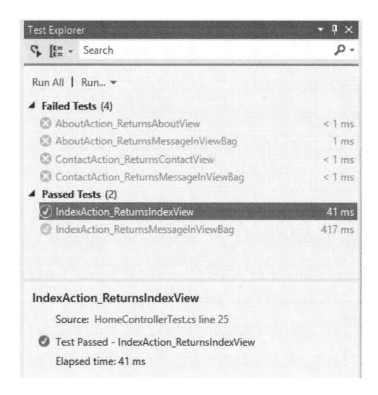

Figure 9-2. *IndexAction_ReturnsIndexView now passes*

The next test that we need to complete is `AboutAction_ReturnsMessageInViewBag`. In this test, we will verify that an object named Message exists and is set to the correct value. In order to test the value of the `ViewBag` property, which is a dynamic type, you need to add a reference to the `Microsoft.CSharp` assembly to your test project—if it does not exist.

To do this, right-click the References folder in Solution Explorer and select Add Reference. Make sure that the Assemblies and Framework nodes are selected, and then use the Search Assemblies text box to search for `Microsoft.CSharp`. Once located, double-click it to select it, and then click OK.

Next, modify the `AboutAction_ReturnsMessageInViewBag` test method so that it resembles Listing 9-5.

Listing 9-5. Completed IndexAction_ReturnsMessageInViewBag Test Method

```
[TestMethod]
public void AboutAction_ReturnsMessageInViewBag()
{
    //Arrange
    string expected = "Your app description page.";
    var homeController = new HomeController();

    //Act
    var result = homeController.About() as ViewResult;

    //Assert
    Assert.AreEqual(expected, result.ViewBag.Message, "ViewBag message incorrect");
}
```

Click Run All from the Test Explorer. You should now see two passing tests. The rest of the tests will appear as Failed since we have not implemented them.

Go ahead and modify the remaining actions in `HomeController` so that it explicitly passes the view name as a parameter, and then complete the remaining tests using the same techniques applied in Listings 9-4 and 9-5.

When you have completed this, you should be able to run all tests and have them pass successfully.

9-3. Understanding Test-Driven Development Strategies
Problem

You have heard a lot about test-first and test-driven development, but are not sure if this approach will work for you. You would like to understand what these strategies are about and how they can be applied to ASP.NET MVC development.

Solution

In most development methodologies, developers write a lot of code, and then if they have time, maybe write a few unit tests. Testing is part of the development process, but it is usually focused on integration testing and occurs toward the end of the development life cycle.

Test-driven development (TDD), on the other hand, is a completely different way of thinking about code. Rather than tests being an afterthought, they are front and center in the design process. In TDD, you always create tests for your code. If you find it difficult to test your code in isolation, you refactor it. The design of your project changes to make it easier to test. Tests drive your application design and development cycles. You do not check your code into source control until all of your unit tests pass.

In the *test-first development* (TFD) methodology, this concept is taken a step further. Tests are written before you write your production code. While this practice may occur in TDD, it is not always the case. In TFD, the first code you create in your solution are your unit tests. You will first write just enough stub code to allow the program to compile. You then run your tests, which will fail. Next, you implement your production code. Once all your tests pass, you can refactor to improve the readability and maintainability of both your production code and your tests.

How It Works

In this section, we will create a simple ASP.NET application using the test-first methodology. We will start by creating a new Visual Studio ASP.NET MVC project with an associated test. We will then create a test class using the MS Test framework and controller actions that we are testing.

The Requirements

All software applications start with the requirements. It is important to have a firm understanding of what is expected in the completed project. For the sake of this example, we need to create an administrative application that allows us to review and edit information about recording artists that have registered in our music collaboration system.

This new application should meet the following requirements:

- The application needs to be secure. If an unauthorized user were to access this system interface, it could potentially be very damaging.

- As an administrator, you need to review a list of new artists to ensure that all the new accounts comply with your web sites' terms of service.

- As an administrator, you need to delete accounts that violate terms of service so that offensive material and unsolicited advertisements are removed from the site.

- As an administrator, you need to be able to confirm that you really want to delete a selected account so that you do not delete valid accounts by accident.

- As an administrator, you should be shown a confirmation screen that confirms the deletion was successful so that you can take action in cases where the deletion fails.

Creating the Design

Based on the requirements, our first priority is security. Security researchers have found that the most effective designs follow a layered approach with many levels of controls. To that end, our first line of defense will be to create a separate web application to host our administrative interface. This allows this portion of the application to be exposed behind the firewall, where it is less likely to be exposed to hackers. This application will use Windows authentication and will be locked down via access control lists (ACLs) as part of our deployment. In production, the site will also use SSL to protect data in transit and to verify that they are connected to a valid server.

This design also frees the developer from most of the responsibility of writing code to handle authentication or authorization.

The next set of requirements roughly describe a set of screens that will list the new artists, view the details of each, and then allow the administrator to delete the artist record and confirm that the deletion was successful.

To meet this requirement, we create a high-level design that consists of a new ASP.NET MVC application with a single controller that we will call the `ArtistAdminController`. This controller will have four actions:

- `List`: Displays the list of new artists.

- `Review`: Displays detailed information on the artist and contains buttons that allow the administrator to either delete the record or return to the list.

- `DeleteConfirm`: Displays the delete confirmation message and allows the administrator to either confirm or cancel the deletion.

- `DeleteCompleted`: Displays a view that shows a delete confirmation message.

- `DeleteFailed`: Displays a view showing a failure message, including the error details that can be used by the administrator to help solve the problem.

Creating the Projects

The following steps will create a new ASP.NET MVC project using the Empty template along with an associated unit test project.

1. Open Visual Studio. Select File ➤ New ➤ Project from the Visual Studio's main menu.

2. Select the ASP.NET MVC 4 Web Application template, name the project **Ch9.R3.Web**, select an appropriate location, and name the solution **Ch9.R3**. Click OK.

3. In the New ASP.NET MVC Project dialog box, select the Empty template, ensure that the Razor view engine is selected, and tick the "Create a unit test project" check box. Keep the default values for Test Project Name, which should be Ch9.R3.Web.Tests, and Test Framework, which should be Visual Studio Unit Test. Click OK.

When you are done, you should have a solution that contains two projects: `Ch9.R2.Web`, which contains your web application, and `Ch9.R3.Web.Tests`.

Expand the references node on the test project. In addition to a reference to your web application project, a number of other assemblies have been added. In particular, there is a reference to `Microsoft.VisualStudio.QualityTools.UnitTestFramework`. This assembly contains the classes that support your unit tests.

Adding the Test Class

Since we are using the test-first methodology, the first thing that we will create is our unit tests. If you have never done this style of development, it may seem bizarre to create a test when you have yet to create the code to be tested.

Since we have not yet written code, we need to refer to our design to decide which tests to write. According to the design, we will have a controller named `ArtistAdminController`. Because we will create the controllers inside the `Controllers` folder in our web project, we will echo that structure in our test project. This will help keep our test classes organized and easy to maintain.

To create the `Controllers` folder in the test project, right-click its project node in Solution Explorer and select Add ➤ New Folder. A new folder will be shown in rename mode in Solution Explorer. Name the folder **Controllers**, and then press the Enter key.

To add a new test to your project, right-click the `Controllers` folder, click Add, and then New Unit Test. A new unit test named UnitTest1 will be added to the project. Rename the test by right-clicking it in Solution Explorer and select Rename. Rename the class **ArtistAdminControllerTests** and press the Enter key. When asked if you would like to perform a rename of all references to the code element 'UnitTest1', click Yes.

In the code editor window, you will see your new test class named `ArtistAdminControllerTests`, as shown in Listing 9-6.

Listing 9-6. New Test Class Created by Visual Studio

```
using System
using Microsoft.VisualStudio.TestTools.UnitTesting;

namespace Ch9.R2.Web.Tests.Controllers
{
    [TestClass]
    public class ArtistAdminControllerTests
    {
        [TestMethod]
        public void TestMethod1()
        {
        }
    }
}
```

Notice that the class has been decorated with the `TestClass` attribute. This tells MS Test that this class contains tests. When you build your solution, Visual Studio's integrated test runner will use reflection to inspect each class that contains this attribute to look for tests. All tests found will then be displayed in the Test Explorer window.

Creating the Test Methods

Now that we have created the test class, we can start adding test methods for each test case. Since our design states that we will have five actions, we can start by deleting `TestMethod1` and then define regions in the class for each action. This helps to keep the tests organized. Inside each region, we will create a test for each use case. Each test name will start with the name of the action. This will help us to identify the tests inside the Test Explorer.

An alternative method for naming the tests is to create a subclass for each action. Both naming schemes are valid, but the subclassing method has grown in popularity because it results in shorter, easier-to-read method names and it is easier to refactor. The downside of this approach is that if you are using Visual Studio's built-in test runner, it may be more difficult to differentiate the test method in the Test Explorer because the class name is not displayed. On the other hand, if you were using a third-party test runner such as the one that comes with NUnit, the tests are organized in a tree view based on the class hierarchy.

The modified test class is shown in Listing 9-7.

Listing 9-7. ArtistAdminControllerTests Modified to Include Regions for Each Proposed Controller Action

```
namespace Ch9.R2.Web.Tests.Controllers
{
    [TestClass]
    public class ArtistAdminControllerTests
    {
        #region List Action

        #endregion

        #region ReviewAction

        #endregion

        #region DeleteConfirm

        #endregion

        #region DeleteCompleted

        #endregion

        #region DeleteFailed

        #endregion
    }
}
```

At this point, you can build your solution to make sure everything compiles.

Next, we will add the test methods, starting with the tests for our List action. First, let's think about the possible execution paths that we can have when retrieving a list of items from a database. You will have your main use case, where one or more results are returned. You may have a condition where no results are found. Beyond this, changes in configuration can result in the action returning an incorrect action result. It is also possible that you may pass the incorrect model to the view.

We will start by creating a test for the main use case. To do this, add a test method named List_ReturnsNewArtistList_ToListView inside the List Action region. The method must be public, have a void return type, and be decorated with the TestMethod attribute, as shown in Listing 9-8. It is also a good practice to add comments to your test method to mark the beginning of each logical section. Each test should have three main parts:

- *Arrange*: Sets up the objects that you will use in your test and the variables that contain the expected result.

- *Act*: Performs the action being tested.

- *Assert*: Verifies the results.

Listing 9-8. The List_ReturnsNewArtistList_ToListView Test Method

```
#region List Action
[TestMethod]
public void ListAction_ReturnsNewArtistList_ToListView()
{
  //arrange

  //act

  //assert

}
#endregion
```

Now that we have added a stub method for the first test, we can follow this pattern and create additional tests for the other execution paths and error conditions. Add the following tests inside the List Action region:

- List_ReturnsListView: This test verifies that we are retuning the correct view.

- List_ReturnsEmptyNewArtistList_ToListView: This test verifies that we send a message indicating that no data has been found.

Notice that each test is looking at a particular use case. Each of the use cases result in a specific execution path in our controller action. Also notice that the method names for the tests are very verbose and descriptive.

If you build your project, the three tests will appear in Test Explorer. If the Test Explorer is not visible, you can open it by clicking Test ➤ Windows ➤ Test Explorer from Visual Studio's main menu. It should look similar to Figure 9-3.

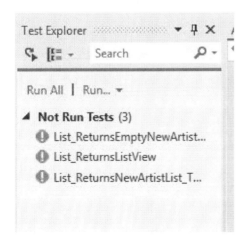

Figure 9-3. *Tests appear in Test Explorer after a test project is compiled*

If you click the Run All link in the Test Explorer, you will notice that all of your tests pass. Your tests pass because you have not yet added any assertions. This is not ideal because if the code is checked into source control in its current form, another developer (or even you) may not know that the tests have not been completed and may mistakenly think that this functionality is fine. To avoid this, you should never check-in an incomplete test.

■ **Tip**   If you have a situation in which you need to check in the code before your tests are complete, you should add an `Assert.Inconclusive` method with a message indicating that the test is still a work in progress. Inconclusive tests show as skipped tests in the Test Explorer and are shown with a warning icon. Alternatively, you can use `Assert.Fail` rather than `Assert.Inconclusive`. This causes the test to show as failed in the Test Explorer, which will make your incomplete tests impossible to miss.

In general, you should avoid checking in unfinished code and should instead use an alternative method such as TFS's Shelving feature. This allows you to update your code to the server without adding it to the source tree.

Next, we need to add the code to our test methods. For the `ReturnsListView` test method, we will arrange the test by first creating a variable that will hold our expected value. Next, we create an instance of the `ArtistAdminController`. For the Act portion of the test, we will execute the controller's List method and write the `ViewResult` of the action to a local variable. Finally, in the assert section, we will compare the view name in the action result to our expected value. We will use the `Assert.AreEqual` method to verify a match. The resulting `ReturnsListView` is shown in Listing 9-9.

Listing 9-9. ReturnsListView Test Method

```
[TestMethod]
public void ReturnsListView()
{
  //arrange
  string expected = "List";
  ArtistAdminController controller = new ArtistAdminController();

  //act
  var result = controller.List() as ViewResult;

  //assert
  Assert.AreEqual(expected, result.ViewName);
}
```

We now have a nearly complete test, but there are a number of problems. First of all, the code will not compile since the `ArtistAdminController` class has not yet been created. It was also somewhat painful to write this test since we did not have Visual Studio's IntelliSense giving us the method name suggestions. To avoid this problem, you can create a stub for `ArtistAdminController` in the web application project.

To do this in Solution Explorer, right-click the `Controllers` folder and select Add and then Controller. Name the controller and make sure that the Empty MVC Controller template is selected, and then click Add.

The `ArtistAdminController` will appear in the code editor window. Rename the Index action to `List`, and then save the file. In the `ArtistAdminControllerTest` file, add a using statement for the `Ch9.R2.Web.Controllers`. Build your solution. In the Test Explorer, right-click the `ReturnsListView` test and then select Run Selected Test. The test should fail.

Return to the `ArtistAdminController` in your web application project. Modify it so that "List" is explicitly passed as the view name when you call the controller's View method. When the MVC Framework executes your controller, if the `ViewName` property is null, it will use the name of the current action in place of `ViewName`. Since your test code does not do this, your test will fail because the `ViewResult.ViewName` property will be null.

Rather than modifying your tests to emulate the behavior of the Framework, we instead change the controller so that it explicitly passes the view name. This is the first example of how our need to test the application is changing the way we write our production code. The modified List action is shown in Listing 9-10.

Listing 9-10. ArtistAdminController Modified to Pass ReturnsListView Test

```
//
// GET: /ArtistAdmin/List
public ActionResult List()
{
  return View("List");
}
```

Build the solution again running the List_ReturnsListView test. This time, the test should pass. Some of you may think that this test passed even though we have not created a view called List. While it is possible to create a unit test that checks for the existence of a view, it is typically not done because it requires that your views be precompiled and it would rely on using subsystems that would compromise the independence of your unit tests. A better way to test this behavior would be inside an integration test, such as ones that can be created using Visual Studio's Coded UI Tests.

Now that our first test passes, we can turn our attention to the List_ReturnsNewArtistList_ToListView test. In order to make this test pass, we need to verify that a model containing a collection of Artist objects is being passed to the ViewResult. However, before we can write this test, we need to solve a number of problems. First, we need to define what an Artist object is. Second, we need to come up with some way to test the behavior of the List action when it is getting data from the external source without actually invoking the external data source.

In this example, our project will leverage another code base. The Artist type and the code to retrieve artist data from a database are contained in an external assembly. We can solve our first problem by adding a reference to the external library in our web application. We will then need to create a layer of indirection that allows the external dependencies to be replaced with a mock implementation of it when used in a test.

We will do this by creating an interface for a repository. We will then create a class that implements this interface using the external APIs. The constructor of our controller class will be modified so that it accepts an instance of our interface as a parameter. In the test class, we will use a mocking framework to create a fake class that can be used in place of the implementation that uses the external API to communicate with the back-end database.

You can see that using the test-driven approach is having a substantial influence on our design.

Add a Reference to the a Shared Library

As mentioned in the previous section, we will leverage an external library that contains the types needed to meet our requirements. This library uses the Entity Framework to retrieve data from an SQL Server database.

This project and the associated database are included in the Shared folder with the source code that can be downloaded from the book's web site. Also included is a database backup file that you can restore to a local running instance of SQL Server. The database contains thousands of records that you can use to test the samples in this book.

To add the reference to the external library in your web application project:

1. Right-click the project node for the Ch9.R3.Web project and select Add Reference.

2. Click the Browse button, which opens a file browser dialog box. Navigate to <booksource code directory>\Shared\References and select SharedAPI.dll and click Add.

3. Click OK on the Reference Manager window.

4. Open the Web.config file and add the connection string section to match the example shown in Listing 9-11.

Listing 9-11. Changes Made to Web.config

```
<connectionStrings>
     <add
     name="DefaultConnection"
     connectionString="data source=.;Initial Catalog=Ch7SharedDatabase;Integrated Security=SSPI;"
     providerName="System.Data.SqlClient"
   />
     <add name="MobEntities"
connectionString="metadata=res://*/Mob.csdl|res://*/Mob.ssdl|res://*/Mob.msl;provider=System.Data.
SqlClient;provider connection string=&quot;data source=.;initial catalog=Ch7SharedDatabase;integrated
security=True;MultipleActiveResultSets=True;App=EntityFramework&quot;"
         providerName="System.Data.EntityClient" />
  </connectionStrings>
```

Defining an Interface for a Repository

We will now create a repository interface that we will use to create an abstraction layer between our external library and our controller. Ideally, you would define the repository as part of the library project so that it can be reused across several projects. In this case, however, let's suppose we are dealing with a black box third-party component that we cannot modify directly. Since the requirements of our admin tool are relatively straightforward, we have made the decision to create an interface as well as a simple implementation of the repository to meets our specific needs. We will add this repository to our Models folder.

To create the repository interface:

1. Right-click the Models folder in the Ch9.R3.Web project, select Add, and then New Item.

2. In the Add New Item window, select Interface. In the Name field, enter **IArtistRepository.cs**, and then click Add. Prefixing an interface name with a capital I is a long-established naming convention and best practice.

3. Modify the IArtistRepository.cs file to look like Listing 9-12.

    Listing 9-12. IArtistRepository.cs

    ```
    using Ch7.SharedAPI;
    using System.Collections.Generic;

    namespace Ch9.R3.Web.Models
    {
        public interface IArtistRepository
        {
            IEnumerable<Artist> GetNewArtistList();
            Artist GetArtistDetails(int id);
            void DeleteArtist(int id);
        }
    }
    ```

Modifying the ArtistAdminController to Support Dependency Injection

One thing that we do not want to do in our unit tests is make calls to a database. In addition to making our unit tests slow, calls to a database will probably not give us consistent results that we could reliably assert in our tests. When your test fails, you will have no way of knowing if the failure was caused by data changing in the database or because of problems with your logic.

In Listing 9-9 we created a simple unit test that creates an instance of our controller and then invokes the List method. If the List method is modified to call to a back-end database, the test will also attempt to make the same call to the back end.

The solution to this problem is to replace the component used in your controller to call the database with another component that implements the same interface. This replacement component which is sometimes called a stub will always return the same results that you supply in the arrange portion of your test. In order for this to work, the controller needs a way to allow you to inject the stub. This is typically achieved by creating a constructor that allows its dependencies to be supplied as a parameter. This technique is known as *dependency injection*.

For our ArtistAdminController, we will do this by creating a new constructor that takes an instance of IArtistRepository as a parameter. An updated version of ArtistAdminController is shown in Listing 9-13.

Listing 9-13. ArtistAdminController Modified with a New Constructor That Accepts an IArtistRepository Instance As a Parameter

```
using Ch7.SharedAPI;
using Ch9.R3.Web.Models;
...

namespace Ch9.R3.Web.Controllers
{
    public class ArtistAdminController : Controller
    {
        IArtistRepository m_repository;

        public ArtistAdminController(IArtistRepository repository)
        {
            m_repository = repository;
        }

        //
        // GET: /ArtistAdmin/List
        public ActionResult List()
        {
            return View("List");
        }

    }
}
```

The first change in Listing 9-13 is to add a member variable that will hold an instance of the repository. We can then create a new constructor that takes an IArtistRepository instance as a parameter. You should now be able to build the web project.

Implementing the ReturnsNewArtistList_ToListView Test

With the interface created and the controller modified to support dependency injection, you can now implement the ReturnsNewArtist_ToListView test. The first thing you will need to do is add a reference to the SharedAPI assembly to the test project. This is required in order for the tests to reference the types defined in the assembly.

Next, you will need to create a concrete implementation of the IArtistRepository interface that you can pass to the constructor of the controller. Visual Studio Ultimate edition has a feature that simplifies this task by allowing you to generate a Fake class that allows you to insert stubs implementation that contain only the code needed to perform your test. If you do not have Visual Studio Ultimate, there are several free add-ins that perform the same function, such as Rhino Mocks and Moq. Please refer to Recipe 9-8 for more information on using Moq.

The IArtistRepository interface that we need to fake resides in the Ch9.R3.Web assembly. To create the Fake, expand the References node for the test project in Solution Explorer, and then right-click the Ch9.R2.Web assembly and select Add Fakes Assembly. After a few moments, a new assembly named Ch9.R3.Web.Fakes will be added to the references list. In addition, a Fakes folder will be added to the project, which also contains a reference to the Fakes assembly that was just created.

We can now implement the ReturnsNewArtistList_ToListView test, as shown in Listing 9-14.

Listing 9-14. ReturnsNewArtistList_ToListView Using a Fake IArtistRepository

```
[TestMethod]
public void ReturnsNewArtistList_ToListView()
{
    //arrange
    IArtistRepository mockArtistRepository =
        new Ch9.R3.Web.Models.Fakes.StubIArtistRepository
        {
            GetNewArtistList = () => { return new List<Artist>{
                new Artist{ CreateDate= new DateTime(2012,5,1),
                            UserName="TestUser1",
                            EmailAddress = "TestUser1@myonlineband.com",
                            ArtistId = 1,
                            WebSite = "http://cnn.com"
                            }
                            };}
        };
    ArtistAdminController controller = new ArtistAdminController(mockArtistRepository);

    //act
    var result = controller.List() as ViewResult;

    //assert
    var model = (List<Artist>) result.ViewData.Model;
    CollectionAssert.AllItemsAreInstancesOfType(model, typeof(Artist));
}
```

In the Arrange section of the ReturnNewArtistList_ToListView test, we create an instance of the IArtistRepository by using an implementation provided by Fakes called StubIArtistRepository. The Fakes framework allows us to inject our own implementation of the GetNewArtistList method defined in the IArtistRepository. For our test, we are verifying the behavior of the action when GetNewArtistList returns one or more records. We simulate this by returning one artist record in our Fakes implementation.

Next, we create an instance of the ArtistAdminController and pass in the mockArtistRepository as a constructor parameter.

In the Act section, of the test we call the List action and attempt to save the results as a ViewResult to the result variable.

In the Assert section, we verify that the model passed to the ViewData contains a collection of Artist objects using the CollectionAssert.AllItemsAreInstancesOfType method.

In order for the code to compile, you will also need to modify the ReturnsListView test so that it also is passing a mock to the contractor. Because we are only verifying that the ReturnsListView method is returning the correct view, the requirements for the stub are minimal. The updated version of the test is shown in Listing 9-15.

Listing 9-15. ReturnListView Updated to Return Mocked IArtistInterface

```
[TestMethod]
public void ReturnsListView()
{
  //arrange
  IArtistRepository fakeArtistRepository =
                    new Ch9.R2.Web.Models.Fakes.StubIArtistRepository { };
  string expected = "List";
  ArtistAdminController controller = new ArtistAdminController(fakeArtistRepository);

  //act
  var result = controller.List() as ViewResult;

  //assert
  Assert.AreEqual(expected, result.ViewName);

}
```

Build the solution and then try running the tests again. The ReturnsNewArtistList_ToListView now fails since no model has been set in the controller action.

Modifying the List Action to Pass the ReturnsNewArtistList_ToListView Test

The ReturnsNewArtistList_ToListView test fails. This is because it is expecting a model that contains a collection of Artist objects, but instead the model is null.

To correct this, modify the List action as shown in Listing 9-16, where the List action now makes a call to the repository and returns a List<Artist> collection.

Listing 9-16. The List Action Using the IArtistRepository

```
public ActionResult List()
{
   List<Artist> artists = m_repository.GetNewArtistList() as List<Artist>;
   return View("List", artists);
}
```

If you build the solution and run the test again, you will find that the ReturnsNewArtistList_ToListView test now passes. Here we demonstrate the value unit testing is good. We've refactored the code by adding the correct model, but our original test still passes—indicating that our changes to the project do not appear to have broken things.

Implementing the ReturnsEmptyNewArtistList_ToListView Test

The last test that we will implement for the List action is the ReturnsEmptyNewArtistList_ToListView test. In this test case, we expect that when no items are found in the list, a message will be sent to the page to notify the administrator that no new artists have been found. To implement this test, we will again use the Fakes assembly to create a stub to pass in for our IArtistRepository. For this test, we will create a version of the GetNewArtist method that returns an empty list. The ReturnsEmptyNewArtistList_ToListView test is shown in Listing 9-17.

Listing 9-17. ReturnsEmptyNewArtistList_ToListView Test

```
[TestMethod]
public void ReturnsEmptyNewArtistList_ToListView()
{
    //arrange
    string expectedViewBagMessage="No New Artists Found";
    IArtistRepository fakeArtistRepository =
        new Ch9.R2.Web.Models.Fakes.StubIArtistRepository
    {
        GetNewArtistList = () =>
        {
          return new List<Artist>();
        }
    };
    ArtistAdminController controller = new ArtistAdminController(fakeArtistRepository);

    //act
    var result = controller.List() as  ViewResult;

    //assert
    Assert.AreEqual(expectedViewBagMessage, result.ViewBag.Message)
    }
}
```

If you build your solution and run the tests, you will notice that ReturnsEmptyNewArtistList_ToListView now fails as expected. You must now modify the List action so that it implements the correct behavior.

Modifying the List Action to Pass the Modifying the List Action to Pass the ReturnsNewArtistList_ToListView Test

If you have been following this example, you should see a pattern emerging. We write the test, the test fails, we adjust the production code so that it passes the test, and then move on to the next test. In order for the ReturnsNewArtistList_ToListView to pass, we must add some logic to the List controller to check to see if the list returned from the repository contains any records. If no records are found, we will pass a message in the ViewBag. The updated List action is shown in Listing 9-18.

Listing 9-18. List View Modified to Pass the ReturnsNewArtistList_ToListView Test

```
public ActionResult List()
{
    List<Artist> artists = m_repository.GetNewArtistList() as List<Artist>;
    if (artists == null || artists.Count == 0)
```

```
    {
        ViewBag.Message = "No New Artists Found";
    }
    return View("List", artists);
}
```

If we build the solution and run the tests, everything should now pass. We see that the code we changed solved the problem and it did not cause a regression. You can see as we build on this that even though it is a lot of work, as your project grows in complexity, this work will pay increasing dividends. Another thing to consider is how much less time we will spend in the debugger.

We can now create a skeleton structure for the List view and verify that it will work in the browser.

Adding the List View

To create the List view, from the ArtistAdminController in the code editor, right-click the List action and select Add View. Ensure that the Razor view engine is selected and that the "Create strongly typed view" check box is unchecked, and then click Add.

A new folder will be added to the web application project under the Views folder named ArtistAdmin. A new view named List.cshtml will be added to the folder. Modify the view so that it contains some basic markup for displaying the list, as shown in Listing 9-19.

Listing 9-19. The List View

```
@model List<Ch7.SharedAPI.Artist>
@{
    ViewBag.Title = "New Artists";
}

<h2>Here is a list of new Artists</h2>
@ViewBag.Message
<table>
    <thead>
        <tr>
            <th>User Name</th>
            <th>Email</th>
            <th>Website</th>
            <th>Create Date</th>
        </tr>
    </thead>

@foreach (var item in Model)
{
    <tr>
        <td>@item.UserName</td>
        <td>@item.EmailAddress</td>
        <td>@item.WebSite</td>
        <td>@item.CreateDate</td>
    </tr>

}
</table>
```

First, `@model List<Ch7.SharedAPI.Artist>` is added to make the List view strongly typed. We then add some basic markup that will display the list of artists in a table.

If we run the project and navigate to `/ArtistAdmin/List`, we will see the following error message:

```
No parameterless constructor defined for this object.
```

The reason that we are seeing this error is because when we added the constructor to the controller, we overrode the default constructor that is required by the MVC Framework. You now need to modify the `ArtistAdmin` controller to include a parameterless constructor. You will also need to pass in a concrete repository instance. To do this, you will need to create a class that implements the `IArtistRepository`. You will then need to add the parameterless constructor to the `ArtistAdmin` controller and ensure that the proper implementation is passed in.

Implementing the IArtistRepository Interface

Next, we will create a class that implements the interface that we will use inside the controller. To create the repository interface:

1. Right-click the Models folder in the `Ch9.R3.Web` project, select Add, and then New Class.

2. In the Add New Item window, confirm that Class is selected. In the Name field, enter **SharedAPIArtistRepository.cs**, and then click Add.

3. Modify the `SharedAPIArtistRepository.cs` so that it implements both `IArtistRepository` and `IDisposable`. Implementing `IDisposable` allows us to dispose of our Entity Framework model when the EF version of the repository is used in the controller. When you are done, the file should look like Listing 9-20.

Listing 9-20. SharedAPIArtistRepository.cs

```
public class SharedAPIArtistRepository : IArtistRepository, IDisposable
{
        private MobEntities m_context;

        public void Dispose()
        {
            if (m_context != null)
            {
                m_context.Dispose();
            }
        }

        public SharedAPIArtistRepository()
        {
            m_context = new MobEntities();
        }

        public IEnumerable<Artist> GetNewArtistList()
        {
            //last 20 Artist records created
            var newArtists = (from m in m_context.Artists
                                orderby m.CreateDate descending
```

```
                               select m).Take(20);
                    return newArtists.ToList<Artist>();
                }

                public Artist GetArtistDetails(int id)
                {
                    var artist = m_context.Artists.Find(id);
                    return artist;
                }

                public void DeleteArtist(int id)
                {
                    m_context.DeleteArtist(id);
                }
        }
```

The repository shown in Listing 9-20 creates a private member variable to hold the DBContext object used to talk to the database. The context is initialized in the repository's constructor and disposed of in the repository's Dispose method. The GetNewArtistList method uses a LINQ query to retrieve the last 20 records added according to the CreateDate property. The remaining methods are straightforward wrappers to the functionality exposed by the API.

Adding a Parameterless Constructor to ArtistAdminController

The last step that we need to perform to get a functioning demo is to add the parameterless constructor to ArtistAdminController. This addition is shown in Listing 9-21.

Listing 9-21. The Updated ArtistAdminController

```
public class ArtistAdminController : Controller
    {
        IArtistRepository m_repository;
        public ArtistAdminController() : this(new SharedAPIArtistRepository()) { }
        public ArtistAdminController(IArtistRepository repository)
        {
            m_repository = repository;
        }

        //
        // GET: /ArtistAdmin/List
        public ActionResult List()
        {
            List<Artist> artists = m_repository.GetNewArtistList() as List<Artist>;
            if (artists == null || artists.Count == 0)
            {
                ViewBag.Message = "No New Artists Found";
            }
            return View("List", artists);
        }

    }
```

After making this change, try browsing the ArtistAdmin/List again to verify the page works as expected.

As an exercise, you should try to complete this application per the requirements specified in the beginning of the How It Works section. If you get stuck, you can see the full source code in the downloadable materials on the book's web site.

9-4. Defining a Naming Convention for Your Unit Tests
Problem

For the last few projects that you have worked on, developers have not been consistent about how they name their test projects, test classes, and test methods. This often leads to confusion and makes the unit tests more difficult to maintain. You would like to create a standard naming convention to use across all of your projects. You would like follow a well-known best practice for your naming convention.

Solution

While there may be some variation in the industry, most companies that perform test-driven development (TDD) or similar methodologies have adopted a similar approach for naming their tests. These conventions are commonly used across many languages and testing frameworks. If done properly, it will make it easy to understand what each test does and what code it is associated with.

How It Works

There are three conventions that you should use in naming your test projects. These include naming conventions for test projects, test classes, and test methods.

Naming Your Test Project

At the project level, the test project name should follow the pattern [project name].Tests. For example, if you have a project named SomeNamespace.SomeProject.Web, the test project should be named SomeNamespace.SomeProject.Web.Tests. You should create one test project for each project in your solution.

This should make it obvious that the test project SomeNamespace.SomeProject.Web.Tests contains tests for SomeNamespace.SomeProject.Web—even for people who are new to the project team.

Naming Your Test Classes

Inside the test project, you should create a class for each class in your production code project that you wish to test. The test class names should follow the pattern [class name]Tests. For example, if you have a class named MyClass, you would create a test class named MyClassTests.

Naming Your Test Methods

For methods, the name of test method should be made up of three distinct parts that include the name of the method under test, the state or condition you are testing, and the expected outcome.

For example, let's say you have a calculator application. The calculator has an Add method that takes any number of float values as parameters and returns a double. The method has three business rules that determine how it will respond to conditions such as negative values passed as parameters, NaN values passed as parameters, and no parameters being passed.

When a negative number is passed as a parameter, the method will throw an `InvalidOperationException`. To test this condition, we will create a test method named `Add_NegativeValue_ThrowsInvalidOperationException`. Underscores are used to separate the three parts of the method name. `Add` is the name of the code under test (CUT), `NegativeValue` is the state or condition we are testing, and `ThrowsInvalidOperationException` is the expected result.

In cases where you are not testing for any specific condition, such as when writing tests for a controller action that always returns the same `ViewResult`, you can omit the state or condition part of the name. For example, if we had a controller action called `About` that always returned a `ViewResult` for the `About` view, you could name it `About_ReturnsAbout`. The problem with this method name is that it is not clear when we are describing the `About` controller action or the `About` view. To avoid this confusion, you should explicitly indicate each. For example, `AboutAction_ReturnsAboutView`.

Another approach that is popular with developers who use NUnit is to create subclasses inside a test class for each method under test. If you use this method, you do not need to include the method name in your test method name. Unfortunately, this method does not work that well with Visual Studio's test runner since it does not display the class name. It works well for NUnit because not only does its test runner show the class name, it also uses a tree view to display the test methods, which allows you to expand and contact each subclass. See Recipe 9-7 for more information about creating tests with NUnit.

9-5. Selecting a Unit Test Framework
Problem

Your team has decided to start using a test-driven development methodology, but you are not sure which unit testing framework is right for you. You know that there is a built-in unit testing framework in Visual Studio, but you are not sure if you should use it or move to a third-party framework such as xUnit.net, NUnit, or MbUnit.

Solution

Visual Studio 2012 has both a built-in unit testing framework (MS Test) and a test runner that provides a user interface for initiating tests and viewing the results. This provides you with all you need to get started out-of-the-box. However, many teams have found Microsoft's framework to be less optimal than third-party frameworks such as NUnit and xUnit.net. For example, since many features of MS Test are tightly coupled and licensed as part of Visual Studio, it requires you to install Visual Studio on your build servers.

Fortunately, in Visual Studio 2012, Microsoft has made it easier to use other frameworks in place of MS Test while maintaining the advantages of being able to perform everything from inside the IDE.

How It Works

Before you can decide on the unit test framework to select, you need to know which frameworks are available and what their main advantages and disadvantages are. In this section, we will briefly review Microsoft MS Test, NUnit, xUnit.net, and MbUnit. We will compare them in terms of simplicity of syntax, capabilities, community support, documentation, and tooling.

MS Test

MS Test is the unit test framework that comes with Visual Studio 2012. The main advantages of MS Test are that it is fully integrated with the IDE and is installed and ready when you install the IDE.

Syntax

The MS Test syntax is relatively simple to use, but some would argue not as elegant as what is offered in competing frameworks. Test classes and methods are marked using a number of attribute classes. The test results are registered with the test runner by using assertion methods. A sample of MS Test syntax is shown in Listing 9-22. The sample shows many of the test attributes in action. Several attributes, such as the TestInitializeAttribute and the ClassInitializeAttribute, allow initialization code to be run before the tests are executed. Likewise, the ClassCleanupAttributes and TestCleanupAttribute allow code to clean up resources.

Other attribute classes can be used to apply metadata to tests methods, as shown with the IndexAction_Is5PM_June_ReturnsDayModel_SoundEffectSummerDay test in Listing 9-22. Metadata such as a description of the test, the TFS Area and Iteration associated with the test, the tests owner, and a test category can be applied to the test. The Visual Studio user interface does not currently make use of these attributes but some teams have used the attributes in custom-build scripts that automatically create work items in TFS and assign them to developers using the attribute values.

Listing 9-22. MS Test Syntax Example

```
[TestClass]
public class MSTestControllerTests
{

  [ClassInitialize]
  public static void RunOnceBeforeAnyofTheTestsInThisClass(TestContext context)
  {
      // this runs once when the class is instantiated before any tests are run.
  }

  [TestInitialize]
  public void RunBeforeAllTestsInClass)
  {
      // run before the test to allocate and configure resources
      // needed. Will be run for each test in the class.
  }

  [TestMethod]
  [CssProjectStructure("UserExperience")]
  [CssIteration("Iteration 1")]
  [Description(@"Tests to verify that when it is 5PM in June that the
            the Summerday sound effect wil be played")]
  [Owner("John")]
  [TestCategory("Controller Tests")]
  public void IndexAction_Is5PM_June_ReturnsDayModel_SoundEffectSummerDay()
  {
    //arrange
    string expected = "SummerDay";
    MSTestController controller = new MSTestController(new DateTime(2012,6,1,17,0,0));
    //act
    var result = controller.Index() as ViewResult;
    var model = result.ViewData.Model as DayModel;
    Assert.IsNotNull(model, "Incorrect model, expected DayModel");
    Assert.AreEqual(expected, model.SoundEffect);
  }
```

```
[TestMethod]
[ExpectedException(typeof(ApplicationException))]
public void IndexAction_Is3PM_Feb292016_ThrowsApplicationException()
{
  //arrage
  MSTestController controller = new MSTestController(new DateTime(2016,2,29,17,0,0));
  //act
  controller.Index();
 }


[TestMethod]
[Ignore]
public void IndexAction_Is3PM_June_ReturnsDayModel_SceenSummerDay()
{
  //arrange
  MSTestController controller = new MSTestController(new DateTime(2012, 6, 1, 14, 0, 0));
  string expected = "SummerDay";
  //act
  var result = controller.Index() as ViewResult;
  var model = result.ViewData.Model as DayModel;
  Assert.IsNotNull(model, "Incorrect model, expected DayModel");
  Assert.AreEqual(expected, model.SceneName);
}

[TestCleanup]
 public void RunsAfterEachTestClassasCompleted()
{
  //runs afer each test in a test class.
  // can be used to clean up resources from the test
}

[ClassCleanup]
 public static void  RunAfterAllTestsInTestClassHaveCompleted()
{
   //use to clean up any resources left over from the test
}

}
```

Documentation and Community Support

There are several official sources of documentation for MS Test, including Visual Studio's integrated help, MSDN, and many Microsoft blogs. There is also quite a bit of community content, including personal blogs and forum responses. Additional information about MS Test can be found in many books, including *Pro Application Lifecycle Management with Visual Studio 2012*, second edition by Joachim Rossberg and Mathias Olausson (Apress, 2012) and *Pro .NET Best Practices* by Stephen Ritchie (Apress, 2011).

MS Test is fully supported by Microsoft as a part of Visual Studio, as well as a large community of developers.

Tooling

The tooling for MS Test is Visual Studio and Visual Studio Team Foundation Server (TFS). When MS Test is used with TFS and MSBUILD, unit tests can be integrated into nightly builds and TFS can generate reports that show build quality statistics, as shown in Figure 9-4.

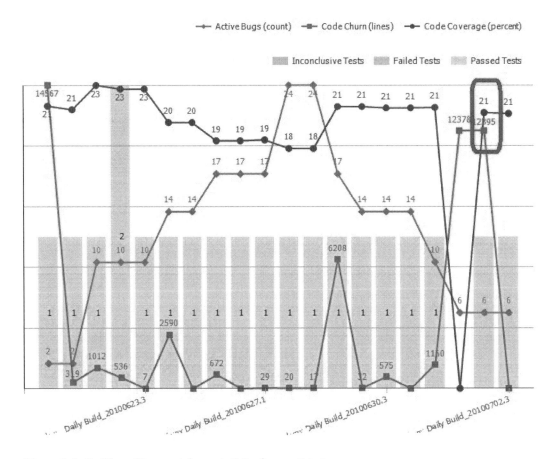

Figure 9-4. *Build quality report shows statistics from unit tests*

NUnit

NUnit is one of the most popular unit testing frameworks for Microsoft .NET. It was originally created as a port of the JUnit Java unit testing framework. In version 2 of the framework, it was rewritten to be a better match for testing .NET applications.

Syntax

The NUnit syntax is relatively simple. Like MS Test, test classes and methods are marked using a number of attribute classes. A sample of NUnit syntax is shown in Listing 9-23. The sample shows many of the test attributes in action. Several attributes, such as the Setup and the TestFixtureSetUp, allow initialization code to be run before the tests are executed. Likewise, the TearDown and TestFixtureTearDown allow code to clean up resources.

Listing 9-23. NUnit Syntax Example

```csharp
using System;
using System.Collections.Generic;
using System.Linq;
using System.Text;
using System.Threading.Tasks;
using NUnit.Framework;
using Ch9.R7.Web.Controllers;
using System.Web.Mvc;
using Ch9.R7.Web.Models;

namespace Ch9.R7.Web.Tests.Controllers
{
    [TestFixture]
    [Category("SampleTestClass")]
    public class NUnitTestControllerTests
    {

        [TestFixtureSetUp]
        public void Init(TestContext context)
        {
            // this runs once when the class is instantiated before any tests are run.
        }

        [SetUp]
        public void RunBeforeAllTestsInClassAssembly()
        {
            // run before the test to allocate and configure resources
            // needed. Will be run for each test in the class.add code that will run before any
            // code in the entire
            //test assembly is executed
        }

        [Test, Explicit]
        public void IgnoredUnlessExplicitlySelectedFoRunning()
        {
            //ignored unless it is explicitly selected for running
            //If encountered in while running tests
            //the test runner will treats  as ignored.
            //The progress bar turns yellow  test listed as not run
        }

        [Test]
        [Platform(Exclude = "Mono,Unix,Linux")]
        public void DontRunIfOnUnix()
        {
            //specifies to include or exclude on certian platforms
            // Case insensitive, multiple values seperated by commas
            // full list of platforms provided here
            // http://www.nunit.org/index.php?p=platform&r=2.2.10
        }
```

```
[Test]
[Category("UserExperience")]
[Description(@"Tests to verify that when it is 5PM in June that the
    the Summerday sound effect wil be played")]
public void IndexAction_Is5PM_June_ReturnsDayModel_SoundEffectSummerDay()
{
    //arrange
    string expected = "SummerDay";
    NUnitTestController controller = new NUnitTestController(new DateTime
(2012, 6, 1, 17, 0, 0));
    //act
    var result = controller.Index() as ViewResult;
    var model = result.ViewData.Model as DayModel;
    Assert.IsNotNull(model, "Incorrect model, expected DayModel");
    Assert.AreEqual(expected, model.SoundEffect);
}
[Test]
[ExpectedException(typeof(ApplicationException))]
public void IndexAction_Is3PM_Feb292016_ThrowsApplicationException()
{
    //arrage
    NUnitTestController controller = new NUnitTestController(new DateTime
(2016, 2, 29, 17, 0, 0));
    //act
    controller.Index();
}

[Test]
[Ignore]
public void IndexAction_Is3PM_June_ReturnsDayModel_SceenSummerDay()
{
    //arrange
    NUnitTestController controller = new NUnitTestController(new DateTime
(2012, 6, 1, 14, 0, 0));
    string expected = "SummerDay";
    //act
    var result = controller.Index() as ViewResult;
    var model = result.ViewData.Model as DayModel;
    Assert.IsNotNull(model, "Incorrect model, expected DayModel");
    Assert.AreEqual(expected, model.SceneName);
}

[TearDown]
public void RunsAfterEachTestClassasCompleted()
{
    //runs afer each test in a test class.
    // can be used to clean up resources from the test
}
```

```
    [TestFixtureTearDown]
    public static void RunAfterAllTestsInTestClassHaveCompleted()
    {
        //use to clean up any resouses left over from the test
    }

}

}
```

Documentation and Community Support

NUnit has strong community support and simple but thorough documentation. The official documentation is available at `www.nunit.org/index.php?p=docHome&r=2.2.10`. There are tens of thousands of blog pages, forums, and other resources dedicated to NUnit.

Tooling

NUnit comes with a test runner GUI and a command-line utility. In addition to the standard download option, NUnit is also available as a NuGet download.

Full integration with Visual Studio is available via a third-party add-in in the Visual Studio extension manager.

9-6. Downloading and Installing NUnit

Problem

You have head many positive things about NUnit and you would like to use it as your unit testing framework. You would like to know how to download it and configure it to work with Visual Studio.

Solution

NUnit is free and available for download at `http://nunit.org`. Once you download the MSI package, you can follow the installation wizard to install it. You can then download a Visual Studio extension using the Visual Studio Extension Manager to provide fully integrated NUnit support inside Visual Studio.

How It Works

The first thing you need to do is download the latest installation package from the NUnit web site. You can do this by;

1. Going to `http://nunit.org`

2. Clicking the download link.

3. On the download page, selecting the "win" download package.

4. Clicking the link will download the MSI package to your computer.

Running the NUnit Installer

Once the download has completed, double-click the NUnit.msi package to launch the installer. On the NUnit Setup welcome screen, click Next. On the End-User License Agreement screen, check the "I accept the terms..." check box (after reading the agreement, of course).

On the Choose Setup Type screen, select Typical. This will install everything except the Unit Tests for NUnit and the PNUnit Runner, which allows you to run parallel distributed tests.

On the Ready to Install screen, click the Install button to begin the installation. If prompted by using Account Control, click Yes.

On the Completed page of the installation wizard, click Finish to close the installer window.

Adding Support for NUnit to Visual Studio's Test Explorer

While many developers prefer to use NUnit's UI, if you wish to allow NUnit to work with Visual Studio's Test Explorer, you can download and install the NUnit Test Adapter, which is available in the Visual Studio Extensions and Updates manager.

To install the NUnit Test Adapter, click Tools in Visual Studio's main menu, and then click Extensions and Updates. Click the Online node in the Extensions and Updates manager window, and then search for NUnit.

Click the Download button next to NUnit Test Adapter. This add-in was in beta at the time of this writing but the pace of improvement has been quick. After a few moments, the Download and Install window will appear. Click the Install button. When installation is complete, restart Visual Studio.

With the adapter installed, unit tests created with NUnit can now be discovered by the Test Explorer when your tests are built. Visual Studio will display all tests it finds, regardless of the framework used. You will also be able to run your tests and view the test results from inside Visual Studio.

The test adapter did not register NUnit as a third-party Unit Testing framework. Because of this, when you create a new ASP.NET project, NUnit does not appear as an option when you opt to create a new unit test project.

9-7. Creating Unit Tests for Controller Actions Using NUnit
Problem

Your team has decided to use the NUnit unit-testing framework as the unit testing standard. You would like to understand how to use it to test a controller action.

Solution

NUnit is a third-party component, which means that it does not come with Visual Studio. If you would like to use it, you must first download and install it, as shown in Recipe 9-5.

Once NUnit and its test adaptor are installed on your PC, you can use it by adding a class library project to your solution and then adding a reference to NUnit assemblies. You can then write tests using NUnit.

How It Works

In this exercise, we will start with an existing project based on the ASP.NET MVC Internet template, and create unit tests for the controllers that are provided out of the box. This is to give you a fundamental understanding of the overall process of creating tests.

Creating a Unit Test Project to Your Solution

To begin, we will launch Visual Studio and open an existing ASP.NET MVC project that does not have any unit tests associated with it. If you have downloaded the source code from the book's web site, you can load the sample project located in the `Chapter9\Before\Ch9.R7` directory. If you wish, you may also create a new project using the ASP.NET MVC Basic template.

Once the project has been opened right-click the Solution node in Solution Explorer and select Add and then New Project. In the New Project window, click the Windows option under the Visual C# node on the left panel and then select the Class library Project template. Name the project `Ch9.R7.Web.Tests` then click OK.

A new class library project should have been added to your solution and class named `Class1` will be opened in a code editor Window.

Next, you will need to add a reference to your ASP.NET MVC Project as well as references to some of the types required such as `System.Web.Mvc`.

To add a reference to your project, right-click the References folder in your test project and select Add Reference. In the Reference Manager window, click Project on the left pane then check the box next to `Ch9.R7.Web` Click Framework on the left pane and then use the Search Assemblies text box to find `System.Web.Mvc` and check the box to the left of `System.Web.Mvc 4.0`. You will also need to add the NUnit assemblies to your project. To do this search for NUnit and then check nunit.framework.

Click OK to add the three references to your test project.

Creating Tests for HomeController

The `HomeController` consists of one action. This action checks the current data and time and then returns a model that contains a theme and sound effect to be used on the page.

Delete the file Class1.cs in Solution Explorer. The file will be removed and automatically closed in the code editor.

Add a new folder called **Controllers** to your test project. Add a new class file to the folder and name it `HomeControllerTests.cs`.

Add the `Public` assess modifier to the `HomeControllerTests` class. Next, add using statements to the beginning of the file for the namespaces `Ch9.R7.Web.Controllers` and for `System.Web.Mvc`. Then add a using statement for `NUnit.Framework`.

Create a new public method called `IndexAction_ReturnsIndexView()`. When you are done, your test class should look similar to Listing 9-24.

Listing 9-24. Unit Test using NUnit

```
using Ch9.R7.Web.Controllers;
using NUnit.Framework; // This is used in place of the MS version
using System.Web.Mvc;

namespace Ch9.R7.Web.Tests.Controllers
{
    [TestFixture]
    public class HomeControllerTests
    {
        [Test]
        public void IndexAction_ReturnsIndexView()
        {
            //arrange
            string expected = "Index";
            HomeController controller = new HomeController();
```

```
            // act
            var result = controller.Index() as ViewResult;

            //assert
            Assert.AreEqual(expected ,result.ViewName);
        }
    }
}
```

Build your solution. After a few minutes, your test should appear in Test Explorer. You can click the Run All button in Test Explorer to run the test.

If you have used MS Test, the syntax should seem very similar. The class is identified as a test class by decorating it with the `TestFixtureAttribute`. Tests methods are identified using the `TestAttribute`.

9-8. Mocking a Repository with Moq
Problem

You are running Visual Studio 2012 Professional and need to create unit tests for a controller that uses a repository class that connects to a back-end database. You want to be able to test this controller without executing any SQL Server code. Since you are not running Visual Studio Ultimate, you do not have built-in support for creating mocks in Visual Studio. You need to know how to install a third-party mocking library and use it to mock the repository.

Solution

There are several free third-party mocking libraries that can easily be added to a test project using the NuGet Package Manager. Assuming that the repository is derived from an interface and the controller is set up to allow for dependency injection, once the mocking library has been added to your test project, you can use it to create a mock of the repository and then use a hard-coded result set that simulates the condition needed for your test.

For this recipe, I have selected Moq—a free open-source mocking framework for .NET. It provides a simple and straightforward approach to creating mocks. In the How It Works section, we will walk through the process of creating an ASP.NET MVC project and associated test project. We will then create a simple repository interface and set up a controller to use it.

In the test project, we will use NuGet to install Moq. We will then write some tests that use Moq to simulate the repository.

How It Works

In this exercise, we will create a simple web site that returns user profiles for members of an enterprise architecture team at a large company. The project will use the Basic MVC template and the MS Test unit test framework. To create the project, do the following:

1.   Open Visual Studio. Select New ➤ Project from the File menu.

2.   In the New Project dialog box, select the ASP.NET MVC 4 template. Name the project **Ch9.R8.Web** and name the solution **Ch9.R8**. Click OK to continue.

3.   In the New ASP.NET MVC 4 project window, select the Basic template. Ensure the Razor view engine is selected. Tick the "Create a unit test project" check box. Keep the default name of `Ch9.R8.Web.Tests`, and then click OK.

Creating the Repository

The repository used in this example will consist of three data classes, an interface, and a stub that will eventually be implemented so that it uses Entity Framework to communicate with a back-end database. The actual full implementation will not be created as part of this exercise.

First, we will define our entity classes, as follows:

1. In Solution Explorer, right-click the Models folder in the web application project, select Add, and then Class.

2. In the Add New Item Window, ensure the Class template is selected, name the file **ArchitectProfileModels**, and then click Add.

3. Modify the new file so that it resembles Listing 9-25.

Listing 9-25. Entity Models Used with Repository

```
using System.Collections.Generic;
using System.Data.Entity;

namespace Ch9.R8.Web.Models
{

    public class Architect
    {
        public int ArchitectId { get; set; }
        public string FirstName { get; set; }
        public string LastName { get; set; }
        public string Department { get; set; }
        public string Country { get; set; }
        public List<Project> Projects { get; set; }
    }

    public class Project
    {
        public int ProjectId { get; set; }
        public string ProjectName { get; set; }
        public List<Document> Documents { get; set; }
    }

    public class Document
    {
        public int DocumentId { get; set; }
        public string DocumentTitle { get; set; }
        public string URL { get; set; }

    }

    public class ArchitectContext : DbContext
    {
        public DbSet<Architect> Architects { get; set; }
    }
}
```

4. Next, we will define an Interface for the repository. To do this, right-click the Models folder, select Add, and then New Item.

5. In the Add New Item window, type **Inter** into the search box in the upper-right of the window. Select the Interface template. Name the Interface **IArchitectRepository.cs**, and then click Add.

6. Modify the new code file so that it looks like Listing 9-26.

Listing 9-26. The IArchitectRepository Interface

```
using System.Collections.Generic;
using System;

namespace Ch9.R8.Web.Models
{
    public interface IArchitectRepository : IDisposable
    {
        List<Architect> GetArchitectList();
        Architect GetArchitectDetails(int id);
        void Create(Architect architect);
        void Update(Architect architect);
        void Delete(int id);
        void Save();
    }
}
```

7. Finally, we will stub out an implementation that eventually will use Entity Framework to talk to a back-end database. To do this, right-click the Models folder, select Add, and then Class.

8. In the Add New Item Window, ensure the Class template is selected, name the **file EFArchitectRepository.cs**, and then click Add.

9. Inside the file, type **IArchitectRepository** after the class declaration.

10. After you are done typing, a small pop-up menu will appear under the interface name. Click it and choose Implement Interface IArchitectRepository. The file will look like Listing 9-27. Note that calling any of the methods will throw a NotImplementedException. This is okay for now.

Listing 9-27. The EFArchitectRepository

```
using System;
using System.Collections.Generic;

namespace Ch9.R8.Web.Models
{
    public class EFArchitectRepository : IArchitectRepository
    {
        public List<Architect> GetArchitectList()
        {
            throw new NotImplementedException();
        }
```

```csharp
        public Architect GetArchitectDetails(int id)
        {
            throw new NotImplementedException();
        }

        public void Create(Architect architect)
        {
            throw new NotImplementedException();
        }

        public void Update(Architect architect)
        {
            throw new NotImplementedException();
        }

        public void Delete(int id)
        {
            throw new NotImplementedException();
        }

        public void Save()
        {
            throw new NotImplementedException();
        }

        public void Dispose()
        {
            throw new NotImplementedException();
        }
    }
}
```

Creating the Architect Controller and Views

Now that we have created an interface and a stub for the repository, we can start working on the controller. We will only build out enough of the controller to allow the code to compile. We will then move on to writing our tests.

To add the controller:

1. From the Visual Studio main menu, select Build ➤ Build Solution.

2. Right-click the Controllers node in the web application project, select Add, and then Controller.

3. In the Add Controller window, name the controller **ArchitectController** and select the "MVC Controller with read/write actions and views, using Entity Framework" template. Select Architect as the Model class and ArchitectContext as the Data Context class. Ensure that the Razor view engine is selected, and then click Add.

4. Visual Studio should have created the new controller with several actions for viewing, updating, and deleting Architects.

At this point, we have stubbed out much of the needed functionality, but nothing is functional. We have a few more steps that we need to do in order to make the controller testable. We can then move on to creating the tests.

The first step will be to modify the code generated by Visual Studio for our controller. We will remove the code that directly invokes the entity framework and replace it with calls to the repository. We will also add a constructor that takes an instance of the repository as a parameter, as well explicitly define a parameterless constructor that will set the repository to an instance of the EFArchitectRepository. The completed code should look like Listing 9-28. The code highlighted in bold are changes made to support testing.

Listing 9-28. Generated Controller Class Modified to Support Testing

```
using Ch9.R8.Web.Models;
using System.Web.Mvc;

namespace Ch9.R8.Web.Controllers
{
    public class ArchitectController : Controller
    {
        //using a repository rather the Entity Framework
        private IArchitectRepository m_Repository;

        //this constructor is required for testing
        public ArchitectController(IArchitectRepository respository)
        {
            m_Repository = respository;
        }

        //constructor required by MVC Framework
        // uses the EFArchitectRepository as the default controller
        public ArchitectController() : this(new EFArchitectRepository()){}

        public ActionResult Index()
        {
            return View("Index",m_Repository.GetArchitectList());
        }


        public ActionResult Details(int id = 0)
        {
            Architect architect = m_Repository.GetArchitectDetails(id);
            if (architect == null)
            {
                return HttpNotFound();
            }
            return View("Details",architect);
        }


        public ActionResult Create()
        {
            return View("Create");
        }
```

```
[HttpPost]
public ActionResult Create(Architect architect)
{
    if (ModelState.IsValid)
    {
        m_Repository.Create(architect);
        m_Repository.Save();
        return RedirectToAction("Index");
    }
    return View("Create", architect);
}


public ActionResult Edit(int id = 0)
{
    Architect architect = m_Repository.GetArchitectDetails(id);
    if (architect == null)
    {
        return HttpNotFound();
    }
    return View("Edit", architect);
}


[HttpPost]
public ActionResult Edit(Architect architect)
{
    if (ModelState.IsValid)
    {
        m_Repository.Update(architect);
        m_Repository.Save();
        return RedirectToAction("Index");
    }
    return View("Edit", architect);
}


public ActionResult Delete(int id = 0)
{
    Architect architect = m_Repository.GetArchitectDetails(id);
    if (architect == null)
    {
        return HttpNotFound();
    }
    return View("Delete", architect);
}

[HttpPost, ActionName("Delete")]
public ActionResult DeleteConfirmed(int id)
```

```
        {
            m_Repository.Delete(id);
            m_Repository.Save();
            return RedirectToAction("Index");
        }

        protected override void Dispose(bool disposing)
        {
            if (disposing)
            {
                m_Repository.Dispose();
            }
            base.Dispose(disposing);
        }
    }
}
```

Creating the Test Class

Now that we have enough controller logic in place, we can write some unit tests to verify the functionality.

1. In the test project, right-click the project node, select Add, and then Folder. Name the new folder **Controllers**.

2. Right-click the Controllers folder, select Add, and then Class.

3. In the Add New Item dialog box, confirm that the Class template is selected and name the class **ArchitectControllerTests.cs**.

4. Inside the class, add a public access modifier to the class and decorate it with the TestClass attribute. You will need to add a using statement to include Microsoft. VisualStudio.TestTools.UnitTesting. The modified class should look like Listing 9-29.

Listing 9-29. Class Converted to a Test Class

```
using Microsoft.VisualStudio.TestTools.UnitTesting;

namespace Ch9.R8.Web.Tests.Controllers
{
    [TestClass]
    public class ArchitectControllerTests
    {
    }
}
```

5. Define a region for the Index action. The regions will help us to keep the test class organized.

6. Inside the region, create a new method named **IndexAction_ReturnsIndexView** and decorate it with the Test Method attribute. This method will verify that the action returns the correct view.

7. Create a second method named **IndexAction_NoData_ViewBagMessageNoData**. This method will test the condition when no data is found.

8. Create a third method named **IndexAction_ModelIsTypeOfArtistList**. This method will confirm the functionality when records are found. It will also verify that the correct model type is being returned.

9. Create one last method and name it **IndexAction_1ArchitectFound_ ViewBagNumberFoundMessage1Found**. It will verify another dynamic property value that shows the number of records found.

10. In the body of each test method, place a call to Assert.Fail. This will prevent unfinished tests from passing or being skipped. The failed tests will remind us to complete the work. The four methods should look like Listing 9-30.

Listing 9-30. Test Method Stubs

```
#region Index Action
[TestMethod]
public void IndexAction_ReturnsIndexView()
{
  Assert.Fail("Incomplete Test Method");
}

[TestMethod]
public void IndexAction_NoData_ViewBagMessageNoData()
{
  Assert.Fail("Incomplete Test Method");
}

[TestMethod]
public void IndexAction_ArchitectsFound_ModelContainsArtistList()
{
  Assert.Fail("Incomplete Test Method");
}
[TestMethod]
public void IndexAction_1ArchitectFound_ViewBagNumberFoundMessage1Found()
{
  Assert.Fail("Incomplete Test Method");
}
#endregion
```

Adding Moq to Your Test Project

The three will require the use of a mock object in order to prevent our test from making calls to the database. Before we can create the mocks and complete the test methods, we will need to add Moq to our test project.

Luckily, with the use of NuGet, it is simple to add Moq to your project and keep it up-to-date. To add Moq:

1. Right-click the references node in your test project and select Manage NuGet Packages.

2. In the search Online text box located in the top right of the window, type **Moq**. After a few moments, Moq should appear in the packages list.

3. Click the Install button to add Moq to your test project.

4. Close the package manager.

Implementing the IndexAction_ReturnsIndexView Test

This is the simplest of the tests. Since all we are testing in this case is that the correct view is being returned, we do not need to provide any setup to the Moq object. In Moq, setup is the way you define how your implementation will behave.

The following steps are required to implement this test method using Moq.

1. Add using statements for the following namespaces:

    a. `Ch9.R8.Web.Controllers`: Required to access your controller.

    b. `Ch9.R8.Web.Models`: Needed for the Entity Types and repository interfaces.

    c. `Moq`: Required for the Moq Library.

    d. `System.Web.Mvc`: Required for accessing classes such as `ViewResult`, which will be used in the test.

2. Create a mock instance of the `IArchitectRepository` using `new Mock<IArchitectRepository>()`.

3. Create an instance of the `ArchitectController` that passes the mock object as a parameter to the `ArchitectController` constructor. The `IArchitectRepository` instance can be accessed through the Mock object's Object property.

4. Complete the test by executing the controller's Index action and then using assertions to validate the result. The completed example should look like Listing 9-31.

    Listing 9-31. IndexAction_ReturnsIndexView Test Method Using Moq

    ```
    [TestMethod]
    public void IndexAction_ReturnsIndexView()
    {
        // arrange
        string expected = "Index";
        var mock = new Mock<IArchitectRepository>();
        ArchitectController controller = new ArchitectController(mock.Object);

        // act
        ViewResult result = controller.Index() as ViewResult;

         // assert
         Assert.IsNotNull(result);
         Assert.AreEqual(expected, result.ViewName);
    }
    ```

To create the mock object, we use `Moq.Mock<T>`. This creates a mock of whatever interface is passed in as T. In this test method, we created a new `Mock<IArchitectRepository>`, which automatically creates an implementation of `IArchitectRepository` and stores it in its `Object` property. Since we have not told Moq how we want this implementation to behave, it will simply return nulls for all methods with return values and it will create empty implementations for methods with void return types. This is fine for this test because we are only testing whether or not the correct view name is being set. We expect that the same view will be returned in all cases.

Click the Run All button in Test Explorer. `IndexAction_ReturnsIndexView` should now pass and the rest should fail.

Implementing the IndexAction_NoData_ViewBagMessageNoData Test

In this test, we are validating that when no results are returned from the call to `GetArchitectList` that a dynamic property named `NoDataFoundMessage` will be written to the `ViewBag` with the value "No architects found". This test requires that we provide some setup for our Moq object. In this instance, we need to ensure that the `IArchitectRepository` `GetArchitectList` method returns an empty `List<Architect>` collection.

To implement this test:

1. Create a `string` named **expected** and provide the value "No architects found".

2. Create a mock instance of the `IArchitectRepository` using new `Mock<IArchitectRepository>()`.

3. Call the Setup method on the mock object and configure it so that the `GetArchitectList` method will return an empty `List<Architect>`.

4. Create an instance of the `ArchitectController` that passes the mock object as a parameter to the `ArchitectController` constructor. The `IArchitectRepository` instance can be accessed through the Mock object's Object property.

5. Complete the test by executing the controller's Index action and then using assertions to validate the result. The completed example should look like Listing 9-32.

Listing 9-32. IndexAction_NoData_ViewBagMessageNoData Using Moq

```
[TestMethod]
public void IndexAction_NoData_ViewBagMessageNoData()
{
    // arrange
    string expected = "No architects found.";
    var mock = new Mock<IArchitectRepository>();
    mock.Setup(a => a.GetArchitectList()).Returns(new List<Architect>());
    ArchitectController controller = new ArchitectController(mock.Object);

    // act
    ViewResult result = controller.Index() as ViewResult;
    string actual = result.ViewBag.NoDataFoundMessage as string;

    // assert
    Assert.AreEqual(expected, actual);
}
```

The Setup method Mock takes a lambda expression as a parameter. The Setup method allows us to supply an implementation for a particular method or property. In this case, we are providing setup for the `GetArchitectList` and then stating that it will return an empty `List<Architect>` collection by calling the Returns method.

If we run the test, it fails with the message:

```
Result Message: Assert.AreEqual failed. Expected:<No architects found.>. Actual:<(null)>.
```

To correct this problem, we need to modify the Index action so that it checks to see if any results are found from the call to `GetArchitectList`, and if not, populate the `ViewBag` `NoDataFoundMessage`. The modified version of the Index action is shown in Listing 9-33.

Listing 9-33. Index Action Modified to Pass Test

```
public ActionResult Index()
{
  List<Architect> architects = m_Repository.GetArchitectList();
  if (architects == null || architects.Count < 1)
  {
     ViewBag.NoDataFoundMessage = "No architects found.";
  }
  return View("Index",architects);
}
```

The refactored method first validates that the architects object is not null. You should always check that an object is not null before trying to access any of its properties. We then check the count property to see if it is less than 1. If so, we add the NoDataFoundMessage property to the ViewBag and set its value to "No architects found".

If we run the test again, both the IndexAction_NoData_ViewBagMessageNoData and IndexAction_ReturnsIndexView pass.

Implementing the IndexAction_ModelIsTypeOfArtistList Test

This test will verify that the Model property of the view result contains the correct type. In this case, we are expecting the model to be of the List<Architect> type. To implement this test:

1. Create a mock instance of the IArchitectRepository using new Mock<IArchitectRepository>().

2. Call the Setup method on the mock object and configure it so that the GetArchitectList method will return an empty List<Architect>.

3. Create an instance of the ArchitectController that passes the mock object as a parameter to the ArchitectController constructor.

4. Complete the test by executing the controller's Index action, and then use the Assert.IsInstanceOf method to validate the type of the Model property. The completed example should look like Listing 9-34.

   Listing 9-34. IndexAction_ModelIsTypeOfArtistList Using Moq

```
[TestMethod]
public void IndexAction_ModelIsTypeOfArtistList()
{
  // arrange
  var mock = new Mock<IArchitectRepository>();
  mock.Setup(a => a.GetArchitectList()).Returns(new List<Architect>());
  ArchitectController controller = new ArchitectController(mock.Object);

  // act
  ViewResult result = controller.Index() as ViewResult;

  // assert
  Assert.IsInstanceOfType(result.Model,typeof(List<Architect>));
}
```

If you run all tests, all should now pass, with the exception of IndexAction_1ArchitectFound_
ViewBagNumberFoundMessage1Found, which still has not been implemented.

Implementing the IndexAction_1ArchitectFound_ ViewBagNumberFoundMessage1Found Test

For the last test in this series, we will again use the Moq to create an implementation of the GetArchitectList
method. This time, however, we will not only create the collection but will pass in one record.

To implement this test:

1. Create a string named **expected** and provide the value "1 architects found".

2. Create a mock instance of the IArchitectRepository using new
   Mock<IArchitectRepository>().

3. Call the Setup method on the mock object and configure it so that the GetArchitectList
   method will return a List<Architect> collection that contains one record.

4. Create an instance of the ArchitectController that passes the mock object as a
   parameter to the ArchitectController constructor.

5. Call the controller's Index action and store the result in the result variable.

6. Attempt to get a string value from a dynamic ViewBag property called
   ViewBag.NumberFoundMessage, and write the results to a variable named actual.

7. Complete the test by using the Assert.AreEqual method to validate that the strings
   expected and actual are equal. The completed example should look like Listing 9-35.

Listing 9-35. IndexAction_1ArchitectFound_ViewBagNumberFoundMessage1Found Test

```
[TestMethod]
public void IndexAction_1ArchitectFound_ViewBagNumberFoundMessage1Found()
{
    // arrange
    string expected = "1 architects found.";
    var mock = new Mock<IArchitectRepository>();
    mock.Setup(a => a.GetArchitectList()).Returns(
            new List<Architect>()
            {
                new Architect { ArchitectId = 1 }
            }
            );
    ArchitectController controller = new ArchitectController(mock.Object);

    // act
    ViewResult result = controller.Index() as ViewResult;
    string actual = result.ViewBag.NumberFoundMessage as string;

    // assert
    Assert.AreEqual(expected, actual);
}
```

For this statement, we have provided an implementation of the GetArchitectList method that returns a List containing a single Architect. The contents of the list are declared inline using the C# shorthand syntax. When using this approach, be sure to use indentation to make your code readable.

When we run this test, it will fail. To correct this, we must modify the Index action to check for the condition, and then provide a value to the ViewBag.NumberFoundMessage. An updated version of the Index action is shown in Listing 9-36.

Listing 9-36. Index Action Updated to Add NumberOfFound Property to ViewBag

```
public ActionResult Index()
{
  List<Architect> architects = m_Repository.GetArchitectList();
  if (architects != null)
  {
    if (architects.Count < 1)
    {
      ViewBag.NoDataFoundMessage = "No architects found.";
    }
    else
    {
      ViewBag.NumberFoundMessage =
              string.Format("{0} architects found.", architects.Count);
    }
  }
    return View("Index",architects);
}
```

If you run all the tests again, they should all pass.

Using Mock to Verify That a Method Has Been Called

In the previous examples, we used the Setup and Return methods of Mock object to simulate a method call that returns a value. You can see how useful this is. What if we are testing to ensure that a method that returns void has been called? Since it does not return a value, how can we verify this?

Moq's answer to this problem is the Mock.Verify method. The syntax to Verify is similar to Setup in that it takes a lambda expression as a parameter. Like the Setup method, you can call mock.Verify(a => a.Method(parameter)), where mock is a Mock object of a given type, a is the interface instance created by the mock and parameter is the value you wish to pass.

If the method had not been called with the given parameter, Verify will throw a Moq.MockException with a message similar to the following:

```
Expected invocation on the mock at least once, but was never performed: a => a.Create(.architect)
```

To demonstrate this let's create some tests for the ArchitectController's HTTP POST Create method. This method expects an Architect object as a parameter. It then checks to see if the ModelState is valid and if so, it will call the update and save methods on the IArchitectRepository.

For our first test, we will validate that the redirect is occurring as expected in the case when we have a valid model.

To implement this test:

1. Create a `string` named **expected** and provide the value "Index".

2. Create a mock instance of the `IArchitectRepository` using new `Mock<IArchitectRepository>()`.

3. Create a new instance of an `Architect` object. You do not need to populate any properties because a test model validation does not occur when running your Action.

4. Create an instance of the `ArchitectController` that passes the mock object as a parameter to the `ArchitectController` constructor.

5. Call the controller's `Create` action with the `Architect` object we created in step 3 as a parameter, and store the result in the `result` variable. Since we are expecting a redirect return type it should be casted to a `RedirectToRouteResult` object.

6. Assert that the result value is not `null`. If the Create action returned a ViewResult rather than a `RedirectToRouteResult`, the result would be null and the test should fail.

7. Complete the test by using the `Assert.AreEqual` method to validate that the strings expected and `result.RouteValues["action"]` are equal. The completed example should look like Listing 9-37.

Listing 9-37. Verifying That You Are Redirected to the Correct Action

```
#region Create(Architect architect)
[TestMethod]
public void CreatePostAction_ModelStateValid_RedirectToIndexView()
{
  // arrange
  string expected = "Index";
  var mock = new Mock<IArchitectRepository>();

  Architect architect = new Architect();
  ArchitectController controller = new ArchitectController(mock.Object);

  // act
  RedirectToRouteResult result = controller.Create(architect) as RedirectToRouteResult;

  // assert
  Assert.IsNotNull(result);
  Assert.AreEqual(expected, result.RouteValues["action"]);
}
#endregion
```

This test validated that we are being properly redirected, but it does not tell us if the save and update methods of our repository have been called. Our next test will use the Validate methods of Moq to check that each of the methods have been called at least once.

To implement this test:

1. Create a mock instance of the `IArchitectRepository` using new `Mock<IArchitectRepository>()`.

2. Create a new instance of an `Architect` object.

371

3. Create an instance of the ArchitectController that passes the mock object as a parameter to the ArchitectController constructor.

4. Call the controller's Create action with the Architect object we created in step 3 as a parameter, and store the result in the result variable.

5. Call Verify on the mock object created in step 1 and pass in a call to IArchitectRepository Create.

6. Call Verify again and pass in a call to IArchitectRepository Save. The completed example should look like Listing 9-38.

   Listing 9-38. Using Moq Verify

   ```
   [TestMethod]
   public void CreatePostAction_ModelStateValid_UpdateAndSaveAreCalled()
   {
     // arrange
     var mock = new Mock<IArchitectRepository>();
     Architect architect = new Architect();
     ArchitectController controller = new ArchitectController(mock.Object);

     // act
     RedirectToRouteResult result = controller.Create(architect) as RedirectToRouteResult;

     // assert
     mock.Verify(a => a.Create(architect));
     mock.Verify(a => a.Save());
   }
   ```

The last test demonstrates how to simulate a model validation error. In the Create action, when model validation fails, we do not save changes and we return the current view rather than redirect to the Index action. To test this, we need to add a validation error to the controller's model state and then verify that it returns the correct Action.

To implement this test:

1. Create a string variable named **expected** and provide the value "Create".

2. Create a mock instance of the IArchitectRepository using new Mock<IArchitectRepository>().

3. Create a new instance of an Architect object.

4. Create an instance of the ArchitectController that passes the mock object as a parameter to the ArchitectController constructor.

5. Use the controller.ModelState.AddModelError method to add an error to the ModelState.

6. Call the controller's Create action with the Architect object we created in step 3 as a parameter, and store the result in the result variable.

7. Call Verify on the mock object created in step 1 and pass in a call to IArchitectRepository Create.

8. Call Verify again and pass in a call to IArchitectRepository Save. The completed example should look like Listing 9-39.

Listing 9-39. Simulating a Model Validation Error

```
[TestMethod]
public void CreatePostAction_ModelStateNotValid_ReturnCreateView()
{
    // arrange
    string expected = "Create";
    var mock = new Mock<IArchitectRepository>();

    Architect architect = new Architect();
    ArchitectController controller = new ArchitectController(mock.Object);
    controller.ModelState.AddModelError("FirstName", "FirstName is required");

    // act
    ViewResult result = controller.Create(architect) as ViewResult;

    // assert
    Assert.IsNotNull(result);
    Assert.AreEqual(expected, result.ViewName);
}
```

If you build your solution and then run all tests, all seven tests should pass. Using the techniques shown here, you can complete the rest of the tests needed for the Architect controller.

The completed example is available in the downloadable samples included on the book's web site.

■ ■ ■

CHAPTER 10

Moving From Web Forms to ASP.NET MVC

10-1. Creating a Simple Data List Using ASP.NET MVC

Problem

You are an experienced ASP.NET Web Forms developer and, in the past, you used the ASP.NET Repeater control when you needed to build a simple data-driven list. You are new to ASP.NET MVC. You have been asked to implement a page that will display a list of the last 20 new members who signed up on your company's web site. You would like to know the proper way to do this using ASP.NET MVC 4. If possible, you would like to leverage some of your existing code.

Solution

In ASP.NET Web Forms, the Repeater control is the least complex of the data controls that came with the framework. It allowed you to define templates for a header, a footer, data items, and separators. To use it, you would place the relevant HTML markup inside each section in conjunction with your ASP.NET data binding statements. If you wanted to inspect your data prior to it being written to the page so that you could have conditional markup displayed, you could implement event handlers such as ItemDataBound.

In ASP.NET MVC, the concept of server-side controls has been deprecated. To achieve functional equivalency with the ASP.NET Repeater control, you need to use a combination of server-side code in the form of Razor loop statements, HTML helpers, and Razor variables in addition to page markup, including HTML, JavaScript, and CSS.

How It Works

In this How It Works section, you will begin by demonstrating a Repeater control in a typical Web Forms scenario and then show how to re-create the functionality using ASP.NET MVC with the Razor view engine.

ASP.NET Web Forms Repeater Control

This example uses a Repeater control to display information about the last 20 users who registered for a web site. Like a lot of real production code, this example uses an HTML table to define the structure of the list. It also uses inline CSS and deprecated HTML attributes to define background colors and spacing between elements.

The example uses the Repeater control's HeaderTemplate property to define the initial structure of the table. It then uses the ItemTemplate and AlternatingItemTemplate to display the data. The item templates are almost identical, the exception being a different background color applied to the table row of each item. A SeparatorTemplate is used to create an empty table row with a dark gray background that is set as 1 pixel high. The FooterTemplate is used to complete the table structure. The one thing about this example that is not typical of most legacy code is the use of the ItemType property and the Item variables used in data-binding expressions. The ItemType property is a new construct added to Web Forms in ASP.NET 4.5 that allows you to use IntelliSense while authoring Web Forms pages. It also offers a simpler syntax than the other data binding syntax styles introduced in previous iterations of Web Forms. The Repeater control is shown in Listing 10-1.

Listing 10-1. Using the Repeater Control in a Web Forms Application

```
<asp:Repeater ID="ArtistsRepeater"
        runat="server"
        ItemType="Ch7.SharedAPI.Artist"
        OnItemDataBound="ArtistsRepeater_ItemDataBound">
    <HeaderTemplate>
        <table width="95%" cellpadding="5" cellspacing="5">
        <thead>
            <tr>
                <th>
                    User
                </th>
                <th>
                    Location
                </th>
                <th>
                    Account Creation Date
                </th>
            </tr>
        </thead>
    </HeaderTemplate>
    <ItemTemplate>
        <tr bgcolor="#AAAAAA" valign="top">
        <td width="150px">
            <asp:Image Height="100px" Width="100px"
                ImageUrl="<%# Item.AvatarUrlSample %>"
                AlternateText="<%# Item.UserName %>" runat="server" />
            <br />
            <asp:HyperLink NavigateUrl="/<%# Item.UserName %>"
                Text="<%# Item.UserName %>"
                runat="server"
                ID="ProfileHyperLink"></asp:HyperLink>
        </td>
        <td width="150px">
            <asp:Label ID="LocationLabel" runat="server"></asp:Label>
        </td>
        <td>
            <%# Item.CreateDate.ToShortDateString()%>
        </td>
        </tr>
    </ItemTemplate>
```

```
<AlternatingItemTemplate>
    <tr bgcolor="#EEEEEE" valign="top">
    <td width="150px">
        <asp:Image ID="Image1" Height="100px"
            Width="100px"
            ImageUrl="<%# Item.AvatarUrlSample %>"
            AlternateText="<%# Item.UserName %>"
            runat="server" />
        <br />
        <asp:HyperLink ID="ProfileHyperLink"
            NavigateUrl="/<%# Item.UserName %>"
            Text="<%# Item.UserName %>"
            runat="server"></asp:HyperLink>
    </td>
    <td width="150px">
        <asp:Label ID="LocationLabel" runat="server"></asp:Label>
    </td>
        <td>
            <%# Item.CreateDate.ToShortDateString()%>
        </td>
    </tr>
</AlternatingItemTemplate>
<SeparatorTemplate>
    <tr>
        <td colspan="3"
            style="background-color:#DDDDDD; height:1px;"></td>
    </tr>
</SeparatorTemplate>
<FooterTemplate>
        </table>
</FooterTemplate>
</asp:Repeater>
```

In the code-behind page, the page load event handler sets the Repeater control's DataSource property to the result of a LINQ query and then calls the Repeater's DataBind method. This causes a loop to be executed, which ultimately generates the combination of data and markup that is displayed in the web browser. The Page_Load event is shown in Listing 10-2.

Listing 10-2. The Repeater Controls Data Source Being Set in a Page_Load Event Handler

```
protected void Page_Load(object sender, EventArgs e)
{
  using (MobEntities context = new MobEntities())
  {
    //last 20 Artist records created
    var newArtistsQuery = (from m in context.Artists
                        orderby m.CreateDate descending
                        select m).Take(20);
    List<Artist> newArtistsList = newArtistsQuery.ToList<Artist>();
```

```
        ArtistsRepeater.DataSource = newArtistsList;
        ArtistsRepeater.DataBind();
    }
}
```

The code-behind page also implements the ItemDataBound event handler for the Repeater control. The event handler takes two parameters, sender which is a reference to the object that generated the event and RepeaterItemEventArgs which contains information about the data bound to that particular row. Inside the event handler, the current DataItem is inspected to see if values have been set for any of the properties that make up the location. The data from the City, Provence, and Country properties are then combined with some markup using a StringBuilder object. The StringBuilder.ToString is called to create the string value, which is written to the text property of LocationLabel (defined in both item templates in the Repeater control). The ItemDataBound event handler is shown in Listing 10-3.

Listing 10-3. The ItemDataBound Event Handler for the Repeater Control

```
protected void ArtistsRepeater_ItemDataBound(object sender, RepeaterItemEventArgs e)
{
    if (e.Item.ItemType == ListItemType.Item || e.Item.ItemType == ListItemType.AlternatingItem)
    {
        Artist currentItem = e.Item.DataItem as Artist;
        Label locationLabel = e.Item.FindControl("LocationLabel") as Label;
        if (currentItem != null && locationLabel!=null)
        {
            StringBuilder builder = new StringBuilder();
            if (!String.IsNullOrEmpty(currentItem.City))
            {
              builder.Append(currentItem.City);
                builder.Append("<br/>");
            }
            if (!String.IsNullOrEmpty(currentItem.Province))
            {
                builder.Append(currentItem.Province);
                builder.Append("<br/>");
            }
            if (!String.IsNullOrEmpty(currentItem.Country))
            {
                builder.Append(currentItem.Country);
            }
            locationLabel.Text = builder.ToString();
        }
    }
}
```

In this example, the code-behind page is filling several roles. First, it is acting in a way similar to an MVC controller in that it is manipulating a model and then passing it to the presentation layer. It is also implementing presentation logic in the Item_DataBound event handler, where it combines data with markup, and then writes the values to a set of page elements.

Migrating the Repeater Sample to ASP.MVC Using Razor

Migrating a Repeater's control code to ASP.NET MVC is a somewhat straightforward process. The simplest approach is to move the code from the Web Form's Page_Load event into a controller action. You could then migrate the Web Form code to Razor syntax inside a view. Let's go through this process step-by-step, and then once the example is functional, we can refactor the page so that it benefits from the increased testability and cleaner separation of concerns offered by ASP.NET MVC. While we are at it, we can also clean up the markup so that inline styles and outdated markup are replaced by more modern techniques.

Locating the Code Samples for This Recipe

Open the Visual Studio solution located in the companion code's Chapter10\Ch10.MvcExamples\Before folder. Once the project is loaded, expand the Controllers folder in Solution Explorer, and then open the DataExamplesController.cs file by double-clicking it. Once the file is open, locate the RepeaterReplacement controller action.

To access the code for the Web Forms sample, open a second instance of Visual Studio and then open the project found in Chapter10\Ch10.WebFormsExamples. In the example Web Forms project, expand the DataControlsExamples folder in Solution Explorer, and then double-click RepeaterExample.aspx to open it. You can right-click anywhere in the open .aspx file in the code editor and select View Code to open the code-behind page for the Repeater example.

■ **Note**   Most of the examples in this chapter are in a single Visual Studio project located in the Chapter10\Ch10.MvcExamples folder. The completed examples are in the Chapter10\Ch10.MvcExamples\After folder. If you wish to follow along with each recipe, you can use the project in Chapter10\Ch10.MvcExamples\Before as a starting point for the exercises in each section.

Migrating the Logic in the Page_Load Event to the Controller Action

Since the LINQ query from the ASP.NET Web Forms project can be reused, the fastest way to get up and running is to copy the code from the Page_Load event handler in the RepeaterExample.aspx.cs, and then paste it into the RepeaterReplacement action in the MVC project's DataExampleController.cs file.

After pasting the code, you will notice that a few lines will have the red squiggly underlining that indicates an error. The first error is that the MobEntities and Artist objects are not recognized. To solve this problem, you can click the MobEntities class name inside the code editor, and then click the small pop-up menu. This will display a list of options that can be performed to resolve the error. Select the Using Ch7.SharedAPI option to add the Using statement to the code project. This will solve the first set of errors.

The next two errors are caused because the object ArtistRepeater does not exist in the current context. Since we do not use Repeater controls with ASP.NET MVC, we can delete the two lines of code that reference the control. In order to pass the query results to the view, change the return statement so that newArtistList is passed as a parameter to the View method.

There is one more problem. Since we have wrapped our MobEntities object in a Using statement, it will be disposed of before the view is rendered. This will cause an error when you try to access the model's data from the view. To solve this problem, we will factor out the MobEntities declaration to a global member variable and initialize it in the controller's constructor. Rename the variable **m_context** to denote that it is a member variable. Also override the Dispose method to the constructor to ensure that the context is disposed as soon as possible, which will return our database connection to the connection pool. You should note that MVC controllers use the "finalizer" implementation of IDisposable, which takes the bool parameter disposing. The DataExampleController is shown in Listing 10-4.

Listing 10-4. DataExampleController's RepeaterReplacement Action

```
using Ch7.SharedAPI;
//..statements removed for brevity
MobEntities m_context = new MobEntities();

public ActionResult RepeaterReplacement()
{
  //last 20 Artist records created
  var newArtistsQuery = (from m in m_context.Artists
                           orderby m.CreateDate descending
                           select m).Take(20);
  List<Artist> newArtistsList = newArtistsQuery.ToList<Artist>();

  return View(newArtistsList);
}

protected override void Dispose(bool disposing)
{
   if (disposing)
   {
      if (m_context != null)
        m_context.Dispose();
   }
   base.Dispose(disposing);
}
```

Migrating the Web Form Markup to a Razor View

Migrating the markup code from a Web Form is hardly ever fun, especially if the code was created by an earlier version of the Visual Studio designer. In most cases, as well as converting the ASP.NET controls to regular HTML elements, you will also need to refactor the code to move inline styles into a separate file.

Another challenge is what to do with the code that was formerly in the ItemDataBound event handler. In some ways, it can be considered view logic since it is altering the way the content describing the user's location is displayed on the page. You could also easily say that this code is modifying a model that includes a property called Location. Another way to look at it is that you do have a Location property, but it is a computed property that includes data from City, Provence, and Country. If it is view logic, then it belongs in the view implemented as a series of control statements. If you are manipulating the model, you should be doing so in the controller. If it is a computed property, you can put this logic in the model. The trick is that if you take either of the latter approaches, you should factor out the need to include HTML break tags in order to maintain separation of concerns.

For this example, we will take the first approach (which considers this a view logic concern). But rather than resort to inline control statements, we will create an HTML helper that concatenates a set of strings. If the string is null or empty, it will be skipped. If a value is found, it will output the string followed by an HTML break tag. For the last string in the set, no line break will be added.

This approach keeps the HTML tags out of the controller logic, increases code reuse, and improves readability and maintainability of the view. Another advantage is that HTML helpers are easy to test, whereas inline control statements in a view are not.

To create the HTML helper, in the MVC Web solution, right-click the Ch10.Shared.Helpers project, and select Add and then Class. In the Add New Item dialog box, ensure the Class template is selected and change the name of the file to Ch10ListHelpers.cs. Inside the file, first designate the class as a static class, and then create a new method named ConcatProperties, as shown in Listing 10-5. ConcatProperties is an extension method that will be accessible by calling @Html.ConcatProperties. The @Html variable is an instance of the HtmlHelper class that is available in all MVC views.

This method uses the params keyword, which allows us to add any number of strings in the parameter list. By using it, we have mirrored the String.Concat method, which should make using this helper easier for developers to learn since it follows a familiar pattern. It also adds flexibility to the helper method, which makes it more reusable.

Listing 10-5. Custom HTML Helper CompositePropertyExtension.cs

```
public static class Ch10Helpers
{
  public static MvcHtmlString ConcatProperties(this HtmlHelper helper, params string[] text)
  {
    if (text != null)
    {
      StringBuilder builder = new StringBuilder();
      for (int i = 0; i < text.Length; i++)
      {
        if (!string.IsNullOrEmpty(text[i]))
        {
          builder.Append(AntiXssEncoder.HtmlEncode(text[i],true));
          if (i < text.Length - 1)
          {
            builder.Append("<br/>");
          }
        }
      }
      return MvcHtmlString.Create(builder.ToString());
    }
    return MvcHtmlString.Empty;
  }
}
```

An important thing to notice about Listing 10-5 is that it returns the type of MvcHtmlString. This is necessary in order for the HTML markup that you have added to be preserved when used in a view. ASP.NET MVC will automatically HTML Encode all strings to help eliminate cross-site scripting vulnerabilities. When using the MvcHtmlString type, the view engine will assume that the string has already been encoded and will not attempt to encode it again. With this in mind, when writing a custom helper, be sure to use AntiXssEncoder.HtmlEncode to encode any string that may have been created from user input.

▓ **Note**　The AntiXssEncoder is similar to the HttpUtility.HtmlEncode method in that it will encode HTML in your data so that it will be shown in the browser as normal text. This prevents potentially harmful input created by a malicious user from executing in another user's browser session. The difference between these methods is that AntiXssEncoder uses a "white list" approach that encodes all characters except the ones that are known to be safe. HttpUtility.HtmlEncode, on the other hand, uses a "black list" approach that only encodes the characters <, >, &, and ". There are several techniques that can be used to get around the simple black list and launch a successful cross-site scripting attack. AntiXssEncoder was formally part of a third-party library created from Microsoft patterns and practices. As of ASP.NET 4.5, it is not included with System.Web, but is accessible from the System.Web.Security. AntiXss namespace.

In order to use your custom helper, you will need to add a namespace entry in the Web.config file located in the Views directory in the MVC Project. This will make this extension and all other extensions you define in this namespace available to all of your views. Make sure that you are making the change to the Web.config file in your views folder and not the one at the root of the site. The change to Web.config is shown in Listing 10-6.

Listing 10-6. Adding a Namespace to the Views/Web.config File

```
<system.web.webPages.razor>
    <host factoryType="System.Web.Mvc.MvcWebRazorHostFactory, System.Web.Mvc, Version=4.0.0.0,
Culture=neutral, PublicKeyToken=31BF3856AD364E35" />
    <pages pageBaseType="System.Web.Mvc.WebViewPage">
      <namespaces>
        <add namespace="System.Web.Mvc" />
        <add namespace="System.Web.Mvc.Ajax" />
        <add namespace="System.Web.Mvc.Html" />
        <add namespace="System.Web.Optimization"/>
        <add namespace="System.Web.Routing" />
        <add namespace="Ch10.Shared.Helpers" />
      </namespaces>
    </pages>
  </system.web.webPages.razor>
```

Next, you will build out the view. You can start by taking the code from the RepeaterExample.aspx page from the Web Forms project and pasting it into your view. You will then need to remove the asp:Repeater tag as well as its child tags, such as HeaderTemplate and FooterTemplate. Next, convert all of the other ASP.NET control tags, such as the asp:HyperLink tag, to regular HTML elements. You can also remove all of the content contained in the AlternatingItemTemplate. This is no longer needed.

Once all the Web Forms control references have been removed, you should add the @model declaration to the top of the page to the type List<Ch7.SharedAPI.Artist>. You can then create a foreach loop around the table body. Inside the loop, convert the Web Forms data-binding tags to Razor variables. For example, you would convert <%# Item.UserName %> to @item.UserName. In place of the label control that contained the location, you will use the HTML helper you created. When you have completed this, your view should look similar to Listing 10-7. At this point, your view should be functional. You should test it by launching your project in the debugger and navigating to DataExamples/RepeaterReplacement.

Listing 10-7. View Created with Code Derived from Content Pasted from Web Forms Project

```
@model List<Ch7.SharedAPI.Artist>
@{
    ViewBag.Title = "Repeater Replacement";
}

<h2>@ViewBag.Title /h2>

<table width="95%" cellpadding="5" cellspacing="5">
    <thead>
        <tr>
            <th>User
            </th>
            <th>Location
            </th>
```

```
                <th>Account Creation Date
                </th>
        </tr>
    </thead>
    @foreach(var item in Model){
    <tr bgcolor="#AAAAAA" valign="top">
        <td width="150px">
            <img height="100px" width="100px"
                src="@item.AvatarUrlSample"
                alt="@item.UserName"/>
            <br />
            <a href="/@item.UserName"
                id="ProfileHyperLink">@item.UserName</a>
        </td>
        <td width="150px">
            @Html.ConcatProperties(item.City, item.Province, item.Country)
        </td>
        <td>@item.CreateDate.ToShortDateString()
        </td>
    </tr>
    <tr>
        <td colspan="3"
            style="background-color: #DDDDDD; height: 1px;"></td>
    </tr>
    }
</table>
```

■ **Note** When you edit the view, Visual Studio's IntelliSense feature should show your custom HTML helper extensions methods in list of properties and methods displayed after typing for the `@Html HtmlHelper` instance in your view. If you do not see your extensions methods make sure that you have added a reference to the project that contains your helper extensions and have rebuilt your web project. If you had the view open in the editor prior to adding the namespace to your `Web.config` file, close and reopen the view.

Refactoring the HTML in Your View

The HTML copied from the Web Forms project is not HTML5 compliant. In fact, it actually violates more than nine rules. In addition, since the revised markup removed the `AlternatingItemTemplate`, the alternate row coloring in the Web Forms version has been lost.

A few other places in the view are using inline CSS styles. Even though this is perfectly legal HTML, it is not a best practice for maintainability and performance reasons. If you are a veteran Web Forms developer, there is a good chance that you only have cursory knowledge of CSS. This is because Web Forms abstracted away HTML and did not necessarily force you to use it. While Web Forms does not prevent you from using external CSS, the tooling around it, especially in earlier versions of Visual Studio, encouraged the use of inline styles and made working with external style sheets more difficult.

To correct these problems, let's start by factoring out the deprecated HTML attributes and inline styles into a separate CSS file.

To add a new CSS file to your project, right-click the Content folder in Solution Explorer, and select New and then Style Sheet. In the Specify Name for Item dialog window, give the item the name **GridStyles**. Click OK to create the file. The new style sheet will open in the code editor window. Next, open App_Start/BundleConfig.cs and modify the "~/Content/css", as shown in Listing 10-8. In cases where you only plan to use a set of styles once, you can explicitly include it in the page by using the HTML <link rel="stylesheet"> tag. In these cases, you will be creating a style that you can use for all grid-type output so that grids will have a consistent look throughout the site. By adding the CSS file to the bundle, its contents will be compressed and combined with the other files listed in the bundle. This will result in a smaller and faster overall download, which will increase the initial load experience of your page.

Listing 10-8. Changes Made to BundleConfig.cs

```
bundles.Add(new StyleBundle("~/Content/css").Include(
            "~/Content/site.css",
            "~/Content/GridStyles.css"
        ));
```

Next, add new styles in GridStyles.css that will define the outer layer of the grid, which in the current HTML is implemented as a Table element, a grid row, an alternating grid row, an avatar image, and a separator grid row. The completed style sheet should look like Listing 10-9.

Listing 10-9. GridStyles.css

```
.grid {
    background-color: #fff;
    margin: 5px 0 10px;
    padding-left: 5px;
    width: 95%;
}
    .grid td {
        color: #717171;
        color: #1a1a1a;
        vertical-align: top;
    }

    .grid th {
        background-color: #333;
        color: #fff;
        font-size: large;
        font-weight: bolder;
        padding-bottom: 5px;
        padding-left: 13px;
        padding-top: 5px;
        text-align: left;
    }

.SeparatorRow td {
    background-color: #C0C0C0;
    border-style: dotted none none none;
    color: #717171;
    height: 1px;
    margin: 0px;
    padding: 0px;
}
```

```
.imgColumn {
    text-align: center;
    width: 100px;
}

.odd {
    background-color: #ebeced;
}

.even {
    background-color: #99acb9;
}
.AvatarImage {
    -moz-border-radius: 5px;
    -webkit-border-radius: 5px;
    border-radius: 5px;
    -webkit-box-shadow: 3px 3px 7px #777;
    -moz-box-shadow: 3px 3px 7px #777;
    box-shadow: 3px 3px 7px #777;
    height: 100px;
    margin: 5px;
    width: 100px;
}

.ProfileLink {
    font-size: 12pt;
    font-weight: bolder;
    letter-spacing: 0.2em;
    text-decoration: none;
    text-transform: lowercase;
}
```

The CSS code in Listing 10-9 provides a substantial upgrade to the styling in the Web Forms example. This style takes advantage of some newer browser capabilities, such as box shadows, which create a drop-shadow effect and border-radius, which can be used to round the corners on otherwise square elements. Moving the style information out of the HTML provides several benefits over using inline styles, including the following:

- Views are much easier to read and maintain.

- Since the visual aspects of your views are defined in one place, it is easy to make global changes to the look and feel of your site without effecting functionality.

- Overall smaller downloads since HTML is simplified.

- Benefits from client-side caching.

- You can use media queries to drastically change the layout of a page based on screen size.

■ **Tip**   If you plan on doing a lot of CSS coding in Visual Studio, I highly recommend installing the Web Essentials 2012 add-in, which is available for free and can be downloaded and installed using the Visual Studio Extensions and Updates manager. It is especially helpful when using CSS 3 constructs such as `box-shadow`. With a single click, it can add all the missing vendor-specific versions of elements, such as `-webkit-box-shadow` and `-moz-box-shadow`.

In ASP.NET MVC and in modern web development in general, understanding CSS and JavaScript are essentially unavoidable. Chapter 11 provides more in-depth coverage on this subject. Now that the styles are defined, we can apply them to our view. Listing 10-10 shows the updated view that is taking advantage of the styles.

Listing 10-10.   Refactored RepeaterReplacement.cshtml

```
@model List<Ch7.SharedAPI.Artist>
@{
    ViewBag.Title = "Repeater Replacement";
}
<h2>Repeater Replacement</h2>
<table class="grid">
    <thead>
        <tr>
            <th>User
            </th>
            <th>Location
            </th>
            <th>Account Creation Date
            </th>
        </tr>
    </thead>
    @foreach (var item in Model)
    {
        <tr>
            <td class="imgColumn">
                <img class="AvatarImage"
                src="@item.AvatarUrlSample"
                alt="@item.UserName" />
                <br />
                <a href="/@item.UserName" class="ProfileLink">@item.UserName</a>
            </td>
            <td>@Html.ConcatProperties(item.City, item.Province, item.Country)</td>
            <td>@item.CreateDate.ToShortDateString()</td>
        </tr>
        <tr class="SeparatorRow">
            <td colspan="3"></td>
        </tr>
    }
</table>
```

Notice how much cleaner and easier to read the code in Listing 10-10 is compared to Listing 10-1. All of the styling has been moved out of the view so that only basic markup and data-binding expressions remain. Run the project and examine how the new version looks. You will notice that although it has been improved visually, it is still missing the alternating row coloring. Stop debugging and return to Visual Studio.

To correct this problem, let's take advantage of some of the capabilities of the jQuery library. This library is included with almost all of the ASP.NET MVC templates and is an essential component for ASP.NET MVC development.

At the bottom of the view, add the code shown in Listing 10-11. This short script uses jQuery's odd and even selectors to select all the even-numbered table rows in the view, with the exception of those with the SeparatorRow class, and then adds the even CSS class to them. In the next line, it performs a similar operation for the odd-numbered rows. The end result is that our grid has alternating colors. This is a nice change from the original version that had the same markup repeated twice, but with a different inline style to denote the background color of the table row.

Listing 10-11. Using JQuery to Add Alternating Item Styles to a Table

```
@section scripts{
    <script>
        $(function () {
            $("tr:not(.SeparatorRow):even").addClass("even");
            $("tr:not(.SeparatorRow):odd").addClass("odd");
        });
    </script>
}
```

In the jQuery code, we define a function inside the $(); construct. This is a shorthand form in jQuery to specify what code we would like executed once the DOM has been loaded. Inside the function, we use jQuery's selector syntax to select all of the tr elements in the document, except those with the .SeparatorRow class assigned to them. We then select the even-numbered items in that subset and add the even CSS class to them. We then perform a similar operation on the odd-numbered rows.

Refactoring for Testability

At this point, you could just check in the code and call it a day. However, if you did, you would be neglecting one of the primary benefits of ASP.NET MVC: testability. The first item that you will create tests for is the custom HTML helper. Even if you are not following a test-driven development methodology, it is still advised that you write tests for your helpers. This is because in most cases, the helpers will be reused. A bug in a helper can have wide-reaching implications because the issue will exist in all pages views that use them.

To create the test for your helpers, right-click the Ch10.Shared.Helpers.Tests project and select Add ➤ Class. Name the new class **ConcatPropertyHelpersTests**.

The Ch10.Shared.Helpers.Tests project used in this example includes a reference to the NUnit unit testing framework. To use this framework, you need to have it installed on your development machine. Instructions for setting this up are in Recipe 9-4.

In order to test the HTML helper, you will need to add the following assemblies to the test project:

- System.Web
- System.Web.MVC
- Ch10.Shared.Helpers

Once you have added the assemblies, you can add test methods for each use case. You should add tests to account for all possible code paths to validate that the code functions as you expect. For this helper, you will test for six possible use cases.

1. Three string values passed as parameters. The expected output will be the three variables concatenated with a break tag <br/> preceding each of them except the last element.

2. Three string values passed as parameters, but with one of the values as a null. The null item should be ignored and no break tag should be added.

3. A single null parameter passed in. In this case, an empty string should be returned.

4. One string value passed as a parameter. Here, the string should be returned with no break tag preceding it.

5. One empty string passed as a parameter. This should behave in a similar manner as the null value, with an empty string being returned.

6. Finally, a single item that includes some HTML. For this one, the element should be encoded.

A fragment of the final result is shown in Listing 10-12. You can view the full example by viewing the sample code downloaded from the book's web site.

Listing 10-12. Unit Testing the HTML Helper with NUnit

```
using NUnit.Framework;
using System.Web.Mvc;
using System.Web.Security.AntiXss;
using Ch10.Shared.Helpers;

namespace Ch10.Shared.Helpers.Tests
{
    [TestFixture]
    public class ConcatPropertyHelpersTests
    {
        [Test]
        public void ConcatProperty_threeValuesNONulls_ReturnsThreeValuesseperatedByLineBreaks()
        {
            // Arrange
            HtmlHelper helper = new HtmlHelper(new ViewContext(), new ViewPage());
            //act
            string expected = "A<br/>B<br/>C";
            string actual = helper.ConcatProperties("A", "B", "C").ToString();
            //Assert
            Assert.AreEqual(expected, actual);
        }
//
// other tests ommited for brevity
//
        [Test]
        public void ConcatProperty_StringContainsHtml_ReturnsHtmlEncodedStringNoBR()
        {
            // Arrange
            HtmlHelper helper = new HtmlHelper(new ViewContext(), new ViewPage());
            string expected = AntiXssEncoder.HtmlEncode("<b>A</b>",true);
            //act
            string actual = helper.ConcatProperties("<b>A</b>").ToString();
```

```
            //Assert
            Assert.AreEqual(expected, actual);
        }
    }
}
```

The next item to make testable will be the controller. To do this, we will move the LINQ query out of the controller and into a repository class in our `Models` folder. This class will implement an interface that defines methods for calling the needed data. The interface will allow us to use a mocking framework in our unit tests to replace the calls to our database with a mocked implementation that always returns a predefined set of values.

The modified `DataExampleController.cs` file is shown in Listing 10-13. Detailed tutorials on creating unit tests for controllers are in Chapter 9.

Listing 10-13. DataExampleController Modified to Support Unit Testing

```
using Ch10.Mvc.Web.Models;
using Ch7.SharedAPI;
using System.Collections.Generic;
using System.Web.Mvc;

namespace Ch10.Mvc.Web.Controllers
{
    public class DataExamplesController : Controller
    {
        private IDataExampleRepository m_repository;
        public DataExamplesController(IDataExampleRepository repository)
        {
            m_repository = repository;
        }
        public DataExamplesController()
            : this(new EFDataExchangeRepository())
        {
        }
        //
        // GET: /DataExamples/

        public ActionResult Index()
        {
            return View("Index");
        }

        public ActionResult RepeaterReplacement()
        {
            List<Artist> newArtistsList = m_repository.GetNewArtistList();
            return View("RepeaterReplacement", newArtistsList);
        }

        protected override void Dispose(bool disposing)
        {
            if (disposing)
```

```
        {
            if (m_repository != null)
                m_repository.Dispose();
        }
        base.Dispose(disposing);
    }

    }
}
```

The first changes are the addition of two constructors. One constructor takes an instance of an object that implements the IDataExampleRepository interface. The second constructor does not take any parameters, but calls the first constructor passing in an instance of the EFDataExampleRepository. This second constructor is the one that will be called by the MVC Framework. Another change removed the global member variable for the MobEntities data context, and instead had a member variable for the repository. The repository is used in the RepeaterReplacement to get the list of Artists that will be passed to the view. We also modified the call to View so that the name of the view is passed in explicitly. This is required in order to write a unit test that can verify that the controller is calling the correct view. That last code change modified the dispose method. It now calls Dispose on the repository rather than on the MobEntities object.

The final result should look like Figure 10-1, which shows how the example will look in the Chrome web browser.

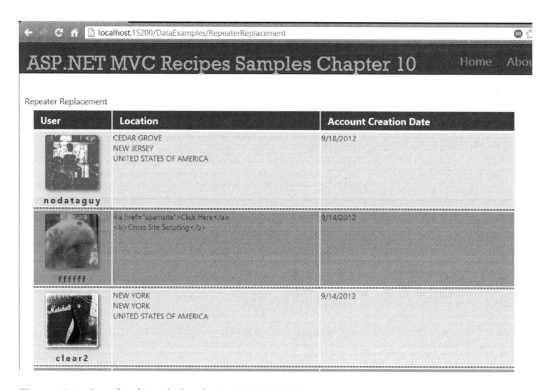

Figure 10-1. *Completed simple data list in ASP.NET MVC*

10-2. Creating a Multiple Column Data List Using a Custom HTML Helper Extension

Problem

You are building a new application using ASP.NET MVC 4. You have requirements to display a list of items in a four-column format. As a veteran ASP.NET Web Forms developer, you would normally accomplish this using a `DataList` control. You would like to know how to do the same thing using ASP.NET MVC with the Razor view engine. You would like to reuse existing code where possible.

Solution

There are a few possible solutions to this problem. One would be to follow the methodology that was used in Recipe 10-1, where you define an HTML table inside a view. The problem with this approach is that you need to replicate this logic in every page you create that has similar requirements.

Another approach would be to use a `foreach` loop in your view to output your template as a series of listing items in an HTML unordered list (`<ul>`). You can then use CSS and JavaScript to dynamically adjust the number of columns displayed based on the resolution of the user's display. This very cool technique is shown in Chapter 11's Recipe 11-1. The only problem with this approach is that it does not support all legacy browsers and will run somewhat slowly on Internet Explorer versions prior to IE 9.

The third approach, shown in this example, is to create an HTML helper that lets you specify the number of columns that you need to create, and then lets you specify the template for each column defined in a partial view.

How It Works

From a straight productivity standpoint, it is hard to argue with the simplicity of being able to drag a `DataList` control to a Web Form, specify the direction and number of columns required, and then bind the list to a data source. For this reason, ASP.NET Web Forms continues to be popular, especially in corporate environments where the deadline is typically the first documented requirement.

It is possible to create a similar level of efficiency with ASP.NET MVC once you learn the correct techniques and build up a library of custom HTML helpers that aid you in your design. In addition to having a highly productive developer experience, you can reap the advantages of clean HTML and increased testability.

This recipe will first show how to create a multi-column data list in ASP.NET Web Forms and then show how to create a functionally equivalent design using ASP.NET MVC. If you wish to follow along, you can use two Visual Studio solutions that can be downloaded from the book's web site. The Web Forms solution is in `Chapter10\Ch10.WebFormsExamples` and the completed MVC version is in `Chapter10\Ch10.MvcExamples\After`. There is also an incomplete version of the project located in the `Chapter10\Ch10.MvcExamples\Before` folder.

Using the ASP.NET Web Forms DataList Control

The ASP.NET Web Forms `DataList` control is very similar to the `Repeater` control in that it will iterate through the items in a data source and output the contents of a specified template. The main difference between the `Repeater` and the `DataList` is that the entire output is wrapped in an HTML table. It then uses the values in its `RepeatColumns` and `RepeatDirection` to determine how to wrap table rows and table columns around your content.

Listing 10-14 shows an example of a `DataList` control being used to output a list of web site users. Each item in the list will have a profile image, a user name, a link to the user's profile page, and information regarding their location. The `DataList` control's `RepeatColumns` has been set to 2 and `RepeatDirection` to horizontal. This will output the items in the list in a table with three columns. After every third item, a new row will be created. On the final row, if there is less than three items in the row, it will create empty columns to complete the row.

Listing 10-14. DataList Control Example

```
<asp:DataList ID="NewArtistDataList"
    runat="server"
    RepeatColumns="3"
    RepeatDirection="Horizontal"
    CellSpacing="3"
    ViewStateMode="Disabled">
        <ItemTemplate>
            <a href="/<%#Eval("UserName")%>">
                <div class="evenbox">
                    <div class="ImageDiv">
                        <img src="<%#Eval("AvatarUrlSample") %>"
                            class="AristImage"
                            alt="Click Image to view full profile" />
                    </div>
                    <div class="ContentDiv">
                        <ul>
                            <li>
                                <%#Eval("UserName")%>
                            </li>
                            <li><%#Eval("Provence")%></li>
                            <li><%#Eval("Country")%>    </li>
                            <li>Joined :
                                <time><%#Eval("CreateDate","{0:d}")%></time>
                            </li>
                        </ul>
                    </div>
                </div>
            </a>
        </ItemTemplate>
</asp:DataList>
```

The code example in Listing 10-14 uses the Data Binding #Eval syntax introduced with ASP.NET 2.0. This syntax offers one-way data binding and allows you to provide some string formatting inline, such as with #Eval("CreateDate","{0:d}") where the created data field is formatted using the default date and time format. Listing 10-14 uses some modern techniques, including HTML5 semantic tags and an ordered list rather than a nested table. An external style sheet is used to format the items, creating an attractive look to the list.

The DataList control's ViewStateMode property has been set to Disabled. This substantially reduces the size of the download and will thus shorten the page's load time. The ViewStateMode property was introduced as part of ASP. NET 4. If you are still using Web Forms for any of your projects, I highly recommend using this property wherever practical. The side effect of not using ViewState with this control is that in a postback, all content in the control will be lost unless you reapply the data binding.

The code-behind page for the DataList example, shown in Listing 10-15, is very simple. It calls an external library to return list and Artist objects, and then sets the list to the DataSource property of the DataList control. It then calls the DataList control's DataBind property.

Listing 10-15. DataList Code-Behind Page

```
public partial class DataListExample : System.Web.UI.Page
    {
        protected void Page_Load(object sender, EventArgs e)
```

```
    {
        using (MobEntities context = new MobEntities())
        {
            var newArtistsQuery = (from m in context.Artists
                                       orderby m.CreateDate descending
                                       select m).Take(20);
            List<Artist> newArtistsList = newArtistsQuery.ToList<Artist>();

            NewArtistDataList.DataSource = newArtistsList;
            NewArtistDataList.DataBind();
        }
    }
}
```

Migrating a DataList Control to ASP.NET MVC

As stated in the Solution section, you shall be creating a custom HTML helper that will allow you to be more productive when implementing views with a multiple-column requirement. The HTML helper will take an ICollection data source and a path to a partial view as parameters. You could then make calls to this helper method using syntax such as @Html.RenderTemplateAsColumns(SomeList, "/SomePartialView", 3). The numeric parameter would be the number of columns.

One problem with this approach is that you need to define the layout of the items in a separate file. This is not that bad, but it definitely adds some minor complexity. On the other hand, this technique allows your view to be very simple. It also allows both the partial view for the template and the HTML helper to be reused in several scenarios. For example, on your home page, you can have a one-column instance, and have a three-column view appear on another page with perhaps an even larger column layout with the same data.

Creating the RenderTemplateAsColumns Helper

To create the HTML helper, in the Ch10.Mvc Solution, right-click the Ch10.Shared.Helpers project node. Select New and then Class. Name the new class **Ch10ColumnHelpers.cs**. Inside the new class file, change the signature of the class file so that it public and static. Inside the body of the class, create a new static method named **RenderTemplateAsColumns** that returns the type of MvcHtmlString. Add Using statements to the top of your file as required.

When writing HTML helper methods, it is important to use the MvcHtmlString return type. If you do not, the Razor engine will automatically HTML Encode the output.

The extension method will perform several actions. First, it will validate the input to make sure that the data source is not null or empty and that the numberOfColumns parameter is within an acceptable range. If the tests fail, it will throw an exception.

Next, the extension will do some calculations to figure out the structure of output. You will need to know the number of table rows, the total number of items, and the number of extra columns that need to be created for the last row. For example, if you have a total of twenty items and want to have three columns, you will need to create a total of seven rows and need to create one empty column in the last row in order to maintain a consistent layout.

After performing the calculations, create the opening table tag, and then begin looping through the items. As you loop through the collection, keep count of the number of table columns that have rendered. Once this count reaches the number of items for the row, close the existing row and create another.

Inside each column, you need to inject your content. Since you wish to use a partial view for our template, you can simply call the Partial helper method, which takes a name of a view and a model as parameters, and then returns the compiled view as output.

Finally, once you get to the final row, append the empty columns to the final row if any are required, and then close the table.

One of the problems that you will find with this initial design of the RenderTemplateAsColumns helper extension is that it is difficult to unit test because of coupling created by using the Html.Partial extension. There are several ways that you can get around this problem. For example, you can create a mock implementation of ViewContext using a mocking framework such as RhinoMock. Another option is to pass an additional parameter that accepts a delegate with the same signature as the Html.Partial. This will also give the developers who are consuming your helper extension additional flexibility.

In order to keep things simple for developers who do not need the flexibility, you can then create a second version of the method that omits this delegate parameter. Listing 10-16 shows the delegate definition for GetStringFromPartial. It takes a string representing a view name and an object that represents a model, and returns an MvcHtmlString object. This is the same signature as the Html.Partial method.

Listing 10-16. RenderTemplateAsColumns Helper Extension for Use in Views

```
using System;
using System.Collections;
using System.Text;
using System.Web.Mvc;
using System.Web.Mvc.Html;

namespace Ch10.Shared.Helpers
{
  public delegate MvcHtmlString GetStringFromAction(string viewName, object model);

  //..
}
```

Listing 10-17 shows a version of the RenderTemplateAsColumns helper extension that does not require the use of the delegate parameter. This will make it slightly easier to use inside your views, but requires the developer to define the template in a partial view. This version of the method simply calls the second version and uses the call to helper.Partial for the GetStringFromAction delegate parameter.

Listing 10-17. RenderTemplateAsColumns Helper Extension for Use in Views

```
public static MvcHtmlString RenderTemplateAsColumns(this HtmlHelper helper,
            ICollection items,
            string partialViewName,
            int numberOfColumns)
{
    return RenderTemplateAsColumns(helper,
                              items,
                              partialViewName,
                              numberOfColumns,
                              helper.Partial,);
}
```

Listing 10-18 shows the version of the method that contains the actual implementation. Notice that it includes an additional parameter named getStringMethod that accepts the delegate GetStringFromPartial.

Listing 10-18. RenderTemplateAsColumns Helper Extension with the GetStringFromPartial Parameter

```
public static MvcHtmlString RenderTemplateAsColumns(this HtmlHelper helper,
        ICollection items,
        string partialViewName,
        int numberOfColumns,
        GetStringFromAction getStringMethod
      )
    {
        //validate input
        if (numberOfColumns < 1)
        {
            throw new ArgumentOutOfRangeException("numberOfColumns");
        }
        if (items == null)
        {
            throw new ArgumentNullException("items");
        }

        if (items == null || items.Count > 0)
        {

            StringBuilder builder = new StringBuilder();
            int columnsInRow = 1;
            int rowsDone = 0;
            int numberOfItemsDone=0;
            int numberOfExtraColumnsInLastRow;

            //calculate the needed table structure
            int numberOfRows = items.Count / numberOfColumns;

            //Create the opening table tag
            builder.Append("<table>");

            //Create the rows and columns
            foreach (var item in items)
            {
                if (columnsInRow == 1)
                {
                    builder.Append("<tr>");
                }
                builder.Append("<td>");
                builder.Append(getStringMethod(partialViewName,item));
                builder.Append("</td>");
                bool isLastItem = (items.Count==numberOfItemsDone+1);

                if ((columnsInRow == numberOfColumns) || isLastItem)
                {
                    if (isLastItem)
                    {
                        numberOfExtraColumnsInLastRow = numberOfColumns - columnsInRow;
                        builder.Append(RenderExtraColumns(numberOfExtraColumnsInLastRow));
                    }
```

```
                    builder.Append("</tr>");
                    columnsInRow = 1;
                    rowsDone++;
                }
                else
                {
                    columnsInRow++;
                }

                numberOfItemsDone++;
            }

            // create the closing table tag
            builder.Append("</table>");

            return MvcHtmlString.Create(builder.ToString());
        }

        return MvcHtmlString.Empty;
    }
```

As you are developing your HTML helper extensions, you should take opportunities to optimize your code as you work. One thing that you should try to avoid is having a single method containing thousands of lines of code. Readability is essential to maintainability and you should try to make the code as easy to understand as possible. Listing 10-19 shows a helper method factored out of the original method that takes an integer as a parameter and then returns a string containing the matching number of opening and closing HTML TD tag pairs. Before the revision, it may not have been as clear to what this loop is doing. Now you know that it responsible for rendering the extra columns that remain after the last full row.

Listing 10-19. Rending the Extra Columns

```
private static string RenderExtraColumns(int numberOfExtraColumnsInLastRow)
{
    if (numberOfExtraColumnsInLastRow > 0)
    {
        StringBuilder builder = new StringBuilder();
        for (int i = 0; i < numberOfExtraColumnsInLastRow; i++)
        {
            builder.Append("<td></td>");
        }
        return builder.ToString();
    }
    return string.Empty;

}
```

Writing Unit Tests

One major advantage to using custom HTML helpers is that you can write a battery of unit tests that can cover every possible execution path for your code. It is almost impossible to do this with manual testing in a reasonable amount of time. It is also very difficult, if not impossible, to do if you had written this same logic into your view. Even with HTML helpers, without some forethought in their design, they can be difficult to test.

In the RenderTemplateAsColumns example, you specifically created a version of the method that allows you to pass in an arbitrary method to generate the string output for the template. This saved the trouble of having to create a mock implementation of the ViewContext object needed to pass into the HtmlHelper constructor in each test method.

The first two tests that you will create for this helper (shown in Listing 10-20) will ensure that the exceptions are thrown as expected. For both tests, you pass in the string "foo" for the name of the view. You are not passing a delegate. You then add a second test that does pass the delegate. This may seem redundant since they are both eventually calling the same code, but the extra tests may prevent an unexpected error if the implementation changes in the future.

Listing 10-20. NUnit Tests for the RenderTemplateAsColumns Method That Verifies Thrown Exceptions

```
[Test]
[ExpectedException(ExpectedException=typeof(ArgumentOutOfRangeException))]
public void RenderTemplateAsColumns_ZeroColumns_ThrowsException()
{
    // Arrange
    HtmlHelper helper = new HtmlHelper(new ViewContext(), new ViewPage());
    List<string> strings = new List<string>();

    //act
    helper.RenderTemplateAsColumns(strings, "foo", 0);
    //Assert

}

[Test]
[ExpectedException(ExpectedException = typeof(ArgumentOutOfRangeException))]
public void RenderTemplateAsColumnsDelegate_ZeroColumns_ThrowsException()
{
    // Arrange
    HtmlHelper helper = new HtmlHelper(new ViewContext(), new ViewPage());
    List<string> strings = new List<string>();

    //act
    helper.RenderTemplateAsColumns(strings, "foo", 0, helper.Partial);
    //Assert

}

[Test]
[ExpectedException(ExpectedException = typeof(ArgumentNullException))]
public void RenderTemplateAsColumns_NullCollection_ThrowsException()
{
    // Arrange
    HtmlHelper helper = new HtmlHelper(new ViewContext(), new ViewPage());

    //act
    helper.RenderTemplateAsColumns(null, "foo", 3);
    //Assert
}
```

```
[Test]
[ExpectedException(ExpectedException = typeof(ArgumentNullException))]
public void RenderTemplateAsColumnsDelegate_NullCollection_ThrowsException()
{
  // Arrange
  HtmlHelper helper = new HtmlHelper(new ViewContext(), new ViewPage());

  //act
  helper.RenderTemplateAsColumns(null, "foo", 3, helper.Partial);
  //Assert

}
```

The next set of tests will validate how the helper behaves when it is passed a collection of strings with various numbers of columns. You will pass in an implementation of the GetStringFromPartial delegate in line as a lambda expression. This way you do not need to rely on an external file for the template contents.

Listing 10-21 shows one of these methods, which tests for a collection of five strings with three columns. The expected result is the creation of a table containing two rows with three columns each. The last column of the last row should be empty. While it is impossible to model every possible input and output for your tests, you should create additional tests for all known code paths. For example, you may want to create a test to show a case where there are nine items and three columns with no extra columns added.

Listing 10-21. Unit Test to Verify That Extra Columns Are Created As Expected

```
[Test]
public void RenderTemplateAsColumns_5StringsCollection3Columns_OneExtraColumn()
{
  // Arrange
  HtmlHelper helper = new HtmlHelper(new ViewContext(), new ViewPage());
  List<string> strings = new List<string> { "1", "2", "3","4","5"};

  //note: there are no line breaks here in the actual code
  MvcHtmlString expected =
  MvcHtmlString.Create( "<table><tr><td><b>1</b></td><td><b>2</b></td><td><b>3</b></td>
</tr><tr><td><b>4</b></td><td><b>5</b></td><td></td></tr></table>");

  //act
  MvcHtmlString actual =helper.RenderTemplateAsColumns(strings, (a, b) => {
            return   MvcHtmlString.Create(String.Format("<b>{0}</b>", b)); },
            "foo",
             3);
  //Assert
  Assert.AreEqual(expected.ToString(), actual.ToString());

}
```

You should note that in the assertion, the ToString method is called on both MvcHtmlString objects. This is because even though the output of the two MvcHtmlString objects are identical, the objects themselves are not. If you compare the MvcHtmlStrings using AreEqual or AreSame, both will always return false. On the other hand, when you use the ToString method, both outputs will point to the same immutable string object, thus returning true.

Adding the Controller Logic

The controller logic in this example is very simple. In this case, it has been refactored for testability with all of the LINQ queries to the data context being factored into a repository. The controller class has a private member variable that holds the repository, which is set in its constructor. The code for the controller is shown in Listing 10-22.

Listing 10-22. DataExamplesController DataListReplacement Action

```
public class DataExamplesController : Controller
{
  private IDataExampleRepository m_repository;
  public DataExamplesController(IDataExampleRepository repository)
  {
    m_repository = repository;
  }

  public DataExamplesController()
            : this(new EFDataExchangeRepository())
  {
  }

  public ActionResult DataListReplacement()
  {
    List<Artist> newArtistsList = m_repository.GetNewArtistList();

    return View("DataListReplacement", newArtistsList);
  }

  //
  //other actions removed for brevity

  protected override void Dispose(bool disposing)
  {
    if (disposing)
    {
      if (m_repository != null)
          m_repository.Dispose();
    }
    base.Dispose(disposing);
  }

}
```

Building the Views

Since the HTML helper requires that the template be placed in a separate view, we will actually need to create two views. The first view contained in DataListReplacement.cshtml is shown in Listing 10-23. It calls the Html.RenderTemplateAsColumns and passes the model, which is a List of Artist objects, a string containing the name of a partial view we will use as our template, and finally, the number of columns we would like to display.

Listing 10-23. DataListReplacement.cshtml

```
@model List<Ch7.SharedAPI.Artist>
@{
    ViewBag.Title = "DataList Replacement";
}

<h2>DataList Control Replacement using a custom HTML Helper</h2>
@Html.RenderTemplateAsColumns(Model, "_ArtistPartial", 3)
```

Next, the partial view needs to be created. To do this, right-click the Views/DataExamples folder, and select Add ➤ View. In The Add View dialog window, name the view **_ArtistPartial**. Make sure the Razor view engine is selected. Check the Create As a Partial View check box. Once you are ready, click the Add button to create the view. Once the view is created, it will appear in the code editor window.

To create the body of the view, take the contents of the ItemTemplate from the Web Forms project and paste it in. You will then need to make some adjustments so that it conforms to the Razor view syntax. The completed partial should look like Listing 10-24.

Listing 10-24. The _ArtistPartial View

```
@model Ch7.SharedAPI.Artist
<a href="/@Model.UserName">
    <div class="evenbox">
        <div class="ImageDiv">
            <img src="@Model.AvatarUrlSample" class="AristImage" alt="Click Image to view
full profile" />
        </div>
        <div class="ContentDiv">
            <ul>
                <li class="ProfileLink">@Model.UserName</li>
                <li>@Model.Province</li>
                <li>@Model.Country</li>
                <li>Joined :
                <time>@String.Format("{0:d}", Model.CreateDate)</time>
                </li>
            </ul>
        </div>
    </div>
</a>
```

The template shown in Listing 10-24 is optimized for touch-first experiences such as Windows 8 tablets and iPads. It makes the entire tile a touch target. Touching or clicking anywhere on the tile will navigate to the artist's profile page. The rest of the magic occurs in the CSS style sheet.

Using CSS to Finalize the Presentation

There are three possible places where CSS can be defined. The first is through creating inline styles. Use of inline styles is not a good practice and usually leads to difficult-to-maintain designs, duplication, and ultimately, visual inconsistency throughout the site.

The second place to add styles is in the head section of the document. You should restrict this to styles that are specific to the page and cannot be used anywhere else in the site. In most cases, however, you should define your styles in an external style sheet. In cases where the page will return a dynamic result, you should always use an external CSS file. This is because even though there is an extra download for the first visit, if users visit this page multiple times, they will benefit from using a cached version of the style.

In this case, all styles used here are split between two files: the Site.css file and the GridStyles.css file. The Site.css file contains styles that are used site-wide, whereas the GridStyles.css are used only for pages that require some sort of data list. The relevant styles from GridStyles.css files are shown in Listing 10-25.

Listing 10-25. Styles Used for the Columns

```
/*used for Data List from GridStyles.css*/
.ProfileLink {
    font-size: 12pt;
    font-weight: bolder;
    letter-spacing: 0.2em;
    text-decoration: none;
    text-transform: lowercase;
}
.evenbox {
    background-color: #f4f5f5;
    font-size: 10pt;
    border: 1px solid #ccc;
    width: 320px;
    height: 90px;
    color: #333;
}

.oddbox {
    border: 1px solid #ccc;
    background-color: #ebeced;
    font-size: 10pt;
    width: 320px;
}

.ImageDiv {
    float: left;
    -moz-backface-visibility: hidden;
    -webkit-backface-visibility: hidden;
    backface-visibility: hidden;
}

.ContentDiv {
    float: left;
    padding: 5px;
    -moz-backface-visibility: hidden;
    -webkit-backface-visibility: hidden;
    backface-visibility: hidden;
}

    .ContentDiv ul {
        list-style-type: none;
        margin: 0;
        padding: 0;
    }
```

```
    .ContentDiv li {
        padding: 2px;
    }
.AristImage {
    height: 75px;
    width: 75px;
    -webkit-box-shadow: 3px 3px 7px #777;
    -moz-box-shadow: 3px 3px 7px #777;
    box-shadow: 3px 3px 7px #777;
    -moz-border-radius: 5px;
    -webkit-border-radius: 5px;
    border-radius: 5px;
    margin: 5px;
}
```

The styles specify the dimensions for each tile and add some visual effects, such as drop shadows and rounded corners. One of the more annoying aspects of CSS is also shown in this example. This is the requirement to add vendor-specific attributes for some of the emerging CSS 3.0 features. The need for this will fade over time as more of the world upgrades to standards-compliant modern web browsers.

The results of all this work, as rendered in the Chrome web browser, is shown in Figure 10-2.

Figure 10-2. *The output of the RenderTemplateAsColumns HTML helper*

Even though it took some effort to create the custom helper, the fact that you will be able to reuse this in many places in your project, and possibly in future projects, makes it worth it.

10-3. Creating a Data Grid with Paging, Sorting, and Filtering Support

Problem

It can be said that the ASP.NET Web Forms DataView control is the bread and butter of most .NET-centric development shops. Many applications have pages that require paging, sorting, and filtering support. In Web Forms, this was as simple as dragging a DataView control from your toolbox to your design canvas, and then adding some declarative data binding statements.

You finally convinced your boss to allow you to do your next project using ASP.NET MVC with Razor, only to discover that there is no DataView control to drag. You need to figure out how to do this and get a prototype working before your next status meeting.

Solution

Data grids are a well-defined pattern. There are literally hundreds of commercial and open-source products that can get the job done. In fact, in modern web browsers, performance of these solutions can be as smooth and interactive as that of native client applications. Some nice examples are at the following web sites:

- Kendo UI (http://demos.kendoui.com/web/grid/index.html)

- jQWidgets (www.jqwidgets.com/jquery-widgets-demo/demos/jqxgrid/index.htm)

If you do not want to invest in a commercial product or if you find that the products offer much more than you need, you can implement some rudimentary, grid-like functionality in ASP.NET MVC using a combination of HTML helpers and action filters.

You will review such a solution in the How It Works section.

How It Works

This example starts by looking at a basic data grid implementation using Web Forms. Next, I show you how to create similar behavior using the MVC Framework. Along the way, we will clean up some issues with the original implementation and convert it into something more readable and easier to test.

The Web Forms GridView Control

This is a fun example adapted from a real-life project, but with variable names changed to protect the guilty. The Web Forms page in this example contains a list of collaboration spaces. It takes advantage of the sorting and paging functionality offered by the GridView control. This default functionality allows the data in the grid to be sorted by clicking the column header, and offers page numbers on the bottom of the grid to allow you to move between pages of result sets. This page was also designed to allow filtering and sorting by passing query string parameters on the URL.

GridViewExample.aspx

The sample page has been divided into two sections: a navigation panel with a list of categories and the data grid that displays the workspace information.

On the left side of the page is the list of categories. If you click a category link, the data grid will be filtered by the selected category. The list of category links is implemented as a Web Forms Repeater control. This Repeater control is shown in Listing 10-26.

Listing 10-26. Repeater Control in GridViewExample.aspx Used to Filter Items in the GridView

```
[some content ommited for brevity]
<nav id="SideBar" class="float-left leftColumn">
   <ul>
     <asp:Repeater ID="CategoriesRepeater" runat="server">
       <ItemTemplate>
         <li>
           <li>
             <a
             href="/DataControlExamples/GridViewExample.aspx?filter=<%# Eval("GenreLookUpId")%>">
                  <%# Eval("GenreName")%>
           </a>
           </li>
       </ItemTemplate>
     </asp:Repeater>
   </ul>
</nav>
```

By default, GridView controls automatically create HTML table columns for each of the columns in your record set. While this is a nice feature for early prototyping and simple result sets, in most cases, you will need to supply your own item templates, as shown in this example.

To disable the automatic column generation, the AutoGenerateColumns property has been set to false. Once this has been disabled, you will need to manually define the fields that you would like to include on the grid.

If you assign a data source to a GridView declaratively by defining an ObjectDataSource and setting it to the GridViews DataSource property, sorting and paging are handled for you automatically. For this example, however, you are populating the GridView from the results of a LINQ to Entities query, which is done in a code-behind page. Because of this, you need to manually create event handlers to programmatically implement sorting and paging. The event handlers have been set using the OnPageIndexChanging and OnSorting properties.

For the majority of the GridView's columns, TemplateField controls have been created. This allows for a more flexible layout inside the grid. Each field defines a SortExpression property. When this is set to a nonempty string, the column headers for that column are set to LinkButton controls that will perform a postback, which fires the OnSorting event with the supplied string bound to the event's GridViewSortEventArgs.SortExpression parameter. The remainder of the GridView properties have been set using a Skin file as part of the application theme, which has been applied to the web site. Listing 10-27 shows the GridView control using custom template fields.

Listing 10-27. GridView Control in GridViewExample.aspx

```
    <h2><asp:Label
        ID="ProjectsFoundLabel" runat="server" Text="50 projects found"></asp:Label>
    </h2>
    <div id="main" class="float-right rightColumn">
        <asp:GridView ID="WorkspaceGridView"
                      runat="server" Width="100%"
                      AutoGenerateColumns="False"
                      GridLines="None"
                      OnPageIndexChanging=" WorkspaceGridView_PageIndexChanging"
                      OnSorting=" WorkspaceGridView_Sorting"
                      AllowPaging="True"
                      EmptyDataText="Cannot find any projects that match your criteria."
        >
```

```
            <Columns>
                <asp:TemplateField SortExpression="ProjectName" HeaderText="Project" >
                    <ItemTemplate>
                        <a
href="/MusicianCollaboration/SongWorkspace/<%# Eval("CollaborationSpaceId") %>"
                            title="Click here to view project."
                            class="CollaborationSpaceTitle">
                        <%# Eval("Title") %></a><br />
                        <%# Eval("Description")%>
                    </ItemTemplate>
                </asp:TemplateField>
                <asp:TemplateField HeaderText="Artist" SortExpression="Artist">
                    <ItemTemplate>
                        <a href="<%# Eval("WebSite")%>"><%# Eval("UserName")%>
                        <br />
                        <img src="<%# Eval("AvatarUrl)%>" class="AristImage"
                            alt="Click the image to view this artist's profile"
                        />
                        </a>
                    </ItemTemplate>
                </asp:TemplateField>
                <asp:TemplateField SortExpression="DateCreated" HeaderText="Created">
                    <ItemTemplate>
                        <%# Eval("CreateDate")%>
                    </ItemTemplate>
                </asp:TemplateField>
                <asp:TemplateField HeaderText="Updated" SortExpression="DateModified">
                    <ItemTemplate>
                        <asp:Label ID="Label1" runat="server"
                         Text='<%# Bind("ModifiedDate") %>'></asp:Label>
                    </ItemTemplate>
                </asp:TemplateField>
                <asp:TemplateField HeaderText="Stats" SortExpression="Stats">
                    <ItemTemplate>
                        <ul class="ItemList">
                        <li>
                            Hits: <asp:Label ID="HitsLabel"
                                runat="server"
                                Text='<%# Bind("NumberViews") %>'
                                ></asp:Label>
                        </li>
                        <li>
                            Posts: <asp:Label ID="PostsLabel"
                                runat="server"
                                Text='<%# Bind("NumberComments") %>'
                                 ></asp:Label>
                        </li>
                        <li>
                            Status: <asp:Label
                                runat="server"
                                ID="Label2"
                                Text='<%# Bind("Status") %>'></asp:Label>
```

```
        </li>
      </ul>
    </ItemTemplate>
  </asp:TemplateField>
</Columns>
</asp:GridView>
</div>
```

GridViewExample.aspx.cs Code-Behind Page

The GridViewExample.aspx.cs file first populates the GridView control containing the data and the Repeater control that contains the filters in its Page_Load event. Since the logic for loading the data and binding it to the grid needs to be called for each of the sorting and paging operations, it has been encapsulated in a method called loadData. A similar method has been created for loading the categories. Both calls are wrapped inside an if statement that checks to see if the page is loading because of a postback. In this case, we do not want to rerun the database queries since it may not be required. The Page_Load event is shown in Listing 10-28.

Listing 10-28. The Page_Load Event Handler in GridVewExample.aspx.cs

```
protected void Page_Load(object sender, EventArgs e)
{
    if (!IsPostBack)
    {
        loadData();
        loadCategories();
    }
}
```

Following the Page_Load event are the event handlers defined for the PageIndexChanging and the Sorting events of the WorkspaceGridView control. Both of these methods are relatively simple and defer the heavy lifting to the loadData method. In the WorkspaceGridView_PageIndexChanging event, the PageIndex property is set to the NewPageIndex property of GridViewPageEventArgs. Once this has been set, the loadData method is called. One of the fatal flaws of the GridView is seen here. Every time you advance to a new page, the grid view will load your entire data set and then move to the first record of your data page. This is very wasteful and can be performance inhibiting when working with large data sets. Although it is possible to work around this issue, the GridView control does not make this process as easy as it should.

For the WorkspaceGridView_PageIndexChanging event, start by setting the page index to 0, and then setting the SortExpression property to the value sent in the GridViewSortEventArgs.SortExpression property. You then call the loadData method again. The events are shown in Listing 10-29.

Listing 10-29. The WorkspaceGridView Event Handlers

```
protected void WorkspaceGridView_PageIndexChanging(object sender, GridViewPageEventArgs e)
{
    WorkspaceGridView.PageIndex = e.NewPageIndex;
    loadData();
}
```

```
protected void WorkspaceGridView_Sorting(object sender, GridViewSortEventArgs e)
{
    WorkspaceGridView.PageIndex = 0;
    SortExpression = e.SortExpression;
    loadData();
}
```

Listing 10-30 shows the definitions of two custom properties. The SortExpression property stores its value in the page's view state. This allows the value to be persisted between postbacks. This property is required to preserve the sort order when a user is clicking between pages. The second property uses a query string to get the values of the filter expression. In this case, we are filtering our list by musical genres using the unique id. The code for the properties are shown in Listing 10-30.

Listing 10-30. Properties for Sort and Filter Expressions

```
private string SortExpression
{
    get
    {
        if (ViewState["SortExpression"] != null)
        {
            return ViewState["SortExpression"].ToString();
        }
        return string.Empty;
    }
    set
    {
        ViewState.Add("SortExpression", value);
    }
}

private int GenreFilterExpressions
{
    get
    {
        if (Request.QueryString["filter"] != null)
        {
            int genreNum = 0;
            Int32.TryParse(Request.QueryString["filter"],out genreNum);
            return genreNum;
        }
        return 0;
    }
}
```

Finally, we get to the data access methods that are populating the GridView and Repeater controls. First, create an instance of the MobEntities class, which represents the data access layer of the application. This is based off the same shared code library that is used throughout much of the book. Since we are defining this object globally, we need to ensure that it is disposed when the page is disposed. We do this by overriding the Dispose method of the Page class.

Once this object has been created, we can call a number of helper methods that call into it to fetch the data needed for the page. The first of these is the loadCategories method. This is a very simple method that makes a call to a data context to retrieve a list of category names and Ids, and then binds the results to the Repeater control, as shown in Listing 10-31.

Listing 10-31. The loadCategories Method

```
MobEntities m_DataContext = new MobEntities();

public override void Dispose()
{
    if (m_DataContext != null)
        m_DataContext.Dispose();
        base.Dispose();
}

private void loadCategories()
{
  var categories = from c in m_DataContext.GenreLookUps
                   orderby c.GenreName
                   select new { c.GenreName , c.GenreLookUpId};
          CategoriesRepeater.DataSource = categories.ToList();
          CategoriesRepeater.DataBind();
 }
```

Now we get to the loadData method. This method uses somewhat complex LINQ query to get a list of workspaces. The query joins data from several objects in the data context. The entity model that is used in this example is based on the same database shown in Chapter 7. In the initial version of this library, the entity data model was generated from the database. It used the default settings, which mapped the tinyint SQL data type to the C# byte data type. In order to make the query more readable, we define several byte const variables that we will use in the query in place of their numeric equivalents.

The fields selected in the base query are required in order to permit the filter expressions to be run. The LINQ query is broken into three separate calls. The first call creates the basic structure of the query, filters out unwanted data, and then selects the result set into a new anonymous type.

If a filter expression is found in the FilterExpression property, a second LINQ query is run against the results of the first one to limit the result set to only workspaces in the specified category.

Next, a group-by query is run to eliminate duplicate results that show up for workspaces in multiple categories. The group-by is used here rather than a distinct clause since the differences in the category ids for each record make each row unique.

Next, a check is made for a sort expression. If a sort expression is found, then another LINQ statement adds sort criteria.

At this point, no queries have been sent to the database. All the LINQ statement has done is generate the query.

The next line of code writes the query result to an IList. We had to use the interface rather than specific implantation in this case since we are using an anonymous type. The list is then set as the data source for the WorkspaceGridView and then the WorkspaceGridView.DataBind method is called.

Finally, a label on the page is updated with the number of records found. The loadData method is shown in Listing 10-32.

Listing 10-32. The loadData Method

```
private const byte PROJECT_STATUS_CANCELED = 6;
private const byte PROJECT_STATUS_PUBLISHED = 4;
private const byte PROJECT_STATUS_ONHOLD = 5;
```

```
private void loadData()
{
    var collabSpacesQuery = from a in m_DataContext.CollaborationSpaces
                            join o in m_DataContext.CollaborationSpaceGenres
                            on a.CollaborationSpaceId equals o.CollaborationSpaceId
                            join p in m_DataContext.ArtistCollaborationSpaces
                            on a.CollaborationSpaceId equals p.CollaborationSpaceId
                            where a.Status != PROJECT_STATUS_CANCELED &&
                            a.Status != PROJECT_STATUS_ONHOLD &&
                            a.Status != PROJECT_STATUS_PUBLISHED &&
                            a.AllowPublicView == true &&
                            p.IsCreator == true
                            select new
                            {
                                a.CollaborationSpaceId,
                                a.CreateDate,
                                a.Description,
                                a.LastPostDate,
                                a.ModifiedDate,
                                a.NumberComments,
                                a.NumberViews,
                                a.RestrictContributorsToBand,
                                a.Status,
                                a.Title,
                                o.GenreLookUpId,
                                p.Artist.UserName,
                                p.Artist.WebSite,
                                p.Artist.AvatarURL
                            };

    if (GenreFilterExpressions>0)
    {
        collabSpacesQuery = from a in collabSpacesQuery
                            where a.GenreLookUpId == GenreFilterExpressions
                            select a;
    }
    //get rid of duplicates
    collabSpacesQuery = from a in collabSpacesQuery
                        group a by a.CollaborationSpaceId into u
                        select u.FirstOrDefault();

    if (!string.IsNullOrEmpty(SortExpression))
    {
        switch (SortExpression)
        {
            case "DateCreated":
                collabSpacesQuery = from a in collabSpacesQuery
                                    orderby a.CreateDate
                                    select a;
            break;
```

```
                        case "DateModified":
                            collabSpacesQuery = from a in collabSpacesQuery
                                                orderby a.ModifiedDate
                                                select a;
                            break;
                        case "ProjectName":
                            collabSpacesQuery = from a in collabSpacesQuery
                                                orderby a.Title
                                                select a;
                            break;
                        case "Artist":
                            collabSpacesQuery = from a in collabSpacesQuery
                                                orderby a.UserName
                                                select a;
                            break;
                        case "Stats":
                            collabSpacesQuery = from a in collabSpacesQuery
                                                orderby a.NumberViews
                                                select a;
                            break;

                }

            }
    IList list = collabSpacesQuery.ToList();
    WorkspaceGridView.DataSource = list;
    WorkspaceGridView.DataBind();
    ProjectsFoundLabel.Text =
        string.Format("{0} Active collaboration spaces found.", list.Count);
}
```

A quick look though this code shows many opportunities for refactoring. We will take the opportunity to do this as we migrate the code to the MVC Framework.

Creating an MVC Grid Infrastructure

Since ASP.NET MVC does not use ASP.NET server controls, we will need a different strategy in order to replicate the functionality shown in the Web Forms example. Our solution should be as reusable as possible and embrace MVC concepts such as clean HTML and separation of concerns.

If you look though some of the grid-type controls available from vendors, you typically see two types of approaches for creating grids that support paging and sorting. On one side, you have a client-centric approach where almost the entire user interface is created using JavaScript. The server's only responsibility in this type of design is to supply data by way of web services. This is not a bad way to go since it will give most of your clients a great experience. However, if you are not planning on buying a commercial product, building a JavaScript grid control can be a difficult task. The ASP.NET MVC Framework does not provide much advantage in this type of design. In fact, with many of the products and frameworks, you can use a RESTful service from any back-end server technology. This technique is shown in Recipe 11-2.

The other approach is to use server-side code to create your grid. ASP.NET MVC can be used to great advantage in this type of strategy. It requires that you create some infrastructure to enable paging and sorting, since it is not built-in by default.

Refactoring the Data Access Code

Whenever you are porting code from an existing system, you should spend some time settling the technical debt. *Technical debt* is a term that refers to bad design choices usually made as a compromise in order to meet a deadline. If you do not settle technical debt, you will propagate problems from the old system to the new one.

The first item that we will correct is the use of the constants in the LINQ expression. Past versions of Entity Framework did not support enum types. This required developers come up with alternative solutions, such as using constants—as done in Listing 10-32.

In Entity Framework 5, converting numeric values to enum is straightforward. It can be done by opening the entity model in Visual Studio, and then right-clicking the property that you would like to convert. You can then choose Convert to Enum from the pop-up menu and supply the required values.

The next change is to factor out the data access code into a repository class. This is a good idea in both Web Forms programming and ASP.NET MVC. It makes your code-behind pages and controllers less complicated and easier to maintain and test. It also fosters code reuse. The first step in any repository design should be to create an interface. In most cases, the interface should derive from IDisposable. This will allow developers that consume your repository to use familiar patterns such as wrapping calls to the repository inside a using block. Listing 10-33 shows the interface for the repository class that now encapsulates the data access logic. For this example, the interface was created in the Models folder of the MVC project. It uses several models classes, including CollaborationSpaceSearchResult defined in the file DataExampleModel.cs and OpenPositionsNeeded, which is defined in WizardModels.cs. For a more complex application, you may want to define this in a separate assembly.

Listing 10-33. Data Access Code Refactored into a Repository

```
public interface IDataExampleRepository: IDisposable
{
  List<Artist> GetNewArtistList();
  Artist GetArtistDetails(int id);
  IList<CollaborationSpaceSearchResult> GetActiveCollaborationSpaces(int page,
          int count,
          string sortExpression,
          int categoryId,
          bool useDefaultSort,
          out int resultsFound);
  IList<GenreLookUp> GetGenreLookupList();

  List<ArtistSkill> GetArtistSkills(int artistId);
  void UpdateSkill(ArtistSkill skill);
  void CreateSkill(ArtistSkill skill);
  void DeleteSkill(int artistSkillId);

  void CreateAds(OpenPositionsNeeded openPositionsNeeded);

  void Save();

  void CreateCollaborationSpace(CollaborationSpace collaborationSpace);
}
```

Now that the interface has been designed, we can create a new class that is derived from it. For this example, we will create the repository class inside the Models folder. You can do this by right-clicking the Models folder, and selecting New and then Class. Name the class **EFDataExampleRepository**.

Once the class has been created and opened in a code editor window, type in **IDataExampleRepository** on the same line as the class declaration. After you have completed typing, you will notice that Visual Studio overlays a small menu icon underneath the first few characters. Click the menu and select Implement Interface IDataExampleRepository, as shown in Figure 10-3.

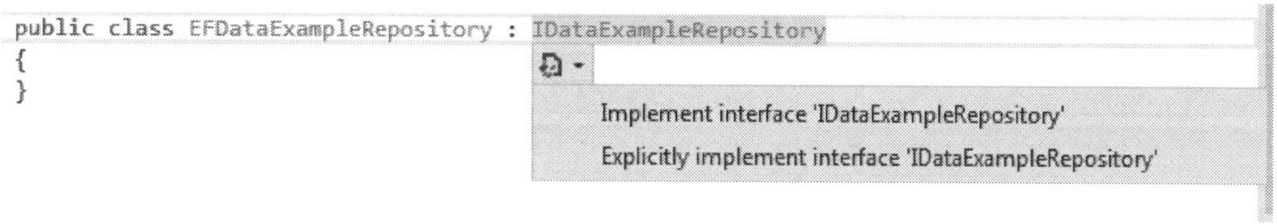

```
public class EFDataExampleRepository : IDataExampleRepository
{
    🔧 ▾
}
              Implement interface 'IDataExampleRepository'
              Explicitly implement interface 'IDataExampleRepository'
```

Figure 10-3. Allow Visual Studio to create method stubs that implement an interface

After clicking the menu item, Visual Studio will create stubs for the methods, which implements both the IDataExampleRepository and IDisposable interfaces. The body of each method will throw a NotImplementedException.

The grid example will fill in an implementation for the GetActiveCollaborationSpaces method. We will base this method on the code from the Web Forms example, but refactor it for maintainability. The cleaned up version of this method is shown in Listing 10-34. The major changes to the LINQ expression are highlighted in bold.

Listing 10-34. The GetActiveCollaborationSpaces Method of the EFDataExampleRepository

```
MobEntities m_context = new MobEntities();
public void Dispose()
{
  if (m_context != null)
     m_context.Dispose();
}

public IList<CollaborationSpaceSearchResult>
    GetActiveCollaborationSpaces(int page,
             int count,
             string sortExpression,
             int categoryId,
             bool sortDecending,
             out int resultsFound
          )
{
    var collabSpacesQuery = from a in m_context.CollaborationSpaces
          join o in m_context.CollaborationSpaceGenres
          on a.CollaborationSpaceId equals o.CollaborationSpaceId
          join p in m_context.ArtistCollaborationSpaces
          on a.CollaborationSpaceId equals p.CollaborationSpaceId
          where a.Status != CollaborationSpaceStatus.Canceled &&
            a.Status != CollaborationSpaceStatus.OnHold &&
            a.Status != CollaborationSpaceStatus.Published &&
            a.AllowPublicView == true &&
            p.IsCreator == true
          select new CollaborationSpaceSearchResult()
```

```
                {
                    CollaborationSpaceId = a.CollaborationSpaceId,
                    CreateDate = a.CreateDate,
                    Description= a.Description,
                    LastPostDate= a.LastPostDate,
                    ModifiedDate = a.ModifiedDate,
                    NumberComments = a.NumberComments,
                    NumberViews = a.NumberViews,
                    RestrictContributorsToBand = a.RestrictContributorsToBand,
                    Status = a.Status,
                    Title = a.Title,
                    GenreLookUpId = o.GenreLookUpId,
                    UserName = p.Artist.UserName,
                    WebSite = p.Artist.WebSite,
                    AvatarURL = p.Artist.AvatarURL
                };
        if (categoryId > 0)
        {
            collabSpacesQuery = from a in collabSpacesQuery
                                where a.GenreLookUpId == categoryId
                                select a;
        }

        //get rid of duplicates and sort
        collabSpacesQuery = (from a in collabSpacesQuery
                             group a by a.CollaborationSpaceId into u
                             select u.FirstOrDefault());

        // First round trip to the database that runs a query to
        // get the count
        resultsFound = collabSpacesQuery.Count();

        int skip = getSkip(page, count);

        // second round trip to the database retieves (count) 10 records
        collabSpacesQuery = collabSpacesQuery.OrderBy(
                sortExpression).Skip(skip).Take(count);
        return collabSpacesQuery.ToList<CollaborationSpaceSearchResult>();
}

private int getSkip(int page, int count)
{
  if (page < 2)
  {
     return 0;
  }
  else
  {
     return page * count;
  }
}
```

You have made four significant changes to this query since the Web Forms version:

- You replaced the use of constants with enums. This simplifies the life of the programmer and increases readability. This change required a change to the entity model.

- Rather than using an anonymous type, you created an explicit type in a separate class file. This change was required for two reasons. First, the Razor views do not have visibility in the definition of anonymous type at runtime and will throw a parsing error if you attempt to reference the properties of that type in your view. The second reason is that using a regular class greatly simplifies the technique used in the third change to this query.

- In the Web Forms version of this query, you used a helper method that looked at the value of the SortExpression property, and then depending on the value, it executed a different LINQ query to sort the list. In this version, you are using a custom extension method that allows you to pass a string (rather than an expression) as the OrderBy clause. This dramatically reduces the amount of code that needs to be maintained for this page. It also increases your flexibility, making it easy to add additional sort options at the view level without needing to make additional changes in either the controller or repository. The down side is that it increases the likelihood of a typo in a property name, resulting in a runtime error.

- Most importantly, you have added the Skip and Take modifiers to the query. This allows LINQ to create database queries that will only return the number of rows needed to render a particular page. This is a major contrast to Web Forms, where you returned the entire result set to the web server even though you only needed 20 rows.

- Since you are no longer pulling back the entire record set, you needed to add another query to get the count by calling collabSpacesQuery.Count().

■ **Tip**   It may not always be obvious which LINQ statements trigger calls to the database. If you are not sure what LINQ to Entities is doing, it is a good practice to use a tool such as SQL Monitor, which is included as part of the SQL Server tools. SQL Monitor allows you to see what queries are being run against your database. If you notice that more queries are being run than you expect, you may need to make adjustments in your code.

The OrderBy Extension Method

One bit of magic used in Listing 10-34 was the consumption of a custom LINQ extension that takes a string as a parameter and then uses it to have LINQ append a sort-by clause to the SQL Server Query that it generates.

To create this custom extension, we will add a new class file named LinqExtensions.cs to the Ch10.Shared. Helpers project. Inside it, we will create a static class that will contain an extension method named OrderBy<T>.

This method will use the classes in the System.Linq.Expression library to create an expression. You can think of this as the long, syntactic, sugarless way to dynamically generate an expression that you would normally create using an inline lambda expression. We will then use this expression in combination with reflection to call the native LINQ OrderBy method with our expression passed as a parameter. This code is shown in Listing 10-35.

Listing 10-35. Creating a LINQ Extension That Uses the System.Linq.Expression Library to Dynamically Create an Expression

```
using System;
using System.Linq;
using System.Linq.Expressions;
using System.Reflection;
```

```
namespace Ch10.Shared.Helpers
{
    public static class LinqExtentions
    {
        //This is the extention that you call in your LINQ code
        public static IOrderedQueryable<T> OrderBy<T>(
            this IQueryable<T> source,
            string property)
        {
            return ApplyOrder<T>(source, property, "OrderBy");
        }

        //this method creates the expression and the uses
        // reflection to construct a method call
        // breaking out into an second method allows us to create varaitions
        // that can use other methods such as OrderByDescending
        static IOrderedQueryable<T> ApplyOrder<T>(
                            IQueryable<T> source,
                            string property,
                            string methodName)
        {
            string[] props = property.Split('.');
            Type type = typeof(T);
            ParameterExpression arg = Expression.Parameter(type, "x");
            Expression expr = arg;
            foreach (string prop in props)
            {
                // use reflection to get metadata for
                // the object we wish to sort by
                PropertyInfo pi = type.GetProperty(prop);
                expr = Expression.Property(expr, pi);
                type = pi.PropertyType;
            }
            //Create the Lambda expression
            Type delegateType =
                typeof(Func<,>).MakeGenericType(typeof(T), type);
            LambdaExpression lambda =
                Expression.Lambda(delegateType, expr, arg);

            // use reflection to call the sort method using the
            // Lambda expression
            object result = typeof(Queryable).GetMethods().Single(
                    method => method.Name == methodName
                            && method.IsGenericMethodDefinition
                            && method.GetGenericArguments().Length == 2
                            && method.GetParameters().Length == 2)
```

```
                    .MakeGenericMethod(typeof(T), type)
                    .Invoke(null, new object[] { source, lambda });
            return (IOrderedQueryable<T>)result;
        }

    }

}
```

In addition to the query for the collaboration sites, our page also needs the list of the genres from the lookup table. This is done with a simple LINQ expression encapsulated in the GetGenreLookupList method from the EFDataExampleRepository, as shown in Listing 10-36.

Listing 10-36. The GetGenreLookupList Method in the EFDataExampleRepository

```
public IList<GenreLookUp> GetGenreLookupList()
{
  var categories = from c in m_context.GenreLookUps
                           orderby c.GenreName
                           select c;
  return categories.ToList();
}
```

Creating the Model

In this example, you will create new class to act as the model. If you have downloaded the sample code, you can find this class inside the file Models\DataExampleModels. The model consists of two classes. The first, CollaborationSpaceSearchResult, represents each row of data in our grid. It replaces the anonymous type used in the Web Forms example. The second class, CollaborationSpaceSearchResultModel, contains a list of CollaborationSpaceSearchResult objects and a list of GenreLookUp objects. The GenreLookUp type is defined in the Ch7.SharedAPI assembly.

The remaining items in the model represent the state of the page, including the number of search results found, the current page number, filter expression, and the sort expression used. Both classes are shown in Listing 10-37.

Listing 10-37. Models Used in the Data Grid Example

```
using Ch7.SharedAPI;
using System;
using System.Collections.Generic;

namespace Ch10.Mvc.Web.Models
{

    public class CollaborationSpaceSearchResult
    {
        public int CollaborationSpaceId { get; set; }
        public DateTime CreateDate { get; set; }
        public string Description { get; set; }
        public DateTime ? LastPostDate { get; set; }
        public DateTime ModifiedDate { get; set; }
        public int NumberComments { get; set; }
```

```
        public int NumberViews { get; set; }
        public bool RestrictContributorsToBand { get; set; }
        public CollaborationSpaceStatus Status { get; set; }
        public string Title { get; set; }
        public int GenreLookUpId { get; set; }
        public string UserName { get; set; }
        public string WebSite { get; set; }
        public string AvatarURL { get; set; }


    }
    public class CollaborationSpaceSearchResultModel
    {
        public IList<CollaborationSpaceSearchResult>
                CollaborationSpaceSearchResults { get; set; }
        public IList<GenreLookUp> GenreLookUpList { get; set; }
        public int NumberOfResults{get;set;}
        public string ResultsDescription { get; set; }
        public int ItemsPerPage { get; set; }
        public int CurrentPage { get; set; }
        public string SortExpression { get; set; }
        public int CategoryId { get; set; }
        public int TotalPages
        {
            get
            {
                if (ItemsPerPage != 0)
                {
                    return NumberOfResults / ItemsPerPage;
                }
                return 0;
            }
        }
    }
}
```

Creating the Controller

With most of the heavy lifting moved out to the repository class, the controller logic is somewhat simplistic. One thing to take notice of is that all of the primitive types passed as parameters to the controller are set as nullable (int ?). This is required so that the MVC data binder can assign null values to properties that are bound to empty fields. If you do not make your primitive types nullable, a runtime error will occur if the parameters are missing.

The first few lines of code in the method body check if the nullable types have values, and if not, assign a default value. We then create an instance of our CollaborationSpaceSearchResultModel model class. This class takes the place of the anonymous type used in the Web Forms example. In addition, this model takes on additional data that was formally expressed as properties in the Web Forms code-behind example. This includes the current sort expression and any filter that may have been applied. After creating the instance of the model, we then make the calls to the repository. The results of the queries are then used to populate the model. The GridViewReplacement controller action is shown in Listing 10-38.

Listing 10-38. Controller Action That Permits Sorting and Filtering

```
public ActionResult GridViewReplacement(int? Page,
                                        string SortExpression,
                                        bool? Accending,
                                        int? CategoryId)
{
    //Set defualt values for all optional  parameters
    int page = Page ?? 1;
    string sortExpression = string.IsNullOrEmpty(SortExpression) ? "CreateDate" : SortExpression;
    bool useDefaultSort = Accending.HasValue ? Accending.Value : true;
    int categoryId = CategoryId.HasValue ? CategoryId.Value : 0;
    int resultsFound=0;

    // set up model
    CollaborationSpaceSearchResultModel model = new CollaborationSpaceSearchResultModel();

    model.CollaborationSpaceSearchResults =
    m_repository.GetActiveCollaborationSpaces(page,
                                              10,
                                              sortExpression,
                                              categoryId,
                                              useDefaultSort,
                                              out resultsFound);

            model.GenreLookUpList = m_repository.GetGenreLookupList();
            model.NumberOfResults = resultsFound;
            model.CurrentPage = page;
            model.ItemsPerPage = 10;
            model.CategoryId = categoryId;
            model.SortExpression = sortExpression;
            return View("GridViewReplacement", model);
}
```

Creating the View

The view is divided into two sections. On the left side of the screen is a list of musical genres. Clicking the Genre name will filter the items in the grid. The rest of the page is made up of the grid itself.

The view is strongly typed with the type Ch10.Mvc.Web.Models.CollaborationSpaceSearchResultModel, which was shown in Listing 10-37. After the title and instructions, a NAV element with the ID SideBar is created. This element contains the list of genres. It has two CSS classes, float-left and leftColumn, associated with it. You can apply multiple CSS classes to an element by using the HTML class attribute, with each class name separated by a space.

The grid is placed inside a DIV element. This DIV element also has multiple styles associated with it. The applied styles make the grid float to the right of the genres list, as well as specify the dimensions of the column.

Inside the table, the first thing defined is the headers. Each header uses the Html.ActionLink helper to create a link to the GridViewReplacement action but with different sort parameters. The links also include a page parameter that notes the current page. It is almost always a good idea to use an action link rather than a standard HTML link. This way, if you want to update your routing tables so that the page number and sort expression are included in the URL rather than the query string, you can do so easily by adding a route in the RouteConfig.cs file.

After the table header, a foreach statement iterates though the record set, rendering each item in a table row. The view is shown in Listing 10-39.

Listing 10-39. The Grid Replacement View

```
@model Ch10.Mvc.Web.Models.CollaborationSpaceSearchResultModel
@{
    ViewBag.Title = "Grid View Replacement Sample";
}


<h2>@ViewBag.Title</h2>
<p>
    This example shows how you could replace the GridView control when used as a read only list that
supports filtering and
paging and sorting.
</p>
<h3>@Model.ResultsDescription</h3>

<nav id="SideBar" class="float-left leftColumn">
    <h4>Genres</h4>
    <ul class="Facet ItemList">
        @foreach (var item in Model.GenreLookUpList)
        {
            <li>
                @Html.ActionLink(item.GenreName, "GridViewReplacement", new {CategoryId=item.
GenreLookUpId, Page=1, SortExpression=Model.SortExpression })
            </li>
        }
    </ul>
</nav>
<div id="main" class="float-right rightColumn">
    <h4>@Model.NumberOfResults records have been found. Page @Model.CurrentPage of
@Model.TotalPages</h4>
    <table class="grid FullWidth">
        <tr>
            <th>@Html.ActionLink("Collaboration Space", "GridViewReplacement", new
{CategoryId=Model.CategoryId, Page=1, SortExpression="Title" })</th>
            <th>@Html.ActionLink("Artist", "GridViewReplacement", new {CategoryId=Model.
CategoryId, Page=1, SortExpression="UserName" })</th>
            <th>@Html.ActionLink("Created", "GridViewReplacement", new {CategoryId=Model.
CategoryId, Page=1, SortExpression="CreateDate" })</th>
            <th>@Html.ActionLink("Modified", "GridViewReplacement", new {CategoryId=Model.
CategoryId, Page=1, SortExpression="ModifiedDate" })</th>
            <th>@Html.ActionLink("Stats", "GridViewReplacement", new {CategoryId=Model.
CategoryId, Page=1, SortExpression="NumberViews" })</th>
        </tr>
        @foreach (var item in Model.CollaborationSpaceSearchResults)
        {
            <tr>
                <td>@item.Title</td>
                <td>@item.UserName</td>
                <td>@item.CreateDate.ToShortDateString()</td>
```

```
                    <td>@item.ModifiedDate.ToShortDateString()</td>
                    <td>
                        <ul class="ItemList">
                                <li>
                                    Hits: @item.NumberViews
                                </li>
                                <li>
                                    Posts: @item.NumberComments
                                </li>
                                <li>
                                    Status: @item.Status
                                </li>
                        </ul>

                    </td>
                </tr>
            }
        </table>
        <nav class="Pager">
        @Html.CreateNumericPager(Model.NumberOfResults, Model.ItemsPerPage, Model.CurrentPage)
        </nav>
    </div>
    @section scripts{
        <script>
            $(function () {
                $("tr:even").addClass("even");
                $("tr:odd").addClass("odd");
            });
        </script>
    }
```

The last interesting line in Listing 10-39 (highlighted in bold) uses an HTML helper called CreateNumericPager to generate the page number URLs that allow you to navigate to through the pages of the result set. This is a custom HTML helper that takes the number of results, the number of items per page, and the current page, and then uses them to generate the appropriate action links.

Creating the Numeric Pager

In order to facilitate paging on the data grid, you need to have a way for the user to navigate between the pages. The CreateNumericPager helper creates a pager that will display a maximum of 20 links at once. In addition, it displays links to the first and last page of the page list. The tricky part is displaying the appropriate links, depending on what page in the list the user is viewing. For example, if you are on page 1, you would need to see the links for pages 1 through 20. If you are on page 15, you may want to see links for pages 6 through 26.

You may want to hide the pager if only a single page of results is displayed. If fewer than 20 pages of results are shown, you may want to hide the first and last page links.

The first problem is easy to solve. You can compare the total number of results to the number of items on a page. If the items per page is less than or equal to the number of pages, then you will return an empty string.

The next interesting bit of logic is determining the first and last pages that need to be displayed. This code has been factored out into the helper methods getStartPage and getEndPage. Once you have these values, you can use a loop to create the list of links, which output as an unordered list. The links themselves are created by using another helper method called buildActionLink. The CreateNumericPager extension method is shown in Listing 10-40.

Listing 10-40. The Numeric Pager HTML Helper

```
public static MvcHtmlString CreateNumericPager(this HtmlHelper helper,
                                               int totalNumResults,
                                               int itemsPerPage,
                                               int currentPage)
{
    if (totalNumResults <= itemsPerPage)
    {
        //no pager needed
        return MvcHtmlString.Empty;
    }
    else
    {
        int numberOfPages = totalNumResults / itemsPerPage;
        int maxNumberOfPagesShown = 20;
        bool showFirstAndLast = numberOfPages > maxNumberOfPagesShown;
        int startPage = getStartPage(numberOfPages, currentPage);
        int endPage = getEndPage(numberOfPages, currentPage, startPage);

        StringBuilder builder = new StringBuilder();
        builder.Append("<ul>");
        if (showFirstAndLast && startPage>1)
        {
            builder.Append("<li>");
            builder.Append(buildActionLink(helper, "...", 1));
            builder.Append("</li>");
        }

        for (int i = startPage; i <= endPage; i++)
        {
            string PageLinkText = i.ToString();
            builder.Append("<li>");
            if (i != currentPage)
            {
                builder.Append(buildActionLink(helper, PageLinkText, i));
            }
            else
            {
                builder.Append(i);
            }
            builder.Append("</li>");

        }

        if (showFirstAndLast && (endPage!= numberOfPages))
        {
            builder.Append("<li>");
            builder.Append(buildActionLink(helper, "...", numberOfPages));
            builder.Append("</li>");
        }
```

```
        builder.Append("</ul>");
        return MvcHtmlString.Create(builder.ToString());
    }
}
```

Listing 10-41 shows the getStartPage and getEndPage methods. In the getStartPage method, you first check the current page. If it is greater than ten, you will place the current page near the middle of the list by making the start page nine less than the current page. If you are nearing the end of the list, you need to make sure that the start page stays 20 pages behind the end page. This prevents us from creating links to pages that do not exist. Lastly, if you are on one of the first ten pages, you will always start your counter on page 1.

The calculation for the end page is less complicated. You might be tempted to think that you can just add 20 to the start page, and then you are done. Unfortunately, this will not work because if you only have 16 pages of results and you started on page one, you would end up creating four extra links to pages that do not exist. The getEndPage solves this problem by checking to see if your calculated last page is greater than the total number of pages. If so, it will subtract the overage.

A final check in getEndPage method determines if you are on one of the last ten pages. In this case, you need to always show all of the remaining pages.

Listing 10-41. Getting the First and Last Page

```
private static int getStartPage(int numberOfPages, int currentPage)
{
    int minToDisplay = 1;
    if (currentPage > 10 )
    {
        minToDisplay = currentPage - 9;
    }
    if(currentPage > (numberOfPages - 10) && (numberOfPages>20))
    {
        minToDisplay = numberOfPages - 20;
    }
    return minToDisplay;
}

private static int getEndPage(int numberOfPages, int currentPage, int startPage)
{
    int maxToDisplay =startPage + 19;
    if (maxToDisplay > numberOfPages)
    {
        maxToDisplay = maxToDisplay - (maxToDisplay - numberOfPages);
    }
    if ((currentPage > numberOfPages - 10) && (startPage!=1))
    {
        maxToDisplay = numberOfPages;
    }
    return maxToDisplay;
}
```

The last bit of this is the method used to create the action links. Since we are inside an HTML helper extension method, we do not know what controller action we need to link to. Luckily, we can derive this information by inspecting the RouteData collection of the ViewContext property of our HtmlHelper instance. Calling helper.ViewContext.RouteData.Values["action"] gives us the name of the current action. We can then use that value to construct the action link.

Also, since we are using the query string to preserve the state of our grid, we will need to copy existing query string values to each link we build. To do this, we first check to see if there are values in the query string by using the HasKeys method. This method returns true if keys are found. We then use the existing query string values to build the query string for the links. The buildActionLink method is shown in Listing 10-42.

Listing 10-42. The Build Action Link HTML Helper

```
private static string buildActionLink(HtmlHelper helper,
                                      string linkText,
                                      int pageParam)
{
  if (helper.ViewContext.HttpContext.Request.QueryString.HasKeys())
  {
    string sort =
        helper.ViewContext.HttpContext.Request.QueryString["SortExpression"];
    string categoryId =
        helper.ViewContext.HttpContext.Request.QueryString["CategoryId"];
    return helper.ActionLink(linkText,
                  helper.ViewContext.RouteData.Values["action"].ToString(),
                  new {
                        SortExpression = sort,
                        CategoryId = categoryId,
                        Page = pageParam }).ToString();
                        }
  else
  {
    return helper.ActionLink(linkText,
                  helper.ViewContext.RouteData.Values["action"].ToString(),
                  new {
                        Page=pageParam}).ToString();
                        }
  }
}
```

The end result of all this hard work can be seen in Figure 10-4, which shows the grid on page 69 of a result set with 695 records.

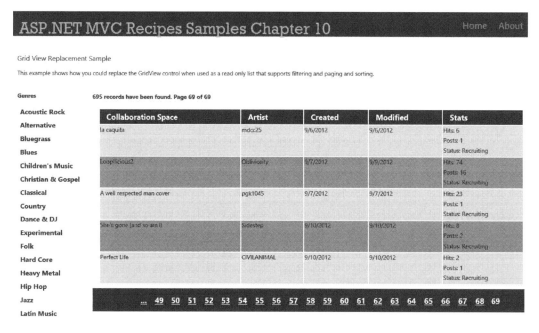

Figure 10-4. *Data grid with paging, sorting, and filtering*

10-4. Creating a Data Grid That Allows Inline Editing

Problem

Coming from a Web Forms background, you normally use a `GridView` control for implementing grids that allow inline editing of rows. You would like to understand how to do this using ASP.NET MVC.

Solution

Since the ASP.NET MVC Framework does not use server controls such as the `GridView` control, you will need to create this functionality. Luckily, with the help of a few HTML helpers, it is a relatively straightforward implementation that requires the following steps:

1. Create a model that represents the data that you would like to view and edit in your grid view. Alternatively, you can use a class or entity defined in an external library.

2. Create an HTML helper that will encapsulate the substitution of read-only rows with editable rows when a row is selected for editing.

3. Create the view that will display the editable grid.

As another option, you can combine the techniques shown in this recipe with the Recipe 10-3 to create a full data grid solution that supports editing, filtering, sorting, and paging.

How It Works

In addition to allowing you to have a read-only data grid with paging and sorting capabilities, the ASP.NET Web Forms GridView control also allowed you to select a row for editing, make changes to the data in the row, and then save the changes. In order to replicate this functionality in ASP.NET MVC, you will need to create a model that not only represents the data needed to display but also allows you to specify which row is selected. You also need to track the changes in the model so that you can make changes to the rows that have changed.

You should also create some reusable components that can be used on several pages. This will simplify your views by removing the need for some conditional logic while increasing your productivity and increasing maintainability for the application.

For this example, you will create several HTML helper extensions that will check to see if a row is selected, and if selected, replace the display with the appropriate editor for the field's data type.

The HTML Helpers

The logic for the inplace editing helpers is pretty simple. You will create a helper method to match the out-of-the-box xxxFor helper methods. For example, for the EditorFor method, you will create a DataGridEditorFor method. Each of the helpers will take two parameters: a bool value that indicates whether or not the item is selected, and an expression that represents the field you wish to display or edit.

If you wish to follow along with this example, open the code example from the code samples downloaded from the book's web site. There is an incomplete version of the project located in the Chapter10\Ch10.MvcExamples\Before\Ch10.Mc folder. The completed version can be found in Chapter10\Ch10.MvcExamples\After\Ch10.Mc.

After opening the project, right-click the Ch10.Shared.Helpers node, and select Add ➤ Class. Name the class **EditInPlaceHelpers**. Since this class will contain extension methods, it must be declared as public static class. Each method must also be declared as public and static, and will return an MvcHtmlString. In order for us to follow the pattern used by the built-in HTML helper extensions, our method signatures need to follow this format:

```
xxxxFor<TModel, TProperty>(this HtmlHelper<TModel> helper,
            Expression<Func<TModel, TProperty>> expression) where TModel : class
```

This ugly signature is the magic that allows HTML helpers to be strongly typed. The TModel represents the type that we are passing to the helper, and the TProperty is the property of that class that we are evaluating. The inclusion of this HtmlHelper<TModel> helper in each helper tells the compiler which class to add the extension to. The expression parameter is what allows a lambda expression to be passed in rather than a static property. This adds the additional flexibility.

In the body of the helper method, first check the value of the isSelected parameter. If it is set to true, call EditorFor, one of the built-in HTML helpers. This helper will render the appropriate HTML input type for the property passed in the expression property. If isSelected is false, then the built-in DisplayFor helper is used to render the property as text.

The completed class is shown in Listing 10-43.

Listing 10-43. The EditInPlace Helpers

```
using System;
using System.Linq.Expressions;
using System.Web.Mvc;
using System.Web.Mvc.Html;

namespace Ch10.Shared.Helpers
{
    public static class EditInPlaceHelpers
    {
```

425

```
        // returns the default editor for the property when isSelected
        // is true
        public static MvcHtmlString DataGridEditorFor<TModel, TProperty>
                            (this HtmlHelper<TModel> helper,
                             bool isSelected,
                             Expression<Func<TModel, TProperty>> expression)
                             where TModel : class
        {
            if (isSelected)
            {
              return
                MvcHtmlString.Create(helper.EditorFor(expression).ToString());
            }
            else
            {
              return
                MvcHtmlString.Create(helper.DisplayFor(expression).ToString());
            }
        }

        // returns a text box for the property when isSelected
        // is true
        public static MvcHtmlString DataGridTextBoxFor<TModel, TProperty>
                            (this HtmlHelper<TModel> helper,
                             bool isSelected,
                             Expression<Func<TModel, TProperty>> expression)
                             where TModel : class
        {
            if (isSelected)
            {
              return
                MvcHtmlString.Create(helper.TextBoxFor(expression).ToString());
            }
            else
            {
              return
                MvcHtmlString.Create(helper.DisplayFor(expression).ToString());
            }
        }
        // returns the default editor for the property when isSelected
        // is true
        public static MvcHtmlString DataGridTextAreaFor<TModel, TProperty>
                            (this HtmlHelper<TModel> helper,
                             bool isSelected,
                             Expression<Func<TModel, TProperty>> expression)
                             where TModel : class
        {
            if (isSelected)
            {
              return
               MvcHtmlString.Create(helper.TextAreaFor(expression).ToString());
            }
```

```
            else
            {
                return
                 MvcHtmlString.Create(helper.DisplayFor(expression).ToString());
            }
        }

    }
}
```

The Model

The model for the solution contains a list of ArtistSkill objects that are defined by the entity data model from a library used by the project. It also keeps track of which item is selected and includes a helper method that allows a test to see if the current item is selected. This was necessary to simplify the view logic. To create the model, right-click the Models folder in the Ch10.Mvc.Web project, and select Add ➤ Class. Name the class **InlineEditingArtistSkillListModel**. The completed model is shown in Listing 10-44.

Listing 10-44. InlineEditingModel

```
using Ch7.SharedAPI;
using System.Collections.Generic;

namespace Ch10.Mvc.Web.Models
{
    public class InlineEditingArtistSkillListModel    {
        public int SelectedRow { get; set; }
        public List<ArtistSkill> ArtistSkillList { get; set; }
        public bool IsSelected(ArtistSkill item)
        {
            if (item == null)
                return false;
            return item.ArtistTalentID == SelectedRow;
        }
    }
}
```

The Controller

The controller requires two actions to support display and processing of the edited results. The first action supports HTTP GET and contains an optional parameter named Selected, which needs to be optional since no item will be selected when the page is first loaded.

The example uses a repository that is located in the Models folder. The repository exposes two methods relevant to this exercise. The first, GetArtistSkill, returns a list of ArtistSkill objects for a given artist specified by the Id parameter. It also contains a method to update a skill, which takes an ArtistSkill object as a parameter. To keep the example a little less complex, the GET action is using a hardcoded Id parameter.

The HTTP POST version of the action, shown in Listing 10-45, takes a FormCollection as a parameter. Unfortunately, this method is not able to take advantage of the model binding since there will not be an exact match between the property names in the model and the names of the form fields being returned from the view. Because of this, we need to perform additional work in mapping the input fields to the property names.

Listing 10-45. GridViewReplacementWithInplaceEditing Controller Actions

```
public ActionResult GridViewReplacementWithInplaceEditing(int? Selected)
{
    //hard code artistId for this example
    var skills = m_repository.GetArtistSkills(2);
    var model = new InlineEditingArtistSkillListModel();
    model.ArtistSkillList = skills;
    if (Selected.HasValue)
    {
      model.SelectedRow = Selected.Value;
    }
    return View("GridViewReplacementWithInplaceEditing", model);
}

[HttpPost]
public ActionResult GridViewReplacementWithInplaceEditing(FormCollection collection)
{
  ArtistSkill skill = new ArtistSkill();
  skill.ArtistId = Int32.Parse(collection["item.ArtistId"]);
  skill.ArtistTalentID = Int32.Parse(collection["item.ArtistTalentID"]);
  skill.TalentName = collection["item.TalentName"];
  skill.SkillLevel = Int32.Parse(collection["item.SkillLevel"]);
  skill.Details = collection["item.Details"];
  skill.Styles = collection["item.Styles"];
  m_repository.UpdateSkill(skill);
  return RedirectToAction("GridViewReplacementWithInplaceEditing");
}
```

The View

The view is strongly bound to the Ch10.Mvc.Web.Models.InlineEditingModel type. It is includes the standard @using(Html.BeginForm()) and @Html.ValidationSummary(), which wrap the grid table in an HTML form and provide an area for validation errors to be displayed.

Inside the grid, a foreach statement loops through each record in the model's ArtistSkillList property. The HTML helper extensions are uses to create our fields.

For the first column in our grid, we use a conditional statement to decide if we should show a link for saving the form or a link to update the view's selected property. For the Edit link, we use a standard ActionLink, but for the Save link, we create an anchor tag that will submit the form when clicked. For the Save link use case, we also include several hidden fields so that we have the rest of the data required to update the field.

At the end of the view is a call to @Scripts.Render("~/bundles/jqueryval"), which provides the validation logic for our form. The view is shown in Listing 10-46.

Listing 10-46. GridViewReplacementWithInplaceEditing Controller Actions

```
@model Ch10.Mvc.Web.Models.InlineEditingArtistSkillListModel

@{
    ViewBag.Title = "Grid View Replacement With In place Editing";

}

<h2>Grid View Replacement With In place Editing </h2>
Click the edit link to edit the row.
 @using(Html.BeginForm()){
     @Html.ValidationSummary()
<table class="grid">
    <tr>
        <th>

        </th>
        <th>
            Talent
        </th>
        <th>
            Level
        </th>
        <th>
            Details
        </th>
        <th>
            Musical Styles
        </th>
    </tr>

@foreach (var item in Model.ArtistSkillList) {
    <tr>
        <td>
            @if(Model.IsSelected(item)){
                <a href="#" onclick="document.forms[0].submit()">Save</a>
                @Html.HiddenFor(modelItem => item.ArtistId)
                @Html.HiddenFor(modelItem => item.ArtistTalentID)
            }
            else
            {
            @Html.ActionLink("Edit", "GridViewReplacementWithInplaceEditing", new {
Selected=item.ArtistTalentID })
            }
        </td>
        <td>
            @Html.DataGridTextBoxFor(Model.IsSelected(item),modelItem => item.TalentName)
        </td>
        <td>
            @Html.DataGridEditorFor(Model.IsSelected(item),modelItem => item.SkillLevel)
        </td>
```

```
        <td>
            @Html.DataGridTextAreaFor(Model.IsSelected(item),modelItem => item.Details)
        </td>
        <td>
            @Html.DataGridEditorFor(Model.IsSelected(item),modelItem => item.Styles)
        </td>
    </tr>
}

</table>
}

@section Scripts {
    @Scripts.Render("~/bundles/jqueryval")
}
```

The last bit of detail is the style sheet information needed to style the form and tables. It is found in the file Content/GridStyle.css. This file is used for several examples in this chapter. The CSS selectors added specifically for this example are shown in Listing 10-47. The style targets only textarea, text and number input types inside a table columns for tables assigned the CSS class grid. It makes the form field stretch to fill the entire horizontal space of the table row and outlines the fields with a thin blue border.

Listing 10-47. CSS Styles in Content/GridStyle.css

```
.grid {
    background-color: #fff;
    margin: 5px 0 10px;
    padding-left: 5px;
    width: 95%;
}
    .grid td {
        color: #1a1a1a;
        vertical-align: top;
    }

    .grid td textarea {
        width:98%;
        border-width:2px;
        height: 3em;
        border-color:lightblue;
    }

        .grid td input[type="text"], .grid td input[type="number"] {
            border: 2px solid lightblue;
            width: 98%;
            height: 2em;
        }
```

The end result of this work can be seen in Figure 10-5. Here we see a total of five rows, with the fourth row selected. Notice how the Level column is rendered as the new HTML5 number type. Clicking the up and down arrows will change the value of the number. The Details column has been rendered as a text area and, in accordance with the styles set in Listing 10-47, is a bit thicker than the other columns.

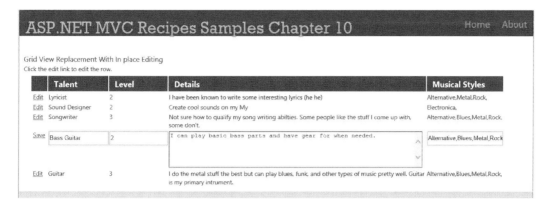

Figure 10-5. *Data grid with inplace editing*

10-5. Creating a Master/Details View in ASP.NET MVC

Problem

In the Web Forms world, it is somewhat simple to create a master/details view page that displays a list of items and allows you to click an item in the list to view details about it. Now that you are using MVC, you would like to create similar functionality.

Solution

Even though ASP.NET MVC does not use the concept of controls, re-creating this functionality is somewhat straightforward. The basic steps are as follows:

- Create a model that consists of a List and a selected object.

- Design a view that consists of a loop that creates a table of items and a section to display the item details. In the table of items, have a link that allows users to select an item. Clicking the link triggers a controller action that updates the selected object property of the model.

- Create a controller action that takes the unique identifier of an object as an optional parameter, and then if that parameter has a value, update the model with the matching details record.

How It Works

We will first review a Web Forms–based solution and then create the equivalent functionality in ASP.NET MVC.

A Master Detail Example in Web Forms

In Web Forms, it is possible to create a master/details view declaratively without writing a single line of C# code. You would start by first creating a new Web Form page and then defining two ObjectDataSource controls. The ObjectDataSource control requires that an object contain a select method that it can call to get the required items. In this example, it was done by creating a simple data source, as shown in Listing 10-48. The repository exposes a single property containing the name of the selected artist and two methods. One method, GetNewArtistList, returns a list of Artist objects, and the other method, GetArtistDetails, returns a single Artist object.

Listing 10-48. Simple Repository Class Used for ObjectDataSource Objects

```
using Ch7.SharedAPI;
using System;
using System.Collections.Generic;
using System.Linq;

namespace Ch10.WebFormsExamples.Web.ObjectDataSources
{
    public class ExampleDataSource : IDisposable
    {
        MobEntities m_context = new MobEntities();

        public String ArtistName { get; set; }
        public List<Ch7.SharedAPI.Artist> GetNewArtistList()
        {
            //last 10 Artist records created
            var newArtistsQuery = (from m in m_context.Artists
                                   orderby m.CreateDate descending
                                   select m).Take(10);
            List<Artist> newArtistsList = newArtistsQuery.ToList<Artist>();
            return newArtistsList;
        }

        public Artist GetArtistDetails(int id)
        {
            return m_context.Artists.Find(id);
        }

        public void Dispose()
        {
            if (m_context != null)
                m_context.Dispose();
        }
    }
}
```

Inside the Web Form page, we can then create two ObjectDataSource controls. Both will use the ExampleDataSource class as their TypeName property, but use different methods for the SelectMethod property.

In the ObjectDataSource for our detail, we define a SelectParameter that maps to the Id parameter of the GetArtistDetails method. We can then drag a GridView control and a DetailsView control to the Web Forms page, and then their DataSourceID properties to the ID of the DataSourceControls. In the GridView control, we set the DataKeyNames property to the ArtistId property.

All that is left to do at this point is wrap the two controls inside HTML section tags, which we style with CSS to define the layout of our page.

The completed page is shown in Listing 10-49. The code linking the ListView and DetailsView controls is highlighted in bold.

Listing 10-49. MasterDetailsView.aspx

```
//some code removed for brevity
<asp:Content ID="Content3" ContentPlaceHolderID="MainContent" runat="server">
    <asp:ObjectDataSource ID="ObjectDataSourceList"
        runat="server"
        SelectMethod="GetNewArtistList"
        TypeName="Ch10.WebFormsExamples.Web.ObjectDataSources.ExampleDataSource">
    </asp:ObjectDataSource>
    <asp:ObjectDataSource ID="ObjectDataSourceDetail"
        SelectMethod="GetArtistDetails"
        TypeName="Ch10.WebFormsExamples.Web.ObjectDataSources.ExampleDataSource"
        runat="server">
        <SelectParameters>
            <asp:ControlParameter
                ControlID="GridView1"
                Name="id"
                PropertyName="SelectedValue"
                Type="Int32" />
        </SelectParameters>
    </asp:ObjectDataSource>
    <section class="MasterList">
        <asp:GridView ID="GridView1" runat="server"
                    DataSourceID="ObjectDataSourceList"
                    AutoGenerateColumns="False"
                    DataKeyNames="ArtistId">
            <Columns>
                <asp:CommandField ShowSelectButton="True" />
                <asp:BoundField DataField="UserName" HeaderText="User Name" />
                <asp:BoundField DataField="Country" HeaderText="Country" />
                <asp:BoundField DataField="Provence" HeaderText="Provence" />
                <asp:BoundField DataField="CreateDate" HeaderText="Create Date" />
            </Columns>
        </asp:GridView>
    </section>
    <section class="DetailsList">
            <h3>Details</h3>
        <asp:DetailsView ID="DetailsView1"
            runat="server"
            Height="50px"
            Width="125px"
            DataSourceID="ObjectDataSourceDetail"
            EmptyDataText="Please select a record">

        </asp:DetailsView>
    </section>
</asp:Content>
```

At this point, you can press F5 and run your project. The page will work. There is no additional code that needs to be written.

433

Creating the Master/Details View in ASP.NET MVC

The first step in this conversion process is to take repository logic and move it to the MVC application. For the most part, this code does not need to change. The example code on the book's web site is included as part of the `EFDataExchangeRepository.cs` file, which can be found in the `Models` folder.

In addition to the repository, a separate model class is required to hold both the data list and the selected item. The model also has a separate property that holds the `id` of the selected artist. The code for this model is shown in Listing 10-50.

Listing 10-50. MasterDetailsModel.cs

```
namespace Ch10.Mvc.Web.Models
{
    public class ArtistMasterDetailsModel
    {
        public Artist SelectedArtist { get; set; }
        public int SelectedArtistId { get; set; }

        public List<Artist> ArtistList { get; set; }
    }
}
```

In the `DataExamplesController` class, there is a new controller action called `ArtistMasterDetailsView`. This action takes an optional parameter, `SelectedItemId`. The action creates an instance of the model class and then fills its `ArtistList` property with the results of a call to the repository. If the `SelectedItemId` contains a value, rather than making a separate database call, it simply uses the `Find` method on the `Artist` list, and then stores that object to the model's `SelectedArtist` property. The `MasterDetailsView` action is shown in Listing 10-51.

Listing 10-51. The MasterDetailsView Action in DataExampleController.cs

```
public ActionResult MasterDetailsView(int ? SelectedItemId)
{
    List<Artist> newArtistsList = m_repository.GetNewArtistList();
    var model = new MasterDetailsModel();
    model.ArtistList = newArtistsList;
    if (SelectedItemId.HasValue)
      {
        model.SelectedArtist =
            newArtistsList.Find(a => a.ArtistId == SelectedItemId.Value);
                model.SelectedArtistId = SelectedItemId.Value;
      }
  return View("MasterDetailsView", model);
}
```

The last piece of the puzzle is the view. To save some coding, you can use Visual Studio's scaffolding generation feature to create a view using the Details template:

1. Right-click the `Views/DataExample` folder in Solution Explorer. Select Add ➤ View.

2. In the Add View window, name the view **MasterDetailsView**. Make sure that the Razor engine is selected.

3.   Click the Create a Strongly-Typed View check box. Select Artist as your model class. Even though we will be using MasterDetailsModel as the model class, we need to use the Artist class to generate the necessary scaffolding.

4.   Select the Details scaffolding template. Ensure that Use a Layout or Master Page is selected and that the Master Page text box is empty.

5.   Click the Add button. Visual Studio will create your new view along with the scaffolding for your details view.

6.   In the code editor, change the first line of code in the view so that it references the MasterDetailsModel rather than Artist.

7.   You will then need to replace all of the instances of model.[SomePropertyName] with model.SelectedArtist.[SomePropertyName]. You can do this easily using Visual Studio's Find and Replace feature.

8.   After the <h2>...</h2> tags at the beginning of the file, define a section to hold your list. You can then add code into the section that uses a foreach loop to create a tabular list of items. To enable the selection of items, use the Html.ActionLink HTML helper in one of the table's columns to create a link back to the MasterDetailsView action with the SelectedItemId as a parameter.

9.   Since you do not want to see the details of this view unless an artist has been selected, wrap the code generated by the scaffolding in an if statement that checks the value of the model's SelectedArtistId property.

Listing 10-52 shows the relevant sections of the MasterDetailsView.

Listing 10-52. MasterDetailsView.cshtml

```
@model Ch10.Mvc.Web.Models.ArtistMasterDetailsModel
@{
    ViewBag.Title = "Master Details View";
}
<h2>@ViewBag.Title</h2>
<section id="ArtistMasterList" class="float-left MasterList">
    <table class="grid">
        @foreach (var item in Model.ArtistList)
        {
            <tr>
                <td>

                    <div class="ImageDiv float-left">
                        <img src="@item.AvatarUrlSample" class="AristImage" alt="Click Image
to view full profile" />
                    </div>
                    <div class="ContentDiv float-right">
                        <ul>
                            <li class="ProfileLink">@item.UserName</li>
                            <li>@item.Province</li>
```

```
                                <li>@item.Country</li>
                                <li>Joined :
                   <time>@String.Format("{0:d}", item.CreateDate)</time>
                                </li>
                                <li>@Html.ActionLink("View Details","MasterDetailsView", new{
SelectedItemId=item.ArtistId})</li>
                            </ul>
                        </div>
                    </td>
                </tr>
            }
        </table>
    </section>
    <section id="ArtistDetails" class="float-right DetailView ">
    @if(Model.SelectedArtistId>0){
    <fieldset>
        <legend>Artist</legend>

        <div class="display-label">
            @Html.DisplayNameFor(model => model.SelectedArtist.OldUserId)
        </div>
        <div class="display-field">
            @Html.DisplayFor(model => model.SelectedArtist.OldUserId)
        </div>

        <div class="display-label">
            @Html.DisplayNameFor(model => model.SelectedArtist.UserName)
        </div>
        <div class="display-field">
            @Html.DisplayFor(model => model.SelectedArtist.UserName)
        </div>
    <!-- Lots of other properties here -->
    </fieldset>
    }
    </section>
```

The results of this view are shown in Figure 10-6. On the left-hand side of the screen, you have a list of artists. For each artist, there is a View Details link. When you click the link, the selected item is shown on the right side of the screen.

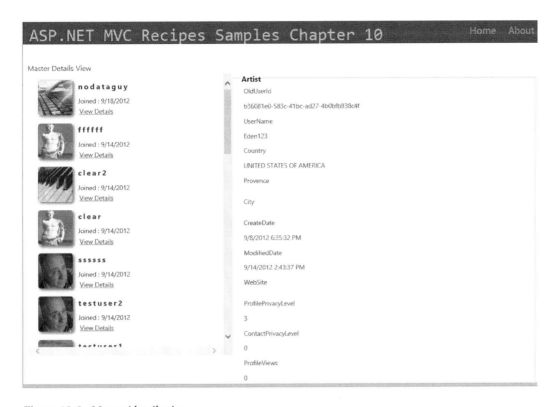

***Figure 10-6.** Master/details view*

10-6. Custom Validators in ASP.NET MVC
Problem

In Web Forms, you created custom validation components that allowed you to verify that a check box had been checked. This was required because, by default, the ASP.NET Web Forms `RequiredFieldValidator` controls could not be applied to a `CheckBox` control. Now that you have moved your project to ASP.NET MVC, you have noticed that adding a `Required` data annotation to a property of your model with a `bool` data type does not have the desired effect of making the property a field on the view. You would like to learn about the ASP.NET MVC equivalent to ASP.NET Web Forms custom validators.

Solution

The `System.ComponentModel.DataAnnotations` library includes an attribute class called `CustomValidation`. This attribute can be applied at either the property level or the class level. It allows you to specify a method name that returns a `ValidationResult` object that will either indicate a successful validation or indicate an error.

How It Works

In the Web Forms world, there are actually two ways to create custom validators. The first is to use the CustomValidator control. Not unlike the data annotations–based version, you needed to pass this control the name of a server-side method, and then implement the validation server-side. In addition to the server-side validation logic, if you wished to have the property validated in the browser prior to postback, you also needed to define a JavaScript method in the browser and configure the control to call the client-side code on validation.

If you wished to create a reusable custom validation control, you could do so by creating a class that extends the System.Web.UI.WebControls.BaseValidator control. A sample of a custom control that verifies that a check box has been ticked is shown in Listing 10-53.

Listing 10-53. A Custom Validation Control That Can Be Used in Web Forms

```
namespace Ch10.WebFormsExamples.ControlLibrary
{
    [DefaultProperty("Text")]
    [ToolboxData("<{0}:RequiredFieldValidatorForCheckBox runat=server>
</{0}:RequiredFieldValidatorForCheckBox>")]
    public class RequiredFieldValidatorForCheckBox : BaseValidator
    {
        private CheckBox _listctrl;

        public RequiredFieldValidatorForCheckBox()
        {
            base.EnableClientScript = false;
        }

        protected override bool ControlPropertiesValid()
        {
            Control ctrl = FindControl(ControlToValidate);

            if (ctrl != null)
            {
                _listctrl = (CheckBox)ctrl;
                return (_listctrl != null);
            }
            else
                return false;    // raise exception
        }

        protected override bool EvaluateIsValid()
        {
            return _listctrl.Checked;
        }

    }
}
```

Custom Validation in ASP.NET MVC Using the CustomValidation Attribute

In this example, by applying the CustomValidation attribute to a property inside a model class, you will add validation logic to verify that a check box has been checked. In addition, you will apply another CustomValidation attribute at the class level. This validator will verify that at least one item in a set of check boxes has been selected.

Listing 10-54 shows the view. Notice that aside from the references to the jqueryval script bundle and the validation summary HTML helper, there is no explicit validation code required.

Listing 10-54. A Razor View That Consumes Custom Validation Defined in the Model

```
@model Ch10.Mvc.Web.Models.CustomValidationModel

@{
    ViewBag.Title = "Index";
}
@Html.ValidationSummary()
@ViewBag.SuccessMessage
@using(Html.BeginForm()){
<h2>Custom Validation Example</h2>
<fieldset>
    <legend>Try and Submit</legend>
    <div> @Html.CheckBoxFor(a => a.IMustBeChecked) @Html.LabelFor(a=>a.IMustBeChecked)</div>
    <section class="RelatedFieldSection">
        <p>Please check one or more of the boxes below.</p>
        <div> @Html.CheckBoxFor(a => a.AtLeastOneShouldBeCheckedOne) @Html.LabelFor(a=>a.
AtLeastOneShouldBeCheckedOne)</div>
        <div> @Html.CheckBoxFor(a => a.AtLeastOneShouldBeCheckedTwo) @Html.LabelFor(a=>a.
AtLeastOneShouldBeCheckedTwo)</div>
        <div> @Html.CheckBoxFor(a => a.AtLeastOneShouldBeCheckedThree) @Html.LabelFor(a=>a.
AtLeastOneShouldBeCheckedThree)</div>
    </section>
    <div><input type="submit" /></div>
</fieldset>
}
@section Scripts {
    @Scripts.Render("~/bundles/jqueryval")
}
```

The controller actions associated with this view does not contain any validation logic. It simply verifies that the ModelState.IsValid property is set to true. You should always verify the value of this property before attempting to perform any work with the posted data. The controller logic is shown in Listing 10-55.

Listing 10-55. Controller That Uses a Model That Includes Custom Validation

```
namespace Ch10.Mvc.Web.Controllers
{
    public class FormsController : Controller
    {
        //
        // GET: /Forms/
```

```
    public ActionResult Index()
    {
        return View();
    }

    [HttpPost]
    public ActionResult Index(CustomValidationModel model)
    {
        if (ModelState.IsValid)
        {
            ViewBag.SuccessMessage = "The form is valid";
        }
        else
        {
            ViewBag.SuccessMessage = "The form is not valid";
        }
        return View("Index", model);
    }

    }
}
```

The model class is where all the magic happens. The CustomValidationModel contains four properties. The first one, IMustBeChecked, has a business rule that requires that it is always selected. A common example of this is the I Accept the Terms and Conditions check box that many applications require you to check before use. The next three properties—AtLeastOneShouldBeCheckedOne, AtLeastOneShouldBeCheckedTwo, and AtLeastOneShouldBeCheckedThree—have a business rule that states at least one of them must be selected.

The IMustBeChecked property has the following attribute:

```
[CustomValidation(typeof(CustomValidationModel), "ValidateIMustBeCheckedTrue")].
```

The first parameter passed to it specifies the .NET type that contains the validation method. This is required even if the methods exist in the same class as the property being validated. The second parameter specifies the name of the method.

The CustomValidationModel class is also decorated with a CustomValidation attribute. In this case, it specifies that the ValidateAtLeastOneIsChecked method is called.

Each of the validation methods defined in the CustomValidationModel class have a return type of ValidationResult. In cases where validation is true, the ValidationResult.Success static property is returned. For the failure cases, the validation methods return a new ValidationResult instance initialized with the error message. The validation methods each take two parameters. The first is the object that the attribute has been applied to. The ValidateIMustBeCheckedTrue method accepts a bool type for its first parameter to match the type of the property it decorates. For ValidateAtLeastOneIsChecked, the first parameter holds an instance of the class CustomValidationModel. The second parameter for each method is a ValidationContext object that contains metadata about the object being validated.

The entire class is shown in Listing 10-56.

Listing 10-56. CustomValidationModel.cs

```
namespace Ch10.Mvc.Web.Models
{
    [CustomValidation(typeof(CustomValidationModel),
                    "ValidateAtLeastOneIsChecked")]
```

```
public class CustomValidationModel
{
    //this Required attribute does not work which is why the custom
    // validator is required
    [Required( ErrorMessage="This box must be checked")]
    [CustomValidation(typeof(CustomValidationModel),
        "ValidateIMustBeCheckedTrue")]
    [Display(Name="I Must Be Checked")]
    public bool IMustBeChecked { get; set; }

    [Display(Name = "You can check me")]
    public bool AtLeastOneShouldBeCheckedOne { get; set; }

    [Display(Name = "Or Me")]
    public bool AtLeastOneShouldBeCheckedTwo { get; set; }

    [Display(Name = "And even me")]
    public bool AtLeastOneShouldBeCheckedThree { get; set; }

    public static ValidationResult ValidateIMustBeCheckedTrue(bool value,
     ValidationContext vContext)
    {
        if (value)
        {
            return ValidationResult.Success;
        }
        return new ValidationResult("IMustBeChecked must be set to true");
    }

    public static ValidationResult
      ValidateAtLeastOneIsChecked(CustomValidationModel cvm,
      ValidationContext vContext)
    {
      if (cvm.AtLeastOneShouldBeCheckedOne ||
          cvm.AtLeastOneShouldBeCheckedTwo ||
          cvm.AtLeastOneShouldBeCheckedThree)
      {
          return ValidationResult.Success;
      }

      return
        new ValidationResult("At lease one of checkboxes must be checked");
    }

}
}
```

10-7. Moving from Master Pages in ASP.NET Web Forms to Layout Pages in Razor

Problem

You have a web site that you created in ASP.NET Web Forms that you would like to convert to ASP.NET MVC. Even though it would be an easier migration if you used the ASPX view engine rather than Razor, you really like the simplicity of the syntax that Razor offers and love the fact that you can use C# code in your view if required.

   The site that you are porting made extensive use of Master Pages. In several cases, you nested the Master Pages. In your site's main Master Page, you execute logic in the code-behind that shows or hides navigation elements. You are wondering how you can port all of this functionality to the ASP.NET MVC Framework with Razor.

Solution

Layout Pages are the Razor view engine equivalent of Master Pages. Both provide the ability to create a page layout template that can be applied across many views, but do so in a slightly different way. Like Master Pages, Razor offers the ability to nest Layout Pages. Razor's only major limitation to nesting is that sections defined in a parent Layout page cannot be accessed within views that use a child layout page.

   Layout Pages and Razor pages do not have code-behinds. If you need to execute code that affects the Layout Pages, you can create partial views that can be embedded in the Layout Page using `Html.RenderAction`. This allows the partial page to have a model and controller that are independent of the parent.

How It Works

Converting a Master Page to a Layout is really a matter of replacing the ASPX syntax with Razor syntax. Table 10-1 shows the Web Form elements coupled with their Razor equivalents.

Table 10-1. *ASPX Master Page Elements and Their Razor Equivalent*

Web Forms	Razor	What It Does
`<pages masterPageFile="~/Main.master">`	`@{ Layout = "~/Views/Shared/_ Layout.cshtml"; }`	Sets the default template for all pages on a site. For the Web Forms example, this snippet is in the `Web.config` file. For Razor, this snippet is from the `_ViewStart.cshtml` file in the root of the Views directory.
`<%@ Page MasterPageFile="~/Main.master" ... %>`	`@{ Layout = "~/Views/Shared/_ Layout.cshtml"; }`	Sets the template that is used for an individual page. It is included at the beginning of the Web Form page or view.
`<asp:ContentPlaceHolder runat="server" ID="HeadContent" />`	`@RenderSection("headContent", required: false)`	Defines a section in the template where the pages that consume the template can inject content. These snippets go inside the Layout or Master page.
n/a	`@RenderBody()`	Defines the placeholder for the main content area of a view. There is no equivalent syntax in Web Forms.

(continued)

Table 10-1. (*continued*)

Web Forms	Razor	What It Does
```<asp:Content``` ``` runat="server"``` ``` ID="HeadContent"``` ```ContentPlaceHolderID=``` ```"HeadContent">``` ``` <link``` ``` rel="stylesheet"``` ``` href="/Content/Wizard.css" />``` ```</asp:Content>```	```@section headContent{``` ``` <link``` ```rel="stylesheet" href="/``` ```Content/Wizard.css" />``` ```}```	Used in the view or Web Form page to designate the content for a placeholder defined in the layout or master page.

Nesting Layout Pages in Razor

A nested Layout Page is very similar to a normal Layout Page, except that it includes a Layout= directive. Just like the parent Layout Page, the nested page needs to call RenderBody once. A nested Layout Page may also define sections. The RenderBody directive defines a placeholder for the main content area for a view.

Listing 10-57 shows a nested layout page that derives from a master layout page named _Layout.cshtml. This is the same Layout Page specified in the _ViewStart.cshtml. Even though it is the default layout for the site, you still need to explicitly include the reference to it.

Listing 10-57. Nested Layout Page Example

```
@{
    Layout = "~/Views/Shared/_Layout.cshtml";
}


<h2>Article About Nested Layout</h2>
<article class="main-content">
    @RenderBody()
</article>
```

This simple layout references the parent using the Layout directive, and then defines a header and a new article. Since this child Layout is not explicitly referencing any sections defined in the parent, the entire body will be output inside the parent layout's @RenderBody.

Views that wish to use this layout can reference it just as they would a normal Layout page. Listing 10-58 shows a view consuming the layout in Listing 10-57.

Listing 10-58. View Consuming the Nested Layout Page

```
@{
    ViewBag.Title = "NestedLayout";
    Layout = "~/Views/Shared/_NestedLayout.cshtml";
}


<h3>Inside Nested Layout Page Body</h3>
```

A more complex example of this technique is shown in the later sections of Recipe 10-8.

10-8. Creating a Multipage Wizard Using ASP.NET MVC

Problem

You have been assigned a new project that requires porting several forms from a legacy ASP.NET Web Forms application to a new application based on ASP.NET MVC 4 that uses the Razor view engine. It seems that the developer who created the legacy project was somewhat fond of the ASP.NET Wizard Control and the project's business owners would like to preserve this functionality moving forward. You would like to understand how this can be done in ASP.NET MVC.

Solution

There are two ways to reproduce the functionality needed in MVC. The first and probably best solution is to create the illusion of a wizard by using JavaScript. This method requires that the entire form be loaded onto a series of HTML containers, which are hidden using a CSS style. As the user clicks though the Next buttons, the form sections are hidden and shown using JavaScript. When the wizard's Finish button is clicked, only then is the data from the wizard posted to the server.

The second approach is a server-centric solution in which the form is submitted to the server to move between pages of the wizard. This approach is probably more comparable to the Web Forms Wizard Control. Unfortunately, this approach is considerably more work to implement. I would avoid using this technique unless the forms you are working on are much too complex to be contained on a single page. An example of a good use for this technique is an application such as TurboTax. In the TurboTax application, a user may need to follow as many as 40 wizard steps in order to complete a tax return. A JavaScript-centric approach to an application would not be practical since it would require a great deal of code to be downloaded upfront. Another problem with JavaScript is that it is very difficult to protect your intellectual property. If your application uses a proprietary tax-calculation engine that provides you with a competitive advantage, you may not want it to be downloadable to the client, where it can be seen by anyone—including your competitors.

How It Works

Two solutions are examined in this section. The first is actually a single form that uses JavaScript to switch between screens of the wizard. The second is a traditional multipage approach. In both cases, the wizard will allow an artist to create a new song collaboration workspace for a musician's collaboration web site. The wizard has four distinct steps:

1. Defining a title and description for the workspace.

2. Applying rules for the workspace, such as who is allowed to contribute and whether the workspace can be viewed by the general public.

3. Seeking help needed for the project. This allows the artist to create classified ads for a set of commonly required skills. For example, a workspace created by a singer/songwriter may seek help from guitarists, drummers, and bass players.

4. Determining whether or not the artist wants to be alerted when items or comments are added to the workspace.

Using JavaScript to Create a Multipage Wizard

The JavaScript solution is based on five files:

- `Controller\WizardController.cs`: Contains three controller actions to display the form, process the form results, and display the wizard completion page.

- Models\WizardModel.cs: Contains the model.

- Views\Wizard\OnePageWizard.cshtml: Contains the entire multipart form.

- Scripts\MVCWizard.js: Contains the JavaScript required for the wizard page.

- Content\Wizard.css: Contains the styles used in the wizard.

The Controller

The first file on our list, WizardController.cs (shown in Listing 10-59), is straightforward. The first action simply displays the form. The second action verifies that the model state is valid, saves the form data, and then redirects to the finished page. The last action method simply displays the finished page. This controller makes use of a repository class that has been used throughout the examples in this chapter.

Listing 10-59. WizardController.cs

```
IDataExampleRepository m_repository = new EFDataExchangeRepository();

public ActionResult OnePageWizard()
{
    WizardModel model = new WizardModel();
    return View(model);
}

[HttpPost]
public ActionResult OnePageWizard(WizardModel model)
{
  if (ModelState.IsValid)
  {
     m_repository.CreateCollaborationSpace(model.NewWorkspace);
     m_repository.CreateAds(model.NeededSkills);
     m_repository.Save();
     return RedirectToAction("OnePageWizardFinish");
  }
     return View(model);
}

public ActionResult OnePageWizardFinish()
{
  return View();
}
```

The Model

The model class, which can be found in the Models\WizardModel.cs file, is also simple. It actually defines two classes, as shown in Listing 10-60. The first class, WizardModel, is the one that will be used in the controller and view. The second class, OpenPositionsNeeded, defines a structure for the open positions and contains a set of bool properties. This object is used by the repository code to create the open position objects, which it then persists to the database.

445

Listing 10-60. WizardModel.cs

```
using Ch7.SharedAPI;
using System.Collections.Generic;
using System.ComponentModel.DataAnnotations;

namespace Ch10.Mvc.Web.Models
{
    public class WizardModel
    {
        public WizardModel() { }
        public WizardModel(List<WizardStep> wizardSteps)
        {
            NewWorkspace = new CollaborationSpace();
        }
        public CollaborationSpace NewWorkspace { get; set; }
        public string OpenPositionDescription{get;set;}
        public int OpenPostionSkillLevel{get;set;}
        public OpenPositionsNeeded NeededSkills { get; set; }
        public bool RegisterForAlerts { get; set; }
    }

    public class OpenPositionsNeeded
    {
        [Display( Name="Bass Guitar")]
        public bool BassGuitar { get; set; }

        public bool Drums { get; set; }

        public bool Guitar { get; set; }

        public bool Keyboards { get; set; }

        public bool Vocals { get; set; }

        public bool Lyricist { get; set; }

        public bool Producer { get; set; }

        public bool Songwriter { get; set; }

    }
}
```

The View

The view for this recipe is made up of three files. There is the view itself, contained in the
Views\Wizard\OnePageWizard.cshtml file. It contains all the data binding statements that you normally
see in a view. In fact, if you take away the JavaScript and CSS, this page would appear as one long form.

The second most important file is Scripts\MVCWizard.js. This script file contains the logic for moving between wizard pages and for ensuring that only the correct buttons are shown and triggering validation between pages. Another important element is the Content\Wizard.css file. Normally, CSS files would not be considered important, but in a client-side-centric application, they play an essential role. For example, it's the CSS file that initializes the wizard pages to not display initially.

Walking through OnePageWizard.cshtml, you will see that it is strongly typed to Ch10.Mvc.Web.Models.WizardModel. It then includes a header content section so that it can place the /Content/Wizard.css into the head section of the document. It is generally a best practice to place all your style link tags in the header section of the HTML document. Since this section is typically defined in your layout page, you will need to define a section that allows you to inject content in the header from your views.

The next section of the view defines the primary navigation that appears on the left-hand side of the screen. This navigation element allows the user to jump back and forth through the various pages of the wizard. Each link used inside the section calls a JavaScript function called ShowWizardStep, which takes an integer as a parameter. In order to maintain separation of concerns, the binding of the click event is done in the MVCWizard.js file. The integer represents the page in the wizard that you wish to jump to. The first section of OnePageWizard.cshtml is shown in Listing 10-61.

Listing 10-61. OnePageWizard.cshtml Part 1

```
@model Ch10.Mvc.Web.Models.WizardModel

@{
    ViewBag.Title = "One Page Wizard";
}
@section headContent{
    <link rel="stylesheet" href="/Content/Wizard.css" />
}
<div class="WizardOuter">
    <nav class="float-left WizardSidebar btn_box_shadow">
        <ul>
            <li class="step" id="WizardStep_0">Title &amp; Description</li>
            <li class="step" id="WizardStep_1">Collaboration Settings</li>
            <li class="step" id="WizardStep_2">Open Positions</li>
            <li class="step" id="WizardStep_3">Alert Settings</li>
        </ul>
    </nav>
</div>
```

The wizard form is the next section of the view. Since we need to manipulate the form from client code, it should be given an explicit id. Even though we can access the form using its indexer, such as documents.forms[0], this is generally not a good idea since it is possible that another form may be added to the layout page or may be injected into the document using JavaScript. By giving our form an id, we can prevent that from causing a problem. To do this using the BeginForm helper, we need to specify the controller and action for the form action, followed by the form method. We can then define the HTML attributes we would like to add by creating a new object and assigning values to it as name/value pairs. Adding new { id = "WizardForm0" } causes the helper to add an id attribute to the form tag with a value of "WizardForm0".

Once the form has been created, wrap each wizard step inside a div tag with an id of WizardStep_Div_x, where x is the index of the wizard step. Each wizard step also contains the CSS class WizardStep. Inside each wizard step is fairly typical Razor markup. The form section of OnePageWizard.cshtml is in Listing 10-62.

Listing 10-62. OnePageWizard.cshtml Part 2

```
<section class="WizardForm float-right">
    @using (Html.BeginForm("Wizard",
                           "OnePageWizard",
                           FormMethod.Post,
                           new { id = "WizardForm0" }))
    {

        <div id="WizardStep_Div_0" class="WizardStep">
            <h2>Title And Description</h2>
            <fieldset>
                <legend>Describe your project</legend>
                <div>
                    @Html.LabelFor(a => a.NewWorkspace.Title)
                    <br />
                    @Html.TextBoxFor(a => a.NewWorkspace.Title)
                </div>
                <div>
                    @Html.LabelFor(a => a.NewWorkspace.Description)
                    <br />
                    @Html.TextAreaFor(a => a.NewWorkspace.Description)
                </div>
            </fieldset>

        </div>

        <div id="WizardStep_Div_1" class="WizardStep">
            <h2>Collaboration Settings</h2>
            <fieldset>
                <legend>
                  Describe the collaboration rules for your project
                </legend>

                <div>
                    @Html.LabelFor(a =>
                      a.NewWorkspace.AllowContributorsToPublish)
                    <br />
                    @Html.CheckBoxFor(a =>
                      a.NewWorkspace.AllowContributorsToPublish)
                </div>
                <div>
                    @Html.LabelFor(a =>
                      a.NewWorkspace.AllowPublicView)
                    <br />
                    @Html.CheckBoxFor(a =>
                      a.NewWorkspace.AllowPublicView)
                </div>
```

```
            <div>
              @Html.LabelFor(a =>
                a.NewWorkspace.RestrictContributorsToBand)
                <br />
              @Html.CheckBoxFor(a =>
                a.NewWorkspace.RestrictContributorsToBand)
            </div>
        </fieldset>
    </div>

    <div id="WizardStep_Div_2" class="WizardStep">
        <fieldset>
            <legend>
                Describe the skills needed for your project
            </legend>
            <h2>Open Positions</h2>
            <div class="CheckBoxGroup">
                @Html.EditorFor(a => a.NeededSkills)
            </div>
            <div>
                @Html.LabelFor(a => a.OpenPositionDescription)
                <br />
                @Html.TextAreaFor(a => a.OpenPositionDescription)

            </div>
            <div>
                @Html.LabelFor(a => a.OpenPostionSkillLevel)
                <br />
                @Html.EditorFor(a => a.OpenPostionSkillLevel)
            </div>
        </fieldset>
    </div>
    <div id="WizardStep_Div_3" class="WizardStep">
        <fieldset>
            <legend>
                Describe the skills needed for your project
            </legend>
            <h2>Alert Options</h2>
            <div>
                @Html.LabelFor(a => a.RegisterForAlerts)
                <br />
                @Html.EditorFor(a => a.RegisterForAlerts)
            </div>
        </fieldset>
    </div>
```

The final sections of OnePageWizard.cshtml contain the Back, Next, and Finish buttons. Back and Next, like the sidebar navigation links, make calls to JavaScript functions. The Finish button, on the other hand, is a submit button that will post back the form to the server.

In the Scripts section, you see that a number of script files have been added. The first are the jQuery validation scripts, which are required for most MVC 4 forms. Next is the jQuery UI library, which is used to add animation for the wizard page transitions. Last, the MVCWizard.js file is included. This is a custom JavaScript file. The code in bold calls a script function that initializes the wizard once the document loads. It uses the jQuery $() function. This function is called when the page's document object model (DOM) has completed loading. After the initialization function has completed, the click events are bound to the navigation buttons using the jQuery on function as shown in bold text in Listing 10-63. The on function binds an event handler to the item or items specified in the selector.

Listing 10-63. OnePageWizard.cshtml Part 3

```
            <section class="WizardButtons">
                <input type="button" value="Back" id="BackButton"/>
                <input type="button" value="Next" id="NextButton" />
                <input type="submit" value="Finish" id="FinishButton" />
            </section>

        }

    </section>

</div>

@section Scripts {
    @Scripts.Render("~/bundles/jqueryval")
    @Scripts.Render("~/bundles/jqueryui")
    <script src="/Scripts/MVCWizard.js"></script>
<script>
 $(function (){
   WizardInit(4);
   $("#WizardStep_0").on('click', function (event) { ShowWizardStep(0); });
   $("#WizardStep_1").on('click', function (event) { ShowWizardStep(1); });
   $("#WizardStep_2").on('click', function (event) { ShowWizardStep(2); });
   $("#WizardStep_3").on('click', function (event) { ShowWizardStep(3); });
   $("#BackButton").on('click', function (event) { WizardBack(); });
   $("#NextButton").on('click', function (event) { WizardNext(); });
  }
  );
 </script>
}
```

The bulk of the front-end functionality is defined inside MVCWizard.js. This file contains a number of functions to show and hide the wizard steps and manage which buttons are shown. In the first function, ShowWizardStep, the string #WizardStep_ is combined with the global variable m_CurrentStep to create a jQuery selector for the link that corresponds to the currently selected step. The jQuery function removeClass is then used to remove the selected CSS class from the element. A similar technique is used to hide the currently active wizard page using the jQuery hide function. It then adds the selected CSS class to the button that was clicked, and shows the new wizard step using the jQuery show method. It then calls the local function, ShowHideButtons. This looks at the current step and then shows or hides the Back, Next, and Finish buttons, depending on the context. For example, we do not need the Back button on the first page of the wizard.

In the WizardNext function, we first call the jQuery unobtrusive validation valid() function against the wizard form. This causes the client-side validation to be executed on the current wizard page. The WizardBack function performs the same function as WizardNext but in reverse. jQuery validation is smart enough not to validate items with the CSS display property set to none, so that only the fields on the current wizard page are evaluated. If validation is successful, as in the ShowWizardStep, the styles in the sidebar buttons are manipulated. It then uses an overload of the jQuery slide function provided by the jQuery UI library. This causes the form to slide from left to right before disappearing from the screen. It then uses JavaScript function chaining to pass an inline function that executes once the first animation completes. This inline function executes a second animation that causes the new wizard step to slide in.

The last interesting function is the WizardInit, which initializes the wizard. It stets the current wizard step to 0, and hides the Back and Finish buttons. The entire MVCWizard.js is shown in Listing 10-64.

Listing 10-64. MVCWizard.js

```
var m_CurrentStep, m_TotalSteps, m_CanShowFinish;

function ShowWizardStep(wizardStepNumber) {
    $("#WizardStep_" + m_CurrentStep).removeClass("selected");
    $("#WizardStep_Div_" + m_CurrentStep).hide();
    $("#WizardStep_" + wizardStepNumber).addClass("selected");
    $("#WizardStep_Div_" + wizardStepNumber).show();
    m_CurrentStep = wizardStepNumber;
    ShowHideButtons();
}

function WizardNext() {
    if ($("#WizardForm0").valid()) {
        $("#WizardStep_" + m_CurrentStep).removeClass("selected");
        $("#WizardStep_Div_" + m_CurrentStep).hide("slide", { direction: "right" },
            function () {
                $("#WizardStep_" + m_CurrentStep).addClass("selected");
                m_CurrentStep = m_CurrentStep + 1;
                $("#WizardStep_Div_" + m_CurrentStep).show("slide", { direction: "left" });
                ShowHideButtons();
            });
    }

}

function WizardBack() {
    $("#WizardStep_" + m_CurrentStep).removeClass("selected");
    $("#WizardStep_Div_" + m_CurrentStep).hide("slide",{direction: "left"},
        function () {
            m_CurrentStep = m_CurrentStep - 1;
            $("#WizardStep_" + m_CurrentStep).addClass("selected");
            $("#WizardStep_Div_" + m_CurrentStep).show("slide", { direction: "right" });
            ShowHideButtons();
        });

}
```

```
function ShowHideButtons() {
    if (m_CurrentStep == 0)
        $("#BackButton").hide();
    else
        $("#BackButton").show();

    if (m_CurrentStep == (m_TotalSteps - 1))
        $("#NextButton").hide();
    else
        $("#NextButton").show();
    if (m_CurrentStep > 2)
        m_CanShowFinish = true;
    if (m_CanShowFinish == true)
        $("#FinishButton").show();
    else
        $("#FinishButton").hide();
}

function WizardInit(numberOfSteps) {
    m_CurrentStep = 0;
    m_TotalSteps = numberOfSteps;
    m_CanShowFinish = false;
    $("#WizardStep_0").addClass("selected");
    $("#WizardStep_Div_0").show();
    $("#BackButton").hide();
    $("#FinishButton").hide();

}
```

That last piece of the puzzle is the CSS file. Highlighted in Listing 10-65 are the styles that are used in the JavaScript file. The WizardStep class is applied to all the div tags that make up the wizard steps. It is set so that none of them are displayed by default. This is an important setting. If you do not do this and try to change this style using JavaScript, the items may appear on the page for several seconds until the DOM has completely loaded and the JavaScript is run.

Another technique that may be of interest to you is the use of CSS gradients applied to several elements, including the sidebar buttons. Notice that it is still required to specifically call out each browser's implementation of the standard. The only browser that does not require a browser-specific version in IE 10. CSS gradients are a new feature introduced in CSS 3, and they only work in new browsers. There are several free tools available on the web that can aid you in using these techniques. Notably, the IE 10 team created a CSS Gradient Background Maker tool (http://ie.microsoft.com/testdrive/Graphics/CSSGradientBackgroundMaker/Default.html) as part of the demos on the developer web site.

Listing 10-65. Wizard.css

```
.WizardStep{
    display:none;
}
.selected {
    font-weight:600;
}
```

```
    .WizardSidebar li ,
    .WizardSidebar a,
    .WizardSidebar a:hover,
    .WizardButtons a,
    .WizardButtons input[type="button"],
    .WizardButtons input[type="submit"]{
        background-color: #6F868C; /*legacy*/
        background-image: -moz-linear-gradient(bottom, #555 0%, #222 100%); /*firefox*/
        background-image: -o-linear-gradient(bottom, #555 0%, #222 100%); /*opera*/
        background-image: -webkit-gradient(linear, left bottom, left top, color-stop(0, #555),
color-stop(1, #222)); /*Safari*/
        background-image: -webkit-linear-gradient(bottom, #555 0%, #222 100%); /*Chrome11*/
        background-image: linear-gradient(to top, #555 0%, #222 100%); /*IE10*/
        padding: 0.4em;
        margin: 10px 0 0 0;
        -moz-border-radius: 3px 4px;
        -webkit-border-radius: 3px 4px;
        border-radius: 3px 4px;
        text-decoration: none;
        color:#fff;

    }

.WizardSidebar {
    padding: 1em;
    width: 20%;
    min-width: 200px;
    min-height: 130px;
}

    .WizardSidebar ul {
        list-style: none;
        margin: 0;
        padding: 0;
        cursor: pointer;
    }
.WizardButtons {
    width: 20%;
    margin: 2em auto 0 auto;
    text-align: center;
    vertical-align:bottom;
    position:relative;
    bottom:0;
}
```

Creating a True Multipage Form

Although the JavaScript example works well in many situations, there are times when you will need to have a true
multipage form. This is usually when the form is very complex and has several paths. For example, depending on
actions taken in step 1, you may need an additional step.

In this version of the solution, you will create a separate controller action for each page in the wizard. A nested layout will be used to contain any UI elements that need to be shared between views. You will also create a base class that the wizard model can inherit.

The Model

The base class can contain all the data regarding the state of the wizard itself, whereas the derived class can contain the properties for the business object. This includes the current wizard step, the list of available step, whether or not to show the Back and Finish buttons, and some basic logic for moving between steps.

The base class for the server-side wizard is shown in Listing 10-66.

Listing 10-66. WizardBase.cs

```csharp
using System;
using System.Collections.Generic;
using System.Linq;
using System.Web;

namespace Ch10.Mvc.Helpers.Models
{
    public class WizardModelBase
    {
        public WizardModelBase() { }
        public WizardModelBase(List<WizardStep> wizardSteps)
        {
            WizardSteps = wizardSteps;
            ShowWizardSteps = true;
        }

        public int CurrentStepIndex { get; set; }
        public bool AllowFinish { get; set; }

        public string CurrentStep(int step)
        {
            if (step == CurrentStepIndex)
                return "selected";
            else
                return "step";
        }

        public bool ShowBackButton
        {
            get
            {
                //hide on first step and on finished page
                return CurrentStepIndex > 0 && (CurrentStepIndex!=WizardSteps.Count - 1);
            }
        }

        public bool ShowWizardSteps { get; set; }
```

```csharp
public bool ShowNextButton
{
    get
    {
        return WizardSteps != null &&
            WizardSteps.Count != 0 &&
            CurrentStepIndex != WizardSteps.Count - 1;
    }
}

public WizardStep FinishAction {
    get
    {
        if (WizardSteps != null)
            return WizardSteps[WizardSteps.Count - 1];
        else
            return null;
    }
}
public List<WizardStep> WizardSteps { get; set; }
public WizardStep LastWizardStep
{
    get
    {
        if (WizardSteps != null)
        {
            if (CurrentStepIndex == 0)
                return WizardSteps[0];
            else
                return WizardSteps[CurrentStepIndex - 1];
        }
        return null;
    }
}

public WizardStep NextWizardStep
{
    get
    {
        if (WizardSteps != null)
        {
            if (CurrentStepIndex == (WizardSteps.Count-1))
                return WizardSteps[CurrentStepIndex];
            else if((CurrentStepIndex == (WizardSteps.Count - 1)) &&
                CurrentStepIndex==0)
                return WizardSteps[CurrentStepIndex];
```

```
                    else
                        return WizardSteps[CurrentStepIndex + 1];
                }
                return null;
            }
        }
    }

    public class WizardStep
    {
        public int StepIndex { get; set; }
        public string Action { get; set; }
        public string Controller { get; set; }
        public string Title { get; set; }
        public bool IsCurrentStep { get; set; }
        public bool HideOnSideNavigation { get; set; }
    }
}
```

The main idea for this base class is to abstract a lot of the rules for the wizard, such as which buttons to display, what action takes place when the Next button is clicked, and whether the Finish button should display.

The WizardModel shown in Listing 10-67 inherits from WizardBase. It then adds several properties similar to the class used in the JavaScript version of the wizard.

Listing 10-67. The Wizard Model Updated to Derive the Base Class

```
public class WizardModel : WizardModelBase
{
  public WizardModel() { }
  public WizardModel(List<WizardStep> wizardSteps) : base(wizardSteps)
  {
    NewWorkspace = new CollaborationSpace();
  }
  public CollaborationSpace NewWorkspace { get; set; }
  public string OpenPositionDescription{get;set;}
  public int OpenPostionSkillLevel{get;set;}
  public OpenPositionsNeeded NeededSkills { get; set; }
  public bool RegisterForAlerts { get; set; }
}
```

The Controller

Listing 10-68 shows the Wizard controller class. For each wizard step, it contains an action for HTTP GET and another for HTTP POST. Having a GET version for each allows a user to start the wizard from any page from a link outside the wizard. If you wish to disable this behavior and force the user to start at page one of the wizard, you can simply remove the actions.

Each method calls a local helper method: GetSteps. This method returns a collection of WizardStep objects. There is one object for each step in the wizard. The WizardStep type was defined in same file as WizardModelBase. It contains the action and controller names associated with each wizard step, as well a bool value that denotes if the step is the current step.

Like most in this chapter, this controller uses the EFDataExchangeRepository class to retrieve and save data from a back-end database. The entire model is passed for each step in the wizard. This is required to maintain state between steps. In order for this to work, all of the model's properties must be represented on each page by either a visible form field or a hidden form field. A helper method named GetSteps is used to define the steps of the wizard. For each step, we define a step index, a title, whether it should be shown in the primary navigation, as well as the action and controller for the step. WizardController is shown in Listing 10-68.

Listing 10-68. The Wizard Controller Class

```
public ActionResult TitleAndDescription()
{
    WizardModel model = new WizardModel(GetSteps(0));
    model.CurrentStepIndex = 0;
    return View(model);
}
[HttpPost]
public ActionResult TitleAndDescription(WizardModel model)
{
    model.CurrentStepIndex = 0;
    model.WizardSteps = GetSteps(1);
    return View(model);
}
public ActionResult CollaborationSettings()
{
    WizardModel model = new WizardModel(GetSteps(1));
    model.CurrentStepIndex = 1;
    return View(model);
}

[HttpPost]
public ActionResult CollaborationSettings(WizardModel model)
{
    model.CurrentStepIndex = 1;
    model.WizardSteps = GetSteps(1);
    return View(model);
}

public ActionResult OpenPositions()
{
    WizardModel m_model = new WizardModel(GetSteps(2));
    m_model.CurrentStepIndex = 2;
    return View(m_model);
}
[HttpPost]
public ActionResult OpenPositions(WizardModel model)
{
    model.CurrentStepIndex = 2;
    model.WizardSteps = GetSteps(2);
    return View(model);
}
```

```
[HttpPost]
public ActionResult AlertSettings(WizardModel model)
{
    model.CurrentStepIndex = 3;
    model.WizardSteps = GetSteps(3);
    return View(model);
}

IDataExampleRepository m_Repository = new EFDataExchangeRepository();
public ActionResult WizardCompleted()
{
    WizardModel m_model = new WizardModel(GetSteps(4));
    m_model.CurrentStepIndex = 4;
    m_model.ShowWizardSteps = false;
    //save data here
    if (ModelState.IsValid)
    {
        m_repository.CreateCollaborationSpace(m_model.NewWorkspace);
        m_repository.CreateAds(m_model.NeededSkills);
        m_repository.Save();
    }
    return View(m_model);
}

private List<WizardStep> GetSteps(int currentStepIndex)
{
    var steps = new List<WizardStep>(){
    new WizardStep{
        Action="TitleAndDescription",
        Controller="Wizard",
        IsCurrentStep= (0==currentStepIndex),
        StepIndex=0,
        Title="Title &amp; Description "
    },
    new WizardStep{
        Action="CollaborationSettings",
        Controller="Wizard",
        IsCurrentStep=(1==currentStepIndex),
        StepIndex=1,
        Title="Collaboration Settings"
    },
    new WizardStep{
        Action="OpenPositions",
        Controller="Wizard",
        IsCurrentStep=(2==currentStepIndex),
        StepIndex=2,
        Title="Open Positions"
    },
    new WizardStep{
        Action="AlertSettings",
        Controller="Wizard",
```

```
            IsCurrentStep=(3==currentStepIndex),
            StepIndex=3,
            Title="Alert Settings"
        },
        new WizardStep{
            Action="WizardCompleted",
            Controller="Wizard",
            IsCurrentStep=(4==currentStepIndex),
            StepIndex=4,
            Title="Wizard Completed",
            HideOnSideNavigation=true
        }
    };
    return steps;
}
```

Custom HTML Helpers Used for the Wizard

One problem with a multipage form is that you need to change the action attribute of the HTML form to point to the correct action. You do this with a set of HTML helper extensions for each button role. Each button is rendered as an HTML anchor tag that calls a JavaScript function that modifies the form action to point to the proper controller action before submitting the form as an HTTP POST. The bulk of the logic resides in the createPostBackLink method. This method first uses the GetVirtualPath method of the RouteData.Route object from the helper's view context to get the URL of the target action. It then uses a string format function to generate the hyperlink. The WizardHelpers helper class is shown in Listing 10-69.

Listing 10-69. HTML Helper Extension Methods for Creating Action Links That Will Post Back to a Target Form

```
using System;
using System.Web.Mvc;
using System.Web.Routing;

namespace Ch10.Shared.Helpers
{
    public static class WizardHelpers
    {
        public static MvcHtmlString WizardBackButton(this HtmlHelper helper,
                                              string actionName,
                                              string controller)
        {
            if (validateAC(actionName, controller))
            {
                return createPostBackLink(helper, "Back", actionName, controller);
            }
            return MvcHtmlString.Empty;
        }

        public static MvcHtmlString WizardNextButton(this HtmlHelper helper,
                                              string actionName,
                                              string controller)
```

```
    {
        if (validateAC(actionName, controller))
        {
            return createPostBackLink(helper, "Next", actionName, controller);
        }
        return MvcHtmlString.Empty;
    }

    public static MvcHtmlString WizardFinishButton(this HtmlHelper helper,
                                        string actionName,
                                        string controller)
    {
        if (validateAC(actionName,controller))
        {
            return createPostBackLink(helper, "Finish", actionName, controller);
        }
        return MvcHtmlString.Empty;
    }

    public static MvcHtmlString WizardSideButton(this HtmlHelper helper,
                                        string text,
                                        string actionName,
                                        string controller)
    {
        if (validateAC(actionName, controller))
        {
            return createPostBackLink(helper, text, actionName, controller);
        }
        return MvcHtmlString.Empty;
    }

    private static MvcHtmlString createPostBackLink(HtmlHelper helper,
                                        string text,
                                        string actionName,
                                        string controller)
    {
        string actionUrl = helper.ViewContext.RouteData.Route.GetVirtualPath(
                helper.ViewContext.RequestContext,
                new RouteValueDictionary {
                    { "controller", controller },
                    { "action", actionName } }).VirtualPath;

        return MvcHtmlString.Create(
            String.Format(@"<a href=""#"" onclick=""WizardSubmit('{0}')"">{1}</a>",
                        actionUrl, text));
    }

    private static bool validateAC(string a, string c)
    {
        if (!String.IsNullOrEmpty(a) && !String.IsNullOrEmpty(c))
```

```
        {
            return true;
        }
        return false;
    }
}

}
```

The View

The view for the wizard is broken into several files. The first piece is a partial view that contains most of the infrastructure for the wizard. There is an additional view for each wizard step.

The partial view can be used with any number of wizards and it does not contain anything specific to creating workspaces. The partial view binds to the WizardModelBase class and has no knowledge of the properties of the child class. _WizardLayout.cshtml's main job is to provide navigation and some user interface elements for moving between view steps. The nested Layout Page _WizardLayout.cshtml is shown in Listing 10-70.

Listing 10-70. The Nested Layout _WizardLayout.cshtml

```
@model Ch10.Mvc.Helpers.Models.WizardModelBase
@{
    Layout = "~/Views/Shared/_Layout.cshtml";
}
@section headContent{
    <link  rel="stylesheet" href="/Content/Wizard.css" />
    <script src="/Scripts/MVCWizard.js"></script>
}
@using(Html.BeginForm()){
    @Html.HiddenFor(a => a.ShowWizardSteps);
    @Html.HiddenFor(a => a.CurrentStepIndex);
     @Html.ValidationSummary(true)
 <div class="WizardOuter">
    @if(Model.ShowWizardSteps){
<nav class="float-left WizardSidebar btn_box_shadow">
    <ul>
        @foreach (var step in Model.WizardSteps) {
        if (!step.HideOnSideNavigation)
        {
         <li
            class="@Model.CurrentStep(step.StepIndex)">
            @Html.WizardSideButton(step.Title, step.Action,step.Controller)

        </li>
        }
    }
    </ul>
</nav>
    }
    <section class="WizardForm float-right">
        @RenderBody()

        <section class="WizardButtons">
```

```
    @if (Model.ShowBackButton) { @Html.WizardBackButton(Model.LastWizardStep.Action, Model.
LastWizardStep.Controller); }
    @if (Model.ShowNextButton) { @Html.WizardNextButton(Model.NextWizardStep.Action, Model.
NextWizardStep.Controller); }
    @if (Model.AllowFinish) { @Html.WizardFinishButton(Model.FinishAction.Action, Model.
FinishAction.Controller); }

</section>
    </section>
</div>

}

@section Scripts {
    @Scripts.Render("~/bundles/jqueryval")
}
```

Each of the views uses the nested Layout page _WizardLayout.cshtml as its layout page. This allows the views to be very simple and clean. Listing 10-71 shows one of the wizard pages.

One thing to be aware of is that since you do not have a ViewState concept in ASP.NET MVC, you will need to store the state of the rest of the objects elements in hidden fields to prevent them from being lost on postback. This can be somewhat cumbersome if you have a very large number of fields. Alternatively, you can store the wizard contents to a temporary repository on each post, retrieve all the values from the temporary storage, and write to the permanent store in the final step.

Listing 10-71. The Title and Description View

```
@model Ch10.Mvc.Web.Models.WizardModel
@{
    ViewBag.Title = "TitleAndDescription";
    Layout = "~/Views/Shared/_WizardLayout.cshtml";
}

<h2>Title And Description</h2>
<fieldset>
    <legend>Describe your project</legend>
    <div>
        @Html.LabelFor(a=> a.NewWorkspace.Title)
        <br />
        @Html.TextBoxFor(a=> a.NewWorkspace.Title)
    </div>
    <div>
        @Html.LabelFor(a=> a.NewWorkspace.Description)
        <br />
        @Html.TextAreaFor(a=> a.NewWorkspace.Description)
    </div>
</fieldset>
<div class="HiddenWizardFields">
    @Html.HiddenFor(a=>a.NewWorkspace.AllowContributorsToPublish)
```

```
@Html.HiddenFor(a=>a.NewWorkspace.AllowPublicView)
@Html.HiddenFor(a=>a.NewWorkspace.RestrictContributorsToBand)
    @Html.EditorFor(a => a.NeededSkills);
</div>
```

The final product of the wizard is shown in Figure 10-7. It shows the Open Positions step of the wizard.

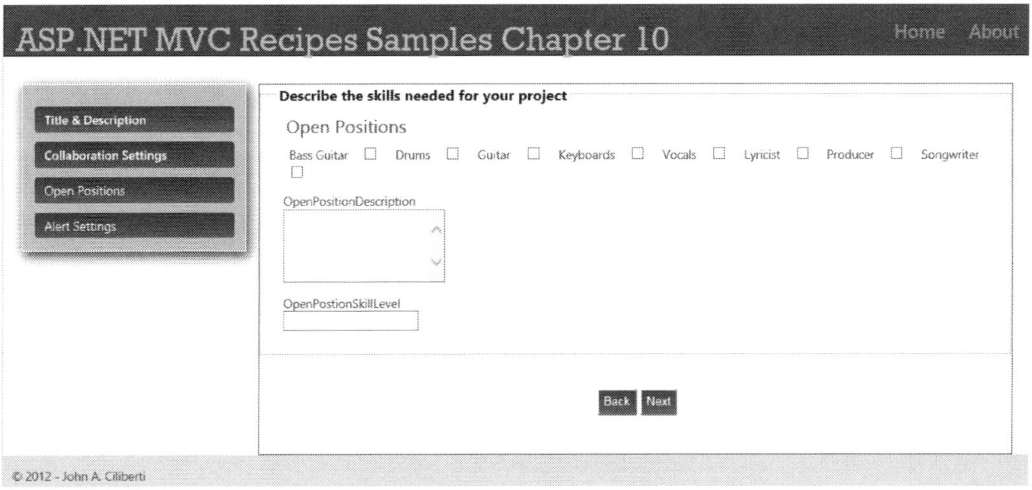

Figure 10-7. *The Wizard page*

Both the JavaScript and the server-side versions of the wizard have the same look and feel. The only difference is that since the JavaScript version does not require a postback for each wizard step, it appears more responsive to the end user. The JavaScript version also supports a slide animation when moving between steps of the wizard.

The downside of the JavaScript version is that nothing is posted back to the server until the Finish button is clicked. This can cause issues, such as all the user's data being lost if the web browser closes unexpectedly or if a major hurricane hits and power is lost while the user is typing. In the server version, the postbacks between each wizard steps can be exploited to save the data on the server. For this to work, however, the data model would need to be designed to tolerate incomplete records. You may also need to devise a way to remove from the system any incomplete records that have been idle for too long.

10-9. Adding MVC to a Web Forms Project
Problem

You are planning a major upgrade for a Web Forms application. In the new version, you would like to take advantage of the patterns and capabilities offered by the ASP.NET MVC Framework, but since your application is very large and complex, you will not be able to do a full upgrade.

You would like to develop the new functionality using ASP.NET MVC 4 while leaving the existing code in place wherever possible. You would also like to use the Razor view engine since you really like the new syntax.

Solution

For a large complex Web Forms application, an all-at-once upgrade is generally not practical. It can be an especially complex task if, in addition to moving to MVC, you are also planning to migrate to the Razor view engine. Creating a hybrid application that allows most of the site to remain in Web Forms while new functionality is created in MVC is one way to approach this problem. Unfortunately, this can ultimately lead to long-term maintenance challenges.

If you plan to go ahead with such a project, the hybrid solution should be considered transitory with existing functionality written using Web Forms—either phased out or upgraded over time. I do not recommend a hybrid application as a long-term strategy.

You can create a hybrid solution by completing the following steps:

1. Upgrade the Web Forms project to support .NET 4.5. After the upgrade, review the application and correct any errors or warnings you discover.

2. Use the NuGet package manager to add the required assemblies to your project using the ASP.NET MVC 4 NuGet package.

3. Modify the project's `Web.config` file as required by ASP.NET MVC 4.

4. Create a subfolder under your project to contain all the new MVC content. An Area for this folder will be defined later. This will help keep the application well-organized and prevent Web Forms and MVC content to comingle in a single directory, which can lead to maintainability issues.

5. Create the MVC folder structure under the new folder.

6. Create an `App_Start` folder and create C# class files for registering, areas, routes, and bundles.

7. Modify your `Global.asax.cs` file so that the required MVC components are registered on project start.

8. Add the JavaScript files required by MVC 4, including jQuery and jQuery Validation, to the proper node in the solution.

How It Works

Before jumping into to migration, you should consider some of the disadvantages of having a hybrid application. If you choose Razor as your view engine, you will need to maintain both ASPX master pages and Razor layout pages. You may also have duplication of effort with shared components such as web user controls and web custom controls. You may end up needing to create custom HTML helpers to fill the functional gap. Much of this effort can be avoided if you used the ASPX view engine rather than Razor. ASPX is still a viable choice for a view engine and it should be seriously considered for this scenario, especially if the migration is planned over many development iterations that may span a year or more.

If you are planning to do a complete migration and would like to move to Razor, you should plan for the extra work—and to realistically set your client's expectations.

Another thing that you should keep in mind is that the hybrid application should be transitory. You should plan an end-to-end conversion of the entire project over time, phasing out obsolete features and upgrading the Web Forms pages to MVC whenever major revisions for these pages are required. In my role as an enterprise architect, I see many homegrown and third-party solutions. In my experience, the ones with mixed architectures are the most difficult to upgrade and maintain. These same applications tend to have reliability and stability issues.

Upgrading Your Project to Target .NET 4.5

ASP.NET MVC 4 requires the latest version of the .NET Framework. The first step in your upgrade process should be to upgrade your project. If you have access to the latest version of Visual Studio and you developed your project using a prior version, now would be a good time to upgrade the solution as well. The following steps describe how to upgrade a project created in Visual Studio 2010 that targeted to .NET 3.5 to ASP.NET 4.5 in Visual Studio 2012.

1. Open Visual Studio 2012. From the File menu, select Open ➤ Projects ➤ Solutions.

2. Browse to the Chapter 10 samples folder and locate the `LegacyWebFormsApp01-before` folder.

3. Select `LegacyWebFormsApp01.sln`, and then click the Open button. Since this project was created using an earlier version of Visual Studio, Visual Studio 2012 will perform a migration on the project and then display a migration report that describes the changes it made. A migration report is shown in Figure 10-8. In this case, there are no errors but a number of warnings and messages. On a real legacy project, you are likely to have many more warnings. It is generally a good idea to read the migration report and understand the changes that have been made.

Figure 10-8. *A migration report for a solution upgraded from Visual Studio 2010*

4. After reviewing the migration report, you should attempt to run the project in the debugger and go through the functionality to see if you come across any errors. In this case, everything worked fine but this may not be true if you are upgrading a large project. If you find problems, you should correct them before moving on to the next step.

5. Once you have reviewed your application and corrected any issues, the next step is to change the target version of the .NET Framework to version 4.5:

   a. Right-click the **LegacyWebFormsApp01** project in Solution Explorer and select Properties. The Properties page will appear in the main Visual Studio window.

   b. Select .NET Framework 4.5 as the target framework.

    c.   Click the Yes button on the Target Framework Change dialog box. This warns you that by changing the target framework, you will likely break your project and will need to manually fix what is broken.

6.   After you have changed the target framework, any open windows in your solution will be closed and the References node in Solution Explorer will be expanded. This is Visual Studio's way of telling you, "Hey, I have added and modified some assembly references in your project!" If you click any of the assemblies, you will see that they have been upgraded to the 4.0 version. Even though you are targeting 4.5, 4.0 will still be the correct version in most cases.

7.   Build your solution (press the F6 key) and check for compilations errors and warnings. In the sample project, you do not get any errors or warnings, but this will probably not be the case in a real project. If you do find errors, you should correct them at this point. For a real project, this can take a significant amount of work.

8.   Run the project and check for runtime errors and other possible regressions. In this sample project, there are no issues, but this may not be the case in a real project.

Adding the MVC Framework Components

The ASP.NET MVC Framework has a number of required assemblies that must be added to the project. Luckily, Microsoft has created a NuGet package that will add all the required assemblies for you. To install the NuGet package:

1.   Right-click the References folder in Solution Explorer. Select Manage NuGet packages.

2.   Click the Online node in the left pane, and then type **MVC** in the search box.

3.   Locate the Microsoft ASP.NET MVC 4 package. Select it and click the Install button. You may be prompted to accept one or more license agreements.

4.   Repeat the preceding steps for the following NuGet packages. These packages are included by default in most ASP.NET MVC 4 templates and are required if you wish to use features such as validation and optimization:

- jQuery
- jQuery Validation
- Json.NET
- jQuery UI (Combined Library)
- Modernizr
- Microsoft jQuery Unobtrusive Validation
- WebGrease
- Microsoft ASP.NET Web Optimization
- Microsoft Optimization—Bundling

5.   Build the solution and verify that there are no errors

Modify Your Web.config File

The ASP.NET MVC templates include additions to the Web.config file that enable features such as unobtrusive validation and add the default namespaces that you need in most of the views. Since the NuGet packages did not add these settings, you will need to add them manually. One way to add these settings is to create a separate project using one of the ASP.NET MVC 4 templates, and then coping these settings into your Web Forms project's Web.config file. For this example, you will port the settings from the one of the other examples created for this chapter and add the entries for appSettings and namespaces. You will not modify any of the default connection strings, Entity Framework, and authentication settings in this example. When you are porting your existing project, you will most likely already have the settings you require. Listing 10-72 shows the required changes.

Listing 10-72. Changes to the Web.config File

```xml
<?xml version="1.0" encoding="utf-8"?>
<configuration>
  <connectionStrings />
  <appSettings>
    <add key="webpages:Version" value="2.0.0.0" />
    <add key="webpages:Enabled" value="false" />
    <add key="PreserveLoginUrl" value="true" />
    <add key="ClientValidationEnabled" value="true" />
    <add key="UnobtrusiveJavaScriptEnabled" value="true" />
  </appSettings>
  <system.web>
    <compilation debug="true" targetFramework="4.5" />
    <authentication mode="Windows" />

    <pages controlRenderingCompatibilityVersion="3.5" clientIDMode="AutoID" >
      <namespaces>
        <add namespace="System.Web.Helpers" />
        <add namespace="System.Web.Mvc" />
        <add namespace="System.Web.Mvc.Ajax" />
        <add namespace="System.Web.Mvc.Html" />
        <add namespace="System.Web.Optimization" />
        <add namespace="System.Web.Routing" />
        <add namespace="System.Web.WebPages" />
      </namespaces>
    </pages>
  </system.web>

  <runtime>
    <assemblyBinding xmlns="urn:schemas-microsoft-com:asm.v1">
      <dependentAssembly>
        <assemblyIdentity name="System.Web.Helpers" publicKeyToken="31bf3856ad364e35" />
        <bindingRedirect oldVersion="1.0.0.0-2.0.0.0" newVersion="2.0.0.0" />
      </dependentAssembly>
      <dependentAssembly>
        <assemblyIdentity name="System.Web.Mvc" publicKeyToken="31bf3856ad364e35" />
        <bindingRedirect oldVersion="1.0.0.0-4.0.0.0" newVersion="4.0.0.0" />
      </dependentAssembly>
      <dependentAssembly>
        <assemblyIdentity name="System.Web.WebPages" publicKeyToken="31bf3856ad364e35" />
        <bindingRedirect oldVersion="1.0.0.0-2.0.0.0" newVersion="2.0.0.0" />
```

```
      </dependentAssembly>
      <dependentAssembly>
        <assemblyIdentity name="WebGrease" publicKeyToken="31bf3856ad364e35" culture="neutral"
        />
        <bindingRedirect oldVersion="0.0.0.0-1.3.0.0" newVersion="1.3.0.0" />
      </dependentAssembly>
    </assemblyBinding>
  </runtime>
</configuration>
```

After making the changes, you should run your project and perform another smoke test to make sure that you do not run into any runtime errors or unexpected behaviors.

Adding the MVC Tooling to Your Project

As you may have noticed, even after adding the MVC assemblies and folders to your project, Visual Studio does not offer any of the normal menu items normally associated with an MVC project. For example, if you right-click the `Controllers` folder, you will not see an Add Controller menu item. This will make creating MVC objects more of a manual effort.

Thankfully, this can be easily corrected by editing the project file and adding the required GUIDs to the `ProjectTypeGuids` element of the solution file.

Normally, we so not edit solution and projects files directly but let Visual Studio manage the files for us. In rare cases, however, such as when there is an error in the file and Visual Studio cannot open it or if we would like to change something that cannot be done by the Visual Studio user interface, we can open this file and manually change the settings.

To modify the project file:

1. In Solution Explorer, right-click the `LegacyWebFormsApp01` project and select Unload Project from the menu. The project will be marked as unavailable.

2. Right-click the project again and select Edit `LegacyWebFormsApp01.csproj`. The project file will open in the code editor.

3. Locate the `ProjectTypeGuids` element. Every Visual Studio project has one or more project types associated with it. Each GUID identifies a specific project type or subtype. For this project, you will see the GUIDs {fae04ec0-301f-11d3-bf4b-00c04f79efbc}, which stands for C#, and {349C5851-65DF-11DA-9384-00065B846F21}, which is the Web Application project type.

4. To get the GUID for the MVC 4 project type, you can open a file for a project created using the MVC 4 template. You will see that, in addition to the Web Application and C# GUIDs, there is an additional {E3E379DF-F4C6-4180-9B81-6769533ABE47} GUID, which stands for MVC 4 Project. A full list of project type GUIDs and what they mean is in the Windows registry under the HKEY_CURRENT_USER\Software\Microsoft\VisualStudio\11.0_Config\Projects key.

5. Modify the `ProjectTypeGuids` element of the `LegacyWebFormsApp01.csproj` project to look like Listing 10-73. Do not add line breaks. They have been added here for readability purposes.

Listing 10-73. LegacyWebFormsApp01.csproj with Modified ProjectTypeGuids Element

```
<ProjectGuid>{1AADC6B3-E831-4582-8103-F838B9B2F801}</ProjectGuid>
    <ProjectTypeGuids>
        {E3E379DF-F4C6-4180-9B81-6769533ABE47};
        {349c5851-65df-11da-9384-00065b846f21};
        {fae04ec0-301f-11d3-bf4b-00c04f79efbc}
    </ProjectTypeGuids>
    <OutputType>Library</OutputType>
```

6. After making the change, save the file and close it.

7. Right-click the project file, and then select Reload Project.

8. If you right-click the project folder, Areas should appear under the Add menu.

Setting Up Areas, Routes, Filters, and Bundles Registration

Another thing missing from your Web Forms project that is included by default with each ASP.NET MVC 4 project template is a directory called App_Start. It contains a set of static classes that are designed to be called in the Global.asax.cs when the web application starts. These methods register the default routes, areas, filters, and optimization bundles used by your MVC files.

While the App_Start folder is not required and you could just write the code to register the routes directly in the Global.asax.cs file, it is a nice convention and will give you consistency with other projects created using the ASP.NET MVC 4 templates and projects created using the new Web Forms templates.

To add the files:

1. Right-click the project node in Solution Explorer and select Add Folder.

2. Name the new folder **App_Start**.

3. Right-click the App_Start folder, and select Add ➤ Class.

4. In the Add New Item window, name the file **RouteConfig.cs** and the click the Add button.

5. Repeat steps 3 and 4 to create class files for BundleConfig.cs and FilterConfig.cs.

6. Modify the BundleConfig.cs file to look like Listing 10-74.

Listing 10-74. Adding a BundleConfig file to a Web Forms Project

```
using System.Web.Optimization;

namespace LegacyWebFormsApp01.App_Start
{
    public class BundleConfig
    {
        public static void RegisterBundles(BundleCollection bundles)
        {
            bundles.Add(new ScriptBundle("~/bundles/jquery").Include(
                    "~/Scripts/jquery-{version}.js"));

            bundles.Add(new ScriptBundle("~/bundles/jqueryui").Include(
                    "~/Scripts/jquery-ui-{version}.js"));
```

```
        bundles.Add(new ScriptBundle("~/bundles/jqueryval").Include(
                "~/Scripts/jquery.unobtrusive*",
                "~/Scripts/jquery.validate*"));

        bundles.Add(new ScriptBundle("~/bundles/modernizr").Include(
                "~/Scripts/modernizr-*"));

        bundles.Add(new StyleBundle("~/Content/css").Include("~/Content/site.css"));

        bundles.Add(new StyleBundle("~/Content/themes/base/css").Include(
                "~/Content/themes/base/jquery.ui.core.css",
                "~/Content/themes/base/jquery.ui.resizable.css",
                "~/Content/themes/base/jquery.ui.selectable.css",
                "~/Content/themes/base/jquery.ui.accordion.css",
                "~/Content/themes/base/jquery.ui.autocomplete.css",
                "~/Content/themes/base/jquery.ui.button.css",
                "~/Content/themes/base/jquery.ui.dialog.css",
                "~/Content/themes/base/jquery.ui.slider.css",
                "~/Content/themes/base/jquery.ui.tabs.css",
                "~/Content/themes/base/jquery.ui.datepicker.css",
                "~/Content/themes/base/jquery.ui.progressbar.css",
                "~/Content/themes/base/jquery.ui.theme.css"));
        }
    }
}
```

▓ **Tip**   You can eliminate some manual effort in creating these files by creating an empty MVC 4 project and then copying the files created from the template into your Web Forms project. You will then need to adjust the namespaces used to match your Web Forms project.

7.   Modify the FilterConfig.cs to look like Listing 10-75.

Listing 10-75. FilterConfig.cs Added to the Web Forms Project

```
using System.Web.Mvc;

namespace LegacyWebFormsApp01.App_Start
{
    public class FilterConfig
    {
        public static void RegisterGlobalFilters(GlobalFilterCollection filters)
        {
            filters.Add(new HandleErrorAttribute());
        }
    }
}
```

8. Modify RouteConfig.cs to look like Listing 10-76. Note that the route definition requires the MVCArea directory name. We are also using a custom controller name rather than the one normally used with the ASP.NET MVC templates.

Listing 10-76. RouteConfig.cs

```
using System.Web.Mvc;
using System.Web.Routing;

namespace LegacyWebFormsApp01.App_Start
{
    public class RouteConfig
    {
        public static void RegisterRoutes(RouteCollection routes)
        {
            routes.IgnoreRoute("{resource}.axd/{*pathInfo}");

            routes.MapRoute(
                name: "Default",
                url: "MVCArea/{controller}/{action}/{id}",
                defaults: new { controller = "NewFeature",
                            action = "Index", id = UrlParameter.Optional }
            );
        }
    }
}
```

9. In the older ASP.NET Web Forms templates, a Global.asax file was not included by default. In a real legacy project, you would need to add one if it wasn't included. If it is not included, right-click the project folder in Solution Explorer and select Add ➤ New Item.

10. In the Add New Item window, locate the template for Global Application Class, select it, and then click the Add button.

11. Modify the Application_Start method to look like Listing 10-77.

Listing 10-77. Application_Start

```
using LegacyWebFormsApp01.App_Start;
using System.Web.Mvc;
using System.Web.Optimization;
using System.Web.Routing;

namespace LegacyWebFormsApp01
{
    public class Global : System.Web.HttpApplication
    {

        protected void Application_Start()
        {
            AreaRegistration.RegisterAllAreas();
            FilterConfig.RegisterGlobalFilters(GlobalFilters.Filters);
```

```
                    RouteConfig.RegisterRoutes(RouteTable.Routes);
                    BundleConfig.RegisterBundles(BundleTable.Bundles);
            }


        }
    }
```

Creating an Area

Now that you have set up all of the required infrastructure, you can begin adding MVC controllers to the project. You will use Areas to isolate the MVC code from the Web Forms code, which will help keep the project maintainable.

1. Right-click the project node in Solution Explorer. Select Add ➤ Area.

2. Name the area **NewFeatures**, and then click the Add button. This will add a new folder at the root of the project called Areas; inside it, you should see a folder named NewFeatures. Inside NewFeatures is a typical MVC project structure.

3. To create a layout page to use in your MVC pages, right-click the Areas\NewFeatures\Views\Shared folder and select Add ➤ View.

4. In the Add View window, name the view **_Layout**. Make sure that the Razor view engine is selected. Uncheck the Use Layout or Master Page check box.

5. Click the Add button.

Adding a Controller to the Area

Now that you have created your Area, you can now add controllers and views to it as you normally would.

1. Right-click the Areas/NewFeatures/Controllers folder. Click Add and then Controller.

2. In the Add Controller window, name the controller **Feature01Controller**. Select the Empty MVC Controller template and then click Add. The new controller will open in the code editor window.

3. To create the view for the generated Index action, right-click anywhere inside the Index action and select Create View from the menu.

4. Keep Index as the view name. Make sure the Razor view engine is selected and check the Use a Layout or Master Page check box.

You should now be able to access your new controller. Click the Debug button on main toolbar to begin debugging. Go to the root of the web site and verify that you can still access your Web Forms pages. Enter the following URL to access the new controller : /NewFeatures/Feature01/. You should see a blank page. If you see a configuration error, go to the next section.

Workaround for Bug in the ASP.NET Web Tools 2012.2 Update

If you have installed the ASP.NET Web Tools 2012.2 Update, you may encounter a regression in Visual Studio that results in a configuration error when you add an Area to your ASP.NET MVC project. This error occurs in both regular MVC projects and hybrid projects such as the one described in this recipe.

If you fall victim to this bug, you will see the following error message when attempting to access an action inside the area:

```
Description: An error occurred during the processing of a configuration file required to service
this request. Please review the specific error details below and modify your configuration file
appropriately.
```

```
Parser Error Message: An error occurred creating the configuration section handler for
system.web.webPages.razor/pages: The given assembly name or codebase was invalid. (Exception from
HRESULT: 0x80131047)
```

This error is caused by a problem with the template used by Visual Studio to generate the Web.config file inside the folder for your area that assigns an incorrect version number when referencing the System.Web.WebPages.Razor assembly.

To correct the problem open the Web.config file in the root of your area. In this example, it is the file located in Areas\NewFeatures\Views. Modify the file as shown in Listing 10-78.

Listing 10-78. Correcting Web.config Error in Code Generated by Visual Studio Template

```
<configuration>
  <configSections>
    <sectionGroup name="system.web.webPages.razor"
            type="System.Web.WebPages.Razor.Configuration.RazorWebSectionGroup, System.Web.WebPages.
Razor, Version=2.0.0.0, Culture=neutral, PublicKeyToken=31BF3856AD364E35">

      <section name="host" type="System.Web.WebPages.Razor.Configuration.HostSection, System.
Web.WebPages.Razor, Version=2.0.0.0, Culture=neutral, PublicKeyToken=31BF3856AD364E35"
requirePermission="false" />

      <section name="pages" type="System.Web.WebPages.Razor.Configuration.RazorPagesSection,
System.Web.WebPages.Razor, Version=2.0.0.0, Culture=neutral, PublicKeyToken=31BF3856AD364E35"
requirePermission="false" />

    </sectionGroup>
  </configSections>
```

After making the change, everything should work as expected. You will need to do this each time you add a new area to your site.

CHAPTER 11

Creating Modern User Experiences Using jQuery, Knockout.js, and Web API

11-1. Creating an Adaptive Multicolumn Layout Using CSS Media Queries

Problem

You have a requirement to create a view that displays a list of photos in a multicolumn format. It needs to support many screen resolutions on several devices including PCs with 24-inch monitors, tablets such as the Microsoft Surface RT, and smartphones such as the Google Nexus 4. You would like to be able to create one view that would work for all of them and can scale up and down and reduce the number of columns when required.

Solution

The easiest way to accomplish this is to have your server-side code render the items in an ordered list and then use CSS3 media queries and other adaptive rendering techniques to enable image scaling based on screen resolution and dimensions.

How It Works

All modern web browsers, including browsers on most mobile devices, support a concept called media queries. *Media queries* allow you to determine the type of device being used to access the site, as well as some of its capabilities, including screen resolution and the number of colors supported. You can use this information to tailor the visual style of your page to best suit the capabilities of your device.

For example, if a user is accessing your blog with an e-reader device such as a Nook or a Kindle, you may want to change your color scheme to one that uses higher contrasts. You may also want to modify the width of your page so that the content can easily fit within the confines of the smaller screen.

On the other hand, if a user is accessing your site on a PC with a huge screen and the browser maximized, you can use media queries to fill in what would normally be unused white space with useful content.

To demonstrate this technique, we show a simple photo page. Depending on the screen resolution or size of the browser window, this example will have between two and ten columns. It will also dynamically change the size of the images based on the same parameters. The solution has added the capability of changing the number of columns and size of the images in real time as the browser window is resized.

The Model

This solution uses an external assembly that uses the Entity Framework to communicate with a back-end database. It is based on the example shown in Recipe 7-5. To simplify the controller logic and to allow for easier unit testing, all the data access code has been factored into a simple repository class, as shown in Listing 11-1.

Listing 11-1. EFArtistRepository

```
public class EFArtistRepository : IArtistRepository
{
    private MobEntities m_context = new MobEntities();
    public IList<Artist> GetNewArtists()
    {
        var results = (from a in m_context.Artists
                        where a.ProfilePrivacyLevel == 0
                        orderby a.CreateDate descending
                        select a).Take(40);
        return results.ToList<Artist>();
    }

        ~ EFArtistRepository()
        {
            Dispose(false);
        }
        public void Dispose()
        {
            Dispose(true);
            GC.SuppressFinalize(this);
        }
        protected virtual void Dispose(bool disposing)
        {
            if (disposing)
            {

                if (m_context != null)
                    m_context.Dispose();
            }
        }
}
```

The code in Listing 11-1 is very simple. It consists of a single method, GetNewArtists. This method returns data from the last 40 people who have created accounts on a web site.

The Controller

The controller in this example is also very simple. Like many of the examples in this book, it uses the repository pattern and constructor injection patterns to allow testability. More information on these patterns can be found in Chapters 7 and 9.

The controller consists of two actions. The Index action does nothing but return the home page and has no controller logic. The NewArtists action gets the list of artists from the repository and then passes it to the NewArtists view. The controller is shown in Listing 11-2.

Listing 11-2. The Home Controller

```
public class HomeController : Controller
{

  public HomeController(IArtistRepository rep)
  {
    m_repository = rep;
  }
  public HomeController() : this (new EFArtistRepository()){}

  IArtistRepository m_repository;

  public ActionResult NewArtists()
  {
    IList<Artist> artists = m_repository.GetNewArtists();

    return View("NewArtists", artists);

  }
}
```

The View

The view is also very simple. It starts by using the @model directive to associate itself with the list of Artist objects. It then makes use of a section called headercontent, which allows it to include a CSS file called Multicolumn.css in the document's header.

The rest of the file is a simple for loop wrapped in a DIV that has been assigned the CSS class DynamicColumns. The code loops through the objects in the model's Artist collection and builds an HTML unordered list. This is normally displayed as a bulleted list of items.

Inside each list item tag is an image (img) tag with the CSS class AvatarImage, which is wrapped in another DIV with the CSS class ImageDiv. Beneath the image is the artist's name, which is wrapped in a set of h3 tags.

The code is shown in Listing 11-3. The CSS class names are highlighted in bold.

Listing 11-3. NewArtist.cshtml

```
@model List<Ch7.SharedAPI.Artist>
@{
    ViewBag.Title = "New Artists";
}
@section headercontent{
    <link href="~/Content/Multicolumn.css" rel="stylesheet" />
}
<h2>New Artists Photos</h2>

<div class="DynamicColumns">
    <ul>
        @foreach (var item in Model)
        {
            <li>
```

```
        <div class="ImageDiv">

            <img src="@item.AvatarUrlSample"
                class="AvatarImage"
                alt="@item.UserName"/>
            <h3>@item.UserName</h3>
        </div>
    </li>
    }
    </ul>
</div>
```

The CSS

Without any styling applied, our example would be displayed as a simple bulleted list of images. The CSS in this example is the star of the show. It alone converts this simple code into a dynamic grid. The first bit of CSS code (see Listing 11-4) shows the styling for the DynamicColumns class. The first selector sets list-style:none to any UL elements that may have been nested inside a DIV element with the DynamicColumns class assigned to it. This removes the bullet from the bulleted list. Also in this same definition, the UL tag is set to display:inline. This removes the line break that would normally be placed after the list.

In the next selector, display:inline is applied to the LI elements. This setting prevents each list item from appearing on its own line.

Finally, a definition is added for H3 tags nested inside a container with the DynamicColumns class. This style removes the margin normally applied to the H3 tag and aligns the text to the center.

Listing 11-4. Multicolumn.css Dynamic Columns Class

```
.DynamicColumns {
margin:10px;
}
.DynamicColumns ul {
    list-style:none;
        display:inline;
}

.DynamicColumns li{
    display:inline;
}

.DynamicColumns h3 {
    text-align: center;
    margin:0;
}
```

Next, we add the class selectors for AvatarImage and ImageDiv. The AvatarImage class, which is applied to image elements in our example, uses percentages rather than a fixed width to define the dimensions of the images. It also adds a fixed, five-pixel margin around each image. If you set the height and width to 90%, the remaining 10% creates a modest amount of space around the images. At 100%, they would be flush against each other. The ImageDiv class selector makes the images float left and then sets the width of the image to be 40% of the screen width. This will size each image to take up almost half of the screen, creating two columns. The selectors are shown in Listing 11-5.

Listing 11-5. Multicolumn.css Avatar Image and ImageDiv Classes

```css
.AvatarImage {
    height: 90%;
    width: 90%;
}


.ImageDiv {
    float: left;
    width: 40%;
}
```

All of the CSS styles shown so far work on all browsers. These techniques are well known and are used in thousands of web sites. Using this technique, you can increase and decrease the number of columns displayed by adjusting the percentage of the `width` attribute on the `ImageDiv` class. For example, if you wanted to display three columns rather than two, you can set the width to 30%.

If you use the CSS shown so far and ran the application, you would notice that if you shrank the browser to the smallest width possible, the images would look fine. If you maximized the browser, however, the images would look stretched-out and pixelated.

It would be better if you could dynamically change the percentage of the `width` attribute of the `ImageDiv` class so that as the canvas became larger, more columns would appear.

This is exactly what we will do using CSS media queries. Five media queries are defined in Listing 11-6. Each uses the syntax `@media all and (max-width: [max number]px) and (min-width: [min number]px)`. This statement says for all device types that have a screen size between a [max number] and [min number], apply the following styles. Inside each media query, we redefine the .ImageDiv selector. As the screen grows larger, the percentage of the screen each image takes decreases. This allows more images to appear in a single row. For the smallest screen, only two images will appear in each row. After the width exceeds 701 pixels, you get three images. On a 1080p or better display with the window maximized, you will get 20 per row.

Listing 11-6. Using Media Queries to Dynamically Change the Width of ImageDiv

```css
@media all and (max-width: 700px) and (min-width: 500px) {
    .ImageDiv {
        width: 30%;
    }
}


@media all and (max-width: 1200px) and (min-width: 701px) {
    .ImageDiv {
        width: 20%;
    }
}


@media all and (max-width: 1500px) and (min-width: 1201px) {
    .ImageDiv {
        width: 15%;
    }
}


@media all and (max-width: 1800px) and (min-width: 1501px) {
    .ImageDiv {
        width: 10%;
    }
}
```

```
@media all and (max-width: 20000px) and (min-width: 1801px) {
    .ImageDiv {
        width: 5%;
    }
}
```

Figure 11-1 shows the page in three different sizes.

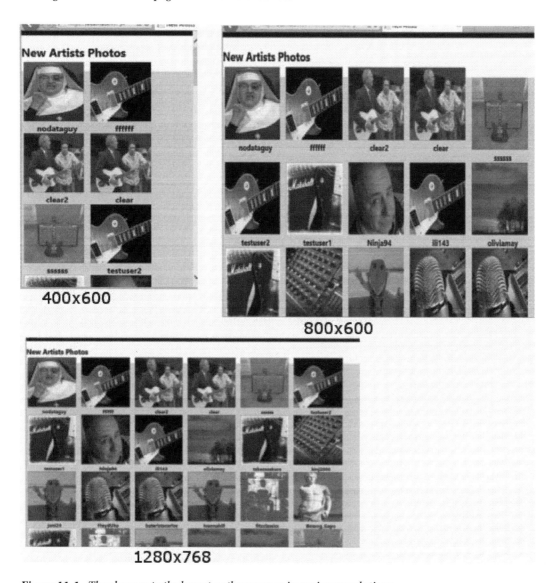

Figure 11-1. *The changes to the layout as they appear in various resolutions*

Supported Web Browsers

CSS media queries, although widely supported, are still a relatively new technology. Many browsers, such as Internet Explorer 8, do not support them. Before deciding whether or not to use this technique, you should know which browsers support it and which do not.

Table 11-1 lists each of the major web browsers and at which version the browser begins providing support for CSS media queries.

Table 11-1. *Browsers with Full Support for CSS Media Queries*

Browser	Minimum Version Supported	Operating System
Microsoft Internet Explorer	9.0	Windows 7, Windows 8, Windows Phone
Mozilla Firefox	3.5	Windows, Mac, Linux
Mozilla Firefox for Android	15.0	Android
Chrome	4.0	Windows, Mac
Chrome for Android	18.0	Android 4.x
Safari	4.0	Windows, Mac, iOS
Opera	9.6	Windows, Linux, Mac
Opera Mini	5.0	Android, Blackberry, iOS
Android	2.1	Android
Blackberry browser	7.0	Blackberry 7, Blackberry 10

If a significant number of your users are using an unsupported browser, it will require some level of additional effort to provide an equivalent experience.

If your site has browser usage statistics similar to the global average, between 15 percent and 20 percent of your users are using unsupported browsers such as IE 7. There are several strategies that you can adopt to deal with unsupported browsers:

1. *Use a fixed set of columns.* If 90 percent of your audience is using an unsupported browser, media queries is probably not for you.

2. *Use a conditional style sheet.* Internet Explorer 5 and up understand conditional statements in the format of `<!--[if lt IE] 9> do this <![endif]-->`. This allows you to specify markup, including HTML link statements that will only be rendered in IE 8 and older browsers. Other browsers will interpret the markup as commented out and will ignore it.

3. *Use an IE polyfill.* A *polyfill* is a workaround for older browser versions. They typically implemented in JavaScript. They allow you to use CSS 3.0 style rules without needing to code IE-specific workarounds inside the style sheet. Polyfills are available for other unsupported browsers but are not as common. A good polyfill that enabled CSS media queries in IE 6, IE 7, and IE 8 is available at `https://github.com/scottjehl/Respond`. If only a small percentage of your users are using unsupported browsers, however, using the polyfill is probably the best strategy.

To apply the polyfill, you can download the file from the web site, include it in your project's script folder, and then include a reference to the file in your view.

Once the polyfill has been added, the unsupported browser will now correctly render the page.

If you decide to use a library such as respond.js, verify that you are downloading the file from a trustworthy source and that the solution has been vetted by the community.

11-2. Creating a Data Grid That Can Page and Sort Without Full-Page Postbacks

Problem

You have a requirement to display a list of records in a grid-like layout. Your company's new user experience guidelines state that you should keep the user on the page and avoid full postbacks whenever possible. In the past, you have created solutions in ASP.NET Web Forms using a combination of a GridView control and an update panel. You would like to know the equivalent technique using ASP.NET MVC.

Solution

In this solution, we will use a combination of ASP.NET Web API to create a RESTful Web Service that will allow us to get our data pages in JSON format from the server. We will then use a combination of jQuery and Knockout to render the user interface on the client. When the user requests a new data page, a web service call will be made to the server.

Knockout is a compact JavaScript library that provides dependency tracking and declarative data binding.

When the response is received, a client-side object array will be updated. The page will then use the Knockout library to automatically update the data grid. We will then add some CSS animations to add some flare to the page transitions.

How It Works

This solution uses the ASP.NET MVC 4 Web API template. The template includes all the required JavaScript libraries and provides some boilerplate code to get started on the web service. Do the following to create the project:

1. Open Visual Studio. Select New ➤ Project from the File menu.

2. In the New Project window, select the ASP.NET MVC 4 Web Application template. Name the project **Ch11.R2.Web** and name the solution **Ch11.R2**. Click OK.

3. On the New ASP.NET MVC 4 Project page, select the Web API template. Make sure that the Razor view engine is selected, and then tick the "Create a unit test project" check box. Keep the default test project name of Ch11.R2.Web.Tests and click OK.

4. Next, add a reference to an external assembly that contains the data access code. If you have followed the instructions for installing the book's code samples, which can be found in Chapter 1, you should have a folder named Shared\References under the root of the code samples directory. Inside that folder, there is a SharedAPI.dll file. Add a reference to this file by right-clicking the References folder in Solution Explorer, and then browsing to the file. Tick the box next to the file name and click OK.

5. Since the SharedAPI.dll connects to an external database, you will need to add the connection string to your Web.config file in order to use it. An example connection string is shown in Listing 11-7. This connection string assumes that you are connecting to a database on your local developer machine.

Listing 11-7. Web.config Connection String Required to Use Shared Library

```
<connectionStrings>
 <add
   name="DefaultConnection"
   connectionString="data source=.;Initial Catalog=Ch7SharedDatabase;Integrated Security=SSPI;"
   providerName="System.Data.SqlClient"
    />

<add name="MobEntities"

connectionString="metadata=res://*/Mob.csdl|res://*/Mob.ssdl|res://*/Mob.msl;provider=System.Data.
SqlClient;provider connection string=&quot;data source=.;initial catalog=Ch7SharedDatabase;integrated
security=True;MultipleActiveResultSets=True;App=EntityFramework&quot;"
          providerName="System.Data.EntityClient" />
  </connectionStrings>
```

6. Add references to an assembly that contains a set of HTML helper extensions created in Chapter 10. This assembly, named `Ch10.Shared.Helpers.dll`, is also included in the `Shared\References` folder.

The Model and Repository

We will now create a repository that we can use to access our data. While using a repository class is not required, it is a good idea. Using the repository pattern allows us to keep our controller logic simple and makes the controllers easier to test in isolation. In the controller, we will use a dependency injection pattern so that we can use a mocked repository in unit tests. This technique allows us to test just the controller logic without needing to worry about the data access code. Separate tests can be set up for testing the repository. First, we will create the interface for our repository:

1. Right-click the `Models` folder in your web application project, and select Add ➤ New Item.

2. In the Add New Item window, search for and then select the Interface template. Name the interface **IAjaxDataGridRepository** and then click Add.

3. Modify the new file so that it defines a single method called `GetActiveCollaborationSpaces` that returns an `IList` of `CollaborationSpaceSearchResult` objects. The method should accept the parameters for the current page, the number of items per page, a sort expression, and an output parameter that will contain the number of items found. In addition to defining the `GetActiveCollaborationSpaces` method, the interface should also inherit `IDisposible`. This makes it easier for developers to clean up after unmanaged resources like database connections. The resulting interface should look like Listing 11-8.

    Listing 11-8. IAjaxDataGridRepository

    ```
    using System;
    using System.Collections.Generic;
    ```

```
namespace Ch11.R2.Web.Models
{
    public interface IAjaxDataGridRepository : IDisposable
    {

        IList<CollaborationSpaceSearchResult> GetActiveCollaborationSpaces(
            int page,
            int count,
            string sortExpression,
            out int resultsFound);
    }
}
```

At this point, the code will not compile because we need to define the CollaborationSpaceSearchResult class, as follows:

1. Right-click the Models folder, and select Add ➤ Class. Name the new class file **AjaxDataGridModels.cs**.

2. Add a using statement to the class for Ch7.SharedAPI. This namespace is defined in the assembly that we added previously.

3. Define the CollaborationSpaceSearchResult, as shown in Listing 11-9.

Listing 11-9. CollaborationSpaceSearchResult Class

```
using Ch7.SharedAPI;
using System;
using System.Collections.Generic;

namespace Ch11.R2.Web.Models
{

    public class CollaborationSpaceSearchResult
    {
        public int CollaborationSpaceId { get; set; }
        public DateTime CreateDate { get; set; }
        public string Description { get; set; }
        public DateTime ? LastPostDate { get; set; }
        public DateTime ModifiedDate { get; set; }
        public int NumberComments { get; set; }
        public int NumberViews { get; set; }
        public bool RestrictContributorsToBand { get; set; }
        public CollaborationSpaceStatus Status { get; set; }
        public string Title { get; set; }
        public string UserName { get; set; }
        public string WebSite { get; set; }
        public string AvatarURL { get; set; }

    }
}
```

In addition to the CollaborationSpaceSearchResult class, we also need a class to use as our model. This class will include a list of CollaborationSpaceSearchResult objects and a number of other properties that will track the various elements of the view, such as the current page number and sort expression. The result should look like Listing 11-10.

Listing 11-10. The Collaboration Space Search Model

```
public class CollaborationSpaceSearchResultModel
{
  public IList<CollaborationSpaceSearchResult> CollaborationSpaceSearchResults { get; set; }
  public int NumberOfResults{get;set;}
  public string ResultsDescription { get; set; }
  public int ItemsPerPage { get; set; }
  public int CurrentPage { get; set; }
  public string SortExpression { get; set; }
  public int TotalPages
  {
    get
    {
      if (ItemsPerPage != 0)
      {
        return NumberOfResults / ItemsPerPage;
      }
        return 0;
    }
  }
}
```

Now that the repository interface and models have been defined, we can create an implementation of the IAjaxDataGridRepository. This implementation will leverage the library defined in the Ch7.SharedAPI assembly to retrieve data from a database. It also leverages a LINQ extension defined in the library Ch10.Shared.Helpers. This extension allows us to use a string to create a sort expression, as follows:

1. Create a new class file by right-clicking the Models folder in Solution Explorer and selecting Add ➤ Class.

2. Name the new class **EFAjaxDataGridRepository.cs**.

3. Inside the new class file, indicate that the class will implement the IAjaxDataGridRepository by typing **: IAjaxDataGridRepository** after the class name.

4. After you have completed typing, Visual Studio will underline the I in IAjaxDataGridRepository. If you hover over the underline, a small menu icon will appear. Click the button to reveal the menu and select Implement Interface 'IAjaxDataGridRepository'. Visual Studio will create method stubs for the methods GetActiveCollaborationSpaces and Dispose.

5. In order to properly implement the IDisposable interface in addition to the public Dispose method, implement a protected virtual version of the method that takes a bool parameter called disposing. You should also create a destructor that can be used to dispose of unmanaged resources. Inside the destructor, call the protected virtual version of the method with the disposing parameter set to false. In the public dispose method, call the protected virtual version of the method with the disposing parameter set to true, and also tell the garbage collector not to call the finalizer for the current instance of the class by calling GC.SuppressFinalize(this).

6. Next, create a global instance of the MobEntities class defined in the Ch7.SharedAPI assembly that we referenced earlier. Make sure that it is disposed in our protected virtual version of the Dispose method when the disposing parameter is set to true.

485

7. Inside the GetActiveCollaborationSpaces method, create a LINQ query that will return a result set with the desired page and sort.

The implementation is shown in Listing 11-11.

Listing 11-11. Repository Implementation

```
using Ch10.Shared.Helpers;
using Ch7.SharedAPI;
using System;
using System.Collections.Generic;
using System.Linq;

namespace Ch11.R2.Web.Models
{
    public class EFAjaxDataGridRepository : IAjaxDataGridRepository
    {
        MobEntities m_context = new MobEntities();

        public IList<CollaborationSpaceSearchResult> GetActiveCollaborationSpaces(
            int page,
            int count,
            string sortExpression,
            out int resultsFound)
        {
            var collabSpacesQuery = from a in m_context.CollaborationSpaces
                                    join p in m_context.ArtistCollaborationSpaces
                                    on a.CollaborationSpaceId equals p.CollaborationSpaceId
                                    where a.Status != CollaborationSpaceStatus.Canceled &&
                                    a.Status != CollaborationSpaceStatus.OnHold &&
                                    a.Status != CollaborationSpaceStatus.Published &&
                                    a.AllowPublicView == true &&
                                    p.IsCreator == true
                                    select new CollaborationSpaceSearchResult()
                                    {
                                        CollaborationSpaceId = a.CollaborationSpaceId,
                                        CreateDate = a.CreateDate,
                                        Description = a.Description,
                                        LastPostDate = a.LastPostDate,
                                        ModifiedDate = a.ModifiedDate,
                                        NumberComments = a.NumberComments,
                                        NumberViews = a.NumberViews,
                                        RestrictContributorsToBand =
                                            a.RestrictContributorsToBand,
                                        Status = a.Status,
                                        Title = a.Title,
                                        UserName = p.Artist.UserName,
                                        WebSite = p.Artist.WebSite,
                                        AvatarURL = p.Artist.AvatarURL
                                    };

            resultsFound = collabSpacesQuery.Count();
```

```
        int skip = getSkip(page, count);
        if (String.IsNullOrEmpty(sortExpression))
        {
            sortExpression = "CreateDate";
        }
        collabSpacesQuery = collabSpacesQuery.OrderBy(sortExpression).Skip(skip).Take(count);

        return collabSpacesQuery.ToList<CollaborationSpaceSearchResult>();
    }

    private int getSkip(int page, int count)
    {
        if (page < 2)
        {
            return 0;
        }
        else
        {
            return page * count;
        }
    }

    ~EFAjaxDataGridRepository()
    {
        Dispose(false);
    }
    public void Dispose()
    {
        Dispose(true);
        GC.SuppressFinalize(this);
    }
    protected virtual void Dispose(bool disposing)
    {
        if (disposing)
        {

            if (m_context != null)
                m_context.Dispose();
        }
    }
  }
}
```

The Controllers

So far, the model and repository code are very similar to other examples that you have seen in this book. There is nothing specific that needs to be done in the model to enable an Ajax-driven, rich user interface.

For the controllers, however, the design needs to be changed. In order to support a rich user experience, we will need to split our controller logic across two classes. The first will be a Web API controller. The primary job of this controller is no different from other controllers you have built. It allows the user to interact with the model. What has changed is the mechanism for updating the view. This class will derive from the `ApiController` base class.

The second controller will fill the role of content delivery. In this case, it only contains enough logic to deliver the view. It will be derived from the `Controller` class.

The Web API Controller

We will start with the API controller. When we created the project, the Web API template added a controller named the `ValuesController` to the project. This controller includes actions that match each of the HTTP verbs—GET, POST, PUT, and `DELETE`. When using the RESTful program style, each verb is associated with a corresponding CRUD operation by convention. For more information on REST, please refer to Recipe 11-8.

In this recipe, we will only implement a read operation and a single action. We will rename this class so that it better matches our business case. Using the following steps, you can convert the API controller included in the template to one that meets the needs of this recipe.

1. Locate the `ValuesController.cs` file in Solution Explorer under the Controllers node of the `Ch11.R2.Web` project. Right-click it and select Rename.

2. Rename the file **CollaborationSpacesController**.

3. Click Yes when prompted to perform a similar rename of all references of `ValuesController`.

4. Open the `CollaborationSpacesController.cs` file and add a using statement for `Ch11.R2.Web.Models`.

5. Delete all the actions in the file.

6. Create a new action with the signature `CollaborationSpaceSearchResultModel Get(int? Page, string SortExpression)`.

7. Modify the contents of this action, as shown in Listing 11-12.

Listing 11-12. CollaborationSpaceController

```
public class CollaborationSpacesController : ApiController
{

    IAjaxDataGridRepository m_repository = new EFAjaxDataGridRepository();

    // GET api/CollaborationSpaces?Page=1&SortExpression=CreateDate
    public CollaborationSpaceSearchResultModel Get(
            int? Page,
            string SortExpression)  {
        int resultsFound;
        int page = Page ?? 1;
        string sortExpression = SortExpression ?? "CreateDate";
        var model = new CollaborationSpaceSearchResultModel();
        model.CollaborationSpaceSearchResults =
            m_repository.GetActiveCollaborationSpaces(
                    page,
                    10,
                    SortExpression,
                    out resultsFound);
```

```
        model.NumberOfResults = resultsFound;
        model.ItemsPerPage = 10;
        model.CurrentPage = page;
        model.SortExpression = sortExpression;
        return model;
    }


}
```

▓ **Tip**   Use the C# null-coalescing operator. This technique provides a very concise way to check for a `null` value and then provide a value. This technique is shown in Listing 11-10. Here we test to see if the nullable `Page` has a value, and if so, assign an `int` variable page to the value of 1. The syntax `int page= Page??1` is equivalent to writing `int page = Page.HasValue ? Page.Value : 1`.

---

8.   In the test project, locate the file `Controllers\ValuesControllerTests.cs` and rename the file **CollaborationSpacesControllerTests.cs**.

9.   Rename the test file **CollaborationSpacesControllerTests**, and then delete all the test methods except `GET`. Comment out the `GET` method. We will write our tests in a later step. For now, we will comment out this test method so that the solution can compile.

10.   Confirm that there are no syntax errors by selecting Build Solution from the Visual Studio BUILD menu.

The action shown in Listing 11-12 takes two parameters. The first is the page number and the second is the `SortExpression`, which should contain the name of a column that the results are sorted by. The `Page` parameter is nullable. This allows the parameter to be omitted from the route without error. When the `Page` parameter is `null`, we return the first page of the result set. The `SortExpression` parameter has a default value of `CreateDate`.

To verify that the API controller can be accessed, click the Start Debugging button in the Visual Studio main toolbar. The site's home page will be displayed in your browser. Append the URL with the path to your service, which will be `/api/CollaborationSpaces`. If you are using Internet Explorer, the browser will prompt you to download or open the file. If you do, you will see that the file contains an error message indicating that it cannot match the URL to a controller.

The reason you are seeing an error is because no routes have been defined with default parameters for the page and sort. In order to get this to work, you will need to specify values for both parameters in the form of a query string; for example, `/api/CollaborationSpaces?Page=1&SortExpression=CreateDate`. If you would like to enable default values for the API controller, you will need to add a new route definition in the `/App_Start/WebApiConfig.cs` file, as shown in Listing 11-13. Detailed instructions and explanation on how to create a custom API route are in Recipe 11-9.

Listing 11-13. Custom API Route

```
using System;
using System.Collections.Generic;
using System.Linq;
using System.Web.Http;
```

```
namespace Ch11.R2.Web
{
    public static class WebApiConfig
    {
        public static void Register(HttpConfiguration config)
        {
            config.Routes.MapHttpRoute(
            name: "PagingApi",
            routeTemplate: "api/{controller}/Page/{Page}/{SortExpression}",
            defaults: new
            {
             Page = 0,
             SortExpression = "CreateDate"
            }
            );
            config.Routes.MapHttpRoute(
                name: "DefaultApi",
                routeTemplate: "api/{controller}/{id}",
                defaults: new { id = RouteParameter.Optional }
            );
        }
    }
}
```

After making this change and recompiling the code, if you enter the full URL, including the query string (for example, http://localhost:3493/api/CollaborationSpaces/Page/1), Internet Explorer will prompt you to download a file—but this time it should contain the data from your request in JSON format. If you are using Chrome, it will return the same data but in XML format.

An alternative technique for reviewing and debugging the output of a Web API response is shown in Recipe 11-10, which describes how to use the Fiddler 4 Web Proxy Application. If you use Fiddler 4, you will see that Internet Explorer and Chrome use slightly different HTTP headers when submitting the request, which results in a different format. Web API supports returning either XML or JSON, according to the HTTP Accept header supplied in the request.

The Content Controller

The controller action used to deliver the content does not need to be sophisticated. For this example, we will add an action to the home controller called WorkspaceList. This controller will simply return a ViewResult. Its view will not be strong typed. In fact, neither the view nor the controller needs to have any knowledge of the model at all. They are simply a content delivery mechanism.

To create the WorkspaceList action, do the following:

1. Open the HomeController.cs file.

2. Add a new action method, as shown in Listing 11-14.

    Listing 11-14. WorkspaceList Action

    ```
    public ActionResult WorkspaceList()
    {
        return View();
    }
    ```

3. Create the corresponding view for the WorkspaceList action by right-clicking the method name in the code editor and selecting Add View.

4. In the Add View window, confirm the default values are as follows, and then click Add:

    a. View name: WorkspaceList

    b. View engine: Razor

    c. Create a strongly-typed view: Unchecked

    d. Create as a partial view: Unchecked

    e. Use a layout or master page: Checked

Creating Unit Tests for Your API Controller

As you are developing your controllers, you should also be creating unit tests for them. The first step in this process is to enable a mocked implementation of the repository to be passed into the constructor of the controller. You do this by defining a constructor that takes an instance of an object, which implements IAjaxDataGridRepository as a parameter. You will also need to create a parameter-less constructor that can be used by the MVC Framework. This technique is explained in detail in Chapter 9. Listing 11-15 shows the CollaborationSpacesController with the modified constructors.

Listing 11-15. Constructor Created to Support Constructor Injection

```
IAjaxDataGridRepository m_repository;

public CollaborationSpacesController(IAjaxDataGridRepository respository)
{
  m_repository = respository;
}


//constructor required by MVC Framework
// uses the EFArchitectRepository as the default controller
public CollaborationSpacesController() : this(new EFAjaxDataGridRepository()) { }
```

This modification allows us to test the controller using a mocked implementation of the repository. For this example, we will use the Moq Framework. A detailed example on how to use Moq to test a controller using a repository is shown in Recipe 9-8.

One of the big differences between Web API controllers and regular controllers is that API controllers can return any C# type. They do not return ActionResult as regular controls do. In some ways, this makes writing tests for API controllers relatively straightforward. Listing 11-16 shows a test for the CollaborationSpacesController Get action. It uses the Moq library to create an instance of a mocked repository that it passes to the controller's constructor. It then calls the Get action and uses the test framework's Assert function to verify that the model contains the expected information.

Listing 11-16. Unit Test That Verifies Default Values for Route Parameters

```
using Ch11.R2.Web.Controllers;
using Ch11.R2.Web.Models;
using Microsoft.VisualStudio.TestTools.UnitTesting;
using Moq;
```

```
namespace Ch11.R2.Web.Tests.Controllers
{
    [TestClass]
    public class CollaborationSpaceControllerTests
    {
        [TestMethod]
        public void Get_PageNullSortNull_ReturnPage1SortedByCreateDate()
        {
            // Arrange
            var mock = new Mock<IAjaxDataGridRepository>();
            CollaborationSpacesController controller =
                new CollaborationSpacesController(mock.Object);

            // Act
            CollaborationSpaceSearchResultModel result = controller.Get(null, null);

            // Assert
            Assert.AreEqual(1, result.CurrentPage);
            Assert.AreEqual("CreateDate", result.SortExpression);

        }

        // Other tests go here
    }
}
```

By using this technique, we can write tests to cover all the expected use cases.

The Workspace List View

The WorkspaceList view will be made up of three files:

- Views/Home/WorkspaceList.cshtml: The view itself.

- Scripts/Home/WorkspaceList.cshtml.js: Contains client-side scripts for the view.

- Content/Home/WorkspaceList.css: Style information specific to this view.

You will need to create each of the required files and then add references to each of them in the view, as follows:

1. Right-click the Script node, and select Add ➤ New Folder.

2. Name the new folder **Home**.

3. Right-click the Home folder, and select Add ➤ New Item.

4. In the Add New Item window, search for the file template by typing **JavaScript** into the search box. When the template is found, select the JavaScript file.

5. Name the file **WorkspaceList.cshtml.js**, and then click Add.

Follow a similar procedure to create WorkspaceList.css in the Content/Home folder, but when creating the file, choose the style sheet template.

In addition to the three custom files, the page also uses the JavaScript libraries jQuery, Knockout.js, and Knockout.Mapping.

jQuery will be used to communicate with the back-end web service and will bind the JSON data to a client-side model. Knockout.Mapping will convert the data received from the web service call into a type that can be used with Knockout.js, which will provide declarative data binding and templating.

Of the three JavaScript libraries, JQuery and Knockout.js are included by default with the Web API Visual Studio template. Knockout.Mapping is not included and must be added using the NuGet package manager, as follows:

1. Right-click the References node in Solution Explorer and select Manage NuGet Packages.

2. Make sure the Online category is selected, and then use the search box to find Knockout.Mapping.

3. Click the Install button next to the package. The package will be added to the project.

4. Click the Close button to close the Manage NuGet Packages window.

■ **Tip** When starting a new project that makes heavy use of client-side scripting libraries such as jQuery and Knockout.js, you should always check to make sure you have the latest version of the NuGet package. To do this, right-click the References node for the web application project in Solution Explorer and select Manage NuGet Packages. In the Manage NuGet Packages window, click the Updates node. Any out-of-date packages will be listed here. You can update them by clicking the Update button for each package.

Inside the WorkspaceList.cshtml file, include the scripts section. Expand the Scripts node in Solution Explorer and then drag the file knockout-2.2.0.js (or current version) into the scripts section. Repeat the procedure for knockout.mapping-latest.js and Home/WorkspaceList.cshtml.js. When you are done, the script section should look like Listing 11-17.

Listing 11-17. Script References Added to WorkspaceList.cshtml

```
@section scripts{
    <script src="~/Scripts/knockout-2.2.0.js"></script>
    <script src="~/Scripts/knockout.mapping-latest.js"></script>
    <script src="~/Scripts/Home/WorkspaceList.cshtml.js"></script>
}
```

Note the order in which the script files are listed. It is important to list them in this order because they depend on one another.

Data Binding After the Page Loads

When creating a traditional MVC View, data bindings occur on the server and the data is sent to the client along with the rest of the page markup. In an Ajax-style page, only the page markup is sent. Because of this, when the page is first loaded, it will contain no data. If this is not desired, it is possible to do a hybrid approach in which the initial page of data is rendered server-side and sent on the initial request along with the markup. For this example, however, we are demonstrating a pure Ajax approach.

In order to populate the page with data, we will use jQuery's Ajax capabilities to call our Web API and then convert the JSON result into a JavaScript array. jQuery's $.getJSON makes this very easy to do. $.getJSON takes two parameters. The first is the URL to the service that you would like to call, and the second is a function that will be executed upon successful completion of the web service call. By convention, most JavaScript programmers will define the function inline.

Inside our completion function, we will need to have code to dynamically generate some HTML in order to display our data. Before the invention of Knockout, you may have done this by looping through the JavaScript object array and using document.write statements to output the content. If you have ever written this type of code, you know that this is not ideal.

Thankfully, the Knockout.js library does all this hard work for us. All you need to do is define a template using plain HTML inside the view, with the addition of a few data-bind attributes. You then make a call to Knockout's applyBinding method. The only tricky part about this is that Knockout.js requires that the data used in its binding expressions are wrapped in a ks.observable object container. This container keeps track of changes made to the data and enables Knockout.js to keep the UI in sync with the data.

Again, we are in luck. The Knockout.Mapping library contains a ko.mapping.fromJS function that takes a JavaScript object and converts it into an observable.

An example is shown in Listing 11-18. The beauty of this example is how little code needs to be written.

Listing 11-18. WorkspaceList.cshtml.js Page Load Code

```
$(function () {
    $.getJSON("/api/CollaborationSpaces/Page/1",
        function (data) {
            var viewModel = ko.mapping.fromJS(data);
            ko.applyBindings(viewModel);
        }
    );
});
```

In the first line of Listing 11-13, we call the jQuery $() function. This function will execute as soon as the page's DOM is loaded. In older versions of jQuery, you needed to use $(document).ready to get the same behavior, but this is no longer necessary.

Inside $() we define another function that calls $.getJSON. This takes the URL /api/CollaborationSpaces/Page/1 as a parameter, which returns a result set that contains 20 rows of JSON-formatted data. The second parameter of $.getJSON is the success callback function. In this case, we implement the function inline. This inline function takes a single parameter called data–a JavaScript object created from the JSON results by the $.getJSON function.

Inside the success callback, we first use ko.mapping.fromJS to create a Knockout observable out of it. We then call ko.applyBindings to bind the data to the view.

Adding Binding Markup to the View

Now that we have set up data binding code that will fire as soon as the document has completed loading, we need to add some HTML elements to our view that will bind to the data.

To bind data to an HTML element, you use the HTML5 data-* attribute syntax to specify the data you are binding and which attribute of the current HTML element you wish to bind to. Let's start by adding an HTML span element that will contain the number of results found. We will bind the NumberOfResults property of the JSON to the text property of the span element, as follows:

1. Open the WorkspaceList.cshtml file in the code editor.

2. Add a span element after the h2 element.

3. Add the following attribute to the span element: data-bind="text: NumberOfResults".

4. Type **Records Found** after the span element.

5. The completed markup should look like Listing 11-19.

Listing 11-19. Using Data-Bind on a Span Element

```
@{
    ViewBag.Title = "Collaboration space List";
}
```

```
<h2>@ViewBag.Title</h2>
<p><span id="ItemsFound" data-bind="text: NumberOfResults"></span> Records Found</p>
<br />
```

```
@section scripts{
    <script src="~/Scripts/knockout-2.2.0.js"></script>
    <script src="~/Scripts/knockout.mapping-latest.js"></script>
    <script src="~/Scripts/Home/WorkspaceList.cshtml.js"></script>
}
```

If you save the file and refresh the page, you should see the text shown in Figure 11-2.

Figure 11-2. *Showing the number of records*

Next, we will add the data grid. To do this, we first define an HTML table including the header rows. We then create a row template. Finally, we add template binding to the table that will loop through the CollaborationSpaceSearchResults array from the JSON result. It is important that you use the THEAD tag for the header rows; otherwise, the header will not display properly.

The HTML table is made up of plain, unremarkable HTML, as shown in Listing 11-20.

Listing 11-20. The Table Definition

```
<table>
    <thead>
        <tr>
            <th>User Name</th>
            <th>Title</th>
            <th>Status</th>
            <th>Create Date</th>
        </tr>
    </thead>
</table>
```

Next, we add the template for the rows. Knockout.js templates are made up of HTML markup with data-bind attributes wrapped inside a script tag with a type attribute of "text/html". The template also requires an ID, which we will later use in the table's data binding expression. The row template is shown in Listing 11-21. The markup for the bindings is highlighted in bold text.

Listing 11-21. The Row Template

```
<script id="CollaborationSpaceTemplate" type="text/html">
    <tr>
        <td data-bind="text: UserName"></td>
        <td data-bind="text: Title"></td>
        <td>
            Views:    <span data-bind="text: NumberViews"></span><br />
            Comments: <span data-bind="text: NumberComments"></span>
        </td>
        <td data-bind="text: CreateDate"></td>
    </tr>
</script>
```

The final piece of this puzzle is the data binding for the table. It uses a slightly more complex binding syntax that binds the table to the template. As with the other bindings, you will add a data-bind attribute to the table element. Inside the binding, you specify that you want to use a template binding, and then inside curly braces, you specify the name of the template followed by a foreach binding expression tied to the CollaborationSearchResults array. Listing 11-22 shows the table definition with the binding syntax added.

Listing 11-22. Table Definition with Data Binding

```
<table data-bind="template: {name: 'CollaborationSpaceTemplate', foreach:
CollaborationSpaceSearchResults}">
    <thead>
        <tr>
            <th>User Name</th>
            <th>Title</th>
            <th>Status</th>
            <th>Create Date</th>
        </tr>
    </thead>
</table>
```

If you run the project, you should see the first page of data.

Adding Paging to the Grid

In order for the user to navigate between data pages, you will need to add some user interface elements to facilitate this. For this example, we will use simple Back and Next buttons placed below the grid.

As users move between pages, they need to keep track of the current page and sort expression being used. The sorting functionality will be added in the next section.

To do this, we will add some global variables to the WorkspaceList.cshtml.js file. We will then add a new function called Move. This function will make a call to the service to retrieve the next page of data and then rebind the results to the web page. The Move function takes a number as a parameter. The number can be positive or negative. To move forward one page, you would call Move(1). To move back, you can call Move(-1). As we do this, we can also refactor the code so that all the back-end calls are moved to a single method called getData. The updated JavaScript file is shown in Listing 11-23.

Listing 11-23. The Move Function from WorkspaceList.cshtml.js

```
var CurrentSort="CreateDate";
var CurrentPage=1;

function getData() {
    $.getJSON("/api/CollaborationSpaces/Page/" + CurrentPage + "/" + CurrentSort,
        function (data) {
            togglePageButtons(data);
            var viewModel = ko.mapping.fromJS(data);
            ko.applyBindings(viewModel);
        }
        );
}
$(function () {
    getData();
});
function Move(pages) {
    CurrentPage = CurrentPage + pages;
    getData();
}

function togglePageButtons(data) {
    if (data) {
        if (data.CurrentPage == 1) {
            $("#back").hide();
        }
        else {
            $("#back").show();
        }

        if (data.CurrentPage == (data.NumberOfResults / data.ItemsPerPage)) {
            $("#next").hide();
        }
        else {
            $("#next").show();
        }
    }
}
```

In addition to the Move function, we also add the togglePageButtons. This function uses the data returned from the web service call to determine the current page and the number of pages there are in total. It uses this information to hide the Back button when we are on the first page and hide the next button if we are on the last page.

In the view, we will update the table definition so it includes a footer section for the Back and Next buttons. The modified table definition is shown in Listing 11-24.

Listing 11-24. Table with Paging Added

```
<table data-bind="template: {name: 'CollaborationSpaceTemplate', foreach:
CollaborationSpaceSearchResults}" class="grid">
    <thead>
        <tr>
            <th>User Name</th>
            <th>Title</th>
            <th>Status</th>
            <th>Create Date</th>
        </tr>
    </thead>
    <tfoot>
        <tr>
            <td colspan="4" class="Pager">
                <span id="back" onclick="Move(-1)">&lt; Back</span>
                <span id="next" onclick="Move(1)">Next &gt;</span>
            </td>
        </tr>
    </tfoot>
</table>
```

If you run the project, you should now be able to move between data pages.

Adding Sorting

The last bit of functionality allows users to change how the data is sorted by clicking the column headers of the grid. To do this, we will add a new function to `WorkspaceList.cshtml.js` called `Sort`. The `Sort` function takes a string containing a sort expression as a parameter. The `Sort` function is shown in Listing 11-25.

Listing 11-25. Adding the Sort Function to WorkspaceList.cshtml.js

```
function Sort(column) {
    CurrentSort = column;
    CurrentPage = 1;
    getData();
}
```

The table definition in `WorkspaceList.cshtml` again needs to be updated so that each of the header columns is a clickable link. Each will have an `onclick` event to call the `Sort` function. The updated table is shown in Listing 11-26.

Listing 11-26. WorkspaceList.cshtml

```
<table data-bind="template: {name: 'CollaborationSpaceTemplate', foreach:
CollaborationSpaceSearchResults}" class="grid">
    <thead>
        <tr>
            <th><a href="#UserName" onclick="Sort('UserName')">User Name</a></th>
            <th><a href="#Title" onclick="Sort('Title')">Title</a></th>
```

```
        <th><a href="#NumberComments" onclick="Sort('NumberComments')">Status</a></th>
        <th><a href="#CreateDate" onclick="Sort('CreateDate')">Create Date</a></th>
    </tr>
  </thead>
  <tfoot>
    <tr>
      <td colspan="4" class="Pager">
        <span id="back" onclick="Move(-1)">&lt; Back</span>
        <span id="next" onclick="Move(1)">Next &gt;</span>
      </td>
    </tr>
  </tfoot>
</table>
```

If you run this page, you should be able to sort and page through the data.

Improving the User Experience

At this point, even though the data grid is functional, it is not user-friendly or attractive. The first problem is that it does not show any indication that something is happening when sorting or paging. When you are developing and testing on a local machine, the pages will load so quickly that you may not notice this as a problem. In production, however, when people are accessing this remotely, network latency will often cause the user to wait several seconds before the data is loaded. It is a best practice to give the user some indication the page is waiting.

For this example, we will use a DIV element that contains the text "Loading....". At the beginning of each web service call, we will show the text block. When the loading has completed, we will hide it. To do this, we add the markup shown in Listing 11-27 to WorkspaceList.cshtml, just below the table.

Listing 11-27. Adding a Data Loading Indicator

```
<div id="LoadingDiv">Loading...</div>
```

To implement the showing and hiding, we will update each of the JavaScript functions that make web service calls. Listing 11-28 show the updated Sort function.

Listing 11-28. Sort Function Updated to Show and Hide the Loading Indicator

```
function getData() {
    $.getJSON("/api/CollaborationSpaces/Page/" + CurrentPage + "/" + CurrentSort,
        function (data) {
            togglePageButtons(data);
            var viewModel = ko.mapping.fromJS(data);
            ko.applyBindings(viewModel);
            $("#LoadingDiv").hide();
        }
    );
}
function Move(pages) {
    CurrentPage = CurrentPage + pages;
    $("#LoadingDiv").show();
    getData();
}
```

```
function Sort(column) {
    $("#LoadingDiv").show();
    CurrentSort = column;
    CurrentPage = 1;
    getData();
}
```

The loading indicator will now be shown briefly whenever the page is fetching data.

The next important thing our grid needs is style. The style sheet should be modified so that it adds shading and formatting to the table. A reference to the style sheet then needs to be added to the view. CSS file references are normally added the header section of an HTML document. Since this page uses a layout page and does not contain its own header section, we must first define a section inside the layout page and then include the section in the view. Listing 11-29 shows the addition of the new section in _Layout.cshtml and Listing 11-30 shows the CSS reference added to page.

Listing 11-29. Adding a Section to Views/Shared/_Layout.cshtml

```
<!DOCTYPE html>
<html>
<head>
    <meta charset="utf-8" />
    <meta name="viewport" content="width=device-width" />
    <title>@ViewBag.Title</title>
    @Styles.Render("~/Content/css")
    @RenderSection("header", required: false)
    @Scripts.Render("~/bundles/modernizr")
</head>
<body>
    <header>
    <div class="content-wrapper">
        <div class="float-left">
            <p class="site-title">
            <a href="~/">Web API Demo</a></p>
        </div>
    </div>
</header>
    @RenderBody()

    @Scripts.Render("~/bundles/jquery")
    @RenderSection("scripts", required: false)
</body>
</html>
```

Listing 11-30. Referencing the CSS File in Home/WorkspaceList.cshtml

```
@{
    ViewBag.Title = "Collaboration space List";
}
@section header{
    <link href="~/Content/Home/WorkspaceList.cshtml.css" rel="stylesheet" />
}

<h2>@ViewBag.Title</h2>
<p><span id="ItemsFound" data-bind="text: NumberOfResults"></span> Records Found</p>
```

```html
<p>Page <span id="PageNumber" data-bind="text: CurrentPage"></span></p>
<br />

<table data-bind="template: {name: 'CollaborationSpaceTemplate', foreach:
CollaborationSpaceSearchResults}" id="DataGrid" class="grid">
    <thead>
        <tr>
            <th><a href="#UserName" onclick="Sort('UserName')">User Name</a></th>
            <th><a href="#Title" onclick="Sort('Title')">Title</a></th>
            <th><a href="#NumberComments" onclick="Sort('NumberComments')">Status</a></th>
            <th><a href="#CreateDate" onclick="Sort('CreateDate')">Create Date</a></th>
        </tr>
    </thead>
    <tfoot>
        <tr>
            <td colspan="4" class="Pager">
                <span id="back" onclick="Move(-1)">&lt; Back</span>
                <span id="next" onclick="Move(1)">Next &gt;</span>
            </td>
        </tr>
    </tfoot>
</table>
<div id="LoadingDiv">Loading...</div>
<script id="CollaborationSpaceTemplate" type="text/html">
    <tr>
        <td data-bind="text: UserName"></td>
        <td data-bind="text: Title"></td>
        <td>
            Views:    <span data-bind="text: NumberViews"></span><br />
            Comments: <span data-bind="text: NumberComments"></span>
        </td>
        <td data-bind="text: CreateDate"></td>
    </tr>
</script>

@section scripts{
    <script src="~/Scripts/knockout-2.2.0.js"></script>
    <script src="~/Scripts/knockout.mapping-latest.js"></script>
    <script src="~/Scripts/Home/WorkspaceList.cshtml.js"></script>
}
```

The very last thing we need to do is add alternating colors to the table rows. jQuery makes this job very simple. Inside the style sheet, we will create styles for odd and even rows, as shown in Listing 11-31.

Listing 11-31. Content/Home/WorkspaceList.cshtml.css

```css
.grid {
    background-color: #fff;
    margin: 5px 0 10px 10px;
    padding-left: 5px;
    width: 95%;
}
```

```css
.grid td {
    color: #1a1a1a;
    vertical-align: top;
}

.grid td textarea {
    width:98%;
    border-width:2px;
    height: 3em;
    border-color:lightblue;
}

    .grid td input[type="text"], .grid td input[type="number"] {
        border: 2px solid lightblue;
        width: 98%;
        height: 2em;
    }

.grid th {
    background-color: #333;
    color: #fff;
    font-size: large;
    font-weight: bolder;
    padding-bottom: 5px;
    padding-left: 13px;
    padding-top: 5px;
    text-align: left;
}
.grid th a{color: #fff; text-decoration:none;}

.odd {
    background-color: #ebeced;
}

.even {
    background-color: #99acb9;
}

.Pager {
    list-style-type: none;
    width: 100%;
    text-align: center;
    background-color: #333;
    padding: 1px;
}

    .Pager td {
        display: inline;
        font-size: large;
        font-weight: bolder;
```

```
        padding-left: 13px;
        text-align: left;
        color: #fff;
    }

    .Pager span {
        color: #fff;
        cursor: pointer;
        padding:5px;
    }
```

Inside the JavaScript file, we will create a function that uses jQuery's even and odd selectors to apply the even style to all even rows and the odd style to the odd rows. For the TR elements contained in the THEAD and TFOOT, the settings from the style sheet override the setting from the added class. If this was not the case, we would need to modify the jQuery selector to include exceptions for these table rows.

We then call the stripe function after each web service call has been completed so that the colors can be applied. Listing 11-32 shows the definition of the stripe function and the modified getData function that now calls it after the bindings have been applied.

Listing 11-32. The Stripe Function

```
function stripe() {
    $("tr:even").addClass("even");
    $("tr:odd").addClass("odd");
}

function getData() {
    $.getJSON("/api/CollaborationSpaces/Page/" + CurrentPage + "/" + CurrentSort,
        function (data) {
            togglePageButtons(data);
            var viewModel = ko.mapping.fromJS(data);
            ko.applyBindings(viewModel);
            stripe();
            $("#LoadingDiv").hide();
        }
    );
}
```

Figure 11-3 shows the finished product.

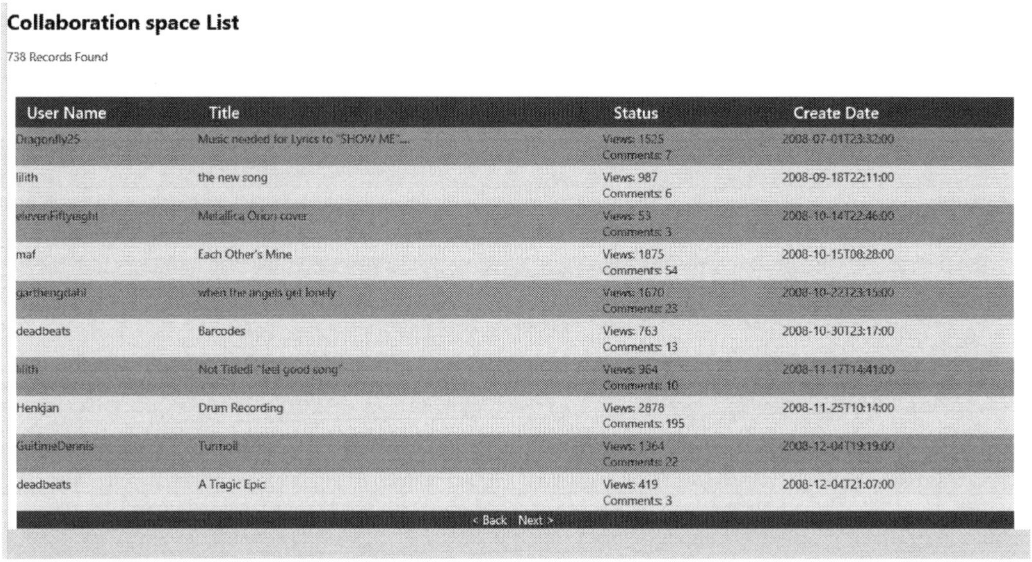

Collaboration space List

738 Records Found

User Name	Title	Status	Create Date
Dragonfly25	Music needed for Lyrics to "SHOW ME"...	Views: 1525 Comments: 7	2008-07-01T23:32:00
lilith	the new song	Views: 987 Comments: 6	2008-09-18T22:11:00
elevenFiftyeight	Metallica Orion cover	Views: 53 Comments: 3	2008-10-14T22:46:00
maf	Each Other's Mine	Views: 1875 Comments: 54	2008-10-15T08:28:00
garthengdahl	when the angels get lonely	Views: 1670 Comments: 23	2008-10-23T23:15:00
deadbeats	Barcodes	Views: 763 Comments: 13	2008-10-30T23:17:00
lilith	Not Titled! "feel good song"	Views: 364 Comments: 10	2008-11-17T14:41:00
Henkjan	Drum Recording	Views: 2878 Comments: 195	2008-11-25T10:14:00
GuitinieDennis	Turmoil	Views: 1364 Comments: 22	2008-12-04T19:19:00
deadbeats	A Tragic Epic	Views: 419 Comments: 3	2008-12-04T21:07:00
		< Back Next >	

Figure 11-3. *A screenshot of the completed example*

11-3. Implementing Two-Way Data Binding Using Web API and Knockout

Problem

You are developing a form in an Ajax-style application. You would like to be able to save data and update your form without needing to make full postbacks. In addition, you would like to work in a semi-connected fashion in order to optimize the use of network resources.

Solution

Implementing Ajax-type forms can give the end user a nicer experience, but it is considerably more work than creating a server-side form. Thankfully, jQuery, Knockout and other libraries can simplify this process. Understanding these libraries and using them effectively can save you countless hours of work and allow you to create rich cross-browser maintainable solutions.

In this recipe, you will do the following:

- Define a simple model that uses Entity Framework Code First to communicate with and a back-end database.

- Take advantage of .NET's data annotations to define the structure of the database and to provide a basis for client-side validation logic.

- Create an API controller that provides read, write, update, and delete functions for the model. The example will only demonstrate the read, write, and update capabilities, but can easily be adapted to perform deleting as well.

- Create a View that uses jQuery and Knockout to provide a rich in-browser application experience.

- Demonstrate advanced features such as how to use Knockout binding handlers to apply custom formatting.

How It Works

This solution uses the ASP.NET MVC 4 Web API template. The template includes many of the required JavaScript libraries and provides boilerplate code to get started on the web service. Do the following to create the project:

1. Open Visual Studio. Select New ➤ Project from the File menu.

2. In the New Project window, select the ASP.NET MVC 4 Web Application template. Name the project **Ch11.R3.Web** and name the solution **Ch11.R3**. Click OK.

3. On the New ASP.NET MVC 4 Project page, select the Web API template. Make sure that the Razor view engine is selected and that the "Create a unit test project" check box is not checked. Click OK.

Creating the Model

We will implement a simple model that represents a list of appointments. Each record consists of some basic information about the person you are meeting and include the date of the appointment. To create the model, complete the following steps:

1. Right-click the Models folder, and select Add ➤ Class.

2. Name the file **AppointmentModels.cs**.

3. Define a class called Person inside the class file.

4. Add four properties to the class:

    a. PersonId: This will use the int data type and represents the unique identifier of the user. It will be used as the primary key for the database.

    b. FirstName: A string represents the person's first name.

    c. LastName: A string representing the person's last name.

    d. AppointmentDate: A nullable DateTime value that represents when you would like to meet this person.

5. Since we plan to use this class to define a database table using Entity Framework Code First, we will need to use data annotations to define the structure of the back end. Without annotations, Code First will resort to using defaults such as varchar(max) data types for string values. To use data annotations, add a using statement for System.ComponentModel. DataAnnotations namespace and then add the following attributes:

    a. Add a Required attribute for each property except PersonId. Use the ErrorMessage parameter of the attribute to add the message that you would like to display to the user when the value is omitted.

    b. Add a MaxLength attribute to the FirstName and LastName properties. The value specified here will be used by Entity Framework to define the length of the field in SQL Server. If the attribute is omitted, the fields will be created as Varchar(max). Set each so that the max length is 50 characters.

     c.   Add `Display` attributes to the `FirstName`, `LastName`, and `AppointmentDate`. This value will be displayed in the view as the label for each field.

6.   Since we will be using Web API to send and receive data between the client, we will need to also include a `DataContract` attribute for the class definition and `DataMember` attributes for each of the properties. A limitation in the JSON serialization component will throw an illegal operation exception if we omit the `DataContract` attributes and apply the `Required` attribute to any value types in our model. To add the attributes, do the following:

     a.   Add a reference to the `System.Runtime.Serialization` assembly to the project by right-clicking the `References` folder in Solution Explorer and selecting Add Reference. Click the Assemblies node and then search for `System.Runtime.Serialization`. Tick the check box for the assembly, and then click the OK button.

     b.   Add a using statement for the `System.Runtime.Serialization` namespace to the `AppointmentModel.cs` file.

     c.   Apply the attributes, as shown in Listing 11-33.

Listing 11-33. PeopleIWouldLikeToMeet Model

```
using System;
using System.ComponentModel.DataAnnotations;
using System.Runtime.Serialization;

namespace Ch11.R3.Web.Models
{
    [DataContract]
    public class Person
    {
        [DataMember(IsRequired = true)]
        public int PersonId { get; set; }

        [Required(ErrorMessage ="First Name is required.")]
        [MaxLength(50)]
        [Display(Name="First Name")]
        [DataMember(IsRequired = true)]
        public string FirstName{get;set; }

        [Required(ErrorMessage ="Last Name is required.")]
        [MaxLength(50)]
        [Display(Name = "Last Name")]
        [DataMember(IsRequired = true)]
        public string LastName { get; set; }

        [Display(Name = "Appointment Date")]
        [DataType(DataType.DateTime)]
        [Required]
        [DataMember(IsRequired = true)]
        public DateTime  AppointmentDate{get;set;}
    }

}
```

Creating the Data Context

In order to use Entity Framework Code First, we will need to define a data context class. To do this, we will define a class that extends System.Data.Entity.DbContext. This class will contain a single public property called People. Do the following to add this class to the project:

1. Right-click the Models folder, and select Add ➤ Class.

2. Name the class **AppointmentsContext**.

3. The completed class should look like Listing 11-34.

   Listing 11-34. The PeepsContext Class

   ```
   using System.Data.Entity;

   namespace Ch11.R3.Web.Models
   {
       public class AppointmentsContext : DbContext
       {
           public DbSet<Person> People { get; set; }
       }
   }
   ```

Creating the Database

To create the database, we will use several commandlets that can be executed via the NuGet Package Manager Console. For more information about using this technique, please refer to Recipe 7-6.

To create the database, do the following:

1. Open the Package Manager Console by clicking View ➤ Other Windows ➤ Package Manager Console.

2. From the BUILD menu, select Build Solution.

3. In the console, run the command Enable-Migrations. Note that if you have more than one project open in Visual Studio, you will need to specify the project name using Enable-Migration -ProjectName Ch11.R3.Web. You should see a class file named Configuration open in the code editor window. You can close this file.

4. After the command completes, enter the command **Add-Migration "First"**. A Migrations folder and classes will be added to the project. A class file should open in the code editor. It should contain a method named Up that contains a CreateTable operation for creating the People table. It should also contain a Down operation that drops the table. If you do not see this and instead have empty Up and Down methods, be sure to first build your project before running the Add-Migration command.

5. Run the Update-Database command to create the database and add the People table. The database will use the default connection defined in the project's Web.config file, which will point to a LocalDB instance. The result of this operation is that a new database will be created under the LocalDB instance associated with your user account named Ch11.R3.Web.Models.AppointmentsContext containing a single table named People. Figure 11-4 shows this database in the Visual Studio SQL Server Object Explorer.

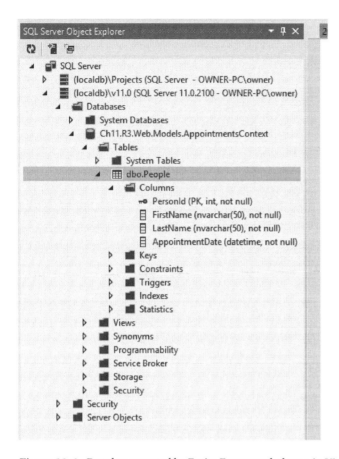

Figure 11-4. *Database created by Entity Framework shown in Visual Studio*

Creating the API Controller

Visual Studio can scaffold an API controller based on a model class and its associated dbContext. Using this feature, you can quickly generate boilerplate code for your API that can perform create, read, update, and delete (CRUD) operations against your data store. The generated code also fills in the HttpResponseExceptions for cases such as when you try to update a record that does not exist in the data source. Even if you plan to factor the data access code to your repository, the generated code is still a great starting point. The following steps explain how to generate an API controller using scaffolding:

1. Right-click the Controllers node in Solution Explorer, and select Add ➤ Controller.

2. Name the controller **AppointmentController**. Select the API controller with read/write actions using the Entity Framework template.

3. For the model class, select Person. If you do not see this class in the list, make sure that you compiled your project.

4. For the Data context class, select AppointmentsContext.

5. Click Add to create the class. For this exercise, we will only be using the GET and POST methods. The generated code for these methods is shown in Listing 11-35.

Listing 11-35. PeepsController

```
namespace Ch11.R3.Web.Controllers
{
    public class AppointmentController : ApiController
    {
        private AppointmentsContext db = new AppointmentsContext();

        // GET api/Appointment
        public IEnumerable<Person> GetPeople()
        {
            return db.People.AsEnumerable();
        }

        //other methods ...

        // POST api/Appointment
        public HttpResponseMessage PostPerson(Person person)
        {
            if (ModelState.IsValid)
            {
                db.People.Add(person);
                db.SaveChanges();

                HttpResponseMessage response =
                    Request.CreateResponse(HttpStatusCode.Created, person);

                response.Headers.Location =
                 new Uri(Url.Link("DefaultApi", new { id = person.PersonId }));
                return response;
            }
            else
            {
                return Request.CreateResponse(HttpStatusCode.BadRequest);
            }
        }

        //delete method ommited

    protected override void Dispose(bool disposing)
        {
            db.Dispose();
            base.Dispose(disposing);
        }
    }
}
```

The generated code follows the REST (Representational State Transfer) architectural style. Each method is associated with a corresponding HTTP verb. Using this API, we can create a client-side state machine where progress is shown via links between operations. Note that in the POST method, a URL is added to the response header. This link can be used by the client to locate the record that we just created.

While this code is good, it does not fully solve the problem stated in the beginning of this recipe. We would like to have a partially connected application that would allow the user to create and modify many records, and then update the server in a batch.

While you could use the API as is and have the client loop through the records and make a separate API call for each, this would not be very efficient from a networking standpoint. In many modern systems, this is very important because users may be using mobile devices such as tablets that have limited battery life and may be communicating over a metered connection.

Looping through the records also creates the risk that if users are on a slow connection, they may halt the operation before it is completed. This would result in some records not being updated.

A better solution would be to modify the POST method so that it accepted an IEnumerable<Person> rather than just a Person. This would allow all records to be updated in a single network call. You can even take this a step further and use the single method for both updates and deletes, and check the value of the PersonId property of each record to determine if it is a new record or an existing record that needs to be updated.

By doing this, however, you would be breaking the REST conventions by combining both update and create operations in the POST method. In fact, it would be more accurate to call this an RPC-style operation. If you are developing a public API, you should avoid this pattern. If the API is intended for use only with your page, however, this technique may be a good compromise. You are getting most of the advantages of using RAW HTTP while decreasing the number of required network operations. The modified POST method is shown in Listing 11-36.

Listing 11-36. Modified Version of PostPerson Renamed to PostPeople

```
// POST api/Peeps
public HttpResponseMessage PostPeople(IEnumerable<Person> people)
{
    if (ModelState.IsValid && people!=null)
    {
        //loop through the collection
        // if PersonId ==0 it is a new record otherwise update existing
        foreach (var person in people)
        {
            if (person.PersonId == 0)
            {
                db.People.Add(person);
            }
            else
            {
                db.Entry(person).State = EntityState.Modified;
            }
        }
        try
        {
                db.SaveChanges();
        }
        catch (DbUpdateConcurrencyException)
        {
                return Request.CreateResponse(HttpStatusCode.NotFound);
        }
```

```
        //return updated people collection in the response
        HttpResponseMessage response =
            Request.CreateResponse(HttpStatusCode.OK, people);
        return response;
    }
    else
    {
        return Request.CreateResponse(HttpStatusCode.BadRequest);
    }
}
```

Adding Other Third-Party JavaScript Libraries

Before we begin construction of our view, we will need to add several additional libraries that will fill a few gaps in the client-side programming model, including the following:

- *moment.js*: This library includes several useful extensions for working with dates in the browser. Since JavaScript does not have any native date formatting functions, this library will be helpful for displaying dates in a human friendly fashion.

- *knockout.mapping*: This library simplifies the process of wrapping normal JavaScript objects into Knockout observables. The Knockout observable provides the magic that allows two-way data binding on the client side.

To add these libraries, we will use the NuGet package manager.

1. Right-click the References node and select Manage NuGet Packages.

2. Click the Online node in the Manage NuGet Package window and search for **knockout**.

3. Select knockout.mapping and then click the Install button.

4. After the install has completed, search for **moment.js**.

5. Select moment.js and then click the Install button.

Creating a New Bundle

Now that we have added several libraries to your project that you will use together, it may be a good idea to create a new script bundle. Script bundles are helpful in a few ways. First, they can help prevent NuGet package updates from breaking your pages. For example, if you drag the Knockout2.2.0.js to your page and then update the package so that it uses Knockout2.2.1.js, your page will break because the original file will be deleted. You can fix this issue when using bundles by defining it using Knockout-{version}.js. This will automatically include the correct version in your pages. You should be careful, however. If you have more than one version of the library in the scripts directory of your project, it will use the first one it finds. For example, if you have knockout.2.1.0.js and knockout.2.2.0.js, the bundle will use knockout.2.1.0.js. For this reason, it is best to manage third-party JavaScript libraries using NuGet and to only install one version of the library at a time.

The other advantage of bundles is that when in release mode, it will automatically minify and combine the scripts included in the bundle.

To create a new bundle that includes Knockout, knockout.mapping, and moment.js, do the following:

1. Open the file App_Start/BundleConfig.cs.

2. Create a new bundle named ~/**bundles/knockout**, as shown in Listing 11-37.

Listing 11-37. New Bundle

```
bundles.Add(new ScriptBundle("~/bundles/knockout").Include(
                    "~/Scripts/knockout-{version}.js",
                    "~/Scripts/knockout.mapping-latest.js",
                    "~/Scripts/moment.js"));
```

Creating the View

The next step is to create the view. The view will be split into the following three files:

- Views\Home\Appointments.cshtml: This contains the HTML markup.

- Content\Home\Appointments.css : This contains the CSS style sheet.

- Scripts\Home\Appointments.js: This contains the view logic that allows the view to communicate with the web service.

Do the following to create the view:

1. Open Controllers/HomeController.cs and create a new action, as shown in Listing 11-38.

Listing 11-38. HomeController with the Appointments Action

```
public ActionResult Appointments ()
{
   return View();
}
```

2. Right-click the Appointments action and select Add View in the pop-up menu.

3. In the Add View dialog box, make sure Razor is selected as the view engine and that create a strongly-typed view is selected.

4. Select Person as the model class and Create for the scaffolding template.

5. Make sure Use a Layout or Master Page is selected, and then click Add.

The resulting generated code adds the basic required functionality for a new item form. It uses HTML helpers to create the form fields, labels, and validation logic that is defined in our model's data annotations. The generated code is shown in Listing 11-39.

Listing 11-39. View Generated from Scaffolding

```
@model Ch11.R3.Web.Models.Person

@{
    ViewBag.Title = "Appointments";
}

<h2>Peeps</h2>
```

```
@using (Html.BeginForm()) {
    @Html.ValidationSummary(true)

    <fieldset>
        <legend>Person</legend>

        <div class="editor-label">
            @Html.LabelFor(model => model.FirstName)
        </div>
        <div class="editor-field">
            @Html.EditorFor(model => model.FirstName)
            @Html.ValidationMessageFor(model => model.FirstName)
        </div>

        <div class="editor-label">
            @Html.LabelFor(model => model.LastName)
        </div>
        <div class="editor-field">
            @Html.EditorFor(model => model.LastName)
            @Html.ValidationMessageFor(model => model.LastName)
        </div>

        <div class="editor-label">
            @Html.LabelFor(model => model.AppointmentDate)
        </div>
        <div class="editor-field">
            @Html.EditorFor(model => model.AppointmentDate)
            @Html.ValidationMessageFor(model => model.AppointmentDate)
        </div>

        <p>
            <input type="submit" value="Create" />
        </p>
    </fieldset>
}

<div>
    @Html.ActionLink("Back to List", "Index")
</div>

@section Scripts {
    @Scripts.Render("~/bundles/jqueryval")
}
```

6. In the scripts section of the view, add references for the jqueryui bundle and the
    knockout bundle we created earlier. You should also add a reference to /Scripts/
    Home/Appointments.js. The updated scripts section is shown in Listing 11-40. Note
    the order that the scripts are added. This is important. They must be added in order of
    dependencies.

Listing 11-40. Adding the Script Bundles

```
@section scripts{
    @Scripts.Render("~/bundles/jqueryui")
    @Scripts.Render("~/bundles/jqueryval")
    @Scripts.Render("~/bundles/knockout")
    <script src="~/Scripts/Home/Peeps.js"></script>
}
```

If you press F5 to begin debugging and then navigate to /Home/Appointments, you should see the form. Clicking the Create button should trigger form validation.

Because we marked the AppointmentDate field as [DataType(DataType.DateTime)] in the model, the field will also be validated to ensure that the input can be converted into a date. To make input easier, we will use the jQueryUI date picker. The date picker, as with most of the jQueryUI user interface extensions, can be applied to normal HTML INPUT elements using a single line of JavaScript. Do the following to add this functionality:

1. Right-click the Scripts node in Solution Explorer and select Add ➤ New Folder.

2. Name the folder **Home**.

3. Right-click the Home folder and select Add ➤ JavaScript file.

4. Name the file **Peeps.js**.

5. Add a JavaScript function that will execute after the page's document object model has been loaded, as shown in Listing 11-41.

    Listing 11-41. Adding a Date Picker to the WhenToMeet Input Element

    ```
    $(function () {
        $("#AppointmentDate").datepicker();
    });
    ```

Now that this has been added, clicking the date field will automatically cause a calendar to be displayed and text will not be permitted to be entered into the text box. Since we did not add any of the styles needed for jqueryui, however, the calendar will lack a background and will look generally unattractive, as shown in Figure 11-5.

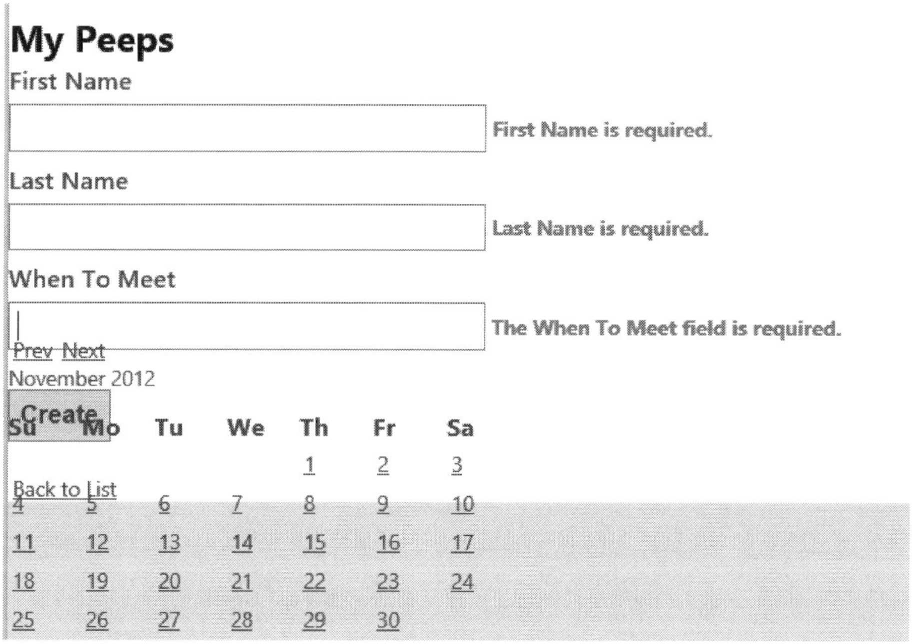

My Peeps

First Name

First Name is required.

Last Name

Last Name is required.

When To Meet

The When To Meet field is required.

Prev Next
November 2012

Create

Su	Mo	Tu	We	Th	Fr	Sa
				1	2	3
4	5	6	7	8	9	10
11	12	13	14	15	16	17
18	19	20	21	22	23	24
25	26	27	28	29	30	

Back to List

Figure 11-5. *The form generated by the scaffolding*

To correct the formatting issues, we will add the `jqueryui-style` bundle to the page, as follows:jqueryui-style bundle.

1. Since the layout page did not contain a section for adding content to the header, we will need to define a section. To do this, open the file `Views\Shared\_Layout.cshtml` and add a section definition, as shown in Listing 11-42.

Listing 11-42. Adding a Header Section to _layout.cshtml

```
<!DOCTYPE html>
<html>
<head>
    <meta charset="utf-8" />
    <meta name="viewport" content="width=device-width" />
    <title>@ViewBag.Title</title>
    @Styles.Render("~/Content/css")
    @RenderSection("header", required: false)
    @Scripts.Render("~/bundles/modernizr")
</head>
<body>
    @RenderBody()

    @Scripts.Render("~/bundles/jquery")
    @RenderSection("scripts", required: false)
</body>
</html>
```

2. Consume the header section inside your view and add a reference to the jqueryui themes file.

3. Add a link statement for the CSS file that will be used for the page. We will create this CSS file later. The header section is shown in Listing 11-43.

4. You can also modify the page title and then use it inside the h2 tag. This is a good technique to use if these will contain the same content.

5. Delete the Back to List link since it is not needed.

Listing 11-43. Header Section in Peeps.cshtml

```
@model Ch11.R3.Web.Models.Person
@{
    ViewBag.Title = "My Appointments";
}
@section header{
        @Styles.Render("~/Content/themes/base/css")
        <link href="~/Content/Home/Appointments.css" rel="stylesheet" />
}
<h2>@ViewBag.Title</h2>
<!-- More code here -->
```

After making these changes, if you refresh the page, the calendar should now have the default jqueryui styling, as shown in Figure 11-6.

Figure 11-6. *Calendar with the jQueryUI default theme applied*

Since we want the view to have the capability to allow users to add and modify a set of records before posting changes to the server, we will need to add a grid that will display each record and allow the records to be selected for editing. Since we all also need to let people know that the page is waiting on server operations such as saving or loading, we also add a loading indicator wrapped in a DIV tag.

The grid will use a Knockout template. For a full explanation of how the templates work, please refer to Recipe 11-2. It will consist of four columns, with the first column containing an Edit link. In order to split the page into two columns, both the table and the form have been wrapped in HTML section tags. The updated markup is shown in Listing 11-44.

Listing 11-44. *Adding a Grid Using Knockout Template Bindings*

```
@model Ch11.R3.Web.Models.Person
@{
    ViewBag.Title = "My Appointments";
}
@section header{
        @Styles.Render("~/Content/themes/base/css")
    <link href="~/Content/Home/Appointments.css" rel="stylesheet" />
}
<h2>@ViewBag.Title</h2>
    <div id="LoadingDiv">Loading ...</div>
<div id="ContainerDiv">
<section id="PeepsList">

    <table data-bind="template: {name: 'PeepsTemplate', foreach: People}" class="grid">
        <thead>
            <tr>
                <th></th>
                <th>First Name</th>
                <th>Last Name</th>
                <th>Date</th>
            </tr>
        </thead>
    </table>

    <script id="PeepsTemplate" type="text/html">
    <tr>
        <td><a href="#" class="edit" data-bind="click: $parent.selectItem">Edit</a> </td>
        <td data-bind="text: FirstName"></td>
        <td data-bind="text: LastName"></td>
        <td data-bind="dateString: AppointmentDate, datePattern: 'MM/DD/YYYY'"></td>
    </tr>
</script>
</section>

<!-- Other Code here -->
```

In order for the layout of the page to look as expected, we will need to add several styles to the Peeps.css file. If you have not done so already, create Peeps.css.

1. Right-click the Content node inside Solution Explorer, and select Create ➤ New Folder.

2. Name the folder **Home**.

3. Right-click the new folder and select Add ➤ Style Sheet.

4. Name the new style sheet **Appointments.css**.

5. Inside Appointments.css, define styles for the HTML elements PeepsList, PeepsForms, and ContentDiv. In CSS (and jQuery) we can select a page element by its ID property by prefixing the CSS selector with a #. The completed style sheet is shown in Listing 11-45.

Listing 11-45. Style Sheet for the Appointments View

```
#PeepsList {
    width: 400px;
    float: left;
    margin-right: 15px;
    margin-left: 15px;
}
#PeepsForm {
    width:600px;
    float:right;
    margin-right: 15px;
    margin-left: 15px;
}

#PeepsForm ul {
    list-style:none;
}

#ContainerDiv {
    display: none;
}
```

Creating a Client-side View Model

In order to enable client-side data binding with Knockout, we need to create a client-side view model for it to bind to. In some cases, such as in Recipe 11-2, this can be done by wrapping a JSON result returned from the server in a Knockout observableArray using the ko.mapping.fromJS command that is available in the knockout.mapping library. In this case, however, this will not work because we are starting with no data. We will also need to add functions to our view model in order to complete this functionality. That cannot be done from JSON.

The view model will be made of two JavaScript classes. The first will be a Person class that will mirror the Person class in our server-side model. This is shown in Listing 11-46.

Listing 11-46. JavaScript Person Model in Scripts/Home/Appointment.js

```
function Person(FirstName, LastName, AppointmentDate)
{
    var self = this;
    self.FirstName = ko.observable(FirstName);
    self.LastName = ko.observable(LastName);
    self.PersonId = 0;
    self.AppointmentDate = ko.observable(AppointmentDate);
}
```

In the client-side person model, we define each of the properties of the object as ko.observable. This allows them to be data bound.

Next, we define a JavaScript class called PeopleModel. This class will act as the view model for the page and will attach to bindings included in the page's markup. This class will consist of an observable array of Person objects that we will call People. People will be bound to the grid. The view model will also consist of another Person object named NewPerson, which will be bound to the form. The NewPerson object will be set to point to the first object in the array. Because we are using observables, this creates an interesting effect. When changes are made to items in the form, the changes are automatically applied to the first item in the grid. This is because the first row of the grid and the form are bound to the same observable object. The PeopleModel is shown in Listing 11-47.

Listing 11-47. The PeopleModel in Scripts/Home/Appointment.js

```
function PeopleModel(People)
{
    var self = this;
    self.People = ko.observableArray([new Person("", "", "")]);
    self.NewPerson = ko.observable(self.People()[0]);
}
```

Now that we defined the class, we add a line of code to the DOM ready function that we created in Listing 11-41, which will create an instance of the class and assign it to variable named viewModel, as shown in Listing 11-48.

Listing 11-48. Creating an Instance of PeopleModel When the DOM Is Ready

```
$(function () {
    $("#AppointmentDate").datepicker();
    var viewModel =  new PeopleModel();

});
```

Using the Appointments Web API

Next, we will add code to our DOM ready function that will try to load a list of existing items using an API call to the GET method on our API/Appointments service. If data is found, it will add the data to the view model. It will also show the loading indicator, and then hide it after the service call has completed. This is shown in Listing 11-49.

Listing 11-49. The Updated DOM Loaded Function

```
$(function () {
    $("#AppointmentDate").datepicker();
    var viewModel =  new PeopleModel();
    $.getJSON("/api/Appointments",
        function (data) {
            if (data && data.length > 0) {
                viewModel.SetPeopleFromJSON(data);
            }
            ko.applyBindings(viewModel);

            $("#LoadingDiv").hide();
            $("#ContainerDiv").show();
        });
});
```

Listing 11-50 uses a helper function added to the `PeopleModel` class called `SetPeopleFromJSON`. This function uses knockout.mapping to wrap the data returned from the Web API call in a Knockout observable collection. It then creates a new empty `Person` object and adds it to the beginning of the array using the JavaScript `unshift` function. We then set the `NewPerson` element to the newly created empty `Person` object.

Listing 11-50. SetPeopleFromJSON

```
function PeopleModel(People) {
//...other code
self.SetPeopleFromJSON = function (jsData) {
        self.People = ko.mapping.fromJS(jsData);
        self.People.unshift(
                new Person("", "", "")
            );
        self.NewPerson(self.People()[0]);
    }
}
```

Adding Buttons That Use Knockout Click Bindings

Next, we will modify the functionality of the buttons on the page so that rather than posting back to the server, they will trigger JavaScript events. To do this, we will first remove the Submit button along with the surrounding P elements. We will then add two Input buttons and then add binding expressions for the click events of the buttons. The updated markup for the buttons is shown in Listing 11-51.

Listing 11-51. New Form Buttons with Click Bindings in Appointments.cshtml

```
@model Ch11.R3.Web.Models.Person
@{
    ViewBag.Title = "My Appointments";
}
@section header{
        @Styles.Render("~/Content/themes/base/css")
    <link href="~/Content/Home/Appointments.css" rel="stylesheet" />
}
<h2>@ViewBag.Title</h2>
    <div id="LoadingDiv">Loading ...</div>
<div id="ContainerDiv">
<section id="PeepsList">
  <!-- Grid code shown in Listing 11-44 goes here -->
</section>
<section id="PeepsForm">
    <form id="NewPersonForm">
    <fieldset>
        <legend title="Peeps Form"></legend>
        <ul>
            <!-- Other form fields shown here -->
```

```
            <li>
                <input type="button" data-bind='click: addPerson' value="Add" />
                <input type="button" data-bind='click: saveAll' value="Save To Server" />
            </li>
        </ul>

    </fieldset>
        </form>
</section>

</div>

@section scripts{
    @Scripts.Render("~/bundles/jqueryui")
    @Scripts.Render("~/bundles/jqueryval")
    @Scripts.Render("~/bundles/knockout")
    <script src="~/Scripts/Home/Appointments.js"></script>
}
```

The bind statements for the buttons are bound to functions that need to be defined in the PeopleModel class. The advantage of using binding rather than normal onclick attributes is that since we are using a binding, the functions will be able to access the current context of the PeopleModel instance. Having this state information available reduces the need for having to pass parameters to the function, which makes the function calls less obtrusive.

Next, we need to add the functions themselves. The first function, addPerson, uses jQuery validation to make sure that the form data is valid. It does this by calling $("#NewPersonForm").valid(). If the form is valid, this function returns true. If false, it will return false and the validation messages will be displayed. If the form is valid, it creates a new ko.observable(person) and adds it to the beginning of the People array using the unshift function of ko.observableArray. The NewPerson property is then assigned to this new object. The addPerson function is shown in Listing 11-52.

Listing 11-52. The addPerson Function

```
function PeopleModel(People) {
    var self = this;
    self.People = ko.observableArray([new Person("", "", "")]);
    self.NewPerson = ko.observable(self.People()[0]);

    self.addPerson = function () {
        if ($("#NewPersonForm").valid()) {
            self.People.unshift(
                new Person("", "", "")
            );
            self.NewPerson(self.People()[0]);
        }
    };

}
```

The second function, saveAll, calls the POST method of the /api/Appointments API and passes it the entire contents of the People array. Note that it uses the jQuery ajax function and sets the content type to application/json; charset=utf-8 and the dataType to jsonData. This lets the Web API know that we are passing it JSON data and will make it invoke its JSON deserialization component that converts the JSON into a .NET object required by the method signature.

If a success code is returned, the success function which is defined inline in the $.ajax call will be executed. This success function expects that the data will contain an updated version of the People array with the unique identifiers assigned from SQL Server. In case of an error, we are adding a simple log entry to the JavaScript console. We will add more robust error handling later. The saveAll function is shown in Listing 11-53.

Listing 11-53. PeopleModel with SaveAll functions

```
function PeopleModel(People) {
    var self = this;
    self.People = ko.observableArray([new Person("", "", "")]);
    self.NewPerson = ko.observable(self.People()[0]);

    self.addPerson = function () {
        if ($("#NewPersonForm").valid()) {
            self.People.unshift(
                new Person("", "", "")
            );
            self.NewPerson(self.People()[0]);
        }
    };

    self.saveAll = function () {
        if (self.People && self.People().length > 0) {

            var jsonData = ko.toJSON(self.People);
            $.ajax({
                url: "/api/peeps",
                type: "POST",
                data: jsonData,
                dataType: "json",
                contentType: "application/json; charset=utf-8",
                success: function (data) {
                    self.SetPeopleFromJSON(data);
                },
                error: function () {
                    console.log('fail!');
                }
            });
        }
    };

}
```

Adding Knockout Bindings Using HTML Helpers

The next thing required to get this form functioning is to add the bindings to the form. The MVC HTML helpers allow us to add miscellaneous HTML attributes to the form elements using the syntax @Html.xxxFor(a => a.Propertyname, new { htmlAttribute="value"}). One problem that you will find with this is that since the data-bind attributes contain a dash, which is a C# operator, trying to add a data-bind attribute using this technique will fail with a syntax error. Thankfully, as of MVC 2 this problem was addressed and you can now use underscores in place of dashes when you need to add an attribute that contains a dash. At runtime, the HTML helper will automatically convert the underscore to a dash. For example, a binding expression for the WhenToMeet property can be added as follows:

```
@Html.TextBoxFor(a => a.WhenToMeet, new { data_bind="value: NewPerson().WhenToMeet,
valueUpdate:'afterkeydown'"}).
```

Here we replace data-bind with data_bind and MVC will automatically convert this to the correct markup. One thing to note is that this capability is not available with the Html.EditorFor method, so we must use Html.TextBox instead.

Another addition to this binding is that it adds a valueUpdate: parameter with the value 'afterkeydown'. This will update the value of the underlying object as well as all the other page elements bound to this object on every key stroke. If this is not added, the value is updated only after focus has left the current input element. As a result, changes made to the form are immediately seen; otherwise, you would not see the changes until you set focus to another form field. The updated form markup is shown in Listing 11-54.

Listing 11-54. Form Markup That Includes Data-Bind Attributes

```
<section id="PeepsForm">
    <form id="NewPersonForm">
    <fieldset>
        <legend title="Peeps Form"></legend>
        <ul>
            <li>
                <label>@Html.LabelFor(a => a.FirstName)</label>
                @Html.TextBoxFor(a => a.FirstName,
                    new { data_bind="value: NewPerson().FirstName, valueUpdate:'afterkeydown'"})

                @Html.ValidationMessageFor(a=>a.FirstName,null)
            </li>
            <li>
                <label>@Html.LabelFor(a => a.LastName)</label>
                @Html.TextBoxFor(a => a.LastName,
                    new { data_bind="value: NewPerson().LastName, valueUpdate:'afterkeydown'"})
                @Html.ValidationMessageFor(a=>a.LastName,null)
            </li>
            <li>
                <label>@Html.LabelFor(a => a.AppointmentDate)</label>
                @Html.TextBoxFor(a => a.AppointmentDate,
                    new { data_bind="value: NewPerson().AppointmentDate,
                        valueUpdate:'afterkeydown'"})
                @Html.ValidationMessageFor(a=>a.WhenToMeet,null)
            </li>
            <li>
                <input type="button" data-bind='click: addPerson' value="Add" />
                <input type="button" data-bind='click: saveAll' value="Save To Server" />
            </li>
        </ul>

    </fieldset>
        </form>
</section>
```

Using the $parent Keyword to Bind a Click to a Child Object

Next, we need to allow an item added to the list to be edited. We will do this by adding a click binding to the Edit links that we have added to the template. One tricky thing about this is that because the table is bound to a child object of the view model, it will not have access to functions defined in the root. This can be addressed, however, using Knockout's $parent keyword inside the binding. $parent allows us to access the next level up in the binding tree. Since our object has only two levels, another option is to use $root. The $root keyword will always allow you to access the top-level object in a nested object hierarchy. In most cases, however, $parent is a better choice because you would not need to recode the binding if additional levels are introduced to the object hierarchy. The updated binding is shown in Listing 11-55.

Listing 11-55. Template Updated with Click Binding Added to the Edit Links

```
<section id="PeepsList">

    <table data-bind="template: {name: 'PeepsTemplate', foreach: People}" class="grid">
        <thead>
            <tr>
                <th></th>
                <th>First Name</th>
                <th>Last Name</th>
                <th>Date</th>
            </tr>
        </thead>
    </table>

    <script id="PeepsTemplate" type="text/html">
    <tr>
        <td><a href="#" class="edit" data-bind="click: $parent.selectItem">Edit</a></td>
        <td data-bind="text: FirstName"></td>
        <td data-bind="text: LastName"></td>
        <td data-bind="test: AppointmentDate"></td>
    </tr>
</script>
</section>
```

Since this binding expects that a function called selectItem will exist in the view model we will need to add this to the PeopleModel class. For this function, we can take advantage of the view model context and set the view model's NewPerson property to this. This property represents the current item being bound, which in this case is a person object associated with the row where the Edit button is clicked. The code for the selectItem function is shown in Listing 11-56.

Listing 11-56. The selectItem Function

```
function PeopleModel(People) {
...

  self.selectItem = function () {
        self.NewPerson(this);
  }
...

}
```

We should now be able to run the code sample. Since we have not saved any data, the table will be empty when run the first time. As you are typing the first record, you will notice that the text will appear in the table as you type. If you click the Add button, you will see the old record move down in the list and now your typing echo in the new row. After you have added several rows, use the Edit link in the table to select a row. It should immediately appear in the form.

If you click the Save To Server button, the working icon should appear for a few seconds, and eventually you will see a message stating that the information was saved. If you refresh the page, you will see that the table is now populated with the records you have saved.

Creating a Knockout Binding Handler to Format Dates

Unfortunately, the data format is shown in the ISO format of 2013-02-01T12:10:23. This is not the most user-friendly way to display a date, and because neither JavaScript nor knockout have any good built-in solutions for displaying dates, we will need to take matters into our own hands by creating a knockout binding handler that takes advantage of moment.js's `format` function.

To define a new binding handler, you define a new function in the format `ko.bindingHandlers.myBindingHandlerName`. Inside the binding handler, you can define two functions: `update` and `init`. The `init` function is called when a binding is first applied to an element. It can be used to set up the initial state of the binding, and to register event handlers and other things you may need to do at this state of the life cycle. The second function `update` is called when the binding is first applied and each time the associated observable is updated. It is used to update the DOM element that the binding has been applied to. The update function accepts several parameters, including the following:

- `element`: The DOM element that the binding is being applied to. In our example, this will be the TD element.

- `valueAccessor`: A JavaScript function that can be used to get the current model property value. In our example, this will be the `AppointmentDate` property of the current item.

- `allBindingsAccessor`: A JavaScript function that allows you to access all of the properties of the model.

- `viewModel`: The current data item. If the binding is at the root, this would be the model passed to `ko.applyBindings`. In nested bindings such as the `foreach` binding used in this example, it is set to the current object. In our case, this would be the `People` array.

This function is shown in Listing 11-57. Comments have been added to explain how the code works line by line. Note that we are not implementing the `init` function in this case because it is not needed.

Listing 11-57. Using a Knockout Binding Handler

```
ko.bindingHandlers.dateFormat = {
    update: function (element, valueAccessor, allBindingsAccessor, viewModel) {
        var value = valueAccessor(),
            allBindings = allBindingsAccessor();

        // unwrap to get value stored in the obserable
        var valucUnwrapped = ko.utils.unwrapObservable(value);

        // if no patten is passed then use mmm d, yyyy as the default
        var pattern = allBindings.datePattern || 'mmmm d, yyyy';
```

```
            // if not data is found, return empty string
            if (valueUnwrapped == undefined || valueUnwrapped == null || valueUnwrapped =="") {
                $(element).text("");
            }
            else {
                //use moment.js create a date object  from the value passed
                var date = moment(valueUnwrapped, "YYYY-MM-DDTHH:mm:ss");

                //apply the formatted text to the text property of the element
                $(element).text(moment(date).format(pattern));
            }
        }
    }
}
```

To use this binding handler, we need to modify the binding for AppointmentDate as shown in Listing 11-58. Instead of calling data-bind="text:.." we now use data-bind="dateFormat: ", which is the name of the binding handler we created in Listing 11-57 To pass in the format string, we specify datePattern: 'MM/DD/YYYY'. This is available to us inside the binding handler's update function via the allBindingsAccessor function.

Listing 11-58. Modified Binding That Using the dateString Binding Handler

```
<section id="PeepsList">

    <table data-bind="template: {name: 'PeepsTemplate', foreach: People}" class="grid">
        <thead>
            <tr>
                <th></th>
                <th>First Name</th>
                <th>Last Name</th>
                <th>Date</th>
            </tr>
        </thead>
    </table>

    <script id="PeepsTemplate" type="text/html">
    <tr>
        <td><a href="#" class="edit" data-bind="click: $parent.selectItem">Edit</a> </td>
        <td data-bind="text: FirstName"></td>
        <td data-bind="text: LastName"></td>
        <td data-bind="dateFormat: AppointmentDate, datePattern: 'MM/DD/YYYY'"></td>
    </tr>
</script>
</section>
```

When this example is run in the browser, the dates should be shown in the expected format. There is a problem, however. When you click the Edit button, the date appears in the ISO format. This is because it is still using the value binding that does not have any date-formatting capabilities. If you update the binding in the form to look like Listing 11-59, you will find that not only is the date not being formatted but the underlying value is no longer being updated.

Listing 11-59. Adding the dateString Binding to the AppointmentDate Field

```
<li>
  <label>@Html.LabelFor(a => a.AppointmentDate)</label>
      @Html.TextBoxFor(a => a.AppointmentDate,
  new { data_bind="dateString: NewPerson().AppointmentDate, valueUpdate:'afterkeydown',
              datePattern: 'MM/DD/YYYY'"})
      @Html.ValidationMessageFor(a=>a.AppointmentDate,null)
</li>
```

To correct this, we will need to update our custom binding so that it updates the underlining observable. We will start by adding an `init` function to the custom binding. In it, we will first check to see if the bound element is an `input` type. If so, we will register an event handler that will fire whenever the bound property of the element changes. In the body of the event handler, we will update the value of the observable.

In the update function, we will also need to perform a check to see if it is an `input` element type. If it is, we will update the contents of the `value` attribute rather than the `text` attribute. We have also added a helper function called `isEmpty` to aid in identifying empty values. The updated `dateString` binding is shown in Listing 11-60.

Listing 11-60. Updating the dateString Custom Binding to Support Input Elements

```
ko.bindingHandlers.dateString = {
    init: function (element, valueAccessor, allBindingsAccessor) {
        if (element.tagName == "INPUT") {
            //register event to update the observable when value changes
            ko.utils.registerEventHandler(element, "change", function () {
                var observable = valueAccessor();
                observable($(element).val());
            });
        }

    },
    update: function (element, valueAccessor, allBindingsAccessor, viewModel) {
        var value = valueAccessor(),
            allBindings = allBindingsAccessor();
        var valueUnwrapped = ko.utils.unwrapObservable(value);
        var pattern = allBindings.datePattern || 'mmmm d, yyyy';
        if (isEmpty(valueUnwrapped)) {
            if (element.tagName == "INPUT") {
                $(element).val("");
            }
            else {
                $(element).text("");
            }

        }
        else {
            var date = moment(valueUnwrapped);
            if (element.tagName == "INPUT") {
                $(element).val(moment(date).format(pattern));

            }
```

```
            else {
                $(element).text(moment(date).format(pattern));
            }

        }
    }
}

function isEmpty(obj) {
    if (typeof obj == 'undefined' || obj === null || obj === '') return true;
    if (typeof obj == 'number' && isNaN(obj)) return true;
    if (obj instanceof Date && isNaN(Number(obj))) return true;
    return false;
}
```

The updated custom binding should now work as expected.

Using Knockout Array Filters

While most of the client-side code appears to be working at this point, you may have noticed that in some cases, exceptions are being thrown at the server when you click the Save To Server button. If you set a breakpoint in the Web API code for the PostPeople method, you will see that the ModelState.IsValid is false, which results in a BadRequest status code being returned. This error is being caused by the fact that when we add a new item, the client-side code is placing an empty Person object to the People array. When the Save To Server button is clicked, the entire array is uploaded to the server, including the empty object. When the empty item is processed, the error is thrown because it violates the rules defined in the data validation attributes applied to the model.

To fix this, we need to remove the empty row from the array uploaded to the server. Knockout offers some useful array functions that can simplify this. Among these is the ko.utils.arrayFilter function. The arrayFilter takes two parameters. The first is the observable array that we wish to process. The second is a function that takes an array item as a parameter and should return true for records that match the condition we are testing. To correct our problem, we will test to see if the required values for our object are set. Incomplete records will be removed from the upload. The updated saveAll function is shown in Listing 11-61.

Listing 11-61. Updated saveAll Function That Removes Incomplete Records

```
self.saveAll = function () {
    if (self.People && self.People().length > 0) {
        var filtered = ko.utils.arrayFilter(self.People(),
            function (person)
            {
                return ((!isEmpty(person.LastName())) &&
                    (!isEmpty(person.FirstName())) &&
                    (!isEmpty(person.AppointmentDate()))
                    );
            }
            );
        var jsonData = ko.toJSON(filtered);
        $.ajax({
            url: "/api/Appointments",
            type: "POST",
            data: jsonData,
```

```
            dataType: "json",
            contentType: "application/json; charset=utf-8",
            success: function (data) {
                self.SetPeopleFromJSON(data);

            },
            error: function (data) {
                console.log(data);

            }
        });
    }
};
```

Using a Custom Binding to Make a Message Appear and Fade Out

The last thing we will demonstrate in this example is how we can use a custom binding to make a message appear once the save operation has completed. The idea is that rather than just having an "Updated Successfully" message appear, and then just sit there while the user is editing additional records, we can instead have this message fade in and then slowly fade out, as follows:

1. Add a new property called Message to the PeopleModel class, as shown in Listing 11-62.

    Listing 11-62. The Message Property

    ```
    function PeopleModel(People)
    {
        var self = this;
        self.People = ko.observableArray([new Person("", "", "")]);
        self.NewPerson = ko.observable(self.People()[0]);
        self.Message = ko.observable("");
        // other properties and functions...
    }
    ```

2. Add a new custom binding called **message**. The binding will contain an update function that will act as a wrapper for the Knockout text bindingHandler. It will first use standard jQuery animation functions to hide the element if it is currently visible, and then fade it in. It will then slowly fade out the message over a four-second period. The custom binding is shown in Listing 11-63.

    Listing 11-63. The Message Custom Binding

    ```
    ko.bindingHandlers.message = {
        update: function (element, valueAccessor) {
            $(element).hide();
            // call to built in text binding handler
            ko.bindingHandlers.text.update(element, valueAccessor);
            $(element).fadeIn();
            $(element).fadeOut(4000);
        }
    };
    ```

3. Add a new DIV element to the Appointment view and bind it to the Message property that you added to your view model in step 1 using the custom binding you created in step 2. The HTML markup is shown in Listing 11-64.

Listing 11-64. Message DIV Element in Appointments.cshtml

```
<h2>@ViewBag.Title</h2>
    <div id="LoadingDiv">Loading ...</div>
    <div id="MessageDiv" data-bind="message: Message"></div>
```

You should now see the message fade in and then fade out slowly after each server update. Listing 11-65 shows the completed Appointment.js file.

Listing 11-65. The Completed Appointment.js File

```
/// <reference path="../jquery-1.8.2.intellisense.js" />
/// <reference path="../moment.js" />
/// <reference path="../knockout-2.2.0.js" />

function Person(FirstName, LastName, AppointmentDate) {
    var self = this;
    self.FirstName = ko.observable(FirstName);
    self.LastName = ko.observable(LastName);
    self.PersonId = 0;
    self.AppointmentDate = ko.observable(AppointmentDate);
}

function PeopleModel(People)
{
    var self = this;
    self.People = ko.observableArray([new Person("", "", "")]);
    self.NewPerson = ko.observable(self.People()[0]);
    self.Message = ko.observable("");
    self.addPerson = function () {
        if ($("#NewPersonForm").valid()) {
            self.People.unshift(
                new Person("", "", "")
            );
            self.NewPerson(self.People()[0]);
        }
    };

    self.SetPeopleFromJSON = function (jsData) {
        self.People = ko.mapping.fromJS(jsData);
        self.People.unshift(
                new Person("", "", "")
            );
        self.NewPerson(self.People()[0]);
    }
```

```
    self.selectItem = function () {
        self.NewPerson(this);
    }

    self.saveAll = function () {
        if (self.People && self.People().length > 0) {
            var filtered = ko.utils.arrayFilter(self.People(),
                function (person)
                {
                    return ((!isEmpty(person.LastName())) &&
                        (!isEmpty(person.FirstName())) &&
                        (!isEmpty(person.AppointmentDate()))
                        );
                }
                );
            var jsonData = ko.toJSON(filtered);
            $.ajax({
                url: "/api/Appointments",
                type: "POST",
                data: jsonData,
                dataType: "json",
                contentType: "application/json; charset=utf-8",
                success: function (data) {
                    self.SetPeopleFromJSON(data);
                    self.Message("Updated Successfully");
                },
                error: function (data) {
                    console.log(data);
                    self.Message("Updated Failed");
                }
            });
        }
    };

}

$(function () {
    $("#AppointmentDate").datepicker();
    var viewModel =  new PeopleModel();
    $.getJSON("/api/Appointments",
        function (data) {
            if (data && data.length > 0) {
                viewModel.SetPeopleFromJSON(data);
            }
            ko.applyBindings(viewModel);

            $("#LoadingDiv").hide();
            $("#ContainerDiv").show();
        });
});
```

```javascript
ko.bindingHandlers.dateString = {
    init: function (element, valueAccessor, allBindingsAccessor) {
        if (element.tagName == "INPUT") {
            //register event to update the observable when value changes
            ko.utils.registerEventHandler(element, "change", function () {
                var observable = valueAccessor();
                observable($(element).val());
            });
        }

    },
    update: function (element, valueAccessor, allBindingsAccessor, viewModel) {
        var value = valueAccessor(),
            allBindings = allBindingsAccessor();
        var valueUnwrapped = ko.utils.unwrapObservable(value);
        var pattern = allBindings.datePattern || 'mmmm d, yyyy';
        if (isEmpty(valueUnwrapped)) {
            if (element.tagName == "INPUT") {
                $(element).val("");
            }
            else {
                $(element).text("");
            }

        }
        else {
            var date = moment(valueUnwrapped);
            if (element.tagName == "INPUT") {
                $(element).val(moment(date).format(pattern));

            }
            else {
                $(element).text(moment(date).format(pattern));
            }

        }
    }
}

ko.bindingHandlers.message = {
    update: function (element, valueAccessor) {
        $(element).hide();
        ko.bindingHandlers.text.update(element, valueAccessor);
        $(element).fadeIn();
        $(element).fadeOut(4000);
    }
};
```

```
function isEmpty(obj) {
    if (typeof obj == 'undefined' || obj === null || obj === '') return true;
    if (typeof obj == 'number' && isNaN(obj)) return true;
    if (obj instanceof Date && isNaN(Number(obj))) return true;
    return false;
}
```

11-4. Creating a Custom Route for an API Controller

Problem

You have an API controller that accepts one or more route parameters. You would like to be able to accept default values for each of the parameters and have a more developer-friendly RESTful interface that does not require query string parameters.

Solution

To solve this problem, you need to add the routes in the App_Start/WebApiConfig.cs file. Web API routes are similar to normal routes, but are defined and handled separately. Routes for Web API are stored inside the HttpConfiguration.Routes collection. You add new routes using the HttpConfiguration.Routes.MapHttpRoute extension method. This method takes several named parameters, including the following:

- name: The name of the route. It must be unique.

- routeTemplate: A format string that is used to generate the URL, which can include a combination of static strings, the controller name, and route parameters. One notable omission is the action name, which is assigned using the HTTP verb rather than the URL.

- defaults: An optional parameter that allows you to specify default values that can be used if one or more sections defined in the route template are not included.

- constraints: An optional parameter that allows you to restrict the strings that can be included in a route parameter.

How It Works

Let's first look at the default route that is included with the Visual Studio Web API template. When you create a new Web API project, a file named WebApiConfig.cs is added to the App_Start folder. In this file, a single route is defined, as shown in Listing 11-66.

Listing 11-66. Default Web API Route Settings

```
public static class WebApiConfig
{
  public static void Register(HttpConfiguration config)
  {
    config.Routes.MapHttpRoute(
        name: "DefaultApi",
        routeTemplate: "api/{controller}/{id}",
        defaults: new { id = RouteParameter.Optional }
        );
  }
}
```

With this route definition, you would access the controller using URLs such as:

- `http://website/api/controllerName`

- `http://website/api/controllerName/12`

- `http://website/api/controllerName/12?SomeOtherRouteParam=value`

- `http://website/api/controllerName?$filter=fieldName%20eq'value'`

The first URL would match the default route and does not include the optional Id parameter. The second URL includes the Id parameter. The third URL includes the Id parameter and an additional parameter added in the query string. The last URL adds OData parameters.

OData is a standard set of query string parameters that allow you to query and modify data using URIs. In order to use OData with Web API, you must include the `Microsoft.AspNet.WebApi.Odata` library in your project using NuGet, create an action that returns an `IQueryable`, and mark your action with a `Queryable` attribute.

Adding a Custom Route

In Recipe 11-2, we created an Ajax-driven data grid that used Web API to return a list of items. In order to allow for sorting and paging, that controller had two route parameters that were passed via the query string. In this example, we will add a route that makes the sort parameters part of the URL, and add a constraint to the sort parameter so that only certain values may be passed.

■ **Note**   A more standard approach to providing parameters for filtering and sorting of the data would be to use OData.

In Listing 11-67, we add a new route called `PagingApi`. In this route, we add a static string `/Page` to differentiate this route from the `DefaultApi` route. We then add a parameter for `SortExpression`. Both parameters are given default values.

Listing 11-67. Adding a Custom Route

```
config.Routes.MapHttpRoute(
           name: "PagingApi",
           routeTemplate: "api/{controller}/Page/{Page}/{SortExpression}",
     defaults: new
     {
         Page = 1,
         SortExpression = "CreateDate"
     }
);
```

With this route added, we can now use the following URLs to access the service:

- `http://website/api/controllerName/Page/1`

- `http://website/api/controllerName/Page/1/CreateDate`

One problem with this current implementation is that it allows any arbitrary string to be used as a sort parameter. If we wanted to constrain what the fields can be sorted by, we can modify this route to include a constraint. Listing 11-68 shows the `PagingApi` route with a constraint that limits the possible sort expression to three fields: `CreateDate`,

NumberComments, and Title. We also ensure that only numeric values are used for the Page route parameter. If either constraint is violated, an HTTP 404 will be returned. One thing to make note of is that when creating the constraint for SortExpression, all the field names must be lowercase. This is required because the constraint will convert the URL parameters to all lowercase characters when performing the comparison. The modified route definitions are shown in Listing 11-68.

Listing 11-68. Adding a Constraint to the PagingApi Route

```
public static void Register(HttpConfiguration config)
{
    config.Routes.MapHttpRoute(
        name: "PagingApi",
        routeTemplate: "api/{controller}/Page/{Page}/{SortExpression}",
        defaults: new
        {
         Page = 0,
         SortExpression = "CreateDate"
        },
        constraints: new
        {
         Page = @"\d+",
         SortExpression= "title|createdate|numbercomments"
        }
    );
}
```

There are two main types of route constraints that can be created. You can use a regular expression, as shown in Listing 11-68 You can read the constraint definition as: "The route parameter Page should match the regular expression "\d+"."

If you need something more sophisticated than a regular expression, you may use an object that implements the IHttpRouteConstraint interface. This interface defines a single method, Match. The MVC Framework includes one implementation, the HttpMethodConstraint, out of the box. This allows you to restrict a route to a single HTTP verb. It is also quite simple to create your own implementations.

Creating Unit Tests for the Custom Route

One problem with creating custom routes is that if they are not tested properly, they can lead to problems that are difficult to diagnose. The reason that these problems are difficult to solve is not because routing is difficult, but more because you may come across the bug when working on something else unrelated to the custom route.

To reduce the likelihood of this occurring, it is highly recommended that you create unit tests for your custom routes. In order to test the route defined in Listing 11-68 we will create four tests. We will validate that the route matches the correct controller and the routes constraints function as expected.

Before we can write a test, we need to modify the global.asax file in the web application project so that routes defined in WebApiConfig.cs can be used inside our unit tests, as follows:

1. In the Ch11.R2.Web project, open Global.asax.cs in the code editor.

2. Inside the Global.asax.cs file, create a public static method called RegisterRoutes that accepts an HttpConfiguration object and a RouteCollection. While we do not need the RouteCollection object for testing the API routes, we add them here so that we can test regular routes as well.

3. Inside the `RegisterRoutes` method add calls to the `WebApiConfig.Register` and `RouteConfig.RegisterRoutes` methods, and pass them the route configuration objects that match their own parameters.

4. Next, add a call to this method inside the `Application_Start` method. We are replacing the two existing calls added to the project from the template. The modified `global.asax.cs` file is shown in Listing 11-69.

Listing 11-69. Global.asax.cs Modified to Simplify Testing Routes

```
public class WebApiApplication : System.Web.HttpApplication
{

        // added to enable unit testing of routes
        public static void RegisterRoutes(RouteCollection routes, HttpConfiguration config)
        {
            WebApiConfig.Register(config);
            RouteConfig.RegisterRoutes(routes);

        }

        protected void Application_Start()
        {
            AreaRegistration.RegisterAllAreas();
            RegisterRoutes(RouteTable.Routes, GlobalConfiguration.Configuration);
            FilterConfig.RegisterGlobalFilters(GlobalFilters.Filters);
            BundleConfig.RegisterBundles(BundleTable.Bundles);
        }
}
```

5. Create a new class named **RouteTests.cs** inside the `Ch11.R2.Web.Tests` project.

6. In the new class, add using statements for `Microsoft.VisualStudio.TestTools.UnitTesting`, `System.Net.Http`, `System.Web.Http`, and `System.Web.Routing`.

7. Decorate the class with the `TestClass` attribute.

8. Add a new method called **PagingApiRoute_TitleAsSortExpression_IsMatch** and decorate it with the `TestMethod` attribute.

9. Set up the method by creating empty `HttpConfiguration` and `RouteCollection` objects, as shown in Listing 11-70.

Listing 11-70. Empty HttpConfiguration and RouteCollection Objects

```
var config = new HttpConfiguration();
var routes = new RouteCollection();
```

10. Add the routes by calling the `WebApiApplication.RegisterRoutes` method with the `HttpConfiguration` and `RouteCollection` objects passed as parameters, as shown in Listing 11-71.

Listing 11-71. Adding the Routes

```
WebApiApplication.RegisterRoutes(routes, config);
```

11. Create a RouteData object that contains the Web API routes by calling `config.Routes.GetRouteData`. This method takes an `HttpRequestMessage` object as a parameter. When we create this object, we can specify the HTTP method as well as the URL, as shown in Listing 11-72.

Listing 11-72. Calling GetRouteData

```
var apiRouteData =
            config.Routes.GetRouteData(new HttpRequestMessage(HttpMethod.Get,
                "http://someurl/api/CollaborationSpaces/Page/2/Title"));
```

Listing 11-73. shows the completed test class so far.

Listing 11-73. Unit Test That Verifies That a URL That Includes a Page Number and Sort Expression Has a Matching Route

```
using Microsoft.VisualStudio.TestTools.UnitTesting;
using System.Net.Http;
using System.Web.Http;
using System.Web.Routing;

namespace Ch11.R2.Web.Tests
{
    [TestClass]
    public class RouteTests
    {
        [TestMethod]
        public void PagingApiRoute_TitleAsSortExpression_IsMatch()
        {
            //arrange
            var config = new HttpConfiguration();
            var routes = new RouteCollection();
            WebApiApplication.RegisterRoutes(routes, config);

            //act
            var apiRouteData =
                config.Routes.GetRouteData(new HttpRequestMessage(HttpMethod.Get,
                    "http://someurl/api/CollaborationSpaces/Page/2/Title"));

            //assert
            Assert.IsNotNull(apiRouteData);

        }
    }
}
```

If no routes are found for the URL specified in the `HttpRequestMessage` object, `GetRouteData` will return `null`. This test only tells us that a match was found. It does not tell is if is matching the correct route.

12. Add a test method that verifies that an invalid sort expression is used and verifies that no matching route will be found. It should resemble Listing 11-74.

Listing 11-74. PagingApiRoute_FooAsSortExpression_IsNotMatch

```
[TestMethod]
public void PagingApiRoute_FooAsSortExpression_IsNotMatch()
{
    var config = new HttpConfiguration();
    var routes = new RouteCollection();
    WebApiApplication.RegisterRoutes(routes, config);

    var apiRouteData =
        config.Routes.GetRouteData(new HttpRequestMessage(HttpMethod.Get,
            "http://someurl/api/CollaborationSpaces/Page/2/Foo"));

        Assert.IsNull(apiRouteData);

}
```

13. Add another test to validate the constraint that requires that the Page parameter be numeric. It should resemble Listing 11-75.

Listing 11-75. PagingApiRoute_FooAsPage_IsNotMatch

```
[TestMethod]
public void PagingApiRoute_FooAsPage_IsNotMatch()
{
    var config = new HttpConfiguration();
    var routes = new RouteCollection();
    WebApiApplication.RegisterRoutes(routes, config);

    var apiRouteData =
        config.Routes.GetRouteData(new HttpRequestMessage(HttpMethod.Get,
            "http://someurl/api/CollaborationSpaces/Page/Foo/Title"));

Assert.IsNull(apiRouteData);

}
```

14. Add one more test to verify that the correct controller is returned by the route. It should resemble Listing 11-76.

Listing 11-76. PagingApiRoute_CollaborationSpaces_ControllerMatch

```
[TestMethod]
public void PagingApiRoute_CollaborationSpaces_ControllerMatch()
{
    var config = new HttpConfiguration();
```

```
    var routes = new RouteCollection();
    WebApiApplication.RegisterRoutes(routes, config);

    var apiRouteData =
        config.Routes.GetRouteData(new HttpRequestMessage(HttpMethod.Post,
            "http://someurl/api/CollaborationSpaces/Page/1/Title"));

    Assert.IsNotNull(apiRouteData);
    Assert.AreEqual("CollaborationSpaces", apiRouteData.Values["controller"]);

}
```

■ **Note** For Web API routes, there is no Action specified in the route data. This is because in Web API actions are associated with HTTP verbs instead of route information.

11-5. Using Fiddler to Debug a Web API
Problem

You have developed a service using ASP.NET MVC Web API and need a browser-independent method of examining the results. You would like to be able to fiddle with HTTP variables such as HTTP methods, URLs, and query string parameters, and then examine the output in a user-friendly way.

Solution

The solution to this problem is to use an HTTP Proxy application such as Fiddler. An HTTP proxy is software that intercepts the data sent between your browser and the server. Fiddler is free and is wildly used by .NET developers. It has a broad feature set and can be used to debug not only web applications, but also Windows Store applications.

Fiddler can be downloaded from `www.fiddler2.com`.

How It Works

Once Fiddler has been installed, you can use it to debug your web application by simply running it. By default, Fiddler will listen to all of your network adaptors for HTTP traffic. With any open browser, you can see each of the requests that you have made. If you are running Windows 8, in addition to the browser requests, you can see all the requests made by Windows 8 applications, such as updates to your live tiles.

Applying a Filter

Although it is nice to be able to access all of this information, it can make your debugging task more difficult because you will need to hunt through all of the request data to find what you are looking for. One solution to this problem is to use a filter.

To apply a filter, read the following:

1.   The Fiddler user interface is divided into two main panels. On the left side is the Web Sessions list. It contains a list of all of the HTTP requests that have passed through the proxy. On the right side are several tabbed windows, which include Statistics, Inspectors, Auto Responder, Composer, Filters, Log, and Timeline. To access the filters, click the Filter tab.

2.   To enable filters, click the Use Filters check box.

3.   To add a filter that will limit what is shown to only the controller you are debugging, under Request Headers, check the Show Only If URL Contains check box, and then enter part of the path to the service you want to debug.

4.   From the Actions menu, on the top-right side of the Filters tab, select Run Filter Set Now. This will apply the filter. A screen capture is shown in Figure 11-7.

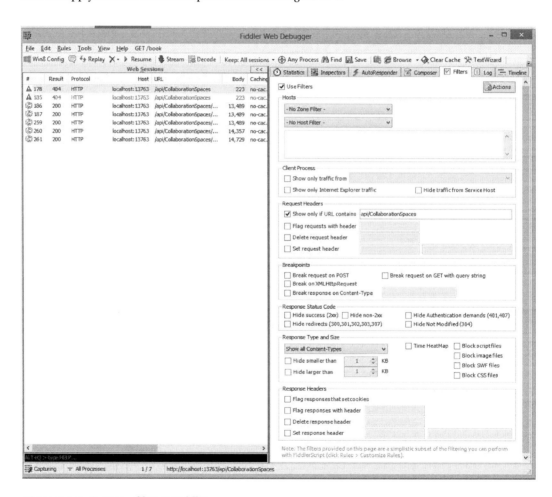

Figure 11-7. *Setting a filter in Fiddler*

Using the Composer

Although it is possible to send your Web API requests in the web browser, it typically involves running it on the context of a view consuming your service. In many debugging use cases, this works well; other times, however, it is beneficial to debug the service in isolation. Do the following to use Fiddler to test the Get action of an API controller:

1. The Fiddler's composer is available as a tabbed document on the right-hand side of the Fiddler UI. Click the tab to access it.

2. After clicking the Composer tab, the Composer's Parsed tab will be selected. This screen allows you to select an HTTP verb, a URL, and the HTTP protocol version to use. Larger text boxes allow you to create custom HTTP headers and a request body.

3. Make sure GET is selected in the drop-down list, and then enter the URL for your service, including protocol and port; for example, `http://localhost:13763/api/CollaborationSpaces/Page/2/Title`.

4. Click the Execute button to execute the request. You should see the request appear in the Web Sessions window along with a 200 response, unless an error occurs.

Using the JSON Inspector to View Your Results

Although it can be useful just to see the status code and size of an HTTP response in most cases, you will also need to view the contents of the response body. When working with Web API, the response will normally be in JSON format. While JSON can be read using any text editor, it is much easier to read if it has been parsed and formatted. If you need to make several calls to a web service and then view the results for each, you can tear off the Composer tab so that it will appear in its own window, and then navigate to the JSON inspector to view the results, as follows:

1. If not selected, click the Composer tab. Click the Options tab.

2. Under UI Options, click the Tear Off button. The Composer will open in a new window.

3. Click the Inspectors tab to view the available Inspectors.

4. Click the JSON Inspector in both the top and bottom panes. The top pane will show any JSON data sent and the bottom pane will show received data.

5. Click any request previously made that is still available in the Web Sessions window. The JSON data will appear in a tree structure.

6. Try executing a new request from the Composer window. The new request will automatically be selected and displayed in the viewer. The results of this exercise are shown in Figure 11-8.

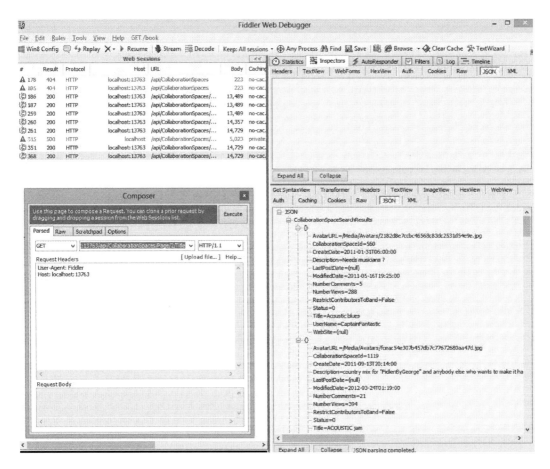

Figure 11-8. *Viewing JSON output in Fiddler*

CHAPTER 12

Mobile, Social, and Cloud Technologies

12-1. Using Facebook As Your MVC Web Site's Identity Provider

Problem

You are planning to create an Internet-facing web application that requires your customers to register and log in to perform certain functions. Since the vast majority of your customers have a Facebook account, you would like to be able to let them use that account to log in to your site. You would also like to allow customers who do not have a Facebook account to create a local account on your web site. You need your web site's local login and the Facebook login to work seamlessly.

Solution

The ASP.NET MVC 4 Internet Application template includes the required code libraries and boilerplate code needed to use Facebook as an identity provider. The `SimpleMemberShipProvider` that is included with the template also permits regular registrations. It even provides the basic forms that allow your customers to associate their Facebook login with your site.

    To use it, you will need to get an application ID from Facebook. This requires that you first create a Facebook account if you do not already have one. You then need to register for the developer program and create an app. Once your Facebook app has been created, you will be assigned a token. Using the token, you can make a few minor changes to a file included in the template, and the integration is complete.

How It Works

We will begin by creating a new Visual Studio project using the ASP.NET Internet Application template:

1.   Open Visual Studio and select New ➤ Project from the File menu.

2.   In the New Project Window, select the ASP.NET MVC 4 Web Application template.

3.   Name the project **Ch12.R1.Web** and the solution **Ch12.R1**. Select an appropriate location, and then click the OK button.

4.   In the New ASP.NET MVC 4 Project window, select the Internet Application template. Make sure that the Razor View Engine is selected and that the "Create a unit test project" check box remains unchecked. Click the OK button.

5.   The project will be created and `HomeController.cs` will be opened in the code editor window. Close this file.

6. Right-click the References node in Solution Explorer and select Manage NuGet Packages.

7. In the Manage NuGet Packages window, click the Updates node. Inspect the list, and if any of the packages for DotNetOpenAuth are out of data, update them. It is good practice to keep all the packages updated if you can; but for now, we will only worry about the packages that we know we will need for our solution. It is important that these libraries be kept up to date because there may be security patches included in the latest version. To update the packages, click the Update button for DotNetOpenAuth OpenID Core. This will automatically update any of the dependent packages.

8. Expand the App_Start node in Solution Explorer and double-click AuthConfig.cs to open it.

9. Uncomment the code for OAuthWebSecurity.RegisterFacebookClient. Notice that there are two empty strings for the appId and appSecret. We will need to get this information from Facebook after we create our Facebook application.

10. Since we are only planning to integrate with Facebook, we can delete the other comments. You can also right-click anywhere on the code file and select Organize Usings, and then select Remove and Sort. The only using statement left will be for Microsoft.Web.WebPages.OAuth. The code for AuthConfig.cs is shown in Listing 12-1.

Listing 12-1. AuthConfig.cs

```
using Microsoft.Web.WebPages.OAuth;

namespace Ch12.R1.Web
{
    public static class AuthConfig
    {
        public static void RegisterAuth()
        {

            OAuthWebSecurity.RegisterFacebookClient(
                appId: "",
                appSecret: "");

        }
    }
}
```

Creating a Facebook Account

In order to create a Facebook login application, you need to have a Facebook account. If you already have an account, you can skip this section and move to the "Create a New Facebook Application Section." If you do not have Facebook account, you can create one following these steps:

1. Open a web browser and navigate to Facebook.com.

2. On the home page, use the registration form to sign up. You will be prompted for your name, your email address, a password, your gender, and your birthday. Click the Sign Up button to proceed.

3. Check your email for a verification message, and then click the link in the email to complete your registration.

4. For now, skip the next three steps of the setup process, which allow you to find or invite friends to connect with your new Facebook account.

Creating a New Facebook Application

Facebook offers several application development models, including the following:

- *Tab Apps for Pages*: This model will run inside the context of the Facebook browser application. These apps can consist of Canvas pages, Social Channels, and analytics. Canvas pages contain the user interface of the application. Social Channels—which include search, notifications, and news-feed stories—allow the application to be discovered and promoted. Analytics give you insight on how your application is being used.

- *Apps on Facebook.com*: This is similar to the Tab Apps for Pages, but with this model, the entire application is hosted on Facebook. This differs from the Tab Apps model, where you are responsible for hosting your content.

- *Mobile Web Apps*: Facebook offers SDKs for building mobile applications for iOS, Android, and mobile web browsers.

- *Facebook for Websites*: For web sites, Facebook offers social plug-ins such as Like buttons, integrated login, personalization, and analytics. For this recipe, we need to create login integration using Facebook for Websites.

Anyone with a valid, verified Facebook account can create a Facebook application. Once you have a Facebook account, the next step is to register as a developer:

1. Open a web browser, navigate to Facebook.com, and then log in.

2. Once logged in, navigate to http://developers.facebook.com. You can do this by scrolling to the bottom of the page and clicking the Developers link or manually entering the URL into the browser. The manual option may be best because Facebook loads additional data as you scroll, which may make it difficult to scroll to the bottom.

3. Once on the Developers page, click the Register Now button in the top-right corner of the page.

   a. If you have not verified your account, you may be prompted to do so. This step may require the use of your mobile phone. You will be required to enter your mobile phone number, and Facebook will send you a text message. The text message will contain a confirmation code that you must enter into a text box on the Facebook web site. You can then navigate back to the Developers page by entering http://developers.facebook.com in the address bar of your web browser.

4. At this point, you should see a screen similar to Figure 12-1. Tick the "I accept the Facebook Platform Policy" check box, and then click the Continue button.

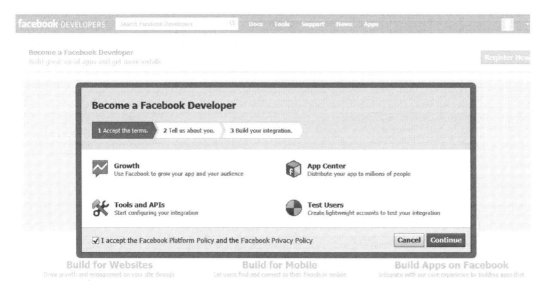

Figure 12-1. *The Facebook developer registration page*

5. Next, you will be asked to answer a quick survey, which you can skip.

6. In the last step, you get a message that says "Yay! You're now a Facebook Developer."

7. Click the Done button to close the pop-up window.

8. Now that you are an official Facebook developer, you need to add the Facebook developer's application to your account. To do this, from the Facebook home page, type **Developer** into the Facebook search bar. Click the Facebook Developers app, as shown in Figure 12-2.

Figure 12-2. *Adding the Developer app*

9. Follow the instructions to grant the Developer account the required permissions on your Facebook account.

10. On the Apps page, click the Create New App button at the top-right of the page.

11. Give the app a name. You can leave the namespace empty. Do not tick the Web Hosting check box.

12. Fill in the required Captcha, and then click Continue.

13. On the new page, check "Website with Facebook Login" under "Select how your app integrates with Facebook."

14. Enter a URL to be used for the login redirects. Since we do not have a web site deployed on the Internet, we need to make up a domain name and then add it to our host file so that we can test this functionality. This needs to be a unique URL that is not being used by any other Facebook account. For example, `johnfacebooktest123.apress.com`. For the rest of this recipe, I will be using the URL `http://aspnetmvcrecipes.apress.com`.

15. Click the Save Changes button to save the changes. Make note of the App ID and App Secret that have been created for your new Facebook application. The values that you will use are inside the `AuthConfig.cs` file. The screen should look similar to Figure 12-3.

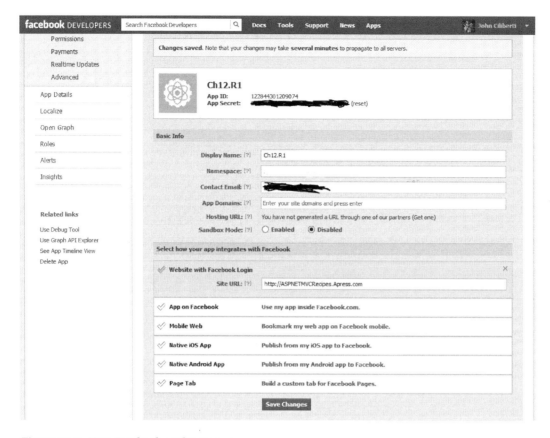

Figure 12-3. *Your Facebook application page*

Configuring and Testing Your Site

Earlier in this recipe, we modified the AuthConfig.cs file so that the OAuthWebSecurity.RegisterFacebookClient was no longer commented out, and we removed some unneeded code. We then created a Facebook account and a Facebook application. In the next steps, we will take the application ID and application secret from the Facebook application, and use it to complete the call to OAuthWebSecurity.RegisterFacebookClient. We will then configure the project and our development environment so that we can test the single sign-on.

1. In Visual Studio, open AuthConfig.cs in the code editor.

2. Copy the App ID and App Secret codes from your application administration page in Facebook. Paste the codes into the appropriate places in the code in AuthConfig.cs. The completed file will look like Listing 12-2. Note that you will need to enter the values generated from your Facebook application page to replace the appId and appSecret.

Listing 12-2. AuthConfig with Codes from the Facebook Web Site

```
using Microsoft.Web.WebPages.OAuth;

namespace Ch12.R1.Web
{
    public static class AuthConfig
    {
        public static void RegisterAuth()
        {
            //Replace the appId and appSecret with values
            // given to you from Facebook as shown in
            // Figure 12-3
            OAuthWebSecurity.RegisterFacebookClient(
                appId: "122844301209074",
                appSecret: "21f37502f363da9bbc0ae0a2a59d5509");

        }
    }
}
```

If you compile and run your site in the debugger, it should compile. If you click the Login link, you should now see a Facebook button under the Use Another Service to Log In section, as shown in Figure 12-4.

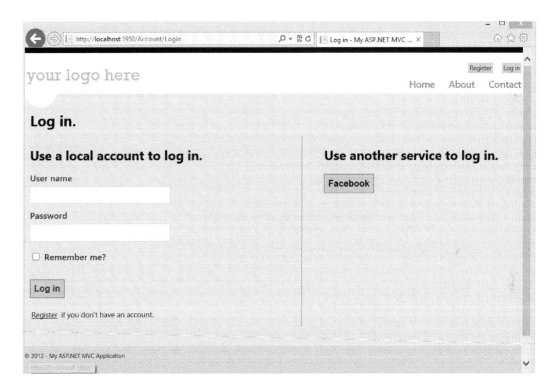

Figure 12-4. *The Facebook link on your web site*

If you click the Facebook button, you will get an error message. The reason you are seeing this message is because your Facebook application is expecting the URL `http://aspnetmvcrecipes.apress.com` and you are browsing to the site `http://localhost:1950`. Since Facebook sees a discrepancy between the URL you are coming from and the one it is set up to redirect to, it throws an error. For security reasons, Facebook will only redirect you to the URL you have specified in the application administration page.

The easiest way to correct this problem is to replace the URL that you had previously entered on the application configuration page on Facebook with `http://localhost:1950`. Since this is address is used exclusively on the client side, you can actually get away with this for some basic testing. If Facebook attempted to make any server-side calls using this URL, it would have problems, however, since it would be calling itself. This would also cause a problem if you or someone else tried to log in to the site from another machine that did not happen to have the site running.

Another option is to add an entry in the host file. The host file is a text file located in the `Windows\System32\Drivers\etc` directory. The Windows DNS client checks this file to see if it contains a match for the requested URL before sending a DNS query to a remote server. You can use this file override DNS so that the address `http://aspnetmvcrecipes.apress.com` will point to your local computer. This option requires additional setup, however. For an explanation on how to do this, please refer to Recipe 3-10.

Once the URL mismatch issue has been resolved, you can run the project and try again. When you click the Facebook button this time, you are taken to the Facebook Login page, as shown in Figure 12-5.

Figure 12-5. The Facebook Login page

After logging in, you are taken to a page that provides information about the application, including who can see posts the app puts on your wall. The screen from our application is shown in Figure 12-6.

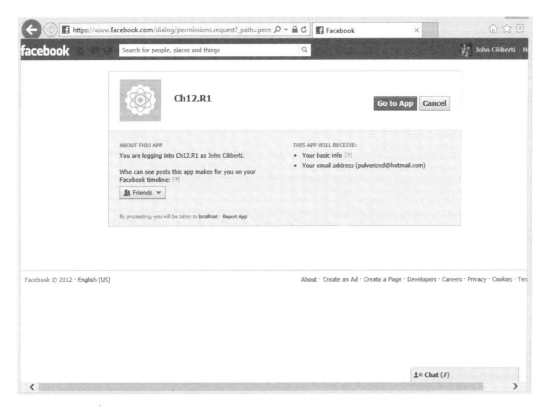

Figure 12-6. *The application information page*

Facebook lets you know that it will be sharing some of your basic information, including your email address, with the application. It also allows you to specify the privacy level of items this application may post to your wall. If you are not comfortable giving the application this information, you can click the Cancel button; otherwise, you can click the Go to App button.

After clicking the Go to App button, you are returned to the site that you have created and you are prompted to provide a username. By default, the email address you are using on Facebook is filled in. If you wish, you may edit this value and replace it with whatever you feel is suitable. After you click the Register button, you are redirected to the home page.

At this point, records have been added to several database tables that are managed by the membership provider, including the webpages_OAuthMembership, webpages_Membership, and the UserProfile table. More information about this schema and the ASP.NET Webpages Simple Membership Provider is found in Recipe 7-10.

12-2. Creating a Facebook Canvas Page Application with ASP.NET MVC
Problem

You would like to create a simple Facebook application that displays some information from your web site and allows Facebook users to share it on their Facebook walls.

Solution

The ASP.NET Web Tools 2012.2 update that was first released at the BUILD conference in October 2012 contains a new Visual Studio template to help you get started in creating a Facebook canvas application. The update can be downloaded from the ASP.NET web site (`www.asp.net/vnext`). The update will only take a few minutes to install and it will not break any existing applications. It is an update to only the tooling and it does not alter the ASP.NET runtime.

Once the update has been installed, several new templates, including the Facebook application, will be available when you create a new ASP.NET MVC 4 project.

Since this project type creates an integration with `Facebook.com`, you will need a Facebook account with the Developer application installed on their profile.

How It Works

This section requires that you first install the ASP.NET Web Tools 2012.2 update. Once this update has been applied, you can create a Facebook canvas application by performing the following steps:

1. Open Visual Studio and click the New Project link from the start page.

2. Select ASP.NET MVC 4 Web Application as the project template.

3. Name the project **Ch12.R2.Web** and the solution **Ch12.R2**, and then click the OK button.

4. On the New ASP.NET MVC 4 Project page, select the Facebook Application template.

5. Make sure that the Razor view engine is selected, and then click the OK button.

6. Visual Studio will create the project and open `HomeController.cs` and `readme.txt`, which contains a link to instructions on how to configure the template. Close the `readme.txt` file and examine the code in `HomeController.cs`, shown in Listing 12-3.

Listing 12-3. HomeController.cs from the Facebook Application Template

```
using System.Collections.Generic;
using System.Linq;
using System.Threading.Tasks;
using System.Web.Mvc;
using Microsoft.AspNet.Mvc.Facebook;
using Microsoft.AspNet.Mvc.Facebook.Client;
using Ch12.R2.Web.Models;

namespace Ch12.R2.Web.Controllers
{
    public class HomeController : Controller
    {
        [FacebookAuthorize("email", "user_photos")]
        public async Task<ActionResult> Index(FacebookContext context)
        {
            if (ModelState.IsValid)
            {
                var user = await context.Client.GetCurrentUserAsync<MyAppUser>();
                return View(user);
            }
```

```
            return View("Error");
        }

        // This action will handle the redirects from FacebookAuthorizeFilter when
        // the app doesn't have all the required permissions specified in the
        // FacebookAuthorizeAttribute.
        // The path to this action is defined under appSettings (in Web.config) with the key
        // 'Facebook:AuthorizationRedirectPath'.
        public ActionResult Permissions(FacebookRedirectContext context)
        {
            if (ModelState.IsValid)
            {
                return View(context);
            }

            return View("Error");
        }
    }
}
```

Note that the file includes two using statements that reference `Microsoft.AspNet.Mvc.Facebook` and `Microsoft.AspNet.Mvc.Facebook.Client`. These namespaces are from the included Facebook NuGet package, which is a C# SDK for Facebook created by Outercurve Foundation. It is an open-source project currently hosted on GitHub. The full documentation for this SDK can be found on `http://csharpsdk.org`. You should also note that it is using the asynchronous programming style, which can be beneficial from a scalability perspective when working with external web services that may experience occasional latency. The asynchronous programming style is described in detail in Chapter 8.

The Index action is decorated with the `FacebookAuthorize` attribute, which states that the application requires access to the Facebook user's email address and user photos. This is used to let the Facebook API know what features the application needs access to. Facebook will alert users to these demands when the users add your application to their profile. By default, Facebook will grant you access to users' public information as well as their friends lists. The public information may consist of the following fields:

- id
- name
- first_name
- last_name
- link
- username
- gender
- local

If your application requires more information about the user, you will need to add the additional fields as strings in the FacebookAuthorize attribute. This can include extended profile properties. A list of these properties are found at `http://developers.facebook.com/docs/reference/login/extended-profile-properties`.

The Index action takes a FacebookContext object as a parameter. The FacebookContext object contains an instance of Facebook.FacebookClient. This client is a proxy class for the Facebook web services. After verifying that the ModelState.IsValid property is set to true, the Index action calls the Client.GetCurrentUserAsync method of FacebookContext. This will attempt to get the information about the current user and pass it into the MyAppUser object. This class is defined in the file Models/MyAppUser.cs shown in Listing 12-4. Make note of the comments included in the code for explanation.

Listing 12-4. The MyAppUser Object

```
using Microsoft.AspNet.Mvc.Facebook;
using Newtonsoft.Json;

// Add any fields you want to be saved for each user and specify the field name in the JSON
// coming back from Facebook
// go to the link below for a full list of fields.
// http://go.microsoft.com/fwlink/?LinkId=273889

namespace Ch12.R2.Web.Models
{
    public class MyAppUser
    {
        public string Id { get; set; }
        public string Name { get; set; }
        public string Email { get; set; }

        [JsonProperty("picture")] // This renames the property to picture.
        [FacebookFieldModifier("type(large)")] // This sets the picture size to large.
        public FacebookConnection<FacebookPicture> ProfilePicture { get; set; }

        // This sets the size of the friend list to 8,
        // remove it to get all friends.
        [FacebookFieldModifier("limit(8)")]
        public FacebookGroupConnection<MyAppUserFriend> Friends { get; set; }

        // This sets the size of the photo list to 16,
        // remove it to get all photos.
        [FacebookFieldModifier("limit(16)")]
        public FacebookGroupConnection<FacebookPhoto> Photos { get; set; }
    }
}
```

Let's pick up from where we left off in creating a Facebook canvas application.

7.   Open the Web.config file and location the appSettings section. There are three values that you need to fill in order to launch the project. The values include Facebook:AppId, Facebook:AppSecret, and Facebook:AppNamespace. To get these values, you need to open Facebook in your web browser and create a new Facebook application. Web.config also contains settings for the properties Facebook:AuthorizationRedirectPath and Facebook:VerifyToken:User. Facebook:AuthorizationRedirectPath, which specifies the path where Facebook will redirect you once you have finished authorization. You do not need to modify this field.

8.   Log in to your Facebook account and type **dev** into the search box at the top section of the site. Select the Developer App. If you have not installed this application on your profile, you will need to do so; otherwise, the Facebook developer dashboard page will be displayed.

9. Click the Create New App button in the top-right corner of the Facebook Apps dashboard page.

10. Name the app **Ch12.R2** and provide a unique namespace name. For this example, I am using apress_asp_recipes. You will not be able to use that as your namespace because I have already taken it. Do not check the box for free web hosting.

11. Click the Continue button and then fill in the required Captcha form. This is a security measure that makes it more difficult for robots to fill in the form to spam the system.

12. On your application's page, copy your App ID and App Security key.

13. Enable the Sandbox Mode check box. If checked, only developers will have access to your app.

14. Click the Save button to save changes to your Facebook application, and then go back into Visual Studio.

15. In Visual Studio, return to the Web.config file and paste in the values you copied from the Facebook page. Your Web.config file should now resemble Listing 12-5. Be sure to save your changes before moving to the next step.

Listing 12-5. Web.config

```
<appSettings>
  <add key="webpages:Version" value="2.0.0.0" />
  <add key="webpages:Enabled" value="false" />
  <add key="PreserveLoginUrl" value="true" />
  <add key="ClientValidationEnabled" value="true" />
  <add key="UnobtrusiveJavaScriptEnabled" value="true" />
  <add key="Facebook:AppId" value="458947667497087" />
  <add key="Facebook:AppSecret" value="573999e60566db72c386b4b40b914080" />
  <add key="Facebook:AppNamespace" value="apress_asp_recipes" />
  <add key="Facebook:AuthorizationRedirectPath" value="Home/Permissions" />
  <add key="Facebook:VerifyToken:User" value="" />
</appSettings>
```

16. Next, you need to add the canvas URL to your Facebook page. This is the URL that the Facebook application will call to display your content. For this example, you will use the home page for the ASP.NET web site that was created as part of the template. By default, Visual Studio uses IIS Express for new projects and launches each site on a random port number. For development purposes, you will use this generated URL as the Canvas page. Open your project's property page and then click the Web tab. On the web, copy the value in the Project URL field.

17. Back on the Facebook app page in your web browser, click the App on Facebook selection under "Select how your app integrates with Facebook".

18. Paste your Project URL into the Canvas URL field. Save your changes.

19. Run the project by clicking the Debug button. After a few minutes, you should see a page similar to the one shown in Figure 12-7.

Figure 12-7. *Facebook application confirmation page*

20. Click the Authorize This Application button. If you are running Internet Explorer, the JavaScript debugger in Visual Studio will break at a JavaScript error that states that accesses is denied. Click the Continue button to move past the error. This error is being thrown because Facebook is using an SSL and your Canvas page is not.

21. Next, you see a page asking you for permission, as shown in Figure 12-8.

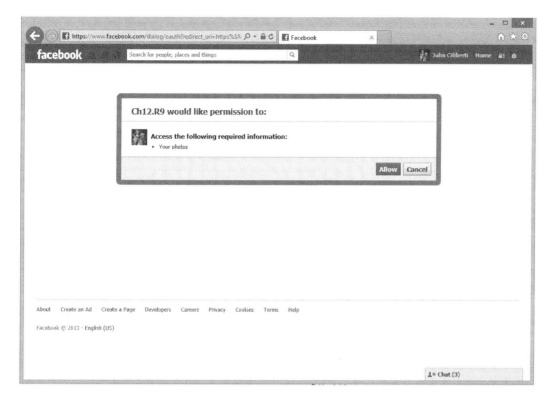

Figure 12-8. *Facebook prompting for permission*

22. After you move past the error, you will see an error on the Facebook page that says the page cannot be displayed. Again, this is normal and caused by your not using an SSL in IIS Express. On the bottom of the screen, there is an Internet Explorer pop-up banner warning you that only secure content is displayed. Click the Show All Content button to dismiss the warning. Note you can avoid these errors if you perform your testing with an alternative web browser such as Firefox. The Facebook page will open with your content displayed. The page will look something like Figure 12-9. It pulls your name, your email address, and your picture. It also pulls similar information for eight of your friends as specified in the [FacebookFieldModifier("limit(8)")] attribute in the MyAppUser class.

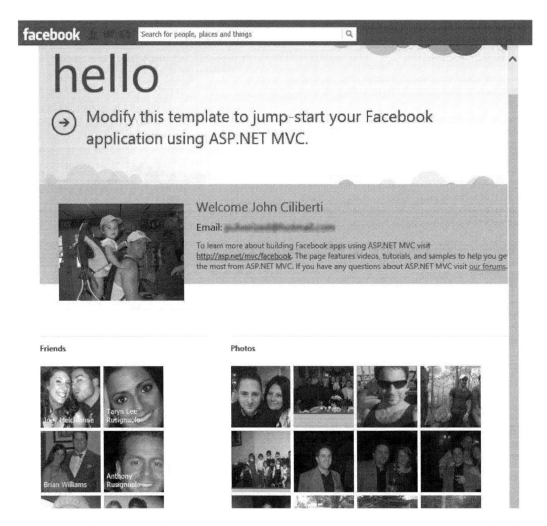

Figure 12-9. *The Facebook Canvas page showing several pictures of your handsome author and his friends*

If you examine the code in `Index.cshtml`, shown in Listing 12-6, you can see how the page is constructed. The page is strongly typed to the `MyAppUser` class which is defined in the `Ch12.R2.Web.Models` folder. The page then uses standard Razor syntax to render the welcome section which shows some information from the current logged in user's profile section. It then uses a pair of loop for loops to display a lists friends and photos.

Listing 12-6. Index.cshtml

```
@using Ch12.R2.Web.Models
@using Microsoft.AspNet.Mvc.Facebook.Models
@model MyAppUser
@{
    ViewBag.Title = "Home Page";
}
```

```
<article class="intro">
    <span id="profilePicture">
        @if (Model.ProfilePicture != null && Model.ProfilePicture.Data != null)
        {
            <img src="@Model.ProfilePicture.Data.Url" />
        }
    </span>
    <h3>Welcome @Model.Name</h3>
    <label>Email: @Model.Email</label>
    <p>
        To learn more about building Facebook apps using ASP.NET MVC visit
        <a href="http://asp.net/mvc/facebook" title="ASP.NET MVC Website">http://asp.net/mvc/
facebook</a>.
        The page features videos, tutorials, and samples to help you get the most from ASP.NET MVC.
        If you have any questions about ASP.NET MVC visit
        <a href="http://forums.asp.net/1146.aspx/1?MVC" title="ASP.NET MVC Forum">our forums</a>.
    </p>
</article>

<article id="content">
    <div class="left">
        <h4>Friends</h4>
        @if (Model.Friends != null && Model.Friends.Data != null && Model.Friends.Data.Count > 0)
        {
            foreach (var myFriend in @Model.Friends.Data)
            {
            <a href="@myFriend.Link" target="_blank">
                <div class="photoTile">
                    <label>@myFriend.Name</label>
                    @if (myFriend.Picture != null && myFriend.Picture.Data != null)
                    {
                        <img src="@myFriend.Picture.Data.Url" />
                    }
                </div>
            </a>
            }
        }
        else
        {
            <p>No friends found.</p>
        }
    </div>
    <div class="right">
        <h4>Photos</h4>
        @if (Model.Photos != null && Model.Photos.Data != null && Model.Photos.Data.Count > 0)
```

```
    {
        foreach (var photo in @Model.Photos.Data)
        {
        <a href="@photo.Link" target="_blank">
            <div class="photoTile">
                <img src="@photo.ThumbnailUrl" />
            </div>
        </a>
        }
    }
    else
    {
        <p>No photo available.</p>
    }
    </div>
</article>
```

Next Steps

This template is an interesting starting point, but it is no way a completed application. Before moving to the next step, you would need to do some clean up from a design standpoint so that the content flows more naturally with the Facebook look and feel. The users of the application should not know that they are looking at an iFrame. Your app should look as if it is part of the site.

You can then modify this sample to do whatever you wish. You can combine it with the technique used in Recipe 12-1 to integrate the Facebook user data with user data from your application. You can also mine Facebook for lots of other interesting data. The Facebook Graph API provides a rich interface for pulling all kinds of information from Facebook's more than 1 billion users.

12-3. Setting Up Your Development for Working with Windows Azure

Problem

You would like to begin using some of the features of the Windows Azure stack, but you are not sure how to configure your development environment to develop and test Azure-dependent components.

Solution

Before you can begin development for Windows Azure, you first need to download and install the Azure SDK for .NET. It includes an add-in for Visual Studio, which contains project and item templates, client libraries, source code samples, and documentation. It also includes simulators that allow you to test your Azure dependent code without needing to connect to the Microsoft data centers.

How It Works

The following steps show how to get the latest version of the SDK:

1. Close any open instances of Visual Studio.

2. Open your web browser and navigate to the Windows Azure download web site at www.windowsazure.com/en-us/develop/downloads/.

3. On the site, locate the .NET section, and then click the link for VS 2012.

4. If running Internet Explorer, when asked to run or save the file, click the Run button. If using Chrome, double-click the downloaded item in the download tray to launch it. When prompted, click Yes in the User Account Control warning dialog.

5. The Microsoft Web Platform Installer will open with the Windows Azure SDK for .NET (VS 2012) – Latest page displayed. Click the Install button.

6. On the Prerequisites screen, click the I Accept button.

7. It will take several minutes for the SDK to be downloaded and installed. Once the download is complete, click the Finish button.

8. Click the Exit button to close the Web Platform installer.

Once installed, you should notice that several items have been added to your Start screen. The items include the Windows Azure command prompt, a compute emulator, and a storage emulator. Additional tools are available from the Start screen's All Apps view, which can be accessed by right-clicking the Start screen and clicking All Apps. In addition to the tools pinned to the Start screen, under the Windows Azure section of All Apps, you can access the Azure SDK documentation, release notes, code samples, and the Windows Azure HPC Scheduler SDK Content. If you are running Windows 7, this content can be found from the Start menu under All Programs.

The Azure SDK tools can help you test and deploy your Azure application by simulating the Azure services. The emulators make up something known as the Development Fabric. These executables emulate the functionally offered by the Azure cloud, but run locally on your development machine. They also offer the ability to monitor and debug your cloud services. The Windows Azure Command prompt launches with the paths to the SDK command-line tools that allow you to package and deploy your services outside Visual Studio.

If you open Visual Studio and create a new project, a new template is available under the Cloud category. If you use this template, the user interface will allow you to select one or more cloud services to include in your project. The available cloud services for Visual C# and Visual Basic include ASP.NET MVC 3 Web Role, ASP.NET MVC 4 Web Role, ASP.NET Web Role, Worker Role, Cache Worker Role, WCF Service Role, Worker Role with Service Bus Queue, and Silverlight Business Application role. For the Visual F# language, only Worker Role is available.

If you open Server Explorer, you will see a number of new items, including Windows Azure Compute, Windows Azure Service Bus, Windows Azure Storage, and Windows Azure Virtual Machines. If you expand the Storage node, you will find a Development node. Inside the Development node, there are containers for Blobs, Queues, and Tables. You can use this interface to browse the files that have been uploaded to your development storage instance.

12-4. Storing and Retrieving Files on Windows Azure from an ASP.NET MVC 4 Application

Problem

You are building an application that allows users to upload documents, and audio and video files. You do not want to move your entire site to Azure because your current hosting plan is meeting your needs. Unfortunately, your hosting plan does not provide enough storage space and does not offer a mechanism for dynamic expansion. You fear that if you run out of space during your peak usage period, it will be very difficult to upgrade your hosting without a noticeable service outage. You would like to have a way to store the files in the Windows Azure cloud without migrating your entire application.

Solution

Using Azure or another cloud provider does not need to be an all-or-nothing proposition. In some cases, it can be cost effective to host most of your web site using a traditional web hosting–provider, but use a cloud provider for features such as BLOB (Binary Large Object) storage.

Azure uses a RESTful web service to permit uploads of files and associated metadata. While it is possible to write your own code to talk directly to the web service, in most cases, you will want to use the Windows Azure Storage API provided by Microsoft. The library abstracts many of the complexities of the file-uploading process and adds additional capabilities, such as automatic retry for failed uploads.

The general pattern for uploading a file to Azure is to first allow the user to upload the file using a typical HTML file input. You then use Azure API to upload the file to Windows Azure Storage.

How It Works

We begin this recipe by first creating a basic ASP.NET MVC Web Application project and then using NuGet to add the required Azure APIs. Since we do not want to host the actual web site in Azure in this scenario, we do not need to use a Windows Azure project template. After creating the project, we will then build a controller that will process the file upload, and then upload the file to Azure. This recipe assumes that you have installed the Windows Azure SDK. We will use the Azure storage simulator for testing and debugging. Instructions on downloading and installing the SDK are found in Recipe 12-3.

Creating the Project

To create the project, you need to do the following:

1. Open Visual Studio and select New ➤ Project from the File menu.

2. Select the ASP.NET MVC 4 Web Application project, name the project **Ch12.R3.Web**, and name the solution **Ch12.R3**. Select a suitable location and click OK.

3. In the New ASP.NET MVC 4 Project screen, select the Basic template, and then click OK to create the project.

4. Right-click the References node in Solution Explorer and select Manage NuGet Packages.

5. Click the Online node in the Manage NuGet Packages window, and then type **Azure Storage** in the Search text box.

6. After a few moments, you should see the Windows Azure Storage library. Click the Install button. In addition to installing Windows Azure Storage, it will also install the required Microsoft OData library and the Microsoft Windows Azure Configuration Manager, which are dependencies.

7. Click the Updates node. Update all the updatable packages. The Azure APIs are updated frequently to keep pace with the new and expanded services.

Now that you have created a project, the next step is to create a controller that will be used to manage your upload.

Creating the Controller

We will create a new controller called Home. We are using Home as the controller name so that we can use the default routes defined in the project template. Inside the controller, we will create actions for uploading the files and for viewing the files inside the container.

To create the controller, perform the following steps:

1. Right-click the Controllers node in Solution Explorer and select Add ➤ Controller.

2. In the Add Controller window, name the controller **HomeController**, select the Empty MVC controller template, and then click Add.

3. Visual Studio will create the file and then open it in the code editor. Modify the file so that it contains the actions Index, UploadFile, and ListFiles.

4. Add using statements for the namespaces Microsoft.WindowsAzure and Microsoft.WindowsAzure.Storage.

5. For now, we will just stub out each action with a return View() statement. We add the logic to the controllers in a subsequent section. The HomeController should now look like Listing 12-7.

Listing 12-7. HomeController with Empty Actions

```
using Microsoft.WindowsAzure;
using Microsoft.WindowsAzure.Storage;
using System.Web.Mvc;

namespace CH12.R3.Web.Controllers
{
    public class HomeController : Controller
    {

        public ActionResult Index()
        {
            return View("Index");
        }

        public ActionResult UploadFile()
        {
          return View("UploadFile");
        }

        public ActionResult FileList()
        {
            return View("FileList");
        }

    }
}
```

Adding Azure Connection Strings to Web.config

In order for the Windows Azure Storage API to connect to the Windows Azure Storage service, it needs to know your account information as well as the URI of the Storage Service end point. This information is provided in the form of a connection string. While it is possible to hardcode this information directly in your source code, in general, this is not a good practice because it would require you to modify and then recompile the code every time you need to deploy it. In a complex project that is likely to have many controller actions that communicate with the storage service, it will also lead to maintainability issues.

The best practice to avoid this issue is to put your connection string in the application configuration file. In an ASP.NET application, the `Web.config` file is used to store this information. To add the connection string to the configuration file, perform the following steps:

1. Locate the `Web.config` file in Solution Explorer, and then double-click it to open the file in the code editor.

2. Under the `appSettings` section, add a new setting with the key `StorageConnectionString` and the value `UseDevelopmentStorage=true`. This is the connection string for the Windows Azure storage emulator. The emulator uses a well-known name and key that is the same for all users. The connection string `UseDevelopmentStorage=true` is a shortcut that the Storage API will replace with the correct parameters for the emulator.

3. Add a second key called **CloudStorageContainerReference** and give it the value **ch12-r4**. This will be the name of the BLOB container that we will use for this project. The modified **Web.config** file should look like Listing 12-8.

Listing 12-8. appSettings Section of Web.config File

```
<appSettings>
  <add key="webpages:Version" value="2.0.0.0" />
  <add key="webpages:Enabled" value="false" />
  <add key="PreserveLoginUrl" value="true" />
  <add key="ClientValidationEnabled" value="true" />
  <add key="UnobtrusiveJavaScriptEnabled" value="true" />
  <add key="StorageConnectionString" value="UseDevelopmentStorage=true"/>
  <add key="CloudStorageContainerReference" value="ch12-r4/>
</appSettings>
```

■ **Caution** Windows Azure has very strict rules about the characters allowed in a container name. These rules are based on the rules for DNS names. This means that no special characters (except dashes) are allowed in a container name and only lowercase letters are allowed. If you attempt to use an invalid name for a container, an exception will be thrown when you try to create it. What makes this difficult to troubleshoot is that the error returned is a very generic HTTP Error 400 (Bad Request) with an `HTTPStatusMessage`: "One of the request inputs is out of range." If you come across this message when using Windows Azure, check the name of your container or BLOB to make sure that it meets the criteria.

In this example, we are using the name "ch12-r4" for the container name. Notice that this name contains no spaces and only contains lowercase letters, numbers, and a dash. Names for containers must meet the following criteria:

- They must be at least three characters long.

- They can be no more than 63 characters.

- They must start with a lowercase letter or number.

- All letters must be lowercase. Uppercase letters are not allowed.

- They may contain a dash (-), but if a dash is used is, it must be preceded and followed by either a lowercase letter or a number.

- With the exception of the dash, no other symbols are allowed.

- Spaces and other white-space characters are not permitted.

Creating the UploadFile Action

Now that we have defined configuration settings for the connection string and storage container, we can use them to create the logic required for storing files in the container. To connect to the storage account and upload a file provided by user input, we add logic to the UploadFile action, as follows:

1. Check to see if the Request.Files collection contains any files and that the uploaded files contain data. If no files are found, we will not invoke the storage container.

2. Use the connection string in Web.config to create an instance of a CloudStorageAccount object.

3. Use the CloudStorageAccount instance to create a CloudBlobClient instance. This is a proxy class for the Azure Storage Web Service.

4. Pull the string defined in the configuration file and use it to create a reference to a storage container.

5. Call the CreateIfNotExists method on the storage container. As the name of the method suggests, this checks to see if the container exists; if it does not, it will create it.

6. For each file in the Request.Files collection, verify that the file is not null and has a content length greater than zero. This prevents us from uploading an empty file.

7. For each valid file, create a block BLOB reference in the storage container using the name of the file as a key. Azure has two types of BLOBs: page BLOBs represented by the CloudPageBlob class and block BLOBs represented by the CloudBlockBlob class. A page BLOB is in conceptually similar to a disk drive. You can programmatically access and write to any sector of the file as you would a disk. A block BLOB is conceptually similar to a file. Block BLOBs are the appropriate choice for the vast majority of the operations you will come across.

8. Once all the files have been processed, redirect to the action FileList. When completed, this action will display a list of files inside our container. The completed code is shown in Listing 12-9.

Listing 12-9. The UploadFile Action

```
using CH12.R3.Web.Models;
using Microsoft.WindowsAzure;
using Microsoft.WindowsAzure.Storage;
using Microsoft.WindowsAzure.Storage.Blob;
using System.Collections.Generic;
using System.Configuration;
using System.Web.Mvc;

namespace CH12.R4.Web.Controllers
{
 public ActionResult UploadFile()
 {

  if (Request.Files.Count > 0)
   {
     //try and connect to storage account
     //connection information and container name are configured in
     //the web.config file
```

```
CloudStorageAccount storageAccount =
CloudStorageAccount.Parse(
                    CloudConfigurationManager.GetSetting("StorageConnectionString")
                    );

//create a storage client instance
var storageClient = storageAccount.CreateCloudBlobClient();

//get a referance to the container
var storageContainer =
storageClient.GetContainerReference(
  ConfigurationManager.AppSettings.Get("CloudStorageContainerReference"));

//create storage container if it does not exist
storageContainer.CreateIfNotExists();
for(int fileNum=0; fileNum<Request.Files.Count; fileNum++)
{
  if (Request.Files[fileNum] != null && Request.Files[fileNum].ContentLength > 0)
  {
    //Get a referance to a new block blob from
    //the storage service using the name of the uploaded file
    var azureBlockBlob =
        storageContainer.GetBlockBlobReference(Request.Files[fileNum].FileName);

    //upload the file to the Azure service
    azureBlockBlob.UploadFromStream(Request.Files[fileNum].InputStream);

  }
}
//view list of files that you have uploaded
return RedirectToAction("FileList");

}
return View("UploadFile");
}
}
```

Creating the UploadFile View

The next step is to create the UploadFile view:

1. In the code editor, right-click anywhere inside the UploadFile action and select Add View.

2. Keep the default view name of UploadFile. Ensure that the Razor View engine is selected and that Use a Layout or Master Page is selected, and then click Add. Visual Studio will create a new file named UploadFile.cshtml and open it in the code editor. Visual Studio will automatically create the file in the correct folder.

3. Repeat this process for the other actions. We will leave these views blank for now.

4. Inside the UploadFile.cshtml file, create the opening and closing Form tags. You can hand-code the tags, but I highly recommend using the @using(Html.BeginForm())

construct instead. The HTML helper is route aware. This will prevent you from needing to change the action attribute in the Form element if you change your page routing logic.

5. Modify the call to BeginForm so that you pass in the action name UploadFile, the controller name Home, the method of FormMethod.Post and a custom attribute enctype="multipart/form-data". In order to upload a file, you must use the Post method and the enctype attribute must be added. This attribute is used to tell the browser how to encode the form data.

6. Next, add an input element of the type file. Ensure the input element has both an id and a name attribute. The name attribute is required for file uploads. If it is missing, the browser will not be able to properly encode the upload data and the Request.Files collection will be empty.

7. Add a Submit button. The completed view is shown in Listing 12-10.

Listing 12-10. UploadFile.cshtml

```
@{
    ViewBag.Title = "UploadFile";
}

<h1>Upload a File</h1>
@using (Html.BeginForm("UploadFile", "Home", FormMethod.Post,
    new { enctype = "multipart/form-data" }))
{
    <input type="file" id="File01" name="File01"/>
    <input type="submit" name="Submit" id="Submit" value="Upload" />
}
```

HTTP ENCODING TYPES

By default, form data uses the application/x-www-form-urlencoded encoding type. If you use a tool like Fiddler 2 to look at the raw HTTP requests generated by your browser, you can see the encoding type set in the Content-Type header. With the application/x-www-form-urlencoded type, the body of the request contains a set of name/value pairs separated by ampersands (&), just like in a query string.

A boundary is defined with the multipart/form-data encoding (in addition to the encoding type itself). It is usually made up of a number of dashes followed by a random character sequence. For example, you may see Content-Type: multipart/form-data; boundary=----WebKitFormBoundaryxFjFO7kV517KsAzW on the Chrome web browser.

In the body of the request, each field is separated by the defined boundary. In the next line, a Content-Disposition is given for each field. This allows the server to know which data is field data and which is form data. For normal form data, you see Content-Disposition with the value of form-data followed by a semicolon and the field name. After a pair of line breaks, the form data is displayed for that field. For files, file name is also listed. In the next line, the content type for the file is shown, followed by two line breaks, and then the file data in binary format.

Testing the UploadFile Action

The way the project is currently configured, it requires the Windows Azure storage emulator to be running. The emulator was installed along with the SDK, but it will not be running by default. If you had built this project using one of the Azure templates, the emulator would start automatically when you began debugging. In this case, because we are using a plain old ASP.NET MVC 4 project, it will not.

There are a few ways to start the emulator. One way is to start it manually by locating it on the Start menu (or Start page if you are using Windows 8). In both cases, you should be able to find it by typing the Windows key followed by **Storage Emu**. You can then launch the emulator by clicking it. You can also launch the emulator from Visual Studio by opening the Server Explorer window, which can be done by selecting it from the Visual Studio View menu. Inside the Server Explorer window, expand the Windows Azure Storage node, and then right-click the Development node and select Refresh.

From Server Explorer, you can browse the BLOBs in your local development store. When expanded, the Blobs node will show all the containers created so far during development. At this stage, if you have not yet developed any solutions that use Azure Storage, the collection should be empty.

You can confirm that the storage emulator is running by looking for its icon in the system tray, located on the far right side of the Windows taskbar. By default, Windows will hide this icon; to view it, you need to click the little white triangle in the left side of the system tray area. The Azure storage emulator icon is shown in Figure 12-10.

Figure 12-10. *The Azure system tray icon*

If you hover the mouse over the icon, the status of the emulator services is shown in a small pop-up window. If you right-click the icon, you can access commands available to shut down the storage emulator or launch the emulator user interface. The emulator UI is very simple. It displays the three services offered by the emulator, which include Blob, Queue, and Table. It shows the status for each service and the end point used. The end point addresses cannot be changed. Even if you did find a way to edit them, it would not be a good idea because the development server connection string shortcut we added to the Web.config file would no longer work.

Once you are sure the service is running, press the F5 key on your keyboard to begin debugging. In the web browser's address bar, append Home/UploadFile to the current URL.

> ▓ **Tip**   You can change the page that opens when the browser is launched in the debugger. This can be done by opening the project's properties, clicking the web tab, and then entering **Home/UploadFile** in the Specific Page text box.

After the page loads, click the Browse button (the Choose File button if you are using Chrome). A file selection dialog window will open. Click a file to select it, and then click the Open button to finalize your selection and close the dialog window. Click the Upload button to begin the upload. After a few seconds, you should be forwarded to a File List page.

To verify that your file was actually uploaded, open the Server Explorer window in Visual Studio if it is not already open. Expand the Windows Azure Storage node, the (Development) node, and then the Blobs node. Right-click the Blobs node and select Refresh to make sure it contains the latest information. Under the Blobs node, you should now see a container named ch12-r2. Double-click the ch12-r2 item. The container viewer window should open with the uploaded file listed.

Adding Multiple File Upload Support

In some situations, you may need to allow users to upload many files at once. The UploadFile controller—as it has been set up in Listing 12-9—can actually process multiple uploads. The view, however, had only a single file upload element. Several approaches can be taken to permit uploading several files at once. One is to add additional file upload elements. You can do this by using either server-side or client-side code to create as many file input boxes as you require. However, this interface would be extremely annoying for most people, especially if they need to upload a large number of files.

If your site targets modern browsers such as Google Chrome or IE 10, the HTML5 specification provides a new multiple attribute for file input boxes. All you need to do is add the attribute, as shown in Listing 12-11.

Listing 12-11. Adding Multiple File Support Using HTML5 Multiple Attribute

```
<h1>Upload a File</h1>
@using (Html.BeginForm("UploadFile", "Home", FormMethod.Post,
    new { enctype = "multipart/form-data" }))
{

    <input type="file" id="File01" name="File01" multiple />
    <input type="submit" name="Submit" id="Submit" value="Upload" />
}
```

Now when you browse for files, you can select more than one file by holding down the Shift key on your keyboard while selecting files. Try selecting a few documents and then clicking the Upload button. If you refresh the Azure Storage Container in Visual Studio, you should now see all the files that you have uploaded.

> ▓ **Tip**   Be careful to click the Refresh button inside the container window—not the Restart debugging symbol on the main toolbar.

Showing the Uploaded Files

For the next part of this recipe, we will display the list of files in the container in the FileList view. This will be done by using the storage container's ListBlobs method. This method returns an IEnumerable<IListBlobItem>. The IListBlobItems in the enumeration can be of several types, including CloudBlockBlob, CloudPageBlob, or CloudBlobDirectory.

In this example, we only want to display a flat list of BLOBs and we do not need to show any directory hierarchies. It is possible to create a directory structure in your storage container simply by naming the files so that they contain forward slashes. We would like to show the BLOB's URL, its short name, and its size. Since these properties do not exist in the IListBlobItem interface, we will need to cast each item into a CloudBlockBlob in order to access the properties. Since it is a good practice to keep the views as clean as possible, we do not want to clutter it up with casts and if statements. We will instead create a new model called FileListModel that will contain a constructor that takes the IEnumerable<IListBlobItem> as a parameter. The constructor will then pass the data into a List<FileInfo>, which is another class that contains the required fields. It should be noted that this is a custom class that has no relation to System.IO.FileInfo. For additional convenience, the FileInfo class has a static method named CreateFromIListBlobItem that accepts an IListBlobItem as a parameter and returns a FileInfo object. Do the following to create these classes:

1. Right-click the Models folder in Solution Explorer and select Add ➤ Class.

2. In the New Item window, name the class file **FileListModel.cs** and click Add.

3. Modify the file to look like Listing 12-12.

Listing 12-12. FileListModel.cs

```
using Microsoft.WindowsAzure.Storage.Blob;
using System.Collections.Generic;

namespace CH12.R3.Web.Models
{
    public class FileListModel
    {
        public FileListModel(IEnumerable<IListBlobItem> list)
        {
            if (list != null)
            {
                Files = new List<FileInfo>();
                foreach (var item in list)
                {
                    FileInfo info = FileInfo.CreateFromIListBlobItem(item);
                    if (info != null)
                    {
                        Files.Add(info);
                    }

                }
            }
        }
        public List<FileInfo> Files { get; set; }
    }

    public class FileInfo
    {
        public string FileName { get; set; }
        public string URL { get; set; }
        public long Size { get; set; }
```

```
        public static FileInfo CreateFromIListBlobItem(IListBlobItem item)
        {
            if (item is CloudBlockBlob)
            {
                var blob = (CloudBlockBlob)item;
                return new FileInfo { FileName = blob.Name,
                                      URL = blob.Uri.ToString(),
                                      Size = blob.Properties.Length };
            }
            return null;
        }
    }
}
```

4. Open HomeController.cs and modify the FileList action to look like Listing 12-13. Here, like in the UploadFile action, we will first create a reference to the cloud storage account and then use it to create an instance of the storage client. We then use the storage client to create an instance of the storage container. We then call the ListBlobs method on the storage container and pass the result from it into the FileListModel constructor.

Listing 12-13. FileList Action

```
public ActionResult FileList()
{
  CloudStorageAccount storageAccount = CloudStorageAccount.Parse(
  CloudConfigurationManager.GetSetting("StorageConnectionString"));

  var storageClient = storageAccount.CreateCloudBlobClient();

  var storageContainer = storageClient.GetContainerReference(
      ConfigurationManager.AppSettings.Get("CloudStorageContainerReference"));

  var blobsList = new FileListModel(storageContainer.ListBlobs(useFlatBlobListing: true));

  return View("FileList",blobsList);
}
```

5. We then return the ViewResult, passing it the model.

6. The final step is to fill in the FileList view so that it displays the list of BLOBs. The Razor code is shown in Listing 12-14.

Listing 12-14. FileList.cshtml

```
@model CH12.R3.Web.Models.FileListModel
@{
    ViewBag.Title = "File List";
}

<h2>File List</h2>
```

```
    <ul>
    @foreach (var item in Model.Files)
    {
        <li>
        <a href="@item.URL">@item.FileName</a> (@item.Size bytes)

        </li>
    }
    </ul>

    @Html.ActionLink("Upload Another File", "UploadFile")
```

Limitations of This Solution

If you try this in several different web browsers, you will see one of the biggest weaknesses of this solution. There is little consistency in the user interface between browser versions. In Chrome and Safari, after selecting more than one file, only the number of files selected is shown in the browser. In Internet Explorer and Firefox, there is absolutely no indication that more than one file has been selected. None of the browsers offer an intuitive way of removing the files once they have been selected. While this constitutes a functional user interface, it is far from ideal.

Another problem with the solution is that the total size of the request can be no larger than 4 MB in size. If the combined size of your files is larger than the 4 MB limit, IIS will throw an error stating that you have exceeded the maximum request size. IIS imposes this limitation in order to protect you from potential denial of service attacks. When uploading a large file, IIS will first buffer the file into memory. If a request size limit were not imposed, it would be quite easy for an attacker to craft an attack that used a large request to take down your web server.

This problem can be somewhat mitigated by increasing the maximum request size in the IIS configurations shown in Listing 12-15, in which the maximum request size has been increased to 60 MB. It also increases the execution timeout. This is often required since it will likely take longer for a user to upload a large file.

Listing 12-15. Increasing the Maximum Request Size and Increasing the Timeout in Web.config

```
<system.web>
 ... other setting ommited
 <httpRuntime targetFramework="4.5" maxRequestLength="61440" executionTimeout="3600" />
</system.web>
```

You should be careful about using this setting. You are increasing the size of the files that you can upload to your service at the expense of scalability and security.

Another problem with this solution is that it does not give the user any feedback on the upload process. Imagine a user has a 30 MB file. Even if he has a relatively fast Internet connection, it may still take several minutes for the upload to complete. If no visual feedback is given on the status of the upload, users of the system will have no way of knowing if the upload is still in progress or if the page has just become unresponsive.

If you are working with small files such as typical Office documents, this may be a good solution for you. If you are allowing users to upload large files, you may want to consider an alternative solution in which the file is broken into chunks on the client side. This be done using the File API, which is built into Google Chrome, or if you need broader reach, a Rich Internet Application (RIA) framework such as Microsoft Silverlight or Adobe Flash. Each chunk is uploaded separately and then reassembled on the server.

Another improvement that you can make to this recipe is to factor out some of the BLOB processing code that would likely repeat often if you were working on a real application; for example, you could create helper functions such as GetStorageAccount and GetStorageContainer.

12-5. Using Fiddler 2 to Help Debug Azure Calls to the Storage Emulator

Problem

You are working on an ASP.NET MVC 4 application that uses Windows Azure BLOB storage. While in development, you are using the Windows Azure storage emulator. While developing a new feature, you ran into issues and the Azure emulator is returning unhelpful generic error messages. You would like to have more insight into what data is being sent to the Azure web service.

Solution

Fiddler 2 is a very popular and powerful tool for debugging HTTP communications. It works by acting as a proxy for all HTTP requests leaving your computer. In Chapter 11, there are several recipes that describe how to download and install the tool, as well as how it can be used to debug Web API calls.

If you run the tool and then access an application that is using the Azure storage emulator, you may be surprised to see that none of the communication between your application and the emulator is logged. This is because the Azure storage emulator is bound to the loop back address (127.0.0.1), which is ignored by Fiddler.

Fortunately, there is a feature built-in the Windows Azure Storage API that will allow you to work around this limitation.

How It Works

When setting up your project to use Azure, you are required to pass in a connection string in order to connect to your cloud storage account. In development, if we need to use the storage emulator, we set this connection string to `UseDevelopmentStorage=true`. This is a shortcut that the API replaces with the well-known connection string for the storage emulator. This shortcut also allows for a second parameter called `DevelopmentStorageProxyUri`, which accepts any valid URI as a proxy address. This allows you to run the traffic through any HTTP proxy. Unfortunately, if you enter the default Fiddler 2 proxy address of 127.0.0.1:8888 for this parameter, it will not work because you would be sending traffic to the loopback address, which would still be ignored.

Thankfully, the Windows Azure Storage API allows you to substitute the loopback address with an alias for Fiddler. Listing 12-16 shows a connection string configured to pass traffic through Fiddler.

Listing 12-16. *Azure Connection String for Passing Communications Through Fiddler 2*

```
<appSettings>
    .. other settings
    <add key="CloudStorageConnectionString"
        value="UseDevelopmentStorage=true;DevelopmentStorageProxyUri=http://ipv4.fiddler" />
</appSettings>
```

The `ipv4.fiddler` address is set up for us automatically by Fiddler; no additional setup or host entries need to be created. When reviewing the traffic in Fiddler, the traffic will not use the address specified in your project (127.0.0.1:8934, for example).

In order for this setting to work, Fiddler must be running. If you no longer require Fiddler and shut it down, you must revert the `Web.config` file back to the original setting.

12-6. Which Is Better: a Mobile Web Application or a Native Device Application?

Problem

You have seen that the MVC Framework 4 comes with a template for creating mobile web applications, but you are not sure if creating a mobile application is worth the effort. You need some help deciding whether you should focus on a mobile web application, move to a native device application, or do a combination of the two.

Solution

Getting into mobile development requires that you make some decisions. The first decision is whether you should build a native application, a mobile web application, or both. The second decision is which devices to support. The third decision is the type of tools you should use to create your application. If you decide to build a native device application, in most cases you will require a back-end service that provides data to your application. ASP.NET Web API is a good solution because this service can work across mobile platforms.

The choice between a mobile web and a native application is usually a question of priorities. What is more important to your service: the richness of the mobile experience or the number of customers that you can reach? With a native device application, you direct access to the capabilities of the mobile operating system. This allows you to take advantage of the unique capabilities of each operating system and the underlying hardware in ways that is not possible with mobile web applications. You are also rendering the user interface using the native device APIs, which will give your application a more native feel that is easier for your customers to learn.

With a mobile application, you have reach. Anyone with a browser can get to your application. Even if the browser does not support the latest standards, you can use polyfills or downgrade certain features using popular JavaScript libraries such as Modernizr. With the mobile web, you have one application to maintain, and everyone gets the latest version as soon as you update your web site.

What many companies do today is to provide native device applications on the most popular platforms, and then provide a mobile web site to fill functional gaps in the native apps and to provide an alternative to the full version of the site for users of less popular mobile devices.

How It Works

As with all software development, you need to start out by trying to understand your customer's requirements. What type of tasks will they want to do on a mobile device? What types of devices are they using? What type of usability problems do they have when using the full version of your application on a mobile device?

In some cases, you can get this information by talking directly to your customers or by having a business analyst interview key stakeholders. While you can get good information from doing this, it is only part of the story.

In addition to talking to your customers, you can also benefit from studying the usage statistics from your web site. While it is possible to get good information from your web logs, tools such as Google Analytics and Adobe Analytics can provide a greater depth of information. These tools collect anonymous data from thousands of your visitors and then present this information in detailed reports.

Of these tools, Google Analytics is one of the most popular. It is free and easy to set up. After creating your account, Google Analytics provide you with a snippet of JavaScript to add to your site. When people visit your site, the script runs and gathers detailed information about the visitor, such as their IP address, device type, screen resolution, and the plug-ins that they have installed.

Using these tools, you can easily get an understating of how people are currently using your site, as well as how these usage patterns have changed over time.

Figure 12-11 shows a report generated by Google Analytics for an average day on MyOnlineBand.com. The chart shows that thousands of people are accessing the site using mobile devices and that the vast majority of them are iOS users. iPhone, iPad, and iPod Touch make up a combined 56 percent of mobile visits, while almost all the rest are running some version of Android. There are other devices in the mix, but they are almost statistically insignificant. The other devices include 0.1 percent running BlackBerry and 0.01 percent running Window Phone.

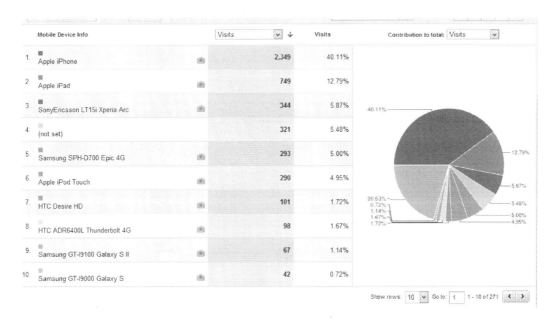

Figure 12-11. *Mobile device distribution from Google Analytics*

Based on this information alone, it seems obvious that the priority should be to improve the experience for iOS users. If I were to build a native mobile application, one targeting iOS would be the highest priority.

The next thing to look at is trending information. Is the data from two years ago the same as today's data? After mining through the data, it becomes clear that even though iOS is still the dominant mobile OS, its popularity is waning in favor of Android. Two years ago, iOS comprised over 90 percent of the mobile users and Android just 5 percent. The overall percentage of users accessing the site using mobile devices has also increased significantly. Two years back, mobile users made up only 2 percent of the total traffic; today, mobile users are almost 10 percent of the total. So, more users are accessing the site with mobile devices and more of them are using Android.

According to Gartner, as of the third quarter of 2012, Android made up 71 percent of all smartphones and tablets, and that 1.2 million new Android devices are being activated each day.

Based on this information, I still consider iOS to be very important, but see Android as the first priority. The strategy will be as follows: first, release a mobile web application that will service everyone, and then a native Android application, followed by an iOS application. I would then take another look at the statistics and decide whether it is worth creating apps for Windows Phone and BlackBerry.

The reason I would like to do a mobile web application first is because I can develop it quickly and I can host it on my current infrastructure. I can also reuse much of its functionality (such as the web services) when creating my other mobile applications.

Other Considerations for Device Applications

One daunting characteristic of native mobile application development is that you have to deal with the bureaucracy of the app store submission process. In web applications, you have total freedom to do whatever you want. You can update your application as often as you like. You can design your application to fit your unique perspective. You can sell your product from your site and keep all the profits. This is not necessarily true with mobile applications that need to be submitted to an app store.

Changing Terms of Service

Apple, Google, Microsoft, and even Research In Motion (RIM) each have a set of rules that govern what is fit to be submitted to their app stores. These rules change from time to time. Some applications that may have met the qualifications last month, will not meet them today.

For example, I know of a developer who built an iOS app that used Google Maps to present some unique information. The app did incredibly well and he had made over $50,000. One day, out of the blue, his application was pulled from the store because it violated some new terms of service in which the logo was misaligned. He was never able to republish the application. Lucky for him that he did not quit his day job.

Exposure and Discoverability

Many people create device applications with the misguided belief that since the mobile OS is used by millions of people, having an application in an application store will give them much greater exposure than having a web application. The reality is that there are hundreds of thousands of applications in the app stores. Your application is possibly even less discoverable than an application published to the web. A recently published statistic from Adeven (a company that specializes in application analytics for iOS applications) showed that as many of 60 percent of mobile-store apps are never downloaded by anyone.[1]

This is not unlike the Web. The Web is used by over 1 billion people. Yet even with a modest advertising budget and dedicated efforts to make your site search engine optimized, you are not guaranteed a significant amount of traffic.

Costs of Deployment

Most application stores require that you pay some sort of fee before you are eligible to submit an application. Apple and Microsoft both charge $99 for the privilege. Google charges $25. The justification for this fee is to cover the cost of the submission review process.

In addition to the entry fee, the app store will take a 30 percent cut of your software license fee. In addition, if you happen to sell a product through your application, most app stores will take a cut of that as well. It should be noted that Microsoft does not charge a fee for in-app purchases like Apple does. Depending on your business model, in-app purchase fees (purchases made inside applications) may be prohibitively expensive. For example, Amazon's business model is to sell a high volume of product at a thin margin. Having to paying an additional fee for each transaction would compromise their profitability. Because of this, Amazon does not allow you to purchase books through their iOS application. They instead force you to exit the application and make your purchase using their mobile web application.

---

[1] PhoneArena.com, "400,000 apps in the App Store have never been downloaded says report,"
www.phonearena.com/news/400000-apps-in-the-App-Store-have-never-been-downloaded-says-report_id32943.

Keeping Your App Updated

One of the biggest factors in the popularity of web applications among developers and businesses is the ease of deployment. There is no need to touch the desktop, and every user gets the upgrade at the same time.

With store applications, you need to submit your update to the store, have it approved, and then hope that your users will download and install it. Since it is up to your users to download and install an update, at any given time you may have many versions of the client code in the wild.

Fragmentation

Device applications are more susceptible to inconsistencies between devices. For example, your app may work fine with Android 4.1 but crashes with Android 4.2 devices. In other cases, you may have two devices running the same version of Android, but because of OEM-specific modifications to the Android OS, your application will not function as expected. With thousands of Android devices on the market, ensuring your application will work across all of them is virtually impossible.

iOS, BlackBerry, and Windows Phone also have some level of fragmentation—with iOS being the least fragmented.

Web applications, on the other hand, are easier to design for resiliency. Minor changes in browser capabilities are abstracted by libraries such as jQuery and Modernizr. The web browser provides an abstraction layer between various operating systems, so in most cases, one set of code will work equally well across many different types of devices.

Tooling

If you plan on creating a mobile web application, Visual Studio may be the only development tool required. After all, a mobile web application is based on the same technology stack as a full-sized application. The main difference is how you design your application. Your design needs to take into consideration the screen size, bandwidth limitations, network latency, the browser capabilities of the targeted devices, and the user input paradigms.

A native application, on the other hand, requires special tooling. In most cases, it requires a combination of an SDK and IDE that is made available from the vendor. In some cases, these tools are only available on certain operating systems; for example, Windows Phone 8 development requires Windows 8.

A number of tools allow you to develop one set of code for all devices. The toolset then translates the code into what is required for each device. Of these frameworks, Apache Cordova (formally PhoneGap) is the most popular. It supports many devices, including Android, BlackBerry, iOS, Symbian, Windows Phone 7, Windows Phone 8, and more. It allows you to create your user interface using HTML5, CSS, and JavaScript. It then adds a number of abstractions for hardware features such as an accelerometer, a camera, a compass, and a geolocation. It also allows for OS-specific modifications so that it is possible to implement user interface guidelines across all devices.

Even if you are using Cordova, you may still need access to a computer running an operating system supported by the target SDK in order to compile your code. For example, to compile an iOS version of your application, you will need a Mac.

Adobe PhoneGap Build offers help for this problem by providing a service that allows you to upload your source files, and it then compiles it for you. You can check out `https://build.phonegap.com` for more information.

Mobile Enterprise Application Platforms

With enterprises, you typically have the challenge of getting data to your mobile applications. In most cases, mobile devices are not able to access web sites and services that sit behind a corporate firewall. Another issue is getting custom corporate applications onto devices.

To meet this need, an emerging class of commercial products known as Mobile Enterprise Application Platforms (MEAP) are rising in popularity. These products are made up of several components that make up an integrated suite of products. The components include the following:

- *Development tools*: Typically based on the Eclipse IDE, development tools provide a graphical user interface for designing forms and reports. They also simplify accessing back-end data via their proprietary gateway technology. Some products, such as SAP's Unwired, allow the use of Cordova to create a more customized interface, in addition to proprietary development tools.

- *Enterprise App Store*: This component is usually available as a free application that your corporate users can download from the consumer app store. When users launch the application and supply corporate credentials, they are able to download your applications. They will later use the Enterprise App Store application to launch individual applications.

- *Gateway*: This component is the middleman between your enterprise data and your mobile application. For example, if the user needs data from an SAP application, the mobile application will send a query to the gateway. If the gateway has the data in its cache, it will return it; otherwise, it will request the data from the back-end store on behalf of the mobile application.

- *Mobile Device Management (MDM)*: This component is typically available separately. It is responsible for provisioning devices and allowing administrators to control which devices have access to corporate data and email systems. It also has capabilities to enforce policies; for example, you can define a policy that blocks jailbroken iPhones from accessing the network.

12-7. Creating a Mobile Web Application Using jQuery Mobile and ASP.NET MVC 4

Problem

You would like to create a web site that targets mobile devices and provides an intuitive, mobile-friendly layout and navigation.

Solution

While most of the templates that come with the ASP.NET MVC 4 tools for Visual Studio support media queries that provide some level of convenience for mobile users, they fall short of creating a true touch-first mobile device interface. The ASP.NET MVC Mobile Web Application template, on the other hand, offers a good starting point for your mobile application.

How It Works

The following explains how to create a mobile application using ASP.NET MVC:

1. Open Visual Studio and click the New Project link on the Start page.

2. In the New Project window, select the ASP.NET MVC 4 Web Application template. Name the project **Ch12.R7.Web** and the solution **Ch12.R7**, and then click the OK button.

3. In the New ASP.NET MVC 4 Project window, select the Mobile Application template. Make sure that the Razor view engine is selected, and then click OK.

Like many of the Internet Application templates, your project, when created, will contain a Home controller with Index, About, and Contact actions. It will also include an Account controller with actions for registering and login.

Unlike the other templates, however, it uses jQuery UI to create a mobile-friendly experience. Figure 12-12 shows a screenshot of the home page created by the template.

Figure 12-12. *The home page of a project created with the Mobile Application template*

If you browse the source code in this project, you will notice that the controller logic is identical to the logic in other templates. All the mobile-specific code is in the views and the layout pages. Listing 12-17 shows the _Layout.cshtml page. Highlighted in the code sample are the parts that are specific to making this a mobile web application.

Listing 12-17. _Layout.cshtml from the Mobile Template

```
<!DOCTYPE html>
<html lang="en">
    <head>
        <meta charset="utf-8" />
        <title>@ViewBag.Title</title>
        <meta name="viewport" content="width=device-width" />
        <link href="~/favicon.ico" rel="shortcut icon" type="image/x-icon" />
        @Styles.Render("~/Content/mobileCss", "~/Content/css")
        @Scripts.Render("~/bundles/modernizr")
    </head>
    <body>
        <div data-role="page" data-theme="b">
            <div data-role="header">
```

```
            @if (IsSectionDefined("Header")) {
                @RenderSection("Header")
            } else {
                <h1>@ViewBag.Title</h1>
                @Html.Partial("_LoginPartial")
            }
        </div>
        <div data-role="content">
            @RenderBody()
        </div>
    </div>

    @Scripts.Render("~/bundles/jquery", "~/bundles/jquerymobile")
        @RenderSection("scripts", required: false)
    </body>
</html>
```

The first highlighted line of code is the `viewport meta` tag. While this tag is not unique to the Mobile Application template, it is important in that it tells mobile web browsers not to zoom out the page but rather have it set to the pixel-width of the device.

The second highlighted line shows the link to the `mobileCss` style sheet bundle. In this bundle, which is defined in `BundleConfig.cs`, all the CSS files under the content directory with the prefix `jquery.mobile` are added to the page. At runtime, the web optimization framework that is included with ASP.NET MVC will combine and compress these files into one small download.

Also important is the inclusion of `data-role` attributes. These are HTML5 attributes that are used by jQuery mobile to convert standard HTML elements into interactive user-interface elements styled to feel natural on a mobile device.

Finally, in the last highlighted line of code, the `jquerymobile` bundle is included. This bundle will include the latest version of the jQuery mobile library, which has been added to your project via NuGet.

The next file of interest is the `Home/Index` view. Here, you can see a jQuery mobile `listview`, which is defined on a standard UL element enhanced using two `data-` HTML5 attributes. The first, `data-role="listview"` tells jQuery mobile that we would like to use this unordered list as a list view widget. The second attribute tells jQuery mobile that we wish to use an inset style list as opposed to full width, which is the default.

Clicking the link within the `ListView` will trigger a navigation as you would expect, but rather than unloading the current page, it will actually make an Ajax call to retrieve the content of the next page and then use an animated transition to display the updated content. Using this technique, the application will have a similar behavior as you may expect from a native device application.

Listing 12-18 shows the markup for `Index.cshtml`, with the jQuery mobile–specific code highlighted.

Listing 12-18. The Home Index View Created by the Mobile Application Template

```
@{
    ViewBag.Title = "Home Page";
}

<h2>@ViewBag.Message</h2>
<p>
    To learn more about ASP.NET MVC visit <a href="http://asp.net/mvc" title="ASP.NET MVC
Website">http://asp.net/mvc</a>.
</p>
```

```
<ul data-role="listview" data-inset="true">
    <li data-role="list-divider">Navigation</li>
    <li>@Html.ActionLink("About", "About", "Home")</li>
    <li>@Html.ActionLink("Contact", "Contact", "Home")</li>
</ul>
```

As you can see, jQuery mobile allows you to create enhanced mobile device experiences with a minimal amount of coding. Full tutorials on how to use the advanced features of this library are found on the jQuery mobile web site (http://jquerymobile.com/demos/1.2.0/).

12-8. Testing Your Mobile Web Application
Problem

You have created a mobile web application based on the ASP.NET MVC 4 Mobile Application template. You would like to test your application across multiple devices before deploying it.

Solution

While it is possible to test your mobile web application using a desktop web browser, it is not optimal. Your desktop browser likely has features and behaviors that are not consistent with mobile browsers and may even render things in a slightly different manner. Unless you are developing on a tablet PC such as a Microsoft Surface Pro, your desktop is likely missing touch support, GPS, and other features commonly found in smartphones.

One solution is to use an emulator. Mobile device emulators are normally made available in mobile device SDKs. The various SDKs are generally free. Emulators come with development tools, code samples, and documentation. They typically use virtualization technology to allow you to run the real device operating system on your PC.

In addition to emulators, you should also test on real devices when possible. Many usability issues are not apparent until you actually use your application on a real device.

How It Works

Once you determine the mobile platforms that you would like to target, you need to acquire a combination of emulators and physical devices for each. In most cases, you can start with acquiring the device emulators.

Testing on Android

Android is the world's most popular mobile OS. It is used on millions of mobile phones and tablets, and it owns over 70 percent of global market share. The latest version of the Android SDK can be downloaded from http://developer.android.com/sdk/index.html.

The SDK is available for Windows, Mac OS, and Linux. Bundled in the SDK is a customized version of the Eclipse IDE, as well as samples, testing tools, and a set of emulators known as Android Virtual Devices (AVD). Via the Android SDK manager, you can download device images for every version of Android starting with version 1.5 (API 3). Unfortunately, if you are targeting a newer version of Android, such as Ice Cream Sandwich, your PC will need to have substantial horsepower. In this section, I discuss a few techniques that can be used to run the emulators. The first is recommended for developers with a high-end Intel i7 CPU with Turbo Boost up to 3.5 GHz or better. If you are running a relatively new i5-based system, you can try the second technique listed here, which shows how to use an x86-based Android emulator. The last technique shows how to use Virtual Box to run the emulator. This technique works well even on older CPUs such as Intel Core 2 Duo processors.

If you happen to have a really fast machine, you can set up a virtual device to emulate a Galaxy Nexus smartphone using the following steps:

1. Download the Android SDK from the Android Developers web site.

2. The SDK is included as a single ZIP file (`adt-bundle-windows-x86_64`). Installing the SDK is as simple as unzipping it. The tools will run from the folder they are unzipped to. The SDKs' total size is around 340 MB.

3. After unzipping the bundle, you can launch the developer tools by navigating to the Eclipse folder and then launching `eclipse.exe`. Eclipse requires that a Java runtime environment (JRE) be installed on your computer.

   a. If you have not installed a Java runtime environment, download the latest package from the Oracle web site (`http://java.com/en/download/manual.jsp`). Make sure that if you downloaded the 64-bit version of the Android SDK, you are installing 64-bit version of Java as well.

   b. If you still get an error message after installing the JRE, you may need to manually add the `java/bin` directory to your computer's PATH environmental variable. You can edit the PATH variable by pressing the Windows key and then typing **env**. If you are on Windows 8, you need to click the Settings category on the Start screen. You can then click the "Edit the system environmental variables" icon. This will open the System Properties window, where you click the Environmental Variables button. On the Environmental Variables window, scroll to find the PATH variable, select it, and then click Edit. Enter a semicolon followed by the path to the Java Bin folder (`C:\Program Files (x86)\Java\jre7\bin`).

4. You will be prompted to select a location to use as a workspace. This is the location that will be used if you decide to develop native Android applications using the SDK. This location will not store the AVDs. They are stored under your Windows user folder.

5. You may also be asked to contribute usages statistics. Tick No unless you want to send your usage data to Google; otherwise, click Yes. Click the Finish button to close the window. The Android Developer Tools welcome page will be shown in the main Eclipse window.

6. In order to create an AVD, you will need to use the Android Virtual Device Manager. To do this from the Eclipse window menu, select Android Virtual Device Manager.

7. Click the New button in the Android Virtual Device Manager window.

8. Name the AVD **NexusGalTest** and select the Galaxy Nexus from the device drop-down menu. This is a predefined template that will create an AVD with similar specifications to the Galaxy Nexus smartphone running Android 4.2 (Jelly Bean).

9. If you wish, you can adjust the settings for the front and back camera. These can be mapped to a real camera, such as a web cam that is connected to your PC, or can use an emulated camera. You may also need to adjust the memory, which is set to 1 GB by default. If you have less than 1 GB of RAM available on your PC, the AVD will fail to load. If your development machine has a good GPU, it is also recommended that you check the Use Host GPU check box.

10. Click OK. You should now see the new AVD listed under the device list. To run the device, click it to select it, and then click the Start button.

11. Click the Launch button in the Launch window to start the AVD.

12. Just like a real Android smartphone, it will take the emulator a few minutes to boot. Once booted, you can dismiss the welcome message and click the browser icon (it looks like a globe).

Solving AVD Performance Issues Using the Intel HAXM Driver

One problem that plagues Android developers is the horrendous performance of the AVDs. If you are running the latest i7 Intel processor with Turbo Boost up to 3.5 GHz, it may run fine for you; otherwise, you may find that the AVD takes a really long time to load, and after it loads, performance is sufficiently unpleasant.

Some of the lag is caused by the fact that, by default, the emulator is not taking advantage of the hardware-assisted virtualization on your machine. It is also adding a layer to emulate an ARM processor. Another flaw is that it is not multiprocessor aware. You may notice that while the emulator is going through its horror-provoking gyrations, that your PC's performance monitor shows that one CPU is at 100 percent while the rest remain near idol.

Luckily, these problems can be mitigated. The first fix is to use an x86-based emulator rather than an ARM-based emulator. This eliminates many of the required CPU cycles that may be choking the emulator. The second fix is to enable hardware-assisted virtualization. This is done by installing a kernel-mode driver that Intel has contributed to the open handset alliance. You can also get some additional benefits from running the emulator from the command line, rather than launching it from Eclipse. This removes some of the debugger overhead, which may not be required for testing a web application. You can also enable GPU acceleration. This will help offload some of the graphical processing required to create the transition animations in the Android OS to your GPU. It does not help with web browsing performance, however, because Android does not use GPU acceleration in its browser.

The Intel HAXM driver requires that you run an Intel processor with Intel VT, EM64T, and Execute Disable Bit features installed and enabled. Most Intel processors sold in the past six years support these features; but in some cases, you may need to manually enable them in your computer's BIOS setting. Unfortunately, at the time of writing, this functionally is not yet available for API level 17 and above. The latest supported version is API level 16.

To install an x86 emulator and Intel driver, you will need to use the Android SDK manager:

1. Run Eclipse.

2. From the Windows menu, select Android SDK Manager.

3. Expand the Android 4.1.2 (API 16) node and select the Intel x86 Atom System Image.

4. Scroll down until you see the Extras node. Expand Extras and select Intel x86 Emulator Accelerator (HAXM). You should also make sure that the Google USB driver is installed. If you do not have this driver installed, your AVD will crash after running.

5. Click the Install Package button.

6. In the Choose Packages to Install window, tick Accept All and then click Install. Any dependent packages will be selected for you automatically. After installation is complete, you may need to repeat this process for the second package.

7. Restart Eclipse to load the changes.

8. You can now create a new AVD for the x86 image. From the Eclipse Window menu, select Android Virtual Device manager.

9. In the Virtual Device Manager window, click the New button.

10. Name the new device **Intel**, select the Galaxy Nexus device template, and select Android 4.1.2 –API Level 16 from the Target. Click OK.

11. Close the Android Device Manager window and then close Eclipse.

12. In the Windows File Explorer, navigate to the directory where you installed the Android SDK. Inside the SDK folder, navigate to the `sdk\extras\intel\Hardware_Accelerated_Execution_Manager` folder.

13. Right-click the `IntelHaxm.exe` file and select Run as Administrator.

14. Follow the instructions to install the driver.

15.   After the driver has been installed, you can confirm its operation by launching a command prompt as an administrator and then typing the following command: **sc query intelhaxm**.

16.   Examine the query results and verify that the STATE property is RUNNING.

17.   If it is running, in the same command window, navigate to the `android sdk\tools` folder.

18.   Enter the following command to launch the AVD: **emulator -cpu-delay 0 -gpu on -avd intel**.

Solving AVD Performance Problems Using Oracle Virtual Box

If you cannot use the Intel HAMX solution because you are not using an Intel processor or are still finding the emulators to run very poorly, there is another way. Members of the Android community have created an Android Virtualization solution that uses Oracle Virtual Box (`https://www.virtualbox.org/`) as an alternative to the SDK tools. To use the Virtual Box–based solution, you first need to download and install the Virtual Box software. Once Virtual Box has been installed, you can download an .OVA from `AndroVM.org`, which has several VMs that you can download. For mobile phones-testing, you can download the latest file with the prefix `androVM_vbox86p`. For tablets, use the file with the prefix `vbox86t` (for example, `androVM_vbox86t_4.1.1_r4-20121119.ova`).

Once the .OVA file has been downloaded, you can run it using the following steps:

1.   Double-click the .OVA file. If you have more than one product installed on your machine that supports .OVA files, you may be prompted to choose one. Be sure to select Virtual Box.

2.   In the Import Virtual Appliance window, click Import.

3.   After the import process has completed, in the Oracle VM VirtualBox Manager, select the AndroVM and then click the Settings button.

4.   Click the Network tab.

5.   For Adapter 1, select Host Only Adapter in the Attached To drop-down list. This adapter is used for management purposes. If you were to create a native Android application, you would configure Eclipse to use this adapter to deploy and debug your application.

6.   For Adapter 2, select Bridged Adapter, and then select a physical network card on your computer.

7.   Click OK to save the changes.

8.   Click the Run button to start the VM.

Unlike the emulators that come with the SDK, Virtual Box does not have the benefit of a hardware skin. To get around this limitation, you will need to use keyboard shortcuts to navigate the virtual machine.

- Escape = Android Back button

- Home = Android Home button

- F1 = Android Menu button

- End = Android Power button

- Delete = Lock button

Figure 12-13 shows an AVD running Android 4.1 inside Virtual Box. By default, this is shown in landscape mode.

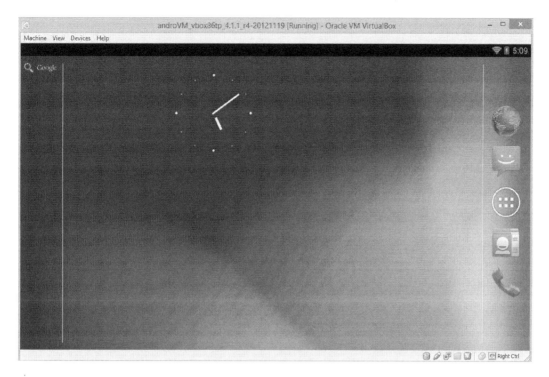

Figure 12-13. *Android emulator running inside Virtual Box on Windows 8*

One problem with using Virtual Box as the emulator is that you do not have the ability to do things like change device orientation, spoof GPS locations, and other fun stuff. It is possible to get around these limitations by installing Android apps such as Rotation Locker on your AVD. The Androvm.org web site provides instructions on how to do this.

Testing Your App on Windows Phone 8 and 7.x

Windows Phone 7 was a major reboot in Microsoft's mobile platform in response to their earlier mobile offerings being decimated by iPhone and Android. After two years of lackluster sales with Windows Phone 7, Microsoft pushed a major upgrade to the platform based on the Windows NT kernel, which is shared by Windows 8 and Windows Server 2012. Unlike previous versions of the mobile OS, which required applications to be developed using Silverlight for Windows Phone or XNA Game Studio, the new Windows Phone 8 SDK is much richer. It allows for native development in C++ and HTML5-based applications similar to Windows 8.

The Windows Phone 8 SDK comes with everything you need to develop on Windows Phone 8 and Windows Phone 7.5 devices. Unfortunately, it is only available for Windows 8 and is not supported on virtual machines. It also requires that your processor supports hardware-assisted virtualization and that this feature is enabled.

If you do not have Windows 8, you can download the Windows Phone SDK 7.1 and the SDK 7.11 Update. Note that there are significant differences in the web browser between Windows Phone 7.x and Windows Phone 8. For this reason, if you are serious about targeting Windows Phone, having a PC running Windows 8 is essential.

The SDK can be downloaded from http://dev.windowsphone.com/en-us/downloadsdk.

The Windows Phone 8 SDK is a whopping 1.6 GB download and the setup requires 5.63 GB on your system drive. Much of this space is required because of the size of the .vhd files that make up the emulator. In addition to the emulators, the SDK comes with add-ins for Visual Studio 2012, a version of Visual Studio Express, XNA Game Studio, and samples and documentation.

The installation will take around an hour to complete, depending on the speed of your Internet connection and your PC. Once installed, you can run the emulators from Visual Studio.

Testing Your Application on iOS

If you wish to run an official iOS emulator, you will need to do so from a Mac with an Intel processor. If you happen to have a Mac, you can use something like VMWare Parallels to run Windows 8 with Visual Studio 2012. You can then run the emulator from the host OS.

Alternatively, you can use a physical iOS device such as an iPhone, iPod touch, or iPad, or run the emulator on a remote Mac that you can access via VNC. The iOS SDK can be downloaded from `https://developer.apple.com/devcenter/ios/index.action`.

If you do not have access to an iDevice, another option is to use the iPhone and iPad simulator from Electric Plum (`www.electricplum.com/simulator.aspx`). While this tool does not emulate the iOS operating system, it does include an embedded version of the rendering engine used by the Safari web browser and it can simulate the iOS browsing experience with some level of accuracy. It's important to be aware that this tool is a simulator, not an emulator. Because of this, testing will not be as 100 percent accurate as a real iOS device. It is, however, somewhat handy for development purposes.

Testing on BlackBerry 10

Like Windows Mobile and Palm OS, BlackBerry OS suffered significant market share loss because of the onslaught of iOS and Android. Even though BlackBerry OS has been in decline, RIM still has close to 70 million subscribers. This is mainly due to their entrenchment in enterprise and government, and their continued success in emerging markets.

BlackBerry 10 is RIM's latest attempt to revitalize their smartphone lineup. It is a major departure from past versions of the BlackBerry operating system. BlackBerry 10 is built on a Linux-based operating system called QNX. With BlackBerry 10, RIM has merged many of the services offered in older versions of their OS, with an upgraded modern interface introduced with the BlackBerry Playbook tablet. The result is an impressive operating system that is surprisingly modern and easy to use, and boasts some of the best security features in the industry.

BlackBerry 10 has several options for developers, including a C++ API—an Adobe Air–based development model, HTML5, and Java development using the Android Runtime. The BlackBerry 10 simulator is a separate download in the form of an .OVA file optimized to run inside VMWare Player. The simulator allows you to use bezel swipe-gestures; supports hardware-accelerated OpenGL for Embedded Systems (GLES) for native gaming; and supports zooming, tilting, GPS, and NFC simulation. Overall, the simulator is very powerful and possibly one of the most complete and easy to use. A separate application named Controller can be used to simulate button presses, changes in device orientation, GPS, and other nonstandard input. Unlike the Electric Plum simulator, which only replicates the functionality of the iOS web browser, BlackBerry's simulator runs a virtualized version of QNX. It is technically considered a simulator because of the ability to generate hardware events such as device rotation.

The BlackBerry simulator can be installed and run by performing the following actions:

1. If you do not have VMWare or VMWare Player installed on your machine, download it from `www.vmware.com` and install it.

2. Download the BlackBerry simulator from `https://developer.blackberry.com/devzone/develop/simulator/simulator_installing.html`.

3. Run the installer. The installer copies the virtual machine file to your `My Documents/Virtual Machines` folder and installs a number of utility programs, such as the controller application.

4. Locate the VMWare Player application on your Start screen (or Start menu) and then launch the VMWare Player.

5. From the VMWare Player menu, select Open, and then navigate to your `My Documents/Virtual Machines` folder and open the `Blackberry10Simulator.vmx` file.

6. After a few minutes, you will see the VNX Unix command prompt begin the boot process. You will eventually be booted into the home screen.

Opening Your MVC Application in the Simulator/Emulators

Once you have installed one or more of the mobile device emulators, you can begin testing your application. Before you do this, however, you will need to make some changes to your Visual Studio project configuration. By default, Visual Studio 2012 uses IIS Express to host your application. While this has the advantage of being convenient, self-contained, and does not require administrative privileges to run on your computer, it has one major issue that makes it unusable with most of the simulators and emulators. IIS Express is configured in such a way that it can also be accessed when the host name is localhost. If you try to access it using any other name, including the IP address of your PC, IIS Express will throw an error complaining of an invalid host name.

The solution is to configure your project to use the full version of IIS. The process for installing IIS on your local PC is explained in Recipe 3-9. Recipe 3-10 shows how to configure your MVC project to use IIS rather than IIS Express.

Once your project has been configured, you will need to access the site using the local IP address of your computer combined with the virtual directory name for your site. You can get your local IP Address by opening a command prompt and typing **ipconfig**.

■ **Note** If you have configured your site to use a host header and you are using a host file on your PC, the simulator will not be able to resolve the friendly name. This is because the host file is local for your PC, and in most cases, the emulator will be a separate virtual machine with its own IP address. A workaround is to create a real DNS entry on your local network or to use a virtual directory, if possible.

Figure 12-14 shows the project created in Recipe 12-8. The Android emulator is shown on the left, the BlackBerry 10 simulator is shown in the center, and the Electric Plum iPhone simulator is shown on the right.

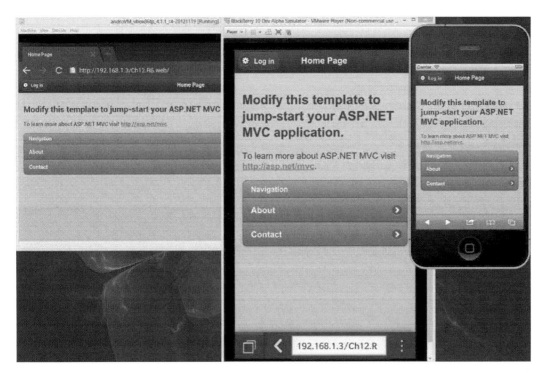

Figure 12-14. *ASP.NET MVC mobile application shown in simulators and the Android emulator*

Index

▓ B

■ N

■ O

■ P, Q

■ R

▓ W, X, Y, Z

22994161R10338

Made in the USA
Lexington, KY
22 May 2013